Communications
in Computer and Information Science 209

Qingyuan Zhou (Ed.)

Advances in Applied Economics, Business and Development

International Symposium, ISAEBD 2011
Dalian, China, August 6-7, 2011
Proceedings, Part II

Springer

Volume Editor

Qingyuan Zhou
Jiangsu Teachers University of Technology
Yuying Road No. 2
Changzhou, Jiangsu Province, 213001, China
E-mail: zqyconference@gmail.com

ISSN 1865-0929
e-ISSN 1865-0937
ISBN 978-3-642-23019-6
ISBN 978-3-642-23020-2 (eBook)
DOI 10.1007/978-3-642-23020-2
Springer Heidelberg Dordrecht London New York

Library of Congress Control Number: 2011933608

CR Subject Classification (1998): H.4, H.3, C.2, I.2, D.2, J.1

Typesetting: Camera-ready by author, data conversion by Scientific Publishing Services, Chennai, India

Printed on acid-free paper

Springer is part of Springer Science+Business Media (www.springer.com)

Preface

It is our pleasure to welcome you to the proceedings of the 2011 International Symposium on Applied Economics, Business and Development (ISAEBD 2011) which was held in Dalian, China. ISAEBD 2011 was the first conference dedicated to issues related to applied economics, business and development. This conference aims to provide a high-level international forum for researchers to present and discuss the recent advances in related issues, covering various research areas including economics, management, education and its applications.

The conference is sponsored by the Hong Kong Education Society, International Material Science Society and Information Engineering Research Institute. Their support is very important for our conference.

The conference was both stimulating and informative with an interesting array of keynote and invited speakers from all over the world. Delegates had a wide range of sessions to choose from.

The program consisted of invited sessions, technical workshops and discussions with eminent speakers covering a wide range of topics in applied economics, business and development. This rich program provided all attendees with the opportunity to meet and interact with one another.

We would like to thank the organization staff, the members of the Program Committees and the reviewers for their hard work.

We hope the attendees of ISAEBD 2011 had an enjoyable scientific gathering in Dalian, China. We look forward to seeing all of you at the next ISAEBD event.

Qingyuan Zhou

ISAEBD 2011 Organization

Honorary Conference Chairs

Chin-Chen Chang	Feng Chia University, Taiwan
Chris Price	Aberystwyth University, UK

General Chairs

Qinyuan Zhou	Jiangsu Teachers University of Technology, China
Junwu Zhu	Yangzhou University, China

Program Chairs

Honghua Tan	Wuhan Institute of Technology , China
Qihai Zhou	Southwestern University of Finance and Economics, China

Publication Chair

Mark Zhou	Hong Kong Education Society, Hong Kong

Local Chair

He Ping	Liaoning Police Academy, China

International Program Committee

Ming-Jyi Jang	Far-East University, Taiwan
Tzuu-Hseng S. Li	National Cheng Kung University, Taiwan
Yanwen Wu	Huazhong Normal University, China
Teh-Lu Liao	National Cheng Kung University, Taiwan
Yi-Pin Kuo	Far-East University, Taiwan
Qingtang Liu	Huazhong Normal University, China
Wei-Chang Du	I-Shou University, Taiwan
Jiuming Yang	Huazhong Normal University, China
Hui Jiang	Wuhan Golden Bridge-Network Security Technocogy Co. Ltd., China
Zhonghua Wang	Huazhong Normal University, China
Jun-Juh Yan	Shu-Te University, Taiwan
Dong Huang	Huazhong University of Science and Technology, China
JunQi Wu	Huazhong Normal University, China

Table of Contents – Part II

Nonparametric Estimator of Value-at-Risk for Stationary Financial Returns

Chu Huang

Department of Mathematics, Zhejiang University,
Hangzhou, China, 310027
huangchu@zju.edu.cn

Abstract. In this paper, it is illustrated that the sample quantiles is a reasonable estimator for VaR when the samples are dependent. The dependence of samples is described by S-mixing which was proposed by Berkes (2009). We obtained the strong consistence of the VaR estimators. We also established a Bahadur representation of the estimator in the sense of convergence in probability, and obtained the asymptotic normality of this VaR estimator as a corollary. The performance of the VaR estimator are evaluated by empirical studies on real financial return series.

Keywords: VaR, Sample quantiles, S-mixing, Strong consistence, Asymptotic normality.

1 Introduction

Value-at-Risk (VaR) is an important measure of market risk associated with an asset or a portfolio of assets in financial literatures, and it has been chosen by the Basel Committee on Banking Supervision as a benchmark risk measure and has been used by financial institutions for asset management and minimization of risk. Suppose $\{Y_k, 1 \le K \le n\}$ is the market value of an asset over n periods of a time unit, and write $X_k = \log(Y_k/Y_{k-1})$. Assume that $\{X_k\}$ is a strictly stationary process with marginal distribution function F, then the $1-\lambda$ level VaR is defined as $\nu_\lambda = -\inf\{u : F(u) \ge \lambda\}$ for a given $\lambda \in (0,1)$. Note that the λ quantile of $F(x)$ is defined as $Q(\lambda) = \inf\{u : F(u) \ge \lambda\}$, then $\nu_\lambda = -Q(\lambda)$, so the estimation of VaR can be attributed to the estimation of quantile.

Remark 1. [1] used an axiomatic approach to the problem of defining a satisfactory risk measure. They defined attributes that any good risk measure should satisfy, and call risk measures that satisfy these axioms "coherent". It turned out that VaR is not a coherent risk measure, in general, as it is not sub-additive. However, as showed in [3], the VaR can be sub-additive within any family of distributions generated by the location-scale transformation of a distribution F_0, that is, $\mathcal{F}(x) = \{F | F(x) = F_0\left(\frac{x-a}{b}\right)$ for any $a, b \in \mathbb{R}\}$, which includes the Gaussian and elliptical families as special cases, as well as the normal inverse Gaussian subfamily within the family of generalized hyperbolic distributions

Q. Zhou (Ed.): ISAEBD 2011, Part II, CCIS 209, pp. 1–8, 2011.

which is closely associated with continuous-time asset pricing models based on Levy processes. In addition, the Expected shortfall (ES) is a closely related risk measure to VaR, which is coherent. So the investigation of estimation of VaR will be helpful to the inference of ES too, because of the close link between the VaR and the ES.

Early estimators of VaR are general based on parametric models for the return distribution F, such as Gaussian or t-distributions, because of its advantages in interpretation. Unfortunately, it is difficult to judge distributions of models in practice, and the parametric method is not suitable for fat-tailed distributions. In recent years, some scholars proposed nonparametric method. The classical nonparametric estimator of quantile, which is called as sample quantiles, is the λ empirical quantile $Q_n(\lambda)$, i.e. the inverse function of the empirical distribution function $F_n(x) = \frac{1}{n}\sum_{i=1}^{n} I(X_i \leq x)$. General speaking, the method of sample quantiles is able to capture fat-tailed distribution of returns automatically, and impose weaker assumptions on the dynamics of the return process. Furthermore, it has a better convergence rate to the VaR when the sample size grew. So it is widely used in practice now. More details about the sample quantiles can be founded in Serfling (1980).

The financial return series are subjected to data dependence is a known reality in empirical finance. The dependence of samples is usually described by strong mixing ($\alpha-$mixing) which was first introduced in [4]. However, the calculation of strong mixing coefficients is generally not easy for nonlinear time series appearing in many economic literatures. Additionally, many well-known processes are not strong mixing. The most prominent example may be that strong mixing fails to hold for the AR(1) process $X_n = \rho X_{n-1} + \varepsilon_n(|\rho| < 1)$ with Bernoulli innovations (c.f. [5]). To overcome these disadvantages, we use the S-mixing which was proposed in [2] to describe the dependence of samples in this paper.

The rest of the paper is organized as follows. Main results are presented in Section 2 and proved in Section 3. Empirical analyses of financial returns series of the stock market of China are carried out in Section 4.

2 Main Results

Let us begin with the introduction of the concept of S-mixing dependent processes. Suppose $\{X_n, n \in \mathbb{Z}\}$ is a stationary process with a representation of the form

$$X_k = f(\cdots, \varepsilon_{k-1}, \varepsilon_k, \varepsilon_{k+1}, \cdots), \tag{2.1}$$

where $\{\varepsilon_k, k \in \mathbb{Z}\}$ is an i.i.d. sequence and $f : \mathbb{R}^{\mathbb{Z}} \to \mathbb{R}$ is Borel measurable. The process $\{X_k, k \in \mathbb{Z}\}$ is said to be S-mixing if it satisfies the following conditions:

(A) For any $k \in \mathbb{Z}$ and $m \in \mathbb{N}$ one can find a random variable X_{km} such that we have

$$\mathsf{P}(|X_k - X_{km}| \geq \gamma_m) \leq \delta_m \tag{2.2}$$

for some numerical sequences $\gamma_m \to 0, \delta_m \to 0$.

(B) For any disjoint intervals $I_1, \cdots, I_r$ of integers and any positive integers $m_1, \cdots, m_r$, the vectors $\{X_{jm_1}, j \in I_1\}, \cdots, \{X_{jm_r}, j \in I_r\}$ are independent provided the separation between I_k and I_l is greater than $m_k + m_l$.

The definition of S-mixing is general, and it contains many important statistical models, such as linear processes with dependent innovations (which includes the ARMA models), Markov processes, augmented GARCH sequences, stochastic Volatility models and so on, hence the results in the article may be applicable. See [2] for more details.

There are some conditions that will be used in our study.

(1) Let $\{X_n, n \in \mathbb{Z}\}$ be a stationary sequence such that $F(x) = \mathsf{P}(X \leq x)$ is Lipschitz continuous of order $\theta > 0$. Assume that $\{X_n, n \in \mathbb{Z}\}$ is S-mixing with $\gamma_m = m^{-A/\theta-\varepsilon}, \delta_m = m^{-A}$ for some $A > 4, \varepsilon > 0$.

(2) For a given $\lambda \in (0,1)$, $f(x) = F'(x)$ is positive and bounded in some neighborhood of $Q(\lambda)$.

(3) $f'(x)$ is bounded in some neighborhood of $Q(\lambda)$.

(4) For any $i \neq j$, $\mathsf{P}(X_i = X_j) = 0$.

Remark 2. Note that $Q'(x) = \frac{1}{f(Q(x))}$, and $Q''(x) = \frac{f'(Q(x))}{f^3(Q(x))}$. Then we know $Q'(x), |Q''(x)|$ is bounded in some neighborhood of λ. The boundedness of $Q'(x), |Q''(x)|$ will be used in Section 3 and Section 4.

Now we present our main results as follows.

Theorem 1. *Suppose conditions (1)-(4) hold. For a given $\lambda \in (0,1)$, as $n \to \infty$,*

$$Q_n(\lambda) - Q(\lambda) = O(n^{-1/2}(\log\log n)^{1/2}) \qquad a.s. \tag{2.3}$$

Theorem 2. *Suppose the conditions (1)-(4) hold. For a given $\lambda \in (0,1)$, as $n \to \infty$,*

$$Q_n(\lambda) - Q(\lambda) + \frac{F_n(Q(\lambda)) - \lambda}{f(Q(\lambda))} = O(n^{-1/2}\log^{-\alpha} n) \qquad a.s. \tag{2.4}$$

Corollary 1. *Suppose the conditions (1)-(4) hold. For a given $\lambda \in (0,1)$, as $n \to \infty$,*

$$\sqrt{n}(Q_n(\lambda) - Q(\lambda)) \xrightarrow{d} N(0, \frac{\Gamma^*(\lambda,\lambda)}{f^2(Q(\lambda))}), \tag{2.5}$$

where $\Gamma^*(\lambda,\lambda) = \sum_{-\infty<k<\infty}[\mathsf{P}(X_0 \leq Q(\lambda)) - \lambda][\mathsf{P}(X_k \leq Q(\lambda)) - \lambda]$, whose existence is guaranteed by Proposition 1.

3 Proof

The following lemmas and propositions are needed in the next section. Now we introduce some notations. Given a sample $X_1, X_2, \cdots, X_n$, let $F_n(x) = \frac{1}{n}\sum_{i=1}^n I(X_i \leq x)$ and $Q_n(\lambda) = F_n^{-1}(\lambda), 0 \leq \lambda \leq 1$, respectively. Define

$$\beta_n(x) = n^{\frac{1}{2}}(F_n(x) - F(x)), \qquad X \in \mathbb{R},$$

$$q_n(\lambda) = n^{\frac{1}{2}}(Q(\lambda) - Q_n(\lambda)), \qquad \lambda \in (0,1),$$

the general empirical and the general quantile process, respectively. With $U_i = F(X_i), i \geq 1$, the uniform empirical distribution and the uniform empirical quantile function are defined by $E_n(\lambda) = \frac{1}{n}\sum_{i=1}^{n} I(U_i \leq \lambda) = F_n(Q(s)), 0 \leq \lambda \leq 1$ and $G_n(\lambda) = E_n^{-1}(\lambda) = F(Q_n(\lambda)), 0 \leq \lambda \leq 1$, respectively. Let

$$\alpha_n(\lambda) = n^{\frac{1}{2}}(E_n(\lambda) - \lambda), \qquad \lambda \in (0,1),$$

$$u_n(\lambda) = n^{\frac{1}{2}}(\lambda - G_n(\lambda)), \qquad \lambda \in (0,1),$$

be the corresponding uniform empirical and uniform quantile process, respectively.

A separable Gaussian process $\{K(s,t); 0 \leq s \leq 1, t \geq 0\}$ is called a Kiefer process if it satisfies $K(s,0) = K(0,t) = K(1,t) = 0, \mathsf{E}K(s,t) = 0$, and $\mathsf{E}K(s,t)K(s',t') = (t \wedge t')\Gamma(s,s')$, for $t, t' > 0$ and $0 \leq s, s' \leq 1$.

Lemma 1. *Assume $K(s,t)$ is a Kiefer process. If $\lambda \in (0,1)$, then*

$$K(\lambda, n) = O(n^{1/2}(\log\log n)^{1/2}) \qquad a.s. \tag{3.1}$$

and there exists $\alpha > 0$, such that

$$\sup_{|s-\lambda|<\delta_n} |K(s,n) - K(\lambda,n)| = O(n^{1/2}\log^{-\alpha} n) \qquad a.s. \tag{3.2}$$

where $\delta_n = n^{-1/4}(\log\log n)^{1/2}$.

This lemma follows from Lemma 3.1 and Lemma 3.5 in [7].

Lemma 2. *Let $\{X_k, k \in \mathbb{Z}\}$ be a stationary S-mixing sequence with $\gamma_m = \delta_m = m^{-A}$ for some $A > 4$. Assume further that X_1 is uniformly distributed on the unit interval. Denote $Y_k(s) = I(X_k \leq s) - s, s \in [0,1]; R(s,t) = \sum_{1\leq k\leq t} Y_k(s), s \in [0,1], t \geq 1$. Then the series*

$$\Gamma(s,s') = \sum_{-\infty<k<\infty} \mathsf{E}Y_0(s)\mathsf{E}Y_k(s')$$

converges absolutely for every choice of parameters $0 \leq s, s' \leq 1$. Moreover, there exists a Kiefer process $K(s,t)$ such that $\mathsf{E}K(s,t)K(s',t') = (t \wedge t')\Gamma(s,s')$ and for some $\alpha > 0$

$$\sup_{0\leq t\leq n}\sup_{0\leq s\leq 1} |R(s,t) - K(s,t)| = o(n^{1/2}\log^{-\alpha} n) \qquad a.s. \tag{3.3}$$

This lemma follows from Theorem 1 in [2].

Proposition 1. *Suppose condition (1) holds. Then the series*

$$\Gamma(s,s') = \sum_{-\infty<k<\infty} \mathsf{E}Y_0'(s)Y_k'(s')$$

converges absolutely for every choice of parameters $0 \le s, s' \le 1$*, where* $Y'_k(s) = I(X_k \le Q(s)) - s$*. Moreover, there exists a Kiefer process* $K(s,t)$ *with covariance* $(t \wedge t')\Gamma(s,s')$ *such that for some* $\alpha > 0$*,*

$$\sup_{0<s<1} |F_n(Q(s)) - s - \frac{1}{n}K(s,n)| = O(n^{-1/2}\log^{-\alpha} n). \tag{3.4}$$

Proof. Let $\{X_{km}\}$ be a random variable sequence satisfying condition (A) and (B) in the definition of S-mixing for $\{X_k\}$. Then by the Lipschitz condition,

$$m^{-A} \ge \mathsf{P}(|X_{km} - X_k| \ge m^{-A/\theta-\epsilon}) \ge \mathsf{P}(|F(X_{km}) - F(X_k)| \ge m^{-A}). \tag{3.5}$$

Easily verify $F(X_{km})$ satisfies condition (B) in the definition of S-mixing. Then our proposition follows from Lemma 2.

Proof of Theorem 1. According to Proposition 1, there exists a Kiefer process $K(s,t)$ such that for some $\alpha > 0$,

$$\sup_{0\le t\le n}\sup_{0<x<1} |K(x,[t]) - [t]^{1/2}\alpha_{[t]}(x)| = O(n^{1/2}\log^{-\alpha} n). \qquad a.s. \tag{3.6}$$

Since $K(\lambda,n) = O(n^{1/2}(\log\log n)^{1/2})$, we have

$$\limsup_{n\to\infty} \frac{1}{(2\log\log n)^{1/2}} \sup_{0<x<1} |\alpha_n(x)| \le C \qquad a.s. \tag{3.7}$$

Recall $\mathsf{P}(X_i = X_j) = 0$ for any $i \ne j$, so

$$X_{(1)} < X_{(2)} < \cdots < X_{(n-1)} < X_{(n)} \qquad a.s. \tag{3.8}$$

then we obtain

$$F_n(Q_n(\lambda)) = n^{-1}\sum_{i=1}^{n} I(X_i \le Q_n(\lambda)) = \lambda + O(\frac{1}{n}), \tag{3.9}$$

it leads to

$$\limsup_{n\to\infty} \frac{1}{(2\log\log n)^{1/2}} \sup_{\lambda\in(0,1)} |u_n(\lambda)| \le C \qquad a.s. \tag{3.10}$$

According to conditions (2) and (3), we have $Q_n(\lambda) = Q(F(Q_n(\lambda))) = Q(G_n(\lambda))$. Recall $G_n(\lambda) = \lambda - n^{-1/2}u_n(\lambda)$, then by the mean value theorem, there exists $\zeta \in (\lambda - n^{-1/2}u_n(\lambda), \lambda)$ such that

$$Q_n(\lambda) - Q(\lambda) = Q(G_n(\lambda)) - Q(\lambda) = Q'(\zeta)(-n^{-1/2}u_n(\lambda)). \tag{3.11}$$

Since $Q'(x) = \frac{1}{f(Q(x))}$ is bounded in some neighborhood of λ, so

$$Q_n(\lambda) - Q(\lambda) = O(n^{-1/2}(\log\log n)^{1/2}) \qquad a.s. \tag{3.12}$$

So the proof is completed. □

Proof of Theorem 2. Recall $F_n(Q_n(\lambda)) = \lambda + O(\frac{1}{n})$, then expand $F(Q_n(\lambda))$ at $Q(\lambda)$, we get

$$F(Q_n(\lambda)) = \lambda + f(Q(\lambda))[Q_n(\lambda) - Q(\lambda)] + \frac{1}{2} f'[Q(\lambda) + \theta(Q_n(\lambda) - Q(\lambda))](Q_n(\lambda) - Q(\lambda))^2, \tag{3.13}$$

where $0 < \theta < 1$.

Proposition 1 together with condition 3, leads to

$$\begin{aligned} & F_n(Q_n(\lambda)) - F(Q_n(\lambda)) + f(Q(\lambda))[Q_n(\lambda) - Q(\lambda)] \\ & = O(n^{-1}) + \frac{1}{2} f'[Q(\lambda) + \theta(Q_n(\lambda) - Q(\lambda))](Q_n(\lambda) - Q(\lambda))^2 = O(n^{-1} \log\log n). \end{aligned}$$

Denote $\delta_n = n^{-1/4}(\log\log n)^{1/2}$, $J_n = \{x : \Big| |F(x) - \lambda| < \delta_n\}$. According to Lemma 1 and Proposition 1, there exists a Kiefer process $K(s,t)$ and $\alpha > 0$, such that

$$\begin{aligned} & \sup_{s \in J_n} |F_n(s) - F(s) - (F_n(Q(\lambda)) - \lambda)| \\ & \leq \sup_{s \in J_n} |F_n(Q(F(s))) - F(s) - \frac{1}{n} K(F(s), n)| + \sup_{s \in J_n} |\frac{1}{n} K(F(s), n) - \frac{1}{n} K(\lambda, n)| \\ & \quad + |F_n(Q(\lambda)) - \lambda - \frac{1}{n} K(\lambda, n)| \\ & = O(n^{-1/2} \log^{-\alpha} n) + O(n^{-1/2} \log^{-\alpha} n) + O(n^{-1/2} \log^{-\alpha} n) = O(n^{-1/2} \log^{-\alpha} n). \end{aligned}$$

Easily verify $Q_n(\lambda) \in J_n$. Therefore,

$$\begin{aligned} & |f(Q(\lambda))(Q_n(\lambda) - Q(\lambda)) + (F_n(Q(\lambda)) - \lambda)| \\ & \leq |F_n(Q_n(\lambda)) - F(Q_n(\lambda)) + f(Q(\lambda))(Q_n(\lambda) - Q(\lambda))| \\ & \quad + |F_n(Q_n(\lambda)) - F(Q_n(\lambda)) - (F_n(Q(\lambda)) - F(Q(\lambda)))| \\ & = O(n^{-1} \log\log n) + O(n^{-1/2} \log^{-\alpha} n) = O(n^{-1/2} \log^{-\alpha} n). \end{aligned} \tag{3.14}$$

So the proof is completed. □

Proof of Corollary 1. Note that $K(\lambda, n)$ is a separable Gaussian process, then our results can get from Proposition 1 and Theorem 2 immediately. □

4 Empirical Studies

In the section we apply the the nonparametric VaR inference procedures to analyze the daily log-return series for the stock markets of China from January 1, 2007 to December 31, 2008. The data were downloaded from the CSMAR Solution (http://www.gtarsc.com). Figure 1 illustrates the return series of Shanghai A share stock market, Shanghai B share stock market, Shenzhen A share stock market, Shenzhen B share stock market, respectively. For there are about 250

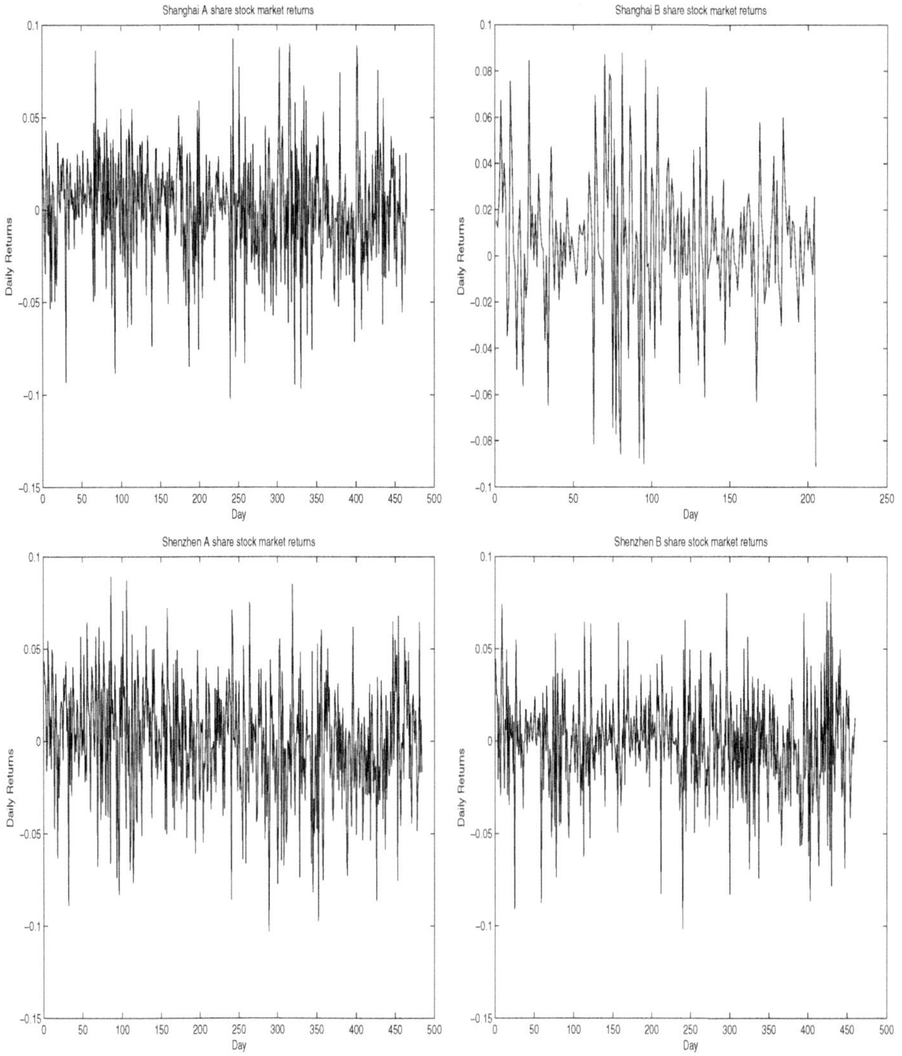

Fig. 1. Daily log-return series for the stock market of China from January 1, 2007 to December 31, 2008

transaction days one year, so we can regard the sample size as 500. We carried out the 99% VaR estimation using the sample quantiles, and obtained the standard error of this VaR estimates by the method introduced in [3]. Due to the Corollary 2.1, we know the interval centered at the VaR estimates whose length is 3.92 times the estimated standard error can be regarded as a kind of 95% confidence intervals for the real VaR. These results are summarized in Table 1.

Table 1. 99% VaR estimate and its 95% confidence interval for the stock markets of China. The VaR estimates are reported without the negative sign.

	99% VaR estimates	95% confidence intervals
Shanghai A share stock market	0.0689	(0.0472, 0.0906)
Shanghai B share stock market	0.0788	(0.0723, 0.0853)
Shenzhen A share stock market	0.0643	(0.0511, 0.0775)
Shenzhen B share stock market	0.0597	(0.0436, 0.0758)

References

1. Artzner, P., Delbaen, F., Eber, J.M., Heath, D.: Coherent measure of risk. Mathematical Finance 9(3), 203–228 (1999)
2. Berkes, I., Hörmann, S., Schauer, J.: Asymptotic results for the empirical process of stationary sequences. Stochastic Processes and Their Aapplications 119, 1298–1324 (2009)
3. Chen, S.X., Tang, C.Y.: Nonparametric inference of Value-at-Risk for dependent financial returns. Journal of Financial Econometrics 3, 227–255 (2005)
4. Rosenblatt, M.: A central limit theorem and a strong mixing condition. Proc. Natl. Acad. Sci. 42, 43–47 (1956)
5. Rosenblatt, M.: Stationary sequences and random fields. Birkhäuser, Basel (1985)
6. Serfling, R.J.: Approximation Theorems of Mathematical Statistics. Wiley Series in Probability and Mathematical Statistics (1980)
7. Wei, X.L., Yang, S.C., Yu, K.M., Yang, X., Xing, G.D.: Bahadur representation of linear kernel quantile estimator of VaR under α-mixing assumptions. Journal of Statistics Planning and Inference 140(7), 1620–1634 (2010)

The Financial Decentralization of the Local Communities in Romania – A Challenge or a Necessity?

Maria-Cristina Ştefan, Constanţa Popescu, and Corneliu Ştefan

Valahia University of Târgovişte, Str. Regele Carol I, nr. 3,
130024, Dambovita, Romania
tantapop@yahoo.com

Abstract. Decentralization is a mechanism by means of which the local administration authorities receive the authority and the resources allowing them to make decisions concerning the provision of public services. The balancing of the local budgets in Romania is the consequence of the financial decentralization, according to which the local communities were entrusted with/allotted their responsibilities and then they were entrusted with/allotted their resources as well. The separation of the attributions of the central and of the local administration conditions the way the revenues and the expenses were distributed between the two levels. This process depends on the degree of regional development, on the concentration of the population on its welfare degree, on the tasks each community has to face, on the possibility of financing the foreseen expenses from local resources.

Keywords: decentralization, local budgets, balancing local budgets.

1 Introduction

The substantiation of an adequate policy for the realization of the financial and administrative decentralization and the balancing of the local budgets in Romania cannot be achieved without respecting several basic principles that the research work and the long-term practical experience of the developed countries have highlighted.

The allotting of the financial resources able to support the decentralization process, the unitary implementation of the logistic resources, the adequate human resource and the objective working standards represent criteria for the realization of the efficiency and quality of the public services provided.

2 Implications of Financial Decentralization on the Local Budgets Balancing Policy

The local budgets of the local public administration authorities in Romania include a section related to functioning (comprising the current expenses needed to realize the attributions and competences foreseen by the law) and one related to development (comprising capital-related expenses), which are approved as annexes of each budget. In the process of local budget balancing shall be analyzed the possibility of covering the

Q. Zhou (Ed.): ISAEBD 2011, Part II, CCIS 209, pp. 9–15, 2011.

section related to functioning from one's own revenues, and only where such is the case, there will be sums proposed for balancing this section so as to assure the minimal cost and quality standards to provide the necessary public services to the population. After that, within the limit of the sums that can be assured from the state budget, shall be established the sums to be included in the local budget development section [1].

In order to assure the vertical and horizontal balancing of the local budgets, the administrative-territorial units have been allotted, from some state budget revenues, certain sums divided on special destinations, namely ratios and sums divided so as to balance the local budgets. The structure and the criteria of allotment of the ratios and sums divided so as to balance the local budgets are established by means of the law of the local public finances. The amount of the sums divided so as to balance the local budgets is established by the state budget law [2].

The realization of this balance is an obligatory condition for carrying out the payments from the local budget whose purpose is to finance certain categories of expenses such as: education, culture, health, social care and protection.

The principles laying at the basis of the allotment of the balancing grants [3] are the following:

- *The principle of correlation* – it supposes that the vertical and the horizontal imbalances should be balanced simultaneously by means of the proposed system, which includes both conditional grants (transfers with special destination), and unconditional grants (transfers with general destination);
- *The principle of adequacy* – it relies on the rule according to which the balancing formula has to assure to the local authorities adequate resources corresponding to the national priorities and assuring local autonomy;
- *The principle of allotment* – it allows a correct resource allotment by assuring higher sums to the administrations with a lower fiscal capacity and higher financial needs;
- *The principle of transparency* – according to which the balancing formula needs to be simple, oriented towards the leveling of the fiscal capacity and/or the fiscal needs, to be understood by all those involved and to be substantiated on the basis of objective factors, so as to have no possibility of exerting manipulations or negotiations concerning it;
- *The principle of the differential approach in order to realize the budget balancing* – it relies on two ways of obtaining the balancing:
  - The first balancing method aims to balance the fiscal capacity per inhabitant, which supposes the measuring of the local tax basis and of the local fiscal effort;
  - The second balancing method concerns the equalization of the differences in needs per inhabitant which supposes the reflection of the differences between the local administrations concerning their demographic, socioeconomic and geographic features.
- *The principle of motivation* – supposes that the balancing formula should not generate negative stimuli in the gathering of one's own revenues (local taxes and tolls) and should not include inefficient choices in the spending of the funds;
- *The principle of the limited use of conditional grants* – it relies on the rule according to which the transfer of new responsibilities to the local authorities and the limited use of conditional grants imposes the increase of the number of indicators contained by the balancing formula.

Although we are talking about decentralization, especially in the financial domain, the available balancing sums are allotted according to a recentralization criterion associated to a strictly statistic sharing. On the one hand, it is not the local public administration authorities that share most of these sums, but the deconcentrated institution that is the General Direction of Public Finances and this happens on the basis of a strict formula that does not take into account the concrete situation in the territory (it is known that we have local communities that are large as area and small as population and, at the opposite end, communities that are large as population and small as area, yet their problems can be identical or different regardless of this quantitative issue).

On the other hand, although it is desired that the administrative territorial units in Romania should build fist of all a budget for functioning, the Departmental Councils can allot 20% of the balancing sums only for co-financing infrastructure projects that concern local development. Under these circumstances, the local administration intervenes mathematically, without considering the needs, the subsidiarity, the decentralization, etc. and allots as well the sums that used to remain until now directly at the local authorities for balancing.

The revenues from the central level have as a main objective the correction of some imbalances intervening locally:

- both vertically (the level of the local taxes and tolls does not cover the necessary expenses for the provision of the public services);
- and horizontally, as not all the local communities have an adequate financial capacity, although they have the obligation of providing equivalent services qualitatively and quantitatively.

The way the local budgets balancing is realized triggers waves of discontent every year. The issue of the impossibility of covering local needs using a mathematical formula has been often invoked, especially by the local public administration authorities, in parallel to the insufficiency of the funds allotted from the central level. However, as a result of the decentralization, the responsibility for assuring sufficient local revenues should be the problem of the local administration authorities, who should be concerned first of all with finding solutions to supplement their revenues locally and only then should they request funds from the central level [4].

A balancing system that does not rely on a transparently used calculation formula cannot be considered an objective and efficient system. Seeing the lack of a clear formula, uniformly applied for all the localities, the balancing policy remains subject to subjectivism and arbitrariness, unable to accomplish its main goal: to reduce the differences related especially to the localities' financial capacity. The revenues from the central level must not be sufficient, but must come as a complement, for the local authorities to be stimulated to realize their own revenues. At the same time, one should assure the balance between the competences of the local authorities and the decentralized resources.

The need to rationalize the spending from the local budgets becomes a must for the local authorities, in the context in which the share represented by contributions from the state budget tends to become increasingly low. The government claims the insufficiency of the state budget resources and asks the local public authorities to make supplementary efforts to increase their own resources.

3 Opportunities of Financing the Financial Decentralization

In the circumstances of the increase of the decisional autonomy and of the limitation of the state intervention, the responsibility for resource management is transferred almost integrally to the local authorities [5]. Insufficient resources compared to the needs implicitly determine the need to implement adequate public policies by rationalizing the local public spending, as well as by attracting supplementary European funds.

The structural funds are funds that the European Union has available for its member states being part of the "Cohesion policy of the European Union". Between 2007 and 2013, the reformed cohesion policy of the EU will try to provide a better answer to the goals established through the Lisbon and Göteborg strategies, namely: competitive economy based on knowledge, research and technological development, sustainable development, employment.

In fact, the correct denomination of these funds is that of structural instruments. The structural instruments are a form of non-reimbursable financing, but they function on the basis of the co-financing principle. The projects are co-financed especially from public funds of the Member State, but they can be drawn from private funds as well.

Among the structural instruments are included community funds meant to reduce the differences in development between the EU member states and between their regions. For ERDF (European Regional Development Fund), ESF (European Social Fund), EAFRD (European Agricultural Fund for Rural Development), and EFF (European Fisheries Fund) the maximum ratio for the EU intervention is of 75%, yet for Romania it will be of 85% of the total eligible costs, while for the CF (Cohesion Fund) it is either of maximum 80% of the total eligible costs or maximum 85% of the total cost. For Romania, the intervention rate of the European Union in the case of the Cohesion Fund will be as well of 85% [6].

The structural funds and cohesion funds are the financial instruments by means of which the EU acts to eliminate the economic and social disparities among its regions, in order to realize an economic and social cohesion, putting the accent on knowledge and innovation, on the creation of more and better jobs, on interregional cooperation and on the transformation of the regions into attractive places for investment and work.

The cohesion policy has three goals:

☞ Convergence – to support the regions left behind from the viewpoint of their economic development;

☞ Regional Competitiveness and Employment – to support the regions, other than those left behind from the viewpoint of their economic development, to attain the targets of the Lisbon Agenda;

☞ European Territorial Cooperation – to promote a balanced development of the whole community area, by encouraging cooperation and good practices exchange among all the EU regions.

The European Regional Development Fund (ERDF) finances mainly the infrastructure, the job-generating investments, the local development projects and the support for SMEs.

The European Social Fund (ESF) promotes the reintegration of the unemployed and of the underprivileged groups on the labor market, by financing professional training acting activities and recruitment support.

The Cohesion Fund – a structural instrument intervening on the entire national territory and on the territory of the member states whose GDP/inhabitant is situated below the 90% threshold compared to the European average, meant to co-finance not programs, but large projects in the domains environment and transport (trans-European transport networks and sustainable development domains bringing benefits to the environmental protection – efficient energy use, renewable energies, intermodal transport, urban transport and ecological public transport).

The European Agricultural Fund for Rural Development (EAFRD) has the following purposes: to increase competitiveness in the agricultural sector, to develop the rural environment and to improve the standard of living in the rural areas by promoting the diversity of the economic activities.

The European Fisheries Fund (EFF) invests in the development of the living aquatic resources, in the modernization of the fishing boats and in the improvement of the processing and trading of fish products.

The main documents substantiating the financial assistance of the EU for Romania during the programming period 2007-2013, and ensuring its management are:

• **The National Development Plan 2007-2013 (NDP)** – a document of strategic and multiannual planning, guiding and stimulating the economic and social development of Romania for attaining the goal of economic and social cohesion of the European Union; it substantiates the access to Structural Funds after Romania's adhesion to the EU, in quality of Member State; it constitutes the basis of the negotiations with the EU concerning the financial assistance provided to Romania during the above-mentioned programming period.

The national priorities established in the NDP are:

➢ To increase the economic competitiveness and to develop the knowledge-based economy;

➢ To develop and modernize the transport infrastructure;

➢ To protect and improve environmental quality;

➢ To develop human resources, to promote employment and social inclusion and to consolidate administrative capacity;

➢ To develop rural economy and to increase productiveness in agriculture.

• **The National Strategic Reference Framework (NSRF)** – a strategic document connecting the national development priorities, established in the National Development Plan for Romania 2007-2013, and the European priorities concerning the economic and social cohesion and the creation of employment opportunities. According to the National Strategic Reference Framework, for the programming period 2007-2013, Romania elaborated 7 Operational Programs within the Goal "*Convergence*" (Increasing economic competitiveness, Environment, Transport, Regional development, Human resources development, Administrative capacity development and Technical assistance) and collaborates with its neighboring countries and other EU member states to elaborate 11 more Operational Programs within the Goal "*European territorial cooperation*".

• **The Sectorial Operational Programs (SOP) and the Regional Operational Program (ROP)** – they constitute strategic documents detailing the development priorities for each sector and for the promotion of regional development. They represent the mutual engagement of both EU and Romania to find solutions to the aspects identified in the National Development Plan and in the regional development plans concerning the development of the high priority domains and the territorial development. For each priority are established measures and eligible actions. Each Operational Program or Operational Sectorial Program is a chapter with its own strategic approach. The strategy of each operational program comprises Priority Axes that include major intervention domains from which the indicative operations and also the beneficiaries that can ask for financing derive.

- **The Complement Programs (CP)** – these are documents detailing the content of the Operational Programs (beneficiaries, activities, grant level etc.) and the implementation system.

The recourse by the Romanian public administration to borrowings, seen as well as the most probable solution for advancing the sums that are to be reimbursed later on within the accessing of the structural funds, raises a series of problems, of which the most significant are related to:

- ➢ the absence of an adequate and favorable legislation;
- ➢ the lack of total clarity concerning the patrimonial problems of the local public authority;
- ➢ the persistence of certain inadequate mindsets among the local representatives and public clerks;
- ➢ the lack of specialists in the carrying out of such operations;
- ➢ the weak operating capacity of the state treasury;
- ➢ the lack of financial credibility of the public authorities in front of the Romanian banking environment (which, in its turn, is quite unstable);
- ➢ the motivation of the population, of the local representatives or public clerks concerning the choice and support of such a financing alternative;
- ➢ the determination of the maximum indebtment level that can be managed, under good conditions, by a local public administration authority, avoiding in this sense an over-indebtment etc. [5]

The local public authorities need to become knowledgeable in the practice of financial planning, in close correlation with the development programs and strategies, in order to know exactly how much, when, and why to allot the public money, in conditions of efficiency.

Making use of the credit market is just one of the solutions that can support local development and can help access structural funds. Another solution, worth considering, is the public-private partnership, a particular interest going to the inter-community development associations, aimed expressedly as potential demanders of international funds [5].

The concept of public-private partnership expresses a way of cooperation between a public authority and the private sector, respectively NGOs, businessmen associations or companies in order to realize a project producing positive effects on the labor market and on the local development. A development of the public-private partnerships will not be possible, in the businessmen's opinion of, without a profound modification of the legislation, which is at present full of gaps and leaves room to interpretations. Moreover, the system application framework is relatively restrained; the actual implementation framework is not motivating enough to attract significant investments and lacks decisional transparency. In the average and long run, this situation will affect the development of the public sector in Romania itself, as it will be unable to take over from the private sector the managerial experience needed for an efficient and coherent management of the public resources.

4 Conclusions

The issue of the administrative and financial decentralization remains an important issue for the actual context of the public policies in Romania. The process of decentralization of the administrative activity has no content and can become dangerous if it is not accompanied by the financial decentralization able to support the accomplishment of the new responsibilities incumbent to the local public authorities.

In order to improve the public services financing and the budget balancing system, by means of the Law no. 273/2006, the criteria of repartition of the balancing sums on the administrative-territorial units of each county were modified, using the principle of the "exclusion" so as to assure a minimum revenue per inhabitant out of the tax on income at least at the level of the average per county.

In the repartition of the balancing sums for the administrative-territorial units in each county, transparency has grown, through the replacement of the county councils, which are a political organism, by the general public finances directions, which are administrative structures.

The access to the Structural and Cohesion Funds will allow Romania to develop in a balanced way the regions left behind, to modernize the transport and environmental infrastructure, to support rural development, to create new employment opportunities, especially in the rural area, to promote social policies leading to the improvement of the standard of living.

At the same time, the public-private partnership introduces a new paradigm in the assurance of social welfare and is a means for the attainment of multiple purposes: savings in public expenses, the improvement of the public services quality, increasing the efficiency of the public administration organs operations and improving the chances of efficiency of the policies chosen and implemented.

References

1. Drăcea, M.: Stadiul descentralizării financiare în România, Revista Finanţe – Provocările viitorului, Anul VI, Nr. 6/2007, p. 92 (2007)
2. Legea cadru a descentralizării nr. 195/2006, Monitorul Oficial al României, nr. 453 din 25.05.2006
3. Tobă, M., Giosan, V., Moraru, A.: Politici de echilibrare a bugetelor locale în România, Institutul pentru Politici Publice, Bucureşti, p. 12 (2005)
4. Onofrei, M., Bercu, A.M.: Implicaţii financiare ale descentralizării activităţii administrative, Analele Ştiinţifice ale Universităţii Alexandru Ioan Cuza din Iaşi, p. 500 (2004-2005)
5. Crişan, L.I., Crişan, G.: Capacitatea administrativă şi financiară a comunităţilor locale – premisă pentru accesarea fondurilor structurale, Studia Universitatis Vasile Goldiş" Arad – Seria Ştiinţe Economice 18/2008, vol. I, p. 204-205, 208 (2008)
6. `http://www.eurobestteam.ro/instrumente-structurale`

Study on the Management and Control Model of Cash Flow in Enterprises

Ying He, Ruihua Bai, and Jiao Dong

School of Economics and Management,
Beijing University of Posts and Telecommunications,
Beijing, China
Heyingcn2001@yahoo.com.cn

Abstract. The gradual promotion and implementation of financial transformation in enterprises has created a more perfect control environment and opportunity for entire management and control of cash flow and value management in enterprises. So this paper tries to establish the management and control model of cash flow in enterprises. The model is composed of two parts: strategic management of cash flow and tactical management of cash flow, concerning four levels: operators, managers, monitors and decision-makers. Its core contents include three parts: strategic planning of cash flow and cash value-added (objective), 'three-dimension' balance of management and control of cash flow and cash flow budget (process) and performance evaluation of cash flow (result). It is a complete self-contained feedback system, which is composed of 'objective- process- result', and the enterprise physical flow, information flow and capital flow provide the support of basic data for the model.

Keywords: Cash Flow, Cash Value-Added, Management and Control Model.

1 Introduction

With the change of the internal and external circumstances in enterprises, profit-oriented model of financial management has break up and the age of financial management which takes cash flow as the core is coming. With the progressive expand of the enterprise business scale, the broadening of the geographical distribution, the gradual extend of the management chain and the constant change of the organizational boundaries, how to manage and control the cash flow of different levels and dimensions to ensure the organic unification of the risk control and value creation has become a burning important issue. So this paper tries to establish the management and control model of cash flow in enterprises, and achieve overall financial management control in enterprises through the management and control of cash flow, so as to promote financial competitiveness continually and finally succeed in fierce competitions.

Q. Zhou (Ed.): ISAEBD 2011, Part II, CCIS 209, pp. 16–23, 2011.

2 The Management of Cash Flow: Literature Review

The Management of Cash flow is the management activities of deploying the direction, amount, process and velocity of cash flow at different times rationally through forecasts and planning, implementation and control, information-sending and reports, and analysis and evaluation to achieve the enterprises' objective of value maximization. The research about the theory of cash flow and cash flow management began in the 1950s in foreign countries, and according to its different fundamental objectives, the theory of cash flow can be divided into four phases: management of liquidity, management of surplus cash, control of cash balance and transnational cash management. The research mainly concentrated in the following aspects. The first is the analysis about the factors influencing cash flow. It's mainly about the internal and external factors in enterprises (such as scale, inflation, exchange rate fluctuations and so on), and the influences of enterprise operation actions (such as the production process, sales behavior, collection management and so on) on the cash flow. The most representative is Denison's study about the induction effects of sales growth and inflation pressure on the cash shortage, and Welsh's study on the influences of enterprise size on cash flow. The second is about the application of cash flow indicators in the financial analysis and evaluation. The most representative is Walter applied cash flow indicators for the financial analysis and crisis early warning at the first time, and this analyzing method led to the establishment of financial warning system. The third is about the study on the relationship between cash flow and enterprise investment and financing conducts. That is, researching the effects of cash flow on investment decisions, financing decisions and policies of the dividend payment. The most representative is Jason's free cash flow theory of results from investment, and Myers and Majluf's pecking order theory. The fourth is the study on the effects of cash flow information on external market efficiency. Its representative is Eugene Fama's effective capital market theory. The fifth is the study on the relationship between cash flow and enterprise value. It's mainly represented by Jason's theory of free cash flow. The study on the management of cash flow in China started fairly late, and the following are some more influential results: First, Zhibin Chen proposed the value-creating management model of cash flow in 2007. This model includes two parts (internal and external), three dimensions (vertical, horizontal and lateral), three blocks (investment activities, financing activities and operating activities), four variables (direction, amount, process and velocity) and five appraisal indicators. It controls cash flow by different levels, blocks and factors, and it's a relatively mature structural framework. Second, Chang Cai put forward an integrated mode of value-promotion in 2007.Taking strengthening cash flow and improving enterprise value as the objective and blended with the relevant policies, measures and methods of the growth of cash flow and value, it found a quick and efficient operation and management mode for creating cash flow and promoting enterprise value. Third, Jiangsu Power Company suggested the "map" model of cash flow in 2005. After investigating, analyzing and testing the factors affecting the scale and the quality of cash flow, it suggested the structural model of the management of cash flow and the analyzing system of cash flow indicators, and finally formed the management and control system of cash flow accommodating to the enterprise development strategy.

3 The Establishment on the Management and Control Model of Cash Flow in Enterprises

The design of the management and control model of cash flow should comply with the ideology of 'structured', 'systematic' and 'combined', and render complex and undetermined information related to cash flow as different dimensions and levels to reflect its completeness, systematicness and importance of value-creation. The management and control of cash flow is a complex process, including several factors such as the direction, amount, process and velocity of cash flow; several levels such as operators, managers, monitors and decision-makers; several dimensions such as growth management, earnings management and risk management. It's too difficult for unsystematic management means and methods to achieve the objective of the management of cash flow, so a comprehensive paradigm of the management of cash flow must be established to take account of all factors, all levels and all dimensions and make them structured, systematic and combined. The basic framework of the management and control model of cash flow is shown as Figure 1.

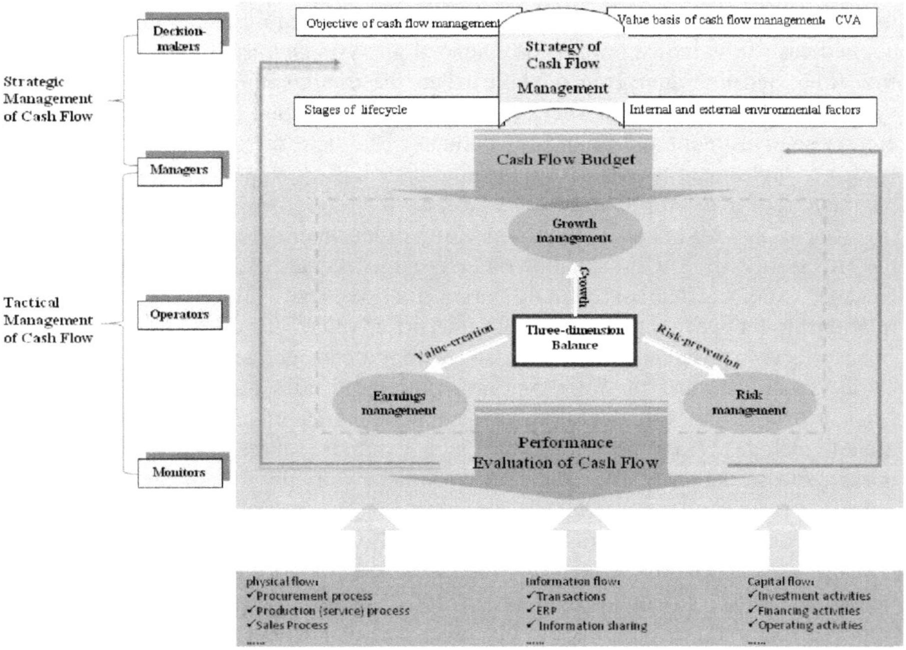

Fig. 1. Basic framework of management and control model of cash flow in enterprises

The model is composed of two parts: strategic management of cash flow and tactical management of cash flow, concerning four levels: operators, managers, monitors and decision-makers. Its core contents include three parts: strategic planning of cash flow and cash value-added (objective), 'three-dimension' balance of management and control of cash flow and cash flow budget (process) and performance evaluation of cash flow (result). It is a complete self-contained feedback system, which is composed of 'objective- process- result', and the enterprise physical flow, information flow and capital flow provide the support of basic data for the model.

3.1 Strategic Planning of Cash Flow and Cash Value-Added —Objective

Strategic Planning of Cash Flow. Strategic planning of cash flow is exploring how to manage and control cash flow to create value appreciation continually from strategic perspective, and it is the dynamic plan and balance between growth, value-creation and risk prevention in essence. The factors influencing the development of management strategy of cash flow include: the stage of lifecycle the enterprise is at, the objective of the management of cash flow, the internal and external environmental factors in enterprises and so forth. ①Different stages of enterprise lifecycle lead to different development strategies, different organization structures and different capital structures. Enterprise financial strategy is based on its overall development strategy, and a financial strategy coordinated with the overall strategy provides financial support for the development of corporation in turn. Cash flow strategy is the core of financial strategy. A successful manager must be able to analyze and identify the enterprise positioning and different corresponding laws of cash flow movements at different stages of lifecycle accurately, and manage the key or leading cash flow of this stage effectively to achieve the enterprise objective of creating value continually. ②The objective of the management of cash flow decides the general direction of making cash flow strategy. The aim of the management of cash flow should be value-creation (CVA). This is decided by the essence of capital, and it is the inevitable result of environmental changes and innate needs of the enterprise development and investors and the stakeholders. The main objective of the management of cash flow includes: safety, profitability and sustainability.③The actual operating condition is the outcome of the comprehensive influences of enterprise various internal and external factors. The management of cash flow in enterprises is not the simple management of internal cash flow, but comprehensively considering the enterprise internal and external environmental influencing factors to improve the efficiency and effectiveness of cash flow management.

Strategic Objectives of Cash Flow—Creating Cash Value-Added. Cash value-added (CVA) is the value basis of the management and control of cash flow in enterprises. It is put forward by Swedish scholars, Erik Ottosson and Fredik Weissenrieder, in 1996, and it is a new value-evaluation model which is based on integrated operating capital flow, risk management of capital cost and operation of investment projects. The purpose of CVA model is using cash flow as a tool to evaluate enterprise performance and provide basis for managers' strategic investment decisions.

The basic formula of CVA model is:

CVA=OCF(Operating cash flow)—OCFD(Operating cash flow demanded)
=EBITDA—Variations of net working capital—Non-strategic investments—Investment capital×Capital cost

=EBITDA—Variations of net working capital—Non-strategic investments—(Current capital + Non-current capital —Interest-free liabilities)×(Rate of return on capital + Investment recovery rate + Tax rate)

Both cash value-added (CVA) and economic value-added (EVA) are very important methods of value management and indicators of value measurement. They measure and evaluate enterprise performance from different angles, and their similarities and differences are shown in Figure 2:

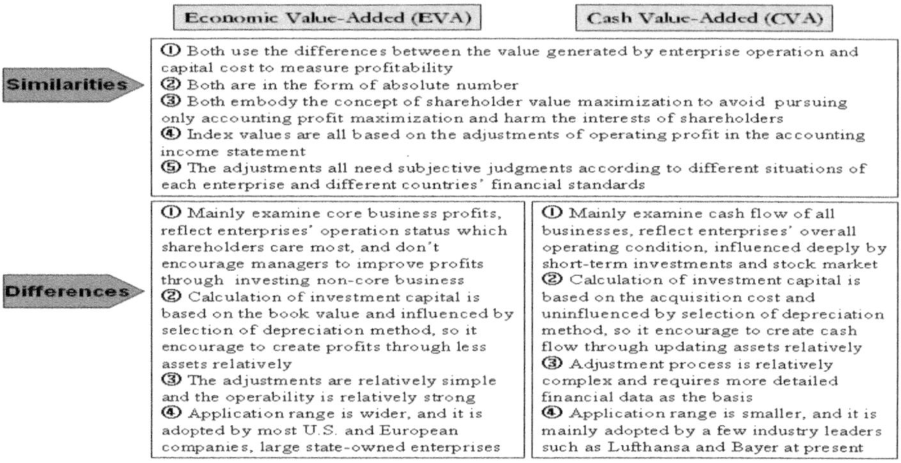

Fig. 2. Similarities and differences between CVA and EVA

In summary, CVA model makes up the defect of traditional net present value (NPV) model. What CVA model based on cash flow choose is the indicators of cash flow. It avoids the local distortion of accounting principles and the subjectivity of accrual accounting, so it's more objective and fair. Meanwhile, CVA model based on cash flow conform to the fact that enterprises' value comes from the cash flow generated by corporations and the ability to return on investment based on cash flow, and it is consistent with enterprise value management. CVA model combine investment decision analysis in the past, operational performance evaluation of the current project with performance evaluation of the project's residual value in the future, and it's propitious to enterprises' project management and value creation.

3.2 'Three-Dimension' Balance of Management and Control of Cash Flow and Cash Flow Budget—Process

The management of cash flow is the balance between growth, value-creation and risk-prevention in essence. The growth of cash flow is mainly to pursue sustainable growth through the outflow of investment cash flow; value-creation is achieved through the management of direction, amount and velocity of cash flow; there are many risks in the process of growth, and we should prevent them through the process optimization of cash flow and internal control. Growth management, earnings management and risk management of cash flow is three aspects which must be focused on to improve the efficiency of the management and control of cash flow and achieve sustainable value creation, and the whole process of the management and control of cash flow is the process of dynamic equilibrium between them.

Growth Management of Cash Flow. Management and operational personnel must attach great importance to the match of strategic cash flow and free cash flow in the management and control of cash flow, so as to achieve sustainable growth of cash flow. These match include: the match of the needs of investment cash outflow and current free cash flow, the match of investment cash flow and free cash flow generated by investment projects in future (the future free cash flow contains future free cash not only generated by new investment projects, but also generated by existing business in future), and the match of financing cash flow and enterprises' financing flexibility in future.

Earnings Management of Cash Flow. Earnings management of cash flow mainly includes the management and control of direction, amount and velocity of cash flow. ① The direction of cash flow investment not only determines enterprises' development direction, but also determines enterprises' investment decisions ; It not only has a long-term effect on enterprises' cash flow, but also decides enterprises' ability to create new cash flow and basic pattern of value-creation. Its influences on enterprises are fundamental. Therefore, the first task of the management of cash flow is to determine the strategy of cash flow direction. Making the enterprises' strategy of cash flow direction is a comprehensive and long-term planning of cash flow direction according to enterprises' internal and external environmental factors and their variation trend. ②The management of amount of cash flow mainly includes two parts: one is the cash inventory------a time-point indicator which reflects the cash amounts of enterprises' entire business or a single value chain at a time; and the other is the cash increment------a period indicator which comprehensively reflects the augmenter of the whole cash flow after cash flow management or implementing a project. The management of amount of cash flow is aimed to balance cash flow inventory of each sector and keep entire best surplus. Its objective is to ensure cash flow can meet the demands of enterprises' day-to-day operation, but meanwhile cash shouldn't overstock so as to waste. ③The management of velocity of cash flow is mainly about the management of efficiency of cash use. The velocity of cash flow is measured by cash turnover period. The shorter the turnover period, the quicker the velocity of cash flow, the larger the amounts of cash participated in production, operation and investment, and the higher the efficiency of cash use. The management of velocity of cash flow is mainly about the management of conversion time between stock, accounts receivable, accounts payable, long-term assets and cash flow. So we should reduce inventory, speed up recovery of accounts receivable, and prolong payment of accounts payable, so as to accelerate the backflow of cash flow and achieve sustainable value-creation.

Risk Management of Cash Flow. Risk management of cash flow mainly refers to the management and control of process of cash flow, and its objective is optimizing the process of cash flow and improving the internal control of cash flow. The process management of cash flow involves many contents, and to be specific, it includes the program of cash circulation and the arrangements of key points of internal control, referring to the organizations, appointment and authorization of cash flow, procedures of cash receipts and payment businesses, the design of internal control institution of cash, the arrangements of credit policy, the recovery of accounts receivable, the withdrawal of sales finance, the arrangements of process, the arrangements of relative cash financing, the responsibility clarify and performance evaluation of each internal control link, and the establishment of relative early warning system. The major risk facing in the management of cash flow includes (Zhibin Chen, 2007): risk based on value, risk based on legislation and risk based on operation, so risk management of cash flow mainly refers to three aspects: decision-making control system of strategic cash flow to prevent risk based on value, internal control system to prevent risk based on legislation and financial early warning system to prevent liquidity risk.

Cash flow budget and the management and control of cash flow are two different conceptions, but they complement each other and are interdependent and integral in the implement of the management of cash flow. In order to achieve the objective of the management and control of cash flow, it must use cash flow budget, this useful tool. If enterprises don't make cash flow budget, their managers can't have a clear knowledge of cash flow they own and will create. So they will be at a loss how to manage and control cash flow, and 'three-dimension' balance and the objective of creating CVA will be impossible to achieve. Cash flow budget is the advance deployment of enterprise resource from the angle of cash. Cash flow budget provides reference standards for the management and control of cash flow, and it also provides evaluation basis for operating performance. The drawing-up, implementation, feedback and adjustment of cash flow budget go with the management and control of cash flow all the way, and they respond to each other with the management and evaluation process of cash flow.

3.3 Performance Evaluation of Cash Flow—Result

Cash flow performance evaluation is the measurement of the results of the management and control of cash flow and it is oriented towards the objective of the management of cash flow. The introduction of performance evaluation index system of cash flow can not only quantizes the management and control model of cash flow to generate financial management and control system centering cash flow, but also coordinates the management objective of cash flow to regulate, guide and appraise the management activities of cash flow in enterprises. The performance evaluation index system of cash flow must be oriented towards the objective of the management of cash flow, and keep consistency with the management and control model of cash flow. The performance evaluation system can be divided into three layers (See Figure 3): The first layer is the objective layer, the subject of evaluation; the second layer is the sub-objective layer, the contents of evaluation; the third layer is the index layer, the specific measurement indicators.

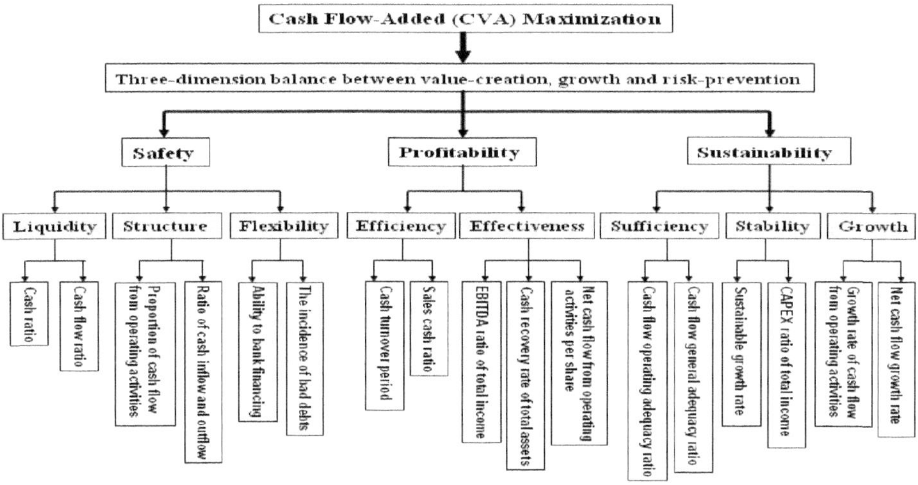

Fig. 3. The performance evaluation system of cash flow

4 Conclusion

Traditional management of cash flow focuses on the tactical level, aims to keep the liquidity of enterprise cash and emphasizes the balance management of cash flow, while modern management of cash flow emphasizes both the strategic level and tactical level in enterprises, and also implements overall management and control of cash flow for different levels and dimensions of organizations to reach the organic unity of risk control and value-creation. In short, if enterprises want to establish the management and control model of financial centralization which takes enterprise development strategy as guidance, optimizing the allocation of financial resources as core, strengthening the comprehensive risk management as protection and continuing to create value-added as goal in word and deed, the management and control of cash flow is the root and guarantee.

References

1. Rajan, G., Zingales: Finance Dependence and Growth. The American Economic Review, 559–586 (1998)
2. King, R.G., Levine, R.: Finance and Growth: Schumpeter Might Be Right. The Quarterly Journal of Economics, 717–738 (1993)
3. Pagano, M.: Financial Markets and Growth: An Overview. European Economic Review, 613–622 (1993)
4. Fama, E.F.: Efficient Capital Markets: II. The Journal of Finance, 1575–1617 (1991)
5. Liu, Q.: Cash Flow Management: Risk Control and Value Creation. Yunnan University Press, Kunming (2010)
6. Chen, Z.: The Value-creation Management Theory of Cash Flow. Nanjing University Press, Nanjing (2007)

The Evaluation Model of Financial Competitiveness in Telecom Enterprises

Ying He, Jiao Dong, and Ruihua Bai

School of Economics and Management,
Beijing University of Posts and Telecommunications,
Beijing, China
Heyingcn2001@yahoo.com.cn

Abstract. With the telecom enterprises' profit being continuously diluted, shareholders haven't yet reduced their request on the return of investment. The duel-pressure of market competition and capital markets has impelled the telecom enterprises to change towards efficient development. The enterprises need to commit the financial transformation, progressively implement the meticulous management and truly put all efficiency management into effect, so that they can continuously improve their performance and financial competitiveness. The current domestic and overseas researches on financial competitiveness of enterprises are most in the phase of concept definition and theoretical explanation, yet to establish normative and practical evaluation model of financial competitiveness. So after summarizing the definitions of financial competitiveness, this paper put forward an evaluation model of financial competitiveness in telecom enterprises. And then use the factor analysis and fuzzy comprehensive evaluation method to make an empirical research on the world top 20 telecom enterprises which are from the Fortune 500 companies, and make a systematical research on the critical path of improving the financial competitiveness of our domestic telecom enterprises.

Keywords: Telecom Enterprise, Financial competitiveness, Factor Analysis Method, Fuzzy Comprehensive Evaluation.

1 Introduction

In recent years, with the saturation of the telecom market, the growth space of telecom business has been rapidly shrinking. The growth of enterprises' performance and value are trapped, and the increase of revenue is in a bottleneck stage with a continuously slowing down growth rate, so they can no longer effectively drive the increase of enterprises' performance. At the same time, the growth of cost and resource consumption seems inevitable in the context of the increasing market competition, service improvement and financial transformation. Therefore, how to maintain a strong financial competitiveness of enterprise in order to ensure sustainable growth in all telecom enterprises has become an important problem. In July 9, 2010, Fortune the website published the Fortune 500 companies of 2009,

Q. Zhou (Ed.): ISAEBD 2011, Part II, CCIS 209, pp. 24–32, 2011.

which includes 23 telecom enterprises. Compared with the previous year, the number had increased by 2 enterprises, while the average ranking had declined. To Chinese telecom enterprises, the reorganization of the telecommunication industry in 2008 brought a dramatic expansion of scale to China Mobile, China Telecom and China Unicom. Especially, China Telecom and China Unicom came into the list of Fortune 500 for the first time in 2008. There is an increase on rankings on all three telecom enterprises, but the Fortune 500 companies list, which based on the operating revenue, can not represent the financial competitiveness of an enterprise. The duel-pressure of market competition and capital market push the telecom enterprises to change toward effective development, actively promoting financial transformation, i.e. to change from traditional accounting and administration to strategic financial management. The strategic financial management is a financial management process which is strategy oriented, and focused on strategy. It is a transformation from focusing on accounting to resource integration, decision supporting and value management (Ying He, 2009). The purpose of financial transformation is to achieve an organic unity of growth management and cost management, and consistently improve the financial competitiveness to support the enterprise's strategy transformation. The correctly evaluating the financial competitiveness and exploring the improving path is the premise and method to objectively assessing enterprise's growth quality and achieve economic value added.

2 Financial Competitiveness: Literature Review

2.1 Financial Competitiveness

In recent years, both academics and practitioners have been paying more and more attention to the financial competitiveness. It is generally believed that the goal to maximize enterprise value is not by enhancing implementation of a particular management targets, but the resources of the enterprise fine management, the integration of the resource capacity to enhance the core competitiveness of enterprise services, business owners and maintain their core competencies in order to increase business value. As part of the core competitiveness of enterprises, improve financial competitiveness of the enterprise value maximization has become an important part. The content of the financial definition of competitiveness has not yet formed a unified understanding in the current academic circles. Research on financial competitiveness is mainly focused on three aspects: the elements, performance evaluation and the value.

The researches on the elements composing financial competitiveness mainly include: Chenglin Hao (2006) put forward the logic relationship among the elements of financial competitiveness: financial competitiveness = (financial Strategy + financial resources + financial management capability) × execution. Jinhao Ou (2006) thought that the competitiveness of its financial mechanism can be divided into two stages, namely: the development of financial capability and access to financial resources, stage of integration of financial resources and financial competitiveness of the financial ability to form stage. Qian Li and Li Zhang (2007) divided the financial competitiveness into five aspects: financial strategy for sustainable development, flexible financial management capacity, financial resources for sustainable growth, sustainable improved financial executive power and continuous financial innovation.

The method used to evaluate the financial competitiveness performance of enterprise are relatively more widely. To take some examples: Xiao Zhu (2007) divided the financial competitiveness into three sub-levels: financial survivability, financial growth and financial potential. He used factor analysis to make an analysis on the listed companies in China. Yi Yang and Yuan Chen (2008) developed a set of evaluation index system from the perspective of cash flow, and then they analyzed the listed companies in liquor and beverage industry, using data envelopment analysis. Huanfeng Liu and Zhe Wang (2009) introduced the concept of entropy and gray theory into the enterprise financial evaluation method. Youtang Zhang (2009) established a three-dimensional evaluation system consists of the financial environment adaptation competitiveness, the financial resources deployment competitiveness and the financial benefits synergy competitiveness.

Ping Wang (2010) defined the enterprise's financial competitiveness, from the perspective of shareholder's value, as the ability to realize the protection to the interests of shareholders during enterprise operation. Its objective is to achieve the investor wealth maximization goal in a long period. In addition, the researches on enterprise's financial competitiveness from the perspective of value also include: Fama and French (1990) proposed when the value-based rate of return of a corporation is greater than the inner rate of return based on the cost, the corporation's investment is effective. The higher the former is than the latter, the stronger financial competitiveness the corporation has. The economic value added put forward by Stern Stewart Inc. is an evaluation method of enterprise's financial as well.

To summary the above definitions of financial competitiveness, we can draw a conclusion: first, most of the current research on the financial competitiveness remain in the general theory level, and the practical operation is relatively poor. We think that when analyzing the financial competitiveness of companies from different industries, the evaluation indicators and criteria should vary with the specific industry's characteristics. Second, in choosing the objective of financial competitiveness, this paper argues that the promotion of financial competitiveness is not only to enhance customer value or shareholder wealth, but rather serve to maximize enterprise value. Third, the above definitions of financial competitiveness did not describe the external representation. This paper believes that the financial competitiveness is routed in the enterprise's financial resources and financial management activities, and whether financial competitiveness of an enterprise is high or low can be reflected by its financial performance is good or poor.

Therefore, this paper defines financial competitiveness as an integrated ability reflected by enterprise's profitability, risk control capability and growth capability, which aims to improve the enterprise's financial performance and service for the maximization of enterprise's value. This paper will take the perspective of financial performance, and use the factor analysis together with fuzzy comprehensive evaluation method to carry out an empirical research on financial competitiveness of telecom enterprises.

2.2 The Evaluation Index System of Financial Competitiveness

On the part of financial competitiveness evaluation index system design, Heqing Wu (2008) decomposed the financial competitiveness into five fist-level indicators: financial activities capacity, sustainable financial profitability, sustainable financial innovation, and adaptability to changes. Then 17 second-level indicators were developed under the first-level indicators. However, some indicators of the evaluation criteria are ambiguous and not suitable for practice. Youtang Zhang (2009) established a three-dimensional evaluation system consists of the financial environment adaptation competitiveness, the financial resources deployment competitiveness and the financial benefits synergy competitiveness. Xiao Zhu (2009) used 17 specific indexes to carry out an empirical research on the companies listed in China, based on the three aspects: financial survivability, financial growth and financial potential.

Taking account of the characteristics and operation position of telecom enterprises, following the five principles in designing an evaluation index system – comprehensiveness, materiality, stratification, maneuverability and practical applicability, we design the evaluation index system of financial competitiveness in telecom enterprises as follows:

Table 1. Evaluation Index System of Financial Competitiveness in Telecom Enterprises

General Objective	First-level Index	Second-level Index
Financial Competitiveness	Profitability	Main Business Profit Margin
		Return of Assets
		Return of Equity
		EVA Margin
		EBITDA Ratio of Total Income
	Solvency	Debt-to-assets Ratio
		Current Ratio
		Interest Protection Multiples
	Assets Management Capability	Total Assets Turnover
		Fixed Assets Turnover
		Receivables Turnover Ratio
	Growth Ability	Total Assets Growth Rate
		Main Business's Growth Rate of Income
		Net Income Growth Rate
		Earnings per Share Growth Rate
		CAPEX Ratio of Total Income
	Cash Support Capability	Cash Flow from Sales Ratio
		Assets Cash Recovery
		Free Cash Flow Ratio of Total Income

3 The Evaluation Model of Financial Competitiveness in Telecom Enterprises

In order to carry out an empirical research on financial competitiveness of telecom enterprises, this paper chooses top 20 from 23 telecom enterprises, which are in the Fortune 500 companies. The data used for calculating the second-level indexes are chosen from the companies' fiscal year 2009 annual reports, which the fiscal year in Japanese companies goes from Apr. 1 this year to next Mar. 31, so Japanese companies' data are selected from their 2010 annual reports. As the second-level indexes calculated, we will use the SPSS 13.0 software to do the data processing.

In methodology, this paper adopts a factor analysis together with fuzzy comprehensive evaluation method. Based on this method, we can integrate the decision makers' subjective judgments into indexes' objective evaluation, thus avoiding the weakness that AHP and principal components analysis can easily be manipulated. The evaluation results can not only evaluate the overall financial competitiveness of enterprise, but also compare each level to in order to explore the financial performance short board of enterprise. The steps are: first, make the factor analysis on each first-level index respectively, calculating the samples' factor scores; then, use fuzzy comprehensive evaluation method to determine the weight of the fist-level indexes; finally, calculate the financial competitiveness score by weighted average.

3.1 Factor Analysis

First, extract the common factors. Generally speaking, for a sample $x_i(i=1,2,...,m)$, and it has a certain volume of m. Because there is a certain correlation between each observed variable, so we usually find n common factors $F_j(j=1,2,...,n)$ to integrate the different types of information existing in various observed variables. The common factors are uncorrelated. So the relationship between common factors and observed variables can be presented by a matrix as follows:

$$X = AF + \varepsilon \quad . \tag{1}$$

Among which: $a_{ij}(i=1,2,...,m; j=1,2,...,n)$ is called factor loading, and it represents the common factor j 's factor loading on the variable i . The bigger the absolute value of a_{ij}, the more variable i can be explained by common factor j. $\varepsilon_i(i=1,2,...,m)$ is called residual factor, the part of observed variables which cannot be explained by common factors. Usually, they are negligible in calculation.

The purpose of factor analysis is to use several factors to replace the original various observed variables. So in practice, we usually chose the first common factors whose cumulative variance contribution rate of extraction is greater than 80%.

Before doing factor analysis on fist-level indexes, we need do KMO test and Bartlett's Test of sphericity on sample data. It shows that all the results of KMO test are bigger than 0.5, indicating that these sample data are suitable for factor analysis. All the results of Bartlett's Test of sphericity are less than 0.05, so we can believe that when the significance level is 95%, the sample data are suitable for factor analysis.

According to the cumulative contribution rate of more than 80% of the variance principle, we make factor analysis on sample data and the common factors of each first-level index are shown in talbe2:

Table 2. The Common Factors and Variance Contribution of Each First-level Index

First-level Index	Common Factor	Eigenvalue	Variance Contribution (%)	Cumulative Variance Contribution (%)
Profitability	F_{1-1}	2.867	38.266	38.266
	F_{2-1}	1.068	30.400	68.665
	F_{3-1}	0.540	20.823	89.488
Solvency	F_{1-2}	1.581	48.909	48.909
	F_{2-2}	0.894	33.618	82.527
Assets Management Capability	F_{1-3}	1.519	50.000	50.000
	F_{2-3}	0.481	50.000	100.000
Growth Ability	F_{1-4}	2.184	42.156	42.156
	F_{2-4}	1.120	21.809	63.965
	F_{3-4}	0.936	20.836	84.802
Cash Support Capability	F_{1-5}	1.652	52.559	52.559
	F_{2-5}	0.949	34.143	86.702

Secondly, calculate the factor score of each first-level index. We choose the rotated variance contribution rate of common factors as the weights, calculating the factor scores by a linear combination of the second-level indexes. The formula is as follows:

$$F = \omega_1 F_1 + \omega_2 F_2 + \cdots + \omega_n F_n \quad (2)$$

3.2 Use Fuzzy Comprehensive Evaluation Method to Calculate the Weight of Each First-Level Index

Assume that the weight of first-level index k is $d_k\ (k = 1,2,3,4,5)$.

First, determine the ranking of importance of the five first-level indexes in evaluating the financial competitiveness. Taking account of the characteristics of telecom industry's current development stage, the relative importance of five first-level indexes is based on the results of expert surveys. Then we get the superiority dual matrix among the first-level indexes:

$$E = \begin{bmatrix} 0.5 & 1 & 1 & 1 & 1 \\ 0 & 0.5 & 0 & 0 & 1 \\ 0 & 1 & 0.5 & 0 & 1 \\ 0 & 1 & 1 & 0.5 & 1 \\ 0 & 0 & 0 & 0 & 0.5 \end{bmatrix} . \quad (3)$$

The matrix above has passed the consistency test, and we can rank the importance of each first-level index to financial competitiveness. The rankings are: profitability, growth ability, assets management capacity, solvency and cash support capability, in a weakening importance.

Secondly, determine the memberships values of each first-level index to financial competitiveness, according to the ranking of first-level indexes. In the last step of analysis, the profitability got the highest importance, therefore, we set the profitability as the standard, and then make comparisons between profitability and growth ability, assets management capacity, solvency, cash support capability one by one. We draw a conclusion after comparison: compared with growth ability, the importance of profitability lays between "obviously important" and "significant important"; compared with the assets management capability, profitability is "very important"; compared with solvency, profitability' importance lies between "great important" and "extremely important"; compared with cash support capability, profitability is "extremely important". Thus, we can use the tone operators to define the superiority mentioned in last step.

Thirdly, normalize the membership values in order to get the evaluation weights of each first-level indexes. According to the above judgments, we can find the membership value of each first-level index's importance to financial competitiveness by looking up the table. Being normalized, the weight vector of first-level index is:

$$d_k' = (0.5311, 0.0759, 0.1328, 0.2013, 0.0589)^T \quad (4)$$

3.3 Calculate the Overall Score of Financial Competitiveness

We use this formula to calculate the sample's overall score:

$$Z = \sum_{k=1}^{5} d_k F_k \quad (5)$$

The scores and rankings are shown in table 3:

Table 3. Overall Score and Rankings of Financial Competitiveness of 20 Telecom Enterprises

Rankings in Fortune 500	Company Name	Profitability		Solvency		Assets Management Capability		Growth Ability		Cash Support Capability		Financial Competitiveness		EVA Margin
		Score	Rankings	Score	Rankings	Score	Rankings	Score	Rankings	Score	Rankings	Score	Rankings	Rankings
1	ATT	-0.24	13	0.18	5	-0.34	14	-0.19	13	-0.02	9	-0.2	14	11
2	NTT	0.02	7	1.78	1	0.11	7	1.02	2	0.97	1	0.42	3	7
3	Verizon	0.30	5	-0.21	14	-0.58	17	-0.07	6	-0.31	17	0.03	9	12
4	Deutsche Telecom	-0.16	10	-0.15	9	-0.19	13	-0.21	16	-0.14	12	-0.17	13	19
5	Telefonica	0.50	4	-0.33	16	-0.05	10	-0.13	10	-0.19	13	0.19	6	5
6	China Mobile	1.09	2	1.11	2	-0.07	12	0.13	6	0.56	3	0.71	1	2
7	Vodafone	-0.14	9	-0.18	11	-0.39	15	0.19	4	-0.23	15	-0.12	11	18
8	France Telecom	-0.28	15	-0.38	17	-0.02	9	-0.27	18	-0.21	14	-0.25	16	10
9	Telecom Italia	-0.22	11	-0.16	10	-0.88	19	-0.20	14	-0.38	18	-0.31	17	8
10	Vivendi	0.12	6	-0.20	12	0.52	3	-0.23	17	0.07	7	0.08	7	13
11	KDDI	-0.25	14	0.50	3	0.30	5	-0.09	7	0.36	4	-0.05	10	9
12	Comcast	-0.23	12	-0.45	19	-0.91	20	-0.12	9	-0.55	20	-0.33	18	16
13	China Telecom	-0.33	16	-0.29	15	-0.44	16	1.54	1	-0.30	16	0.04	8	14
14	BT	-0.56	19	-0.96	20	0.21	6	-0.92	20	-0.43	19	-0.55	20	3
15	Sprint Nextel	-0.68	20	0.10	6	0.06	8	-0.36	19	0.07	8	-0.41	19	20
16	Softbank	-0.39	17	-0.03	7	0.52	4	-0.09	8	0.16	5	-0.15	12	15
17	America Movil	1.24	1	-0.14	8	0.59	2	-0.14	11	0.13	6	0.71	2	1
18	China United Telecom	-0.49	18	0.41	4	-0.72	18	0.54	3	-0.03	10	-0.22	15	17
19	DirectTV Group	-0.11	8	-0.38	18	2.34	1	-0.16	12	0.60	2	0.23	5	6
20	Telstra	0.80	3	-0.21	13	-0.05	11	-0.21	15	-0.13	11	0.35	4	4

3.4 Results

By analyzing the above calculation results we can find that China Mobile, China Telecom and China Unicom locate in 6, 13, 18 respectively in the list of Fortune 500 companies, and their financial competitiveness rankings are 1, 8 and 15 respectively, indicating that our nation's three telecom enterprises are comparatively more financial competitive. In terms of five first-level index of financial competitiveness, three telecom enterprises all have a low asset management capability, which China Mobile,

China Telecom and China Unicom ranks 12, 16 and 18 respectively. The three enterprises' average and below ability of total assets turnover and fixed assets turnover are directly affected by our country's telecom policy and current telecom market competition position. China Mobile's total assets have arrived 751,386 million Yuan, including 360,075 million Yuan fixed assets. The annual report shows that the fixed assets investments are most about telecom transceiver machinery and equipment, switching center, transmission and other network facilities. China Telecom's net property, plant and equipment arrived 283,628 million yuan by the end of 2009, of which plant and equipment, communication network reached 216,349 million yuan. China Unicom's fixed assets arrived 285,035 million yuan by the end of 2009, of which only one entity, communication device, occupies 233,172 million yuan. The three operators' investments on communication devices account for almost 80% of their fixed assets investments. Since our country reorganized telecom industry and decided to develop 3G network in 2008, the three capital intensive telecom enterprises have a further expansion on the scale by merger and acquisition. Meanwhile, three operators invest heavily to 3G's network construction and business promotion, hoping to occupy a certain market share and more competitive advantage in the 3G era. However, the rapid expansion of the scale hasn't resulted in a significant improvement in operating income. Therefore, poor assets management capability is a common problem of Chinese telecom enterprises, i.e. the telecom enterprises in China have strong hard power, while lack of soft power.

Financial competitiveness of China Mobile ranks 1st, and its efficiency of value creation, EVA rate, ranks 2nd, while profitability, solvency and cash support capability are all at a high level. But its growth capability is lower than China Telecom and China Unicom, while the main difference comes from the capital expenditure. Affected by the economic development level, the telecom industry in some developed countries has stepped into mature sage, with characteristic that the average capital expenditure maintains between 10-15%. However, in order to develop 3G businesses, the Chinese operators' CAPEX ratios of total income are relatively higher; especially China Unicom's CAPEX ratio of total income in 2009 was as high as 71.02%, of which 60% were invested to 3G, infrastructure and transmission network. China Mobile didn't make such drastic investment.

China Telecom fluctuates widely on the ranks of five first-level indexes. Its growth capability ranks 1st, while its profitability, solvency, assets management capability and cash support capability are at a low level. Such a high growth capability is mainly driven by an extraordinarily high growth of net profit. After reorganization, China Telecom expanded its business from fixed voice to mobile voice. Compared with 2008, there is only a small decline on 2009's fixed voice revenue, but in terms of mobile voice, the revenue realized an increase from 2,955 to 20,027 million Yuan, and there also has a big growth in the value added services driven by mobile business. In terms of profitability, China Telecom's business cost is too high, leaving its main business profit margin is only 10.82%, and the return of assets is only 3.47%. Its EVA rate is still negative, meaning that it hasn't created value. To improve profitability, China Telecom must implement fine management and strengthen its cost control. The increase on capital expenditure resulted in a lower free cash flow, cash support capability and liquidity.

China Unicom has a similar situation as China Telecom, and it has a poor performance on profitability, assets management capability and cash support capability. The main business profit margin of China Unicom is only 7.75%, and EVA rate is -5.74%. Therefore, it must strengthen the cost efficiency, focusing on the control of administration and selling expenses. At the same time, China Unicom must endeavor to attract high-end customers, carry out value added service, and improve return on investment. China Unicom made a high capital investment in 2009, making a negative free cash flow. While maintaining a positive free cash flow is the premise and protection to achieve sustainable development and financial risk prevention.

4 Conclusion

With the gradual promotion and implementation of financial transformation, it becomes a universal agreement among telecom enterprise that we can achieve the value management by improving financial competitiveness. For the evaluation of financial competitiveness can be based on different aspects, such as: cash flow, value creation and comprehensive performance and etc, this paper mainly builds a comprehensive performance-based evaluation index system of financial competitiveness, and then carry out an empirical research using factor analysis fuzzy comprehensive evaluation method. Being scientific and objective, telecom enterprises can find the main path to improve financial competitiveness by analyzing the results. And this paper has a significant practical value to the deepening of financial transformation and maximization of enterprise's value.

References

1. Gode, D., Mohanram, P.: Inferring the Cost of Capital Usingthe Ohlson-Juettner Model. Review of Accounting Studies (2003)
2. Leech, N.L., Barrett, K.C., Mohan, G.A.: SPSS for Intermediate Statistics Use and Interpretation. Publishing House of Electronics Industry, Beijing (2009)
3. Hitt, M.A., Duane Ireland, R., Hoskisson, R.E.: Strategic Management; Competitiveness and Globalization; Concepts. Tsinghua University Press, Beijing (2006)
4. Fama, E.F., French, K.R.: The Corporate Cost of Capital and the Return on Corporate Investment. Journal of Finance 54 (1999)
5. Hao, C., Qi, R., Guo, J.: Study on Enterprise's Financial Core Competence. Accounting Communications Academic Edition, (3), pp. 70–72 (2006)
6. Ou, J., Liu, X.: Study on Enterprise's Financial Competitiveness under the New Financial View. Finance & Economy (12), 178–179 (2006)
7. Zhu, X.: Research and Analysis about Standardization of Financial Competitiveness of Listed Companies. Accounting Communications Academic Edition (7), 17–19 (2007)
8. Wang, P.: Capital Cost, Protection of Shareholder's Interests and Enterprise's Financial Competitiveness. Accounting Communications, Comprehensive Edition (10), 6–7 (2010)

Multiple Perspective of Public Administration Development Strategy of NGOs

Weigong Du[1], Yujie Song[1], and Yanfang Li[2]

[1] College of Business Management, Wuhan Polytechnic University, China
[2] Military Economics Academy, Wuhan, China
wgd48551@yahoo.com

Abstract. Public management is the governmental and non-governmental public organizations in the use of public power have handled the process of social and public affairs, to the effective promotion and fair distribution of social and public interests. From the resulting sense is a function of public organizations, including government-led public organizations and the public interest to point to the non-governmental organizations to achieve public interest, to provide public goods and services activities.

Keywords: Public management, Non-governmental organizations, Strategy.

1 Introduction

Social needs of the diverse and changing government functions so that activities of Chinese non-governmental organizations the field of diversity. Through the construction of non-governmental organizations can effectively promote the efficiency of governmental organizations, responsibility, democracy, legal system, the effective realization of public interests and collective interests or the interests of individuals with diverse, non-governmental organizations, integration is conducive to reducing government's administrative costs, building service-oriented government to promote and facilitate the role. Since reform and opening, the development of Chinese non-governmental organizations faces unprecedented opportunity. Of course, in the face of opportunities, also faces many problems and challenges.

2 The Meaning of Non-governmental Organizations and Being in Public Management Position in the Subject

Non-governmental organizations, the English full-called "non-government organization", the English abbreviation for "NGO", refers to a specific legal system, which government departments not to be regarded as associations, societies, foundations, charitable trusts, companies or other non-profit corporate, not-for-profit non-governmental organizations. United Nations non-governmental organization is defined as: at the local, national or international level organized non-profit, voluntary civic organizations. They provide a

Q. Zhou (Ed.): ISAEBD 2011, Part II, CCIS 209, pp. 33–39, 2011.

wide range of services and play a humanitarian role, to the Government the concerns of citizens, monitor policies and encourage political participation on the community level.

In many areas of public administration, the government has not enough energy to meet, close to the grassroots non-governmental organizations rely on to understand the feelings of superiority, with a more professional capacity, through a variety of ways to participate in public administration, make up deficiencies, to provide public goods and public services.

3 Our Wide Range of Defects in Non-governmental Organizations and Confusion

NGOs are diverse body of social media management, buffer zone, safety valves, regulators, and mediation. Non-governmental organizations to establish a dialogue between government and citizens, consultation and communication mechanisms, bringing together the views from all walks of life, as communication with the masses of the party and state relations between the bridge and link. NGOs in China is still a new thing, most people's understanding of NGOs is also very limited, coupled with some understanding of the errors, now there are still many obstacles that could sweep away - most of which are caused by bureaucracy - is a serious impediment to its development.

3.1 Non-governmental Organizations Set Up More Stringent Conditions

Currently, to become NGO (non-governmental organizations) in the non-profit organization, which are most unable to meet the official application to the high standards required for registration. These include "the size of funds shall not be less than 100,000 yuan," "must employ at least two full-time staff," and so on, in this context, most organizations can not be officially recognized as a "non-governmental organizations", to achieve such high barriers to entry, only after becoming only more channels NGO funding to achieve the standards set by the government.

3.2 Not Included in the List of Officially Licensed, Non-governmental Organizations, a Platform and Space Is Very Limited

Despite public become more aware of the potential of non-profit organization, we need to step up publicity to enable it to more effectively bring about positive change for the country. Many insiders point out that a considerable number of grassroots groups want to be the voice of social progress, but most organizations can not meet the prerequisites for difficult to do so.

3.3 Lack of Funds, Poor Operation Mechanism

Lack of funding for NGOs is a common problem worldwide, China is much more prominent. This is because, despite the reform and opening up China's economic development has made great achievements, but overall, China is still a poor and backward countries. So far, the Government encourages individuals and businesses donator's measures also extremely limited.

3.4 NGOs Human Resources, Lack of Relevant Knowledge and Experience

From the investigation, China's NGOs are fewer full-time, the more the lack of volunteers. Many of China's existing NGOs or government agencies from the former separate institutions, and even been called the "second government" or "quasi-government." Some of them retained the original of a bureaucracy, not to understand the management skills of NGOs, NGOs lack of innovation, flexibility, lack of resolution of social problems, to meet the needs of the community experience and means.

4 Hinder the Development of Multiple Causes of Non-governmental Organizations

China's non-governmental organizations has been widely active in technology, law, education, culture, health, employment, sports, environmental protection, social services, economic services in all areas of social life for the people involved in economic, political, cultural and social life to provide an important carrier and means. In the preceding analysis, how many actually have been involved in obstruction of the reasons for multiple non-governmental organizations, as follows:

4.1 The Market Mechanism Is Imperfect

Driving force of economic growth as the market mechanism, market-oriented reforms in China since the 90s of last century, while rapid advance, the market system has not increased at the same maturity. Overall birth of non-governmental organizations in China, but the mechanism is not perfect as the current non-governmental organizations will play an active role in the restriction of production. This inevitably makes the current of non-governmental organizations play an active role which has been greatly restricted.

4.2 The Lack of Community Supervision

Although there are specialized non-governmental organization and management agency, a very limited number of institutions, regulatory authorities can register non-governmental organizations, and the annual inspection as the main form of supervision, and operations departments have their own main business, usually without too much effort or do not want to manage the daily activities of non-governmental organizations, and the competent authorities and non-governmental organizations often have a joint relationship, it is difficult to play a supervisory role.

4.3 Serious Lack of Funds

Various types of donors (such as foundations, overseas-funded institutions) funded projects tend to focus only, not for non-government organization's own capacity building. Non-governmental organizations in the daily administrative expenses, the lack of internal staff training funds, some donors are only used to subsidize disadvantaged groups, rather than the operation of projects funded public institutions themselves. People tend to ignore the implementation of project activities is also a non-governmental organizations need funding to maintain its operations, the implementation of the project only when the ability of NGOs, the donor contributions are to play a greater role.

4.4 Government Functions Blocked

Our Government monopoly in many aspects of the implementation of direct production model, the proportion of monopolistic state-owned enterprises is too large, bureaucratic system, control the color of relatively strong type of government, the government in China's economic development process of society as a whole played a too strong (and low efficiency co-exist) role, and this is bound to suppress, including non-governmental organizations outside the government system, including the development of other organizations, so the smooth transition of government functions not greatly restricted the non-governmental organizations play an active role.

4.5 Social Capital Is Missing

The market economic system being adapt to the current of nature and the ideology has not been a fundamental change in the cultural; the foundation of market economy is still relatively weak, an important aspect of improving the social environment. The development of non-governmental organizations and environmental requirements of society is out of tune; this social environment is not suited to conversion of the hysteretic and also greatly restricted the non-governmental organizations play an active role.

4.6 The Legal System Is Not Perfect

Although the Chinese government is actively concerned about non-governmental organizations to establish registration and management framework of the legal system more complete, that does not mean that the hair of non-governmental organizations have been active in promoting the rule of law or protection. At this stage, because of the lack of institutionalized channels to protect the communication between the NGO and the government in terms of producing results which rely on the personal and media elite.

5 The Development of China's Strategy of Non-governmental Organizations

With China's reforming and opening up to unprecedented opportunities for development, while the healthy development of NGOs and the reform and opening up are the boosters. However, from the current status of NGOs, China's NGOs are still inadequate, weak independence and other issues, it is difficult to undertake the functions of government transfers to meet the needs of the community. Therefore recommended that:

5.1 With the Partnership Established by the Government to Form a Good Interactive Response Mechanism

China's state-dominated society in political behavior, although the governance of public affairs, non-governmental organizations have open borders, but the government as the most powerful social organization, the community still have the most powerful force to interfere. Effective crisis management is necessarily a selective retreat government, non-governmental organizations have chosen to enter, the two mutual trusts, mutual support, interdependence, to carry out a variety of contractual, institutional alliances, establishes good and friendly partners' relationship to achieve effective governance of public crisis.

5.2 To Promote Freedom of Opinion, the Establishment of Public Oversight Mechanisms

A good public opinion environment must meet the need for democratic politics. Improve the environment of public opinion in public opinion, for the promotion of democratic political construction of great benefit. Echoes with them to achieve this role, it also depends on the "social trust" this accumulation of social capital. Non-governmental organizations in order to pursue the area of governance in public affairs and government organizations, equality, cooperation, legal system and the system must be designed with two clear areas of governance in public affairs, rights, responsibilities and obligations, that is, define their own governance margin.

5.3 To Increase the Government's Economic Investment, and Low the Threshold of the Establishment of Non-governmental Organizations

"Financial" pointed out: "China does not register much larger than the number of NGO registered with the NGO". This led to the current situation, and it is relevant to the NGOs "misreading" a relationship. All along, the "non-government sector" lack of real understanding. Rather than let a large number of NGO legal statuses in a clear state, the establishment of NGO is lower than the real threshold, so that each volunteer can do the work in the public service, people can be easy to form a legitimate organization. Government should not go to block, but more is going to lead.

5.4 The Right of Guiding the Development of Non-governmental Organizations

Role of non-governmental organizations are in the function of public services and so there is still a wide gap between the Governments which should vigorously strengthen legislation and actively cultivate non-governmental organizations, to reduce direct government intervention, let assume the Government is unable to provide or provide good public services. The Government should be based on the needs of society and government management, comprehensive use of economic, legal, public opinion, and necessary administrative means, planned, guided and focused the development of non-governmental organizations, regulating development, grasp the pace of development, will guide the development of non-governmental organizations into the overall economic and social development planning.

5.5 Strengthening Capacity Building and Continuous Improvement of Social Environment

Sustainable development strategy, vigorously promote resource-saving and environment-friendly society, and promote economic, social and environmental development of comprehensive, coordinated, well-off society steadily improve environmental quality. In short, we should by all means work in all directions, forming together, cause with the economic system, political system reform deepening and transformation of government functions, the gradual development of non-governmental organizations on track, and its ability to continue to strengthen.

5.6 Expedite the Development of NGOs Legal Regulations

Chinese non-governmental organization representatives and maintenance of the rights and interests of the diverse demands of conducting self-management, development services on behalf of the group's overall interests and rights of appeal, on behalf of the marginalized social aspirations and voices involved in the development and monitoring of political decision-making. In short, crisis management of the law to define the powers and responsibilities of each of the main boundaries of the law regulate and restrict the power of running.

6 Conclusion

China's official non-governmental organizations, etc. establish the governance structure of the Council, but a considerable part of the organization's Governing Council is useless. China's non-governmental organizations have achieved some development, but still in its infancy, especially in building an effective non-profit organization to promote the cultivation, development and management of the Legal System, is still a need for long-term efforts of systems engineering. The face of a market economy, the inevitable trend of pluralistic governance, we need a good system conditions to promote the healthy development of non-governmental organizations, and gradually establish a mature civil society.

References

[1] Zhongze Wu. Development of NGO status and its management, non-profit organization set out in China Management Training report set. Tsinghua University NGO Research Center, ed., Beijing (1999)

[2] Dongmin, W., Dong, X.: Non-Profit Organization Management. China Renmin University Press, Beijing (2003)

[3] Zhao, L.: Non-governmental organizations and sustainable development. Economic Science Press, Beijing (1998)

[4] Gu, J.: Non-governmental organizations and their role in the rise of. Shanghai Jiaotong University (Social Science Edition) (2003)

[5] Road winds. Unit: a special social organization. "Social Science" 1989, No. 1. Nonprofit organization management cadre training class in China Report Set, Internal (1989)
[6] Lebanon. Public Management. Higher Education Press, Beijing (2003)
[7] Zhang, J.: The Government's role in economic development. Economic Management Press, Beijing (2001)
[8] Gong, P.: The process of legal modernization in China. On the volume. China People's Public Security University Press, Beijing (1991)

Case Teaching in the Course of Water Economy*

Yuqiang Wang, Qunge Hu, and Yinghua Wang

Zhejiang Water Conservancy and Hydropower College,
Zhejiang Hangzhou 310018
wangyq@zjwchc.com

Abstract. Water Economy course is a professional basic course for the course with the characteristics and the training goal, a detailed analysis of the current situation and the teaching of hydraulic engineering economic problems in teaching on the teaching method conducted in-depth thinking, put forward several recommendations for the relevant officers.

Keywords: case teaching, hydraulic economic programs, present situation, recommendations.

Since the end of the century, along with the continuous development of market economy and improve people's concept of engineering economy gradually. Society to adapt with the times and the economy made by people at the same time, the industry with its own characteristics, but also made the project a new understanding of the economy, evaluation and measurement criteria. Water economy of which is a typical example.

In recent years, as the country's drag on the water industry continues to increase, natural resources --- water resources development, utilization and protection are more and more people value, followed by a growing water conservancy construction tasks increase, which makes the project with a water feature Water economy in the entire economy ----- Status during construction is more important.

Water Economy course is an important water conservancy professional basic course is to study how to make the project technology to achieve maximum economic benefits practice a discipline of how to select the project technology from the economic point of view the best or satisfactory The principle method of the program.

1 The Current Status of the Teaching Water Economy

1.1 Hydraulic Characteristics of the Economic Program

Water courses and other professional economic foundation course there are obvious differences, it has a practical hydraulic engineering, integration, independence and accuracy of economic, seriousness and so on.

---

* The ministry of water resources demonstrations specialized funding ; Zhejiang Characteristics and specialized funding; Zhejiang Water Conservancy And Hydropower College Key professional funding; Zhejiang Province in 2010 to enhance the level of local institutions of special funded projects; School Education project in 2011 funded projects of Zhejiang Water Conservancy and Hydropower College (XGJ-201103).

Q. Zhou (Ed.): ISAEBD 2011, Part II, CCIS 209, pp. 40–46, 2011.

(1) Practical

Water itself is a practical engineering economic course practice and experience, should be used on reality. The main elements are mostly for the project investment, project income, calculation methods and the actual project evaluation methods, and highly practical.

(2) Comprehensive

Course contains theoretical knowledge related to the economy, water conservancy, electric power, irrigation, navigation, resources, environment and systems and knowledge management theory and other disciplines, with strong comprehensive. To learn this course, we must understand and master the basic theories related to knowledge.

(3) Independence

Water economy and efficiency of the investment program includes two parts content. The terms of investment in water conservancy projects, are relatively simple and easy, but involves the investment share, the more difficult, to be considered relatively comprehensive; the terms of the benefits, considering the financial benefits and economic benefits both to make effective calculation more difficult.

(4) Accuracy

Water economy continue to be among the areas of economics, and in the field of economics, anything related to the contents related to the economy, the relative requirements more stringent, requiring that their very high accuracy, in order to serve the economic purposes of the calculation. Therefore, the use of hydraulic economic knowledge to be able to build water conservancy projects in the early stage of construction and building sufficient to provide reasonable after the convincing theoretical basis for the decision makers with a strong theoretical basis.

(5) Seriousness

Water economy in the process of applying to all aspects of involving the knowledge and content and data, are to be treated seriously, makes the whole process of construction, time and effectiveness of the project to evaluate the investment constraints to play a project management role in cost control.

2 Water and Economic Status of the Teaching Problems [1]

2.1 The Equipment of Teachers

As a practical hydraulic engineering economy courses, comprehensive, independence, accuracy, and the seriousness of the theory of large span, the reality of the teaching requirements and the needs of society have a certain talent gap, and the teachers teaching in the lack of practical engineering Economic calculation and evaluation experience, and the resulting two problems: first, ideas problems. Important theory in the teaching process, light practice, the teaching process scripted, too much emphasis on systematic knowledge, consistency, comprehensiveness and rigor, can not meet the requirements of education and training purposes. Second, the lack of practical ability. Most of the teachers after graduating from school directly to the podium, from school to school, but as a shift, the lack of calculation and evaluation of actual project experience, it is difficult competent skills training requirements.

2.2 The Teaching System and Materials

Traditionally, we refer to the teaching system of elite education, but by the traditional educational thinking, teaching system, water system and the knowledge re-instill discipline, light ability and overall quality of education still exists. Elite education teaching materials are used, many materials are rather biased towards the elaboration of theoretical methods and formulas are derived. Although the economic evaluation of water conservancy projects covering all aspects of content, but can not meet the training model and educational requirements and completion of this course, students can not understand the reality of the actual operation project, still not solve the water conservancy construction in the process of cost control and economic evaluation of the practical problems.

2.3 Ways and Means of Teaching

Outdated teaching content, methods are backward, Comparison of single, divorced and engineering practice. Traditional teaching methods and the basic method is the use of classroom teaching, and course there is a lot of theoretical knowledge and other knowledge Deriving formula doctrines taught entirely through the way teachers teach to students, less effective; and because teachers lack practical engineering and economic calculations Evaluation of work experience, a lack of lively lectures, we can not attract the attention of students; although students have some professional basis, but the lack of comprehensive analysis and practical knowledge, so that students in the learning process can only passively accept the theory of knowledge, can not take the initiative participation in learning and practice.

Application of knowledge in teaching, innovative spirit and practice ability inadequate attention, expertise, training is also relatively weak, it is difficult to make students develop proficient knowledge, skills and ability to adapt to changing knowledge, did not fully reflect the essence of education quality and capacity characteristics. In the teaching process, are more theoretical teaching, practical teaching relatively small, so students only a rough hydraulic theory of economic knowledge, not to mention a particular method, an evaluation of content and in-depth evaluation understanding and skilled master.

3 Hydraulic Engineering Case Study of Economic Programs

Currently, research on and interpretation of case teaching more, but these explanations have a common characteristic, that is, the characteristics of case teaching are the actual life of society, or is there a problem that we want included in the occurred within the typical real things or events to be used in the teaching process, in the hope to enhance the students about the things that impression, so as to achieve a clearer understanding of the purpose. Will be the use of actual cases is different from other methods of case teaching the key.

Often the case that we use is a description of the actual event, in this case, we want to contain or explain the issues implicit, and sometimes also contains solutions to these problems, in discussing the use of the process of teacher education case when Richart (Richert, A.. E), said: "Teaching Case describes teaching practice, it is to enrich the narrative form, to demonstrate some of the teachers and students includes the typical behavior, thoughts, feelings The story included [2]. "

In order to make our economy in the teaching of hydraulic engineering students are more profound understanding of its important content, we need the teaching of this course the use of case teaching, and the economic content of the case involving hydraulic often have the following characteristics:

(1) Is the project itself, there really is in real life, not hypothetical or imaginary. In these cases, often through the entire event actually happened, to enhance the students throughout the implementation process of building water conservancy projects, the occurrence or possible dynamic economic control or understanding of economic management activities of the event more clearly.

(2) Construction of the project which involves all aspects of the economy there are some problems or difficult, or difficult each of these issues there is some connection between and constraints, there are problems, conflicts, mutual promotion and mutual restraint, which requires After a reasonable economic comparison, a careful analysis, to make the right judgments, through such case, the students will have a vivid idea, if they own, how to handle these things.

(3) The use of the teaching process has some typical cases. Water project construction by this typical case, can explain a certain type of problems, giving students the inspiration and guidance. Teaching through a typical case, the whole case in detail according to different nodes separately, when necessary, can in turn use to illustrate a contrast problem.

It can be seen, often from teachers directly involved in the case of research subjects,theproduction of a variety of related issues and cases scattered books, the information in the literature selected, processed and sorted out the typical case, write the information into case teaching counseling, establish a case base [3]. In fact it is teachers will be involved in the actual water conservancy construction in the economic issues to show students, teachers guide students in the classes, based on the active conduct of its own reading, research, guide the class through the teacher to understand. Shows the case of hydraulic engineering economic course instructor teaching is not only a special choice of teaching materials, but also the use of these materials, the instructor of special skills and tools.

4 Case Study Teaching on the Economic Role of Hydraulic

(1) The use of case teaching, making the teaching process is no longer hydraulic boring economy, greatly stimulated the enthusiasm of students.

(2) Case study, the actual project's economic problems are often a large variability exists, which virtually increase the teachers during the process of case teaching, to improve their practical ability to solve problems, to cope with the teaching that may occur when "was asked.

Case teaching is training teachers to develop innovative and practical problem solving ability and quality

(3) The use case can also be training teachers to promote good theoretical knowledge and expand their knowledge of teachers.

(4) The use of case teaching, and more easy to form a dialogue and interaction between students and teachers, for teachers in the teaching process control emotions play a positive role in the classroom.

(5) Are often taken from actual cases the actual problems in construction, therefore, it allows students to master the theoretical knowledge of the events which occurred during the process easier to form links between, making the theory and practice of the "distance" greatly shortening [4].

(6) Water economy through the use of case teaching is more likely to accept the economic concepts, making economic analysis more deeply, become a potential sense of educating people.

5 Case-Based Teaching on Water Economy Suggestions for Teaching

Teaching for the hydraulic status of the economy and problems in teaching, to make a few suggestions:

5.1 The Case Study Will Apply the Concept of Integration into the Construction of Teachers, Improve Teacher Practice Teaching Ability and Level

(1) Teachers actively participate in the economy actually works in practice and training, drawing on practical experience in production, improve professional skills.

(2) The units involved in the actual works in practice, the situation will be involved in practical projects related to economic issues, the introduction of the daily teaching process, and take in the wild, the actual engineering of engineering economy to move to class, which will Theory and practice of teaching contents of the organic combination of teaching.

5.2 In the Teaching System and Teaching Materials Reflect the Concept of Case Teaching

(1) Education and training objectives by adaptation of the teaching system and materials. In the case of students studying engineering in the process of teaching the theory of the economy, improve their comprehensive ability and quality. The teaching system used in education and teaching should be the characteristics of students to apply their knowledge and learn something with; implement the theory with practice and focus on the overall requirements of practical ability; highlight specific and practical, convenient for students to learn, and actively cultivate creativity in our students.

(2) Using a wide range of materials. Materials to be readable and teachable, and satisfy students and teachers bilateral expectations[5]. Organization of teaching materials is the main basis is the main tool for teaching and learning, good teaching materials on the guarantee and improve the quality of teaching is very important [6]. This single book Water economy should be hydraulic type materials and similar materials Selected economic case replacement guide students through a case study of

theoretical knowledge. These materials also enhance the student's intuitive ability to accept and deepen the economic control of the construction process, the evaluation of the understanding.Energy and the actual project using a combination of teaching resources, and effective integration into the actual engineering aspects of teaching and the process to.

5.3 Will Be Fully Applied to the Case Teaching Method and Means of Teaching

(1) The use of behavior-oriented method, focusing on teaching, creating a teaching and learning, interaction between teachers and students of social interaction situations. By around a topic,problem or project to carry out teaching and learning activities, the individual capacity for culture. Composed of specific teaching methods: the project approach, role-playing method. These methods are different from the emphasis on teaching the theory of the method.

(2) Project site teaching, strengthen practical links. Practice teaching focus on students ability to apply technology, innovation and practice of quality [7]. The students are more interested in practical projects, so this is an effective way to enable students to abstract water conservancy economy has an intuitive sense of the whole. The minds of the students will be abstract, fragmented knowledge and image of the overall integration of the actual system up and a firm grasp of the knowledge.

(3) The problem of teaching and inspire students to thinking [8]. In teaching, teachers will be the case in the Water as the medium of the economy the main line, on the case analysis, followed by a question raised another issue raised by the continuous and constant problem solving to enable students to master knowledge, as well as other related the intrinsic link between knowledge and the implication of the contradictions, to open up their horizons, and to enlighten the students thinking. This question teaching, but also can improve the enthusiasm of students, so students have learned so much more solid and the consolidation of [9].

(4) The combination of Jing Jiang and go into detail. According to certain teaching requirements, a professor in the curriculum process, analyze the contents, for the basics, to explain the deep, thorough, detailed, and strive to enable students to understand profoundly and grasp. Jing Jiang and go into detail with the combination of both can improve the quality of classroom teaching, but also gives students time to leave more independent thinking, ability to exercise independent thinking of students [10].

At present, the hydraulic status of the economic teaching there is a certain problem, and social skills on the economics and quality talent more and more attention in the innovation and other aspects of the comprehensive ability of relatively high demand, therefore, we should further deepen teaching reform, the theoretical and practical works closely further and actively implemented by relying on the case teaching method works, both to enhance the students knowledge, understanding and consolidation, but also help train students to analyze and solve problems. Water economy of education on ways and means of course a positive improvement and innovation.

References

1. Wang, Y., Du, L., Wang, Y., Chen, B.: Based on CDIO Pattern in Higher Vocational Colleges. Teaching Reform and Study on Hydraulic Engineering Construction. Frontiers of Manufacturing and Design Science 12, 3559–3563 (2010)
2. Richert, A.E.: Case methods and teacher education: vsingcases to teach teacher reflection. In: Tabachnich, B.R., et al. (eds.) Issues and Practices in Inquiry-Oriented Teacher Education (1991)
3. Zhang, X.: Case teaching courses in investment project evaluation in the application. Economist 6, 132–133 (2006)
4. Zheng, J.: Case Study: New way of teacher professional development. Educational Theory and Practice 7, 36–41 (2002)
5. Li, M., Zhang, M.: Engineering economics Reflections on teaching effectiveness. Economist 7, 125–126 (2009)
6. Wang, Z., Hou, Q.: Teaching content and construction of water conservancy construction of Practice Reform. Jilin Water Resources 10, 40–41 (1997)
7. Jiang, M.R., Tan, Y.: Motivation of the construction project cost management, the effect of education. Jiangsu Institute of Education (Social Sciences) 3, 42–43 (2008)
8. Jiang, G., Li, Y., Zhang, Z.: Teaching to improve the quality of water conservancy construction of. Higher Agricultural Education 6, 57–59 (2006)
9. Guo, X.: Can improve the effectiveness of several methods of teaching. Finance Teachingand Research 5, 61–62 (2001)
10. Li, M., Zhang, M.: Engineering economics Reflections on teaching effectiveness. Economist 7, 125–126 (2009)

Virtual Organization of Construction Project Based on Project Life Cycle

Lei Jiang[1], Xiaodong Chen[2], and Xiaohong Zhang[3]

[1] Department of Civil engineering and Architecture, Dalian Nationalities University, Liaoning Dalian, P. R. China
[2] Facilty of Infrastructure Engineering, Dalian University of Technology, Liaoning Dalian, P. R. China
[3] Department of Management, City Institute, Dalian University of Technology, Liaoning Dalian, P. R. China
{jianglei0310,xiaodong1122,sarah0217}@163.com

Abstract. The organizational structure of construction project determines quality of construction and efficiency of management. This paper combined virtual organizational theory with modern construction project management, and established virtual organization of construction project (VOCP) based on project life cycle. The organizational structure of VOCP is a characteristic horizontal organization, which has only two managerial levels, project management team (PMT) and project team (PT). The management of VOCP is a complex and integrated process, which includes: communication management, cost management, schedule management and quality management. The work process was designed in the consideration of the complexity and interaction of VOCP based on project life cycle.

Keywords: Virtual organization of construction project (VOCP), Project life cycle, Information technology (IT), Management.

1 Introduction

Globalization and information revolution have become two important characteristics of world economy development since 1990s. In a certain time of 21 century, the globalization based on information revolution will still be the main characteristic, and construction industry with no exception. Globalization leads to more and more cooperation which refers to complex communication and cooperation, while information revolution provides an effect platform and foundation for this kind of project. Many scholars have made researches in project management of virtual organization [1, 2] and supply chain management [3, 4], which considers both information flows and different participants.

In this paper, virtual organization theory is presented, and construction project life cycle is taken into account in the organization design. The organization structure is proposed and finally the management of organization is discussed.

Q. Zhou (Ed.): ISAEBD 2011, Part II, CCIS 209, pp. 47–53, 2011.

2 Virtual Organization of Construction Project (VOCP)

Virtual organization is a new type of organization appeared in the 1990s, which is first proposed by Kenneth Preiss , Steven L. Goldnan and Roger N.Nagel [5].It aimed at manufactory and put forward the smart manufacture mode based on virtual organization. After this, numerous scholars made further study in this area, for example, organization design of virtual enterprise based on agent, SME networking coordination operation frame and case study of virtual enterprise [6-8].Most people think that the most important stage in construction project is construction, but other stages which interact with each other in project life cycle are as important as construction. Therefore, a successful construction project doesn't only mean good construction, but also includes excellent planning, design and operation. In this paper, we take project life cycle into consideration, so the conception of VOCP needs to be clear and specific.

2.1 Definition

In this paper, the definition of VOCP is as follows:

It is a dynamic organization for the purpose of successful construction project in the life cycle, which is supported by information and computer technology integrating the advantages of all the participants to form core competence.

On the base of project life cycle, all the participants in different stages should be included in VOCP. The construction project can be divided into four stages, planning, design, construction and operation. Different participants take part in different stages, and the success of the project needs the cooperation of all participants. Therefore, VOCP includes owner, consultant, designer, general contractor, subcontractor, supplier, supervisor and operator.

2.2 Characteristic

There are mainly four characteristics of VOCP which play important roles in the project life cycle, and they are as follows:

Objective. VOCP exists for the project, and when the project life cycle ends, VOCP is disbanded. The organization is compounded by many participants, and they may have complex interest relationship and confliction. The most important thing is there is only one objective of the organization, success of the project. The participants rely on each other and share resource, information, technology as well as core capacity, which will help them all win in the end. Every decision is made from the view point of the whole organizational benefit, but from any participants' benefit. The organizational objective may be based on communication of organization, which influences efficiency and performance of VOCP.

Dynamic. The project life cycle is a dynamic process which has different stages. Therefore, VOCP is not changeless, but dynamic based on the specific situations in different stages. In the project life cycle, new participant can join in at any moment, and old participant can exit if his work is finished. But when engineering problem happens, all participants should reorganize again and solve the problem together as quickly as possible. Therefore, the organization limit is blurred and uncertain. All the participants in the project life cycle can be classified into two categories, fixed participant, who has important task in a certain stage and have to stay in the organization, and dynamic participant, who just has assisted task and can exit in a certain stage.

Flexibility. VOCP is composed by different participants, who are not only integrated into an organization for a project, but also independent relatively in the market. The scale of VOCP is decided by the nature, scale and emergency of the project. Since there are less management levels in VOCP, personnel can take part in the project deeply. The decision-making is quickly, so it could response to changeable environment as soon as possible. Since the organizational culture is highly compatible, all the organizational culture could coexist in VOCP. The atmosphere in VOCP is benefit for cooperation of all participants, which is based on the fluency of information flow.

Supported by information technology (IT). VOCP relies on the sharing of information, experience, technology and resource, which base on fluent information flow. Therefore, information technology (IT) is one of the key capacities of VOCP, which couldn't operate without the supporting of IT. The information platform should be constructed as soon as VOCP establishes. The main effect of IT is as follows:

Share information, resource, experience and technology.
Understand the project in detail and different perspective.
Strengthen communication between different participants.
Make the objective more clear and acceptable.
Solidarize and cooperate more effectively.

2.3 Structure

With the development of IT, the organization structure changed greatly in the past thirty years, more and more new types of organization emerged, and the structure of which is becoming flatter and flatter. This decentralizes the power of organization, makes it more flexible and responds to the environment as soon as possible. The VOCP is a typically flat organization, which has less managerial levels. The VOCP has two layers, project management team (PMT) and project team (PT), as shown in Fig.1.

Project Management Team (PMT). Project management team (PMT), the leadership of VOCP, is in charge of the project life cycle. It answers for the result of the project to guarantee that the project can be optimized in whole. It also has the ultimate authority to make all important decisions and keep the control of cost, timeliness and quality. Owner is the hard core of project management team, which is consists of personnel representing all participants. The members of PMT contact with each other by information platform, and they can also discuss face to face.

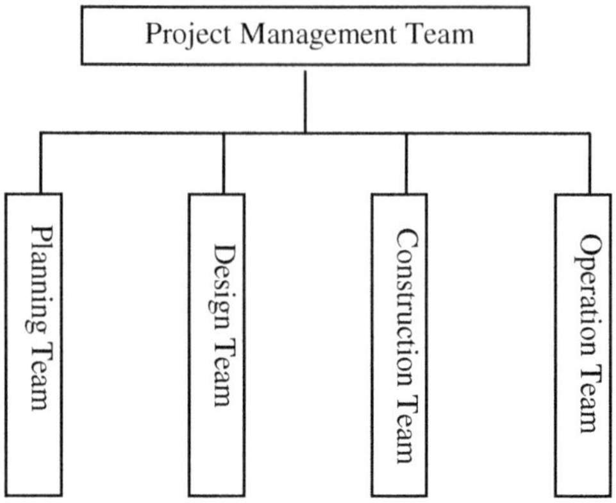

Fig. 1. Structure of VOCP

Project Team (PT). Project team (PT) which takes charge of the implement process is the implementation layer of project. It answers for a certain stage of project, has different core capacities, and accepts the leadership of PMT. PMT makes decisions and plans, organizes and gives order to PT, which should implement the order and report the result to PMT. According to project life cycle, VOCP should have four PTs: planning team, design team, construction team and operation team. The members of PT come from all participants, but different participants are in charge in different stages. They communicate with each other by information platform mainly, and as well as face to face discussion.

3 Management of VOCP

As a brand-new type of organization mode, traditional manage method and technique can't get satisfied effection when applying to VOCP. Through cooperating with different participants, virtual organization responds quickly to changeable environment, but organization management is more difficult and complex, for all the participants that are relatively independent should be integrated in a whole. The management of VOCP based on project life cycle can be classified into communication management, cost management, schedule management and quality management. The four parts are not isolated, but interact with each other. A problem happened in one part will cause problems in other parts. On the basis of effective communication management, cost, schedule and quality management can be integrated to perform an important role in the project life cycle. The integrated management process is shown in fig 2.

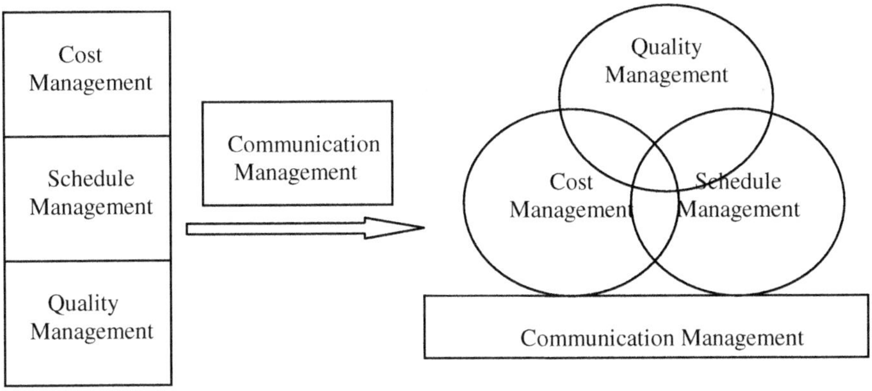

Fig. 2. Integrated Management based on Communication Management

3.1 Cost Management

Cost determines profit, so every organization tries to minimize project cost, and VOCP with no exception. As previous stated, VOCP can integrate the core capability of all participants, so it could reduce direct cost. Meanwhile, cooperating with so many participants will increase indirect cost. The cost management tries to complete the project with minimize cost in the perspective of project life cycle, not only in a certain stage. The task of cost management is as follows:

Establish project cost plan based on project life cycle.
Minimize cost in the project life cycle.
Supervise the cost timely.
Discover and transmit cost problems in progress.
Analyze cost problems and find the reason.
Try to solve the cost problems as soon as possible.
Adjust cost schedule when situation changes.

3.2 Schedule Management

Completion on time is a main objective of all projects. The direct consequence of work behind schedule will cause delayed completion, which will disturb the planning, and lead to stagnation if serious. There are also other consequences, such as cost overrun and rejectable quality level. The task of schedule management is as follows:

Establish project schedule plan based on project life cycle.
Complete project on schedule.
Supervise the schedule timely.
Discover and transmit schedule problems in progress.
Analyze schedule problems and find the reason.
Try to solve schedule problems as soon as possible.
Adjust schedule plan when situation changes.

3.3 Quality Management

Quality is the life of project. The unique nature of each facility, the variability in the workforce, the multitude of subcontractors and the different quality standards of participants make quality management difficult. Quality problem will cause cost and schedule problems. Therefore, quality management should be concerned as early as possible. The most important decisions regarding the project quality are made during the planning and design stage rather than construction. The task of quality management is as follows:

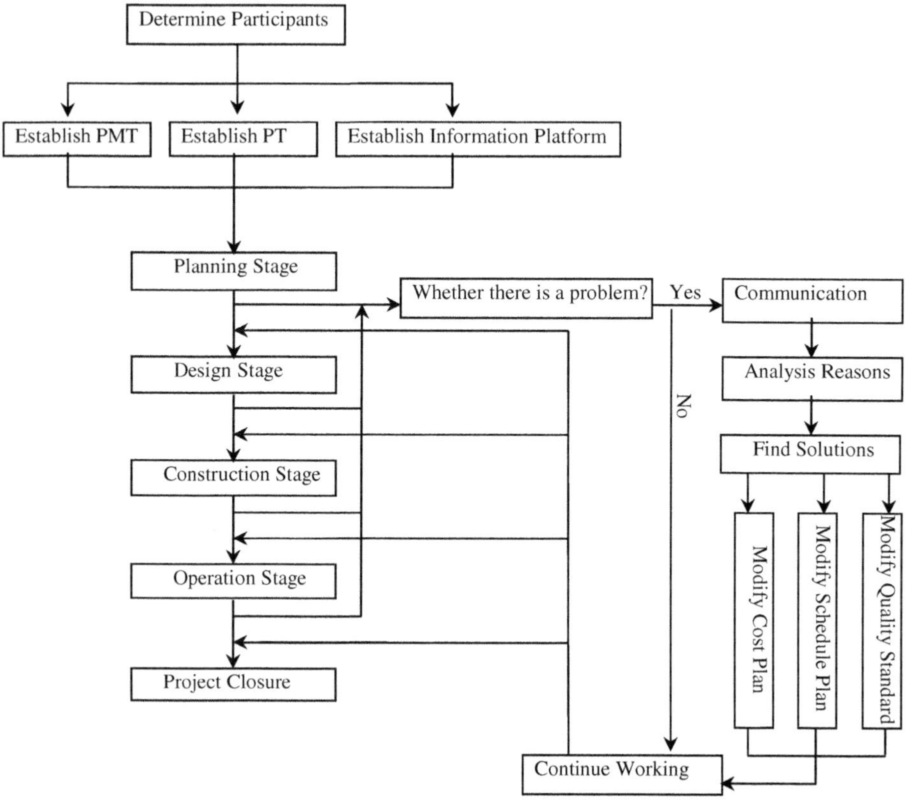

Fig. 3. Work Process of VOCP based on Project Life Cycle

Establish project quality standard based on project life cycle.
Complete project according to quality standard.
Supervise the quality timely.
Discover and transmit quality problems in progress.
Analyze quality problems and find the reason.
Try to solve quality problems as soon as possible.
Adjust quality standard when situation changes.

3.4 Work Process

In the work process, a problem in one part may cause the change of other parts since four parts of management interact with each other. The communication, cost, schedule and quality management should be integrated and considered synthetically based on project life cycle. The work process is shown in fig.3.

4 Conclusion

This paper presents the organization and management of VOCP that is suitable for information age. Four characteristics are determined and the structure of VOCP is established. The management of VOCP includes communication management, cost management, schedule management and quality management, which are integrated into a synthetical process. The work process is designed, which shows the interaction of different management based on project life cycle. This paper can assist owners, consultants, designers, general contractors, subcontractors, suppliers, supervisors and operators to understand the management of VOCP better and cooperate with each other more effectively in the future. Currently the author is focused on the evaluation of VOCP. Future research aims to propose evaluation method, evaluation index and improvement of VOCP. Ultimately, a whole management and evaluation system will be made available.

References

1. Levitt, R.E., Thomsen, J., Christiansen, T.R., Kunz, J.C., Jin, Y., Nass, C.I.: Simulating Project Work Processes and Organizations: Toward a Micro-Contingency Theory of Organizational Design. Management Science 45(11), 1479–1495 (1999)
2. Jin, Y., Levitt, R.E.: The Virtual Design Team: A Computational Model of Project Organizations. Comp. and Math. Organ. Theory 2(3), 171–196 (1996)
3. Cooper, M., Lambert, D., Pagh, J.: Supply Chain Management: More than a New Name for Logistics. Int. J. Logistics Manage 8(1), 1–14 (1997)
4. Lewis, I., Talalayevsky, A.: Logistics and Information Technology: A Coordination Perspective. Bus. Logistics 18(1), 141–157 (1997)
5. Crawford, S., Binmore, K., Axelord, R.: Competition by Cooperation. Liaoning Education Publications, China (1998)
6. Jung, U.M., Hans, C.B.: Agent-Based Construction Supply Chain Simulator (CS^2) for Measuring the Value of Real-Time Information Sharing in Construction. Journal of Management in Engineering 24, 245–254 (2008)
7. Kluschl, M.: Information Agent Technology for the Internet -A Survey. Journal on Data and Knowledge Engineering, Special Issue on Intelligent Information Integration 36(3), 337–372 (2001)
8. Liz, L., Tim, S.: Global Virtual Teams for Value Creation and Project Success: A Case Study. International Journal of Project Management 26, 51–62 (2008)

Research on Risk Aversion of Human Resources Outsourcing

Yuanxun Li[1] and Rui Li[2]

[1] Business School, Shandong University at Weihai, Weihai, 264209, China
[2] Business School, Nanjing University, Nanjing, 210093, China
sdlyx@yahoo.com.cn

Abstract. During recent years, although Human Resources Outsourcing becomes popular in china, risks contained in the process of Human Resources Outsourcing restrict its further development and prospect, so Outsourcing Risks become an important research subject in the field of Human Resources Outsourcing. Currently, most of the researches are concentrated on the demanding party of Human Resources Outsourcing service market, without considering the risks caused by supplies. This paper analyzes Human Resources Outsourcing Risks from the perspective of service providers and raised the measures to reduce risks.

Keywords: human resources outsourcing, risk aversion.

1 Introduction

Recently, Human Resources outsourcing has become a tideway of the world globalization. According to one of American famous research institutes, Yankee Group's investigation, compound annual rate of growth of global Human Resources Outsourcing market is more than 12% in recent years[1]. With the popularity of Human Resources Outsourcing, service industry of Human Resources Outsourcing becomes an emerging industry which grows rapidly.

In china, Human Resources Outsourcing grows speedily in recent years. But compared with the developed countries, it still has a long way to go. Then its lagging development restricts Chinese enterprises' enthusiasm to develop core competitive strength through Human Resources Outsourcing to reduce the cost.

2 Human Resources Outsourcing Risk Is the Main Obstacle Which Restricts the Development of Human Resources Outsourcing Service

Resources Outsourcing Risk is the main obstacle which restricts the development of Human Resources Outsourcing service. Resources Outsourcing Risk restricts the expected effect Human Resources Outsourcing Risk, even causes the failure of it. An investigation of American enterprises' Human Resources Outsourcing indicates that

Q. Zhou (Ed.): ISAEBD 2011, Part II, CCIS 209, pp. 54–59, 2011.

35% of Human Resources Outsourcing failure is caused by Human Resources Outsourcing risk [2]. Although there is still no quantitative study of Human Resources Outsourcing in our country, Human Resources Outsourcing risk should be higher in china according to the imperfect market of other countries' Human Resources Outsourcing.

So that, only reducing Human Resources Outsourcing risk can enhance the development of service industry of Human Resources Outsourcing, reduce the cost and improve core competitive strength [3].

Although Human Resources Outsourcing risk attracts general attention from business circles and academic circles, current researches are limited to demands aspect. That is from the aspect of Human Resources Outsourcing enterprises to do research and to give strategy recommendations which often require Human Resources Outsourcing enterprises to enhance self-monitoring and management of Human Resources Outsourcing risk, to establish consciousness of risk prevision, to set up risk early warning system, and to maintain powerful monitoring and control in order to prevent Human Resources Outsourcing risk to the utmost. However, there is rare research considering from the aspect of supplies. It is well known that Human Resources Outsourcing enterprises have no choice but to prevent the Human Resources Outsourcing risk. According to this paper's analysis in the following, Human Resources Outsourcing risk origins from the imperfect market of Human Resources Outsourcing which can causes Information asymmetry. It is necessary to consider from the aspect of industry supplies and to perform the power of industry organization in order to reduce the Human Resources Outsourcing risk caused by the Information asymmetry. On the basis of these, this paper studies Human Resources Outsourcing risk's hedging mechanism from supplies aspect.

3 Human Resources Outsourcing Risk and Its Manifestations

Scholars in and abroad have a wide spectrum of opinions on the definition of Human Resources Outsourcing risk.

Some scholars generalize Human Resources Outsourcing risk into five kinds as follows: Risk to choose subcontractors, or risk of choice. That is, when enterprises carry on the process of Human Resources Outsourcing, they must meet the risk caused by the choice of Outsourcing contents and subcontractors; Risk of relationship. That is, the risk is produced during dealing with the relationship with subcontractors. During the outsourcing business, enterprises should find a balance point to supervise subcontractors. So that they can avoid being in passive place or uncooperative from subcontractors. Of course, all these are due to the enterprises' awareness of subcontractors' service ability; Risk of business security. In the process of Human Resources Outsourcing, enterprises will leak out certain information to subcontractors. Because of the imperfect of laws and regulations to ensure activity of Human Resources Outsourcing, it is hard to protect the privacy of enterprises' information; Risk of operation. It contains two aspects. One is the Extraordinary Expenditure caused by the enterprises' incomprehension of outsourcing service's price and quality. The other is the misleading management caused by subcontractors' incomprehension of enterprises. Enterprises should exchange information with subcontractors to avoid this kind of risk which also raises the operational cost; Risk of the decline of business efficiency. The uncooperative between the internal part of enterprises and subcontractors will lead to the decline of business efficiency.

Generally speaking, we can divide the above risks into two categories according to their origins. One category is originated from the risk of outsourcing market, containing risk of choice, risk of relationship, and risk of operation. Risks of this category are due to the imperfect market of Human Resources management service and the Information asymmetry between enterprises and subcontractors. The other category is originated from the risk of the internal part of enterprises. Risk of this category is caused by the enterprises' incomprehension of outsourcing service which can be lower with the further understanding of Human Resources Outsourcing management by business circles and academic circles.

4 The Generative Mechanism of Human Resources Outsourcing Risks

In the above, this paper generalizes outsourcing risks into two categories: One category is originated from the risk of outsourcing market. The other category is originated from the risk of the internal part of enterprises. The author thinks that the risk of outsourcing market and suppliers is caused by the outsourcing market's Information asymmetry.

4.1 Definition of Information Asymmetry

Theory of Information Asymmetry is raised by Professor James Merles in Cambridge University and Professor William Vickrey in Columbia University. Mishkin (2001) says that Information Asymmetry is the insufficiency of information of the other party during the process of transaction.Meanwhile, the author believes that the outsourcing risk of market is created by Information Asymmetry of outsourcing market which contains three aspects. Firstly, none of the transactional parties obtains the completely clear information. Secondly, transactional information is distributed anisomerously between transactional parties. Thirdly, transactional parties know each other's relative place in information occupation very well.

4.2 Reasons of Information Asymmetry and Its Manifestations in Human Resources Outsourcing Market

In real life, Information Asymmetry is due to informed players' different information which is on the basis of the asymmetry of people's ability of information acquisition.

Scholars in and abroad have a wide spectrum of opinions on the reasons of Information Asymmetry. Some scholars believe that Information Asymmetry has objective reasons and subjective reasons. Objective reasons: information's social division, high cost of information retrieval, and persons'limited rationality. Subjective reasons:enterprises' insufficient information of outsourcing market and credibility of main parts of market. Reasons of Human Resources Outsourcing industry's information asymmetry contain the following aspects.

Social division of labors develop into different professional fields in which knowledge gap between specialist and non-specialist becomes wider and wider. Even two specialists in the same field would not understand other's professional knowledge completely.

Because of different qualities and recessive knowledge of outsourcing facilitators, outsourcing facilitators will spend much time and capital cost to collect relative information when they choose outsourcing service facilitators. However, many enterprises don't do sufficient research in order to avoid high cost that will create information asymmetry.

Outsourcing facilitators often hide the information of their qualification prerequisites, capital structure, industrial strength, and service level or provide false information to the market in order to obtain maximum economic interests. This situation also intensifies outsourcing facilitators' difficulty to collect information and enlarges information asymmetry between two parts.

If people have reasonable rationality, they may obtain useful information. However, they also may not accept, recognize or understand the information because of their shortage of abilities to choose, to judge and to calculate the information. This situation can cause information asymmetry, too.

On one hand, after making a contract, many outsourcing facilitators wrongly believe that outsourcing business has nothing to do with enterprises themselves and give the complete power to outsourcing facilitators to control, so that they can not supervise outsourcing facilitators effectively. On the other hand, many outsourcing facilitators' workers lacking of relative special knowledge of outsourcing service, then they can not supervise outsourcing facilitators, too. According to the above, outsourcing facilitators may use their advantages of information to damage the interests of outsourcing facilitators.

5 Hedging Mechanism of Human Resources Outsourcing Risk from Business Perspectives

Risks of Human Resources Outsourcing service market are caused by Information asymmetry. Industrial Association can play an important role in reducing the risks through following measures.

5.1 Setting Up Industrial Standardization

Nowadays, the starting point of Human Resources Outsourcing facilitators is low. The service quality of Human Resources Outsourcing institutions is various. The Human Resources Outsourcing market is still imperfect. Then we can see that facilitators' total quality of Human Resources Outsourcing is not high which is apt to provide basic service s. So that industrial association of Human Resources Outsourcing should set up different levels of service standardization for various outsourcing projects according to its member-enterprises' service quality and give them different formworks. Then outsourcing facilitators can make more scientific decision and choose convenient outsourcing more easily.

Imperfect market of Human Resources Outsourcing, various qualities of outsourcing facilitators and the performances of setting their own charges all make the outsourcing facilitators harder to seize the precise price of service products. So that industrial association can provide relative indicative prices of different levels of service, indicative prices of the costs of information retrieval, decision, negotiation, and supervision of outsourcing facilitators. Benefiting from the above indicative prices, outsourcing facilitators can reduce their cost risks.

5.2 Building Information Platform of Public Service

Outsourcing facilitators may meet many problems at any node in the process of outsourcing which would lead to outsourcing bottleneck problems and block the process of outsourcing. Then industrial association can set up information network, such as on-site counseling, telephone counseling and network counseling, to solve outsourcing facilitators' problems. The problems may contain which kind of service will be chosen according to their own business and what details should be paid attention what kinds of demands should be proposed when sign an outsourcing contract; the information network should provide profound counseling about how to supervise outsourcing facilitators and how to share relative knowledge and techniques with outsourcing facilitators.

If outsourcing facilitators only catch unreal and incomplete information, they will meet enormous risks when they choose outsourcing facilitators. Then industrial association can provide outsourcing facilitators relative information about its member-enterprises and set enterprise records of outsourcing facilitators which contains both member and non-member outsourcing facilitators. Outsourcing facilitators can obtain precise information about outsourcing facilitators' background, creditworthiness, professional competence, corporate culture, management philosophy, price factors, price of outsourcing service products and client's public praise.

5.3 Establishing Industry Code of Conduct

In order to improve relative information of outsourcing facilitators, industrial association should establish client feedback system. Then outsourcing facilitators can send problems happening in the process of outsourcing and information about whether outsourcing facilitators reveal outsourcing enterprises' business secret or not after termination of contract back to industrial association who will add these problems and information into existing outsourcing facilitators' records. In this way, other outsourcing enterprises can reduce their worries when they change facilitators.

In China, there are not perfect laws or regulations to punish outsourcing facilitators' conduct of breach of confidence, conduct of nonobservance of contracts, and conduct of arbitrary charges. However, industrial association can write down the list of outsourcing facilitators, who have the above problems, into blacklist. Then outsourcing facilitators will not choose outsourcing facilitators in blacklist. In this way, outsourcing facilitators have to improve their own level of professional ethics.

Specialists for Human Resources management can supervise outsourcing facilitators' conducts in order to avoid opportunism and immoral actions during the process of outsourcing and to prevent the reveal of outsourcing facilitators' business secrets. Besides, industrial association can set up credit point card for outsourcing facilitators to encourage these outsourcing facilitators whose feedback evaluations are high and to enhance their activities and initiative.

6 Conclusion

Human Resources outsourcing Service industry's development is the product of outsourcing of Human Resources management which is due to enterprises' purposes for improvement of self-competition, optimization of resource allocation, reduction of business cost. It is also the result of social division of labors and the development of specialism. In order to keep healthy and rapid development of Human Resources outsourcing Service industry, the Human Resources outsourcing risks which are basically caused by Information Asymmetry must be avoided. Then this paper proposes measures of hedging Human Resources outsourcing risks from the aspect of industrial association on the basis of analyzing Information Asymmetry's causes.

Acknowledgment. This paper is Supported by "educational reform project of Shandong University at Weihai" and "Social Science Program of Shandong Province"(10DJGJ04).

References

1. Shen, G.z.: The strategic value of human resources outsourcing. Journal of Human Resources 4, 48–53 (2006)
2. Liu, X.: Risk identification and prevention of human resources outsourcing. Journal of Economist Forumt (China Economist) 7 (2008)
3. Bi, X., Yan, R.: The overview of research on tempdespatch in China. Journal of Technoeconomics & Management Research 6 (2007)

Study on Influence Mechanism of Knowledge Value Chain on Service Innovation of Service Enterprise

Yuanxun Li and Zhenhai Mei

Business School, Shandong University at Weihai, Weihai, 264209, China
sdlyx@yahoo.com.cn

Abstract. The arrival of knowledge economy era, makes the enterprise promote innovation through the knowledge and improves the ability to use and manage knowledge, so that it can obtain sustainable competitive advantage. This paper, through analyzing the knowledge value chain including knowledge input, knowledge activities, knowledge output and knowledge innovation of service enterprise, studies the influence mechanism of knowledge value chain on service innovation of service enterprises. The thinking of service innovation based on knowledge value chain is advantageous for enterprise to make full use of internal and external knowledge resources, so as to promote competitive ability of the enterprise, is also helpful for the exploration of enterprise service innovation in knowledge management field.

Keywords: influence mechanism, knowledge value chain, service innovation.

1 Introduction

With the change of technology revolution, "Knowledge Economy" began to appear. Knowledge has become the most important strategic resources and production factors, the vitality, competitiveness and development of enterprise, more and more depend on the ability of knowledge acquisition, storage, propagation, using, developing innovation and organizational management.

The study on knowledge value chain is in the initial phase currently, related research achievements at home and abroad are few, and it focus on knowledge chain rather than knowledge value chain. Hollsopple C.W. and M.Singh, American scholars, put forward the concept of system knowledge chain in 1998. This knowledge chain is constructed from the relationship of knowledge within the organization and core competitive ability of the organization.Later many scholars had improved and enriched the theory, made the knowledge chain theory become more typical. The enterprise knowledge value chain model proposed by Ching chyi Lee & Jie Yang(2000)[2], Hollsopple C.W.(2001) and Allard S. & Hollsopple C.W.(2002) included five kinds of main activitiesand four kinds of auxiliary activities.

The main activity functions of knowledge chain are that:(1)knowledge acquisition: acquiring knowledge from the external organization and making it easy to use for the organization;(2)knowledge selection: choosing knowledge resources from internal organization, and making it easy to use for the organization;(3)knowledge creation:

Q. Zhou (Ed.): ISAEBD 2011, Part II, CCIS 209, pp. 60–65, 2011.

discovering and splitting apart the new knowledge from existing knowledge; (4)knowledge internalization: systemizing knowledge which has been "got", "chosen" and "generated" through the mode of Figure1. Enterprise knowledge value chain distribution and storage, so as to change knowledge resource status of the organization;(5)knowledge exteriorization: putting knowledge into the output of the organization. The auxiliary activity functions of knowledge chain are that:(1)leadership: constructing conditions to make the guidance work of knowledge management more effective;(2)coordination and cooperation: in knowledge management, strengthening cooperation management, at the right time taking appropriate processes and resources to the right place to make full use of; (3)control: making the quality and quantity of the knowledge satisfy requirement and conform to the security requirement; (4)evaluation: assessing the value of knowledge resources, knowledge generation and knowledge metabolism.

The knowledge value chain of enterprise is system tool of managing the internal knowledge of enterprise, it is a system where the enterprise operator takes knowledge as scarce resource, under the guide of related theory, takes knowledge input, knowledge activities and knowledge output as a whole, so as to get the maximum of knowledge value transferring. In the traditional industry value chain, the basis value-added activities of enterprise are "production and operation" in the ordinary sense, the value of the enterprise is composed by value activities such as design, production, marketing, delivery and product support and so on, which is a visible value chain. But the knowledge value chain is formed by all kinds of knowledge and intangible property, which is a virtual value chain and contains more innovative elements. The knowledge value chain is as well as the traditional industry value chain, including the basic and auxiliary activities. Its basic activities include acquisition, processing, accumulation, storage, dissemination, sharing, using and innovation of knowledge. Its auxiliary activities are formed by organization structure, information technology, enterprise culture and human resources. The knowledge value chain, taking knowledge activity as the core and innovation as the goal, takes the people who possesses knowledge as a unique competitive knowledge node, the human system is the most critical part. Only activating each node of enterprise knowledge value chain, it will be possible to make the enterprise's core competitiveness improve continuously. At the same time the knowledge storage capacity decides the ability of enterprise innovating activities, what finally performs sustainable competitive advantage in production and market force of the enterprise.

2 The Analysis of Knowledge Value Chain of Service Enterprise

The enterprise knowledge value chain refers to the whole links with shared knowledge and added value in the enterprise, which includes the knowledge input, all knowledge activities produced in the enterprise, the knowledge output contributed to enterprise by knowledge and the knowledge creation utilized by the enterprise to produce knowledge value finally. The enterprise establishes adaptive and unique system with shared knowledge, which make knowledge adapt to the environment and create wealth constantly in circulation and transferring, so as to become effective knowledge delivering and transferring system of the enterprise.The knowledge activities in service enterprises mainly spread along the chain of "input→activity →output→ innovation".

In service enterprises, customer demand is the guidance of enterprise producing, therefore it is particularly important for the enterprise to get information of customer and market by various methods (such as internet). In the process of understanding competitors and investigating customer demands, enterprise realizes the knowledge input. The knowledge input is the upstream of the knowledge value chain, by which external knowledge is gradually internalized implicit knowledge of staff through the processing of the organization, finally is accumulated experience of staff. The knowledge input is the basic of innovation, it can inject new blood and bring new energy to the enterprise, so many enterprises spare lots of expense to investigate market to obtain the timely and accurate information, or employ outside experts to train employees so as to update the old knowledge of staff.

The knowledge activity is intermediate link of the knowledge value chain. Service enterprises, through the ways of knowledge sharing such as team communication, authorization, organization learning, transfer individual experience of employee into the explicit organization knowledge, or transform the external knowledge into internal knowledge gradually. In this process, the dominant knowledge and recessive knowledge interact to form innovative service products. But in the process of knowledge sharing, the enterprise needs to adjust management mechanism and organization structure, such as establishing fairness personnel appointment and removal system and rewards and punishment. Enterprise knowledge value chain system, taking straight organizational structure instead of flat structure so as to facilitate knowledge flow, and cultivating right enterprise culture to promote employees to share the individual knowledge with others actively. The knowledge sharing can maximize the knowledge benefit, so as to maximize the customer value.

After above activities such as knowledge input, knowledge sharing and knowledge storage, under the help of internet, information or other technology measures, service enterprise has formed stable organization knowledge which can be transformed into the convenient standardizing service products to bring economic benefits directly for them.

Knowledge innovation is the downstream link of the knowledge value chain, it is the critical process of maintenance and appreciation of knowledge value. Regardless of its quantity, quality and efficiency, if enterprise knowledge isn't transformed to knowledge that satisfies customer demand, it won't have value. Starting from the enterprise value, this process reflects the transformation and materialization of knowledge, service, relationship, ability and so on. After the links of knowledge input, activity and output, dominant and recessive knowledge constantly interact each other, complete four basic modes of creating knowledge in any organization. (1)socialization: from recessive knowledge to recessive knowledge; (2)comprehension: from dominant knowledge to dominant knowledge; (3)externalization: from recessive knowledge to dominant knowledge; (4)internalization: from dominant knowledge to recessive knowledge. Finally, through accumulating, developing and innovating constantly, individual service can be formed.

3 The Mechanism of Knowledge Value Chain in Affecting the Service Innovation of Service Enterprises

Through the analysis of the knowledge value chain, it can be known that service enterprises generate knowledge innovation after input, activity and output of knowledge.

Knowledge input of service enterprise, refers to that service enterprises, through the stages of knowledge identification, collecting, sorting, storage, transform the knowledge in external environment into internal knowledge of enterprises, thus to be used by the enterprise. Knowledge input makes internal and external knowledge environment of the enterprise communicate dynamically, so as to create conditions for knowledge management of the enterprise. Knowledge input of service enterprises is that collects internal and external information of enterprise through various channels to acquire knowledge. Knowledge sources are extensive, including scientific research institutions, upstream suppliers, customers, consultants, competitors, the noncompetitive companies and individuals who possess knowledge. Additionally, the enterprise, through the mode of production-study-research cooperation, setting up a learning strategy alliance and allowing customers to participate in developing of new product, establishes knowledge network and connects the physical network and relationship network with internal knowledge system of the enterprise, to form knowledge alliance, all these are the effective sources of knowledge. In the process of collection information, the enterprise can realize the new knowledge input through the ways of market surveys, communicating with exterior. In a fast changing society, the enterprise should actively capture external information through the modes of internet, e-commerce, the qualified enterprises can establish internal local area network to form internal information exchange platform, so as to further facilitate the communication of external knowledge in internal organization. In this process, experienced employees are recruited from other enterprises and experts are employed to carry professional training to the staff, it is an important measures for enterprises to realize old and new knowledge replacing.

After knowledge input, the enterprise can adjust self strategy according to requirements, improve the organizational structure and management approach through strategic innovation, management innovation and organization innovation, foster the healthy, active and fair enterprise culture, the establishment of new organizational structure and organizational culture is helpful for sharing and learning of employee experience, as well as transforming, stabilizing and updating of organization knowledge. By smooth execution of the above work, it is easy to make employees highly satisfy with their enterprises, so employees provide high quality services for the customer voluntarily, and in the service process carry consciousness innovation consciously, apply the new service concept to service, so as to produce new service products. For example, when employees recognize that they are the "masters" of the enterprise, they will take customer satisfaction as the guide of their action, even initiatively innovate service product or optimize service process to provide greater value for the enterprise.

Knowledge output is that presenting the high quality and efficient services formed in earlier stage to customers, so as to get customer satisfaction and loyalty. In this process, service quality of employees is of crucial importance, although currently some standardized service can be realized by computer and internet, the individuation of service products is a general developing trend, many products need customers involved in, then by using the rich experience of staff the products are tailor-made for customers, so the staff 's one-onone services are very important to win more customers and markets.

Knowledge innovation of the enterprise, is the process that enterprise develops and creates new knowledge on the basis of existing knowledge resources. The new knowledge is probably a new knowledge system or new idea, also only a new 3035 concept. The knowledge innovation is the fundamental force of enterprise development. Yang Yehua, Qian Jun point, currently the key of improving productivity is not manual worker, but the production of knowledge and the using of knowledge to production. Enterprise's knowledge innovation is realized by the process of knowledge management such as system innovation, management innovation and technology innovation, so as to realize the sustainable development of the enterprise. Knowledge innovation is produced by the combined action of input, activities and output of knowledge, namely the loyalty of customer to service enterprises not only stabilize the customer source, but also because of the formation of public praise of customers and brand effect, the enterprise will have more customers and markets. To sum up, the input of external knowledge generates a strong impact on internal knowledge and organizational structure, in order to adapt to the development needs of information exchange, transformation and sharing, the enterprise should reform organization structure and management approach, cultivate active opening organizational culture, and make full use of technology measures to realize knowledge output and innovation. In the process of knowledge innovation, the internal value chain of enterprise------ employee satisfaction, employee loyalty, customer satisfaction and customer loyalty is gradually realized. Enterprise's knowledge activities has entered a virtuous circle track.

4 Conclusion

This paper discusses the effect and mechanism of service innovation based on the theory of the knowledge value chain, thinks that enterprise service innovation is realized through the process of knowledge input, knowledge activity, knowledge output and knowledge innovation, then competitive advantage of enterprises is built. This research is beneficial to the practice of service innovation. From the analysis of service innovation mechanism based on the knowledge value chain, it can be seen that knowledge plays an important role in the process of the enterprise service innovation, which should be emphasized. The thinking of enterprise innovation based on knowledge value chain, is not only advantageous for enterprise to fully utilize internal and external knowledge resources so as to enhance competitiveness in the industry, but also is helpful for enterprise to explore service innovation in knowledge management field. However, how to make the influence mechanism model really play the role in enterprises, how to form sustainable competitive advantage of enterprises and industry, still face many problems. The study on this problem will put forward higher requirements to enterprise management, this is also the future research issued for scholars who are engaged in the service innovation research.

Acknowledgment. The authors gratefully acknowledge the financial support of Sociological Research Program of Shandong Province (10DJGJ04).

References

1. Hollsopple, C.W., Singh, M.: The Knowledge Chain Model: activities for competitiveness. Expert System with Applications 20, 77–98 (2001)
2. Lee, C.c., Yang, J.: Knowledge value chain. The Journal of Management Development 19, 783–794 (2000)

A Model of Labor Demand in Technical Change: Based on Combination of Marxism and Neo-Classical Theory

Rundong Luo and Weiwei Wu

Business School, Shandong University at Weihai, P.R. China, 264209
rundong_luo@163.com

Abstract. Based on current situation about the mixture of industrialization and informatization in the developing countries such as China, a model of labor demand in the technical change is built up. By describing the structure and change of capital-labor ratio, The author describes the theoretical trend and type of technical change in industry sector.

Keywords: Technical Change, Labor Demand, Employment.

1 Introduction

After 1990s, the development of information technology sweeps across the world. At the same time the employment structure in most countries has changed significantly, in which the increasing demand for the skilled labor highlights most. And the technical change is also widely known as the "skill-biased technical change" during this period. What is interesting is the nature of the contemporary technical change with informatization as its center. Is it an independent stage beyond the industrial technology stage or does it still remain subordinate to the framework of the traditional industrialization? If it's too early to define the exact boundaries between the two types of technical advances. At least from the practical point of view it's necessary to show the influence on the demand of labor and employment with the extensive use of information technology.

As noted, the earlier relative literatures on this topic have made some achievements. For example, Kennedy(1964), Schmookler (1966) and Hayami and Ruttan (1970), all of them predicted that the technological innovation will inevitably arise in order to make GDP increase along with the capital-labor ratio.

The recent representative research proved that a profit-maximizing firm might adapt capital-augmenting or labor-augmenting technical change. However the economic growth showed a "pure labor-augmenting technical change" in the long term, meanwhile the labor share in GDP was a constant (Acemoglu, 2000). Machin and Jon Van Reenen(1998)did positive studies on the labor market change in the demand pattern in seven countries of OECD. They described the role that SBTC played in the countries with mature industrialization and information technology, and confirmed the tendency that labor demand turned to skilled ones. As a large developing country whose Dual Economy is very prominent, China has continued the process of industrialization and also integrated lots of informational factors. The intertwined

Q. Zhou (Ed.): ISAEBD 2011, Part II, CCIS 209, pp. 66–72, 2011.

development pattern of "industrialization" and "informatization" has become a unique landscape in China and some other developing countries as well as a special type in global technological progress.

Based on current background, this paper just builds up a labor demand model corresponding to the situation and uses the Chinese data from 1985 to 2002 to validate the assumptions.

2 The Model

2.1 Assumptions

The assumptions of the model in this paper come from the features of the development of information technology. The prominent features of the information technology which has significant impact on the economic growth are the extremely high research and development (R & D)cost of the product and its almost zero marginal cost(Shapiro and Varian , 2000).

The main reasons why the change in cost structure could become an important hastening factor to promote birth of the new growth theory are the differences between the information products and the industrial products which are as follows. Firstly, the innovation. From the development process of information products in the world, it can be seen that such products are developing towards the way to show the innovation achievements of the labor. Secondly, the inheritance (Luo, 2003). Different from the general products which take entities to update, the information-based products use the upgrade of the old versions to the new ones as the major means. What's more, the new versions not only largely inherit the old ones, but also expand, improve and rewrite the codes on the basis of the old versions. Meanwhile, the inherited part is only a copy and its cost is zero. Thirdly, part failure of the law of diminishing marginal reward. Because the information products can be shared, used repeatedly and replicated with low cost, the spillover effort of such knowledge will mitigate or offset the diminishing reward of other factors, so as to achieve the same or even increased remuneration receipts. Considering the basic features of the information technology mentioned above and the following positive analysis, the following assumptions for the model are very necessary:

1) the labor is divided into two types, the highly skilled and the non-skilled. The former has the feature of investment in human capital and the latter doesn't have such feature.2) the marginal reward to the skilled labor is unchanged, that is MPS=constant.3) there is diminishing marginal return to the non-skilled labor whose supply is unlimited .4) both types of labor are of full employment in the initial state.

2.2 The Connotation of Capital-Labor Ratio (K/L) and Its Form

The capital-labor ratio (K/L) which means the firms' demand rate of capital to labor can be used to measure the degree of technological progress, because the progress is always closely linked to the investment of special factors. Through the perspective of neo-classical economic growth theory, the changes in output and employment depend on the ratio of the two factors (K/L) whose changes reflect the degree of technological progress and its direction. This shows that K / L can be used as a basic indictor to describe the relation between the technical advances and the changes in output and employment.

Then the logic of the neo-classical theory is used to prove that as technology advanced from the stage of industrialization to that of informatization, there will be a theoretical equilibrium point for output and employment with the change in K/L.

Now consider a Cobb - Douglas production function

$$Y = f(K, L) = AK^{\alpha}L^{\beta} \qquad (0<\alpha,\ \beta<1), \tag{1}$$

which has two basic factors—capital (K) and labor (L), and α and β are their elasticity separately.

In a perfectly competitive condition, the firm's long-term profit will fall to 0, which will make the marginal product of each input the same, that is $MP_K = MP_L$. So we also get

$$\alpha AK^{\alpha-1}L^{\beta} = \beta AK^{\alpha}L^{\beta-1}, \text{ i.e. } \alpha L = \beta K,$$

and the long-term equilibrium of capital-labor ratio(K / L) is

$$\omega^* = K/L = \alpha/\beta. \tag{2}$$

It's better to start from the Lewis model (Lewis, 1954) to understand the change in capital-labor ratio. His model describes the expansion path of capital in developing countries in the early industrialization period with unlimited supply of labor, that is to say, with the increase of capital accumulation, the labor will be absorbed by economic growth gradually. In Lewis' model, the technical advance is apparently based on the investment in physical capital, and the remuneration to the owner of the labor who doesn't make physical or human capital investment just maintains the simple production themselves. So in this case, we get K/L>> * ω.

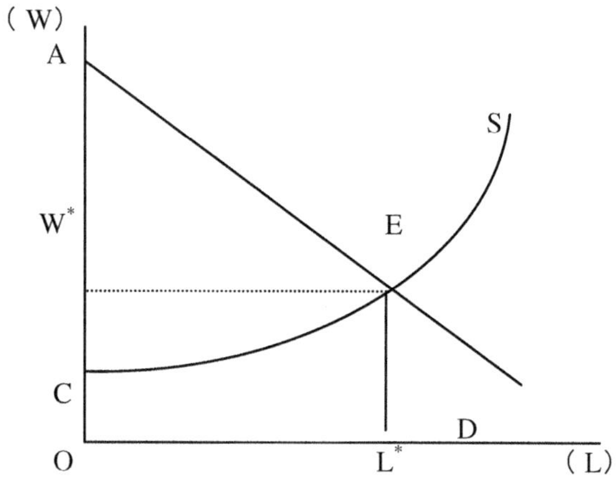

Fig. 1. The capital-labor ratio and the decision of employment

As to the neo-classical theory, in addition to meeting the maintenance of consumption expenditure S_{L*ECO}, there is still surplus S_{CEW*} for human capital investment, as shown in Figure 1. Finally, with the full development of technical change and the emergence of increasing marginal return to labor, the demand curve of capital to skilled labor is horizontal or positive. In this case we get K/L $<<\omega^*$(Acemoglu, 2001). From the "unlimited supply of labor" in the early stage of technological advance to the "unlimited demand for skilled labor" later, this change just reflects that the impact of technical change on the K/L declines after rising at first.

In Figure 1 the horizontal axis is the number of labor while the vertical axis is its prices. The curve AD stands for the marginal product of the labor factor while CS is the supply curve of labor. E is the equilibrium of employment and wage. Furthermore, from the rental income area of the factors, we can get capital-labor ratio K/L:

$$K/L = S_{AEW*}/(S_{CEW*} + S_{L*ECO}) = k/(h + l_0), \qquad (3)$$

Where k is the profit that the firm gets after investment in physical capital; h + 10 is the return to the labor factor. We define $\Sigma W = h + l_0$, l_0 is the survival wage to maintain the daily life, and h is the additional investment in human capital of the workers themselves. Consolidated (2.2.2) and (2.2.3)we can further get the physical capital-human capital ratio

$$k/h = \alpha k/[\beta k - \alpha l_0]$$

When the technical change reaches a certain stage, the returns to capital will exceed the survival wage, that is $K>>l_0$, and the relative share of the return to physical capital α will decrease gradually with the increasing prominent of human capital, so we get $\alpha l_0 \rightarrow 0$, and the previous function will be equal to

$$k/h = \alpha/\beta \qquad (4)$$

From (4) and (2)we know that when there is a high rate of technical change, the ratio of physical capital to human capital tends to be the same as the ratio of capital to labor. So k/h can be understood as a specific form of K/L under the advance of information technology, namely

$$k/h = K/L = \omega^* \qquad (5)$$

Through the above analysis on the capital-labor ratio(K/L) , it is clear that the expansion of the human capital and its impact should be emphasized when we study the output growth and employment under the condition of technical change. Based on this view the labor demand model is developed in the following part.

2.3 Basic Model

First of all we use the Edgeworth Box to describe the relative changes of employment of the two types of labor under the conditions of information technological advances. In Figure 2, O and O' stand for the origin point of employment of unskilled and skilled labor and the wage rate separately. The horizontal axes are the total labor force, the skilled labor $L_S = L_SO'$, the unskilled labor $L_u = OL_u$, so the total labor force is $L_S + L_u$. The two vertical axes are the relative wage of the two labors, i.e. $W_U/OW + O'W_S/OW = 1$. According to the previous assumptions, we see that the demand and supply curves for unskilled labor are WL and W_UW_S, while for skilled labor are W_SW_U and L_SL_u. So the point E becomes the initial equilibrium of the two labor markets. The technical change will bring about two effects on the employment: one is that many posts in the traditional industry will decrease or even disappear; the other is that new positions will appear because of the new industries and the involved services caused by technological advances. The ultimate influence technology has on employment depends on the net increase after the offset of the two effects. Further analysis is shown by Figure 2.

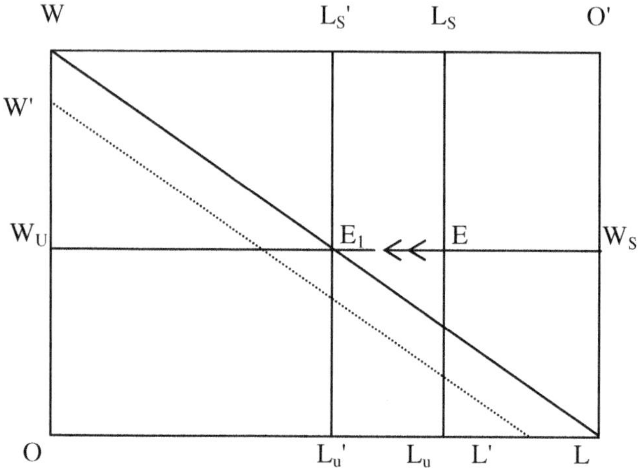

Fig. 2. The relative changes of the employment of skilled and unskilled labor under technical change

Since the information technology came out and was widely applied, the innovation of products and technology has become the main sources of profit for the firms. A representative enterpriser would like to pay O'WS to a skilled labor and the demand is unlimited (in this case, the curve W_SW_U is almost horizontal and the demand elasticity is $+\infty$). However, for the unskilled labor the demand curve will move to the left from WL to W'L', so there will be unemployment directly at the original wage levels and the amount is $\Delta L = L_uL_u'$, which belongs to structural unemployment of technology. So in this situation, in order to maintain the original goal of full employment, there should be $\Delta L = L_S'L_S$ units of skilled labor. In other words, there must be investment in human capital to produce skilled labor. Then it should be made clear how to determine the border and way of human capital investment theoretically, and how to choose the intensive mode for the combination of technology and labor as well as capital. The questions will be discussed as follows:

To increase the employment of skilled labor by ΔL means that the equilibrium point should move from E to E1. Hence training is needed to improve the human capital of the unskilled labor. And the amount of this investment is$\Delta H = \Delta L(O'W_S - OW_U) = \Delta L \cdot \Delta W$, in which ΔW is the wage difference between the skilled and unskilled labor, namely $\Delta W = w_S - w_U$. With technical change, the additional requirement for investment in human capital to achieve full employment is

$$\Delta H \begin{cases} \text{Upper bound}: \ \Delta H_2 = \Delta L \cdot w_S \\ \qquad = \Delta L \cdot \Delta W = \\ \text{Lower bound}: \ \Delta H_1 = \Delta L \cdot \Delta W \end{cases} \tag{6}$$

Following the above analysis and transforming the function $\Delta H = \Delta L(w_S - w_U)$, we get

$$\Delta H = \Delta L(w_S \cdot L_S / L_S - w_U \cdot L_U / L_U) = (\Delta L / L_S)\, w_S \cdot L_S - (\Delta L / L_U)\, w_U \cdot L_U,$$

Where $\Delta L / L_S$ and $\Delta L / L_U$ stand for the creation rate of new posts($\pi 1$)and the recession rate of traditional posts ($\pi 0$) separately; $w_S \cdot L_S$ is the part of the labor reward for human capital investment, h , and $w_U \cdot L_U$ is the part for survival, l0. Then the equation becomes

$$\Delta H = \pi_1 \cdot h - \pi_0 \cdot l_0 , \tag{7}$$

The relationship between investment in human capital and the replacement of the old and new posts is made clear in (2.3.2)under the conditions of technical change. Consolidating (2.2.2), (2.2.5) and (2.3.2), the investment model for full employment can be divided into three types: First, the "technology-capital intensive model" at pure industrialization phase, at which, for a representative firm, the ratio of physical capital to human capital $k/h \gg \omega^*$, and the economic growth will be mainly maintained by investment in physical capital, while investment in human capital $h \rightarrow 0$, and at this time the investment in capital for full employment $\Delta H = -\pi 0 \cdot l0$. Second, the "technology-labor intensive model" at pure informatization phase. At this stage $k/h \ll \omega^*$,that is to say if the return to investment in human capital is big enough, then the additional investment $h \gg l0$ and the return to capital $k \rightarrow r$, i.e. $h = r/\alpha$, and the additional investment in human capital$\Delta H = \pi 1 \cdot (r/\alpha) - \pi_0 \cdot l_0$. Third, the transitional stage from industrialization to informatization. At this phase the ratio of physical capital to human capital , k/h is near to the steady value ω^*. In this case, both the physical capital and the human capital make contributions to the economic growth and employment augment, and in some industries they are alternatives. In order to balance the creation rate of the new posts and the recession rate of the traditional posts that is$\pi 1 = \pi_0 = \pi^*$, the additional external investment in human capital should be$\Delta H = \pi^* \pi^* (h - l_0)$. From the previous analysis on Figure 2, it can be seen that the labor reward $\Sigma W = h + l_0$. Both sides are divided by ΣW and we get

$$\Delta H / \Sigma W = \pi^* \cdot (h / \Sigma W - l_0 / \Sigma W) .$$

Then, the new equilibrium posts creation rate in technical change is

$$\pi^* = (\Delta H / \Sigma W) / (h / \Sigma W - l_0 / \Sigma W)$$

where the endogenous growth rate of investment in human capital $\Delta H / \Sigma W$ is recorded as g_H. And $h/\Sigma W$ and $l_0/\Sigma W$, which meet $h/\Sigma W + l_0/\Sigma W = 1$, are the proportions of the labor wage invested in human capital and in basic consumption, and they are recorded simply as λ_H and λ_L. Then the equilibrium of the creation rate of the new posts with technical change can be further written as

$$\pi^* = g_H / (\lambda_H - \lambda_L) \tag{8}$$

With technical change, the growth rate of investment in human capital to balance the new and old posts as well as the internal structure of labor reward is described in formula (2.3.3). Both of them are the key variables which impact whether full employment can be achieved during this process. And this formula also reflects the interactional relationship between the creation rate of new posts, growth rate of investment in human capital and the reward structure of labor. In the next section the change in employment as well as the investment patterns will be discussed positively in the industrial sector with technical change when China is in the process of industrialization and informatization from late 20th century to now.

3 Conclusion

The basic understanding of technical change in this paper are as follows:The current wave of global informatization has had great impact on China's industrial growth and employment. However this information-oriented process of technical change is not a completely independent stage beyond industrialization. It actually reflects the "incremental" part of the contemporary technological advancement, and in the view of "stock" it is still subordinate to the basic framework of industrialized society. Just as so far the human power and animal power have not been completely replaced by industrialization, informatization will not thoroughly remove scale and standardization which represent the industrial production. Therefore the mixed development of industrialization and informatization will be a long-term phase rather than a short period of time in the technological change. The the equilibrium and the trend of China's "capital-labor ratio" during the advances of industrial technology can provide a reference to understand industrialization and informatization. From the employment situation in China's industrial sector, it can be seen that informational-based technical change as well as industrialization is a "double-edged sword". Therefore, on the one hand China should seize timely the opportunities for economic growth brought by the development of informatization and accelerate investment in human capital so as to improve the creation rate of new posts under the technical change; on the other hand with the dual development of informatization and industrialization, we need to avoid investing blindly for the sole purpose of rapid growth. Only in this way, will China not lose the significant advantages that labor-intensive industries bring to the economic growth and employment.

Acknowledgment. This paper is Supported by "Project Fund of Shandong University at Weihai" and "Program for New Century Excellent Talents in University"(NCET-10-0523).

References

1. Acemoglu, D.: Labor- and Capital- Augmenting Technical Change, NBER Working Paper, No.7544 (2000)
2. Acemoglu, D.: Induced Innovation. In: Directed Technical Change and Human Capital. In: Edmund Phelps' Conference, October 1-2, New York (2001)
3. Kennedy, C.: Induced Bias in Innovation and the Theory of Distribution. Economic Journal LXXIV, 541–547 (1964)

Impacts of Minimum Wage on Employment of Migrant Workers in China

Rundong Luo, Min Zhou, and Weiwei Wu

Business School, Shandong University at Weihai, P.R. China, 264209
rundong_luo@163.com

Abstract. Using balanced panel data on 27 regions for the years 1995 to 2008, this paper empirically analyzes the employment effects of minimum wage. Based on the varying coefficient mode with fixed effects, we select Generalized Least Square Method to estimate the coefficients. According to the regression results, we conclude that employment effects of the minimum wage vary from region to region. In addition, we use unbalanced panel data to formulate the fixed effect variable intercept model to analyze the employment effects. Different from other empirical results, our results show that it has a negative effect in manufacturing industry, while positive effects in construction, wholesale and retail and catering industry.

Keywords: minimum wage, migrant workers, employment.

1 Introduction

The minimum wage is that employers should provide the minimum labor remuneration according to law, on the premise of labors providing normal work during the work hour ruled by law or the labor contract. From 1940s, the employment effects of minimum wage continued to be hot topic of research. There are a large number of literatures which focus on the impacts of minimum wage on income distribution, employment and eliminating poverty, etc. Among these research fields, the employment effects become the core question in theoretical and empirical researches. In early studies, Stigler (1946) proposed the unemployment effects model of minimum wage[1]. He pointed out if the minimum wage was higher than equilibrium wage, in perfectly competitive labor market, it would decrease employment. On the contrary, if below equilibrium wage, although no impacts on employment, it would severely damage the interests of laborers. The domestic research on minimum wage has just started in recent years. Many scholars such as Lin Xingzhi(2002), Xue Zhaofeng (2004) [2], etc, think that the minimum wage has a negative effect on employment. In other words, increasing the minimum wage will push labor cost and reduce competitiveness, resulting in the unemployment of unskilled labor. Cai Fang (2005) also put forward that we should implement the minimum wage system further. Therefore, the impacts of minimum wage on employment of migrant workers, along with industry and regional characteristics, needs to be further studied.

Q. Zhou (Ed.): ISAEBD 2011, Part II, CCIS 209, pp. 73–77, 2011.

2 Empirical Analysis

Most empirical studies use time-series analyses to test the impacts of the minimum wage on the employment. However, time-series studies on Chinese labor markets have several limitations. There are small amount of the time-series observations which are not in dependent. Different regions have different levels of minimum wage and different executive frequencies. Another limitation is that it is difficult to distinguish the effects of a change in the minimum wage from the effects of other structural changes. By contrast, the panel dada have advantages such as describe heterogeneous individuals, increase degree of freedom, revise multicollinearity, and provide more information and so on. Based on balanced panel data, we analyze the impact of the minimum wage both in time and cross-section dimensions, in order to eliminate deviation, provide more comprehensive and precise estimation.

Key model: EMP= F (MW, GDP′)

Where EMP is the amount of migrant workers' employment, MW is the minimum wage, GDP' is the added value of the Second and Third Industry.

In some provinces of China, the minimum wage system was put into effect in 1993. Two years later, the scope of implementation expanded to the whole country. So we use 27 selected provinces and cities of 1995-2008 panel data from China Statistical Yearbook, China labor Statistical Yearbook, analysis report on supply and demand condition in urban labor market and the website of ministry human resource and social security of different regions.

EMP denotes the amount of employment of migrant workers. The migrant workers are defined as persons working in the city who have agricultural registered permanent residence. In quantity, they equal the amount of employees with agricultural registered permanent residence deducting practitioners in the farming, forestry, animal, husbandry and fishery. As a whole, The data calculated with this method agree with the figures in report on migrant workers in China 2009, especially in 2003,2004 and 2005.

We choose the high level of minimum wage in different regions. Because different regions have different schedules when the minimum wage is put into effect, we calculate the data again using time as factor weight. GDP' denotes the added value of the Second and Third Industry. The main reason is that the Second and Third Industry are directly influenced by the minimum wage.

To ensure the estimation validity, we apply unit root stationarity test and cointegration test theory to study the relationship of these variables. Panel data stationarity test includes the common root process and individual root process.

According to the results, as to the EMP series, we can't reject the null hypothesis and accept unit root hypothesis. So we conclude that the origin series are not stable while the first order difference series are stable. Though the first order difference series with the method Breitung are not stable at 10% level, it will not have obvious influence on the conclusion. The MW series and GDP′ series are the same as the EMP. They are non-stationary series of unit root which are integrated MW of order one.

In order to explore their long-term equilibrium relationships, we need to apply the co-integration test. With Johansen Fisher Panel Co-integration Test, we analyze these variables. Because the statistic p is less than0.05, we reject the null hypothesis. So that, the results show that there are long-term balanced relationships among the three series.

3 Regression Estimates

3.1 Regression Model and Results

We can formulate the pooled regression model in three ways: Pooled Regression Model, Individual—mean Corrected Regression Model and the Varying Coefficient Model. Though the method of hypothesis testing, we can choose the most appropriate one. The two hypothesizes below should be tested.

$$H_1: \alpha_1 = \alpha_2 = \ldots = \alpha_N \; ; \; H_2: \alpha_1 = \alpha_2 = \ldots = \alpha_N, \beta_1 = \beta_2 = \ldots \beta_3 = \beta_N$$

The results for the hypothesis testing show that the Varying Coefficient Mode with fixed effects should be formulated. In this paper, the model might appear as:

$$EMP_{it} = \alpha_i + \beta_{1i} MW_{it} + \beta_{2i} GDP_{it} + u_{it}, i = 1, 2, \cdots, 27, t = 1, 2, \cdots, 14$$

Where u_{it} is a random error term. In order to reduce heteroscedasticity, we select Generalized least Square Method to estimate the coefficients:

β1 means the impact of the minimum wage on employment. Results show that there are significantly correlations expect Beijing, Hei Longjiang and Sichuan Province.β2 means the impact of GDP′ on the employment of migrant. Every province but Shandong has significantly correlation. Among these provinces, GDP′ has negative effects in Jiangxi, Guangxi and Sichuan, which shows that the "no-employment-growth" in the three provinces is more significant than others. Since 1990s, both rapid economic growth and high rate of unemployment exist in China. At present, China is at stage of industry structural upgrading, from labor-intensive industrialization to capital-and technology-intensive industrialization. The labor is gradually replaced by the capital and technology which may reduce the ability to absorb labor. Consequently, economy growth pays a diminuendo role in employment promotion.

3.2 Results for Analyzing the Employment Effects by Industry

In China, migrant workers mainly in sub-manufacturing, construction and wholesale and retail and catering industry do the unskilled job. Taking the three industries above as samples, based on unbalanced panel data, we analyze the employment effects of the minimum wage. The fixed effect variable intercept model is formulated and it appears as:

$$EMP_{it} = \alpha_i + \beta_1 MW_{it} + \beta_2 GDP_{it} + u_{it}, i = 1, 2, \cdots, 27, t = 1, 2, \cdots, 14$$

Where u_{it} is a random error and the assumption of zero–mean, homoscedasticity and strict exogeneity of MW, GDP′ can be guaranteed. Individual effect is α_i. Thus, β1, β2 respectively embody the impact of MW, GDP′. The estimations are listed in Table 1.

Table 1. Regression Results for the Equation above

Explained variable	Manufacturing Industry	Construction Industry	Wholesale and Retail and Catering Industry
β_1	-0.2358	0.1087	0.1338
Std. Error	0.0385	0.0204	0.0231
Prob.	0.0000	0.0000	0.0000
Result	☆☆☆	***	***
β_2	0.0438	0.0122	0.0133
Std. Error	0.0038	0.0014	0.0015
Prob.	0.0000	0.0000	0.0000
Result	***	***	***
Fixed Effects	the first three JS:244.8905 ZJ:232.9069 JX:154.1474 the last three LN:-100.4254 JL:-97.1327 BJ:-93.0824	the first three HN: 207.6900 SD:177.3351 AH:118.2141 the last three SH:-111.0922 BJ:-87.4648 TJ:-80.7237	the first three ZJ:100.2695 HN:95.6809 JX:65.7335 the last three SH:-88.8144 BJ:-59.5965 TJ:-46.0257
Weighted Statistics	R2 = 0.8228 Adj-R2= 0.8079 F =55.2246 P= 0.0000	R2 = 0.9454 Adj-R2= 0.9408 F =208.8990 P = 0.0000	R2 = 0.8880 Adj-R2= 0.8786 F =93.5211 P = 0.0000

Note: *** means significantly positive correlation at p=0.1 and ☆☆☆ means significantly negative correlation at p=0.1.

From Table 1, we conclude that the employment effects of the minimum wage vary with different industries.

(1) The minimum wage has a negative effect in manufacturing industry. The absolute value of the coefficient is less than 1, which indicates that the influence is limited. In China that is a manufacturing power, the labor cost affects the labor-intensive manufacturing industry. Raising the minimum wage means the cost of enterprise is pushed. As a result, many workers especially migrant workers may be fired. The negative effect in manufacturing industry can be explained by elasticity of employment. When the minimum wage is raised, if the elasticity of employment in manufacturing industry is less than1, capital deepening may occur in this industry. Capital substitutes labor, as a result that the growth rate of employment is lower than that of output and that the growth of employment is curbed. Though raising the minimum in manufacturing industry may cause unemployment, it may necessitate restructuring and upgrading industries.

(2) The minimum wage has a positive effect in construction industry. In some provinces, underdeveloped regions of China, a good many migrant workers are engaged in the construction industry for more revenue. These migrant workers cross area to flow in forms of diverse organizations, or flow among different construction projects. Because the wage is an important factor of labor mobility, the minimum wage is an important reference for payment. In addition, the primary purpose of old migrant workers, more than forty years old, lack of skill, is to earn more money. The phenomenon that these old migrant workers are long engaged in construction projects can explain why the minimum wage has a negative effect in construction industry.

Thus, raising the minimum wage in construction industry may not reduce employment but increase migrant workers' income.

(3) The minimum wage has a positive effect in wholesale and retail and catering industry. Statistics show that the migrant workers' employment percentage of service industries, such as wholesale and catering, has the rising trend in recent years. In addition to industrial policies and continuous development of the third industry, low minimum wage and inadequate enforcement are two other important reasons for the positive effect. Thus, we think it is necessary to increase the minimum wage in these industries and to guide the labor force for purpose of further promoting economic development.

4 Conclusions

The empirical analysis shows that the minimum wage has positive effects in the eastern and western regions. However, it is just the opposite in the central China. In the eastern region, because of higher economic development level, faster speed of development, it has a strong demand for labor. In addition, the consumer spending and prices of these areas are high, but the minimum wage is relatively low. So the minimum wage of the eastern region can increase to higher level. As for the central region, it almost has the same minimum wage level as the west region does. However, its price level is higher than the west, which causes the outflow of labor. So in the central region the adjustment should be postponed. As for the western region, the industrial structure of the primary and excavation industries is helpful to absorb the low-end labors. In recent years, with the development of the west region, more and more labors flow to these areas. Thus, raising the minimum wage in the west region is feasible and beneficial.

Further more, employment effects of the minimum wage differ by industries. In China, the minimum wage system is implemented according to the regions. Because there are differences among industries at the aspects of labor demand and productivity, etc, employment effects of the minimum wage differ by industries. According to the empirical results, it has a negative effect on the manufacturing industry and positive effect on construction, wholesale and retail and catering industry. Therefore, it is necessary to set different minimum wage levels for different industries, in order that the minimum wage can play a positive effect on employment.

Acknowledgment. This paper is Supported by "Project Fund of Shandong University at Weihai" and "Program for New Century Excellent Talents in University"(NCET-10-0523).

References

[1] Stigler, G.J.: The Economics of Minimum Wage Legislation. The American Economic Review 36, 358 (1946)
[2] Xingzhi, L.: Cautious in the minimum wage system. Finance 19 (2004) (in Chinese)

Employment Effect of Minimum Wage in China – Research Based on Construction and Manufacturing

Juan Shi

School of Economics and Management, Huangshi Institute of Technology, Huangshi, China, 435003
shijuanju@sina.com

Abstract. This paper adopted panel data model from 1996 to 2007 to study the effect of the minimum wage standard on employment of construction and manufacturing in China. The empirical results showed that the improvement of minimum wage standard last year had significant positive effect on the employment of construction, the improvement of minimum wage standard current year had significant negative effect on the employment of manufacturing. This paper finally proposed a more detailed minimum wage standard should be for required format.

Keywords: Minimum wage standard, Employment Effect, Construction, Manufacturing.

1 Introduction

Since the reform and opening-up policy in 1978, China achieved rapid economic development, but at the same time, some contradictions have gradually come out, of which the contradiction represented by labor and capital got the most concern. The minimum wage system was first introduced in 1994, as one of the policy measures in reducing labor and capital contradictions, its establishment or not, whether the minimum wage standard is reasonable or not and its possibility of negative impact on employment all have always been the debate focus of domestic scholars. The author believe that, for a developing country like China who is in a period of economic transition, the establishment of minimum wage system is very necessary.

This study estimates the effects of the minimum wage standards on employment of construction and manufacturing using panel data model and Chinese data from 1996 to 2007. The empirical results showed that the improvement of minimum wage standard last year had significant positive effect on the employment of construction, the improvement of minimum wage standard current year had significant negative effect on the employment of manufacturing. The main policy implication from our findings is that a more detailed minimum wage standard should be for required format. The main contribution of this paper to the literature and policy debate is to present new empirical evidence on the effect of the minimum wage for a key developing country, China.

Q. Zhou (Ed.): ISAEBD 2011, Part II, CCIS 209, pp. 78–82, 2011.

In Western countries, the early debate about the impact of minimum wage on employment were mainly focused on Stigler□ 1946□ and Lester□ 1947□ . The former considered that the low-skilled labor market and perfect competitive labor market was close, therefore, increase the minimum wage will reduce the employment of low-skilled workers. But Lester considered that the low-skilled labor market was not perfectly competitive, thus the unemployment model proposed by the latter one was not consistent with the reality, so the resulting conclusion was not valid. By the 80s, the employment effect of minimum wage in academic circles was basic consensus, they thought that the increasing of minimum wage had statistical significant negative effect on employment. However, the coefficient of elasticity was relatively small, they were generally concentrated in the range of 0.1-0.3. Then with further research, different point of views also gradually emerged. They can generally be divided into two factions: One was represented by Neumark, they thought the increasing of minimum wage has a negative effect on employment; The other was represented by Card, they thought the increasing of minimum wage will not have negative effect on employment.

For this problem, scholars in China also have obvious divergence. Economist Zhang Wuchang(2004) had always been strongly opposed to the implementation of minimum wage system, he considered minimum wage system will weaken the competitive advantage of China's labor force and affect economic growth. And Yang Tao, Zhang Libin, Chang Kai(2006) believed that the current China is in transition period to a socialist market economic system, the implementation of minimum wage policy will not increase unemployment. Practice also showed that after the implementation of minimum wage policy in each regions, the unemployment rate had not significantly increased.

The empirical research about the impact of minimum wage on employment had experienced a development process from time series data, cross-sectional data to panel data in the selection of data. Early in the study, because of measurement tools and data limitations, economists typically used time series or cross-sectional data to perform research. In recent years, with increased access to data sources, many scholars began to study by the using of panel data to overcome the defects of purely using time series data and cross-sectional data.

Machin and Manning(1994) adopted the panel data model of 80's and 90's in UK and concluded that the increasing of minimum wage will not reduce employment. Lemos(2004) adopted the monthly survey data of Brazil residents from 1982 to 2000 to study the impact of minimum wage on the employment of formal sector and informal sector in Brazilian, the conclusion showed that the formal and informal sector in Brazil all had negative employment effect, and the negative effect of the latter is stronger than that of former. Luo Xiaolan(2007) adopted the time series data of Shanghai from 1993 to 2005 to study and found that raising the minimum wage will have a positive impact on the employment of migrant workers. Zhou Peihuang, Zhao Lukuan(2010) adopted the panel data from 1995 to 2006 to study the impact of minimum wage on the employment of construction in China, and found that there was a significant negative effect and the coefficient of elasticity was -0.13.

2 Model Specification and Empirical Analysis

2.1 Model Specification

When performing empirical analysis on the impact of minimum wage on employment in China, combining with China's actual situation and based on the experience of Neumark and Dickens model, this paper specifically set the model as:

$$\ln Eit = \beta 0 + \beta 1 \ln MWit + \beta 2 \ln MWit-1 + \beta 3 \ln GDPit + \beta 4 \ln LSit + \mu i + \varepsilon it \quad (1)$$

Where Eit is our measure of employment, MWit is the real minimum wage, MWit−1 is the past real minimum wage, GDPit is labor demand shifter, LSit is labor supply shifter, μi is region fixed effect; andεit is the error term in region i and year t, i = 1, ..., 27, and t = 1, ..., 12. To get the employment elasticity of minimum wage and reduce the volatility of variable data, this model used a log-linear form, in addition, we estimated the model with the using of EGLS to overcome the impact of heteroscedasticity brought by cross-sectional data.

2.2 Empirical Analysis

For labor-intensive enterprises, since the labor cost accounts a relatively large proportion in its entire production cost, we can know that the increasing of minimum wage standard should have a greater impact on the employment of labor-intensive enterprises. In view of this, we chose construction and manufacturing of more labor-intensive enterprises to inspect. When inspecting the impact of minimum wage standard on the employment of construction and manufacturing, constrained by the statistical data, the time series data can not only meet the requirements of a large sample when conducting econometric analysis, which may affect the accuracy of estimates, so this paper will use the annual panel data covering 27 provinces, municipalities and autonomous regions in China from 1996 to 2007 to solve the problem of small size samples. Hunan, Fujian, Hainan and Tibet were not included because of their incomplete minimum wage data collection. The minimum wage data in this paper is from China's Labor and Personnel Network and Labor Advisory Network, other data is from "China Statistical Yearbook" of State Statistics Bureau in each year and the Statistical Yearbook of each region. Regression results are in Table 1.

The employment elasticity coefficient of minimum wage in construction is not statistically significant, while the employment elasticity coefficient of minimum wage's first episode lagged term is significantly positive at the statistical level of 1%, the coefficient is 0.285. In other words, the increasing of minimum wage this year will not generate significant impact on the employment of construction, but the increasing of minimum wage last year will have a significant positive impact on the employment of construction. The minimum wage last year increased by 10%, construction employment will increase 2.85%. The actual total output value of construction will also generate a significant positive impact on the employment of construction, the elasticity coefficient is 0.268, which is consist with the theoretical expectations. The employment elasticity coefficient of labor supply is statistically significantly negative as -1.414.

We then take a look at the case of manufacturing. Employment elasticity coefficient of minimum wage in manufacturing is statistically significantly negative, the coefficient is -0.587, while the employment elasticity coefficient of minimum wage's first episode lagged term is not statistically significant. This indicated that the increasing of minimum wage standard in current episode will have a significant negative impact on the employment of manufacturing, and the impact strength is relatively large. Minimum wage increased by 10%, the manufacturing employment will decrease 5.87%, but the increasing of minimum wage in last episode will not have significant impact on the employment of manufacturing. As with the construction, the increasing of real total output value in manufacturing has significant positive impact on its employment, but the employment elasticity coefficient is relatively small as only 0.140. This shows that, although in recent years the improvement of labor productivity in manufacturing promotes the rapid development of manufacturing, at the same time limiting its ability to create jobs. Increase the supply of labor will not have a significant impact on the employment of manufacturing, indicating that labor supply of manufacturing may be a more relaxed, so the increasing in labor supply will not increase the level of employment in this industry.

Table 1. The impact of minimum wage on employment – inspection on construction and manufacturing

independent variable	construction		manufacturing	
	coefficient	P value	coefficient	P value
lnMW	−0. 128	0. 210	−0. 587	0. 000
lnMW(-1)	0. 285	0. 008	−0. 095	0. 298
lnGDP	0. 268	0. 092	0. 140	0. 000
lnLS	−1. 414	0. 000	−0. 014	0. 938
Hausman test	85. 333	0. 000	95. 660	0. 000
LLC test	−5. 208	0. 000	−9. 422	0. 000
IPS test	−1. 735	0. 041	−5. 866	0. 000
ADF-Fisherχ^2 test	80. 324	0. 012	136. 563	0. 000
the adjusted R^2	0. 947		0. 971	
sample size	297		297	

Apparently under the above empirical results can be seen, the employment elasticity coefficient of the minimum wage in construction and manufacturing is different, which we thought the possible explanation was: First, different industries have different labor supply curve, labor demand curve, labor productivity, wage levels and the production cycle, and thus their sensitivity to changes in the minimum wage standard will be different. However, the minimum wage standard is oriented to the whole industry in the same area, the same standard applying to all industries and employees is excessively simplex and broad, it ignores the differences between industries, the result is if the established minimum wage standard deviates from the nature of the industry, the minimum wage standard will naturally have different effects on the employment of various industries; Second, the coverage of minimum wage between industries and the actual implementation are different, which will lead to its different effects on employment.

3 The Policy Recommendations

The minimum wage system is a effective tool for nation in achieving the reasonable regulation of income distribution, but also a necessary requirement to maintain social stability. Since the minimum wage system in China has only established for a relatively short time, there are still some problems to be perfected. Based on the previous research and analysis, we propose the formulation of minimum wage standard should be more refined. At present, all 31 provinces, municipalities and autonomous regions in China have implemented the minimum wage system, when local governments formulate the minimum wage standard, according to local circumstances, different urban areas have also developed several grades of minimum wage standard. But the whole industry and all stuff in the same area are implementing a uniform minimum wage standard, ignoring the differences between industries and job categories, which makes the practical implementation of the minimum wage system often runs into a blank wall due to issues of industries, job categories and other issues, which not only causing part of the workers' wage level deviating from the nature of the industry, the real pay off and job performance of workers, but also objectively providing an opportunity for various covered infringement of enterprises. In view of this, we should learn from the practice of western countries, the formulation of minimum wage standard not only varies with time and place, but also varies with industries and jobs, that is different wage minimum wage standards are formulated based on their own characteristics of industries and job categories.

References

1. Lemos, S.:The Effects of the Minimum Wage in the Formal and Informal Sectors in Brazil. University of Leicester Discussion Paper (2004)
2. Lester, R.A., Marginalism: Minimum Wages,and Labor Markets. American Economic Review 37, 135–148 (1947)
3. Machin, S., Manning, A.: Minimum Wages, Wage Dispersion and Employment: Evidence from the UK Wages Councils. Industrial and Labor Relations Review 47, 319–329 (1994)
4. Stigler, G.J.: The Economics of Minimum Wage Legislation. American Economic Review 36, 358–365 (1946)
5. Low, X.: Analysis of the Employment Effect ofM in imum Wages in China's Monopsony Labor Market. Finance and Trade Research 4, 1–5 (2007)
6. Zhang, L., Chang, K.: Setting minimum wage won't lead to job losses, `http://www.theory.people.com`
7. Zhang, W.: Evaluation of China's minimum wage policy, `http://blog.sina.com.cn`
8. Zhou, P., Zhao, L.: The Employment Effect of Minimum Wages and mechanism Based on Construction. Journal of Zhong Nan University of Economics and Law 1, 22–28 (2010)

Does Globalization Benefit Developed or Developing Country? – Case Studies on Chinese and Australian Construction Industry

Peng Zhang and Kerry London

School of Property, Construction and Project Management, RMIT University
Melbourne, Australia
zhangpeng2222@hotmail.com

Abstract. Globalization has penetrated deeply into all areas of the world. The researches on this topic have been never stopped in recent years. The debate on globalization's benefits and concerns for develop and developing countries is still intense in recent years. This paper adopts Chinese and Australian construction industry as case studies to explore the answer for that debate. The International Advanced Index is used for the measurement of a certain country's construction industry's performance and position in the international market. The key findings are: both the developing and developed countries could be benefits from the process of globalization. However, because the advantages such as technology, education, finance and management, the growth rapid of developed country is much higher than developing country. It could lead to extend the gap between them.

Keywords: Globalization, Construction Industry, International Advanced Index.

1 Introduction

As one of the main trend of today's world, globalization has developed deeply in all the economy and society fields. Many researchers have hammered at this topic. Some of them believe globalization could benefit the whole world. However, some others state the globalization could bring plenty of concerns, especially for the developing countries. This paper will adopts Chinese and Australian construction industry as cases to explore the question of "does globalization only benefit developed countries". The trend of Chinese and Australian construction industry's performance and position in the international market with the development of globalization will be explored to answer this question. In addition, the International Advanced Index [1] [2] will be used for the measurement of a certain country's construction industry's performance and position in the international market.

Q. Zhou (Ed.): ISAEBD 2011, Part II, CCIS 209, pp. 83–90, 2011.

2 Literature Review

Since its inception, the concept of globalization has inspired numerous competing definitions and interpretations, with antecedents dating back to the great movements of trade and empire across Asia and the Indian Ocean from the 15th century onwards [3]. Globalization is not a new phenomenon. It began towards the end of the nineteenth century, but it slowed down during the period from the start of the First World War until the third quarter of the twentieth century [4].

Globalization describes the process by which regional economies, societies, and cultures have become integrated through a global network of political ideas through communication, transportation, and trade. The term is most closely associated with the term economic globalization: the integration of national economies into the international economy through trade, foreign direct investment, capital flows, migration, the spread of technology, and military presence [5]. However, globalization is usually recognized as being driven by a combination of economic, technological, socio-cultural, political, and biological factors [6]. The term can also refer to the transnational circulation of ideas, languages, or popular culture through acculturation. An aspect of the world which has gone through the process can be said to be globalized.

Globalization has various aspects which affect the world in several different ways, such as industrial, financial, economic, job market and political [7] [8]. There is little common ground between proponents and opponents of globalization. The benefits of globalization have been addressed by various scholars. For example, firstly, globalization is a very positive force that lifts countries out of poverty [5]. Secondly, globalization causes a virtuous economic cycle associated with faster economic growth. Next, workers in developing countries now have more occupational choices than ever before. Educated workers in developing countries are able to compete on the global job market for high paying jobs. Production workers in developing countries are not only able to compete; they have a strong advantage over their counterparts in the industrialized world [8]. In addition, the global economy provides a market for the products of cottage industry, providing more opportunities [5].

Globalization has generated significant international opposition over concerns that it has increased inequality and environmental degradation [9]. For the inequality issues, the first point should be addressed is the income inequality. This has resulted in a growing gap between the incomes of the rich and poor. This trend seems to be greater in the United States than other industrial countries. Income inequality in the United States started to rise in the late 1970,'s, however the rate of increase rose sharply in the 21st century; it has now reached a level comparable with that found in developing countries [10]. The next one could be called "brain drains". Opportunities in rich countries drive talent away from poor countries, leading to brain drains. Brain drain has cost the African continent over $4.1 billion in the employment of 150,000 expatriate professionals annually [11].The Associated Chambers of Commerce and Industry estimates that the brain drain of Indian students cost India $10 billion per year [12]. In addition, the issue of sweatshops is widely discussed in recent years. In many poorer nations, globalization is the result of foreign businesses utilizing workers in a country to take advantage of the lower wage rates [13].

From the perspective of environmental, the rapid increasing of emitter of CO_2, reducing of tropical rainforests and nearly running out of minerals, such as zinc, indium, hafnium, and terbium, could be caused by globalization [14]. Next, with the development of globalization, the financial interdependency could increase. In addition, some illegal activities could be promoted by globalization, such as drug and illicit goods trade. Some also view the effect of globalization on culture as a rising concern. Along with globalization of economies and trade, culture is being imported and exported as well. The concern is that the stronger, bigger countries such as the United States, may overrun the other, smaller countries' cultures, leading to those customs and values fading away. This process is also sometimes referred to as Americanization or McDonaldization [15].

As discussed above, globalization could affect all the fields of today's world. There is no different in construction industry. The benefits and concerns of globalization have been debated for long a time in many fields. But most of them are focused on the nation or country level [16]. This research will focus on the construction industry to explore the developing country (China) and developed country (Australia)'s construction industries' performance and position in the international market in hence to explore whether the globalization only benefit developed countries, for the perspective of construction industry.

3 Model and Methodology

When the performance, development level or position in the world is discussed, there are two kinds of measurement are used commonly. The first one could be called the one-dimensional financial measurement. For example, GDP and GNP are commonly used to measure a country's development level, performance and position in the world. For the industry or firms, the measurement could be financial issues, like total revenue, international revenue, Return On Assets, Return On Sale [17], this kind of one-dimensional measurement couldn't reflect the whole picture and could lead to misunderstanding [18].

The other measurement could be called complex method. This method is used for comparison between countries by various researchers. They compare all the aspects separately. It is a good comparison strategy to find the gap and difference in each element, in hence to generate an appropriate further development strategy [16]. However, this complex comparison couldn't quantitatively measure all the elements and indicators they mentioned. In addition, this kind of comparison couldn't generate a standard used for the entire participant in this field. It only could be used in small group and samples. Also it is difficult to tell the real position of the sample in the entire participant in this field, because this method could not provide a standard quantitative index or indicator. In this sense, a proper measurement for a certain country's construction industry's performance and position in the international market should be proposed.

Therefore, Zhang and London generated a multidimensional quantitative measurement model in 2010, called the International Advanced Index, according to the characteristic of construction industry [1]. The International Advanced Index (IAI) is a quantitative measure and index system which could intuitively reflect the performance and position of certain country's construction industry in the international market. The International Advanced Index for construction industry is proposed by the following index:

- Depth Index (DI): is defined as the ratio of overall international revenue of all companies of the country to total international revenue of all the companies of all the countries.
- Height Index (HI): is defined as the quantity and quality of a certain country's top enterprises. It is not only measured in the ratio of the number of a certain country's enterprises in the top international constructors list, which is only the quantity issue. In order to consider the quality issue, a "weight" index should be mentioned, which also could reflect the distinction between the different rankings in the top list.
- Width Index (WI): is defined as a certain country's enterprises' market involvement in different specialized fields of the construction industry. It could be measured in terms of the average of the ratio of the number of specialized fields that a certain country's each construction firm is involved with to the total number of specialized fields within the construction industry. However, the specialization and diversification are two different development strategies. Firms could be successful in either way. In order to reflect this issue, in this paper, the influence in international market of a company listed in the top 10 of any specialized fields could be considered as the same with a company involved in all the fields of construction industry. It means if there are nine fields in construction industry and a company is only involved in one field, but it is listed in the top ten of this field. The number of its involved fields will be counted as 9 not 1.

In summary, the International Advanced Index of a certain country's international construction industry is the sum of DI, HI and WI.

This research will calculate the International Advanced Index of Chinese and Australian construction industry in 2000 and 2009, in hence to explore the trend of Chinese and Australian construction industry's performance and position in the global market. Based on this trend, the question of "does globalization only benefit developed countries" in construction sector could be answered.

4 Data Collection

In this paper, the analysis is limited to the Chinese and Australian multinational construction enterprises. It is difficult to overemphasize the importance of multinational enterprises. It has been acknowledged by various researchers and social institutions in the world (United Nations, International Monetary Fund, etc.) because of their massive financial, technological, human, intellectual, and organizational resources [19][20]. In the international construction sector, most of the direct participants are multinational enterprises. In this sense, the level of multinational enterprises' development could be considered as the indicator of the country's level of development. Therefore, in this paper, the multinational enterprises will be studied as cases.

The annual report about the top 225 international contractors provided by Engineering News-Record (ENR) will be adopted in this paper. However, some limitations should be discussed. Firstly, the quality of the data depends on the willingness of firms who wish to participate in the ENR's survey. If some firms do not wish to participate, the data and the rank will be different. For example, because the British contractors-Trafalgar House PLG in 1996 and Kvaener Groupand Bovis Construction Ltd in 1999 did not participate in the ENR survey, all the data changed dramatically. In addition, the authenticity of data depends on the firms' honesty. However, the data provided by ENR are also the most comprehensive data set currently available.

For the International Advanced Index of Chinese and Australian construction industry in the international market, it is difficult to gather data for the Depth Index. Therefore, adopting the ENR's statistics, Depth Index is generated as the ratio of overall international revenue of all Chinese or Australian companies to total international revenue of all companies in the list. In addition, Height Index could be measured in the number of certain country's construction enterprises in the top 225 international constructors list and the "weight", which is the value of the average international revenue in the top 100 international constructors to the average international revenue in the rest 125. The "weight" could be called Gap index (GI) which is the indicator of the gap between the top international constructors. The smaller value indicates the smaller gap between these top companies, and vice versa. So, the formula of HI can be written as:

$$\mathrm{HI} = \frac{\text{No.of CCCEs in top the 100 ICs list} \times \text{GI} + \text{No.of CCEs in the rest 125}}{225} \tag{1}$$

$$\mathrm{GI} = \frac{\sum_{i=1}^{100} f(Ti)}{\sum_{i=101}^{225} f(Ti)} \times \frac{125}{100} \tag{2}$$

Though the International Advanced Index realizes the difference between the top 100 and the rest 125 construction companies by using the Gap Index, the difference between each companies should be measured, not only in groups. Therefore this paper will give a rank score to reflect this issue. According to the rank of these companies listed in the top 225 international constructors, the first one could get 225 scores, the second one is 224 scores, until the last one is 1 scores. The High Index of a certain country's construction industry is the average rank score to the total number of companies in the list, 225. The higher value of High Index shows the better performance of the country's construction industry in the global market. So, the High Index could be calculated by the formula below.

$$\mathrm{HI} = \frac{\text{Average Score of CCCEs in the top 225 ICs list}}{225} \tag{3}$$

Furthermore, according to the classification of ERN, there are 10 specializations in the construction industry. However, the data of Industrial sector and Petroleum sector are put in together. Therefore, in this research, they are recognized as one field in construction industry. In this sense, there are nine fields totally in construction industry. ERN also provides the number of Chinese enterprises listed in the top 10 of each specialized fields. The formula for generating WI will be:

$$\mathrm{WI} = \frac{\sum_{i=1}^{N} f(W'i)}{N} \tag{4}$$

$$\mathrm{N} = \text{No. of CCCEs in top 225 IC list} \tag{5}$$

$$f(W'i) = \frac{W'i+(9-1)M}{9} \tag{6}$$

$$W'i = \text{No. of fields each CCCE involved} \tag{7}$$

$$M = \sum \text{NO. of CCCEs listed in top 10 of each field} \tag{8}$$

5 Results and Discussion

As a traditional developed country, Australian economy plays an important role in the Asia Pacific area, even the world. Many sectors of Australia are at the forefront of the world. Australian construction industry has also got great achievement and development in the international market. For example, there are four Australian construction enterprises listed in the ERN top 225 international constructors in 2009. Hereinto, two of them are listed in the top 25. Their total international revenue is more than 12 billion USD, which is 3.13% of total international revenue of the top 225 international constructors [21], compared with 0.8 billion USD for the total international revenue of Australian construction enterprises listed in the top 225 in 2000 and 0.7% for the percentage in total international revenue of the top 225 international constructors [22].

Although China is one of the most ancient civilizations in human history, it has recently in the last decade made dramatic moves towards modernization and marketization. After the implementation of the "reform and opening-up policy" in the 1980s', China embarked on a road of revival. In 2007 the GDP of China was ranked fourth in the world after the United States, Japan and Germany, whereas previously it was tenth in 1990 [23]. In 2007, Foreign Direct Investment (FDI) in China reached 83.52 billion U.S. dollars, ranking No. 6 in the world, accounting for 16.7% of the total of developing countries. China's level of FDI ranks first among developing countries for the last 17 years consecutively [24]. It has often been claimed by both the popular business media and academic experts alike that the 21st century will be the Chinese century [25] [26] [27][28][29].

Regardless of the rhetoric it is important for us to understand these most recent changes on construction industry performance. The Chinese construction industry has undergone a dramatic change caused by internationalization in recent years, and as a result become integrated into the world economy to a greater extent. Chinese construction enterprises have accounted for 54 among the world's top 225 international constructors in 2009 [21]. The total international revenue has change from 5.4 billion USD in 2000 to 50.6 billion USD in 2009 [21] [22].

From Table 1, the International Advanced Index of both Chinese and Australian construction industry are increased from 2000 to 2009. However, the growth rate of Chinese construction industry is only about 10%. For contrast, the Australian construction industry has achieved 25% growth in 2009, compared with 2000 in the

International Advanced Index. This means both the developing and developed countries could be benefits by the globalization in a certain degree. However, under the current situation and environment, developed countries could be easier to use the advantages of globalization and get more rapid growth. It could extend the gap between developing and developed countries. Therefore, the developing countries should learn from developed countries to make full use of the advantages of globalization, at the same time, reduce the negative effect of globalization by making appropriate strategy and policy.

Table 1. Compurgation of Chinese and Australian construction industry

Index	Chinese construction industry		Australian construction industry	
	2000	2009	2000	2009
DI	0.046	0.132	0.007	0.0313
HI	0.4518	0.4339	0.6756	0.6911
WI	0.4412	0.467	0.5556	0.8611
IAI	0.939	1.0329	1.2382	1.5835

6 Conclusion

Globalization has become one of themes of today's world. The debate on the advantages and disadvantages of globalization has never been stopped. This research adopts Chinese and Australian construction industry as cases to explore whether globalization only benefits developed countries, based on the International Advanced Index. The result shows both the developing and developed countries could be benefits from the process of globalization. However, because the advantages such as technology, education, finance and management, the growth rapid of developed country is much higher than developing country. It could lead to extend the gap between them. In this sense, the developing countries should make appropriate strategy and policy to make full use of the advantages of globalization, at the same time, reduce its negative effect. Developed countries should help developing countries in the process of globalization. In addition, a new international economic and social new order should be built, based on the cooperation of developed and developing countries, which is an important issue for the future research.

References

1. Zhang, P., London, K.: A comparison research on the international performance of Chinese construction industry between before and after entry into the WTO. In: Zhou, Q.Y. (ed.) Applied Social Science, vol. 1, pp. 127–129. Information Engineering Research Institute, Delaware (2011)
2. Zhang, P., London, K.: Chinese construction industry performance after entry into the WTO. In: Wang, Y.W., Wang, J., Shen, G.Q.P., Wong, J. (eds.) Proc. of 2010 International Conference on Construction & Real Estate Management, vol. 1, pp. 93–99. China Architecture & Building Press, Beijing (2010)
3. Hopkins, A.G. (ed.): Globalization in World History. Pimlico, London (2002)

4. United Nations Economic and Social Commission for Western Asia: Summary of the Annual Review of Developments in Globalization and Regional Integration in the Countries of the ESCWA Region, New York (2002)
5. Bhagwati, J.N.: In Defense of Globalization. Oxford University Press, New York (2004)
6. Croucher, S.L.: Globalization and Belonging: The Politics of Identity a Changing World. Rowman & Littlefield, Lanhamp (2004)
7. Reich, R.: The Work of the Nations, Preparing Ourselves for 21st Century Capitalism. Alfred A. Knopf, Toronto (1992)
8. Lorenz, A., Wagner, W.: The birth of China's special economic zones, http://www.spiegel.de/international/spiegel/0,1518,465007-3,00.html
9. Krishn, A.G.: Impact of Globalization on Developing Countries (With Special Reference To India). Int'l. Research Journal of Finance and Economics 5, 166–171 (2006)
10. Noah, T.: The United States of Inequality, Introducing the great Divergence. Slate (September 3, 2010), http://www.slate.com/id/2266025/entry/2266026/
11. Karim, R.: Global Standards for Justice in the era of Globalization. World Universities Congress, Canakkale, Turkey (2010)
12. IANS: Students' exodus costs India forex outflow of $10 bn: Assocham, http://www.thaindian.com/newsportal/business/students-exodus-costs-india-forex-outflow-of-10-bn-assocham_100147339.htm
13. Slaughter. J.M., Swagel, P.: Does globalization lower wages and export jobs? International Monetary Fund, Washington, D.C (1997)
14. Cohen, D.: Earth's natural wealth: an audit. New Scientist 2605, 34–41 (2007)
15. Steger, M.: Globalization. Sterling Publishing, New York (2009)
16. Wei, X.Y., Han, C.F.: Comparative Analysis of the development level of United States and Chinese construction industry. Construction Economy, 239, 19–21
17. Loncan, T., Nique, W.M.: Degree of Internationalization and performance: Evidence from Brazilian multinational firms. GCG Geoggetown University-Universia 4(1), 40–51 (2010)
18. Sullivan, D.: Measuring the degree of internationalization of a firm: A reply. Journal of International Business Studies 27(1), 179–192 (1996)
19. Kanter, R.M.: World class: Thriving locally in a global economy. Simon & Schuster, New York (1995)
20. Korten, D.C.: The Post-Corporate world: Life after capitalism. Berrett-Koehler Publishers, San Francisco (1999)
21. Reina, P., Tulacz, G.J.: The top 225 international Contractors. Engineering News Record 265(6), 44–48 (2010)
22. Reina, P., Tulacz, G.J.: The top 225 international Contractors. Engineering News Record 247(8), 66–76 (2001)
23. IMF: World Economic Outlook. International Monetary Fund, New York (2008)
24. National Bureau of Statistic of China, China Statistical Year Book-2008. China Statistics Press, Beijing (2008)
25. Dyer, G.: Bumps on the pitch queer the Chinese century. Financial Times, London (2009)
26. Thayer, C.A.: Peace Studies in the Chinese Century: International Perspectives. Asian Studies Review 33(1), 136–138 (2009)
27. Chan, G.: Peace Studies in the Chinese Century: International Perspectives. Peace Review 20(3), 404 (2008)
28. Smith, P.G.: Book Reviews - The Chinese Century - Doing Business in the New China: A Handbook and Guide. The Journal of Product Innovation Management 23(3), 295 (2006)
29. Hines, A.: The coming Chinese century. The Futurist 31(5), 8–10 (1997)

Study on Incentive Mechanism of BOT Financing Model for Low-Renting Public Housing

Fangqiang Liu[1,2], Jiansheng Dai[3], and Liming Wang[3]

[1] College of Construction Management and Real Estate, Chongqing University, Chongqing 400044, P. R. China
[2] Chongqing Traffic & Tourism Investment Group Co., Ltd, Chongqing 400021, P. R. China
[3] College of Economics and Business Administration, Chongqing University, Chongqing 400044, P. R. China
lfqcq@163.com

Abstract. The fact that private capital does not will to invest projects of low-renting public housing dues to the low return on investment and the uncontrollability of risks. Therefore, it is necessary to build up the mechanism of economic incentive, property right incentive and allocation of risk to propel BOT financing model in the field of low-renting public housing so as to deal with the shortage of funds. In this way, it can make sure investors can get normal profits and consequently improve the healthy development of the construction of low-renting public housing in China.

Keywords: low-renting public housing, BOT, incentive mechanism.

1 Introduction

As one of the most important ways widely used for housing security internationally, low-renting public housing plays an important part in dealing with the housing problems for "Sandwich layer"(Yang Huakai, 2009). However, it is not enough to rely on financial investment merely, which results in the shortage of the construction funds of low-renting public housing (Li Dezheng, 2010) so that the achievement of the construction of low-renting public housing is far away from satisfaction.

As one financing way for attracting private or international capital, BOT plays a great role in the construction of infrastructure, especially road construction (NOMBELA G、GINES DR, 2004; Yang Hongwei, He Jianmin, 2003) and power facility construction (S.Q Wang、 L.K Tiong, 2000 ; Nigel Smith、 Hao Zhang, 2004). In recent years, some regions have started to explore to bring private capital into the construction of low-renting public housing actively by borrowing ideas from the experience of BOT of road, bridge and other infrastructures (Beijing Municipal People's Government, 2009). So far, some domestic scholars have discussed about BOT financing model for low-renting public housing primarily (Li Zhiqing, Tian Jinxin, 2009; Deng Wei, 2009), but their research is not deep enough which mainly focus on the feasibility and effectiveness of BOT financing model. Some foreign scholars research the supply and demand of low-renting public housing in terms of tax

Q. Zhou (Ed.): ISAEBD 2011, Part II, CCIS 209, pp. 91–98, 2011.

preference(Michael D、Eriksen, 2009), energy cost(Peter Gresche, 2010), the sell of low-renting public housing(Urmi Sengupta, 2006)and others. However, there are fewer literatures to research BOT financing model for low-renting public housing. Different from other infrastructures like road, as a non-profit project with security, it is hard for low-renting public housing to get normal benefits by depending on reasonable operation of projects merely even we treat whole life cycle of projects as concession period. Therefore, it is necessary to bring in many kinds of incentive mechanism to draw social capital into the construction of low-renting public housing, including private capital, in order to promote the healthy development of the construction of low-renting public housing in China.

2 Payoff Function of BOT Financing Model for Low-Renting Public Housing

2.1 Payoff Function of Low-Renting Public Housing

Payoff function of low-renting public housing can be showed like this:

$$\pi = \sum_{t=T_0}^{T_t} \left(\frac{(P_t - b_t)Q - f_t}{(1+r)^t}\right) - \sum_{t=T_b}^{T^r} \frac{Di}{(1+r)^t} - \frac{D}{(1+r)^{T_r}} - (I(Q) - D) \tag{1}$$

In this formula, T_b represents beginning period of construction, T_o is beginning period of operation, T_t is transfer moment and T_e is last junked moment of projects. We suppose that P_t is rental price at the time of t, Q is construction areas of low-renting public housing, b_t is maintenance cost per unit to maintain normal running during operation period of projects, f_t is the cost during the period of t except financing cost and maintenance cost, including revenue cost, I is total cost of the construction of low-renting public housing (including land cost and building cost) and r is required rate of return of investors. Investors of low-renting public housing can take full advantage of other financing channels to enhance the availability factor of own funds. To simplify the discussion, we suppose that investors obtain a loan from a bank at the early days of the construction and length of maturity is T^r and the repayment way of the loan is: investors should pay the interest during the maturity and pay the principal back at the end of the maturity. We suppose D is total loan amount of low-renting public housing, $I-D$ is own funds of investors to development low-renting public housing and i is loan interest rate of projects.

According to formula (1), payoff function π is the profits on the premise of considering about opportunity cost of units but not the usual accounting profits. $\pi > 0$ shows that investors can obtain much more profits in the construction of low-renting public housing; $\pi = 0$ expresses investors can get the compensation of opportunity cost in the construction of low-renting public housing, that is, there is no difference for investors whether to take part in projects or not. Sum up, $\pi \geq 0$ is one necessary condition to attract private capital into the construction of low-renting public housing.

2.2 Example

We can calculate the benefits of investors taking part in the construction of low-renting public housing by formula (1). One project of low-renting public housing has total investment of 3,200,000,000. The areas of it are 954,700 square meters. The rent is 10 RMB/year*square meter. We suppose that 80 % of the total investment is from the bank's credit with 6% annual interest. We assume that operation period of low-renting public housing is 20 years, maintenance cost is 2 RMB/year*square meter and required IRR by the investor is 10%. According to those given data, the maximum profits the investor can get are -859,000,000, which is less than zero far and away. So if the private capital undertakes this project of low-renting public housing, it will face a huge sum of loss.

3 To Construct Incentive Mechanism to Improve the Construction of Low-Renting Public Housing

Different from other BOT financing models of road and others, low-renting public housing is the project with the security which aims at low-income residents. The rent of it is limited by spending power of residents so that it is hard for investors to obtain normal profits through effective operation even we extend the concession period of low-renting public housing to whole life cycle of the project. Therefore, the government is supposed to adopt some measures like economic incentive, property right incentive and allocation of risks to advance the application of BOT financing model in low-renting public housing. In this way, it can deal with the trouble of funds in the construction of low-renting public housing.

3.1 Economic Incentive Mechanism

One main reason for private capital unwilling to participate in the construction of low-renting public housing is the low return on investment. So the government should research some economic measures like interest rate preference, land assignment, guarantee support (including financing guarantee, etc), the adjustment of concession period, subsidy support (including construction subsidy and running subsidy) and tax relief to increase private capital's return on investment of low-renting public housing.

The Adjustment of concession period

Under the condition that rent is greater than maintenance cost, the longer operation period is, the more profits investors obtain (according to formula (1), there is $\partial\pi/\partial T_t > 0$). For BOT projects, rent and concession period are two main factors which determine the income that investors get from the construction and operation of low-renting public housing. For non-profit of low-renting public housing, the rent of it is restricted by many economic and social factors so that it is hard for it to rise by a large margin. Besides, the aim to construct low-renting public housing is to solve housing problem of low-income people. So from the point of view of the maximization of social welfare, the government will also control the rent of low-renting public housing. In this situation, the government should take some measures, one of which is to adjust concession period flexibly. Despite of it, the length of concession period is also limited by whole life cycle of projects. If the government treats whole life cycle of the project as its concession period, investors still can not achieve $\pi \geq 0$. Therefore, we should consider some other incentive measures.

Land assignment

From the point of the view of cost structure of current housing market, land cost takes more than 50% of total sum of house construction (Wang Weiguo, 2009). This proportion is very high. At this stage, there has been no definite rule to regularize whether the government can supply the land in the way of land assignment by free to low-renting public housing projects, which contains private capital. However, the way of land assignment will be able to decrease aggregate investment of low-renting public housing by a large margin and increase the profits of projects (form formula (1), there is $\partial\pi/\partial I < 0$). Hence, the policy of land assignment is beneficial to drawing much more private capital into the construction of low-renting public housing.

Interest rate preference

We suppose that the government supplies preferential loan interest rate i_0 to investors of low-renting public housing and $i_0 < i$. If other conditions don't change, the benefit of units is:

$$\pi|i_0 = \sum_{t=T_0}^{T_t} \frac{(P_t - b_t)Q - f_t}{(1+r)^t} - \sum_{t=T_b}^{T^r} \frac{Di_0}{(1+r)^t} - \frac{D}{(1+r)^{T^r}} - (I(Q) - D)$$

Because of $\partial\pi/\partial i < 0$, it is easy to prove $\pi|i_0 > \pi$. Preferential interest rate can increase the profits of low-renting public housing. The larger preferential extent of interest rate is, the more investors can get. However, interest rate preference is also limited by capital cost of commercial banks, which means preferential loan interest rate is not able to lower than deposit rate at the same time. Actually, the extent of interest rate preference is limited by many factors so that it is difficulty for projects of low-renting public housing to get positive profits only by this measure. We should think about other incentive measures.

Financing guarantee

Financing guarantee can increase the profits of low-renting public housing in many ways. One is to decrease financing cost of units through government guarantee, like getting relatively preferential interest rate or decreasing fund raising cost relevant to loan. The second one is to shorten the time when units get the credit as well as construction period of projects through the government guarantee so as to increase the profits of units indirectly (for $\partial\pi/\partial T_o < 0$). The third one is to increase loan limit for units through government guarantee in order to reduce the pressure of own funds and improve the efficiency of own funds (we can prove that if $r > i$, $\partial\pi/\partial D > 0$, that is, the larger loan limit is, the more profits low-renting public housing can obtain).

Direct subsidies

To supply economic subsidies to low-renting public housing directly can reduce building cost or increase running income of projects undoubtedly. The subsidies for low-renting public housing contain construction subsidies and running subsidies. Construction subsidies are that the government supplies various kinds of economic subsidy to units which undertake the construction of low-renting public housing. For example, the government can give monetary subsidies directly according to the construction areas and quality. And running subsidies are that the government gives various kinds of subsidies during the process of running after projects of low-renting public housing are constructed and put into operation.

Tax preference

Tax preference is that the government offers many kinds of tax preference or deducts and exempts some kinds of tax to investors of projects during the building or running process of low-renting public housing. For example, the government can reduce tax rate of income tax and carries out tax relief within three to five years of running.

3.2 Property Right Incentive Mechanism

Payoff function for allowing investors of projects to develop part of commercial projects.

Compared with commercial projects, projects of low-renting public housing have low return of investment since the rent is controlled by the government. If we allow investors of projects to run commercial projects by a certain proportion during the construction of low-renting public housing, they can take back the cost as well as obtain normal profits. Based on the features of low-renting public housing the government can think about some incentive measures. For example, property right of matched garages, business facades and even the houses of low-renting public housing can go to investors conditionally after concession period comes to an end. In this way, it can form complete property right incentive mechanism and legal framework of the government under the BOT of low-renting public housing. To simplify our discussion, we suppose that the government permits investors of projects to develop business facades according to a certain proportion (like a) of development capacity of low-renting public housing Q and gives property right to units after offering certain land price compensation. We suppose external sales price of commercial projects after the completion is P^0 and additional commitments for commercial projects are I^0 which include land price compensation. Furthermore, we suppose that commercial projects can begin the sale at the time of T. After considering about those factors, payoff function of units is:

$$\pi^0 = \sum_{t=T_0}^{T_t} \left(\frac{(P_t - b_t)Q - f_t}{(1+r)^t}\right) + \frac{aP^0Q}{(1+r)^T} - \sum_{t=T_b}^{T^r} \frac{Di}{(1+r)^t} - \frac{D}{(1+r)^{T_r}} - (I(Q) + I^0(Q) - D) \quad (2)$$

Among it, as long as $\frac{aP^0Q}{(1+r)^T} - I^0(Q) > 0$, there is $\pi^0 > \pi$.

According to the roaring trade of current real estate market, we can make sure considerably that $\pi^0 > \pi$ works. Moreover, as the proportion a of commercial projects and non-profit projects grows bigger and bigger, $\Delta\pi = \pi^0 - \pi$ will rise. And units are allowed to develop commercial projects in the construction of low-renting public housing as well as to enjoy tax preference, interest rate preference, direct subsidies and other economic benefits offered by the government so that investors can get more profits in this kind of project development than pure commercial one. In addition, different from pure commercial project development, in the construction of low-renting public housing, the proportion taken by commercial projects is controlled by the government seriously, so the output facing the market is smaller, which means market risk this kind of projects face is less than those of pure commercial development and capital risk can be controlled much better.

Example (continuous)

Based on example (1), if the government permits investors to develop commercial projects as well as low-renting public housing, we might as well suppose the areas of commercial project as 179,900 square meters and the selling price on the market is 18000/square meter. To develop this project, the investor should invest 1,767,000,000 in addition. And we also suppose the houses can sold out in one year after the completion and the tax rate is 25%. According to those given data, we can calculate the investor's profits by formula (2) as 239,000,000 RMB, which means that the investor has made profits.

3.3 The Mechanism of Allocation of Risks Incentive

Another important reason why private capital is not willing to enter into the field of low-renting public housing is the uncontrollability of various risks. In terms of the characteristics of low-renting public housing, we should design the mechanism of allocation of risk like risk of rent fluctuations, financing risk and risk of taxes and dues fluctuations. Through those reasonable measures of allocation of risks, the stability of the return of investment for low-renting public housing can be increased.

Under the environment of market economy, economic fluctuation is extremely nature because inflation and deflation always happen periodically and bank rate also changes because of the need of national macro-control and the influence of international financial market. In payoff functions (1) and (2) of projects, we don't consider the influence of inflation and interest rate fluctuation on investor' profits of projects. If so, payoff function of investors can be showed as:

$$\pi = \sum_{t=T_0}^{T_t} \left(\frac{(P_t - b_t)Q - f_t}{\prod_{j=T_b}^{t}(1+r+g_j)}\right) - \sum_{t=T_b}^{T^r} \frac{Di_t}{\prod_{j=T_b}^{t}(1+r+g_j)} - \frac{D}{\prod_{j=T_b}^{T_r}(1+r+g_j)} - (I(Q) - D) \quad (3)$$

Among it, g_t is inflation rate at period of t. Because we can not predict inflation rate g_t completely in advance, the profit of low-renting public housing is uncertain actually (even other factors of payoff function are certain). And i_t is interest rate during the period of t, which is uncertain either as same as the factor of inflation.

To build up the mechanism of allocation of rent fluctuation risks

From formula (3) we can see that the profits of low-renting public housing will be uncertain even under the same rent because of some uncertain factors like inflation. As usual the profits of investors will decrease with the rise of inflation rate. Therefore, the government should raise the rent of low-renting public housing in inflation period in order to guarantee the normal profits of investors. However, compared with changeable inflation, the adjustment of rent always seems slow relatively because of some limiting factors. For this reason, it is necessary to set up the mechanism of allocation of risks. When the rent would not be raised with market fluctuation or not in time, the government should take certain rent compensation to investors into account so as to reduce the loss of them.

To build up the mechanism of allocation of interest rate risks

Interest rate fluctuation is also frequent in the society today. When loan interest rate is adjusted, financial costs of investors of low-renting public housing will also changed with it, which raises the income risk of investors to some extent. If interest rate fluctuation is slow or not big, investors of projects can still bear it. However, on the contrary, if interest rate fluctuation is frequent relatively and fluctuation range is big, the result would be opposite. Different from real estate market, running period of low-renting public housing is longer so that interest rate risk that investors will suffer is much bigger. Therefore, it is necessary to build up the mechanism of allocation of interest rate risks. One feasible way is to control loan interest rate of low-renting public housing in certain range (like in the range of 50% of normal fluctuation of commercial loan interest rate) and the government offers interest subsidies to commercial banks so as to reduce interest rate risks of investors.

To build up the mechanism of allocation of expenses and taxation fluctuation risks

Expenses and taxation reflect the will of the nation and local government. In the nations with mature market economy, expenses and taxation should maintain relative stability to guarantee the continuity of policies. For all this, any modern country will adjust the levy of expenses and taxation in good time according to the need of economic development and national macro-control. In order to control the influence of expenses and taxation fluctuation on investors, the nation and local government should try their best to decrease the impact of policy changes on profits of investors in terms of expenses and taxation levy of low-renting public housing and other non-profit projects as well as carry out various preferential policies to improve the healthy development of low-renting public housing.

4 Conclusion

To draw social capital, including private capital, into the construction of low-renting public housing, the government is supposed to build up the mechanism of economic incentive, property right incentive and allocation of risk and so on, adopt various measures like land assignment, interest rate and tax preference, direct subsidies, etc, allow investors to develop part of matched commercial projects, set long operation period, adjust the rent according to economic fluctuation and control risks of interest and expenses and taxation fluctuation so as to guarantee investors can take back costs and obtain normal profits.

Acknowledgment. This work is supported by The Chongqing Soft Science Research Program (CSTC,2010CE0120).

References

1. Beijing Municipal People's Government, Beijing Municipal Administration of Public Rental Housing (Trial) (EB/01) 09-16 (2009), http://bj.9ask.cn/fangchanjiufen/fwzlsifajieshi/200909/232996.html
2. Drew, W.: Discuss about the Establishment of Rental Housing Security System. Construction and Economics 4, 81–83 (2009)
3. Li, D.: The Introduction of the Construction of Low-renting public housing by BOT financing model. Economic and Social Development 8, 8–11 (2010)
4. Li, Z., Tian, J.: Research on Forecast in Indemnificatory Housing Supply in Beijing. Journal of Harbin Institute of Technology(Social Sciences Edition) 11(5), 89–94 (2009)
5. Eriksen, M.D.: The market price of Low-Income Housing Tax Credits. Journal of Urban Economics 66(2), 141–149 (2009)
6. Smith, N., Zhang, H.: Yiran Zhu The Huaibei power plant and its implications for the Chinese BOT market. International Journal of Project Management 22(5), 407–413 (2004)
7. Nombela, G., de Rus, G.: Flexible-term, On tracts for road franchising. Transportation Researeh Part A 38(3), 163–179 (2004)
8. Gresche, P.: Housing, energy cost, and the poor: Counteracting effects in Germany's housing allowance program. Energy Policy 38(1), 93–98 (2010)
9. Wang, S.Q., Tiong, L.K.: Case study of government initiatives for PRC's BOT power plant project. International Journal of Project Management 18(1), 69–78 (2000)
10. Sengupta, U.: Liberalization and the privatization of public rental housing in Kolkata. Cities 23(4), 269–278 (2006)
11. Wang, W.: Does the Land Secret let it Hard to Make Housing Cost Available to the Public? It is Difficult to Measure and Calculate the Profits of Developers (EB/01) 09-16 (2009), http://www.fdch.com.cn/xinwen/Class309/200609/590530.html
12. Yang, H.: Think over the Development of Low-renting public Housing in Shanghai. Shanghai Real Estate 9, 4–8 (2009)
13. Yang, H., He, J., Zhou, J.: Game Decision-Making Model on Toll Road Pricing and Investment under a BOT Scheme. Chinese Journal of Management Science 11(4), 30–33 (2003)

Measurement of Carbon Emissions Based on Energy Methods

Zhongwen Liu[1,2], Jinghui Zhao[2], and Pengzhao Gao[2]

[1] Research Institute of Shandong Women's University, Shandong Jinan, China
[2] College of Economic and Management, Shandong University of Science and Technology, Shandong Qingdao, China
Lzw3541@sohu.com

Abstract. Climate change, which was caused by economic development, has become attract the national concerns. In this context, low carbon economy development model came into being, and it's becoming the main trend. This paper is based on the energy consumption statistics, the sample of raw data is between 1990 and 2009, analyze the characteristics of carbon dioxide emissions from the point of view of energy consumption, and the influencing factors, and tries to use the knowledge of statistics and econometrics to determine the measurement model for carbon emissions through the establishment of mathematical model and statistical tests. Finally, in the existing technology level, predicts carbon emissions in the next five years, and gives several proposals to promote low carbon economic development, such as impose carbon tax, readjust the industrial structure, and control energy consumption and so on.

Keywords: Carbon emissions; Energy consumption; Measurement; Low carbon economy.

1 Introduction

Intergovernmental Panel on Climate Change (IPCC) thinks that the incremental concentration of CO_2 is the main reason for global climate change, and fossil energy consumption is the most important factor [1]. The accelerated process of urbanization in China led to a large number of fossil energy consumption and carbon emissions increase, besides, the current energy consumption structure is still based on coal, oil and other traditional fossil fuels, as the main fuel source, therefore, both coal and oil are the main causes to increase carbon emissions, and this "coal-based" energy consumption structure is difficult to change in a short time. So, it is becoming the main topic to how to improve energy efficiency and the energy consumption structure.

Neil Strachan (2007) summarized and developed a hybrid energy system model MARKAL-MACRO, and then analyzes that it is feasible for UK to reduce CO_2 emission by 60% in the long-term by mandatory ways[2];Xiangzhao Feng and Ji Zou (2008) have decomposed the Chinese CO_2 emissions using ka identity, the result

Q. Zhou (Ed.): ISAEBD 2011, Part II, CCIS 209, pp. 99–105, 2011.

shows that the energy efficiency helps to reduce the CO_2 emissions[3]; Xin Zheng .etc.(2009) predicted the 2007-2020 coal, oil, natural gas consumption used the gray metabolic model, based on the data of fossil energy consumption, then they analyzed fossil energy consumption and CO_2 emission trends in the next 10 years[4];Sen Bao .etc.(2010) proposed two-component model about the energy structure. And predicted that the carbon emissions has an upward trend by 2012 [5].

2 Status of Carbon Emissions Based on Energy Research

According to the data provided by The Chinese Academy of Sciences,"China Energy Report 2008: Carbon Emissions",in the year of 1997-2005, China's carbon emissions increase is mainly due to accelerated growth in industrial added value, leading to substantial growth in final energy consumption.

To be faced with the tension trend of the change of global climate, our government has put forward the strategic goal of developing a low carbon economy in the "Chinese sustainable development strategy report by 2009", its objective is that the unit of CO_2 of every GDP reduces to 50% by the year of 2020. The Report estimates that China has adopted more stringent emission reduction technologies and corresponding policies and measures, Chinese carbon emissions from 2030 to 2040 will go to the peak, then fall into the stable phase after a period of time.

However, China is a developing country, and it always meeting many bottlenecks to realize the goal above. First of all, coal-dominated energy structure is a long-term constraint for China to change to a low-carbon development model. Second, between the Chinese stage of development and the development of low-carbon economy, there exists a sharp contradiction. Third, the mainly lower level of technology is the serious carrier for China to develop low-carbon economy. Low-carbon economy is an important way to protect the climate, but to realize a low carbon economy needs the support of advanced technologies.

3 Model and Empirical Analysis

In this paper, we choose several major energy consumptions, the time is from 1990 to 2009. And the data comes from the "China Statistical Yearbook 2010" and EIA.

3.1 Variable Selection

According to the IEA, the global CO_2 emissions in 2008 was about 30.4 billion tons, and about 99.7% came from fossil fuels, therefore we choose coal, oil, natural gas and hydropower, nuclear power, wind power and other new types of energy consumption as explanatory variables.

China's total energy consumption in 1990 was 9.87 billion tons, while in 2009 the total amount was 3.066 billion tons, the increase as much as 300%. Among them, the coal consumption of fossil fuels had the largest proposition, and it had a rising trend. Oil as an important fossil energy, its consumption also showed an upward trend. In addition, hydropower, nuclear power, wind power as the new renewable energy, all had a certain proportion in the energy consumption structure, and showed a growth trend.

3.2 Stationarity Test and Cointegration Test

(1) Time Series Unit Root Test
In this paper, we take Augmented Dickey-Fuller Test, which is the null hypothesis is: there is a unit root; and alternative hypothesis is: there is no unit root. If the ADF is greater than the absolute value of the absolute threshold, then reject the null hypothesis that the variable is stationary, there is no unit root; the contrary, that the existence of unit root.

Next, by Eviews6.0 ,we analysis five variable time series trend respectively, and we find that they all have tendency, so we should choose the time-series model with the time trend to make the unit root test. Upon examination, at 1%, 5% and 10% significance level, the original series are non-stationary, but after the first difference they are stable ,that is to say they are all first-order single whole sequence, and the data can be Cointegration test. Below table 1:

Table 1. Time Series unit root test

variable	ADF	1%	5%	10%
CO_2	0.258835	0.216000	0.146000	0.119000
Coal	-1.811389	-4.571599	-3.690814	-3.286909
Petr	-1.712968	-4.532598	-3.673616	-3.277364
Gas	0.287236	-3.857386	-3.040391	-2.660551
Power	-1.633515	-3.77000	-3.19000	-2.89000
ΔCO_2	0.108241	0.216000	0.146000	0.119000
Δ Coal	-3.466792	-4.800080	-3.791172	-3.342253
ΔPetr	-3.798513	-4.571559	-3.690814	-3.286909
ΔGas	-6.730057	-4.571559	-3.690814	-3.286909
ΔPower	-4.298710	-3.77000	-3.19000	-2.89000

(2) Time Series Cointegration Test
Based on this regression model:

$$CO_{2t} = \beta_0 + \beta_1 Coal_t + \beta_2 Petr_t + \beta_3 Gas_t + \beta_4 Power_t + e_t \quad (1)$$

In this model, CO_{2t} represents the CO_2 emissions in the t year, $Coal_t$ represents Coal consumption in the t year,$Petr_t$ represents Petr consumption in the t year,Gas_t represents Gas consumption in the t year,$Power_t$ on behalf ofPowerconsumption in the t year; β_0 is the regression intercept coefficient, β_1, β_2, β_3, β_4 are the correlation coefficients of each variable; t represent the year.

Augmented Dickey-Fuller Unit Root Test on RESID01

Null Hypothesis: RESID01 has a unit root
Exogenous: Constant
Lag Length: 3 (Automatic based on SIC, MAXLAG=4)

		t-Statistic	Prob.*
Augmented Dickey-Fuller test statistic		-4.341160	0.0045
Test critical values:	1% level	-3.920350	
	5% level	-3.065585	
	10% level	-2.673459	

*MacKinnon (1996) one-sided p-values.
Warning: Probabilities and critical values calculated for 20 observations and may not be accurate for a sample size of 16

Fig. 1. Unit Root Test on the residual series

According to Fig.1.the test result showed that when the critical value is -4.341160, the residual sequence is significant, the residual sequence can reject unit root hypothesis. Then, those variables all through cointegration test, that is, in the long-term their relationship can be described by the equation cointegration regression.

3.3 The Measure Model of Carbon Emissions

Hypothesis: The above factors are rational, based on the data of energy consumption from 1990 to 2009, we can do regression analysis in CO_2 emissions.

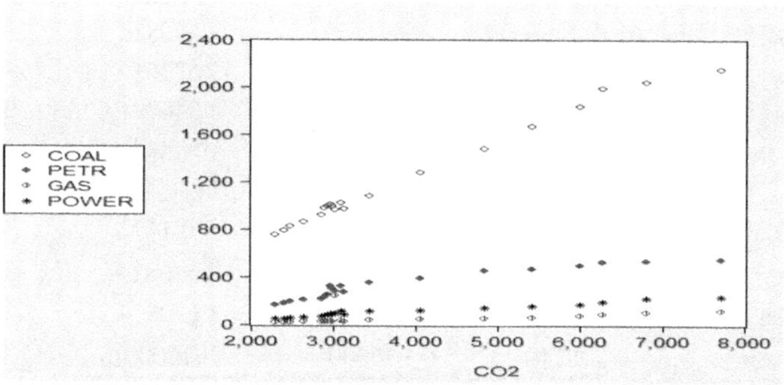

Fig. 2. The scatters about CO_2 and energy consumption

From Fig.2.We can get several possible regression function models :

① Linear function:

$$CO_{2t} = \beta_0 + \beta_1 Coal_t + \beta_2 Petr_t + \beta_3 Gas_t + \beta_4 Power_t + e_t \quad (2)$$

②Power function:

$$LnCO_{2t} = \beta_0 + \beta_1 LnCoal_t + \beta_2 LnPetr_t + \beta_3 LnGas_t + \beta_4 LnPower_t + e_t \quad (3)$$

③Logarithmic function:

$$CO_{2t} = \beta_0 + \beta_1 LnCoal_t + \beta_2 LnPetr_t + \beta_3 LnGas_t + \beta_4 LnPower_t + e_t \quad (4)$$

④Exponential function:

$$LnCO_{2t} = \beta_0 + \beta_1 Coal_t + \beta_2 Petr_t + \beta_3 Gas_t + \beta_4 Power_t + e_t \quad (5)$$

As can be seen from Table 2, models pass the T statistic test and F statistic test and goodness of fit values were greater than 0.9, then the results are effect. However, when combining the actual situation in 1990-2009, we can find that the amount of CO_2 has a largest proportion in the CO_2 emissions from energy consumption, and in reality, CO_2 emissions growth rate and coal consumption has a strong correlation; In the past those years, the clean energies, Hydropower, nuclear power, wind power, has a slowly increase, and have a small share in energy consumption. Therefore, we reject models ①③④, and consider the model② can reflect the trend of carbon emissions.

That is, we take the follow equation as the measure model of carbon emissions.

$$LnCO_{2t} = 0.914 + 1.036LnCoal_t + 0.096LnPetr_t + 0.036LnGas_t + 0.085LnPower_t \tag{6}$$

Table 2. The Results of Those Models

	model①	model②	model③	model④
β_0	-105.95(0.477)	0.914(1.395)	-21209.63(-5.02)	7.109(151.4)
β_1	2.979(5.776)	1.036(7.78)	4241.224(4.94)	0.00075(6.853)
β_2	-1.76(1.174)	0.096(0.94)	-2014.48(-3.07)	0.00029(0.929)
β_3	3.751(0.461)	0.036(0.49)	1149.05(2.45)	-0.00469(-2.728)
β_4	6.808(1.29)	0.085(0.79)	564.502(0.81)	0.00246(2.207)
R^2	0.9937	0.9941	0.9871	0.9946
R^2_1	0.9920	0.9925	0.9837	0.9932
F	591.8153	632.839	287.084	694.477

Note: Figures in brackets are t-statistic in 1%.

3.4 The Projections of Carbon Emissions

Markov model applies the basic principles and methods of Markov chain to analysis things, and Markov model is a technology to predict the trends.

In this paper, we put the data of the 1998 as base period, in the view of energy consumption structure; calculate the amplitude of the energy consumption from 1990 to 2009 respectively. We divide the datum into three grades:

The low-amplitude: $y \le 0.02$ The middle level: $0.02 < y \le 0.05$ The high level: $0.05 < y$ .According to its data, there are 20 years, namely ,N=20; Hypothesis: S_1、S_2、S_3show the above three grades. Accordingly, we get: N_1=8, N_2=5, N_3=7.

And the initial probability vector is: $S^{(0)} = (1 \quad 0 \quad 0)$

And its transition probability is:

$$P = \begin{pmatrix} 5/8 & 3/8 & 0 \\ 1/5 & 2/5 & 2/5 \\ 2/7 & 0 & 5/7 \end{pmatrix}$$

After 5 times like this, we get the coal consumption in the next 5 years:

$$S(5) = S^{(0)}P^5$$

$$= (1 \quad 0 \quad 0) * \begin{pmatrix} 5/8 & 3/8 & 0 \\ 1/5 & 2/5 & 2/5 \\ 2/7 & 0 & 5/7 \end{pmatrix}^5 = (1 \quad 0 \quad 0) * \begin{pmatrix} 0.42 & 0.3 & 0.32 \\ 0.41 & 0.25 & 0.36 \\ 0.41 & 0.24 & 0.34 \end{pmatrix}$$

$$= (0.42 \quad 0.3 \quad 0.32)$$

It can be predicted that in the next five years, the consumption of coal is probable at a low potential growth rate, which is consistent with the reality. Similarly, we can get the prediction of Petr, Gas, and Power. In the next five years, the consumption of oil will maintain a certain growth, while the demand for new energy sources will also rise. This shows that clean energy began to replace traditional energy sources, energy consumption changes to the high efficiency, low-carbon.

Finally, we get the prediction of CO_2 emissions in the next five years: The CO_2 emissions will be more likely to remain a low growth rate. Because any new energy or new technologies are not completely replace the traditional energy in a short time, the mature development of new technology needs sufficient time. But in the long run, the new energy will replace the fossil fuels, and then the CO_2 emissions will gradually decrease which consistent with creating a low-carbon energy-saving society.

4 Measure to Reduce Carbon Emissions

4.1 The Introduction of Carbon Taxes, and the Improvement of Market-Oriented Energy

The carbon tax is a tax to CO_2 emissions, and it is an economic means to prevent increasing carbon emissions. The government should take the resource taxes, environmental pollution taxes, carbon tax on energy consumption enterprises, and establish carbon funds for new energy development and low carbon technology development using those taxes. Market economy is more effective and rational than the planned economy to use energy[6], therefore, on the view of regimes and policies, we should promote the process of energy market vigorously and take effective ways to remedy the situation of market failure to reduce carbon dioxide emissions.

4.2 Optimizing the Industrial Structure, Promoting the Development of Tertiary Industry

We must improve the "carbon" industry' barriers to entry, prevent duplication of low value-added industries, promote the development of the profit curve at both ends [7].Through merger, recombination, strategic cooperation, etc., we can realize the industrial intensification strategies. Strengthen the circulation of commodities, transportation, post and telecommunications development, and focus on developing market potential, high value-added financial, insurance, business consulting, tourism, entertainment and other smoke-free, low carbon emissions of the service sector. Only then will it be possible to achieve lower energy demand growth.

4.3 To Adjust Energy Consumption Structure

What the development of social economy needs is resources but not carbon. We have to give priority to the development and selection of clean coal, natural gas and renewable energy and new energy technologies, encouraging development and promotion of the use of the renewable energy in Hydro, wind, solar and biomass energy. These energy sources are carbon-free energy, and the use of these energy sources does not produce CO_2. Adjusting the energy structure will not affect the social and economic goals, but can reduce carbon emissions [6].

4.4 Improving Energy Efficiency

Improved energy efficiency is equivalent to using a small amount of energy consumption to get more material wealth, to achieve better economic development. From the technical point, we should take clean coal technology to improve the efficiency of coal utilization, and CO_2 capture, utilization and storage technologies to reduce pollution and emissions of coal. We can enhance energy efficiency from the points of market and law, for instance, raising the price of energy consumption; encouraging practitioners to participate in market competition; lastly, property rights could encourage enterprises to efficient use of energy.

4.5 Control Energy Consumption Growth Rate

On the base of keeping the development of economy, the growth rate of greenhouse gases can been controlled. During the boom times, we need to guide rational investment into low-power industries. Promoting the low carbon development concept, encouraging people stop the traditional luxury and waste habits to establish the concept of saving and consumption to promote green, civilized, healthy and low-carbon lifestyle, so that we can achieve the purpose of controlling the energy consumption, but also makes the low-carbon economy get a good development.

Acknowledgments. The initial result of common item (2010LC54) of 2010 annual national statistical research plans.

References

[1] Intergovernmental Panel on Climate Change(IPCC). Climate change 2007: The physical science basis. Contribution of Working Group I to the Fourthassessment Report of the Intergovernmental Panel on Climate Change. Cambridge University Press, Cambridge (2007)

[2] Neil, S.-c., Ramachandran, K.: Hybrid modelling of long-term carbon reduction scenarios for the UK. Energy Economics 30, 2947–2963 (2006)

[3] Feng, X., Zou, J.: The economic analysis in China CO2 emission trend. China Population Resources and Environment 18, 43–47 (2008) (in Chinese)

[4] Zheng, X., et al.: The projections of CO2 emissions by fossil fuels. Water Resources and Power 10, 224–227 (2009)

[5] Bao, S., et al.: The trend prediction of Chinese energy production and consumption and carbon emissions study. Natural Resources 8, 1248–1254 (2010)

[6] 2050 China Energy and CO_2 Emissions Task Force, 2050 China Energy and CO_2 Emissions Report. Science Press, Beijing (2009) (in Chinese)

[7] Xu, H., Yang, G.: Green turned around: Low-carbon development in China. China Electric Power Press, Beijing (2010) (in Chinese)

Grey Correlation Degree Analysis on the Operating Performance of the Tourism Listed Company in China

Caifeng Ma

#17 Shandong Jiaotong University, No. 5001 Haitang Road, Changqing District, Jinan, 250357 China
cfhorse@163.com

Abstract. In order to reveal company's strengths and weaknesses, identify key financial indicators affecting the operating performance, evaluates each company performance. Through grey correlation degree analysis, I selected 18 financial indexes and comprehensively reflected the operating performance of the tourism listed company six items : Profitability, solvency, asset management, growth capacity, capital expansion, and cash flow. The operating performance of the 14 tourism listed company of our country is carried out a comprehensive evaluation and sorting. From the analysis to evaluation results, we obtain the tourism operating performance of listed company is no differences on grey correlation degree, need to further tap the potential of the industry, also find enough reasons of insufficient operating performance after analyzing single index affect operating performance by the grey correlation degree analysis.

Keywords: Tourism listed company, Grey correlation degree, Operating performance.

1 Introduction

Presently, the listed tourism companies in China have become a new force in the capital market. However, the investment income of these companies usually fluctuates, and it is impacted obviously by the economic development and people's consumption. Gradually our country is walking out of the bottom of the financial crisis, besides the economic stimulus package goes into effect. Under this circumstance, it is necessary to study the growth of the listed tourism companies and to evaluate their performances, which can positively guidance the scientific program of the investment focus, and the timely adjustment of micro-business strategy. There are many common methods of evaluating the performance of the companies, e.g. principal component analysis and factor analysis. In this paper, we will use the Grey Relational Analysis (GRA) method to evaluate the performance of listed companies.

2 Literature Review

Qingsong Wang and Li Cheng carried out the empirical research on the impact that the technology innovation exerting on the performance of the enterprise. The

Q. Zhou (Ed.): ISAEBD 2011, Part II, CCIS 209, pp. 106–112, 2011.

empirical results showed that the gray relation between the technical innovation and the economic performance was weaker than that between the fixed assets and economic performance of the enterprises.Runfang Liu regarded reflecting the financial indicators of operating performance in listed real estate companies as the core. She abstracted 11 indicators from 5 aspects which are the following profitability, solvency, asset management, ability to grow, and the capacity of capital expansion. Liu evaluated and ranked the performance of the 53 listed real estate companies by the GRA model, and made a further analysis of evaluation results. Ji-an Wang and Ping Li also applied the GRA model to analyze the relationship between the inbound factors of tourism industry system and the foreign exchange earnings of tourism in Shandong Province. They proposed the ideas of adjusting the inbound tourism industry structure of Shandong Province.

3 Models of Evaluation

3.1 Evaluation Method

Economic operating system contains a great deal of identifying information and non-identifying information. Relationships between many factors in the system are complex and grey. It is rather hard to judge the relationship between primary and secondary factors, especially for the randomness of change on the surface. Because it directly obscures the essence of things, it makes the description of essential features very difficult. Principles of GRA take the uncertainty system, which is called "some of the information clearly, some information is unknown" and "small sample, poor information", as research object. Through the generation and development of the "partial" information, researchers extract the valuable information, and realize the correct descriptions and the effective monitoring of the system operation behaviors and the evolution law. Principles of GRA provide an effective method for solving these problems. The basic idea of this approach is measuring the relation between factors in the two systems. The relation changes as time or objects change, and it is called correlation. In the process of system development, if trends of the two factors are consistent with each other, i.e. a higher degree of synchronization change, which can be described as a higher degree of correlation between the two; and vice versa. Thus, the GRA method, based on the similar or different trends of factors, is a method to measure the degree of correlation between factors. The grey system theory proposes to do gray correlation analysis for each subsystem concept, and to seek the relationships between each subsystem (or each factor) via a certain method. The GRA, therefore, provides a quantitative measure for the trends of system changes. It is quite suitable for dynamic process analysis.

3.2 Evaluation Index

The evaluation index system for the performance of listed companies is a certain group of indicators that are internally related and mutually complementary. This system can fully reflect a wide range of capabilities, e.g. the company's profitability, solvency, management ability and ability to develop. In this system, questions which to set up and how to set up are related to both the scientific, accuracy and practicality of the evaluation, and also related to the enhance of the competitiveness of enterprises. Therefore, the scientific selection of the design evaluation index is the premise and basis of the correct evaluation of corporate performance.

Considering the comprehensive reflection of the listed companies competitiveness, combined with the index from the "Rules of Performance Evaluation of State-owned Capital" issued by the Ministry of Finance, we comprehensive select six aspects, which are profitability, solvency, asset management capacity, growth capacity, capital expansion and cash management respectively. And then we determined the weight respectively (see Table 1).

Table 1. Listed Company Competitiveness Evaluation Index Selection

Evaluating Object	Aspects & Weight	Selected Index	Weight	Index Code
Performance Evaluation	Profitability 0.3	Asset Margin	0.05	Z_1
		OPE	0.05	Z_2
		ROE	0.1	Z_3
		Earnings per share	0.1	Z_4
	Solvency 0.2	Asset Margin	0.05	Z_5
		Current Ratio	0.05	Z_6
		Quick Ratio	0.1	Z_7
	Asset Management 0.2	Total assets turnover	0.05	Z_8
		Inventory Turnover	0.05	Z_9
		Accounts receivable turnover	0.1	Z_{10}
	Growth 0.1	Growth rate of total assets	0.04	Z_{11}
		Growth rate of main business	0.05	Z_{12}
		Net profit growth rate	0.01	Z_{13}
	Capital Expansion 0.12	Net assets per share	0.05	Z_{14}
		Retained earnings per share	0.02	Z_{15}
		Capital reserve per share	0.05	Z_{16}
	Cash Management 0.08	Cash flow from operating activities per share	0.04	Z_{17}
		Cash and cash equivalents per share	0.04	Z_{18}

3.3 Evaluation Process

Firstly, On the basis of qualitative analysis of the research questions, we identify a group of comparative sequence and a reference sequence. Then the comparative sequence and the reference sequence are put together to constitute the order (m+1) ×n matrix. Secondly, dimensionless Processing the Sequence Data. Generally the original variables have different dimensions or orders of magnitude. To easily compare objects and to reliably ensure the results, it is necessary for us to dimensionless process the sequence data. Finally, calculating the correlation. Sorting the comparative sequence and the reference sequence in descending order. The higher correlation is, the more consistent, this is the trend that sequence changes with the reference sequence.

4 The Empirical Analysis

4.1 The Sample Series

This sample data come from the Reset database which provides the 2008 annual report data of the tourism listed companies. According to classification standards of China Securities Regulatory Commission, there are resources and integrated listed companies, but only a small number of hotels listed companies in the Shenzhen and Shanghai Securities Market lists. We exclude the ST companies and some companies with the default index. Then we take 14 listed companies as the objects of the study. According to the annual financial statements of listed companies and the 18 selected indexes, ultimately we build the original data of the 14 tourism listed companies in 2008, X_i' (k)(i=0, 1,2…14;k=1,2…18;), Please see Table 2.

Table 2. The financial indicators of the tourism listed companies in 2008

Sequence Code	Name of Co.	Z_1	Z_2	Z_k	Z_{17}	Z_{18}
X_0'	Reference Sq.	0.0776	0.7595	…*	0.6936	1.7189
X_1'	OCT	0.0695	0.3571	…	0.4294	0.339
X_2'	Huatian Hotel	0.049	0.4747	…	0.6936	0.5798
X_3'	Xi'an Tourism	0.0158	0.3017	…	0.1857	0.3965
X_4'	Beijing Tourism	-0.0523	0.5318	…	0.1289	0.0957
X_5'	E-mei Mount	0.0205	0.3213	…	0.5657	0.3679
X_6'	Guilin Tourism	0.0255	0.4158	…	0.2282	0.5426
X_7'	Lijiang Tourism	0.0776	0.7595	…	0.4535	1.6846
X_8'	Horti-Expo Co.	0.0216	0.2854	…	-0.0539	1.7189
X_9'	Sante	0.015	0.5027	…	0.2137	0.7318
X_{10}'	CYTS	0.0282	0.2018	…	0.5556	0.8102
X_{11}'	CUTC	0.0251	0.5455	…	0.0339	0.1318
X_{12}'	Dalian Shengya	0.006	0.4442	…	0.3987	0.2344
X_{13}'	Tibet Tourism	-0.0695	0.1619	…	-0.0324	0.4897
X_{14}'	CITS	0.0755	0.2068	…	0.2868	0.3856

Source: Resset Financial Database listed companies.
Note:* The reference of the liquid ratio is 1 and the reference of quick ratio is 0.5.

4.2 Grey Relational Analysis of Samples

Reference sample data sequence of selected. We regard the tourism listed companies in our country as a gray system, and regard each company as a factor in the system. We construct a reference index. Because the reference values are taken from the original sequence data, the series posed by its maximum or optimum value of the financial indicators can be used as a reference sequence X0′. Specific options are as follows: the quick ratio and the asset-liability ratio are the modest targets, they are not too high or too low and the best financial criteria are 1 and 0.5 relatively. Thus, the index values are selected in the sample 1 and 0.5.Other indicators are positive ones, the bigger the better, so the maximum value of the original data are selected. Then the reference sequence is listed as X_0 '=(X_0' (1), X_0' (2)... X_0' (k)), (k=1, 2...18). And we take the sequence of the companies 'financial indicators as the comparative sequence, which is listed as X_i'=(X_i' (1), X_i' (2)... X_i' (k)), (i=0, 1, 2...14; k=1, 2...18), where i is the number of the companies, and k is the number of financial indicators.

The selected reference sequence data is always in the optimal value of evaluation in the selected period. It can reflect comparisons between the various evaluation data and rule out the gray components, besides it also can avoid the changes on the evaluation criteria because of the subjective factors and time changes. So it plays a better effect in comparison.

Dimensionless Processing of Sample Data. As the indicators of the same company vary widely in Table 2, and the unit of measurement is different for each index, to facilitate the analysis, it is necessary to dimensionless deal with the data.

The reference sequence X_0'and the comparative sequence X_i' are both divided by the reference sequence X_0', and a new set of sequence can be generated, which are shown in Table 3.

Table 3. Dimensionless series after processing

Sequence Code	Name of Co.	Z_1	Z_2	Z_k	Z_{17}	Z_{18}
X_0	Reference Sq.	1	1	···	1	1
X_1	OCT	0.8956	0.4702	···	0.6191	0.1972
···	····	···	···	···	···	···
X_{14}	CITS	0.9729	0.2723	···	0.4135	0.2243

Analysis of the Sample Correlation Coefficient. First we need to calculate the absolute difference of financial indicators at each point between $X_0$and X_i (see Table 4), ΔX_i (k)= | X_0 (k)-X_i (k) | . Second we obtain the following:

$$\min_i \min_k \left|X_0(k) - X_i(k)\right| = 0, \quad \max_i \max_k \left|X_0(k) - X_i(k)\right| = 25.1017$$

Table 4. The absolute difference between X_0 and X_i

Sequence Code	Name of Co.	Z_1	Z_2	Z_k	Z_{17}	Z_{18}
$\triangle X_1$	OCT	0.1044	0.5298	···	0.3809	0.8028
···	····	···	···	···	···	···
$\triangle X_{14}$	CITS	0.0271	0.7277	···	0.5865	0.7757

Third we substitute the result into the correlation coefficient formula. As the smallerρcan increase the larger difference between correlation coefficients, so we take ρ=0.2, then find the correlation of each point, e.g.

$$\xi_1(1) = \frac{0+0.2\times 25.1017}{0.1044+0.2\times 25.1017} = 0.9796$$

Lastly we calculate the correlation of each point, combined with the weight of each index (weight in Table 1), we get the weighted-rating correlation and the weighted correlation (see Table 5).

Table 5. The correlation coefficient of each company

Sequence Code	Name of Co.	Z_1	Z_k	Z_{18}	r^1	r^2	Rank*
ξ_1	OCT	0.9796	...	0.8621	0.9126	0.9077	4
ξ_2	Huatian Hotel	0.9316	...	0.8834	0.9111	0.9143	2
ξ_3	Xi'an Tourism	0.8631	...	0.8671	0.8762	0.8709	11
ξ_4	Beijing Tourism	0.7499	...	0.8417	0.8236	0.8458	13
ξ_5	E-mei Mount	0.8722	...	0.8646	0.8701	0.8784	9
ξ_6	Guilin Tourism	0.8820	...	0.8800	0.8782	0.8915	8
ξ_7	Lijiang Tourism	1.0000	...	0.9960	0.9239	0.9326	1
ξ_8	Horti-Expo Co.	0.8743	...	1.0000	0.8596	0.8702	12
ξ_9	Sante	0.8616	...	0.8974	0.8783	0.8923	7
ξ_{10}	CYTS	0.8875	...	0.9047	0.8967	0.9011	5
ξ_{11}	CUTC	0.8812	...	0.8447	0.8735	0.8749	10
ξ_{12}	Dalian Shengya	0.8447	...	0.8532	0.8998	0.8985	6
ξ_{13}	Tibet Tourism	0.7259	...	0.8753	0.7877	0.8123	14
ξ_{14}	CITS	0.9946	...	0.8662	0.8994	0.9135	3

Note: The correlation $\mathbf{r}^1$ is weighted-rating correlation, the correlation $\mathbf{r}^2$ is the weighted correlation (weight see Table 1), rank * is based on the weighted correlation.

5 Conclusion

5.1 The Gray Correlation Difference Is NOT Obvious, So the Potential of the Industry Is Still Needed to Tap

We select 14 tourism listed companies in the Shanghai and Shenzhen Security Market. There are 2 hotel travel listed companies like OCT and Huatian Hotel; 4 resources travel listed companies like E-mei Mount, Guilin tourism, Beijing tourism, Lijiang tourism; 8 Miscellaneous tourism listed companies like Tibet Tourism, CYTS, CUTC, CITS, Dalian Shengya, Xi'an tourism, Sante and Horti-Expo Co. ,Ltd.. After the correlation analysis of 14 companies, we find the weighted gray correlation of Lijiang tourism is 0.9326, which is ranked 1. While the weighted gray correlation of Tibet Tourism is 0.8123, which is ranked 14th. The results indicate that performance gap between different companies is not obvious in tourism industry, and also shows resource travel listed companies have no particular advantage. Compared with other industries, although the tourism demand grows continuously in recent years, tourism companies still need to adjust the operating mode. The main industry has potential for full development, and the market can be further expanded. Therefore, tourism companies should seize the opportunity, strive to conduct business innovation, enhance core competitiveness, and reduce uncertainty risk factors adversely affecting on our business.

5.2 GRA Can Help to Find the Root Causes of Inadequate Performance

On one hand, for the objective listed companies in the study, GRA ranks scores based on comprehensive correlation of each company and then evaluates each company performance, which can help to achieve the purposes that the front edge companies find advantages to mountain and the behind ones rectify and improve by analyzing the reasons. On the other hand, GRA can also rank the company's financial indicators, and reveal company's strengths and weaknesses. It helps to identify key financial indicators affecting the operating performance. Appropriate measures can be taken according to different information reflected in financial indicators, and the key factor influencing and restricting the company's development can be seized. For example, the calculation of the correlation of operating cash flow per share (Z17) shows that index of Huatian Hotel is 1.000 ranked first while the same indicator of Horti-Expo Co., Ltd. is 0.8233 ranked last. This index underlines the Horti-Expo Co., Ltd. has the weak capacity of cash supply by the main business, so this company need to further highlight the main industry and strengthen the cash collection management to improve efficiency.

References

1. Liu, R.F.: Grey correlation degree analysis on the performance evaluation of the real estate listed company. Industrial Technology & Economy 12, 148–150 (2009)
2. Wang, J., Li, P.: Grey correlation degree analysis on the industrial structure of inbound tourism in Shandong Province. Journal of Shandong Teachers' University 6, 118–121 (2009)
3. Xu, L., Li, X.P., Dai, Y.H.: Grey correlative degree analysis on the employee satisfaction evaluation. Chinese Journal of Management Science 10, 68–70 (2009)
4. Wang, Q., Cheng, L.: Grey correlation degree analysis on technological innovation and economic performance. Forum on Science and Technology in China 12, 64–68 (2009)
5. Yang, L.H.: The establishment of index system of tourism enterprise performance evaluation. Economic Research Guide 8, 206–207 (2009)

Model of Human Resource Management Based on Psychological Contract

Caifeng Ma

#17 Shandong Jiaotong University, No. 5001 Haitang Road, Changqing District, Jinan, 250357 China
cfhorse@163.com

Abstract. In order to explore better human resource management mode, through studying the relationship between psychological contract and human resource management, we find the psychological contract, as a psychological ties of employees and organization, is very important to the effective human resource management. It influences employee's behaviors and attitudes, and determines employee's motivation from organizations and employee's devotion to organizations. It also exerts huge effects on organizational commitment, job performance, job satisfaction, career satisfaction and employee's demission, etc. In order to construct the innovative human resource management mode, on basis of people-oriented organizational culture, the organizations should start the creation of the psychological contract from recruiting. And then they should formulate the win-win career plan, and establish effective training mechanism, fair appraisal mechanism and impartial salary based on psychological contract.

Keywords: Psychological Contract, HRM mode, Incentive Mechanism.

1 The Content of Psychological Contract

Organizational psychologists Argyris (1960) showed the relationship between employees and employers by psychological contract in the "Understanding Organizational Behavior", but he did not interpret what was psychological contract. Levinson et al (1962) clearly proposed that psychological contract is sum of implied mutual expectations between the organization and employees. Schein (1965) defined it as the expectations, without express provision, that is always present between individuals and organizations. Kotter (1973) explained that psychological contract was a tacit agreement between individuals and organizations, which specified what one party paid to and got from the other party in it. How to define the psychological contract generated controversy. "Rousseau School" (American scholar Rousseau, Robinson and Morrison, et al.) commended the research of psychological contract should be limited to the employee, which was also called unilateral relationship; whereas the "classical school"(British scholar Guest, Herriot and Pemberton, etc.) thought psychological contract research should include both the individual and the organization, which was also called bilateral relationship. We describe that the psychological contract is the implicit and unwritten psychological expectations and

Q. Zhou (Ed.): ISAEBD 2011, Part II, CCIS 209, pp. 113–119, 2011.

commitments which are exchanged and recognized between employees and the organization in the process of organizational behavior. It is the subjective beliefs accepted and recognized by both sides, which include the psychological expectations, organizational commitment, satisfaction, responsibility, perception and other core components between organization and staff.

2 The Relationship between Psychological Contract and Human Resources Management

2.1 The Dynamic Relationship between Psychological Contract and Human Resources Management

Human resources management is to effectively manage people's thoughts, psychology and behaviors by modern scientific methods and to make full use of subjective initiative to achieve organizational goals. Psychological contract, as the psychological bond of employees and organizations, is part of the staff's mental activity, and is the object of human resource management, the dynamic changes of psychological contract determines the dynamics of human resources management. The dynamic changes of human resources determine the dynamic character of psychological contract. Whenever psychological contract changes, the human resources management system should quickly find the changes and timely response to them. Therefore, there is a mutual adaptive dynamic equilibrium relationship between the psychological contract and human resource management.

When the psychological contract and human resource management matches, human resources management system in companies has a clear understanding of the staff's psychological contract, timely realize the reasonable expectations of employees, and guide the employees' psychological contract to the direction that is benefit to organization. It is in this moment that the enterprises have the higher employees' satisfaction, the lower turnover and the higher productivity. Changes in social and economic environment are bound to impact traditional thinking and cultures. Under this circumstance, people have new-understanding of the relationship between employees and organization, which leads to changes of the psychological contract. The changes of psychological contract include two aspects. On change is that of employees' expectations of their dedication to the organization, and the other one is that of employees' expectations of their rewards from the organization. Some change is good for business, e.g. as the competition intensifies, employees' expectation changes from a stable occupation to self-achievement. Employees have this changes are more interested and more involve in work, which is beneficial for enterprise. On the contrary, some changes are bad for enterprise, and they adversely affect the stable development of the enterprise. According to the changes of psychological contract, human resource management system in enterprise should make the appropriate adjustments to meet the staff new demands in the new situation, and to guide employees' psychological contract to the benefit direction. The psychological contract and human resource management restore to the new balance after human resource management adapt to this change in the psychological contract.

2.2 The Relationship between Psychological Contract and Human Resources Management Functions

Psychological contract is the psychological bond of employees and organizations, which is crucial for effective human resources management, and it is closely related to various aspects of human resource management.

Recruitment and Psychological Contract. Recruitment is a channel that company attracts and access talent, is of vital importance to human resources management. The establishment of psychological contracts starts from recruitment, and is based on the real and effective transfer of information in the recruitment process. The pre-publicity and the work introduction of recruitment offer applicants with many expectations for their scope of future work, which has an important impact on future work. These expectations form part of the psychological contract between employers and employees. The key of the satisfaction of both sides is they are consistent with the understanding of the scope of future work, or at least a similar understanding with the nature of the work.

Training and Psychological Contract. Staff training is indispensable to organizations that would like to achieve lasting competitive advantage in the harsh competitive environment. Almost all kinds of organizations do various training for staff. They use training as an important initiative to attract staff, but in reality it is not effective. An important reason is there is no effective psychological contract about training established between organizations and employees. The organization may reduce training if the expected effects are not achieved. And for the employee, if they don't get the desired effects in training, such as improving skills or enhancing promotion opportunities, they may be negative or even in a hostile attitude to training. Therefore, it is very important to understand the content of the employees' training, especially their needs, and to understand the training method.

Motivation and Psychological Contract. Psychological contract and employee motivation are closely combined. According to the Western incentive theory, the meet of people's need is incentive for the employee's hard-working. These needs are divided into different levels. Basic needs such as survival needs can be satisfied by wages, welfares and other financial means, and these basic needs can be constrained through the signing of formal labor contracts. However, there are very few relevant contents about the needs of the higher level like self-realization and respect need in the labor contract. Only these high-level needs are met, would people feel the greatest satisfaction, and mobilize the greatest possible enthusiasm for work. In the intangible psychological contract, the employer and employee may agree to relevant content which can meet the employee's high-level needs and motivate employee.

3 A New Model of Human Resource Management Based on Psychological Contract

The psychological contract is subjective and dynamic. The violation of psychological contract will lead the employee to re-evaluate relationship between individual and organization, and will result in very adverse effects on organizational commitment, job performance, job satisfaction, career satisfaction and employee turnover rates. Managers should recognize that psychological contract violation may be resulting in very serious consequences as formal contract violation. Raise awareness of the psychological contract can help companies retain talent, improve job performance, make employees obtain their professional success as the business development.

3.1 Establish People-Oriented Organizational Culture Based on Psychological Contract

A new model of human resource management based on psychological contract must be on basis of capacity-oriented organizational culture. The capacity-oriented organizational culture, refers to the organization's cultural values should build on paying attention to and making full use of the human ability. The aim is to let people do their best and to develop employee's capability and potential. The building of capacity-oriented organizational culture, will undoubtedly create a good atmosphere and space for reaching and maintaining the "psychological contract", and will enhance employee's work enthusiasm and belief, and inspire organization and employee to honor their own "commitment" implied by the "contract". The organizational culture should ensure employee effectively service for the organization development in the long run, avoid employee to lose morale as the growth of organization changes, and maintain a dynamic balance of the "psychological contract "between organizations and employees.

3.2 The Creating of Psychological Contract Should Start from Recruitment

The sources of psychological contract formation are diverse. Some contract may be generated before formal contact between employee and organization through some channels. For example, employee has a rough preliminary cognition of the organization's responsibility through public media, networks, or acquaintances. Recruitment process is the course when individual and organization firstly contact with each other, and is the formal stage when the psychological contract of employees formed. Many channels can make job seekers produce many expectations for the organization and future work, such as the preaching on the mobilization meeting, the slogan on recruitment manual and the introduction by the interviewer. For the recruitment organization, they can not be too brag to exaggerate their advantages and too modest to avoid their disadvantages. They should make an objective introduction of the organization's real situation to attract the best talent. In the recruitment process, the recruiters should know clear about what kind of message passing to the candidates, and understand what is the real expect of the candidates, and what the organization can provide for the recruiters. The recruiters should accurately describe the current system and institutions of enterprises, the rights and responsibilities of staff as well as the specific requirements of job. Especially some sensitive issues like compensation and development are better put forward earlier, which can help new employees form a more comprehensive and realistic impression of organization. Or else, after employees' entry into the organization, they find the actual and expectations are very different, which may cause severe violation of psychological contract, and exert negative impacts on job performance, employee satisfaction and other aspects, and also the high turnover rate happens.

3.3 Develop a Win-Win Career Development Plan Based on Psychological Contract

The organization guides and involves in employee's career plans, which not only makes employees more clear about the relationship between work environment characteristics and their self-positioning, but also effectively coordinates the individual specialty and the job demand to improve performance and satisfaction in the matching process. The combination of employee's career plan and human resource planning benefits the rational use and the reasonable flow of human resource, and achieves the best combination of human and resources. On the moment of organizational goals' completion, individual employees achieve their fulfillment of career. Link the personal career plans with the organizational career management, it can reach the balance between human resources needs and personal needs through the organization career development system, and then create an efficient work environment. Staff selects an organization often based on the pursuit of career development. If an excellent employee does not develop well, he will find another job. The maintenance of good "psychological contract" rests with the organizations' respect for this right. Organizations should make a clear and systematical preview of their future role within organizations for the new and old employees. On the one hand, it benefits the socialization of new employees, and conducts older employees to the understanding of the content on the employer and employee commitment; on the other hand, it can also reduce the manager's intent violation of the psychological contract.

3.4 Establish an Effective Training Mechanism Based on Psychological Contract

In order to help the staff adapt to various needs of work, the organization should pay attention to staff training program. The discussion and consultation are suggested to carry out before the start of training, which will be discussed and decided by the trainees' immediate supervisor and the training department. But the better approach is that the trainees put forward their own demand. In fact, this discussion determines a contract between the organization and the trainees. The employees have opportunities to contact a variety of business and to be promoted and accordingly extend their career scope through job rotation. The combination of employee training and career design is good method, which can strengthen the employee's achievement, the job satisfaction, the organizational loyalty and a brain drain. The enterprise should raise employees' awareness of training's importance and provides them with multi-channel, multi-ways of training, and then do the pre-job training, on-the-job training, job-transfer training and so on. In particular, it can encourage them to fully utilize the network training to improve, enrich them in work and then enhance operational capacity and work performance. For excellent employees, the company can give those more material awards and spirit awards, or even exceptional promotion.

3.5 Establish a Fair Assessment Mechanism Based on Psychological Contract

Getting employees involved in the establishment and assessment of target plans can help employees know supervisor's trust, attention and recognition, and can satisfy the demand of belonging and appreciation. Thus, employees can experience the responsibility that is produced from the close relationship between their own interests and the group's interest. The contents of the employee's assessment should focus on job performance. In order to motivate and drive employees, those who fulfill their duties, complete tasks, work efficiently, and work effectively should be given necessary substance rewards and spiritual rewards. The staff assessment is according to discipline that leader's assessment should be combined with general staff's assessment and daily assessment should be combined with annual assessment. The objective assessments to staff are required to reduce the affects from subjective factors. The assessment results should be linked to personal promotion and compensation. The fair assessment brings fair treatment, and it enhances the impartiality and authority of assessment. Performance assessment can be used as the intermediary between the value creation and reward distribution. Contents associated to the result of performance assessment can be established in various systems such as salary, bonus, training and staff development.

3.6 Establish Fair Compensation Incentives Mechanism Based on Psychological Contract

Providing employees with a decent salary and welfare that are corresponding to their capability and contributions can not only get recognition of employee efforts, but also supply him with the basic survival material conditions. According to Maslow demand theory, if the basic survival needs of people are not satisfied, they are generally lack of motivation. Therefore, we must appropriately raise the level of employee's compensations and establish the normal growth of wages mechanisms. Equity theory indicates that staff motivation is not only affected by the absolute rewards, but also the relative rewards. People's feelings of fair reward exert more influence on employee behaviors. On the one hand, the external fairness of employees' compensation levels should be remained. The level of employees' compensation should be consistent with other local organization levels. The brain drain and erosion caused by low salary should be avoided. On the other hand, the internal fairness of employees' compensation levels should also be remained. The level of Employees' compensation should be adapted to their position, work, ability, responsibility and job performance. The low productivity resulted from psychological unbalance should be prevented. Therefore, the fair of distribution results and the fair of allocation process both should be highlighted. In the meanwhile, the short-term incentives (such as salary and bonus) should be organically combined with the long-term incentives (such as stock and options). In addition, diversified compensation system should contain both economic awards and other compensations, e.g. promotion opportunities, honor, information sharing and social status improvement, etc. In conclusion, employee motivation should be impartial according to individual contribution. Diversity compensation systems can be adopted. On basis of material incentive, spiritual incentive should be strengthened to reach twice the result with half the effort.

Acknowledgments. This is the initial results of important scientific research subject 2010(10-ZZ-KY-14) sponsored by Shandong Social Sciences Association and Research Fund subject 2010(R201003) sponsored by Shandong Jiaotong University.

References

1. Shen, Y.: Comparing Four Employees' Psychological Contract Relationships. Psychological Science 27, 958–960 (2004)
2. Fengyu, W.: Research on the Imbalance and Reconstruction Model of Librarian's Psychological Contract. Library Work and Study 155, 28–31 (2009)
3. Mingde, L.: Management Psychology. Chengdu University of Science and Technology Press, Chengdu (2002)
4. Shuming, Z., Ziyan, F., Hong, L.: New Progress of Human Resource Management Research Editors. Nanjing University Press, Nanjing (2002)
5. Caifeng, M., Zhongli, Z.: Staff Incentive Based on Psychological Contract. Economic Herald 144, 38–39 (2010)
6. Jie, Y.: The effective recruiting. China Textile & Apparel Press, Beijing (2003)

A Practical Approach of Hierarchy Process Analysis in Modeling MICE City Brand Attributes System*

Sheng Ye[1] and Xi Li[2]

[1] Lecturer, Faculty of International Tourism Management,
Macao University of Science and Technology, Taipa, Macao SAR
chariceye@gmail.com
[2] Associate Professor, Faculty of International Tourism Management,
Macao University of Science and Technology, Taipa, Macao SAR
liximust@gmail.com

1 Introduction

In this research, a system model is proposed to assist the formation of MICE city brand from all-around sustained attributes, and this can be a crucial contribution to future related studies. Based on the literature review of the definition of MICE city [1-2], and city branding [3-5], this paper concludes MICE city brand conception as a city establishes its MICE brand by possessing differentiate city attributes for MICE industry development from other competitors and moreover be authorized by commonalty.

2 Methodology

Proposed Attributes System. In order to model the proposed system, the empirical study performed is concerned with an analysis of the explanatory factors of MICE city branding by the means of literature review, expert interviews, the analytic of hierarchy process (AHP) and SPSS were facilitated to data analysis of the model. From May 2010 to August 2010, a number of experts and senior managers were included in this in-depth interview part. The selection of interviewees was based on convenience, authoritative, and industry-oriented criterion.

MICE City Branding Attributes. The author and the research team sorted the interview section into 2 parts: Part1. Author and the research team wanted to get opinions from interviewees by asking: "what necessary attributes do you think a city should have as so-called a city of MICE"; Part 2. The Image comparison method was used in this step by comparing 10 selected MICE city samples [9] with each other to recognize their own unique characteristics this part was designed as an attributes complementary process. Based on the in-depth interview, 35 attributes suggested by interviewees were city infrastructure, urban transportation, the supportiveness of local government, exhibition halls, MICE Brand, image of the city, etc. The author and the research team concluded them into five categories by considering influence factors on

* Macao Foundation: This paper is a stage achievement of Branding Construction Strategy of Macau as a MICE Destination project supported by Macao Foundation.

Q. Zhou (Ed.): ISAEBD 2011, Part II, CCIS 209, pp. 120–126, 2011.

perception of MICE city image [7-8]: City External Environmental Attributes, City Production Attributes, City Supporting Industries Attributes, City Foundation Attributes and City Image Attributes were the five categories. The elementary attributes and their components are depicted in Table 1.

Table 1. MICE City Branding Attributes & Components

Attributes Categories--City External Environmental: Components under Categories: Economic Environment, Political Environment, Location Condition, Development Opportunity, Social Environment, Cultural Environment, and Nature Environment
--City Production: Policy Support, Industrial Base, Human Resources, Exhibition Pavilion, Convention Facilities, MICE Enterprises Scale, MICE Development History,
--City Supporting Industries: Travel Industry, Hotel Industry, Retail Industry, Logistic Industry, Business and Insurance Industry, Convention and Exhibition Industry Association, Exhibition Professional Organizations
--City Foundation: Developed External Transport, Convenient City Traffic, Road Infrastructure, High Accessibility for Enter or Exit the Country, Modern Urban Facilities, Developed Communication Services, Efficient Administration Service,
--City Image: City Image, City Features, City Internationalization, Urban Attraction, City Popularity, City Reputation, Residents Attitudes Towards Tourists

MICE City Classification. A variety of city types generate diverse attributes for each unique branding case. A city classification theory review [9] was employed to produce MICE city assortment, indicating function and size were used as two major criterions for classifying urban areas. Detailed classification results are presented in Table 2.

Table 2. City Functional Classification & City Size Classification

Functional Classification------Integrative Function City Multi-functions, Diversification Economy Forms, Diversification Industrial Structure, Abundance City Resources, Suitable for all Types of Exhibition Activities
Functional Classification ------Specific Function City Single Function, Specific Industrial Structure, Relatively Concentrated City Resources, Industry Obvious Advantages, Type of Exhibition and Convention
Size Classification ------Large-sized City Domestic Definition: population more than or equal to 200 million Foreign country definition: population more than or equal to 100 million
Size Classification -------Small & Medium City Domestic Definition:population less than or equal to 200 million Foreign country definition: population less than or equal to 100 million

In order to model attributes system, this paper will assign weight value to each attribute and sort those attributes importance degree in accordance with their contribution to the city brand establishment, and using ration concept to figure out components weighting value under each categories.

Weight Score of the Attributes. The study gathered attributes weight score from over 15 depth-structured interviews with MICE industry experts from May 2010 to August 2010. A mixed approach of interviews and AHP was chosen to identify general attributes weight scores and those specific weight scores in response to each four city classifications.

AHP Analysis Application. Generally, AHP consists of three main steps, including developing criteria hierarchy framework, allocating weights to previously framework by using pair wise comparisons analysis and lastly assigning numerical scores to the attributes on our evaluation scale [9-11].

Step 1: Hierarchy Framework. According to the city classification four hierarchy frameworks (Figure1) were indicated and all frameworks are the same. The objective goal for this paper was the certain class of city classification. Structuring Criteria hierarchy into sub-criteria (city's five attributes categories) helps MICE cities to set priorities among attributes, which were sorted within the same layer.

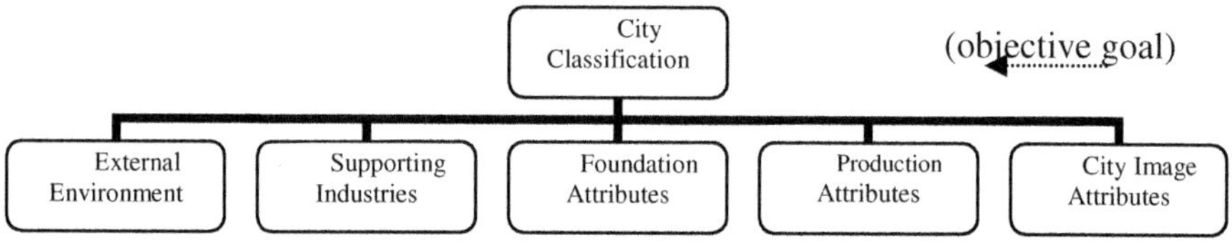

Fig. 1. Hierarchy Framework

Step 2: Pair Wise Comparison allocating Relative Weights. The experts were asked to give weighting values among the five main attributes categories of the hierarchy by making a series of judgments based on pair wise comparisons. Weighting values represent the relative weights of the attributes in every pair wise comparison. In every pair we assigned the degree of dominance of one element over another. The exceptional supremacy of one criterion over another can be assessed at 5, equality at 1. The guidelines for assessing the pairs can be found in Table 3.

Table 3. Value of Criteria

Value	Definition	Description of comparison
1	Equal importance	Equality
2	Somewhat greater Importance	Somewhat greater importance of one criterion over another
3	Strong importance	Strong superiority of one criterion over another
4	Very Strong Importance	Very strong superiority of one criterion over another (clearly seen in practice)
5	Absolute Importance	Absolute (highest possible) superiority of one criterion over another

Step3: Assigning numerical scores to the attributes. The experts were asked to give their numerical rating evaluation on the five main attributes for example: External Environment Attribute- Production Attribute score: 1. it means external environment attribute contributes the equivalence value as production attribute to MICE city branding in the case of this city class. The priorities of the attributes always add up to 1.000. Ratio Scale was put into Positive Reciprocal Matrix and was assigned relative weights across attributes by Weighting score Principle. The criteria were compared in pairs (values from 1/5 to 5), and these subjective assessments were recorded into a matrix of dimensions [i, j]. (Table 4) Based on the Positive Reciprocal Matrix Weighting Principle, the process of calculating the priority of each criterion in terms of its contribution to the overall achievement of the objective goal (city classification) has been processed.

Table 4. A Matrix to Evaluate Criterion Importance

Criteria	1	2	...	n
1	1	a_{12}	...	a_{1n}
2	a_{21}	1	...	a_{2n}
.	.	.		.
j	$1/a_{1n}$	$1/a_{2n}$	...	1

At the end of this stage, this paper do test the consistency of the pair wise judgments by using AHP calculation software Formula 1). according to CR=CI (Consistency Index, C.I.)/RI (Random Index, R.I.), the ration of was 0.031 for large-sized city; 0.013 for Small-medium sized city; 0.021 for Integrative Function city; 0.028 for Specific Function city, all CR value were less than 0.01 showing the good consistency of the judgments.

$$W_t' = \frac{1}{n} \sum_{j=1}^{n} \frac{a_{ij}}{\sum_{i=1}^{n} a_{ij}} \quad i.\ j = 1, 2, \ldots\ldots, n. \qquad (1)$$

Analysis and calculation of the attributes indicated external environmental attribute is the Absolute Importance one accounts the highest weighting score among four city classifications ranging from 0.265 to 0.307. (See Table 5 for detailed weighting score, and the scores present each score of large city, small& medium city, integrative function city, specific function city, in that order). Although the scores were slightly different between each other, the rest of other attributes categories indicate no obvious difference in MICE branding contribution.

Table 5. Large Sized City Attributes Weighting

Sorting	Attribute	Weighting Score (order)
1	City External Environment Attribute	0.307; 0.289; 0.300; 0.265
2	City Production Attribute	0.214; 0.211; 0.248; 0.232
3	City Supporting Industries Attribute	0.183; 0.206; 0.171; 0.194
4	City Foundation Attribute	0.163; 0.152; 0.143; 0.170
5	City Image Attribute	0.133; 0.142; 0.139; 0.140

3 Modeling MICE City Brand Attributes System

This study also validated the weight for each seven components under the main categories. The seven components of external environmental attribute were: economic environment, political environment, location condition, development opportunity, society environment, cultural environment, and nature environment. According to four city classifications, Table 6 indicates the specific case for Integrative Function & Small-medium sized city attributes weighting score. To understand of the score, it means that External Environmental Attributes contains 29.45% of total attribute weighting that means external environment attributes take up 29.45% of priority when establishing MICE city brand in integrative functional small medium sized city and so forth for the other three type city classification.

Table 6. Integrative Function & Small Medium Sized City Classification Attribute Weighting Score

Sorting	Attributes Category	Weighting Score	Averaged Weighting Score
1	City External Environment	0.289+0.300=0.589	0.2945
2	City Production Components	0.206+0.248=0.454	0.227
3	City Supporting Industries	0.211+0.171=0.382	0.191
4	City Foundation	0.152+0.139=0.291	0.1455
5	City Image	0.142+0.143=0.285	0.1425

$$\text{Economic Weighting Ratio} = \frac{\text{Economic Component Total Value Score}}{\text{External Environmental Attributes Value Score}} \tag{2}$$

In addition, for the case of external environment attribute, external environment attribute as the object Goal accounts for 1.00, hence, the ratio between component and attribute is displayed as Formula 2 (The Ratio of Economic component and External environmental attribute) which equals to the weighting score of the component. The economic component weighting percentages of External Environmental Attribute equals to the ratio of economic component multiple attributes percentage. (Table 7 illustrates 35 components weighting score '7 components x 5 attributes categories 'percentage from the perspective of their weighting score towards attributes category).

Table 7. Components Weighting Score in Terms of each Attributes Category

Attributes Category	Components	Total weighting Score
External Environment	Economic Environment	0.167 *0.2945=4.9182
	Political Environment	0.151*0.2945=4.447
	Location Condition	0.147*0.2945=4.3292
	Development Opportunity	0.143*0.2945=4.2114
	Society Environment	0.138*0.2945=4.0641
	Cultural Environment	0.133*0.2945=3.9169
	Nature Environment	0.122*0.2945=3.5929
Production Components	Policy Support	0.152*0.2770=4.2104
	Industrial Base	0.146*0.2770=4.0442
	Human Resources	0.143*0.2770=3.9611
	Exhibition pavilion	0.143*0.2770=3.9611
	Convention Facilities	0.143*0.2770=3.9611
	MICE Enterprises Scale	0.139*0.2770=3.8503
	MICE Development History	0.152*0.2770=3.6841
City Supporting Industries	Travel Industry	0.148*0.191=3.0369
	Hotel Industry	0.159*0.191=2.8268
	Retail Industry	0.124*0.191=2.8268
	Logistic Industry	0.148*0.191=2.7504
	Business and Insurance Industry	0.135*0.191=2.7122
	Convention and Exhibition Industry Association	0.144*0.191=2.5785
	Exhibition Professional Organizations	0.142*0.191=2.3684
City Foundation	Developed External Transport	0.154*0.1455=2.2407
	Convenient City Traffic	0.148*0.1455=2.2407
	Road Infrastructure	0.135*0.1455=1.9643
	High Accessibility for Enter or Exit the Country	0.143*0.1455=2.0807
	Modern Urban Facilities	0.137*0.1455=1.9934
	Developed Communication Services	0.155*0.1455=2.2553
	Efficient Administration Service	0.146*0.1455=2.1243
City Image	City Image	0.150*0.1425=2.0805
	City Features	0.146*0.1425=2.1375
	City Internationalization	0.143*0.1425=2.0378
	Urban Attraction	0.141*0.1425=2.0378
	City Popularity	0.143*0.1425=2.0093
	City Reputation	0.139*0.1425=1.9808
	Residents Attitudes towards Tourists	0.137*0.1425=1.9523

4 Conclusion and Suggestion

In the present study, MICE city branding attributes system was preliminary constructed, it may provide theoretical and reference value for future studies. In the current study, Macao, the city where research was processes still needs long way to reach the mature development station of MICE industry. Brand system can be used to explore the priority attribute that Macao possesses and its adverse attributes that need to be investigated with mixed local conditions, and to formulate an optimization brand attributes strategy in strengthening Macao's diversified future development for Macao.

References

[1] DaKe, L., Te Jing, W.: Introduction to exhibition activities, p. 14 Tsinghua University Press (2004)
[2] Jianlin, C., Chunling, A.: Convention & Exhibition Economy, Urban Competitiveness and Functions Promotion. City Planning Review 32(10), 15–20 (2008)
[3] Hai, J., Jianxin, C.: On the Mechanism of Creating Well-Known Images of Cities. Journal of South China University of Technology (Social Science Edition) 6(2), 50–55 (2004)
[4] Rainisto, S K.: Success Factors of Place Marketing:A Study of Place Marketing Practices in Northern Europe and the United Sates. Doctor Dissertation, Helsinki University of Technology, institute of Strategy and International Business (2003)
[5] Kotler, P., Haider, D., Rein, I.: Marketing Places. In: Kotler, P., Haider, D., Rein, I. (eds.) Attracting investment, industry and tourism to cities, states, and Nations. Maxwell Macmillan Int., New York (1993)
[6] Anholt, S.: Editor's foreword to the first issue. Place Branding 1(1), 4–11 (2004)
[7] Shumin, L., Zhi, Y., Jinping, S.: Discussing the Design and Construction of the Concept of the Brand of Tourist Attractions. Journal of Northwest University (Philosophy and social sciences Edition) 32(3), 39–42 (2002)
[8] Li, X., Ma, Y.: A Review of Study on Foreign MICE Tourism. Tourism Tribune 23(3), 85–89 (2008)
[9] Lee, M.J., Back, K.J.: A review of economic value drivers in convention and meeting management research. International Journal of Contemporary Hospitality Management 17(5), 409–420 (2005)
[10] Palcic, I., Lalic, B.: Analytical Hierarchy Process as a Tool for selecting and Evaluating Projects. Int. J. Simul. Model 8(1), 16–26 (2009) ISSN 1726-4529
[11] Saaty Thomas, L.: Fundamentals of decision making with the analytic hierarchy process. RWS Publications, PA (1994)

Empirical Study of Treasury Auction Formats

Yanping Bai[1] and Yu Zhang[2]

[1] College of Resource Environment and Tourism, Capital Normal University, Beijing, China
[2] School of Computer Science, Beijing University of Civil Engineering and Architecture, Beijing, China
yibaibaby@126.com, zhangyubit@gmail.com

Abstract. The revenue between Dutch auction, American auction and hybrid auction can not be compared by auction theory. The paper establishes a statistical empirical model and uses the data of China's treasury auction market to examine the revenue between Dutch auction, American auction and hybrid auction. The paper has three important conclusions and the hybrid auction can prevent the winner's course and collusion. It is the better treasury auction format for the seller.

Keywords: Treasury auction format; Dutch auction; American auction; Hybrid auction; Statistic analysis.

1 Introduction

In the modern market economy country, treasury has become the important macro modified tool for the governments. Since China began to issue the first treasury in 1981， the scale rise quickly. Vickrey(1961) presents the famous Revenue Equivalence Theorem(RET), from that on, economists are very interested in that which auction methods can bring the highest revenue to the seller. The RET states that any allocation mechanism/auction in which (i) the bidder with the highest type/signal/value always wins, (ii) the bidder with the lowest possible type/value/signal expects zero surplus, (iii) all bidders are risk neutral and (iv) all bidders are drawn from a strictly increasing and atomless distribution will lead to the same revenue for the seller. After Vickrey(1961), a lot of literatures loose the assumptions and rank the revenue of auctions (Filiz (2005), Roseenkranz (2007)). But the theory of single-unit auction can not be applied to the treasury auction, because the treasury belongs to multi-units auction. Daripa (2001), Wang and Zender (2002) established model and compared the revenue gap between Dutch auction and American auction, they get different conclusions; Florens and Sbai (2002)'s empirical study on the revenue of treasury auction is uncertain. Experiment economists study the revenue between different auction methods, but which auction method can bring the highest revenue to the seller is still uncertain. (Kagel, 1995; Sade 2006).

Due to the revenue among Dutch auction, American auction and Hybrid auction can not be compared by auction theory. The paper establishes a statistical empirical model and uses the data of China's treasury auction market to examine the revenue

Q. Zhou (Ed.): ISAEBD 2011, Part II, CCIS 209, pp. 127–132, 2011.

between Dutch auction, American auction and hybrid auction, and then draw conclusions.

2 Basic Model

The theoretical argument with regards to differences in revenue between Dutch auction and American auctions stems from the winners' curse argument (Friedman, 1960).

$$B_i = V + \rho + \varepsilon_i \tag{1}$$

Where B_i represents the bid placed by bidder i, V is the true common value of the asset being auctioned, ρ represents intervening market factors due to the type of auction format, and ε_i is a random error term for each individual bid's variance from the true bid. The bidder with the largest positive error term will have the winning bid. Thus, if the winning bidder has bought the asset in order to resell it, as is the case with most financial securities, the winning bidder will have paid more than the market consensus price for the asset. Therefore, the winner is actually cursed because by winning the auction, the winner has mispriced the asset relative to the other bidders and will have to sell the asset at a loss in the secondary market. In an American auction, the bidders who place the highest bid will have a large winner's curse than those who bid close to the auction clearing price.

The Dutch auction is not subject to a winner's curse. Each bidder pays the same amount for the securities being auctioned. The winning bidder who placed the highest bid will not be penalized for his/her bid. Thus, the auction clearing price should be close to if not equal to the market consensus value. In this case, ρ will be equal to zero. If bidders collude in the Dutch auction and shade their bids down, the ρ will be a negative amount representing the downward shading of bids due to collusion.

The differences in revenue for the seller form the two different auction formats will be a function of the increase in the level of prices in the Dutch auction less the revenue lost from the lack of price discrimination in the Dutch auction. This relationship can be seen in a graph which Reinhart (1992) uses. This graph is depicted in figure 1.

From **Fig. 2**, the increase in revenue from a Dutch auction is the difference between the two triangles A and B. If the gain from added demand is greater than the loss from inability to price discriminate, then the Dutch auction will prove to be superior with regards to revenue. However, if the loss from ability to price discriminate exceeds the gain from added demand, then the American auction will prove to be revenue superior to the Dutch auction. If the two triangular areas are identical, there will be no discernible difference between the American auction and Dutch auction. Because of this trade-off between the ability to price discriminate and the gain in demand, the issue of profit maximization with regards to different auction techniques is largely an empirical issue.

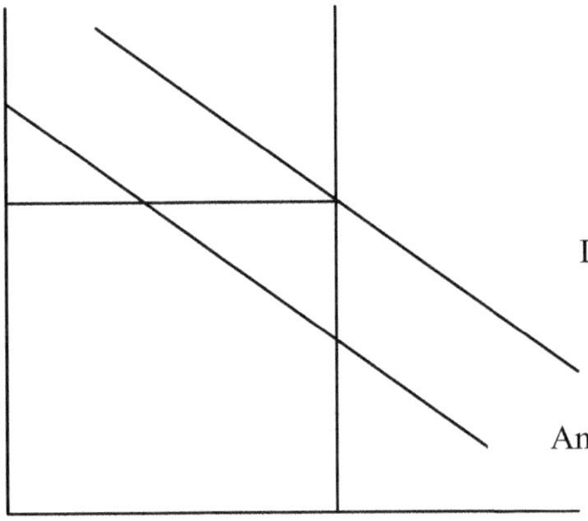

Fig. 1. Revenue comparison between Dutch and American auction

One method to isolate the presence of a downward shading of bids due to the winner's curse or collusion of market participants is to compare the average auction price to the secondary market price for both the American and Dutch auction. If there is a downward shading of bids in the American auction but not in the Dutch auction, then there will be a larger difference between the average auction price and the secondary market price under an American auction than under a Dutch auction. Alternatively, if there is downward shading of bids with both auction types then there will be a difference between the average auction price and the secondary market price for both auctions. This proposal leads to the following set of testable hypotheses:

$$H_1 : \pi_{sp} > 0$$
$$H_2 : \pi_{mp} > 0 \qquad (2)$$
$$H_3 : \pi_{mp} > \pi_{sp}$$

π_{sp} refers to the profit that bidders could earn in the Dutch auction market, equals to the price in the secondary minus the price in the auction market. π_{mp} refers to the profit that bidders could earn in the American auction market, equals to the price in the secondary minus the price in the auction market. If the first relationship holds, this will indicate the presence of a downward shading of bids in the Dutch auction. That means in the Dutch auction, bidders have collusion. If the second relationship holds, it will indicate the presence of a downward shading of bids in the American auction. That means in the American auction, bidders have winner's curse. If the relationship in the third hypothesis holds, it will indicate that there is an increase in the level of demand with the Dutch auction, which could lead to an increase in revenue for the Treasury.

Comparing the Hybrid auction and the Dutch auction, which auction format has winner's curse or bidders' collusion, we also use the above hypotheses.

3 Data, Empirical Results and Analysis

3.1 Data

In order to test the proposed hypotheses, the author collects the auction data form 2000 to 2009. The data was obtained from the Department of the Treasury's home page. The data include 127 Dutch auction, 36 American auction and 48 Hybrid auction.

3.2 Test of Winner's Curse and Collusion

3.2.1 Test of American Auction's Profit Larger Than Zero

The distribution of American auction's profit is unknown, but it is large sample. We use U test. The null hypothesis and the alternative hypothesis are as following:

$$H_0 : \mu_1 = 0$$
$$H_1 : \mu_1 > 0 \tag{3}$$

Here μ_1 is the population mean of the American auction. μ can be got as the followings:

$$\mu = \frac{\overline{x} - \mu_1}{s_1 / \sqrt{n_1}} \tag{4}$$

Here $\overline{x}$ is the sample mean of the American auction. S_1 is the sample variance. Through calculation, we can have $u = 2.932333793$, the significance level is 0.05, $u_{0.05} = 1.645$, $u > u_{0.05}$, so we can not accept H_0, the profit of American auction is larger than zero, it proves that American auction exits winner's curse, so there is a downward shading of bids in the American auction.

3.2.2 Test of Dutch Auction's Profit Larger Than Zero

We use the statistical methods of 3.3.1 to test whether Dutch auction or Hybrid auction can bring larger profit, and through calculation, we can have u=2.93220, the significance level is 0.05, $u_{0.05} = 1.645$, $u > u_{0.05}$, so we can not accept H_0, the profit of Dutch auction is larger than zero, it proves that Dutch auction exits the bidders' collusion, so there is a downward shading of bids in the Dutch auction.

3.2.3 Test of American Auction's Profit Larger Than Zero

We use the statistical methods of 3.2.1 to test whether Dutch auction or Hybrid auction can bring larger profit, and through calculation, we can have $u = -2.1$, the significance level is 0.05, $u_{0.05} = 1.645$, $-u < -u_{0.05}$, so we accept H_0. The profit of Hybrid auction is equal to zero. Because the Hybrid auction improves the American auction and the Dutch auction, it prevents the winner's curse and bidder's collusion so there is not a downward shading of bids in the American auction. From above, we can see that the Hybrid auction is the best auction method for the sellers.

3.3 Comparison of the Revenue

3.3.1 Test of Whether Dutch Auction or American Auction Can Bring Larger Profit

The population 1 is American auction and the population 2 is Dutch auction; the sample 1 is American auction and the sample 2 is Dutch auction.

(1) Supposed the variance of the two populations is equal, we use F test to test whether it is equal or not.

$$H_0 : \sigma_1^2 = \sigma_2^2 \tag{5}$$

Here σ_1^2 is the population 1's variance, and σ_2^2 is the population 2's variance.

We use $F = S_1^2 / S_2^2$ to test the equal variance. Here S_1^2 is the sample 1's variance and S_2^2 is the sample 2's variance.

Through calculation, F=0.316749. The significance level is 0.05, $F_{0.025}(35,126) = 1.614$, $F < F_{0.025}$, so we accept H_0.

(2) The population 1 and the population 2 's variances are equal, we can use the t test.

$$H_0 : \mu_1 = \mu_2$$
$$H_1 : \mu_1 < \mu_2 \tag{6}$$

Here μ_1 is the population 1's mean and μ_2 is the population 2's mean.

$$t = \frac{\overline{x} - \overline{y}}{\sqrt{\frac{(n_1 - 1)s_1^2 + (n_2 - 1)s_2^2}{n_1 + n_2 - 2} * (\frac{1}{n_1} + \frac{1}{n_2})}} \tag{7}$$

Here $\overline{x}$ is the sample 1's mean and $\overline{y}$ is the sample 2's mean, n_1 is the number of sample 1 and n_2 is the number of sample 2.

Through calculation, t=-0.62. The significance level is 0.05, $t_{0.05}(161) = 1.6449$, $-t_{0.05}(161) < t < t_{0.05}(161)$, so we accept H_0. Because the American auction exits winner's curse and the Dutch auction exits collusion, the two auction format can bring profit for the bidder, but the two auction's profits have not significant different.

3.3.2 Test of Whether Dutch Auction or Hybrid Auction Can Bring Larger Profit

We use the statistical methods of 3.3.1 to test whether Dutch auction or Hybrid auction can bring larger profit, and through calculation, t=-0.32. The significance level is 0.05, $t_{0.05}(104) = 1.6449$, $-t_{0.05}(104) < -t < t_{0.05}(104)$, so we accept H_0. Because the Hybrid auction can prevent winner's curse and collusion, so the bidders can not make profit; the Dutch auction exits collusion, the bidders can make profit, but the two auction's profits have not significant different.

4 Conclusions

The paper establishes a statistical empirical model and uses the data of China's treasury auction market to examine the revenue between Dutch auction, American auction and hybrid auction. The paper has three important conclusions:

(1) the American auction exits winner's curse and the Dutch auction exits collusion, the two auction format can bring profit for the bidder, but the two auction's profits have not significant different.

(2) The Hybrid auction can prevent winner's curse and collusion, so the bidders can not make profit; the Dutch auction exits collusion, the bidders can make profit, but the two auction's profits have not significant different.

(3) The Hybrid auction improves the American auction and the Dutch auction, it prevents the winner's curse and bidder's collusion so there is not a downward shading of bids in the American auction. From above, we can see that the Hybrid auction is the best auction method for the sellers.

References

1. Vickrey, W.: Counter-speculation, auctions, and competitive sealed tenders. Journal of Finance 16, 8–37 (1961)
2. Milgrom, P.R., Weber, R.J.: A theory of auctions and competitive bidding. Econometrica 50, 1089–1122 (1982a)
3. Filiz, E., Ozbay, E.Y.: Auctions with Anticipated Regret, Working Paper, New York University (2005)
4. Roseenkranz, S., Schmit, P.W.: Reserve Prices in Auctions as Reference Points. The Economic Journal 520, 637–653 (2007)
5. Back, K., Zender, J.F.: Auctions of divisible goods: on the rationale for the Treasury experiment. Review of Financial Studies 6, 733–764 (1993)
6. Daripa, A.: A Theory of Treasury Auctions. Journal of International Money and Finance 20, 743–767 (2001)
7. Wang, J., Zender, J.: Auctioning Divisible Goods. Economic Theory 19, 673–705 (2002)
8. Barker-Rogers, T.M.: The Auction of Financial Securities: A Study of the Treasury Auction Market, PhD Dissertation, Texas Tech. University (2001)
9. Florens, J.P., Sbai, E.: Identification in Empirical Games, Working Paper, University of Toulouse (2002)
10. Alvarez, F., Mazon, C., Cerda, E.: Treasury Auctions in Spain: a Linear Approach. Spanish Economic Review 5, 25–48 (2003)
11. Kagel, H.J.: Auctions: A Survey of Experimental Research. In: John, K.H., Alvin, R.E. (eds.) The Handbook of Experimental Economics, pp. 501–585 (1995)
12. Sade, O., Schnitzlein, C., Zender, J.F.: Competition and Cooperation in Divisible Good Auctions: An Experimental Examination. Review of Financial Studies 19, 195–235 (2006)
13. Simon, D.P.: Markups, quantity risk, and bidding strategies at Treasury coupon auctions. Journal of Financial Economics 35(1), 43–62 (1994)
14. Feldman, R.A., Reinhart, V.: Auction format matters: evidence on bidding behavior and seller revenue. International Monetary Fund Staff Papers 43, 395–418 (1996)
15. Chatterjea, A., Jarrow, R.A.: Market manipulation, price bubbles and a model of the U.S. Treasury securities auction market. Journal of Financial and Quantitative Analysis 33(2), 255–290 (1998)

Anti-monopoly Analysis of Tencent QQ vs. 360 Dispute

Weiwei Hu and Yimeei Guo

School of Law., Xiamen University; 361005, China
helusi420hw@163.com,
ymguo@xmu.edu.cn

Abstract. Anti-monopoly concerns are becoming more and more frequent for Internet industries competiting all over the world. This paper makes a case analysis of Tencent QQ vs. 360 dispute, then has some further thought from such dispute.Finally, it is hoped by this paper that China's Anti-monopoly Law be healthily and perfectly enforced in the future.

Keywords: Anti-monopoly, Internet industries, Case analysis.

1 Introduction

Anti-monopoly concerns are becoming more and more frequent for Internet industries competiting all over the world.For example, in February 2011,Apple launched a new service that allows for magazine and newspaper subscriptions for its popular devices, might draw claim from publishers that Apple dominates the market for consumer tablet computers and that it has allegedly used that commanding position to restrict competition.[1] Also in February 2011,Hudong.com, an online encyclopedia, is alleging that Baidu unfairly blocks its Web pages from search results in favor of its own encyclopedia service, Baidu Baike.[2] On April 1,2011, Microsoft plans to file a complaint with the European Commission demanding action against competitor Google on competition law grounds. Microsoft claims that Google stops other companies from accessing the information needed to run effective search operations.[3]

Notably, in 2010 in China which has more than 400 million Netizen, [4]a "war" called "Tencent QQ vs. 360 battle" happened in front of the desktop of tremendous Internet users and was well-known both inside and outside the industry. 360 , which relys on its 360 free anti-virus software become world-renowned, is a top company of security software services company chiefs, and Tencent QQ, which is an "overlord" of instant messaging supported by 600 million users, these two desktop client software giants revealed a typical case of Chinese Internet industry ' s competition. Indubitablebly , this case is regarded as an anti-monopoly law issue, however, compared to the tranditional anti-monopoly cases, it has its own feature i.e. it took place in Internet area.

Under the frame of analysis on anti-monopoly law to prohibit abusing the market dominance position, frist of all, we must identify whether or not Tencent owns the dominant market position, and secondly to identify whether or not it carries on the action of abusing the dominant market position. But to identify the dominant market

Q. Zhou (Ed.): ISAEBD 2011, Part II, CCIS 209, pp. 133–141, 2011.

position, we have to begin from defining the relevant market (including commodity market and geography market).

In ordinary market, the definition of relevant market is a complex question, involving substitutable demand and supply analysis of alternatives, sometimes even having the hypothetical monopolist test. And in Internet market, it's even more complex. It's temporal and spatial boundary is difficult to determine. Internet market is in dynamic development because of the rapid technology innovation and Internet industry's vivid characteristic of network externality. Thus, the traditional definition method for relevant market is limited in its application.

Moreover, a dominant market position in Internet market is more complex to determine either the market share or market entry barriers , all of this exhibited some characteristics different from the ordinary market. For example, Internet market entry barriers are mainly expressed as the network effects and intellectual property (IP), technical standards or other non-price factors.

For this reason , although the public tend to make sure that Tencent QQ has a conduct of violating the anti-monopoly law , but it's difficult to convict legally that Tencent QQ violates anti-monopoly law, this article thinks that this issue is very complicated and has a long way to go , it still wants to provide an analysis on the captioned Tencent QQ vs. 360 case according to China's Anti Unfair Competition Law (AUCL) and the Anti-Monopoly Law (AML)and brings forward some further thought and suggestion.

2 Anti-monopoly Analysis of Tencent QQ vs. 360 Dispute

2.1 Fact Summary

Tencent Technology (Shenzhen) Limited is an Internet service provider (ISP) – its most well known product, however is an instant messaging system known as "QQ" (Tencent QQ).

Beijing Qihoo Technology Limited supplies security software – its most well known line of products, are its "360" line of security software (including software which protects user's privacy on the Internet and anti-virus software) (Qihoo 360).

In September 2010, Qihoo 360 launched a software called "360 Privacy Protector". This product is used to keep tabs on other software on a user's computer and is able to detect a number of things, for instance the type of data that another software extracts from a user's computer. The objective of this product is to shield a user from software which illegally extracts or retains a user's personal data; in other words, to protect a user's privacy.

On September 26, 2010, Qihoo 360 published an article on their website entitled "360 Privacy Protector 1.1 Beta – new function – privacy clean up function" . In this article, Qihoo 360 alleged that its 360 Privacy Protector software had recently detected that a "certain instant messaging software" was found to be "peeping" at the private files and data of users, without first obtaining the approval of those users. The article itself did not name which instant messaging software Qihoo 360 was referring to. However a screenshot in the article bore the logo of the Tencent QQ instant messaging software.

On October 14, 2010, Tencent Technology (Shenzhen) Limited and Shenzhen Tencent Computer System Limited (hereinafter Tencent QQ) filed an application with the Beijing Chaoyang District People's Court, alleging that:

Beijing Qihoo Technology Limited (manufacturer and copyright holder of 360 Privacy Protector; and owner of www.360.cn); Qizhi Software (Beijing) Limited (company which supplies 360 Privacy Protector software); and Beijing 3G Wireless Internet Technology Limited (operator of www.360.cn) (hereinafter Qihoo 360) have fabricated or spread false facts about Tencent QQ's instant messaging software resulting in the Tencent QQ's business reputation or "commodity fame" being damaged. This conduct was allegedly in breach of Article 14 of the AUCL.

Further in Tencent QQ's court application, they claimed that they could properly be construed as a competitor to Qihoo 360 as the latter also manufactures and supplies their own anti-virus or security software (i.e. called "QQ Computer Housekeeper"). In its complaint, Tencent QQ requested that the Court: injunct Qihoo 360 from fabricating or spreading false facts about Tencent QQ's instant messaging software; that Qihoo 360 apologise to Tencent QQ for the conduct described above; and that Qihoo 360 pay damages of RMB 4 million.

On November 3, 2010, the Court accepted this case (the AUCL allegation).

On the same day, Tencent QQ issued a newsletter to all its users entitled "A letter to all users of QQ". Through this newsletter, Tencent QQ informed all users that they have made the "difficult" decision of making the use of QQ instant messaging service incompatible with the use of 360 privacy or anti-virus software. In other words, QQ users who choose to use 360 privacy or anti-virus software will no longer be able to use QQ instant messaging in the same instance. Tencent QQ explained that this was mainly because they were not confident that they could continue to protect their user's privacy (including data such as chats and passwords), if they continued to use the 360 line of security software. In its newsletter, Tencent QQ also requested that users use its "QQ Computer Housekeeper" or other antivirus or security software in place of the 360 line of security software.

Notably, from November 3, 2010, users of QQ reported that they weren't able to use the 360 line of security software and QQ at the same time. However, a few days later, reports suggest that government agencies intervened and users reported that their QQ and 360 softwares were able to be used concurrently.

On November 4, 2010, Li Changqing (a Beijing based lawyer) filed a complaint with the State Administration of Industry and Commerce (SAIC) requesting that the SAIC should commence an Anti-Monopoly investigation against Tencent QQ. In his application, Li alleged that Tencent QQ had abused its dominance by restricting QQ users or "forcing" QQ users to uninstall 360 software, without a valid reason (in breach of Article 17(4) of the AML). Li also submitted a study report issued by Research Consulting Group – this report showed that Tencent's market share in the instant messaging software market was approximately 76.2%. Li requested that the SAIC impose an appropriate penalty on Tencent QQ for its alleged breach of Article 17(4) of the AML (the AML allegation). [5]

This paper then discusses and analyses the AUCL allegation and the AML allegation outlined above in some detail as follows.

2.2 The Anti Unfair Competition Law (AUCL) Allegation

As mentioned above, Tencent QQ's allegation is that Qihoo 360 is in breach of Article 14 of the AUCL. Article 14 of the AUCL prohibits entities from fabricating or spreading false facts to damage the business reputation or commodity fame of a competing entity.

In order to prove that a breach of Article 14 has occurred, Tencent QQ would need to prove the following elements:

- that Tencent QQ and Qihoo 360 are "competing" entities (first element);
- that Qihoo 360 has undertaken conduct amounting to "fabricating or spreading false facts" about Tencent QQ (second element); and
- that the business reputation or "commodity fame" of Tencent QQ has been damaged (third element).

In respect of the first element, we note that a lot would depend on what the Court would construe as the "relevant market". If the Court construes the relevant market to be a broad "market for Internet services" , for instance, then it is likely that Tencent QQ and Qihoo 360 could be construed as "competitors". However, if the relevant market is more narrowly drawn, it might be more challenging for Tencent QQ to prove that they should rightly be considered "competitors" to Qihoo 360.

As mentioned above, Tencent QQ's primary business is in providing QQ instant messaging software to users; whereas Qihoo 360's primary business is in providing the 360 line of anti-virus or security software to users. In Tencent QQ's court application, they have argued that they are competitors to Qihoo 360's line of anti-virus or security software, because Tencent QQ also provides similar software in the form of "QQ Computer Housekeeper".

The second and the third elements would depend on whether the Court is satisfied that Tencent QQ has provided sufficient evidence to prove that Qihoo 360 has "fabricated false facts" and that this has resulted in "damage" to the former's business reputation.

2.3 The Anti-monopoly Law (AML) Allegation

As mentioned above, Li's allegation is that Tencent QQ breached Article 17 of the AML.

Article 17 of the AML prohibits entities which hold a dominant position to abuse their dominance by engaging in several specified acts, including by restricting other entities to transact only with the original entity or only with specified entities, without a valid reason (Article 17(4), AML).

In order to prove that a breach of Article 17 has occurred, Li would need to prove or the SAIC would need to be satisfied that the following elements have been fulfilled:that Tencent QQ is "dominant" in the relevant market (the first element); that Tencent QQ has abused its dominance in the relevant market by restricting other entities to transact only with Tencent QQ or only with specified entities (thereby excluding others), without a valid reason (the second element).

With regards to the first element, Article 19 of the AML is instructive. Article 19 of the AML outlines three scenarios in which an entity would be considered a dominant entity, most relevant of which is an entity would be deemed dominant where the entity holds half of the market share (i.e. more than 50%) in the relevant market. However, this is a rebuttable presumption – in other words, an entity which has been "deemed" as dominant may provide evidence that it is not dominant in the relevant market.

As mentioned above, Li submitted a study report which alleged that Tencent QQ is dominant in the instant messaging software market (with a market share of 76.2%). It remains to be seen if a court or the SAIC would be of the view that the report provides sufficient evidence that Tencent QQ is dominant in the instant messaging software market.

Another issue is, that, if indeed the allegation is that Tencent QQ is dominant in the instant messaging software market but that the alleged "abuse" has resulted in effects in the security or antivirus software market; would a court or authority still consider this to be an abuse of dominance? In other words, if an entity is dominant in Market A but the alleged abuse has taken place in Market B – would such conduct still be construed as an abuse of dominance? If so, what are the factors which a court or authority would consider as relevant in proving such a case?

The allegation appears to be that Tencent QQ has somehow "made use of" or "leveraged" its dominance in the instant messaging market to influence another "market", arguably the "anti-virus" or "security" software market. Whether an entity has "leveraged" its dominance in Market A to influence conduct or outcomes in Market B is a complex issue – in overseas jurisprudence (such as the EU), there is conflicting jurisprudence on whether Market A and Market B have to be "related" markets, for an abuse of dominance breach to be made out.

In addition, even if a court or authority was willing to accept that an "abuse" may occur in a separate market, then the next step would be to prove the second element or nature of the abuse. In this case, it appears that the allegation is that Tencent QQ has restricted users from transacting or using the 360 line of anti-virus software, without a valid reason – in breach of Article 17(4) of the AML.[6]

2.4 Brief Comment

Nevertheless, having a dominant market position itself is not illegal. Only the abuse of such a status falls under the jurisdiction of anti-monopoly laws. Although in the above analysis , Tencent was suspicious of abusing dominant market position, but the concrete determination requires adequate reasons and evidence. In fact, the foregoing China's Anti-Monopoly Law , Article 17 (4) provides the condition that corresponding actions constitutes an abuse of dominant market position is "not justified" , so obviously , there is need for an application of rule of reason , whether the relevant conduct of Tencent QQ is justified, it is not only a fact-finding problems, but a standard for judgement .

From the Tencent QQ vs. 360 dispute, the relevant facts here can not be fully established , now the parties just act on their own, thus it requires the fact to be identified by presiding agencies. There are different opinions about the nature of relevant conduct acted by Tencent QQ ,whether or not it is a legitimate defensive conduct or a abuse of dominant market position also need further judgement after relevent facts are clear. If it can support that Tencent is"justified" to act this conduct in relevent fact-finding, then the behavior does not constitute abuse of dominant market position.

Obviously, even though all the captioned analysis supports that Tencent QQ constitutes the act of abusing dominant market position, going through the whole investigation and analysis must be a very complicate procedure and long process. Furthermore, in fact,Tencent QQ stopped such suspicious conduct immediately under the strong public opinion pressure and after presiding agency's intervention. Therefore, the problem of prohibiting such suspicious conduct to continue does not exist any more.Certainly, it does not influence the attribution and enforcement of panelty etc. punishment against such happened conduct,only the level of punishment will be different.

3 Further Thought Arising from Tencent QQ vs. 360 Dispute

3.1 Need We different Anti-monopoly Law in Internet Area

Despite the Anti-Monopoly issue in Internet area has its own characteristic,this paper thinks that it doesn't mean the application of law must be totally different.

The above analysis shows that, related to anti-monopoly in traditional markets, the anti-monopoly enforcement of Internet area is much more complex and difficult. Comparing with the traditional economy, the Internet economy has the characteristics on faster innovation, easier market entry, market share instability, as well as first-mover advantage, network effects , two-sided markets and so on.

On the one hand, technical renovation brings impact on the maintenance of the dominant market position and can reduce the demand of rapid anti-monopoly action, but on the other hand, network effects, especially combined with intellectual property , allows the enterprises to rely on its customers , who have already been locked in the use of many existing products and services , to prevent new competitors and high-tech challenges.

Therefore, we must think over these characteristics when enforcing anti-monopoly law in Internet area and developing the analytical methods of anti-monopoly law enforcement, but not completely confined to the traditional anti-monopoly law. For example, such as "price discrimination", "tying", "predatory pricing" and other conducts, which is concerned by the anti-monopoly policy, it's a strategy for the companies that have considerable market power in the traditional economy, however , in the Internet economy , it becomes just one way to survive for the enterprises and it's a necessary way to keep the most of them survived, so the rationality of "tying" conduct problems requires further research combining with the characteristics of the industry. But these characteristics of the Internet economy has not shaken the basic principles and institutional mechanism of Anti-Monopoly Law, it just needs to consider its distinctive feature when making a concrete analysis.

In this respect, There can be specific guides or regulations aiming at the Anti-Monopoly law enforcement in Internet area, which come into being based on fundamental principle and system by State Council Anti-Monopoly Committee or relevant legal authority of anti-monopoly enforcement.

3.2 Accurate Understanding on Anti-monopoly Law in China Is Required

Undoubtedly, the public pay close attention to the Tencent QQ vs. 360 dispute is in favor of popularizing and propagating the Anti-Monopoly Law in China, but it requires an accurate understanding on this Law.

The Tencent QQ vs. 360dispute caused universal public concern and widely reported by the media, had a strong influence on the society. For the feverish comments and discussions, in addition to refer to concern for right and wrong and resentment between the two companies in China's Internet industry, it also involves a large number of monopoly and anti-monopoly issues. This makes China's Anti-Monopoly Law which has implemented more than two years, become the focus of public attention again. Whether or not they look forward to the anti-monopoly law enforcement agencys' intervening in the dispute effectively and dissatisfy with reality, or the discussion of applicable law and the assumption of improving law concerning the specific conduct, all of these have played a very important role in publicizing the konwledge of anti-monopoly law, but there are some condition that seemingly right but actually wrong even misread the law in the feverish comments and discussionst here.

For example, several reports mentioned that the supervision agency considers to split the Tencent company, this is a unfounded claim. As a private enterprise and listed company, Tencent does not have a responsibile supervision agency like state-owned enterprises. Although administration regulator can supervise the conduct of their operations, but it's without foundation to split. Even the anti-monopoly enforcement agencies of a few countries like the United States can apply to the court to split companies which made monopolistic conduct, but the anti-monopoly law enforcement agencies in China have no power in this regard.

Except the operators who conduct illegal concentration, the State Council Anti-Monopoly Law Enforcement Agency can order to stop conducting concentration, disposing stocks or assets for duty by the prescribed time and taking other necessary measures to restore the status before the concentration. Except which belong to structural relief measure, for relief measures of the other monopolistic conduct (including abuse of dominant position) are behavioral, that is to say , the Anti-Monopoly Enforcement Agency can order to stop illegal conducts, confiscating illegal gains, and fining more than 1%, fewer than 10% sales last year.

Therefore, even if Tencent is convicted of having the monopolistic conduct to abuse dominant market position , according to the laws of China, although they have to receive the appropriate punishment, but the situation to be split is impossible. In a word, intratype competition is a good thing, it's terrible without it; but we need to regulate competition in order to ensure its free and fair.

360 and Tencent are all Internet industries, although thair main business scopes are different , but there are many intersected areas, and they both take the business model of free services like advertising or add-service , to attract users and dominate the market quickly , then to be profitable, so there is an obvious competition between them. Under the condition of market economy, an intratype competition in the market is a normal thing, which is the market mechanism to play a role in the fundamental mode. Technological progress, economic development , as well as the rational allocation of resources, all of which can only be achieved in this competition . If there is no competition between the parties (for exemple, according to plan instruction to

manufacture to produce under the Planned Economy), and even restrict competition artificially (for exemple, in a case of one party has a monopoly or the both parties conspire to make a plan for monopolize), that have problems and are more terrible.

Therefore, it is a normal phenomenon that fierce competition between the operaters in order to survive and develop themselves under the condition of market economy, from another standpoint, this is a proof of China's market economy status. Of course, the market competition have a difference both in intensity and even in means. Even though competition is a good thing, it has advantages and disadvantages of the means and results. Not all of people like competition in any conditions, on the contrary, the tendency to distort and limit competition is always exsistent.

For this reason , despite the competition of spontaneous market can't guarantee its fairness or even freedom, it becomes necessary to ensure free and fair competition in modern society by enacting and enforcing of competition laws and regulations. [7]

4 Conclusion

As we know, the promulgation in August 2007 and implementation in August 2008 of the Anti-monopoly Law is a milestone in the history of China's legislation. However, the implementation of anti-monopoly law has been accompanied by endless controversies in every country just as several cases we mentioned in the begianning in this article. Anti-monopoly is an exotic area in China's legal system, so it lacks sound local resources for self-growth and independent improvement. China's legislative, law enforcement and judicial sectors are all quite unfamiliar with anti-monopoly law and have virtually no independent experience. They mainly depend on foreign experiences and theoretical research at the literary level. Anti-monopoly is a complex issue involved with legal, policy, economic and social factors and should be considered thoroughly from various perspectives. [8] Nevertheless, it is hoped by this paper that China's Anti-monopoly Law be healthily and perfectly enforced in the future.

References

[1] Koppel, N.: Apple's Subscription Rules Raise Possible Antitrust Issues (February 16, 2011), http://online.wsj.com/article/SB10001424052748704409004576146613997208194.html
[2] Xing, W.: Baidu accused of abusing dominant position, http://www.chinadaily.com.cn/bizchina/2011-02/23/content_12063335.htm,2011-2-23
[3] Microsoft files EU competition complaint against Google, http://www.out-law.com/page-11844,2011-3-31
[4] According to "the 27th Statistical Report on Internet Development in China" released by CNNIC on January 19, 2011, up to the end of December 2011, the number of netizens in China has reached 457 million.Such Report (in Chinese) is available at http://www.cnnic.net.cn/dtygg/dtgg/201101/P020110119328960192287.pdf

[5] Ning, S., Liang, D., Ng, A.: The QQ / 360 Disputes - Who, What, Where, When and Preliminary Anti-Monopoly Analysis, http://www.chinalawinsight.com/2010/11/articles/corporate/antitrust-competition/the-qq-360-disputes-who-what-where-when-and-preliminary-antitrust-analysis/,2010-11-12
[6] Anti-Monopoly Law Needs to Be Correctly Understanded: the Plausibility of Tencent Monopoly cCase(in Chinese), http://www.legaldaily.com.cn/economical/content/2010-12/31/content_2424660.htm?node=21506
[7] You, M.: To Understand Abuse of Market Dominance in Anti-Monopoly Law. Chinaipmagazine (36) (2010-7-5), available at http://www.chinaipmagazine.com/en/journal-show.asp?id=593

A Comparative Study between the Investment in China's Urban and Rural Public Infrastructure*

Xiang Yinghui[1,2] and Wen Tao[1]

[1] School of Management, Shenyang Jianzhu University
[2] School of Economics, Liaoning University,
Hunnan East Road 9 110168 Shenyang, P.R.C
xyhlrb@sohu.com

Abstract. What are the trend of public infrastructures' inventory and investment in China? What differences are existing between the urban and rural area in this field? Use data from "China Urban-Rural Construction Statistical Yearbook", aided by excel, this paper studies on inventory status and investment in urban, township, and village public infrastructure, and makes a comparison. It is found both the investment in and the actual inventory of urban public infrastructure have trended up significantly; the actual inventory of township's roads and bridges has trended down; the investment in village's public infrastructure has increased significantly, while the actual inventory of village roads and bridges has not increased obviously. The dualization characteristic between urban and rural area is apparent, and it is urgent to increase the investment scale in rural public infrastructure, and to improve investment's efficiency. It is originally pointed out although both as "rural area", the township area and the village area are taking on apparently different characteristics in public infrastructure development. Moreover, the huge gap of public infrastructures development between urban and rural area is convincingly and empirically manifested.

Keywords: urban and rural area, public infrastructure, investment, comparison.

1 Introduction

The term of "infrastructure" was introduced to the field of economics in the 1940s, however, economists have much earlier realized the importance of public facilities such as the navigation, port, warehouse, and water conservancy project. With the rapid development of China's economy and the increasing demand from urban and rural inhabitants for the quality of their livelihood and their surrounding environment, infrastructures' role as the carrier of social and economical activities is paid more and more attention.

* "A study on new financing models of rural infrastructures construction", Research project sponsored by Ministry of Housing and Urban-Rural Development, P.R. China (2009-R2-03); also sponsored by Education Department of Liaoning Province (2009A595).

Q. Zhou (Ed.): ISAEBD 2011, Part II, CCIS 209, pp. 142–147, 2011.

2 The Empirical Study on the Construction of and Investment in Public Infrastructure in Urban and Rural Areas

2.1 The Analysis of Fixed-Asset Investment in Urban Public Infrastructures

According to "China Urban-Rural Construction Statistical Yearbook" (2008), we obtain the statistic data of fixed-asset investment in China's urban public infrastructure from 1990 to 2008,and we get the price index of infrastructure investment (based on 1990's price) from "China's Statistical Yearbook (2008)" and "China's Fixed-asset Investment Statistical Yearbook(2008)", and then we come up with the development trend of both normal and actual investment in China's urban public infrastructure.

Figure 1 indicates the change trend of fixed-asset investment in China's urban public infrastructure, from 1990 to 2008 the increase of normal fixed-asset investment in urban public infrastructure was clear, from 12.12 billion yuan of 1990 to 736.82 billion yuan of 2008. Even if the inflation effect was deducted, the increase of actual fixed asset investment volume was still apparent, from 12.12 billion yuan of 1990 to 292.505 billion yuan of 2008. The main reason may lie in that accompanying China's rapid urbanization process, the state has paid more and more attention on the construction of urban public infrastructure, and the related fiscal input has simultaneously increased.

Figure 2 indicates the increase rates' change of actual investment in urban public infrastructure. From 1991 to 2008, although the average increase rate was as high as 20.09%, the increase rates' variation among different years was acute. The highest increase rate appeared in the year of 1993, which was 45.5%, while the lowest increase rate appeared in the year of 2004, which was 1.03%. This sharp fluctuation somehow suggests that it is necessary to ensure the stability and sustainability of urban fiscal investment.

2.2 The Analysis of China's Urban Roads and Bridges

According to "China Urban–Rural Construction Statistical Yearbook (2008)", we get the statistical data of the inventory of China's urban roads and bridges. Based on this, we calculate increase rates of urban roads length, urban roads area, and per capital urban roads areas, and thus make a comparison of these rates.

From figure 3 we can see that the increase rate of each urban roads index is rather evident. From 2000 to 2008 the average increase rate of urban roads length was 6.18%, the average increase rate of urban roads area was 8.28%, and the average increase rate of per capital urban roads area was 8.53%. But among different years, these indexes varied a lot. The increase rates of indexes in 2003 were the highest, while these rates were at the lowest level in 2006 and 2007. When comparing different index, the relationship of contrast among different index varied a lot. For example, the increase rate of per capital urban roads area in 2003 was the highest, while the same index in 2006 was much lower than that of total urban roads area. The possible reason that the general increase rates among different years varied a lot may be the effect of the change of state's macro policy. On the other hand, the fact that the average increase rates are obvious indicates that along with the rapid urbanization process and the population shift from rural to urban area, both the general level and per capital level of urban roads have stepped up significantly, which is in line with the urbanization process.

2.3 The Analysis of China's Township Public Infrastructures

According to the "China Urban-Rural Construction Statistical Yearbook (2008)", we get the statistical data of the inventory of China's township various public infrastructure. And based on this, we are able to describe the change trend of their quantity.

From figure 4, we can see that from 1990 to 2008, the township roads length had taken on a trend of gradual drop; the number of township bridge had also decreased slightly; the length of drainage pipelines before 2005 had increased, but since 2006, this number had also decreased; the area of public green space had raised before 2005, but since 2006, this number had also dropped off; the number of special vehicles for environmental sanitation had increased. Possible reasons may be as the following: statistic errors exit; the state fiscal input on township roads and bridges is not enough, while the township government's fund-raising ability after "the reform of rural taxation system" has been weakened, which hinders the construction of township roads and bridges; the utilization efficiency of fiscal input is low; the population outflow from rural to urban area has caused that the increasing rate of the demand for rural infrastructure slows down; the fiscal input on township environmental equipment has increased as a result of the state's more and more concern with environment issue.

2.4 The Analysis of the Construction of and Investment of Villages' Public Infrastructure

From "China Urban–Rural Construction Statistical Yearbook(2008)", we get the data of investment volume in china's villages construction (including the house construction investment and public infrastructure investment), investment in villages' public infrastructure, and villages' road length. Based on this, we begin with describing the change trend of investment volume in villages' construction, then we describe the change trend of increasing rate of investment in villages' construction, public infrastructures and road length.

From figure 5, we can see that the investment scale in villages' construction has taken on a trend of stable increase, simultaneously the investment scale in villages' public infrastructures has also increased steadily, especially in recent years. The possible reason may lie in that along with the gradual propelling of the "construction of new rural area", the state's fiscal input on "Agriculture Rural areas and Peasantry" has increased gradually, meanwhile, the construction of rural public infrastructure has also been placed importance.

From 1990 to 2008, the average increasing rate of construction investment for the year was 9.68%, the average increasing rate of public infrastructure was 24.55%. However, the increase of physical inventory was not apparent. For example, the average increasing rate of road length was negative 0.68%. From figure 6, we can see that the increasing rates of villages' construction investment for the year, villages public infrastructure investment, and villages road length took on obvious difference with each other or in different period. Making a comparison among different index, we can find that the increasing rate of villages public infrastructure was the highest, followed by the increasing rate of villages construction investment, and the increasing rate of villages' road length was the lowest. When making a comparison among different year, the related increasing rates in 1995 and 2002 were most eminent. In recent years, the investment volume in villages' public infrastructure has increased significantly, but the villages' road length has not increased remarkably. The possible reasons may be as the following: although the normal investment volume has stepped up significantly, the actual investment volume has not increased to the same extent; The physical inventory of villages' other public infrastructures except roads may have increased more significantly; The increasing investment may bring us not only the increase of road length, but also an improvement of road quality; The efficiency of fiscal input is low; Statistic inaccuracies exist.

3 Conclusion

As far as the urban public infrastructure is concerned, both the investment scale and physical inventory have taken on an trend of increasing in recent years; As far as the township public infrastructure is considered, the physical inventory of township's road and bridge has decreased to some extent; As far as villages public infrastructure is considered, the fixed-asset investment in villages' public infrastructure has increased significantly, while the physical inventory of villages' road and bridge has not changed obviously.

The final conclusion will be: the dualization characteristic of the public infrastructure's construction and investment between urban and rural area is apparent, and it is urgent to increase the investment scale in rural public infrastructure, as well as to improve investment's efficiency.

References

1. Department of Planning, Financing and Foreign Affairs Ministry of Housing and Urban-Rural Development, P.R. China, China Urban-Rural Construction Statistical Yearbook (2008)
2. Naude, A., Mashiri, M., Nchabeleng, A.: New roads are not enough.: Planning and delivering more integrated, intelligent and sustainable rural access systems. In: 24th Annual Southern African Transport Conference, pp. 598–610 (2005)
3. Narayanan, A., Jain, A., Bowonder, B.: Providing. rural connectivity infrastructure: ICT diffusion through private sector participation. International Journal of Services, Technology and Management 6(3-5), 416–436 (2005)
4. Hossain, M., Romanoschi, S.A., Emig, L.W.: Rural Transportation Infrastructure Preservation in Kansas: Issues and Challenges. Transportation Research Record I(1819), 30–38 (2003)
5. Czuczman, K.: Promoting the sustainability of rural transport infrastructure. In: Proceedings - Conference of the Australian Road Research Board, vol. 21, pp. 517–531 (2003)
6. Xiang, Y.: A design for derivative model of rural infrastructure BOT. Engineering and Business Management 3, 205–208 (2010)

Appendix

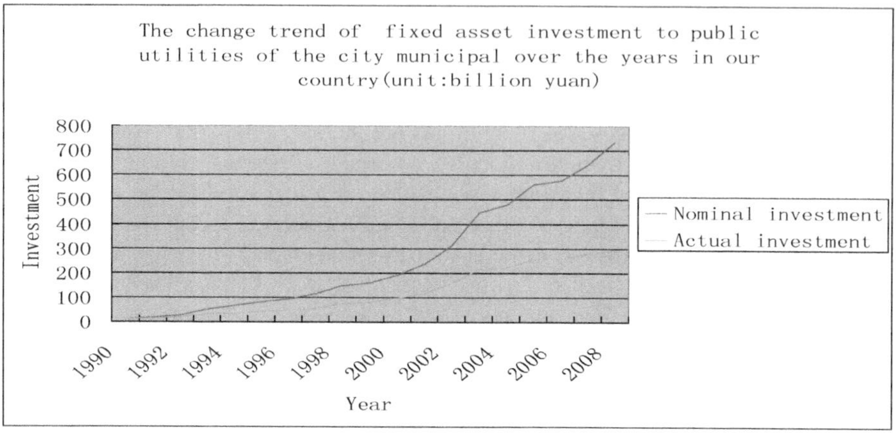

Fig. 1. The development trend of normal and actual fixed asset investment in China's urban public infrastructure

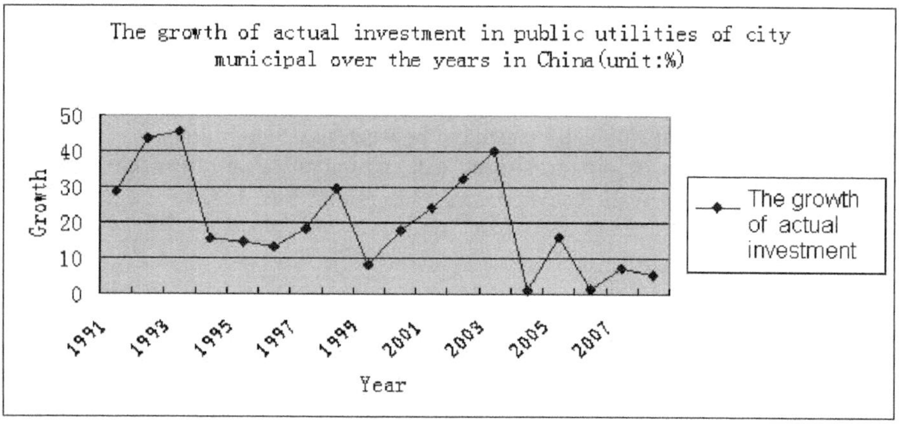

Fig. 2. The growth of actual investment in public utilities of city municipal over the years in China

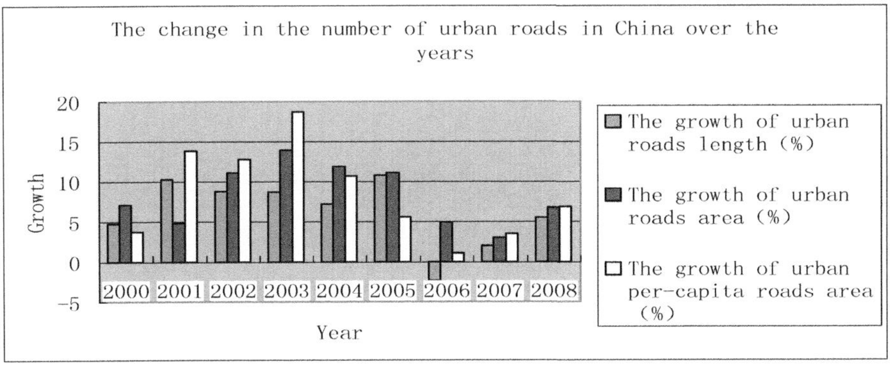

Fig. 3. The change in the number of urban roads in China over the years

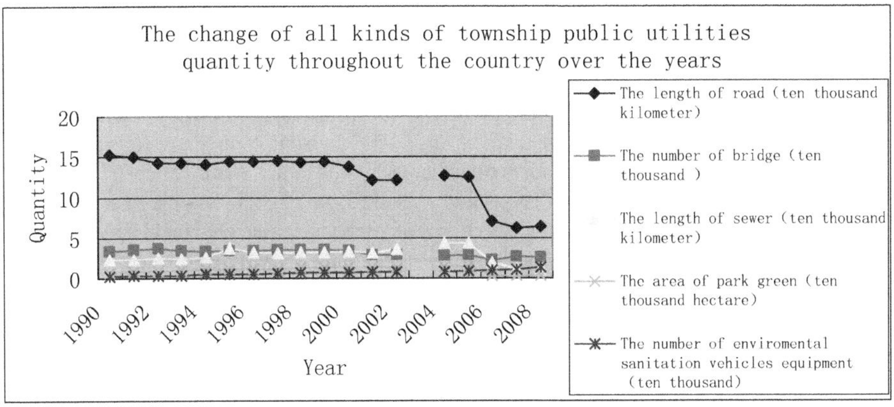

Fig. 4. The change of all kinds of township public infrastructures quantity through the country over the years

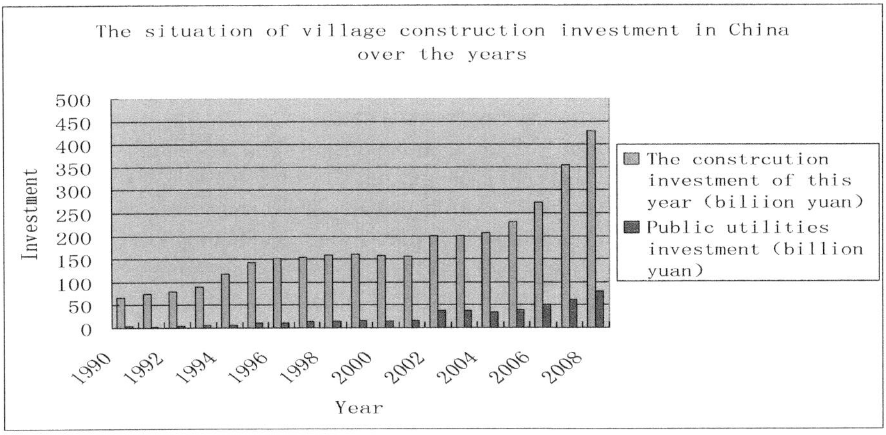

Fig. 5. The situation of village construction investment in China over the years

Evolution Mechanism of Fresh Agri-Product Circulation Pattern: An Analysis from the Angle of Labor Division

Lin Li and Xijian Quan

College of Management, Ocean University of China, 238 Songling Road, 266100 Qingdao, China
capricorn_lilin@yahoo.com.cn, qxj@ouc.edu.cn

Abstract. This paper aims to study the evolution mechanism of fresh agricultural products (FAP) circulation patterns and predict the evolution trend. We investigated the development process of FAP circulation patterns in chronological order and brought up six basic modes. Each basic mode has various specific patterns. Then we explained the evolution mechanisms from the angle of labor division and put forward two concepts: involution of labor division and externalization of labor division. The circulation process includes both involution and externalization of labor division which are opposite processes. Involution of labor division increases administrative costs but decreases transaction costs. This study showed FAP circulation pattern is the result of waxing and waning affections of externalization and involution of labor division. The pattern which can minimize total cost will be prevalent.

Keywords: Agricultural products circulation, Labor division, Involution, Externalization.

1 Introduction

In addition to food crops, fresh agricultural products (FAP) are the main nutrition sources for people, which include fresh vegetables, fruits, aquatic products, poultries, livestock, meat, eggs and milk. These fresh foods take a very important position in daily consumption, so it's of great significance to improve their circulation processes. For this purpose, we analyzed their circulation patterns.

Many researches studied on FAP circulation patterns. Yunfu Ma and Jun Yang [1], Jun Yang and Luqing Li [2] and Bin Dan and Jun Chen [3] analyzed FAP circulation patterns from the perspective of the dominant firm. Their researches can be used in supermarket-oriented FAP circulation pattern for reference. Weihua Liu et al. [4], Tao Tan and Yihua Zhu [5], Junmiao Deng and Pengjun Dai [6] and Yingli Qiao et al. [7] analyzed FAP circulation patterns from the point of view of supply chain. Most researches classified existing modes although the classification standards were confusing and incomplete. Jusheng Yu and Peihong Zhang [8] and Fei Meng and Xianzhi Fu [9] studied FAP circulation patterns of main developed countries. Feixiang Liu et al. [10] and Bin Cui [11] studied FAP logistics patterns. Aiqun Wang et al. [12] and Yajing Sun [13] researched on agriculture industrialization which can give reference to circulation pattern studies.

Q. Zhou (Ed.): ISAEBD 2011, Part II, CCIS 209, pp. 148–152, 2011.

The organization of the remainder of this paper is as follows. Section 2 lays out the circulation patterns chronologically and basic modes are classified and described. Section 3 discusses the evolution mechanism of basic modes. Section 4 concludes.

2 Classification of FAP Circulation Patterns

By investigating the development and changes of the production part, retail area and the middle part of FAP circulation process in chronological order, six basic modes are as follows:

- "Farmer" + "farmer's market" mode (mode 1). Early in the FAP circulation system reform, government deregulated country fairs allowing farmers to sell their surplus produce. This is the primary form of FAP circulation. In this mode, the production scale is small, and the purpose of production is mainly self-sufficiency but not trading. A trade happened only when there is surplus. A country market's coverage is small because of small-scale production and poor transportation. In this mode, farmers are producers, sellers and transporters. There is not specialized division of labor at all.
- "Farmer" + "wholesale market" + "farmer's market" mode (mode 2). As demand for FAP increased and technology developed, production scale expanded gradually, so production for trading purpose appeared. The local farmer's market could not absorb a large number of agricultural surplus, so bigger markets (wholesale markets) were needed. Wholesale market, long-distance transporters and vendors in farmer's market appeared subsequently. At that point, specialization division in the FAP circulation chain established basically. Specific realization modes are listed as below: "farmer" + "rural broker" + "wholesale market" + "farmer's market", "farmer" + "transporter" + "wholesale market" + "farmer's market", "farmer" + "rural broker" + "transporter" + "wholesale market" + "farmer's market" and "farmer" + "wholesaler" + "wholesale market" + "farmer's market". Wholesale markets include origin wholesale markets and terminal wholesale markets which are not distinguished in this paper. In the above modes, there are substitution and complementation relations among rural broker, transporter and wholesaler, because some rural brokers probably don't have long-distance transport capacity, some transporters probably don't know local planting, and some wholesalers might be competitive in local agricultural information and transportation capacity.
- "Farmer" + "intermediary organization" + "wholesale market" + "farmer's market" mode (mode 3). Due to market information asymmetry in the second pattern, interests of scattered and small-scale farmers were often squeezed by merchants. In order to enhance anti-risk ability and profitability, small farmers tended to come together to respond to volatile market, so all kinds of intermediary organizations such as farmer professional cooperative, research institution and agrotechnical station gradually developed. In this mode, intermediary organizations provide services such as seed supplying, production guidance, acquisition, sales and so on. Professional division appears in production and sales area and then splits away. Intermediary organization is the result of recombination and incorporation of professional division.

- "Farmer" + "intermediary organization/supermarket supplier/wholesale market" + "supermarket" mode (mode 4). As people's living standards improved, they paid attention to good shopping environment and food safety. In order to satisfy customer demand, supermarket became increasingly popular and tended to replace farmer's market. Supermarket procured FAP through wholesale market, specialized supplier or intermediary organization. The specific modes are as follows: "supermarket" + "scientific research institute" + "farmer" mode, "supermarket" + "village committee" + "farmer" mode, "supermarket" + "pre-existing cooperative" + "farmer" mode and "supermarket" + "third-party logistics center" + "farmer" mode. In this mode, no matter what kind of procurement channel is used, there are huge differences compared with previous modes: Supermarket as the retail part is stronger than vender of farmer's market, more compatible with expanding large-scale production and has the ability and potential demand of contract farming.
- "Farmer" + "supermarket" mode (mode 5). In order to further reduce transaction costs between organizations, it's necessary to reduce middle links and make a single organization cover more circulation functions, which is called involution of labor division in this paper. As long as the administrative costs arising from the reduction of trade links between organizations are less than decreasing transaction costs, involution of labor division will happen. As circulation chain is shortened gradually, in the end, farmers deal with retailers directly. The specific modes are as follows: "supermarket" + "big farmer" + "small farmer" mode, "supermarket" + "co-founded cooperative" + "farmer" mode, "supermarket" + "production base" + "farmer" mode and "supermarket" + "owned agricultural company" + "farmer" mode.
- Vertical integration mode (mode 6). Vertical integration means mergence of upstream and downstream of agriculture industry into one enterprise. This mode is the ultimate form of involution of labor division.

3 Evolution Mechanism of FAP Circulation Patterns

The evolution mechanism of FAP circulation patterns was analyzed from the angle of labor division according to the development process of the six basic modes.

During the process from mode 1 to mode 2, specialized wholesalers, brokers, vendors and other market participants emerge. The process of separating from existing organization and forming new market participants is called externalization of labor division in this paper. Both mode 2 and mode 3 are the results of externalization of labor division.

Difference of mode 4 from mode 3 is the emergence of supermarket which responds to changes in consumer demand. The large-scale retail organization does not match scattered small producers. It requires merger and recombination of original circulation organizations to form stronger market organizations. We call this process involution of labor division.

Mode 4, mode 5 and mode 6 are results of involution of labor division which shortens circulation chain, helps to reduce transaction costs, but increases administrative costs as shown in the following diagram:

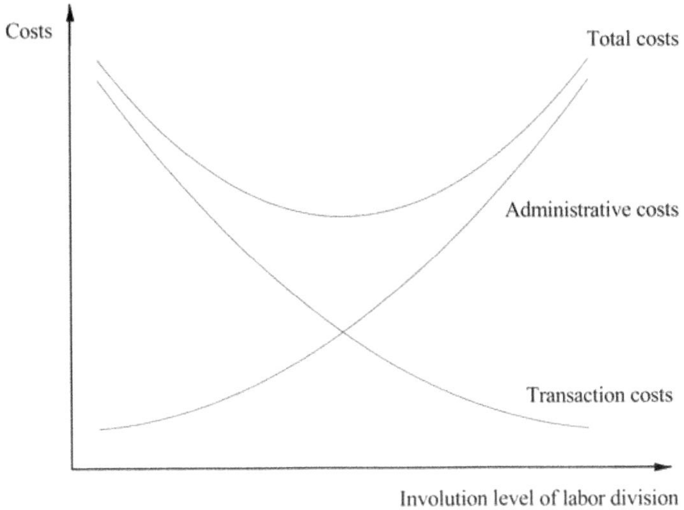

Fig. 1. Relationship between costs and involution of labor division

Involution of labor division is the opposite process of externalization of labor division, so we can derive the relationship between cost and labor division status by analyzing the relation of cost and involution level of labor division. According to figure 1, whether the retailers deal with producers directly depends on variation trend of total cost. Mode 6 is the extreme status of involution of labor division which is not widespread right now. In this mode, administration costs are very high and only strong and competitive enterprise can apply it successfully.

4 Conclusions

According to the level of labor division, there are six basic patterns for FAP circulation and many variant of each basic mode. From the time perspective, circulation chain first becomes long from short and then cut short as the division of labor changes. The evolution of circulation patterns mainly depends on the combination of involution and externalization of labor division which can influence circulation costs directly. Involution of labor division increases administrative cost but decreases transaction cost. It's just the reverse for externalization of labor division. In the past, we only considered the advantages of detailed division of labor and neglected the disadvantages. In this paper we considered advantages and disadvantages of detailed division of labor synthetically. In addition, we considered changes in retail sectors which arise from new consumer demand and promote the evolution of upper reaches of circulation process.

References

1. Ma, Y.F., Yang, J.: Necessity, Principles and Modes for Transformation of Traditional Farmer's Market. Rural Economy 2, 109–111 (2005)
2. Yang, J., Li, L.Q.: China's Circulation Mode Reform of Agricultural Terminals. Journal of Chongqing Technology and Business University (Western Forum) 15(4), 11–14 (2005)
3. Dan, B., Chen, J.: Third-party Sophisticated Processing Mode of Fresh Agricultural Product of Supermarket. Business Economics and Management 5, 18–22 (2008)
4. Liu, W.H., Xiao, J.H., Jiao, Z.L.: Study on Typical Operation Model and Cost Control in Agricultural Product Closed Supply Chain. Soft Science 23(11), 58–63 (2009)
5. Tan, T., Zhu, Y.H.: Research on Organizational Model of Agricultural Supply Chains. Modern Economic Research 5, 24–27 (2004)
6. Deng, J.M., Dai, P.J.: Fresh Agricultural Prodcut Circulation under Supply Chain Management. Commercial Research 23, 185–187 (2006)
7. Qiao, Y.L., Li, Y.X., Ji, X.G.: Stage Feature Analysis of Regional Fresh Agricultural Industry Chain Evolution. Journal of Hebei North University (Natural Science Edition) 25(5), 56–60 (2009)
8. Yu, J.S., Zhang, P.H.: Agricultural Market Models of Three World-Class Cities. World Agriculture 10, 29–31 (2004)
9. Meng, F., Fu, X.Z.: Comparison of Agricultural Product Distribution Channels between the USA and Japan and Its Significance for China. China's Rural Economy (Special Issue), 141–146 (2007)
10. Liu, F., Li, Z., Guo, J., Chen, Y.: Analysis on Fresh Produce Self-Run Logistics Pattern. Taiwan Agricultural Research 4, 59–61 (2006)
11. Cui, B.: Research on Optimization of Fresh Food Logistics Model. Modern Business 6, 14–15 (2008)
12. Wong, A.Q., Jian, Q., Teng, R.G.: Establishment and Development Strategies of Agricultural Industrialization–Based on Institutional Economics Perspective. Agricultural Economics 3, 12–15 (2007)
13. Sun, Y.J.: Research on Development Model of Agricultural Industrialization. Theory Journal 12, 38–40 (2006)

Resource Characteristic, Transaction Characteristic and Agriculture Organization System: The Case of Laoshan District of Qingdao

Lin Li and Xijian Quan

Department of Management, Ocean University of China, 238 Songling Road, 266100 Qingdao, China
capricorn_lilin@yahoo.com.cn, qxj@ouc.edu.cn

Abstract. The purpose of this study is to explore the determinants of agriculture organization system and the relationships among resource characteristic, transaction characteristic, agriculture organization system and production and marketing mode (PMM). This paper derived eight types of transaction characteristics and four broad categories of PMM. Different transaction types correspond to different PMM. However, resource characteristic is also important for production and marketing modes. Given that PMM are determined, organization system rests with institutional efficiency. Accordingly, this paper established an agriculture organization system decision model and applied it to agricultural industry of Laoshan district in Qingdao. The results show that our theoretical model can explain the case well and provide meaningful guidance to construct efficient organization system.

Keywords: Resource characteristic, Transaction characteristic, Organization system, Institutional efficiency, Production and marketing mode.

1 Introduction

Many researches studied on agricultural production and marketing modes and agriculture organization system, but few of them mentioned resource characteristics. Xiaoli Wu [1] studied agriculture organization system, resource characteristics of Hainan farm. Shujin He et al. [2] studied development and utilization mode of mudflats based on resource characteristic. Agriculture organization system depends on not only institutional efficiency, but also resource characteristics. This paper reveals the relationship of resource characteristic, transaction characteristic, system efficiency and agriculture organization system by establishing and applying a theoretical model.

2 Theoretical Model

We established an agriculture organization system decision model by analyzing the following four sides.

Q. Zhou (Ed.): ISAEBD 2011, Part II, CCIS 209, pp. 153–157, 2011.

2.1 Resource Characteristic

Resource characteristic includes production characteristic and consumption characteristic. Production characteristic refers to natural conditions, asset specificity of production factors, intensity and controllability of production and uncertainty. Consumption characteristic refers to demand structure, amount of consumption, guarantee period and identifiability.

2.2 Production and Marketing Mode

Production and marketing mode means the organization method of production and marketing activities, which determines products how to reach consumers. We propose integration model and non-integrated model. According to Qunlin Fan et al. [3], there are three integrated models: full integration, contract integration, integration led by cooperatives. Non-integrated model mainly refers to smallholder production, with farmers selling products by themselves in country fairs or just waiting mongers in the fields.

2.3 Transaction Characteristic

According to O.E. Williamson [4], transaction characteristic was understood from three dimensions: asset specificity, transaction uncertainty and transaction frequency. Generally, the higher the asset specificity is, the more difficultly the asset participates in other transactions, which is called "asset locked". It is thus more inclined to adopt the form of enterprise to conduct a transaction. Greater transaction uncertainty means higher market transaction costs, so it's also more inclined to take corporate form. Transactions with high frequency tend to occur within the enterprise. On the contrary, common assets usually mean transactions through market. Transactions with low frequency are also often taken through market to avoid the cost brought by establishing risk-avoidance mechanisms. Therefore, we can speculate: a specific type of transaction should be taken by adopting corresponding type of transaction mode.

We derived eight types of transaction characteristics according to permutation and combination of three transaction dimensions shown as follows:

Table 1. Types of transaction characteristics

Transaction characteristic	Asset specificity	Uncertainty	Transaction frequency
Type 1	High	High	High
Type 2	High	High	Low
Type 3	High	Low	High
Type 4	High	Low	Low
Type 5	Low	High	High
Type 6	Low	High	Low
Type 7	Low	Low	High
Type 8	Low	Low	Low

2.4 Institutional Efficiency

According to Biliang Luo et al. [5], institutional efficiency of organization is affected by the following factors:

- Property rights structure implied in organization system refers to the distribution of bundle of rights in space and time, and determines whether there are sufficient incentives for transaction participants. It has impacts on both production costs and transaction costs.
- Measurement capability of organization system depends largely on organizational incentive and restraint mechanisms, in particular the monitoring mechanism and its implementation costs. If the measurement ability is low, the productivity will be low. Productivity can be increased through perfecting measurement capability of an organization.
- Transaction environment of organization includes at least institutional environment, resources environment and market environment.

2.5 Mathematical Expression of Model

According to above analysis, the theoretical model can be expressed by formulas as follows:

$$PMM = f[RC(PC, CC), TC(AS, TU, TF)] . \tag{1}$$

$$OS = g[IE(PRS, MA, TE) \mid PMM] . \tag{2}$$

Production and marketing mode (PMM) is a function of resource characteristic (RC) and transaction characteristic (TC). Resource characteristic depends on production characteristic (PC) and consumption characteristic (CC). According to O.E. Williamson, transaction characteristic (TC) is determined by asset specificity (AS), transaction uncertainty (TU), and transaction frequency (TF). Organization system (OS) is a function of organizational institutional efficiency (IE) and PMM. Institutional efficiency is decided by property rights structure (PRS), measurement capability (MA) and transaction environment (TE) of an organization.

3 Model Application – The Case of Laoshan District in Qingdao

Laoshan district of Qingdao city has developed economy and convenient transportation, which are suitable for developing urban agriculture. The diversity of landforms, terrain and many small ecological environments lay a good foundation for developing eco-agriculture [6], landscape agriculture and characteristic planting. Good water, air and appropriate climate are very suitable for high quality fruits, tea, vegetables and other efficient cash crops. In this paper we took the local well-known cherry industry as an example, and analyzed this industry using the model mentioned in section 2.

3.1 Resource Characteristic and Transaction Characteristic

We analyzed resource characteristic from two dimensions: production characteristic and consumption characteristic.

Production characteristics are as follows. First, cherry production relies on the land and producers largely, so asset specificity of production factors is high. Secondly, from the view of concentration and controllability of production, the seedling breeding, construction of plantation, fertilizer and water management, pruning, fruit management, harvesting and post-harvest handling, pest management and other operations are all scattered field work, which are inconvenient to be quantified, therefore, its concentration and controllability degree are very low. Thirdly, cherry production is affected by natural conditions largely. Rain weather, frost, and other severe weather all have great impacts on the output. According to the above analysis we can infer, cherry production relies on the land and labor, so it requires a relevant stable land system; Supervision cost of cherry production is very high; high uncertainty requires that the production organization system must match the production characteristic to reduce risks.

Consumption characteristics are as follows. It is difficult for cherry to store and transport, so its market radius is small. However, limited by the spending power and low volume production, the market is in short supply situation.

Due to small production per household, it's no need to enter wholesale market, and there are few mongers coming to buy. Therefore, farmers can sell their products at roadside or in farmer's market which belongs to non-integrated production and marketing mode. According to the foregoing, the integration modes are also possible. Therefore, the optional production and marketing modes are: roadside sales mode, fully integration mode, contract integration mode, and integration led by agricultural cooperative mode.

Transaction characteristics are as follows. First, the asset specificity of transaction is low. Secondly, the uncertainty of transaction is very high. Finally, the transaction frequency is low because many of them are one-shot deal. According to the classification of transaction characteristic types, cherry transaction belongs to type 6. The type 6 transaction is suitable for tripartite agreement production and marketing mode. Incorporate mode led by agricultural cooperative and non-integrated mode involving wholesale market are both tripartite agreement modes, but resource characteristics have excluded the latter mode. Then we could determine the appropriate production and marketing mode is integration mode led by agricultural cooperative which is just consistent with the reality, so formula 1 has been verified.

3.2 Institutional Efficiency and Organization System

We have identified that the suitable production and marketing model for this case is integration mode led by cooperatives. Further study on institutional efficiency of cooperative organizations is helpful for establishing efficient organization system.

We have deduced that if the property rights structure implicit in organization system is clear, the measurement capability of an organization is strong, and the compatibility between an organization and transaction environment is good, the efficiency of organization system will be high. Through field research, we find organization systems of existing cooperatives are as follows. Cooperatives are usually co-funded by leading companies who provide capital and farmers who provide land or labor. Persons in charge of cooperatives usually serve as village cadres or the village committee members. Leading companies are generally village-run enterprises which know well local situations, so they are able to work conveniently. Cooperatives have general meeting of commune members, council and board of supervisors, and set up an account for each member.

There are three representative allocation modes of equity in cooperatives. The first mode is that members only provide land for rent. The second mode is that members who own the income grow their own garden according to the requirements of cooperatives that are responsible for sales, providing water and infrastructure, and cooperatives deduct a certain percentage of management fees from income. The third model is that cooperative members provide land for rent and labor for salary monthly.

Thus, cooperatives' property rights are clear. Model 1 and model 2 don't have measurement problem. Measurement difficulties caused by the third model are not obvious, because cooperatives are managed by village cadres and organization systems are compatible highly with transaction environment. This is consistent with the reality as the investigation indicates the three models have roughly the same proportion.

4 Conclusions

Through the above analysis, we can draw the following conclusions:

Agriculture organization system not only depends on the institutional efficiency of organization, but also closely relates with production and marketing patterns. Production and marketing patterns are decided by resource characteristics and transaction characteristics. If resource characteristics are not considered, the production and marketing patterns must be infeasible. It's difficult to change resource characteristics, so it's crucial to improve transaction characteristics in order to establish efficient agricultural organization systems.

References

1. Wu, X.L.: Resource Characteristics, Structure of Property Rights and the Efficiency of Agriculture Organization System. Special Zone Economy, 113–114 (2007)
2. He, S.J., Li, X.B., Liu, S.H.: Beach Resource Characteristics and Development Model in Bohai Rim. Progress in Geography 21(1), 25–34 (2002)
3. Fan, Q.L., Shao, Y.F., Wu, H.P.: Research on Modern Agricultural Production Mode and Multiple Supporting Systems. Guangxi University of Finance and Economics 24(1), 92–96 (2011)
4. Williamson, O.E.: Capitalist Economic System. Commercial Press, Beijing (2002)
5. Luo, B.L., Wang, Y.R., Wang, J.: Efficiency Decisions of Agricultural Products Circulation Organizational System: an Analytical Framework. Issues in Agricultural Economy 8, 26–31 (2000)
6. 11th Five-year Development Plan for Urban Agriculture of Laoshan District in Qingdao City, http://www.laoshan.gov.cn

Network Audit Mode Based on Electronic Commerce and Carried Out

Bin Wang, Chengfeng Huang, and Kanxiong Nie

School of Finance and Economics, Chongqing Jiaotong University, Chongqing 400074, China
wangb404000@sohu.com, huangcf@cquc.edu.cn, NKX_888@163.com

Abstract. The beginning of this article made a book about a network audit, discussion on the enterprise operation of the network audit in e-commerce environment, analysis of network audit is different from traditional audit. Network audit is divided into three working modes, deals with the characteristics of network audit mode, explains how to implement network audit. Proposed network audit process of the five steps, should pay attention to the problem, to help enterprises improve the quality of audit work and audit integrity.

Keywords: Electronic Commerce, Network, Audit Mode, Carry out.

1 Introduction

Electronic commerce is all enterprises using the Internet to engage in business activities, Forms of business transaction and service activity is no longer rely on paper documents and transfer documents, but the use of computer and Internet technology and electronic trading and settlement process, e-commerce business management not only changed the model, also changed the traditional accounting business mode, change the accounting information processing and output. Accounting from the traditional accounting, computerized accounting developments to the network accounting, auditing, also from the traditional audit, computerized audit development to a network audit. More and more enterprises to develop e-commerce activities, economic activities, review of these networks, resulting in network audit requirements.

Network Audit is the comprehensive use of networks and related technology by means of the Internet economy and network accounting information system review of new audit .It is to audit the standards, technologies and requirements of the Internet economy itself, to audit the process of economic operation of the network economy of the main financial accounting, reflection, supervision and control of the process, review and evaluate the results and make judgments and analysis. It includes two aspects: First, the network unit being audited accounting information system development process and its own audit, the information systems audit; Second, the network being audited accounting information systems audit process and results of operation, but also is based on the audited accounting information units the authenticity and legality of the audit. Based on network audit under electronic commerce and traditional audit what's the difference? How to conduct network audit it?

Q. Zhou (Ed.): ISAEBD 2011, Part II, CCIS 209, pp. 158–163, 2011.

2 Network Audit Is Different from Traditional Audit

Emerged with e-commerce network finance, based on the mode of financial management of the Internet, accounting work, including internal financial synergy with the business, purchase online sales from the Web, from online payment online payment from circulation;Enterprise collaboration with suppliers, online inquiries, online reminder account, online banking, online insurance, online tax returns, all of which require network audit, Audit object hidden, digital, network, network audit to promote the development of traditional audit, network to shorten the parties to the transaction time and space, remote reimbursement, remote checkout and remote reporting, also remote query and network audit, audit methods and techniques audit information storage medium, audit scope change. Statement of the basis of the traditional audit model, system-based audit model and risk-based audit model based on the survival of lost, network audit and audit of the difference between traditional performance in four areas:

(1) The audit of different objects and clues. Object not only has the Internet economy business network auditing, network system itself also, audit trail from paper into digital information, network audit is still on the nature of the financial management activities relating to the revenue and expenditure and its confirmation.Traditional audit to review the paper books based on credentials, plus search, audit methods such as retrogradation, playing the role of error-checking correct disadvantages. Based on e-commerce audit object and clue of different auditors face is enterprise's system of computerized accounting information system and network accounts, Main internal control systems have changed the network economy occurred based on the information technology enterprise resource planning ERP, customer relationship management CRM, and supply chain management SCM and other management software, audit objects is more complex. Business information to electromagnetic signal transmission and preservation of the Internet, the loss of traditional audit trails.

(2) Different tools and methods. Network Audit introduced computer-based network equipment and network audit software as a tool. Tools make network audit both the different computer-assisted audit, financial audit of the network, there are different methods, including real-time monitoring, electronic circularization, remote review, real-time testing of audit techniques. Real-time monitoring of any selected part of the audit staff information in the data processing system Beishendanwei run compared with manual calculation to determine the accuracy of data processing; e-circularization, the remote review of the audit staff by e-mail remote circularization, confirm the authenticity; real test is to check the data communication and recording situation.

(3) Different requirements for auditors. Network audit is based on knowledge of computer skills, network and comprehensive application of auditing theory, requires auditors in addition to professional quality, must also have some knowledge of computers, networks, and other aspects of electronic commerce, to master theories and methods of network audit, have the capacity for lifelong learning and innovation, meet the needs of development of network audit.

(4) Audit work and reporting requirements are different. Network systems certification, periodic review and audit of online business posed by the three audit work by the different audit agencies. Network system certification and annual audit by the Government or by the general delegate of the social audit; or social audit in the government auditing license, under the supervision of the commission receiving enterprise. Online business audit commissioned by the receiving authority or government audit or public audit to complete. Compatible with the audit work, first, by the operational audit report and its annexes constitute the necessary results of the audit are borne by the three audit units; Second, the network should Confirmation periodic review of network systems and operational audits given the key recommendations; Third, the network system to regularly review network services should be given the focus of the audit recommendations. Three closely cooperate with the audit results, complete forensic audit and supervision of economic activities, on the network.

3 Network Audit Mode and Characteristics

The subject of electronic commerce into traditional enterprise and network enterprises, traditional enterprise has its own industry support, network audit was the principal into traditional businesses and virtual enterprises, traditional enterprises e-commerce in two ways: Enterprises building their own e-commerce Web site and join the third-party trading platform. Their financial system may be manual or computerized financial system, the books may also be on the Internet, so it is necessary to use the network audit software, network audit the financial accounts of units and the operations audit, but also on-line e-commerce unit activities and systems of audit, Thus the network audit can be divided into three modes: the audit of the network economy, network system audit, audit of use of the network. Network so that audit information gathering, processing, output of transmission changes, has the following characteristics:

(1) Changes in network audit the collection of audit information, the audit trail from the visible into the invisible. Collection of audit information is to collect audit evidence, audit evidence obtained by auditing standards methods include inspection, observation, inquiries, confirmation and calculation. Save the credentials in the form of electronic information based on e-commerce, and online delivery, preparation of registration of accounting vouchers, account books, should have the computer automatically. Cash, inventory and other fixed assets, materials and the physical network in real time by a dynamic management, Documents, books, reports and other information through the network of electromagnetic media inquiries and to refer to, Various calculations and analysis carried out by computer to increase the collection of audit information in real time, reliability, reduce collection costs.

(2) Network audit change audit information processing methods, audit of Web test tools. Certificates, account books paper media disappear, information system check, inspection and internal audit control function so that there is no longer necessary, but the inventory, logistics still need people to monitor disk, observed.

(3) Network audit to change audit information output, transmission, storage and retrieval, etc., Audit reports, audit findings more timely and accurate. The output of the use of audit information network, so that the audit office automation work itself is its own network audit, network audit reflects another layer of meaning.

4 How to Develop the Network Audit

Based on the audit of e-commerce division three: online transaction audit, audit of electronic payments, virtual enterprise audit. Virtual Enterprise is a special e-commerce is the main, it is composed of different areas rely on a network of business entities, through the network to disclose their operating results, financial situation, financial flows of electronic money.

How to develop the network audit? First, establish and perfect the audited units and the related information in a network to review, monitor and audit organizations providing forensic services; Second, by the auditor to do e-commerce audit services, to provide users with a professional e-commerce security; Third, build a complete computer systems and network systems. Audit institutions to establish Center for network auditing platform, equipped with powerful hardware devices such as servers, switches and network system auditing software. The process of building the platform include software development, network infrastructure and back-end database development center platform, so that the required audit of the financial data from the original direct access to the computer network system, with units at the same time the formation of the original data backup. Division of auditing organizations including: the network environment for the financial system's hardware review, review of system operation, operational review and coordination to complete audit assignments.

Based on e-commerce network audit process can be divided into five steps: the audit plan, the network's internal control reviews, Compliance testing and substantive testing, Audit evidence collection, evidence evaluation and issue a comprehensive report, with particular emphasis on the internal control review and audit of the database. Including: project management and implementation of audit, audit planning on the Internet, distribution audit tasks, review working papers, understand project progress, viewing audit records, prepare audit reports, collecting audit evidence, preparation of working papers, review system features□ sample reviews of the accounting information, to electronic letter permits banks, customers, suppliers, and so on.

Network auditing the introduction of new auditing techniques. (1) the application of network auditing software, to network systems related to the field trace. First, the evaluation of network systems, and compared using the audit software is stored in the database with a different address in the comparison of the data to form the corresponding log file, and there are differences in the detailed review of file data; Secondly, the use of the audit interface software for the original data, the use of audit software for sample extraction and so on. (2) the use of database technology to analyze, audit using audit expert system reasoning and judgments, through data mining, sample extraction, abnormal item survey, data analysis and processing methods for testing, check.

Collection of information on the terms of the internal audit units, from within the financial, labor, storage, marketing, production and other departments to collect data audit information, the establishment of audit data warehouse, External audit institutions can access through the firewall audit information, audit the economic activities of real-time monitoring, to discover problems and solve them, to play the role of audit and supervision, If you embedded in system development audit program, the computer can automatically to economic business monitoring in real time to complete some audits; In terms of external audit information collected through the Internet to collect the relevant laws, policies and other information, Through Enterprise Extranet collection of enterprise vendors, customers, payment settlement and receivable, accounts payable, advance payments and other audit information.

5 Carry Out Network Audit Should Pay Attention to the Problem

Network audit should note the following aspects of the issue. Audit the network to distinguish between two types of financial mistakes: First, their errors of economic activities, such as vouchers error, omission man, etc. Second, there is a network of financial system bugs or security holes, the results of the operation generated errors. To consider when auditing the contents of the test cases test the electronic signing, delivery, handling of testing, billing and payment transaction testing, scenario testing transactions, monitoring the situation test. Insecurity when the audit review of the operator whether the program and data files by manipulating accounting data led to false, unreliable, inaccurate, or to achieve some illegal purpose; Review network counterfeiting; review of illegal modification, destruction, access to private interests output of insecurity. Audit of electronic payment can be by viewing the electronic wallet management, electronic transactions, online banking for reconciliation between the balance sheet, or to online banking for circularization, to review customer transactions on the bank account number of the currency accounts, lists and data.

In addition, computer viruses and hacker attacks can be from any corner of the threat of accounting information system through the network data security, Auditing of risk increases, you can firewall, data authentication, data encryption and other security technology in network audits, establishment of security mechanisms, Including access management, security monitoring and security recovery, etc., the auditor must use risk-based audit in the audit related to the implementation of the concept of risk in order to ensure audit quality.

6 Summary

In short, the network audit is engaged in economic supervision, evaluation, verification activities, Not only the audit of the financial condition and business enterprise numbers themselves, but also the formation of the audit figures. Auditors from the above analysis of several aspects, gradual development of network audit to meet the needs of e-commerce network economy, otherwise, the audit agency will lose the audit qualifications.

References

1. Zhou, D.: Gold audit engineering application development to achieve the three development. Chinese Audit (January 2003)
2. Wu, L.: Internet and network audit.Shanghai Accounting (June 2002)
3. Liou, X.: Audit of e-commerce environment. Business Times(May 2005)
4. Jian, J.: Analysis Network Audit. Monthly Financial (May 2003)
5. Bin, W.: Research on the application and development of computer audit software. Financial Communications (Academic Edition) (September 2004)

Study on Hotel Outsourcer Evaluation Based on ANP Model

Jing Sun and Liying Liu

Harbin University of Commerce
Harbin China
sunjing1230@sohu.com, liuliying0539@163.com

Abstract. Rational evaluation of outsourcer can help select outsourcer and enhance hotel's core competitiveness, reduce costs, and improve service quality. In this study, ANP (analytical network process) model has been adopted in order to evaluate the right hotel outsourcer. By constructing hotel's outsourcer evaluation model, many factors, such as quality, price and time, which will impact the evaluation of hotel outsourcer, are judged and compared, and then Super Decisions software is used to deal with the Matrix in order to find the priority of alternative outsourcers and to make the best decision for hotel.

Keywords: ANP; Hotel, Outsourcer evaluation, Super decisions software.

1 Introduction

Outsourcing can provide a lot of benefits to an enterprise, such as improving the core competitiveness, streamline institutions, cost reduction, obtain the professional service and fast response market demand change etc[1]. Hotel industry is becoming the focus of the implementation of outsourcing industry. Hotels, in order to reduce costs and improve core competitiveness, often outsource non-core businesses. After determining the outsourcing content, the evaluation of outsourcers has become an important part of the outsourcing process. Selection a right hotel outsourcer can improve hotel flexibility, improve service quality and enhance hotel's competitiveness [2].

Nowadays, AHP (analytic hierarchy process) is always used in literature to evaluate hotel outsourcer. During this method, all aspects of outsourcer are judged by experts, and then are handled in clusters, so the priority will be found after elements are compared and taken into account [3]. However, as AHP assumed that all the elements are independent and non-interact, it will no longer accurate when used in a more complex system. Hotel outsource selection is a complex multi-criteria evaluation problem, which involves quality, time, price technical ability etc., and the factors are often connected with each other and mutual influence. ANP (The Analytic Network Process), based on AHP, solves the problem that elements are interconnected and interactivities, and is more suitable for the evaluation of hotel outsourcer. Since the ANP has these advantages, in this paper, we develop an effective method based on the ANP to help hotel evaluate outsourcer.

Q. Zhou (Ed.): ISAEBD 2011, Part II, CCIS 209, pp. 164–171, 2011.

2 ANP Theory and Its Steps

ANP is introduced by the Professor Thomas L. Saaty in Pittsburgh University in USA. It generalizes a widely used multi-criteria decision-making tool, the AHP, by replacing hierarchies with networks [4]. It is a practical and useful technique for ranking and selecting a number of externally determined alternatives in those problems where there are interactions and dependencies among the elements of a system. So, it was applied widely in decision areas such as society, enterprise and nation.

Followings are the steps of ANP model to make decisions:

Step 1. Establishing the clusters and identifying the relationships
As shown in fig.1, ANP model consists of two layers. Control layer is the first layer, including evaluation goal and decision-making criteria. The network layer, according to control layer, is an interrelated feedback network structure. In Fig.1, C_i means cluster, e_{ij} means element. The relationship between clusters includes internal and external dependencies and feedback relations.

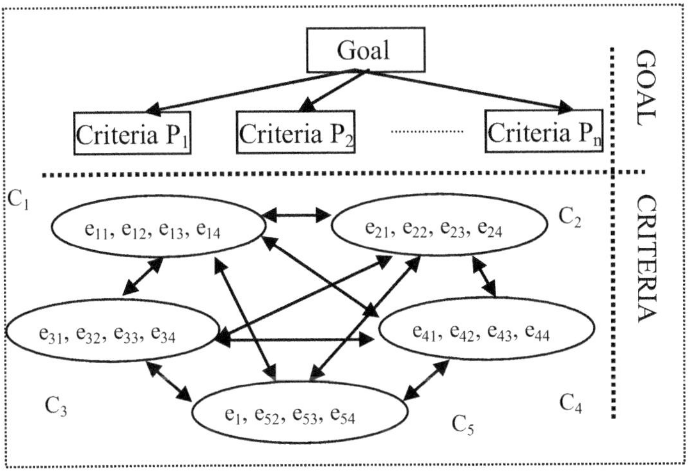

Fig. 1. Typical ANP model [5]

Step 2. Building the unweighted super-matrix
Asher ANP model control layer are $P_1, P_2, \ldots P_m$, network layer are $C_1, C_2, \ldots C_N$, and C_j has elements $e_{i1}, e_{i2}, \ldots e_{in}$. Under each control rule, by applications pair-wise comparison method, constructing unweighted super matrix W_{ij}.

First, make the criteria $P_S\left(s=1,2,\ldots m\right)$ selected when building the network as the main criterion, and make an element $e_{jl}\left(l=1,2,\ldots,n_j\right)$ in the cluster C_j as a sub-criterion, construct a comparison matrix in accordance with the elements e_{jl} on each element in the cluster C_i to determine the degree of influence. And then obtain the normalized eigenvector $(W_{i1}^{jl}, W_{i2}^{jl}, \ldots W_{in}^{jl})^T$.

Second, do pair-wise comparison of elements in cluster C_i and in cluster C_j one by one to construct comparison matrix. And put all the normalized eigenvectors of every comparison matrix in matrix W_{ij}, and then the matrix W_{ij} denotes the sub-matrixes which mean that cluster C_j influences cluster C_i .

$$W_{ij} = \begin{Bmatrix} W_{i1}^{j1} & W_{i1}^{j2} & \cdots & W_{i1}^{jn_j} \\ W_{i2}^{j1} & W_{i2}^{j2} & \cdots & W_{i2}^{jn_j} \\ & & & \\ W_{in}^{j1} & W_{in}^{j2} & \cdots & W_{in}^{jn_j} \end{Bmatrix}$$

Similarly, take other criterion as the main criterion, do pair-wise comparison of elements in every cluster of internal and external relations in turn, unweighted super-matrix W_s can be obtained. When the elements in cluster C_j does not affect the element in cluster C_i, $W_{ij}=0$.

$$W_s = \begin{pmatrix} W_{11} & W_{12} & \cdots & W_{1n} \\ W_{21} & W_{22} & \cdots & W_{2n} \\ \vdots & \vdots & \cdots & \vdots \\ W_{n1} & W_{n2} & \cdots & W_{nn} \end{pmatrix}$$

Step 3. Construction of the weighted super-matrix

Make P_s as the main criteria and cluster C_j as the sub-criteria, do pair-wise comparison, so comparison matrix a_j is constructed. After normalized matrix a_j, normalization eigenvector $(a_{1j}, a_{2j}, \ldots a_{nj})^T$ will be obtained, and weight matrix A_s, which reflects the relationship between clusters under one criterion, will also be obtained.

After the weighted matrix A_s multiplies the unweighted super-matrix W_s, weighted super-matrix $W_s^{(W)}$ can be obtained ($W_s^{(W)} = A_S \cdot W_S$) .

Step 4. Solving the limit super-matrix

Limit super-matrix $W_s^{(W)}$ will be obtained after normalizing the weighted matrix ($W_s^{(l)} = \lim_{k \to \infty} W_s^{(k)}$). Value of each column in limit super-matrix $W_s^{(l)}$ is the limit relative priority under the principle P_s of corresponding elements of each element.

Step 5. Choosing the priorities

Sum up all the limit eigenvector of control layer in accordance of the criteria control vector. Finding the priorities among alternatives and choosing the best alternative.

3 Evaluation System of Hotel Outsourcer Based on ANP Model

There are many researches on manufacturing outsourcing, which always takes quality, price and time as important evaluation criteria. In addition, factors, like geographical location, production capacity, technical capability, reputation and the possibility of long-term cooperation, are often necessary to be taken into consideration of the evaluation criteria [6]. And because of the acceleration of globalization and the complex competitive environment, flexibility has become an important criterion. By drawing on research results related to outsourcing and the characteristics of the hotel industry itself, in this paper, we take the quality, price, flexibility and other factors as the evaluation of hotel outsourcer selection criteria.

3.1 Quality

Quality means the hotel outsourcing product or service quality. The quality provided by outsourcer directly affects the hotel service quality and hotel reputation. In order to ensure that outsourcing does not damage the reputation of the hotel, the hotel must control and supervise the outsourcing process.

3.2 Price

The price of the hotel outsourcing is an important motivation, for outsourcing is to reduce operating costs and unnecessary spending. Without affecting the quality of the premise, price becomes an important factor in selection of hotel outsourcer.

3.3 Flexibility

Variety. Hotel management policy always changes with the management strategy, so the outsourcing product or service must meet the changed demand, sometimes even need to completely change the content of outsourcing. For example, if the hotel service quality has been improved, the hotel human resources outsourcing business training requirements may be replaced to the service team skills training or customized training service training.

Quantity. The flexibility in quantity means that the outsourcer has the ability of adapt to change in quantity demand. Hotel always increase its service reception because of meetings or exhibitions, then the number of outsourcing providers must have the flexibility to meet the hotels business outsourcing increase or decrease demand.

Time. If the outsourcing business can not be completed in time, it tends to affect the normal management and operation of the restaurant, the hotel's reputation and image will damage., It is better to choose those outsourcers with high speed.

3.4 Other Factors

Geographical Position. If the outsourcer's geographical position near the hotel, the total cost will reduce, and the delivery time will also be saved. On contract, with far geographical position, the cost of outsourcing is bigger and the speed will be much slower. So, the geographical position is always relevant to time and cost.

Production Capacity. The production capacity of outsourcer has great relevance with quality, price, time, etc., generally, with strong production capacity; there will be more assured quality, lower prices, and faster delivery time.

Technical Capacity. Technical skills are usually embodied in advanced machinery and equipment, the level of outsourcing of information technology aspects. The enterprise with better technical ability often has higher flexibility, better brand reputation, and big possibility for restaurants to establish long-term partnership. Of course, under normal circumstances, the price may be higher.

Brand&Reputation. As we all know, it is better to choose hotel outsourcer with good brand and reputation. General, the brand and reputation of outsourcer has big relationship with the product quality, delivery time, and possibility of long-term cooperation. Hotel can improve the image of brands by select better outsourcer, while the outsourcer can maintain its own brand through the hotel.

Stability. Stability includes the financial situation stability of the outsourcer and the outsourcing product quality stability. Stable financial situation of outsourcer will help make long-term relationship with restaurant, while stable products or service provided by outsourcer will help hotel control the service quality.

Possibility for Long-term Corporation. Hotels should select outsourcer with big possibility to establish long-term cooperation in order to reduce unnecessary transaction costs by frequent replacement of outsourcers. Meanwhile, the outsourcer with strategic partnership can provide more favorable prices and reduce the operating costs of the hotel.

According to the above criteria and the interactivities relationship between them, we can establish evaluation of hotel outsourcer based on ANP model in Figure 2 using SD (Super Decisions) software.

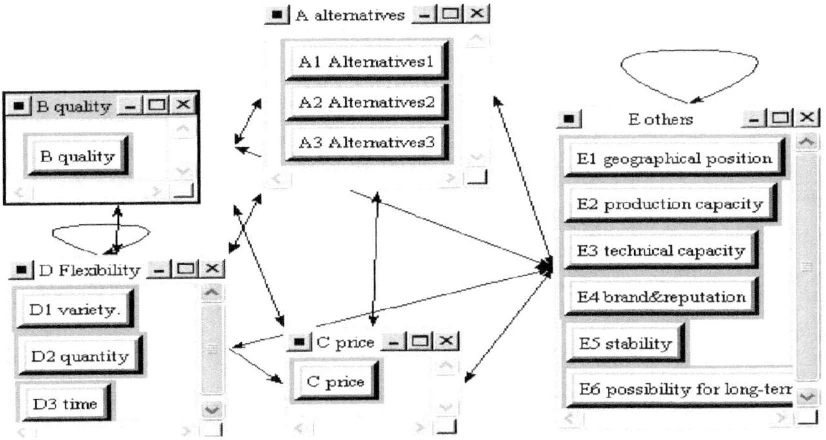

Fig. 2. The hotel outsourcer evaluation model based on ANP

4 Case Study

Here we choose S hotel as the ANP model case hotel. As the hotel's laundry section need to invest the relatively high operating costs, and it need many professional staff to do normal work, that will cost flow cash and human resource, so the hotel decide to outsource laundry business. After an initial screening found in the city, there are three alternative outsourcers: outsourcer 1, outsourcing 2, and outsourcers 3. For the scientific selection of the outsourcer, ANP model is used to evaluate laundry outsourcer.

First, through the questionnaires made by hotel outsourcing decision-makers and experts, the unweighted pair-wise comparison has been established in the ANP model outsourcer selection of 16 elements in the normalized. For example, do pair-wise comparison of A1 and the other elements; we can construct Table 1 - Table 2 Matrix. Similarly, other groups of elements can be obtained in order pair-wise comparison of Judgment. Thus, we can construct outsourcer unweighted super matrix.

To enable the expert's score does not appear logical error, CR (Consistency ratio) is defined in ANP model to measure the reliability of the questionnaire by scholars Saaty. If the CR value is less than or equal to 0.1, consistency of the questionnaire is of high degree, if CR Value is greater than 0.1, the consistency of the questionnaire is poor.

Table 1. Pair-wise comparison matrix of cluster D based on cluster A (CR=0.0516)

A1	D1	D2	D3	**priority**
D1	1	1/3	1/3	0.139642
D2	3	1	1/2	0.332525
D3	3	2	1	0.527833

Table 2. Pair-wise comparison matrix of cluster E based on cluster A (CR=0.1660)

A1	E1	E2	E3	E4	E5	E6	priority
E1	1	3	2	3	1	1/3	0.122405
E2	1/3	1	3	4	1/3	2	0.121411
E3	1/2	1/3	1	3	2	1/2	0.167224
E4	1/3	1/4	1/3	1	1	1/2	0.244795
E5	1	3	1/2	1	1	2	0.094179
E6	3	1/2	2	2	1/2	1	0.099160

Table 3. Pair-wise comparison matrix of clusters

	A	B	C	D	E
A	0.000000	0.232662	0.303512	0. 153094	0.214795
B	0.301117	0.000000	0.518995	0.199221	0.490368
C	0.268625	0.203903	0.000000	0.223617	0.189124
D	0.144216	0.498015	0.344850	0.000000	0.105712
E	0.286043	0.064420	0.177494	0.079210	0.000000

Table 4. Limit super-matrix

	A1	A2	A3	B C D	E
A1	0.054149	0.054149	0.054149	As the matrix	0.054149
A2	0.093581	0.093581	0.093581	is	0.093581
A3	0.056555	0.056555	0.056555	normalized,	0.056555
B	0.251435	0.251435	0.251435	so each column	0.251435
C	0.195401	0.195401	0.195401	is the same	0.195401
D1	0.030026	0.030026	0.030026	to others	0.030026
D2	0.091400	0.091400	0.091400		0.091400
D3	0.094681	0.094681	0.094681		0.094681
E1	0.008898	0.008898	0.008898		0.008898
E2	0.013948	0.013948	0.013948		0.013948
E3	0.019105	0.019105	0.019105		0.019105
E4	0.024451	0.024451	0.024451		0.024451
E5	0.032004	0.032004	0.032004		0.032004
E6	0.025599	0.025599	0.025599		0.025599

Second, the pair-wise comparison matrix of the four clusters is construct by expert's opinions, using SD software can easily re-obtained matrix elements of the priority groups, as shown in Table 3. According to the weight matrix that has been obtained, the weight matrix and the unweighted super matrix multiplication, can get a weighted super-matrix. Normalized the weighted matrix, limit super-matrix can be obtained (the limit super-matrix shown in Table 4).

Finally, after a comprehensive calculation of the relative priority of the limit, the final results of the comprehensive priority order options can directly sort using SD software, as shown in Figure 3.

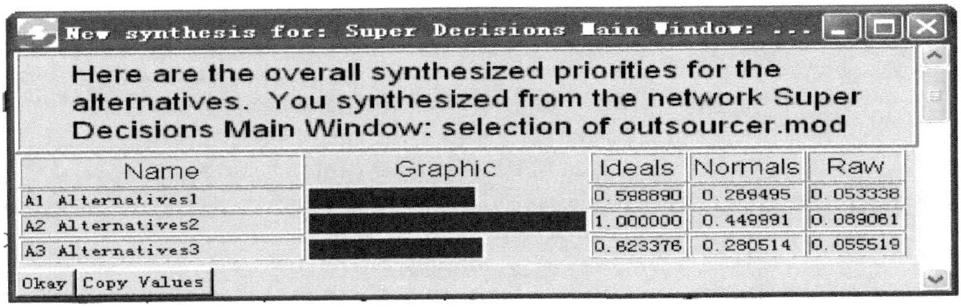

Fig. 3. Synthesized priorities for the alternative using SD software

Based on the above results, the final ranking results show that, A2 has highest priority, followed by A3; the last for the A1, therefore, S hotel should select A2 as the outsourcing laundry.

5 Conclusion

There are many decision-making methods which have been developed in literature. But these methods do not deal with the interdependence among elements. ANP is relatively a new method which can be used as an analysis tool in those problems where there are interactions and dependencies among the elements of a system.

In this paper, we attempt to propose a decision-making model to choose hotel outsourcer and applying ANP as a decision-making tool. At the end, the detailed implementation process of the proposed ANP model is examined and demonstrated through a real case study. The results obtained from the case reveal that how to select a hotel outsourcer by the priorities among alternatives. The direction for future research can be considering some quantitative data into the model.

References

1. Venkatesan, R.: Strategic Sourcing: to make or not to make. Harvard Business Review, 98–107 (1992)
2. Long, H., Chen, X.: Study on the hotel core capability of outsourcing strategy. Guilin Tourism University Journey, 84–87 (2005)
3. Liu, T.: Study on Chinese hotel outsourcing process. Qingdao University master's degree paper, 6 (2006)
4. Saaty, T.: The analytic hierarchy process. McGraw-Hill, New York (1980)
5. Saaty, T.: Decision making with dependence and feedback: the analytic network process. RWS, Pittsburgh (1996)
6. Sun, J.: Study on the problems of Chinese economic hotel. Dongbei Forestry university doctor's degree paper 6, 102–103 (2006)

Reputation-Based Incentive and Restraint Mechanisms for Fund Managers

Chang Liu[1] and Yuemei Zhou[2]

[1] Quantitative Economics, Economics and Management School,
Wuhan University Wuhan, P.R.China, 430072
liuchang@foxmail.com
[2] Department of Statistics and Mathematics, Zhongnan University of Economics and Law,
Wuhan, P.R.China, 430000
ymzhou@qq.com

Abstract. This paper deals with the incentive and restrictive mechanism based on the principal-agent relationship between the fund companies and fund managers. Through the establishment of multi-phase dynamic game model, we analyzed and compared the excitations under explicit contract mechanisms with and without considering the reputation effect. We have come to the conclusion that reputation has better incentive and restriction effect on fund managers' behavior and will improve the economic efficiency. On this basis, we analyzed the internal mechanism of the long-term incentive role which the reputation effect plays, and then made a number of recommendations on how the reputation effect can operate to motivate fund managers effectively.

Keywords: explicit contract, incentive mechanism, reputation effect, fund managers, fund company, Dynamic Game.

1 Introduction

In the explicit contract excitation, as substance incentive, provided by fund companies, like equity, fund management fees and other incentives play the explicit role of basic security to fund managers, in the actual operation, explicit contract excitation may be invalid to some extent. In the long run, reputation can raise fund managers' future value on the one hand; on the other hand, according to Maslow's hierarchy of needs theory, the human beings' need rise from low to high. When their monetary income reaches a certain degree, the fund managers will make every effort to protect their reputation to win respect. The establishment of an incentive mechanism combined of reputation effect and the explicit incentive is particularly important to form a sound market environment for fund managers, which could promote the whole economic efficiency.

2 Basic Functions Preparing

(1) Linear function of a fund company's return on investment. Assuming in phase t, the fund manager's proceeds of operating the fund is $y_t = e_t + \theta + \varepsilon_t$. e_t is the monetary

Q. Zhou (Ed.): ISAEBD 2011, Part II, CCIS 209, pp. 172–178, 2011.

level of fund manager's effort, and θ is the monetary operating capacity(assumed to be independent of time) of the fund manager, ε_t is the random disturbance caused by external factors (such as technical and market uncertainty). We made the assumption that e_t is the private information of fund manager and y_t is the common information between the fund manager and the fund company. θ and ε_t are both subject to normal independent distribution, with the same mean 0. Their variance are $\sigma_\theta^{\ 2} = \tau\sigma^2$ and $\sigma_{\varepsilon_t}^{\ 2} = (1-\tau)\sigma^2$, and here $\tau = \dfrac{\sigma_\theta^{\ 2}}{\sigma_\theta^{\ 2} + \sigma_\varepsilon^{\ 2}}$. We also assume that random variable ε_1 and ε_2 are independent. e_t and ε_t are independent.

(2) Linear contract function. Fund managers and fund companies have signed compensation contracts before operating investment, and they agreed if certain business goals are achieved, the fund companies need to pay the fund manager according to the reward function $w_t = a + by_t$. Here a is a fixed remuneration, including wages and basic benefits. b represents incentive coefficient or performance share, satisfying 0 < b < 1. by_t is the performance-related compensation, including bonuses, profit sharing, stock options.

(3) Fund manager's effort cost function $c(e_t) = \frac{1}{2}e_t^{\ 2}$, which is a strictly increasing convex function. The cost of his efforts is increasing, as $c'(e_t) > 0, c''(e_t) > 0$

(4) Net profit function.: $x_t = w_t - c(e_t) = a + b(e_t + \theta + \varepsilon_t) - \frac{1}{2}e_t^{\ 2}$ For the fund manager. $\pi_t = y_t - w_t = (1-b)(e_t + \theta + \varepsilon_t) - a$ for fund the company

(5) Utility function. Assuming that the risk of the fund company is neutral, that is $E(u(\pi_t)) = u(E(\pi_t))$, then the utility function of the fund company's expected net income in a single phase is $E(\pi_t) = E[(1-b)(e_t + \theta + \varepsilon_t) - a] = (1-b)(e_t + \theta) - a$

We assume that fund managers are risk aversion investors, who prefer income with certainty. The utility function of fund manager's single-phase net income could be set as $u(x_t) = e^{-rx_t}$. Here r is coefficient of risk aversion, reflecting the fund manager risk aversion. As the fund manager's expected net income function in a single phase is $E(x_t) = a + b(e_t + \theta) - \frac{1}{2}e_t^{\ 2}$, which is normally distributed with the variance $\mathrm{var}(x_t) = b^2\sigma^2$, the fund manager's net income is certainty equivalence

That is $$CE_t = a + b(e_t + \theta) - \frac{1}{2}e_t^{\ 2} - \frac{1}{2}rb^2\sigma^2$$

The certainty equivalence refers to the certain income, which the fund manager is willing to accept, brings the same utility with the case in uncertain situation.

3 Dynamic Model of Explicit Incentive without Reputation

In the Principal-Agent Relationship between fund companies and fund manager, the following two conditions are required to achieve stable equilibrium. One is the maximization of fund companies' utility and the other is the maximization of fund managers' utility. As in this principal-agent relationship, the fund companies have the right to select venture capitalists, according to the traditional framework of principal-agent theory, when incentive compatibility constraint and participation constraint are satisfied for fund managers, the fund companies will design contract to gain their maximum utility. Then, the optimal contract model could be established.

$$\Pi=\max_{a,b}\sum_{t=0}^{\infty}\rho^t[(1-b)(e_t+\theta)-a] \tag{1}$$

S t. (IC) $$X=\max_{a,b}\sum_{t=0}^{\infty}\rho^t[a+b(e_t+\theta)-\frac{1}{2}e_t^{\,2}-\frac{1}{2}rb^2\sigma^2] \tag{2}$$

(IR) $$\sum_{t=0}^{\infty}\rho^t[a+b(e_t+\theta)-\frac{1}{2}e_t^{\,2}-\frac{1}{2}rb^2\sigma^2]\geq\sum_{t=0}^{\infty}\rho^t\overline{u}_t \tag{3}$$

Let $$L=\sum_{t=0}^{\infty}[a+b(e_t+\theta)-\frac{1}{2}e_t^{\,2}-\frac{1}{2}rb^2\sigma^2], \tag{4}$$

$$M=\sum_{t=0}^{\infty}\rho^t[(1-b)(e_t+\theta)-a] \tag{5}$$

Take the derivative of equation (4) to e_t, $$\frac{\partial L}{\partial e_t}=\rho^t(b-e_t)=0 \tag{6}$$

Then $$e_t^{\,*}=b,\ \frac{d(x_t)}{de_t}=\frac{dc(e_t)}{de_t}, \tag{7}$$

The marginal cost of fund manager's effort equals to his marginal monetary benefits.

Take equation (6) to (5), $M=\sum_{t=0}^{\infty}\rho^t(1-2b-\theta)$

Take the derivative of the above to b.

$$\frac{\partial M}{\partial b}=\rho^t(1-2b-\theta)=0,\ \text{then}\ b^*=\frac{1-\theta}{2} \tag{8}$$

Put equation (8) to (3), and take the equal mark

$$a^* = (1-\rho)\sum_{t=0}^{\infty}\rho^t[\overline{u}_t - b^*(e_t^* + \theta) + \frac{1}{2}e_t^{*2} - \frac{1}{2}rb^2\sigma^2] \tag{9}$$

So the optimal incentive contract is (a^*, b^*). Then $w = a^* + b^* y_t$ (10)

We can draw the conclusions based on the above analysis that explicit contract incentives cannot work effectively without the effective implementation of the contract. If the contract cannot be effectively carried out, or non-cooperative behavior cannot be detected or punitive measures are incredible threat, the fund manager may take opportunistic behaviors.

4 Optimal Dynamic Contract Model

According to the assumption in the front, the fund investment income function $y_t = e_t + \theta + \varepsilon_t$; θ and ε_t are independent normal-distributions, with the means 0 and variance $\sigma_\theta^2 = \tau\sigma^2$, $\sigma_{\varepsilon_t}^2 = (1-\tau)\sigma^2$, where $\tau = \dfrac{\sigma_\theta^2}{\sigma_\theta^2 + \sigma_{\varepsilon_t}^2}$. We can get:

$E(y_t) = E(e_t) + E(\theta) + E(\varepsilon_t) = e_t$ and $\text{var}(y_t) = \text{var}(e_t) + \text{var}(\theta) + \text{var}(\varepsilon_t) = \sigma^2$

In the phase *t*, if the effort level higher than the fund company's lowest expected return at the probability $F(y_0, \hat{e}_t)$, then the fund manager's reputation will increase by *R* (expressed as monetary value); contrarily, if the effort level is higher than the minimum expected return at the probability 1-$F(y_0, \hat{e}_t)$, the fund manager's reputation will reduce by *R*. The expected utility of the fund manager's reputation is

$$E(R) = F(y_0, e_t) * R - (1 - F(y_0, e_t)) * R = 2F(y_0, e_t) * R - 1$$

The cost of the reputation incentive provided by the fund company is assumed to be 0.Under repeated games in steady state, following optimization model exists

$$\Pi' = \max_{a,b}\sum_{t=0}^{\infty}\rho^t[(1-b)(e_t + \theta) - a] \tag{11}$$

S,t (IC)

$$X' = \max\sum_{t=0}^{\infty}\{\rho^t[a + b(e_t + \theta) - \frac{1}{2}e_t^2 - \frac{1}{2}rb^2\sigma^2] + \rho^t F(y_0, e_t)R\} \quad (\pi \ge \pi_o) \tag{12}$$

$$X' = \max\sum_{t=0}^{\infty}\{\rho^t[a + b(e_t + \theta) - \frac{1}{2}e_t^2 - \frac{1}{2}rb^2\sigma^2] - \rho^t(1 - F(y_0, e_t))R\} \quad (\pi < \pi_o) \tag{13}$$

$$\text{(IR)} \quad \sum_{t=0}^{\infty}\{2\rho^t[a+b(e_t+\theta)-\frac{1}{2}e_t^{\,2}-\frac{1}{2}rb^2\sigma^2]+E(R)\}\geq\sum_{t=0}^{\infty}\rho^t\overline{u}_t \tag{14}$$

Obtains the derivatives of (12) and (13) to e_t, and let $\frac{dX'}{de^t}=0$,

$$\text{Then } b+R\frac{dF(y_0,e^{**}{}_t)}{de_t}=e_t^{**}\text{, or } \frac{dx_t}{de_t}+R\frac{dF(y_0,e_t)}{de_t}=\frac{dc(e_t)}{de_t} \tag{15}$$

That is to say, the marginal cost of effort equal to the marginal monetary revenue and marginal reputation. Here $\frac{dF(y_0,e_t)}{de_t}>0$. That is, the higher level the fund manager takes effort, the higher income could be gained from the fund investment, which will lead to a higher probability of the minimum expected return.

Put (15) to $M=\sum_{t=0}^{\infty}\rho^t[(1-b)(e_t+\theta)-a]$, and take its derivative to b

$$b^{**}=\frac{1}{2}(1-R\frac{dF(y_0,e_t)}{de_t}-\vartheta) \tag{16}$$

$$a^{**}=(1-\rho)\sum_{t=0}^{\infty}\{\rho^t[\overline{u}_t-b^{**}(e_t^{**}+\theta)+\frac{1}{2}e_t^{**2}-\frac{1}{2}rb^2\sigma^2]-E(R)\} \tag{17}$$

We can get that the optimal contract combining reputation effects and explicit contract mechanism is (a^{**},b^{**}).

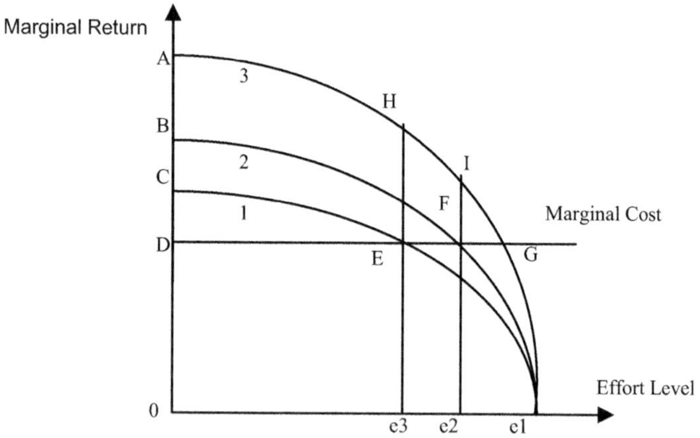

Fig. 1. Marginal return - Marginal cost curves

It can be seen from Figure (1) that, without reputation effect, the efficiency loss of the fund manager in curve 1 is the area of EHIG; a reputation effect. However, in curve 2, the fund manager's efficiency loss is the area of IFG under reputation effect, which reduces the loss by an area of HIEF. Obviously, reputation effect brings a less efficiency loss IFG, as an efficiency optimization.

5 The Internal Mechanism of Long-Term Incentive by Reputation

Considering a two-phase game model, different from normal dominant contract mechanism, the fund manager's return in phase 2 depends on the his expected operational capability, which is affected by e_1's action to y_1. It is assumed that fund companies have rational expectations, observed income of the fund is y_1, and it is known that $\theta+\varepsilon_1 = y_1 - e_1$. But, fund companies cannot identify θ and ε_1, which means it's unknown the income of the Fund in phase 1 is the result of the fund manager's operating ability or the result of exogenous random factors.

Following relation could be drawn from previous assumption

$$w_1 = E(a+by_1) = E[a+b(e_1+\theta+\varepsilon_1)] = a+b\bar{e}_1$$

Here, $\bar{e}_1$ is the expected effort level of the fund manager.

$$w_2 = E(y_2 \mid y_1) = E(a \mid y_1) + b[E(e_2 \mid y_1) + E(\theta \mid y_1) + E(\varepsilon_2 \mid y_1) = a + bE(\theta \mid y_1)$$

As $E(e_2 \mid y_1) = 0, E(\varepsilon_2 \mid y_1) = 0$, $\text{var}(y_2 \mid y_1) = (1-\tau^2)\sigma^2$

According to the formula of rational expectations

$$E(\theta \mid y_1) = (1-\tau)E(\theta) + \tau(y_1 - e_1) = \tau(y_1 - e_1) \tag{18}$$

For given y_1, the expected value of θ is the weighted average of priori expectation $E(\theta)$ and observation value $\tau(y_1 - e_1)$, that is, the fund company adjusts its judgment to the fund manager according to his observed ability. For given τ, the equilibrium wage income $w_2 = a + b\tau(y_1 - \bar{e}_1)$ indicates that more fund income in phase 1 will lead to higher return of fund manager in phase 2. The fund manager's utility in phase 1 and 2 is

$$CE_{1,2} = CE_1 + CE_2 = E(y_1) + \text{var}(y_1) + E(y_2 \mid y_1) + \text{var}(y_2 \mid y_1)$$

$$= [a + b(\bar{e}_1 + \theta) - \frac{1}{2}e_1^2 - \frac{1}{2}rb^2\sigma^2] + [a + b\tau(y_1 - e_1) - \frac{1}{2}\bar{e}_1^2 - \frac{1}{2}rb^2(1-\tau^2)\sigma^2]$$

The condition of the fund manager's optimal utility in phase 1 is $\frac{\partial CE_{1,2}}{\partial e_1} = e_1 - b\tau = 0$

The fund manager's effort level in phase 1 is strictly positive, and the incentive effect of reputation will be greater with greater τ and b.

The two-phase model can be easily extended to phase T. Except the last phase, the efforts of all the previous T-1 phases are positive. Furthermore, if operational capability θ_t subjects to the theory of random walk, when $r \to \infty$, the first-order conditions in steady-state satisfy $e_t = \frac{r\tau}{1-(1-\tau)r}$. If $r = 1, \tau = 1$, then $e_t = 1$, and the Pareto optimum can be achieved. Although there are no explicit contract incentives, reputation effect can play an implicit role of incentives.

6 Proposal for the Improvement of the Incentive Effects

(1) Ensure that fund managers have long-term expectation. As the premise of incentives of reputation effect is repeated game theory, only if the game is expected to be repeated in the long run, fund managers would be motivated to invest on his reputation for future return, or, opportunistic behavior may occur.

(2) Create fund manager's complete historical record. As a "quality" signal, reputation reflects the fund manager's ability to manage fund successfully in the long run which makes the fund manager has long-term expectations.

(3) Foster a fully competitive market for fund managers to ensure their reputation.

(4) Combination of complete legal regulations and moral ideology.

References

1. Zhang, W.: Game Theory and Information Economics. Shanghai Joint Publishing House, Shanghai (1996)
2. Sun, W., Xu, C.: Optimization Methods. Higher Education Press, Beijing (2004)
3. Securities Association of China. Securities Investment Fund. China Financial and Economic Publishing House, Beijing (2010)
4. Zheng, C.: The Effectiveness of Stock Options Incentives. China Management Science 9(5), 74–80 (2001)
5. Liu, H., Zhang, S.: Dynamic Incentive Model Based on Reputation Effect. China Management Science 13(4), 78–86 (2005)
6. Lin, Z., He, J., Liu, H.: Reputation Effect for Professional Managers. Chang'an University Journal (Social Science Edition) 8(1), 29–42 (2006)
7. Li, Y.: Incentives for Fund Managers – In The View of The Agency Relationship. Tongling Polytechnic University Journal, 28–29 (2010)
8. Geng, P.: Analysis of The Reputation Incentive for Fund Managers.Entrepreneurs World, 35–36 (2009)
9. Li, X., Jing, H.: The Establishment of Incentive Mechanisms of Reputation For Fund Managers. Accounting Monthly, 19–21 (2010)
10. Ke, J.: Game Analysis of Incentive Mechanism in Venture Company. Liaoning Normal University Journal (Social Science Edition) 33(1), 33–36 (2010)

The Labor Process of Chinese Knot Industry: Ethnicity-Based Research and Investigation of Rural Migrant Workers in Huashui, Dongyang

Xiaoyun Yan[1,2]

[1] School of Public Administration, Zhejiang Gongshang University, Hangzhou, P.R. China
[2] Department of Sociology, Shanghai University, Shanghai, P.R. China
Yxy504@yahoo.com

Abstract. Chinese knot industry reflects the development of eastern china handicraft industry and the social mobility of rural migrant workers. The ethnicity research of labor process theory provides a theoretical view of studying rural migrant workers, and reflects the labor and social relationship between rural migrant workers and Chinese knot industry. Through the field investigation, this dissertation analyzes the living and working conditions of migrant workers in Chinese knot industry and concludes its features and proposes suggestions to improve social policies.

Keywords: Rural Migrant Workers, Labor Process, Ethnicity, Social Mobility.

1 Introduction

Labor process theory provides "from abstract workers to concrete workers" perspective to investigate rural migrant workers, which not only focuses on how workers convert raw materials into product through labor, but also on the study of revealing the social relationship through this process. This theory was first proposed by Karl Marx' description of "Labor process of capitalism" that capitalist have an effective control of living labors. Braverman(1974) observed that with the development of science and technology, vocational skills in handicraft or technical occupations become vestigial. Burawoy(1979) emphasized subjective factors of labor, his investigation found out that consensus on game rule could effectively regulate production order, then he put up with "The Politics of Production" [1]. Besides the class category, the subsequent researchers introduced the categories of gender, ethnic and civil right. Jingjun Li (2006) introduced gender into labor process research. Yuan Shen (2007) explained construction workers labor process from the respective "Relation Hegemony". Xiang Wen (2007) introduced ethnicity based on native place to observe how ethnicity influences working relationship[2].

Now there are a few researches on rural migrant workers in eastern china. "leaving the farmland but not hometown, entering the factory but not the city" are characteristics of the social mobility of these workers. The Chinese knot industry (Huashui town, Dongyang city,Zhejiang Province) provides such opportunities for investigating rural migrant workers. Since the 80's of last century, the growing

Q. Zhou (Ed.): ISAEBD 2011, Part II, CCIS 209, pp. 179–185, 2011.

specialized and professional industries in Huashui town like clothing, embroidery, plastic and Chinese knot that not only help local peasants to cast off poverty and become better off but also attract a large number of migrant workers. Rural migrant workers who take part in this industry have two characteristics: one is that they are relatively older with less schooling, the other one is that most of them come from Sichuan and Guizhou provinces and three quarters among them are Guizhou people. It should be pointed out that the place of source of rural migrant workers in Chinese knot industry is intensive so that the ethnicity is very obvious. Ethnicity means in the large social and culture system, people have common origin and culture objectively, recognize and differ from other ethnic groups subjectively. Generally ethnicity is related with race and complexion, and related with sub-ethnic group in narrow sense. In this dissertation, ethnicity is based on native place and genetic relationship, and used to investigates the labor and social relationship developed in Chinese knot industry.

2 Basic Information of Chinese Knot Industry and Rural Migrant Workers

2.1 Basic Information

Chinese knot industry grew up from last 90's, more than 60 villages in Huashui town are in this business, around 63% peasants take part in this production and process, which contributes about 60% national output. With the development of this industry, rural migrant workers become the main labor force in knitting, and those who previously worked in this process has retreated and focused on organization, design and sales. We have done a questionnaire survey among 400 rural migrant workers in Huashui town, with 389 valid returns, and interviewed some relevant workers.

The survey shown that male works takes 57.0%, because some types of Chinese knot are manual labor. The average age of survey samples is 32, those younger than 30 takes 41.1%, 30-39 takes 44.2%,40-49 takes 12.3% and above 50 is 2.3%. Married takes 85.3% and singles 14.7%. 16% of them live alone and 84% live with their family. Workers are lack of education, majority of them graduated from primary or junior high school. And most of them are from Guizhou, Chongqing, Sichuan, Hunan and Hubei provinces, and Guizhou people takes 76.9% which ranks the first.

2.2 Working Conditions

Chinese knot products include shapes like ring, fish ,doll, tassel. Except knit, there are other type of work in production like stencil, spray paint, strings template making, sewing and so on. People in knit takes79.2%, in fish knit takes 12.1%, the rest are auxiliary stuff. Workers treat the difficulty variously, 32.9% thinks that Chinese knot requires high techniques, 33.9% thinks its normal, and the rest thinks it's not hard.

The wage is paid by piece, the size of Chinese knot is determined by knot which normally are 16 knots, 20 knots, 24 knots, larger ones like 48 knots, or even 80 knots. The thickness of string would also determine the size, both of number of knots and thickness are factors of piecework wage. Skilled workers can earn 80 RMB per day at peak seasons.

The average work hour for knitting workers are 11 hours per day. Normally the commuter time is not explicitly stipulated, it is more flexible than other industries. In summer, the work lasts less than 8 hours, but during peak seasons that start from September, work time increases obviously, especially in November and December, workers knit all day except dining and sleeping.

3 The Labor Relationship between Ethnicity and Chinese Knot Industry

3.1 Bound with Labor

The main purpose for rural migrant worker to leave native place and go out to work is to earn money, which takes 85.6%, the native place and relative based "ethnicity" plays a very important role. 80.3% workers are introduced by fellow-villagers or relatives, only 15.9% come to Huashui town by themselves. Fellow-villagers, relatives, friends play a leader part at the initial period of Chinese knot industry. The ethnicity based on native place and relatives forms information network before they go out of their village, the one who has settled down would be one node of the network and pass work information to people in his hometown. For example ,A young man from Guizhou province told us that he brought some fellow-villagers when he went home, and there are 300 to 400 Guizhou fellow-villagers around Huayang village[3]. The investigation shows 74% of them contact with relatives, friends and fellow-villagers more than others.

There are 4 or 5 large scale Chinese knot factories in Huashui town with dozens of stuff unequally. The majorities are small scale family workshops; most dealers arrange workplace at home. Because knitting needs certain tools especially for large Chinese knot, 82% migrant workers choose to works at the workshop, 18% will take them (small size) home. Generally there are 6 or 7 workers in the workshop and among them 2 or 3 people keeps years of employment relations with the employee. The boss and relatives trust them for their skill and trustiness. If there are vacancies in the workshop, the boss will let them introduce fellow-villagers or relatives into workshop. The leader in the workshop is also the supervisor. One of the questions in the survey is "who taught you to make Chinese knot when you first come to Huashui town", 56.6% are by fellow-villagers, saw and learned takes 26.7%, by relatives 9.3% and by boss 5.9%.

3.2 Gender-Based Division of Labor

Rural migrant workers not only have a tight contact with fellow-villagers, but more with their families. They usually come as a family. Question in the survey "Are you live with your families now?"73.0% choose "the whole family", 11.1% "just the couple", 1.8%"live with siblings", and only 13.6% work alone. This phenomenon is greatly different from city workers because Huashui town provides various jobs with less education requirements. Men can take job of cement carrying, transportation, plastic and women take job of clothing, Chinese knot, handicraft and the old and children can help with string of beads. The piecework system of handicraft gives certain freedom, "I can do the handicrafts and look after baby at the same time" "my parents are here, I could do some to help".

Chinese knot knitting requires not only skills but also strength. from the interview we knew that at the primary period ,Chinese knot knitting are mostly done by women, and male workers came together work in other businesses. With the knitting technology gets more sophisticated, the circumference become longer, they are draw into this industry. And it is turned out that male are more effective than female workers. Since then, Chinese knot industry has the division of labor between male and female, male workers take large scale knot while female works with middle-small sized. Although female earn less but save physical strength so that pay more attention to family and children. The ethnicity shaped by the labor division in working process leads to the coming of more family to the Chinese knot business.

3.3 Seasonal Work

Interviews with dealers shown when they employ workers, apart from interpersonal relations, skill are a very important factor. "We value their skills, if it is not perfect, we don't hire them". workers realize that only if they improve their skills can maintain a longer relation with the employee. Chinese knot is usually paid by piece, so workers prefer to work over time because work more and get more, someone said "The more I made the more money I can get, so we are willing to knit". If workers can not finish their work at the workshop or the family need to be taken care of, they would take middle-small sized knot back home, under the nightlights, every household come into "overtime rush game".

Chinese knot industry is seasonal; usually employee pays 500 RMB living expenses per month and settle all wage at the end of the year. The first half of the year is a period of slack sales; there is not much or even no work to do. Rural migrant workers have to find other temp-job to support their family; the head of the household will divide labor. When the peak season comestible, migrant workers will go back to the work shop. It is found in a workshop that July is not busy, 3-4 work hours, but from September, work hour will last from 6 a.m. to 9 p.m, some workers said that around Spring Festival, they even work 13 or 14 hours a day.

4 The Social Relationship of Ethnicity and Chinese Knot Industry

4.1 Labor Reciprocity and Terminal Market

Freidrich pointed out that in a comprehensive society system, the positive bond of several ethnic groups determines group complementarities[4]. Chinese knot industry has formed an interdependent labor structure; migrant workers support the development of Chinese knot industry and also boosted three main industries. Employee will treat workers well especially those with skills and contact with hometown workers. In the survey, 96.9% workers said employees would not arrears of wage; they can overdraw living expenses, if the employee is easy going, and they can easy going more. Question of "How many workshops have you worked for?" 83.0% choose "Regular one" and 17.0% with "Multiple". as a whole the relations between employee and employer is good. One respondent said that he can make at least tens of yuan for one day, some skilled worker can make hundreds, all work are done indoors and they do not expose to harsh weather, so they are fairly satisfied.

With the different control of resources, local and migrant ethnic groups take part in different economic activities. Rural migrant workers are complementary to local economic activities. Local elite are in charge of production organization, sales and design, purchase stores at Yiwu Commodities City. In Chinese knot industry rural migrant workers only takes the end of production line. Question "Did you compete with local people and do what they do?" 96% choose "No". On the other hand, low wage is far enough to accumulation of capital and they can not involve themselves in the operation at a foreign place, question "Have you ever thought of starting your own Chinese knot business?" 69.7% choose "No" and 30.3% have thought about it but they all acknowledged that it is difficult and many locals are doing it, the risk is too high.

4.2 Subculture and Social Segregation

Ethnicity represents ascribed social relation by same native place. The most frequently association with rural migrant workers are fellow-villagers, relatives and friends. When facing difficulties, what is the first thing come in mind, "ethnic groups" takes 85.3% in the survey. Though the workers, come from the same district, live in different villages, they communicate with other frequently. Some said: "We often talk about recent life, how is the wage". New comers can adapt the living environment more easily, they said"We have not been to big cities, there are too much pressure, here is better, there are farmland like hometown". Rural migrant workers usually come from remote villages, they have exposed to relatively modern material civilization at Huashui town, and migrant workers also take part in some entertaining activities. By the survey 35% of them have expend their social network.

Generally speaking, the mobility of migrant worker has formed into "sub-culture" and it gets along with local cultures but not fully merged into it. Natives still hold a certain degree of exclusion, so far, there is a village that only the native people can do chinese knot. Manufactures design new fancy that knitter cannot pass it to his won countryman. Above from that, there are some rural culture differences among Huashui town, Guizhou and Sichuan provinces, so it is even harder for migrant workers to fit into local culture. Quote of one interviewee: "frankly speaking, lots of natives look down upon us rural migrant workers " . It is especially typical in residential seperation. In Huashui town, more and more villagers have moved out of original houses and constructed new buildings. And shabby old houses are leased to migrant workers. The survey shows that 89.2% migrant workers rent houses, 8.5% live in the factory or boss' house. The resident area is obviously devided by native place or relative relations. For example, there is one Guizhou Building because all migrant workers are from Guizhou province.

4.3 Difference among Towns and Group Needs

Huashui town has become well developed in Zhejiang province, The 2002 annual production of the origin, Yanxia, is more than 40 million RMB[5].Rural migrant workers evaluate the local hygiene, public security, and commercial services is above average. The floating population registered in recent three years: 3434 of 2007, 3900 of 2008, and 4210 of 2009, 1500 migrant workers are in Chinese knot industry. The flow of Guizhou, Sichuan people keep coming here tests push and pull theory which shows regional development difference, 87.2% of them work out of home town all year round, occupation mobility is unitary or lower, with 389 samples, 169 have gone to other places to find jobs, the reasons they come to Huashui town are : " cannot search a job in big city and cannot used to city living " "do not have kids, wife is better to work in the factory" " cannot find job because of low education" "quite old to find a proper job". In Huashui town they always find the same job, question "How many times have you changed your job", 55.6% choose"0", 17.0 choose"1", 15.7% choose "2" and the rest are 3 times or above.

From large scale industries of big cities to township industries, the mobility of rural migrant workers in Chinese knot industry is spontaneous and compelled, but they have find a proper job through the help of ethnic groups, some said "economy and living are improved" "not much change actually" "still poor, but staying with family is better ""the better education here is better for the children". Question" How are policies for rural migrant workers by local governance?", most workers give a high evaluation "temporary residence permit is free" "children can enjoy the same schooling as local kids" "local police station conducts well", 33.4% choose "they have pay more attention on us",36.8% choose "Normal",13.1% choose "they neglect our needs",16.7% choose "hard to say".12.3% respondent wish they could settle down here, but more people are living in Huashui town temporarily.

5 Conclusions

The Chinese knot industry of Huashui town represents labor intensive industry characteristics. Ethnicity reveals the problems during social fusion and labor process of western rural migrant workers coming to eastern towns. As many other handicraft industries, when the Chinese knot industry of Huashui town develops to a certain period, problems emerge. The financial crisis of 2008 made a great pressure on businessman and migrant workers, many of them have to go back home and be a farmer. Apart from industrial policy making, we should pay more attention on interests of workers. From ethnicity perspective, we realized the basic requirements of workers in Chinese knot industry: jobs and staying with family. When the rights of rural migrant workers in big cities is risen to a new industry stage, the workers in eastern Chinese townships also need practical social policies. A balanced development of eastern and western china is the most important task. Governments should foster Chinese knot industry in Guizhou province and redistribute economic benefits, gives rural migrant workers more social welfare, and organize Chinese Knot Trade Union to help labor process become more complete and perfect.

References

1. Shen, Y.: Society Transaction and Reformulation of Working Class. Sociological Studies (February 2006)
2. Wen, X.: Western Labor Process Theory and Chinese Experience: a Critical Review. Social Sciences in China (April 2009)
3. Dongyang news center, http://www.zj.xinhuanet.com/df/2008-03/14/content.htm
4. Sun, J.: Ethnic Group and Ethnic Group Relation of Foreign Enterprises. Journal of Guangxi University Nationalities (March 2001)
5. Dongyang daily, http://dyrb.zjol.com.cn/html/2009-04/content_6781.htm

Study on Current Situation and Development Strategies for Rural Tourism in China

Zhibo Diao

Tourism and Cuisine School, Harbin University of Commerce Harbin, China
dzb1977@sina.cn

Abstract. The paper aims at analyzing the current situation of rural tourism in China and providing relevant development strategies. By means of careful field observations and in-depth interviews of tourists, farmers and experts, the achievements and problems of rural tourism have been shown. The facts and findings lead to the following conclusions: the current situation is very encouraging; rural tourism is being converted from extensive growth to intensive growth; development strategies include scientific programming, marketing strategies, consumer protection and guidance, environmental protection and sustainable development. The study is helpful to official and commercial decision-making.

Keywords: Rural Tourism, Current Situation, Development Strategy, China.

1 Introduction

From 2004 to 2010, China Central Government had issued a series of official documents and policies, which aimed at promoting agricultural development, increasing farmers' income and building new villages. Those are not only long-term goals but also an urgent task of China. The governments of all levels are now more competent to ensure the improvement of agriculture and rural areas. Rural tourism is considered as an important and effective means to fulfill the task, balance the economic and social development between urban and rural areas, and finally narrow the gap. For those under-developed regions, rural tourism means prosperity and modernization in addition to financial support.

As the result of urbanization, rural tourism has a history of over 100 years. It first turned up in Europe [1]. During the process of urbanization, rural tourism became a solution to urban disease, and people escaped to rural areas. Consequently, rural tourism began to boom, esp. after World War II.

The initial rural tourism in China emerged in the 1980s after China's reform and opening up. The factors to promote rural tourism are different between China and Europe for their different levels of urbanization. The original forms of rural tourism are country inns and rural recreation. It is widely accepted that Chengdu City was the first one in China where rural tourism arose [2]. From then on rural tourism began to blossom around the whole country. More and more citizens began to experience and enjoy rural tourism. Now rural tourism has become an indispensable part of China's tourism industry.

Q. Zhou (Ed.): ISAEBD 2011, Part II, CCIS 209, pp. 186–190, 2011.

2 Methodology

The study was based on available literature, field observations and in-depth interviews. It made full use of qualitative analysis. Fifteen villages in the suburbs of four large cities were intentionally selected. They are located in three different regions. Specific notes will be taken during the fieldwork. The interviewees consisted of 90 local residents, 30 urban residents (tourists), and 5 experts. The samples were collected by random sampling. When interviewing residents, it required no more than three interviewees each time. It took about 20 minutes to answer open-ended questions in each interview. The questions are related to the current situation and development strategies for local tourism industry. All the interviews were on a voluntary basis. All the findings and facts were summarized based on the available literature and fieldwork.

3 Current Situation of Rural Tourism in China

The current situation is financially encouraging. All the parties (governmental agencies, businesses, farmers, mass media, etc) involving in the rural tourism have made a great contribution. Rural tourism has got a rapid and comprehensive growth.

3.1 Official Support and Regulation

In 2006, China National Tourism Administration (CNTA) declared the "Year of Rural Tourism". Its slogan was "new countryside, new tourism, new experience, new trend." Then in 2009, CNTA declared the "Year of Eco-tourism". Meanwhile, local governmental agencies have made a determined effort to promote local tourist attractions. The governments planned to develop rural tourism rapidly and regard it as the main part of domestic travel markets. They have invested in roads, garbage disposal, forestation, water and power supply, pollution prevention and other infrastructures construction. They have formulated policies to rate country inns, design travel routes, and construct new villages featuring local folklore. Their efforts lead farmers and other participants to improve and upgrade their accommodations. For example, Heilongjiang Province had planned to help building 1000 villages suitable for rural tourism. During the process, mass media play an important role. Their push helps citizens to find a new recreation.

For example, Beijing Tourism Administration (BTA), a functional department of the Beijing Municipal Government, took action to support local rural tourism. In 2009, BTA cooperated with Ctrip.com (the largest Internet distributor in China's tourism market) to deliver free entrance tickets for citizens to enjoy rural tourism. The number of free entrance tickets was 700,000 and all of them were publicly provided through the Internet. Local residents with the identification card could get a free tourist handbook. The total number of the handbooks was 800,000[3]. By means of those efforts, millions of citizens flooded into the rural areas.

3.2 Scale and Scope of Rural Tourism

As of the end of 2010, it was estimated there were 1.5 million country inns and other accommodations in addition to 18 thousand farms. The annual rural tourists amounted to over 400 million, and the annual revenue was over 120 billion RMB. About 15 million farmers benefited from rural tourism. [4]

After development and growth for 20 years, China's rural tourism has spreaded to the whole country covering 31 provinces and municipalities. Rural tourism involves agriculture, animal husbandry, fishery, forestry, and processing industry. Usually one large city is surrounded by many special villages featuring kinds of rural tourism, esp. in the suburbs of cities like Guangzhou, Shanghai, Beijing, Shenzhen, Chongqing, and Chengdu. Many parks and farms were built in the countryside for their nearby citizens. Rural tourism has better performance in eastern areas and coastal areas than in inland areas. Therefore there are more farmers and investors engaged in rural tourism in those coastal provinces, such as Liaoning, Shandong, Jiangsu, Zhejiang, Fujian, Guangdong, Hainan, Guangxi, etc.

3.3 Types of Rural Tourism

A large amount of citizens as well as foreign travelers are attracted by beautiful scenery, folklore, food, regional specialties, and recreational activities. Not only villages but also some towns become attractive destinations. Usually outdoor activities are very popular, including sightseeing, fishing, picking fruits (strawberry, apple, peach, pear, etc), cultivating and picking organic vegetables, camping, ornamental horticulture, experiencing folklore and traditional festivals, riding horses, water activities (e.g. rowing, drifting), etc. Generally speaking, rural tourism can be classified into several types: countryside inns, farms and gardens for sightseeing and picking, ecological fishery, folklore exhibition and performance, health care and leisure.

There are several parties involved in the development and business of rural tourism, esp. local governments, businesses, banks, farmers, etc. Some business projects are controlled by outsiders other than local farmers. Rural tourism has become an independent sector in some developed areas. Rural tourism as a whole is becoming more and more standardized and normalized.

4 Development Strategies for Rural Tourism in China

4.1 Making a Comprehensive Program

Rural tourism relates to farmers, agriculture and villages, hence a comprehensive and scientific program is essential for each village and each development project. Those programs involve in land use, housing, transportation, environmental protection and other important items. All the relevant parties need to participate in the drawing up of a plan and decision-making, esp. the active involvement of farmer families[5]. The local governments and those companies are often in a dominant position. By comparison, farmer families are decentralized and independent.

Now the central government and provincial governments have provided relevant policies and goals. Each town or village needs to decide their local program according to their own advantages and disadvantages. There is great difference between coastal areas and inland areas, also between developed areas and under-developed areas. There is no fixed model or program to ensure profit and success, although some experience can be shared. If possible, professional institutions and experts should be invited to the program.

Usually the assignment of interest is the focus, and it should be established in advance. The farmer families need to get their appropriate portion. Usually they provide their houses, land and money to support the development of rural tourism, and they work as employees to provide service.

4.2 Marketing Strategies

As far as the operation of rural tourism, marketing strategies is key factors [6], and they should adjust to the habits of citizens. Marketing strategies involve in four factors: product and service, price, distribution channel, sales promotion. Firstly, the product and service need to be upgraded and classified so that each group of citizens can find their favorites. Secondly, electronic distribution channels should be main sales channels, esp. by Internet websites and call centers. Some local governments and businesses have established some websites. However, only few of them are operated and invested by those villages. Thirdly, more attractive price, flexible service package, and detailed information are necessary.

4.3 Consumer Protection and Guidance

Rural tourism often takes the form of one-day tour. Some business dealers and operators do illegal activities. Some citizens got unlawful infringement during their tour. However, they are reluctant to complain to local government department for the high cost. Therefore local government departments should cooperate with each other in harmony. They need to provide efficient and convenient channels to receive complaints from those tourists, and provide essential guidance. When the cost of safeguarding rights is cut, those tourists will be encouraged to report. Sometimes necessary reward can be a choice. Besides, those law-breakers should get well-deserved punishment.

4.4 Environmental Protection and Sustainable Development

When rural tourism booms around the country, environmental protection and sustainable development become very urgent. It is easy to find kinds of pollution and destruction. People care too much about economic growth and return on investment. However, they got their return at the cost of pollution, destruction and welfare of the coming generations. Therefore all the parties involved should be aware of their activities and impact. What is an ideal situation of rural tourism? Someone said that it would be ideal if the environment did not get worse 100 years later.

5 Conclusions

The rural tourism in China is going through a new phase. The development of rural tourism is at a crucial turning point. It is going to be converted from extensive growth to intensive growth. The rural tourism in China is greatly different from it in Europe and the other developed countries. It is involved in economic growth and social development. The development strategies for rural tourism are as followings: making a comprehensive program, marketing strategies, consumer protection and guidance, environmental protection and sustainable development.

References

1. He, J.: A Study on Rural Tourism Overseas. Tourism Tribune 1, 76–80 (2003)
2. Guo, H., Han, F.: Review on the Development of Rural Tourism in China. Progress in Geography 12, 1597–1605 (2010)
3. Rural Tourism in Beijing, `http://www.ctnews.com.cn`
4. The Chengdu Declaration of Rural Tourism in China, `http://www.chinadaily.com.cn`
5. Guo, L.: Rural Governance in Rural Tourism Development: Reconstruction and Interaction. Journal of Sichuan Normal University (Social Sciences Edition) 3, 16–22 (2008)
6. Fang, Z., Guo, Y.: Marketing of Rural Tourism Product of France and Its Lessons — A Case of Le Relais de Chenillé. Human Geography 5, 76–79 (2007)

Research on Value and Approaches of Tourism Aesthetic Construction

Peiyin Zhang and Chao Ma

Tourism and Cuisine School, Harbin University of Commerce,
Heilongjiang Province, China
zhangpeiyinharbin@126.com,
mybestchris@yahoo.com.cn

Abstract. The tourism aesthetic culture belongs to aesthetic cultural level of tourism culture and it refers to design tourism products by the application of the principle of art and aesthetics. Human being's aesthetic faculties, the aesthetic attributes of traveling and traditional Chinese tourism cultural tastes combine to lay the foundation of tourism aesthetic construction. The value of construction of tourism aesthetic culture lies in the promoting aesthetic through travelling, making up the humanism loss in the tourism product creation and relieving the spiritual exhaustion of life and working. The effective way to construct tourism aesthetic culture is to establish the tourism aesthetic culture system by creating tourism aesthetic behaviors, tourism aesthetic system and tourism aesthetic products.

Keywords: tourism aesthetic culture, construction, value and approach.

1 Connotation and Value of Tourism Aesthetic Culture

The nature of aesthetic culture is to guide and change peoples' tastes and ways of thinking, lifestyles, ethics and education by penetrating into all aspects of life. Just as Nie zhen bin wrote in Artistic Survival , "Aesthetic culture is a in a higher stage of cultural development, at this stage, as the degree of autonomy and perfect of the art and aesthetic part increasing, its underlying principle begins to go to the culture of the autonomous region, "know" and "moral" in the field work to the people's ethical and know and social life and production and consumption of the field and wait for them and to other areas is esthetics and art of the principles of the instruction and training, to be aesthetic or allowed to taste, as an artistic or allowed to art, and thus, the esthetics and art to breaking their "autonomy" or "isolated" and to promote the culture of the aesthetic distillation to make contributions. When people's mode of thinking, lifestyle and educational means all show artistic, the culture is aesthetic culture. [1]

In theory, art is a way of dominating the world and in this way, the aesthetic qualities of a culture refers to the aesthetic relationship between the aesthetic activities and aesthetic object. Aesthetic is able to beyond to a higher level from the

Q. Zhou (Ed.): ISAEBD 2011, Part II, CCIS 209, pp. 191–195, 2011.

present object. In this concept of the framework, we can regard the tourism aesthetic culture as the aesthetic level of tourism culture. It includes not only the cultural realm and effect created by tourists in the tourism activities but also material and cultural production made by tour operators in order to achieve this objective.

By entering the 21st century, consumers receive a variety of information by different channels everyday, and media are eager to promote commercial and vulgar movies. Books are replaced by cyber games; the spiritual life has been changed into short excitement. Most people are neither really serious in reading nor read books in spirit, let alone achieve spiritual growth by learning from great figures form masterpieces, therefore, the spirit of true art and aesthetics are becoming the history of memory as curios. At this time, tourism globalization is gradually drawing the curtain, travelling is becoming a fashion chased by more and more people since they can spend discretionary time and money in travelling. Today, travelling is by no means isolated events, the short moment of individual life but the development of the mass behaviors, even the part of the regular manner. Everyone is equal and a lot of people can be converted into a kind of the decisive factor to lead a common social quality. Therefore, tourism will play an important role by the unprecedented force in the development of human society. Tourism activities are becoming the gene of the human social development by impacts to the individual mind and the whole intelligence structure. It is not difficult for us to notice that the mass tourism has become a cultural phenomenon covering the whole society and a dominant tourism phenomenon since its bulk production aiming at vulgar tastes. It is in pursuit of visual exciting, illegible over show, strengthening of the perceptual immediacy in commercial purposes. "The travel experiences to lifelong regret, regret is life-long" has been the consensus for many tourists. Because many tourism products are secular and commercialized, they generate negative impacts on tourists' values and aesthetic orientation.

Tourism aesthetic construction aims to make traveling as a sublimation of human life and art and a change of space travel during the temporary aesthetic by applying "rule of beauty " in the landscape design, the arts presentation of material and cultural tourism resources. Tourism activities can improve human aesthetic perception of the exhibits in life experiences as a study of the leisure and tourist activities of the human life to the humanistic spirit of compensated by a state — the spirit of the soul free with them, a human cultural evolution has actively promoted optimization of factors.

2 Multi-angle Reflection on the Possibility of Tourism Aesthetic Cultural Construction

2.1 Tourism Aesthetic Cultural Construction Is the Instinct Aesthetic Need of Human Beings

People can get pleasure from the beautiful things no matter where they are. Although we have varied aesthetic standards based on individuals and groups, people without exception all like beauty. Just as the American writer Dissanayake mentioned in Aesthetic People, we concerned about the man is upright, able to use language, utility, but ignore human as aesthetic.

In the millions of years ago, our forefathers were confused about birth, disease, death, natural disasters and other weather phenomenon. They felt the danger or fear, distress and invented to do something with full original passion and mysterious ceremony to know how to explain the nature and life, try to contain them, or to carry them through totems, dance, special costumes, ornaments, visual show in order to overcome fear and obtain console. It is worth a great deal of attention that in the history of human's development, scientific knowledge of world history is short, the history of unscientific and irrational exchanges with nature is long. As Dissanayake mentioned in Aesthetic People that, in the 3 million years of evolution process, aesthetic and art are not individual's behaviors but most serious and important part of human beings. Looking at the world by feelings and emotions has been the human spirit and emotion genes. [2]

2.2 Change Living Space and Contain Aesthetic Values

Travelling is a short experience and purchasing travelling is to buy a "dream" and "special feeling" which is difficult to realize in the life. The charm and value of traveling are to provide the chances of escaping from daily routine, break the chain between human and worldly affairs, create living space transformation .The spirit of tourists reaches the sacred "high" through a unique exile. A daily life is changed into a more independent and free state, it can reveal some aspects that are usually hidden and provide space of the theory and practice for the aesthetic object. Maslow (1968) called these aesthetic appreciation activities as the "peak experiences" which is the highest performance of human being's spiritual production.

As the material and cultural development of the society, aesthetic factors of human material life and cultural life are increasing. There is a continuous artistic tendency in the reality and aesthetic factors and implications are increased in people's living. Meanwhile, the human's physical survival of artistic and aesthetic factors are growing, and in a certain extent reduce the distance between the mental and material fields. In this field and in cultural life continually to the existence of artistic, this modern material in the process of cultural fact change greatly expand the aesthetic theory and practice, though in the modernization process of such material just beginning to talk about artistic country life are far too luxurious, but the space of survival as a means of unique aesthetic do her own leisure activity, it can lead a culture of a separate kingdom within aesthetic.

2.3 The Existence of Aesthetic in the Traditional Chinese Tourism Culture

In ancient China, it was easy to find the importance attached by traditional Chinese culture meaning and the fields and spaces to the travel activities are extensive. The ancient Chinese classical literature told us about this particular enthusiasm to mountain and rivers seems to be very strong and complex. The Chinese saying "sightseeing mountains and waters " means travelling, it is not only the Chinese tourism cultural tradition, but also a sense of humanity.

Human's real like for mountains and waters can be regarded as the origin of the desire to undertake a trip for most people ranging from heroes, great figures to normal citizens. The human spirit of this inclination is a kind of a human society, so the first man of sentiment and human cultures are different types of psychological and common practices and cultural identity, it may be furthered as artificial, urbanized and graduated intelligent of human's environment but it will not loose forever. In Chinese tourist cultural tradition, the "enjoy mountains and waters" of the Confucius is the statement of Confucianism and the perfect personality .The philosophy of Zhuangzi, paying attention to talk with nature, makes up the moral and ethnic loss. After the Confucius and Zhuangzi, the basic conception of traveling for scholars is the combination of nature and human beings.

To personalize all natural segments and make them elegant is an important feature of Chinese culture. In the aesthetic context of China, everything has a life, strange hills, rocks and trees and flowers are showing a natural charming with the human spirit and cultural meaning. Only in china, transforms between physical and human beings are so obvious so that we can easily find that when Chinese scholars are representing the landscape, they are representing both traveling experiences and artistic activities. The aesthetic consideration is no doubt a very noble sublimity of feeling and also an active exercise and a soul clean. However, "romantic gaze" tendency to the nature had been one of the cores of the traditional Chinese tourism culture, rather than the thinking of modern traveler's or group tours. Because the circumstances are different, there was a fundamental change. In the past, most travellers are scholars with different degrees, but at present, it is totally different. For today's mass tourists, travelling is a simple sense of pleasure; the object and the process of the main part of today are physical, emotional feeling. The tour of the objects of beauty, and bitter insights mind and spirit of today, in general is not the results for most popular tourist voluntary initiative to seek. Traditional Chinese scholars a scene in the face of nature than the responsibility of introspection and philosophy to explore the modern tourist group, the more remote and for heavy and dry, today, the public become the main, it should be a great historical progress, At present, we will discuss and think, as if the bridge and fishing as merely an interesting occupation, so the cost of the tourists and tourist development and human environment for the damage is worth? We are based on traditional Chinese tourism culture in aesthetic exist, there is reason to believe in human culture of the holistic approach to the evolution and in need of the aesthetic cultural forms that we must solve the culture of the strategic task.

3 Approaches to Construct Tourism Aesthetic Culture

Establishing a tourism aesthetic cultural system is an effective approach to construct tourism aesthetic culture. Based on the structure of aesthetic culture, we can define the framework of tourism aesthetic cultural system as follows:

3.1 Tourism Aesthetic Manners

Tourism aesthetic activities include at least two aspects, the production and exchange. On the one hand, in terms of material production and exchange, the tourist destination and travelling activities supply should integrate the aesthetic value intention into practical needs based on meeting the needs of the functions. It is required to be applied into the whole process of food, accommodation, transportation, sightseeing, shopping and entertainment to realize the production and creation of material culture.

On the other hand, in terms of spiritual culture of the aesthetic manner, the fundamental is a pleasure to have a mind for the purpose of procedure and enjoy himself. As an intermediary, tour operators aim to stimulate the context of the aesthetic consciousness and tourists in aesthetic knowledge by building an aesthetic sense. The final goal is the realization a rational heroic sentiment between human beings and the soul by the value created by tourists' "romantic gazing" and "meaning".

3.2 Tourism Aesthetic Conception System

Manner is the reflection of aesthetic ideas system, however, the aesthetic culture ideas system includes the concept of the aesthetic values, aesthetic ideas produced by travel agents. Aesthetic value sense regards the aesthetic needs as creation evidence, aesthetic conception as value sense; it is a practical behavior, which is different from non-aesthetic value sense.

3.3 Tourism Aesthetic Production Series

Based on the "rules of beauty", the tourism aesthetic cultural system includes the architecture, transportation, infrastructure and souvenirs harmonized with the nature in the tourist destinations. It also includes tour guide narration with artistic sense, the promotion of aesthetic connation of tourist objects. Tourism aesthetic cultural construction is the integration of truth-seeking, moral-establishing and artistry in the high-tech era which will lead to a new travelling method with more intelligence. In these travelling experiences, tourists can not only obtain rich and deep tourism aesthetic pleasure but also get enlightenment in the process of tourism aesthetic and enjoy the freedom of life and the world to observe the deep meanings.

References

1. Nie, W.B.: Artistic Living, vol. 12, p. 527. Sichuan People's Publish (1997)
2. Dissanayake, E.: Aesthetic People, p. 65. Commercial Press (2004)

New Definition and Related Research of Telecommunication Universal Service under the Broadband Divide Phenomenon in China

Yan Li and Shoulian Tang

Mailbox 164#, School of Economics and Management, Beijing University of Posts and Telecommunications, Xi Tu Cheng Road 10, Haidian District, Beijing, China
soec_casey@sina.com

Abstract. Universal service can be a good solution for information differences brought by the digital divide among different countries and regions. Yet in the world, modern telecommunication technology is experiencing a great revolution, the "digital divide" has begun to be "broadband divide", and this makes the universal service also produce a corresponding change and development. Therefore, this article would use the methods of contrast, induction and deduction to analyze different cases, combined with the view of broadband penetration, access and convergence of the three-network. Finally, we propose a new definition &standard of universal service for China, and we also make several suggestions about amendment and supplement on the category &scope change of universal service, which is based on our new definition.

Keywords: Telecom, Universal service, Digital divide, Broadband divide, Penetration, New definition, Scope & category.

1 Introduction

Universal service can be a good solution for information differences brought by the digital divide among different countries and regions. Yet in the world, the "digital divide" has begun to be "broadband divide" with popularity of the broadband and internet access, the universal service also produced a corresponding change and development. Therefore, this article would use the methods of contrast, induction and deduction to analyze different cases from the telecom industry and authoritative reports &papers. In the end, we propose a new definition of universal service for China, combined with the view of broadband penetration, access and convergence of the three-network. And we also make several suggestions about amendment and supplement on the category &scope change of universal service, based on our new definition.

2 Digital Divide Begin to Change into Broadband Divide

With the rapid development of telecommunication industry and its convergence with broadcast and information technology, the penetration of new business and facilities based on broadband internet access is getting more and more attention by developed

Q. Zhou (Ed.): ISAEBD 2011, Part II, CCIS 209, pp. 196–202, 2011.

and developing countries. It also prompts people to reconsider the scope and the obligation essence of the universal service, expecting it constantly getting modified and supplemented in step with the fast development of network and technology to narrow the information disparity for diverse social groups, caused by the divide of internet access.

The most obvious feature is that "digital divide" begins to change into "broadband divide ", which refers to the information difference between the groups of those who use broadband to enjoy interactive video and audio service at home and those who could only use narrowband to enjoy service based on data and text transmission. *Information Society Statistics Profiles 2009*[1] shows that the penetration of fixed broadband in developed countries is far higher than those in developing countries, making the phenomenon of "broadband divide" so obviously.

This so called disparity between developed and developing countries shows multiple growths in broadband access and penetration. Beside the country differences, the broadband divide[2] also appears between urban and rural areas in each country of the world; we further summarized the data from *Chinese Internet Development Report 2009*[3], *FCC Universal Service Monitoring*[4] *Report 2010, ITU Information Society Development Report 2010*[5] and related website and obtained the broadband access condition of several major countries worldwide, as Fig.1 shows.

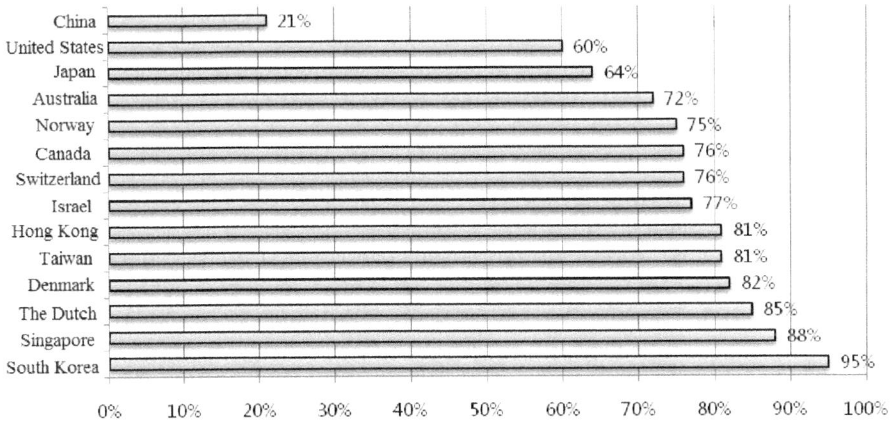

Fig. 1. Urban family broadband popularizing rate per 100 inhabitants (2009) . This shows a figure that the unban family broadband rate in China is only 21%, which is much lower than it in developed countries, even lower than the average level of them.

The report also shows that the coverage rate of administrative villages is higher, but there are still many remote, scattered rural areas, which are not connected with broadband service. Overall, other countries' data show the basic development direction for universal service: broadband internet access. Take European for example, *OFCOM Universal Service Survey Report 2010 Edition* shows that EU's goal is about to let all the European people to use broadband Internet by the end of 2010. In order to observe the relevant data selected toward broadband growth rate of

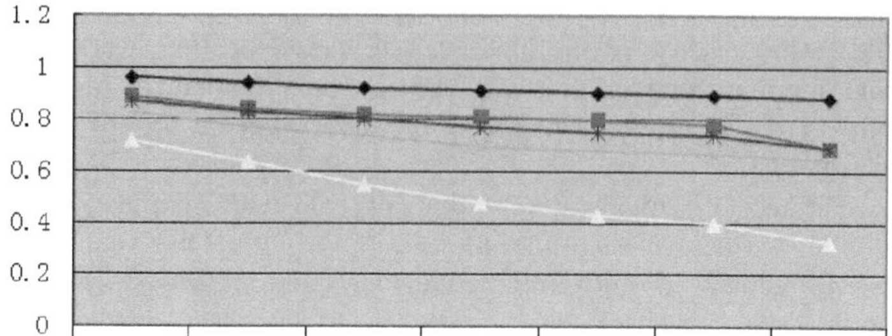

	2001	2002	2003	2004	2005	2006	2007
C&U DDI- PC	0.96	0.94	0.92	0.91	0.9	0.89	0.88
C&U DDI- Internet	0.89	0.84	0.82	0.81	0.8	0.78	0.69
C&U DDI- Phone	0.72	0.64	0.55	0.48	0.43	0.4	0.33
C&U DDI- M. Phone	0.83	0.77	0.74	0.7	0.68	0.67	0.65
C&U DDI	0.87	0.83	0.8	0.77	0.75	0.74	0.69

Fig. 2. Changes in Digital divide index between China and EU(C&U DDI means China and European Digital Divide Index, M. Phone Means mobile phone). The rapid internet development of Europe, from 2001 to 2007, prompted the internet penetration rate increased by 2.25 times. Though Chinese Internet penetration rate reached 16 % from the original 2.64%, 6.06 times' growth, Chinese overall development level is still less than the level of Europe in 2001. On the other hand, although the digital dividend index between Europe and China reduced from 87% to 69%, the broadband divide appears with the development of new telecom technologies.

European changes as reference and contrast to our country, we found some data from *White Paper on China's Informatization 2009——China Digital Divide Report 2008*[6], as Fig.2 shows.

In summary, as worldwide broadband internet access is getting popularity increasingly, there are two "how" problems need to solve: how to adjust the universal service policies to ease the "broadband divide" phenomenon, which brings Chinese urban and rural information differences, and how to improve broadband network coverage and penetration[7]. Solution to these problems will become the focus of our future study for the development of telecom industry in China.

3 The New Definition of Universal Service under the "Broadband Divide" Phenomenon for China

Facing the convergence and the broadband dividend phenomenon, China needs to have a new definition of universal service, so in order to help us define it, experience learning is indispensable. We chose three world telecom development powers' definition of universal service to observe as representative examples, such as the United States, France and Britain.

United States' latest definition of universal service is from the *Internet Bill of Universal Service 2006*, which is that: providing fast, efficient, national and global wire line, wireless and broadband internet access service with reasonable charges and completed facilities to the United States, who are treated equally, regardless of race, color, religion, national origin or gender.

French latest definition of universal service is from the *Universal Service Regulations for Europe 2003*, which is that: providing quality services at affordable price to everyone, including free access to emergency calls, number directory inquiry service, delivering print electronic phone book, nationwide public pay telephone and broadband internet access.

British latest definition of universal service is also from the *Universal Service Regulations for Europe 2003*, which is basically the same as France.

Chinese existing definition of universal service is based on the *Implementation Scheme of Village Phone Project and Countryside Informatization Activities 2010*[8] (short for the Scheme), which was promulgated by Ministry of Industry and Information Technology of the People's Republic of China in April 2010. This scheme puts forward the goal of universal service 2010: 100% administrative villages can make phone calls, 100% villages and towns can connect to the internet, that is what we mean two hundred goals, short for every village can make phone calls, every town can connect to internet(Cun cun tong dian hua, xiang xiang neng shang wang). At the same time, early in 2010, the State Council Executive Meeting hosted by Premier Wen Jiabao said that China will accelerate the convergence of telecommunication network, broadcasting network and internet network for the triple play. We could find that most of the arrangements and deployments are based and focus on broadband construction and penetration, so the two hundred goals become the form of three hundred goals: every village can make phone calls, every town can connect to the internet, every township can receive the TV programs (cun cun tong dianhua, xiang xiang neng shang wang ,cun cun tong dian shi) .

When the convergence of three-network brought by new telecom technologies' appearances, no matter the telecommunication companies or internet companies, who provides users with service based on broadcast, television and video programs, or broadcasting &television department provides users with IPTV, digital radio and two-way interconnection VOD programs, or some related information communications and internet information services, these services they provide need to establish on the connection of broadband network with the feature of stable and fast.

Therefore, we can make the new definition of universal service for China under the broadband divide phenomenon: providing all people with fast, efficient, nationwide wired, wireless communications and broadband internet access service, which contains low and reasonable charges, comprehensive facilities. Especially, in order to meet the needs of users watching online video programs, the speed of broadband network connection should be no less than 768Kbps ~ 1.5Mbps. The requirement for broadband connection speed is based on the report: *Review of the Universal Service Obligation from OFCOM*[9]. It says that 768Kbps is the lowest limit for users downloading video programs, running applications on the internet, applying broadband data services and communications. If broadband connection speed is below the limit, the user cannot simultaneously apply these data communication business and service, even no mention of the convergence.

Compare to the previous basic three hundred goals of universal service in China, based on solving the informatization differences between urban and rural area caused by broadband dividend phenomenon, the new definition of universal service for China could be concentrated as one goal for all: every village and township can connect to broadband(xiang xiang shang kuan dai).

4 The Scope Change of Universal Service under the "Broadband Divide" Phenomenon for China

Relevant scope of the universal service contain the basic content, cost accounting principles, related management mechanism, policy and obligation undertakers. In this part, we also choose the United States, British and France as our standard of summarizing and analyzing.

The responsibility distribution mechanism[10] of universal service in U.S. are classified into four different items, responsible by different types of service providers or network operators, charged with different level of the universal service fund. In the United States, all the internet service providers, mobile operators, VoIP providers and access providers, they must pay the universal service fund, regardless of whether they are eligible to receive the fund. On the other hand, the Universal Service Management Committee and Company[11], which are independent with the government, are in charge of the obligations and the fund. We need to note that current laws related to universal service in the United States do not explicitly point out the broadcasting &television companies should take the obligations and pay the fund, but we argue that all the members that pay the fund in the United States have one thing in common: the business they provide are taking up the bandwidth to communicate. Therefore, we boldly speculate that after the convergence, the broadcasting &television companies in the U.S. need to use bandwidth resources, so they must pay the universal service fund and undertake the relevant obligations.

The responsibility distribution mechanism of universal service in France is similar to the United States. The French government binds the universal service obligations and the operator license together. It means that all the operators providing telecom services, must take the universal service obligations, and pay the fund. The Management Committee and the Fund Management Committee, which are independent with the government, constitute the universal service management system. Just like the United States, the relevant laws in France are not clear about the universal service obligations of internet and broadcasting &television companies, but we can anticipate that they must undertake the relevant obligations and pay the fund, as long as their services are using the broadband resources.

As well as the telecommunication universal service in Britain, which is affected by the *Universal Service Regulations for Europe 2003,* makes the provisions of broadband internet access as its basic content. While the British government also binds the universal service obligations with operator license, and claim that all citizens can connect to the broadband internet by 2010. As for the mechanism of responsibility distribution, British Telecom (BT) is now the main discharger of the universal service obligations for United Kingdom. And for the surveillance and implementation, OFTEL (Office of Telecommunications) is mainly responsible. The aspect of paying universal service fund is similar with France telecom.

Therefore, the amendment and supplement of the universal service scope under the broadband dividend phenomenon mainly contain the following three aspects:

Add the obligations of universal service implementation to the telecom operators' licenses. Under the premise of the convergence, if the enterprise's services use the broadband resources, then it must take the basic obligation of universal service. Meanwhile, any fixed-line operators, mobile operators, internet providers, VoIP providers, and related SP, AP,EP, they should be considered as the obligatory providers of universal service, regardless of whether they are qualified to accept the fund or not.

Add broadband access and broadband internet into the basic content of universal service.

With the new technologies and the broadband penetration, it remains need to have regulators that are independent with the government departments, which is in charge of the regulatory and implementation of the universal service obligations. The regulators should still use the mode of universal service fund to implement and distribute the relevant obligations.

5 Conclusion

If we review the modern convergence of telecom, we'll find that broadband access become the basic content of the universal service. Table 1 ("O" means "Yes") shows that the United States, Britain and France have modified their range and definition of universal service since 2004 to increase the broadband penetration. Therefore, we can be sure that in the future, the focus on development of telecommunication universal service in China will be on the broadband penetration and promotion.

Table 1. Changes of universal services in U.S, Britain and France

Details / Country	Modify the laws of universal service for broadband access after 2004	Broadband access as the basic content of universal service	Universal service fund system	Pay universal service fund on using broadband resources	Universal Service/ Universal Access (US/UA)
U.S.	O	O	O	O	US
UK	O	O	O	O	US
France	O	O	O	O	US

References

1. ITU In preparation for the World Telecommunication Development Conference. ITU : Information Society Statistics Profiles 2009 (May 7, 2009)
2. Zhang, X., Lin, T.: Telecommunications Universal Service and Informatization in Rural Areas. Research Commissioned by Advisory Committee for State (February 14, 2005)
3. China Internet Association: China Internet Development Report 2009 (July 1, 2010)
4. FCC's Reference Information Center: Universal Service Monitoring Report (August 2010)
5. ITU In preparation for the World Telecommunication Development Conference. ITU : Information Society Development Report 2010 (March 23, 2010)
6. Chinese State Information Center: White Paper on China's Informatization 2009——China Digital Divide Report 2008 (April 10, 2009)
7. Laffont, J.-J., Zhang, X.: Universal Service Obligations in Developing Countries. China Economic Quarterly (February 2004)
8. Ministry of Industry and Information Technology of the People's Republic of China: Implementation Scheme of Village Phone Project and Countryside Informatization Activities 2010(Cun Cun Tong Dianhua Project and Informatization Xia Xiang Huo Dong Implementation Opinions). S. MIIT Management Function [2010] No.118 (April 2010)
9. OFCOM (Office OF Communications): Review of the Universal Service Obligation (March 14 ,2009)
10. FCC's Reference Information Center: Universal Service Monitoring Report (August 2009)
11. THE EUROPEAN PARLIAMENT AND OF THE COUNCIL: On Universal Service and Users' Rights Relating to Electronic Communications Networks and Services (Universal Service Directive). J. Official Journal of the European Communities (March 7, 2002)

The Impact of Customer Participation on Service Quality Improvement – An Empirical Study in Tianjin Hotels

Jiaxin Wang[1,2]

[1] School of Management, Tianjin University, Tianjin 300072, China
[2] College of History and Culture, Tianjin Normal University, Tianjin 300387, China
sylvia_wong6@163.com

Abstract. This paper proposed four dimensions of customer participation in service purchase. They are information collection, participation in service design and standard build-up, interaction with employees, and word of mouth delivery. The paper analyzed how these customer participative behaviors shorten the gap between customer expectation and perception. To test the theoretical analysis this research distributed questionnaires in Tianjin hotels China. Using 185 completed surveys from hotel customers, the paper did an empirical study to explore the relationship between customer participation and service quality. Independent-samples T test and path analysis confirmed that the more participation a customer devoted in a service process, the shorter the gap between his expectation and perception. That is active customer participation helps to improve service quality.

Keywords: Customer behavior, Participation, Service quality, SERVQUAL.

1 Introduction

In the field of service management, the study of service quality has been well researched because both the operators of the enterprises and researchers have clearly realized the impact of service quality on enterprise performance. At present service quality depends mainly on the gap between customer expectation and perception. Thus, the two factors determine the gap in service quality. However, customers not only expect and perceive service quality; they also participate in the whole service process. In this process, the attitude and behavior of the customer also impacts service quality. So the author argues that customer participation, as an important factor influencing service quality, cannot be ignored. Nonetheless, throughout more than 20-year evolution of service management literature, the research about the relationship between customer participation in service and service quality has received much less attention than has each of these concepts separately. Alternatively, the exact manner and magnitude of the influence of customer participation on service quality has been less fully developed, theoretically, and essentially ignored, empirically.

The aim of this study was to assess the impact of customer participation on service quality and how they shorten the gap between customer expectation and perception. In order to certify the theoretical analysis, the paper used an empirical study in hotel industry which is typical in service industry.

Q. Zhou (Ed.): ISAEBD 2011, Part II, CCIS 209, pp. 203–210, 2011.

2 Literature Review

2.1 Service Quality

The most common definition of service quality is the comparison customers make between their expectations and their perception of the service received (Berry, Zeithaml and Parasuraman, 1985; Berry, Parasuraman and Zeithaml, 1988; Grönroos, 1984; Lewis and Boom, 1983). Lehtinen and Lehtinen (1982) define quality as a two dimensional concept of process and output. Grönroos also defines two dimensions of service quality; namely, technical quality or what is received by the customer and functional quality or how the service is provided. This latter dimension of service quality is seen as the more important aspect, as there is a psychological interaction taking place during the service transaction.

Through their pioneering research work, Parasuraman, Berry and Zeithaml (1990) have developed their widely quoted gaps model. In this model five gaps affecting service quality, they were gap1= Customer Expectation – Management Perception Gap; gap2= Management Perception – Service Quality Specification Gap; gap3= Service Quality Specification – Service Delivery Gap; gap4= Service Delivery – External Communication Gap; and gap5= Expected Service – Perceived Service Gap. Gap 5 was the function of the other four gaps, namely gap5=f (gap1, gap2, gap3, gap4). The lower the value of gap5 indicates the higher service quality.

In this research we adopt the most common definition of service quality that the comparison customers make between their expectations and perceptions of the service received. Based on the conceptual model of service quality we analyzed causes of formation of the gaps and how customer behaviors can make them shorter, namely, improving service quality.

2.2 Customer Behaviors

Customers engage in preparation behaviors to ready themselves for service encounters. These behaviors include seeking referrals, researching alternative providers, and gathering information prior to the encounter. By managing relationships and providing social support (Adelman et al., 1994), customers act as partial employees (Bowen, 1986) or even supervisors in motivating service providers to perform. Information exchange involves exchanging relevant information (Hanser and Muchinsky, 1978) to clarify requirements and other service parameters.

When relating the various behaviors to effort and satisfaction, Youngdahl and Kellogg (1997) found that relationship building correlated most strongly with both high levels of satisfaction and low levels of effort. Preparation, involving moderate levels of effort, also correlated strongly with high levels of satisfaction. Information exchange relate to about an even mix of satisfied and dissatisfied service customers while involving moderate levels of effort. Interventions seldom led to a satisfactory outcome, and customers expended high levels of effort when they intervened in service delivery. The researchers provided several prescriptions for service design and delivery to accommodate the desirable behaviors of relationship building and preparation , improve upon organizations' ability to exchange information, and detect early warning signs to trigger recovery before customers feel the need to intervene.

Zeithmal and Bitner (2004) customer behavior can be divided into five categories, they are (1) requirement recognition; (2) information collection; (3) assessment of alternatives; (4) purchase and consume; and (5) after consuming assessment.

Therefore, in this paper customer participation can be divided into four dimensions: information collection, participation in service design and standard build-up, interaction with employees, and word of mouth delivery.

3 Analysis of Customer Participation Shorten the Gap of Service Quality

3.1 The Impact of Information Collection on Shorten the Gap

Gap 1 is the difference between management perception and customer expectation of service. Several factors may contribute to gap1, such as the insufficient market survey about customer demands, inaccurate market analysis; lacking of the knowledge about customer requirements and expectations; the unsmoothed communication system, as well as failing to retain the customer and strengthen the relationship between service supplier and customer, namely the relationship marketing is unsuccessful.

If customers cooperate during market research actively may lead gap 1 greatly shorten or even eliminate. In addition, building up relationship with customer and keeping in touch with them will help to catch the changing trend of customer requirements and expectations. Thus, information collection can shorten the gap between management perception and customer expectation of service, which will improve service quality.

3.2 The Impact of Participation in Service Design and Standard Build-Up on Shorten the Gap

Gap 2 is the difference between service quality specification and management perception. The main reasons causing gap2 lie in: lacking of customer definition about service standard and the process management focused on customer, which induce the hotel cannot provide the satisfied service to customers.

To make use of customers' knowledge and outside resources, one of the effective ways is that let customers participate in designing and developing service products under the essential support provided by service supplier. The customers can design the function, quality standard and providing time of the service products that they need. This process not only satisfied customer, but also help to design the service products accord with the customers' needs. Customer participation could form customization in a certain degree as well. For instance, the restaurant of a hotel allows customers to choose the salad and Pizza size according to their needs, and the cook could bake the popular size Pizza continuously. Actually, it is a way to provide products which satisfy customers. By doing so, gap2 can be greatly shortened. Meanwhile, service quality can be improved a lot.

3.3 The Impact of Interaction with Employee Actively on Shorten the Gap

Gap 3 represents the difference between service delivery and service quality specification. Customers and employees cannot fulfill their duties during the service process and the confliction between customers and employees may lead to gap3.

Customer affirmation and commendation can motivate employees of service enterprises. Friendly interaction between customers and employees will promote the service level to a better state. Active cooperation and communication from customers with employees can make the employees much happier to serve for the customers. During service process customers play a dual role, both receiver and coadjutant of the service. Cooperating and communicating with employees make the service experience memorable, thus gap 3 will be effectively shortened.

3.4 The Impact of Word of Mouth Delivery on Shorten the Gap

Gap 4 indicates the difference between external communication and service delivery. Propagandas like advertisements may make customers overestimate service levels that cause customers form extortionate expectations in their minds.

Positive word of mouth is most welcomed and important in marketing. Word of mouth is one of the most important decisive factors which affects customers choose a certain service supplier. Customers prefer to get the recommendation from those who have certain experiences in a specific service supplier, but not only from the advertisements. Moreover, the introduction from friends and relatives can be more close to the reality of the service supplier. This will reduce the customers' overestimation and shorten the gap between customer expectation and perception of service quality.

Gap 5 is the function of gap1, gap2, gap3, and gap4. Therefore the four dimensions of customer participation can make the gap5 much closer according to making gap1, gap2, gap3, and gap4 shorten. Thus service quality is improved.

4 Methodology

4.1 Survey Instruments

The questionnaire included three sections: SERVQUAL, customer participation scale items, and basic personal information.

SERVQUAL scale is one of the few tested instruments available to measure service quality developed by Parasuraman et al. in 1985 and later refined. It has been widely used to measure service quality in different service contexts, such as health care (Lam, 1997), tourism (Tribe and Snaith, 1998) et al. It has also been widely tested for its validity and reliability (Babakus and Boller, 1992; Bolton and Drew, 1991; Cronin and Taylor, 1992, 1994). Fick and Ritchie (1991) applied the SERVQUAL instrument to hotels and restaurants. Their findings demonstrated the usefulness of the instrument in measuring service quality in hotels. In this part the respondents were asked to evaluate their perceptions and expectations on 22 service attributes with a 5-point Likert scale (1=strongly disagree, and 5=strongly agree).

The second section of the questionnaire is customer-participation scale items which were used to test the extent of the customer's effort when they are involved in the service process. The questionnaire addressed the customer's participative behavior framework with respect to information collection, participation in service design and standard build-up, interaction with employees, and word of mouth delivery. After modifying the questionnaire by pilot study, KMO value in factor analysis of the modified questionnaire was 0.743 and the significance level of Bartlett's test was at 0.000. All of these data indicate that validity of customer participation questionnaire is good. Customer participation was measured with a series of 18 items on a 5-point Likert scale (1=strongly disagree, and 5=strongly agree).

The third section of the questionnaire is the measures designed to collect demographic information, such as gender, age and education background.

4.2 Sample

The data for this study were collected from Tianjin hotel industry. 300 questionnaires were distributed in four hotels. A total of 217 questionnaires were returned. Before recording the data, the author visually inspected all questionnaires for missing items and haphazard answers. And a total 185 cases remained (i.e. response rate was 61.67%) after excluding the unusable questionnaires.

Of the 185 respondents, 53.5% were male and 46.5% were female. 57.3% of the respondents were between 19-35 years old, followed by 36 to 59 (about 37.3%). Only 2.2% were 18 years of age and under, and 3.2% were 60 and over. Majority of the respondents (57%) had college or above education, followed by high school and vocational education graduates (38%). Only 5% of respondents had some or no high school education.

4.3 Reliability and Validity

The reliability of the instruments was tested by using Cronbach's alpha. Nearly all of the Cronbach's alpha scores (see Table 1 and Table 2) were above 0.70(except reliability of customer expectation, which the Cronbach's alpha values was 0.68), ranging from 0.68 to 0.80 for customer expectation of SERVQUAL, 0.72 to 0.82 for customer perception of SERVQUAL, and 0.76 to 0.91 for the dimensions of customer participation scale. And the synthetically Cronbach's alpha of SERVQUAL was 0.82 for customer expectation, 0.90 for customer perception, and 0.92 for customer participation questionnaire. These alpha scores indicate sufficient reliability for the study (Nunnally and Bernnstein, 1994).

Table 1. Reliability of SERVQUAL

Dimensions	Items	Alpha Value of Customer Expectation	Alpha Value of Customer Perception
Tangibles	4	0.73	0.82
Reliability	5	0.68	0.73
Responsiveness	4	0.76	0.77
Assurance	4	0.80	0.77
Empathy	5	0.80	0.72
Synthetical Cronbach's alpha		0.82	0.90

Table 2. Reliability of customer participation scale

Dimensions	Items	Alpha Value
Information collection	4	0.81
Participation in service design and standard build-up	7	0.91
Interaction with employees actively	4	0.83
Word of mouth delivery	3	0.76
Synthetical Cronbach's alpha of the measures		0.92

Validity of the SERVQUAL instrument was not tested in this research, because it has been widely tested by former researchers in many areas including in hotels. And for customer participation scale, although this section has been pre-screened, a scale validation was still accomplished by using factor analysis. The result of the analysis showed that all the items of the instruments had a good fit and KMO value in factor analysis was 0.838 and the significance level of Bartlett's test was at 0.000.

5 Result

This study made a comparison between two different groups of high participation and low participation customers. High participation customers are who scored the customer participation scale above 4(include 4), and low participation customers are who rated the questionnaire below 4. The result of independent samples T test (Table 3) showed 2-tailed significance value was at p<0.001 level, which indicated there was significant difference between two groups on service quality.

Meanwhile, Path analysis (Table 4) showed significant negative effect of the four dimensions of customer participation on the gap: information collection with a path coefficient of -0.248 (t = -3.831, significant at the p< 0.005 level); joining in service design and standard building-up having a path coefficient of -0.182 and a corresponding t value of -2.736, significant at the p<0.01 level; active interaction with employees on the gap between customer expectation and perception, yielding a path

Table 3. Difference in service quality between high and low customer participation

	Levine' Test for Equality of Variances		T-Test for Equality of Means				
	F	Sig.	t	df	Sig. (2-tailed)	Mean Different	Std. Error Different
G Equal variances assumed	15.863	.000***	10.472	183	.000	.6714	.06412
Equal variances not assumed			9.916	118.049	.000***	.6714	.06770

Notes: G=Service Quality; Significance Level: ***<0.001.

Table 4. Results of path analysis

Dimensions	β	SE β	Standardized β	t value	P
Information collection	- 0.174	0.047	-.248	-3.831	.000
Joining in service design and standard building-up	- 0.147	0.052	-.182	-2.736	.005
Active interaction with employees	- 0.243	0.047	-.322	-5.023	.000
Word of mouth delivery	- 0.148	0.044	-.197	-3.305	.001

Dependent Variable: The service quality gap between customer expectation and perception.

coefficient of -0.332 ($t = -5.023$, significant at the $p<0.005$ level); and word of mouth delivery with a path coefficient of -0.197 ($t = -3.305$, significant at the $p< 0.01$ level). That is the higher customer participation, the shorter the gap between his expectation and perception of the service.

6 Conclusion

The purpose of this study is to discuss the influence of customer participative behaviors on service quality improvement. A theoretical analysis has been developed at first to understand the issue better. Support has been found in the literature review of service quality, customer behaviors and the analysis of the effect of customer participative behavior on the service quality improvement, which allow the author to propose an empirical analysis for testing.

The empirical analysis of the relationship between customer participation and the gap between customer expectation and perception of service quality has been done. Different dimensions of customer participation have been identified including information collection, participation in service design and standard build-up, interaction with employees and word of mouth delivery. Furthermore, we divided customer participation into two groups, high participation and low participation. The result of independent samples T test suggested that there was significant difference between two groups on service quality. And path analysis showed that customer participation has a direct and negative relationship with the gap, indicating that the more customer participation in service process will lead to higher service quality. But different aspects of customer participation do not contribute equally to service quality. For example, the effect of participation in service design and standard build-up on service quality is not as strong as other customer participation behaviors. Anyway, however, the results of this research suggest active and high level of customer participation is considerable significant to service quality improvement. Thus customer participation in service should be encouraged and inspired.

References

1. Adelman, M.B., Ahuvia, A., Goodwin, C.: Beyond smiling, social support and service quality. In: Rust, R.T., Oliver, R.L. (eds.) Service Quality, pp. 139–171. Sage, Thousand Oaks (1994)
2. Babakus, E., Boller, G.W.: An empirical assessment of the SERVQUAL scale. Journal of Business Research 24, 253–268 (1992)

3. Berry, L.L., Zeithaml, V.A., Parasuraman, A.: Quality Counts in Business, Too. Business Horizens 31, 46 (1985)
4. Bolton, R.N., Drew, J.H.: A Longitudinal Analysis of the Impact of Service Changes on Customer Attitudes. Journal of Marketing 55, 1–9 (1991)
5. Bowen, D.E.: Managing customers as human resources in service organizations. Human Resource Management 25, 371–383 (1986)
6. Cronin, J.J., Taylor, S.A.: Measuring Service Quality: A Reexamination and Extension. Journal of Marketing 56(3), 55–68 (1992)
7. Cronin, J.J., Taylor, S.A.: SERVPERF versus SERQUAL: Reconciling Performance-Based and Perceptions-Minus Expectations Measurement of Service Quality. Journal of Marketing 58(1), 125–131 (1994)
8. Fick, G.R., Ritchie, J.R.B.: Measuring service quality in the travel and tourism industry. Journal of Travel Research, 2–9 (Fall 1991)
9. Grönroos, C.: A Service Quality Model and its Market Implication. European Journal of Marketing 18(4), 36–44 (1984)
10. Hanser, L.M., Muchinsky, P.M.: Work as an information environment. Organizational Behavior and Human Performance 12, 50–76 (1978)
11. Lam, S.K.: SERVQUAL: a tool for measuring patients' opinions of hospital service quality in Hong Kong. Total Quality Management 8, 145–152 (1997)
12. Lehtinen, U., Lehtinen, J.R.: Service Quality: A Study of Quality Dimensions, Service Management Institutes, Helsinki (1982)
13. Lewis, R.C., Boom, B.H.: Customer care in service organizations. In: Johnston, R. (ed.) The Management of Service Operations: Proceedings of the UK Operations Management Association Annual International Conference, pp. 183–194. IFS Publications, Bedford (1983)
14. Nunnally, J.C., Bernstein, I.H.: Psychometric Theory, 3rd edn. McGraw-Hill, New York (1994)
15. Parasuraman, A., Zeithaml, V.A., Berry, L.L.: A conceptual model of service quality and its implications for future study research. Journal of Marketing 49, 41–50 (1985)
16. Parasuraman, A., Zeithaml, V.A., Berry, L.L.: An empirical test of the extended gaps model of service quality. Marketing Science Institute working paper, pp. 90-122 (1990)
17. Tribe, J., Snaith, T.: From SERVQUAL to HOLSAT: Holiday satisfaction in Varadero, Cuba. Tourism Management 19(1), 25–34 (1998)
18. Youngdahl, W.E., Kellogg, D.L.: The relationship between service customer's quality assurance behaviors, satisfaction, and effort: A cost of quality perspective. Journal of Operations Management 15, 19–32 (1997)
19. Zeithaml, V.A., Bitner, M.J.: Service Marketing: Integrating Customer Focus Across the Firm, 3rd edn. McGraw-Hill, New York (2003)

Choice Preferences on Tourist Resorts in Northeast China

Guangyong Zou and Jianhua Zhang

Department of Ecotourism, Shanghai Business School, P.R.China, 201400
zouguangyong@gmail.com

Abstract. The paper filled the empirical gaps in the study of market choice in Northeast China. At first, we designed a survey questionnaire based on four main characteristics of tourist resorts. Then we made the investigation for interviewees who are chosen with random sampling at Pudong Airport, Capital Airport and Longjia Airport, and we drew the differences and similarities on choice preferences of local market and remote developed market in China (See Figure). Furthermore, we tested our conclusions by generalizing related characteristics of tourist resorts in Northeast China. Finally, we raised classification and planning advices on tourist resorts in Northeast China.

Keywords: Northeast China, Tourist resort, Choice preference.

1 Introduction

Tourism research in northeast mainly focused on industrial tourism as well as rural tourism tourism development for the resource-based city, colonial relic tourism. Now exploitation mode had been transferring from resource or products-oriented to modularization-oriented. So tourist resort should initiate and participate in the division so as to release innovative potential among modules to a deeper degree. Empirical analysis tested that tourism products circulation is notability influence. Obviously, tourist resorts in northeast need consider their tourism products plan from that standpoint. The paper analyzes the selection differences, so that the empirical study on the selection differences to Northeast tourist resorts is filled.

2 Investigation and Data

2.1 Investigative Methods and Process

The study conducts on-the-spot investigation of questionnaire. The markets are mainly divided into northeast, developed areas, overseas areas and others. Between August 2009 and March 2010, we gave the questionnaires of 528 for survey in random at Shanghai Pudong Airport, Beijing's Capital Airport and Changchun's Longjia Airport respectively, among which, a total of 162 usable responses were received out of an eligible of 180 at Longjia Airport, representing a 90% response rate, and 336 done out

Q. Zhou (Ed.): ISAEBD 2011, Part II, CCIS 209, pp. 211–217, 2011.

of 348 at Pudong Airport and Capital Airport, representing a 97% one. Furthermore, 44% from Jing-Jin-Tang and 38% from Yangtze Delta.

2.2 Investigating Findings

2.2.1 Basic Statistical Characteristics of the Poll

Table 1. Basic statistical characteristics of the poll

Individual Characteristic	Category	Percentage	
		Northeast China	Area Surrounding the Bo Sea and Yangtze Delta
Gender	male	63%	53%
	female	37%	47%
Age	Under 18	6%	2%
	19-30	49%	41%
	31-50	33%	47%
	51-60	6%	5%
	Above 61	6%	5%
Occupation	National Public Servant	6%	7%
	Business Executives	17%	23%
	Employees in Enterprises and Institutions	11%	25%
	Small Shopkeepers and Owners of One-man Business	27%	11%
	Freelancer	6%	9%
	Student	27%	16%
	Retired Person	6%	9%
Monthly Profit	Under 5000	87%	11%
	5000-6000	15%	35%
	6000-10000	0%	38%
	Above 10000	0%	16%
Plan on Vacation Time	Frequently	11%	39%
	Within 1 to 2 Years	63%	31%
	Within 2 to 5 Years	5%	5%
	A Great Deal of Uncertainty	21%	25%

2.2.2 Preferences Analysis about Market Choice

(1) Tourist cognitive preferences for tourist resort

We can conclude that the first is general in 'famous scenic spots' and the second does in 'town surrounding them. There aren't big difference between both markets .

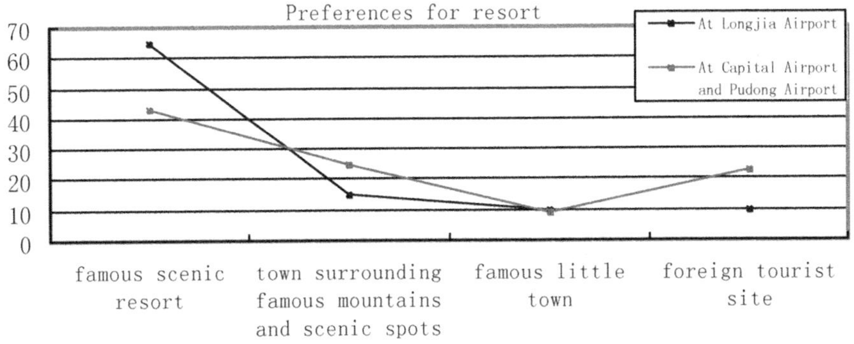

Fig. 1. Cognitive preferences for regional tourist resorts

(2) Tourist preference for characteristics of tourist site in northeast china

Tourists like general in 'ice-snow landscape', especially the tourists of the developed area. Cool mountains and waters, local historical human rank first three.

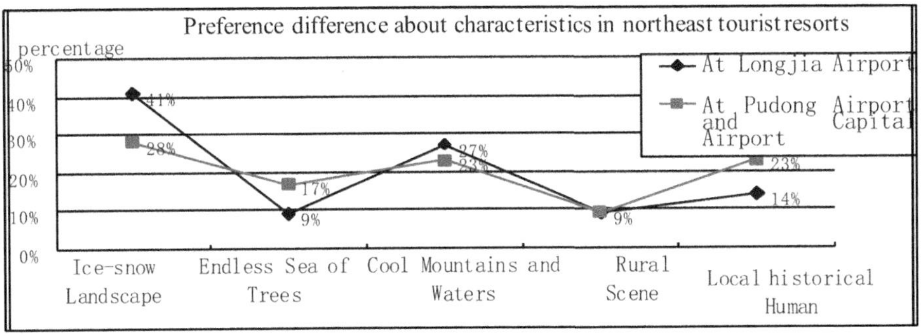

Fig. 2. Cognitive difference of tourism program in Northeast China

(3) Program preference for tourism town in Northeast China

Tourists like general to 'taste local characteristic foods' and 'health preserving and body-building'. There aren't obvious cognitive differences between two markets

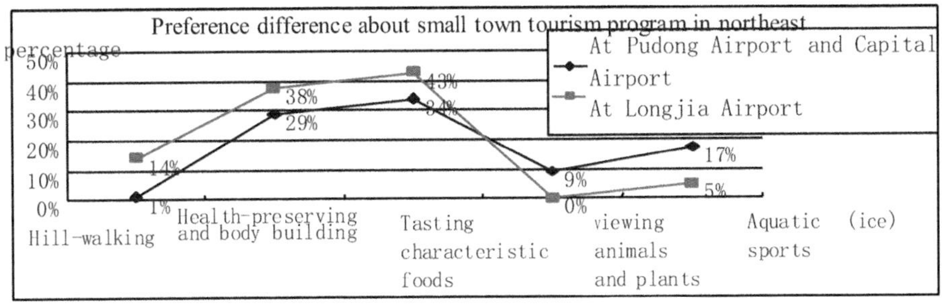

Fig. 3. Cognitive difference about small town tourism program in Northeast China

(4) Preferences for styles of tourism town

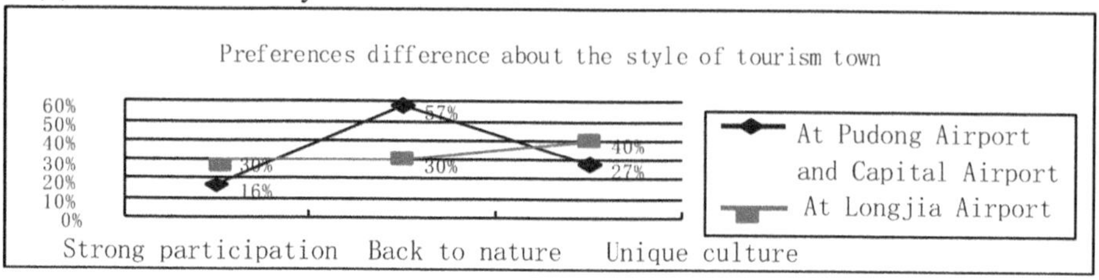

Fig. 4. Cognitive difference about tourism town in Northeast China

From Figure 4, there are obviously cognitive differences between two markets. Tourists from developed area mostly choose 'back-to nature', which account for 57%, however, tourists from the northeast mostly do 'unique culture'.

3 Difference Comparison about Preferences for Market Choice

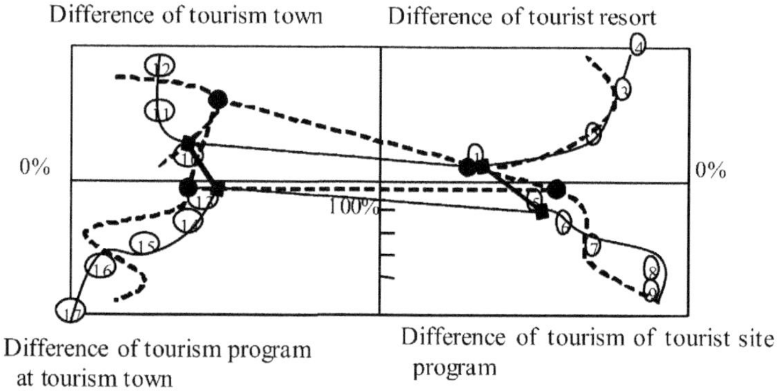

Note : —— shows interviewees at Longjia Airport, --- shows interviewees at Pudong and Capital Airport, Horizontal axis = percentage, Vertical axis (top right) = difference of tourism resort, Vertical axis (top left) = difference of tourism resort of small town in Northeast China, Vertical axis (bottom right) = tourism program difference in Northeast China ; Vertical axis (bottom left) = tourism program difference of small town in Northeast China, 1 = famous scenic sites, 2 = tourism town surrounding famous mountain resorts, 3 = foreign tourist sites, 4 = well-known characteristic tourism town, 5 = ice-snow sightseeing, 6 = cool mountains and waters, 7 = local historical human, 8 = endless sea of forests, 9 = rural sightseeing, 10 = unique culture, 11 = back-to nature, 12 = frequent anticipation, 13 = tasting local foods, 14 = body building and health preserving, 15 = hill-walking, 16 = aquatic (ice) sports, 17 = viewing animals and plants

Fig. 5. Difference matrix of market preference

3.1 Preference Difference of Market Choice

From Figure 5, solid portions indicate market choice preferences in Northeast China, among them related high parts are within solid boxes—quadrangle1-10-13-5, which represents it's most popular for famous scenic spots with ice-snow sightseeing and unique culture and unique foods. Dotted portions indicate market choice preference in Yangtze Delta and the area surrounding Bo Sea, among them related high parts are within dotted boxes—quadrangle 1-11-13-5, which represents it's most popular for famous scenic spots with ice-snow sightseeing and back-to nature and unique foods.

So there are more similar preferences than difference between them. Similarity consists in: it's most popular for famous scenic spots with ice-snow sightseeing and unique foods. By its side is: it's second popular for small town surrounding famous mountains and scenic spots, which has health preserving and body building, cool mountains and waters. Difference consists in: interviewees in Northeast China like tourism resorts with unique culture, however, interviewees in developed market prefer back-to nature tourism resorts. In addition, interviewees in Northeast China don't have any interest of viewing animals and plants, and which in developed market don't one of hill-walking.

3.2 Further Test

At the present time there are seven AAAAA scenic spots, 75 AAAA, 1 world culture heritage, 2 world geological parks and 1 member of Man and Biosphere Programme in Northeast China, many of which are tourism resorts, including 7 tourists sites directly named tourism resorts. (see Table 2).

Table 2. Characteristic of typical tourism resorts (vacation village) in Northeast China

Typical tourism resorts(vacation village)	Grade	Main characteristics
Jinshitan National Holiday Resort	AAAAA	Famous scenic spot、cool mountain and water、back-to nature
Lvdao Holiday Resort in Shenyang	AAAA	Cool mountain and water、back-to nature
Weihai Dingxiang Ecological Holiday Resort at Panjin	AAAA	Cool mountain and water、back-to nature、unique foods
Chagan Lake Holiday Resort at Songyuan	AAAA	Cool mountain and water、unique foods and culture
Yabuli Skiing Holiday Resort	AAAA	Ice-snow sightseeing、back-to natuer
Xingkai Lake Holiday Resort at Dangbi Town	AAAA	Back-to nature、cool mountain and water、unique foods
Meihua River vacation village at Yichun	AAAA	Cool mountain and water、ice-snow sightseeing、back-to nature

Source from : www.lntour.gov.cn, www.jlta.gov.cn, www.Hljtour.gov.cn and above-related websites.

Above all belong to back-to nature tourism resorts, furthermore, some of which excel at ice-snow sightseeing, some of which do at cool mountain and water, some of which are famous scenic spots, and a few of them have unique foods or culture Furthermore, in spite of a few of them named tourism resorts, many of which surrounded by tourism resorts. E.g. Changbai mountain national-level nature reserve lies in the boundary of counties of Changbai, Fusong and Antu, small-size tourism resorts of which accord to our analysis too (see Table 3).

Table 3. Typical tourism resorts' characteristics at counties surrounding Changbai Mountain

County	Typical tourism resorts	Main characteristics
Dunhua	Xiaoshan Holiday Resort	Cool mountain and water, back-to nature
Changbai	Ethnic Chao Folk Custom Village	Unique culture and foods
Fusong	Spring Holiday Resort	Body building and health preserving, Back-to nature
	Biquan Lake Holiday Village	Cool mountain and water, unique foods

Source from : http://gov.dh.jl.cn/ , www.jl.gov.cn/zt/lygj/ , www.fusong.gov.cn/ , and above-related websites.

4 Basic Conclusions

Obviously, there are two sorts of tourism resorts in Northeast China. One is scenic area with certain popularity, which are all above AAAA and back-to-nature, however, with special emphases respectively on perception degree ice-snow sightseeing, unique foods and unique culture. The other, being little town surrounding famous mountains and scenic spots, which rank lower than the first, however, with characteristics based on famous mountains and scenic spots, can be divided into three categories : Landscape, health preserving and body building, unique culture.

As we know, regardless of whether it's within famous scenic spots or little town surrounding famous mountain and scenic spot, more and more tourism resorts will be built, which need to be in light of Figure 5. As for famous scenic spots, the emphasis is to attract developed market. However, as for little town surrounding famous mountains and scenic spots, the one is to do local northeast market.

There are some basic unique characteristics based on Figure 5, which shouldn't be disobeyed. At the same time, they face cut-throat competition. So every tourism resort should realize the value impetus of regional tourism cooperation and position very well based on Figure 5. Only doing that, the tourism resort market can be trending towards sound development.

Nowadays government needs to develop evaluation system for competitive strength of tourism resorts, and create better environment to decrease regional circulation obstacle by systematically optimizing forward circulation institution of regional tourism capital and products based on Figure 5. At the same time, every tourism resort need be more forward-looking, especially in allocation plan of regional tourism products, and work over market choice preference, and clearly define the position in regional modularity of tourism resorts, and try to explore related rules among modularity, so that they can speed up knowledge innovation and rapidly enlarge network effects and positive effects among regional tourism industry chain. By doing that, the average cost of the whole tourism industrial chain will be lower with the more of tourism products increasing, so tourism value will maximize and the effects of winner-take-all will be gained.

5 Concluding Remarks

By and large, the research can keep related mind open, especially it's helpful for tourism resorts in Northeast China to plan well. At the same time, every related enterprise should realize the analogies and dissimilarities in Northeast China, and do a good job in coping with future development.

In addition, the survey exists a few inaccuracies, for example, the places we choose can't present all visitors in Northeast. Furthermore, more than 20% don't have plan for a holiday, whose choice preferences don't be representative enough. Moreover, the questionnaire just selects four main characteristics of tourism resorts, which is not enough to clear all characteristics in Northeast China.

Acknowledgement. Creative Project founded by the Shanghai Education Commission (No. 11YS265).

References

1. Zou, G., Zhang, J.: Industry Chain Integration in Regional Tourism Cooperation、Value Impetus and Strategy planning for Regional Tourist Destinations. M&D Forum (Australia), p. 70 (2010)
2. Zou, G.: An Empirical Analysis on Problems Relating to Regional Tourism Cooperation Based on the Theory of Circulation. Information Engineering Research Institute (USA), p. 366
3. Tian, X., Song, B., Yan, J.: A Study on Cognition and Choice Preference on Tourism Scenic Spots in Large-Scale Region Based on a Perspective of Tourist Groups. Resources Science 5, 13 (2010)
4. Hu, P., Yang, J.: An Empirical Research on the Economic Impact of MICE Industry. Tourism Tribune 11, 81 (2006)
5. Chen, X.: On the Selection and Evaluation of Convention Tourism Destinations—Taking Shanghai as an Example. Tourism Tribune 1, 82 (2005)

Empirical Analysis on the Treatment and Working Conditions of Grass-Root Agricultural Technique Extension Personnel: A Case Study on Grass-Root Agricultural Technique Extension Personnel in Hubei Province

Zaizhou Liu[1] and Fayuan Wang[2]

[1] Research Institute for University Development, Yangtze University, Jingzhou, China 434025
[2] College of Economics, Yangtze University, Jingzhou, Hubei China, 434025
lzz@yangtzeu.edu.cn, wangfayuan315@sina.com

Abstract. This paper gives a survey to the treatment of the agricultural technology extension personnel and analyzes its degree of the work secure minds, which can provide foundation for formulating the corresponding policy. This paper gives a corresponding correlation regression analysis through Eviews software among the treatment of the agricultural technology extension personnel, the work satisfaction of the agricultural technology extension personnel, the correlation degree of the work satisfaction. It shows that the salary is significantly positive with degree of the work secure minds of the agricultural technology extension personnel and the degree of the work satisfaction, but has significant negative correlation with the second career personnel.It is an important measure of promoting the agricultural extension system development in China's grass-root agricultural to promote the system, to solve the job establishment of the agricultural technology extension personnel, to implement the performance management, to introduce the quality management.

Keywords: agricultural technology extension personnel, salary, work condition, correlation.

1 Introduction

It shows from the SHRM's large scale investigation, salary is the primary factor to affect work satisfaction. [1] The degree of satisfaction plays an important positive role in the working enthusiasm, teaching effect and work performance of the college teachers. [2] In the eyes of scientific and technical personnel, salary represents not only the income from his work, but also his self-valuation to a certain extent, the organization identification to the individual, even personal ability and future development. [3] Most scholars believe that the degree of the satisfaction is significantly positive with the individual work performance, that is to say, the higher the degree of the individual satisfaction, the higher the organizational commitment

Q. Zhou (Ed.): ISAEBD 2011, Part II, CCIS 209, pp. 218–223, 2011.

level will be. The individual will sustain a better work attitude, a stronger sense of ownership of the group, which can encourage the individual to work effectively and achieve the better work performance; otherwise, the lower the degree of the individual satisfaction, the lower the organizational commitment level will be, the work performance will decrease. As a primary means to the organizational incentive, salary is the main effect factor to the scientific and technical personnel's degree of satisfaction. So, salary is the mainly factor to the organizational incentive, which affects deeply to the quality of technical personnel's material and spiritual life.

With the development of the society, it has been becoming the keystone for the individual to pay much attention to the deep psychological feeling, such as, the self-valuation, work environment and so on. The organization with its prosperous future which can provide a good platform for the individual, strong cultural atmosphere, moderate pressure, and reasonable organization management can better win the trust of the individual and its positive work attitude. Furthermore, it will increase the individual degree of the satisfaction. Non-economy salary has becoming more and more important to the effect factor of the science and technology personnel's degree of the salary satisfaction. [4] However, the agricultural technical extension personnel in China with the ambiguous public service position, the technology extension system has no incentive mechanism, no close hook between the extension work performance and the income, a serious shortage of investment in technology extension. It is difficult to carry out a substantive meaning of the technical extension. [5] Up to now, no systemically research has been made about whether the salary, pension and other treatment factors have a significance positive influence to the agricultural technology extension personnel. Thus, this paper makes a survey to the salary and work condition of the agricultural technology extension personnel in Hubei province, intends to give a correlation research by the quantitative method, to provide a reliable basis for the decision-making sector to check the agricultural technology extension personnel's salary.

2 Empirical Analysis

2.1 Investigation Method

The grass-root agricultural technique extension system in this paper refers to the agricultural technique extension service institutes in county and town. Since only the agricultural technique extension institute in county and town carries out the reform "use money to foster things", we only investigate and analyze the situations of agricultural technique extension personnel in county and town. We adopt random sampling method and investigate the situations in 15 cities or states in Hubei Province. In each city or state, 5 agricultural technique extension centers in towns are randomly selected and in each center, 4 agricultural technique extension personnel are chosen for investigation. In this way, there are total 300 agricultural technique extension personnel investigated.

2.2 The Basic Characteristics of Personnel Investigated

The basic characteristics of the 300 agricultural technique extension personnel are as follows. In terms of gender, there are 260 male personnel accounting for 86.7% and 40 female ones accounting for 13.3%. As for the age, 17 personnel are under 30 years old, accounting for 5.7%; 148 personnel are between 30 and 40 years old, accounting for 49.3% and 135 ones are between 40 and 50 years old, accounting for 45.0%. It can be seen that most of the personnel are between 30 and 50 years old and there are fewer personnel under 30 years old. From the educational level point of view, there are 63 personnel with bachelor degree, accounting for 21.0%; 141 personnel with associate degree, accounting for 47.0% and 96 personnel graduated from technical school, accounting for 32.0%, as illustrated in Table 1. It indicates that most of the agricultural technology extension personnel graduate from junior colleges. There are much fewer personnel with bachelor degree.

Table 1. The Basic Characteristics of the personnel investigated

Gender				Composition of the age						Composition of the education level					
Male		Female		Below 30		30 40		40 50		Bachelor Degree		Associated Degree		Technical Secondary School	
Number (people)	%	Number (people)	%	Number (people)	%	Number (people)	%	Number (people)	%	Number (people)	%	Number (people)	%	Number (people)	%
260	86.7	40	13.3	17	5.7	148	49.3	135	45.0	63	21.0	141	47.0	96	32.0

2.3 Analysis of Investigation

2.3.1 The Basic Data of the Treatment of the Grass-Root Agricultural Technology Extension Personnel and Its Degree of the Work Satisfaction from the Questionnaire Survey

We investigate the situations of grass-root agricultural extension personnel in townships of Hubei province by questionnaire. The elements investigated include annual salary, office expense, insurance premium, job satisfaction, whether to do a second job, whether focus on one's own work, the most urgent need and why graduates from agricultural schools would not like to work in grass-root agricultural technique extension system etc.

Investigation results show that the average annual salary per person of grass-root agricultural technique extension personnel is 15 827 Yuan, the average annual office expense per person is 2 553 Yuan and the average annual insurance premium is 3 246 Yuan. The total average of these three elements are 21 626 Yuan. The salary varies with great difference in difference areas. There are 4 cities where the annual salary per person is over 20 000 Yuan. In other cities, the annual salary per person is between 10 000 and 20 000 Yuan. The highest annual salary per person in all the cities investigated is 26 000 Yuan and the lowest one is 10 000 Yuan. In average, 36.7% of the personnel are satisfied with their salaries, 19.3% of them are basically satisfied and 44% of them are unsatisfied. In the most satisfying city, only 50.0% of the personnel are satisfied with their salaries and in the worst one, only 25% of them are satisfied. In the most unsatisfying city, 55.0% of the personnel are unsatisfied with their salaries and in the worst one, 15.0% of them are unsatisfied. Personnel with a second job account for 58.4% in average, with the highest percentage 75% in some area and the lowest one 45% in another area. Personnel without a second job account for 41.6%. 36.7% of the personnel can focus on their work, 26.0% are hesitating and 37.3% are uneasy about their work. As for the most urgent problem that needs to be solved, 254 persons consider it to be the improvement of salary, which account for 84.7%; 30 persons choose the problem of social security, accounting for 10% and others consider it to be the improvement of working environment. To the question that why graduates from agricultural schools wouldn't like to work in grass-root agricultural technique extension system, 43.3% of the personnel think that it is because the job is not officially authorized and unstable while 41.8% of them consider that the salary is low and there is no social security.

2.3.2 The Theoretical Analysis of the Salary and Job Satisfaction of the Grass-Root Agricultural Extension Personnel

From the questionnaire, we can see that most agricultural extension personnel are not satisfied with their treatments. The treatment of agricultural technique extension personnel mainly refers to salary, office expense and various types of insurance premiums. In these three items, salary is the most sensitive. Office expense is also important but it is not the direct payment, so it has little impact on the job satisfaction of agricultural technique extension personnel. Insurance premium is directly related to the life guarantee when they are dismissed, the pensions after their retirement, and the medical care when they are sick, so there should be some correlations.

2.3.3 The Regression Analysis on the Salary of the Agricultural Extension Personnel and Its Degree of the Satisfaction

In order to obtain the impact of salary, office expenses and insurance premiums on job satisfaction of grass-root agricultural technique extension personnel, we adopt the software Eviews to analyze the correlation between each treatment and job satisfaction and get their correlation coefficients as illustrated in Table 2. X_1, X_2 and X_3 represent salary, office expenses and insurance premiums respectively.

Table 2. The correlation coefficient table of the salary and its degree of the satisfaction of the agricultural extension personnel

	X_1	X_2	X_3
X_1	1	0.198 6	-0.010 1
X_2	0.198 6	1	-0.376 8
X_3	-0.010 1	-0.376 8	1

From Table 2, it can be seen that there are no strong linear correlations among them, which is consistent with the expectation. That is because the three elements form the total treatment of agricultural technique extension personnel. Without considering multicollinearity, we adopt ordinary least square (OLS) and obtain the following regression results.

$$\hat{S} = -0.1916 + 0.9090X_1 + 0.1375X_2 + 0.2072X_3 \quad \overline{R}^2 = 0.8886 \quad se = 0.3338$$
$$(-2.1700) \quad (9.9612) \quad (1.3957) \quad (2.1459) \tag{1}$$

From (1), we can see that the fitting level is very high and it is 88.86% after adjustment. The coefficients for the three explanatory variables are all positive, which is consistent with expectation. Except X_2, the other two variables have obvious impacts. The standardized coefficient of X_1 is the largest and that of X_2 is the smallest. It shows that at present, the improvement of the office expense for grass-root agricultural technique extension center is not enough to affect the job satisfaction of agricultural extension personnel. Increasing salary is the most significant and direct factor for the work enthusiasm and job satisfaction of agricultural technique extension personnel. Agricultural technique extension personnel have urgent demand of raising their salary.

2.3.4 The Regression Analysis of the Annual Total Payment and the Job Satisfaction of the Agricultural Extension Personnel

Investigation results show that the total treatment of grass-root agricultural technique extension personnel consists of salary, office expenses and various types of insurance premiums. Let P denote the total treatment after standardization. Theoretically, the higher the total treatment is, the more they can focus on their work rather than do a second job.

The regression results of the standard ratio of engaging in a second job (Y_1) and the standard ratio of focusing on one's own job (Y_2) related to the standard treatment are given respectively as follows. Considering that personnel are from different cities or states and the differences of region, economic level and job opportunity in these areas may lead to the heterogeneous of doing a second job or focusing on one's own job, we do not take into account these external environment factors in our model. Therefore, in order to avoid heteroscedasticity, we adopt the weighted least square (WLS) to make regression analysis. The weighted regression results are as follows.

$$\hat{Y}_1 = 0.0228 - 0.6047P \quad \overline{R}^2 = 0.8076 \quad F = 41.0235 \quad se = 0.3727$$
$$(0.2650) \; (-6.4049) \tag{2}$$

$$\hat{Y}_2 = -1.94E-10 + 0.9528P \quad \overline{R}^2 = 0.9079 \quad F = 128.1195 \quad se = 0.3150 \tag{3}$$
$$(0.0135) \; (6.6548)$$

From (2) and (3), it can be seen that the fitting level is very high. The coefficient of P is negative in (2) and positive in (3), which conforms to the anticipation. The results indicate that the higher the total treatment of agricultural technique extension personnel is, the more they can focus on their own work and do not do a second job. Therefore, it is significantly important to improve the treatment of agricultural technique extension personnel, especially their salary, which has been shown in (1).

3 Conclusion and the Further Study Issues Are Needed

We investigate the situations of agricultural technique extension personnel in townships of Hubei province by random sampling and obtain the questionnaire results of 300 personnel. With regression analysis, we get the following conclusions. The treatment has an obvious impact on job satisfaction of agricultural technique extension personnel. The improvement of salary is the most critical and direct factor for enhancing the work activity and job satisfaction of them. It is very common for agricultural technique extension personnel to engage in a second job. Most of them are uneasy or hesitating about their work, which has influenced the effect of grass-root agricultural extension seriously. There are obvious correlations between the total treatment and whether they do a second job and the degree of focusing on their work. The higher the total treatment is, the higher the job satisfaction is and the more they can focus on their own work and do not engage in a second job. Otherwise, the lower the total treatment is, the more they do not focus on their own work and engage in a second job. Under the condition of market economy, what is the suitable salary that can encourage grass-root agricultural technique extension personnel to focus on their own work? How to adopt a scientific performance measurement method so as to improve the quality of agricultural technique extension personnel and their work enthusiasm? These questions are not mentioned in the paper and need further study.

References

1. Hao, Z., Lirong, L.: An Experimental Study of the Influence of Social Comparisons on Pay Satisfaction. East China Economic Management 4, 156 (2010)
2. Chen, J.: University Teachers' Compensation Satisfaction effect on their work performance and effect. Human Resource Development of China 8, 103 (2009)
3. Xianli Chen, D.: Empirical Research and Strategy on the Core Members' Satisfaction of the Neusoft Cooperation. Northeastern University, Shenyang (2005)
4. Zhang, J., Lai, P.: Empirical Research on the Impact Factors of Pay Satisfaction of the Scientific and Technological Personnel. Journal of Hohai University (Philosophy and Social Scienes) 4, 53 (2008)
5. Huang, J., Hu, R., Zhi, H.: 30 Years' Development and Reform for the Grass-roots Agricultural Technology Extension System: Policy Assessments and Recommendations. Journal of Agro technical Economics 1, 8–9 (2009)

On the Function and Basic Assumption of Value Chain Accounting in the IT Environment

Mengzhu Wu, Hui Fang, and Xiaohong Xie

Military Economic Academy Wuhan Hubei
wmzqh@yahoo.com.cn

Abstract. Value chain accounting is product of the combination of the value chain management theory, accounting theory and information technology and is the new area of the accounting to adapt to economic development. This paper discussed the functions and basic assumptions of value chain accounting. It puts forward the functions of value chain accounting which includes: real-time reflecting, real-time multidimensional controlling and predicting, decision-making and so on; the assumptions of value chain accounting includes: main body assumption of accounting, the elastic stage accounting assumption under the continuous operating, value measurement hypothesis and so on.

Keywords: IT environment, value chain accountings, function, assumption.

1 Introduction

Since 1985, Michael porter have brought in the concept of the value chain, the idea have rapidly adapted to enterprise's management, which plays an important role in the aspect of promoting the enterprise competitiveness. Along with the development of information technology, the traditional accounting increasingly doesn't adapt to economic development, Chinese deceased professor Yan Dawu makes a combination with value chain management theory, accounting theory and information technologies and puts forward the concept of value chain accounting. As a new field of accounting, many theory and practice problems of the value chain accounting is in the discussion, this paper mainly talks about some views of the functions and basic assumptions of value chains accounting.

2 Value Chain Fiscal Function

Function, refers to the inherent function of objective things. Accounting function is inherent function of accounting and is the embodiment of the accounting essence. The realization of accounting goal needs to perform accounting functions. But there is a close relation between accounting functions and accounting environment, accounting environment will restrict playing the accounting function through the accounting objects, accounting target, etc. Value chain fiscal function is the function which the value chain accounting plays in the enterprise and value chain management of the

Q. Zhou (Ed.): ISAEBD 2011, Part II, CCIS 209, pp. 224–230, 2011.

value chain alliance. Value chain accounting by means of information technology, sets financial accounting and management accounting in the integration, the nature of this kind of value chain management activities determines the multi-function of accounting value chain.

2.1 Real-Time Reflect Function

Reflecting is a primary and basic accounting function. It makes the currency as the units of measure, through currency recognition, measurement, records and report, reflects the enterprises' ongoing, already happened, completed economic activity in a period from the number.

The one characteristic of value chain accounting reflect function is real-time, which doesn't been restricted by the accounting period ruled by accounting system, but will reflect value activities' information of each node in the value chain alliance on real-time, such as enterprise inflows, creating, outflow and so on. The real-time reflect function includes simple reflection and reflection based on evaluation. Simple reflection refers to processing, handling and reflecting information of value creation and value realization for the using of managers making decisions and real-time controlling. But the reflection based on evaluation is a kind of reflection by comparing, analyzing and judging and is the more senior reflection. Through the value chain accounting, it can evaluate various activities of creating value and value realization process, can identify value-added activities, non value-added activities and value-added amplitude, and according to the result of identification, can judge the key link of value chain operation, decide which activities is suitable for doing by the enterprise itself, which ought to outsource to other enterprise to do, in order to realize the vertical management of the value chain.

Another characteristic of value chain reflecting accounting functions is the expanded range. In addition to reflecting economic activities of enterprise itself, it still can reflect the economic activity of the value chain' upstream suppliers and downstream customers. From the present, this function will not be possible, but along with the development of information technology, each node of the value chain alliance can realize seamless links with network technology someday, the function of reflecting other enterprise value creation and value realization situation in the value chain can be easily realized.

2.2 Real-Time Multidimensional Control Function

Accounting controlling function is refers to the accountant control and dominate production and operating activities of accounting subject according to a certain rules and standards and applying a certain method, namely through commanding, regulating and supervising, etc, to complete the desired objectives. Compared with the traditional accounting controlling function, the controlling function of value chain accounting performs comprehensive multi-dimensional controlling based on the real-time evaluation. Namely, the relevant personnel using modern information technology and related information make real-time contrast and real-time analysis of each node enterprise of value chain alliance and the whole business activities process of enterprise itself, and through the link of commanding, coordinating and restricting, etc, to intervene enterprise business to improve its operation efficiency and benefit, so as to achieve the ultimate goal of value maximization.

Compared with the traditional enterprise management, value chain management pays more attention to the decomposition and integration of each value creation activity of each enterprise in value chain alliance, through integration value activities, to realize the maximization of the value added. While the basis of integrating value activity is the coordinating and controlling the value creation and value realization activities, namely it is to coordinate and control the value creation activities and the performance management, cost management, capital budgeting, salary, etc, of each enterprise in value chain alliance. Because of the value chain accounting with hyperspatial multidimensional view, it can achieve the financial and business coordination treatment by information technology, it reaches every corner of the value chain alliance, and it is possible to do real-time control of any value activities or business of each enterprise. Under the condition of information technology, except the enterprise internal value chain, the object will also extend outward, performance for the vertical and horizontal crisscross value network. The value chain controlling made by the value chain accounting served in the value chain management can realize the comprehensive multi-dimensional control based on the real-time evaluation.

2.3 Prediction Function

The meaning of accounting prediction function is: accounting, through reflected economic business, provides accounting information, according to the accounting information, finds out the accounting elements and changing rules among elements to predict the future development trend of financial position, operating results and cash flows. Compared with the traditional accounting the prediction function' range of value chain accounting is broader, on the one hand, it will predict various possible value creation and value realization activities in the value chain, on the other hand, it also needs to predict the value effect of these value activities, namely it will predict which links will appear value-added effects and the possible value appreciation; and which links may appear zero value-added effects and negative value effect and the influential degree on the enterprise total value appreciation, etc.

2.4 Decision-Making Function

The main basis of accounting decision is accounting prediction, which is the process according to analyzing prediction results and choosing the best scheme to achieve management goals. In the concrete decision-making process, value chain accounting management goal can be decomposed into many objectives, the realization of the total goal relying on realization of these sub-targets, so that the decision-making view changes from abstract total goal to specific objectives. For the value chain accounting, each objective should be set respectively based on the different value chain of enterprises. For example, the aim of managing the money activities on longitudinal value chain is to guarantee the funds flow smoothly from the customer to suppliers, the aim of managing the purchasing activities and sales activities is to ensure product flow smoothly from suppliers to customers; the aim of analyzing competitive advantage on horizontal value chain is to make sure enterprise maintaining and enhancing its competitive advantage; the aim of managing the cost activities on internal value chain is to guarantee the lowest cost of production and continuing to reduce, the aim of managing the value added activities is to make sure each management unit gains the maximum added value, strengthens value-added activities with a positive value effect and eliminates value activities having zero value effects and negative value effect on the enterprise, etc. the goal of value chain accounting decision is based on the predicted results, combining possible influencing factors in the future, putting forward optimal scheme which can make these objectives realized, so as to ensure the total aim implemented [1].

3 The Basic Assumption of Accounting Value Chain

Accounting assumption is to make reasonable judgment and assumption for the economic environment the accounting in, is an idealized, standardized accounting environment in essence. When the reality changing and making assumptions away from the accounting economic environment, the assumptions must make corresponding modification and supplement to adapt to the changing environment. The same with other scientific system, the value chain accounting must rely on some assumptions to build its knowledge system. The basic assumptions of traditional accounting include accounting subject, sustained operation, accounting periodicity and monetary measurement. Under the condition of information technology, accounting assumption suffers a certain impact and influence, comparing with the traditional accounting, the basic assumptions of value chain accounting has a certain change and development.

3.1 Accounting Entity Assumption

Accounting entity is the particular unit reflected by accounting information, also called accounting subject and accounting unity. Its main effect is: ruling the transactions accounting should handle and the range of events, which provides the content and boundary of financial report, that is namely who listen to the report and whose economic activities should be reported.

Under the condition of information technology, the main body assumptions of value chain accounting still exist, just both the content and extension has been expanded. An accounting entity is not only an independent accounting enterprise, but is also multi-level and multi-dimensional. Firstly, value chain accounting accounts economic activities within the scope of the enterprise of a node on value chain, and provide related accounting information for the relevant aspects, carring on the management. In this level, the meaning of that is consistent with the traditional accounting entity. Secondly, the value chain accounting needs to reflect the other firms' economic activities on the value chain. Finally, the value chain accounting is still to reflect the overall economic activity of value chain alliance. In the three levels, the first level is a foundation, leaving the first level, the second and third level is nonexistent. Under the condition of information technology, by the network, each node enterprise of the value chain alliance can realize completely seamless links, can understand the economic activity of other enterprise and the whole value chain alliance in real time, and can implement management activities of an enterprise according to the information provided by the value chain accounting.

3.2 Non-periodical Accounting Assumptions Under Continuous Operating

Sustained operation is point to that accounting entity will continue to its normal business activities in the foreseeable future and won't face the condition of ending the normal business operations such as disintegration, liquidation and so on, it provides the time spans of accounting activities. Accounting period assumptions is based on the assumption of continuous operating, in order to meet regularly decision-making of decision makers; it is divided into several periods by people in order to provide regular financial report. In the traditional accounting theory, the assumption of continuous operating and accounting period assumption are very important two basic assumptions.

Under the condition of information technology, the changing of accounting environment brings in great impact for the two assumptions of ongoing operation and accounting periodicity, and its content also should be changed. For the value chain accounting, because of the multilayered accounting entity, the assumption of continuous operating can not only point to a single organization, but also should include the value chain alliance. Expanding the assumption of continuous operating to the broader value chain alliance, the enterprise on node of value chain can judge which links may threaten the normal business ability through longitudinal analysis of each link, thus can take corresponding measures to avoid risk. When a part of the value chain alliance appearing bankruptcy, the assumption of continuous operating still holds true.

Because the accounting period assumptions is the outspread of the continuous operating assumption, accounting period assumptions in the value chain accounting still stands, but there is a litter different from the tradition. Traditional financial accounting generally taking "year" as the accounting period, the enterprise provides the year's report reflecting the operating performance and financial status at the end of each year. But with the people's higher requirement of timeliness and real time about financial reporting, the correlation of this kind of traditional providing financial report by year is dying out. Providing real-time information for decision is one of the main characteristics of value chain accounting. Along with the development of information technology, real-time providing the required information has become possible. We can use modern information technology to collect and extract relevant data from the relevant data at any time and automatically, generating out financial reports and statements being related to decision-making. The balance sheet in every point and hour and the income statement in the different periods can be generated timely by the computer system, making the interval of accounting periodicity can continuously shorten, changing "historical information" into "real-time information".

As long as the enterprise doing continuously operation, users of the information can get financial report in every hour or period according to their different needs, which makes the accounting periodicity of value chain accounting have the characteristic of irregularity [2].

3.3 Value Measurement Assumption

Measurement unit is that it must adopt uniform measuring unit to the enterprise happening trade. Accounting has quantitative character and has strict requirements for choosing the measuring tool. Traditional monetary measuring unit is currency, namely, the currency measuring assumption. This assumption incidental includes two incidental assumptions: the functional currency (uniqueness); secondly, the currency stable invariant (consistency). This assumption has defect which is difficult to overcome by it, and suffers a strong impact under the condition of information technology. On the one hand, in real life, it is not the true of the currency stable assumption. In different times, the purchasing power of money is different; the currency in different countries does not exist ratio relationship of stability. Therefore, taking the unstable currency as the only unit of measurement is unfair. On the other hand, along with the development of information technology, network breaking the restrictions of time and space, it is become very easy to do cross-border financial tools deal and different currency transaction on the internet, especially the rise of "online banking", the appearance of "electronic money", making the currency accumaccumulation no longer uniqueness.

In the framework of the value chain accounting, measurement unit not only includes monetary unit, non-monetary unit, but also includes many non-financial information, such as customer preferences and satisfaction and so on. So that, the view of accounting management is expansive, financial information and non-financial information is unified value information, and the currency measurement extended to value measurement. This measuring unit assumption breaks the single currency measurement assumption of the traditional financial accounting, and is a kind of three-dimensional, multidimensional metering way. In the value information, financial information is still using money to measure and non-financial information is measured with standardized non-monetary information. The selection of value information based on the materiality principle, as long as it is conducive to analyze and evaluate the value-added situation of the value chain, the value information should be included in the value chain accounting framework. According to these measuring units, each node on the value chain alliance builds its own database. All total information databases, total information databases and son information databases, and all son information databases; can exchange value information freely between them. Enterprises should establish a unified standard for these value databases to ensure the smoothness of value information exchanging.

References

1. Yu, F., Zhang, M.: On management framework of the value chain accounting. The Proceedings of the Third "Value Chain Management and Value Chain Accounting" symposium (2005)

2. Guo, M.: The research of value chain accounting. East China normal university, degree papers of master graduate student (2005)
3. Zha, Y.: On the importance of accounting prediction function. Economist 6, 175 (2003)
4. Yu, F., Min, Z.: On basic assumptions of the value chain accounting. Journal of Shandong Finance College 1, 3 (2006)
5. Li, X.: Innovation and development of financial accounting theory, pp. 230–233. China business press, Beijing (1999)
6. Luo, C.: The research of manufacturing enterprises value-chain accounting. Central south university, master degree papers (2005)
7. Li, X.: The theoretical research of the value chain accounting. Finance and accounting monthly, 5 (2006)
8. Zhang, X.: Constructing theory framework of value chain accounting based on the scientific development. Commercial Times, 18 (2006)

Institutional Investors and Management Incentives: the Empirical Evidence from Chinese A-Share

Beibei Chang

School of business and management, NCEPU
1042355005@qq.com

Abstract. According to the date from the listed companies on China ' s A stock market for the period 2006-2009, we examined wether there was a relationship between institutional investors and executive incentives of listed companies. Our empirical study found that in China, institutional ownership concentration was positively related to the level of executive compensation and negatively related to executive shareholdings proportion. These results suggest that the institutional investors do not serve a monitoring role in mitigating the agency problem between shareholders and managers; they do not restrict the level of executive compensation, and just depress executive shareholding proportion to some degree. Institutional investors do not improve the merchanism of executive incentives.

Keywords: Institutional Investors, Management Compensation, Corporation Governance.

1 Introduction

After three decades later, the institutional investors have developed rapidly, coupled with the guidance and the contribution of the relevant laws, and their market shares have grown bigger. So far institutional investors have become dominant position on the stock market. As shares holding by institutional investors continue to rise, institutional investors have developed mature increasingly .In terms of institutional investors in the United States ,which are the most developed in the world, the overall size of fund assets in 1993 is 2.08 trillion dollars, 3.3 trillion in 1994, and in 1997 it reached 4.49 trillion dollars, an increase rate of 116.3% in five years. In 1999, some institutional investors hold 30% share of the stock market, of which 18% held by the Fund (Tang Zhengqing and Gu Chiyang, 2005).Meanwhile, in China, with the opening of capital markets, institutional investors ,in particular,with the rapid growth of securities investment funds and enterprise annuity, the insurance company entered directly into the stock market and increased the proportion of participating in stock market ,which have prompted Chinese extraordinary development of institutional investments. According to China Securities Regulatory Commission, as of October 2009, professional institutional investors have hold the A-stock market value of about 2.25 trillion yuan,which account for the proportion of the total market value from 12% by the end of 2003 to 17.2% in 2004 ,and all institutional investors holding the share of the market value reached 69.13%.

Q. Zhou (Ed.): ISAEBD 2011, Part II, CCIS 209, pp. 231–238, 2011.

Many researchers consider institutional investors as positive "voting by hand," shareholders. Through positive intervention approach,such as exerting pressure on the board of directors, forcing the board of directors to replace inexperienced CEO to completely change the company's development strategy and key personnel, institutional investors achieve active participation and improve corporate governance, so it will effectively solve the problem of internal control and other agents. Xie Zhihua (2003) pointed out that institutional investors had two characteristics. At first, institutional investors is principal parts of expert, representing natural personal investors' right or ownership; secondly, institutional investors collect the capital from many natural people, correspondingly having a larger proportion of shares of the company and a higher ownership concentration, so that institutional investors realize that the "voting with their feet" is undoubtedly a low-efficiency constraint way.

2 Paper Review

Wether institutional investors can affect corporate governance has attracted a great attention of western scholars, but their research angle and conclusions are not uniform. While in China, the development of institutional investors has a short history, but the future development space is still big, so the research paper about the Chinese investors are few. Paper review will also start from the following several aspects.

2.1 Motivation and the Style of Institutional Investors Participating in Corporate Governance

There is much debate about whether institutional investors should involve in corporate governance, which controversy is that institutional investors investment objectives is short-term or long-term and wether institution is able to participate in the company management. Zhong Jiyin (2000) summarized the institutional investors' motivation of participating in corporate governance, said "speak after the hold-up , institutional investors are not easy to withdraw their capital from companies, having to participate in corporate governance". Li Weian and Li Bin (2008) thought institutional investors actively participating in corporate governance was due to the self-interest motive under the cost of efficiency consideration , which was brought by the sustainable growth of the market value of stock invested in , and the returns had greatly overweighted their input. In the process of institutional investors participating in corporate governance, institutional investors accumulate expertise in the system, greatly reducing the cost of participating in corporate governance, and make participating in corporate governance a profitable business.

The goal of Institutional investors participating in corporate governance is mainly to improve stock price, implement incentive mechanism, limit the anti-takeover measures and improve governance structure. Gillan and Starks (2000) found that institutional investors' proposal often got more support than the personal proposal, therefore the result of the vote was closely related to the status of the sponsors. Institutional investors usually get more support in proposals such as the restrictions to executive officer's salary, director's stock right, director's condition,etc. Institutional investors can exert larger pressure on administration and supervision authorities. Guercio(2008) has studied proxy voting right behaviour of institutional investors in the board of directors , who thought "casts the opposite ballot" activity were a low cost to mobilize the enthusiasm of the shareholders attending, therefore it could act as a tool to express the discontent of management performance and corporate governance.They pointed out that adequate voting incentives drove the superintendent takeing the prompt action to avoid the further awkwardness, prompting business performance enhancement and incompetent executives for replacement, and institutional investors "casts the opposite ballot" campaign prompted board of directors on the behalf of shareholders'interests to take action.

2.2 The Study of the Effect of Institutional Investors in Corporate Governance

The papers make empirical researches for institutional investors participating in corporate governance from the performance of takeovering markets, long-term investment plan, the executive compensation, corporate performance and other aspects, evaluating all aspects of institutional investors affecting companies.

Florou and Pope (2008) pointed out that the performance of takingover the market compared to the disclosure of accounting information was more negatively correlated with stock returns, when institutional investors are in high ownership concentration. They thought the reason was that institutional investors often acquire richer information than the disclosure of accounting information. Wahal and McConnell (2000) refuted that institutional investors who would increase the argument of company's short-sighted .They found no evidence to prove institutional investors leading to the short-term behaviour of managers, Instead, they found that the proportion of shareholding of institutional investors were positively related with the long-term investment. Hartzell and Starks (2000) found that the level of executives' salaries and the equity of institutional investors was in significant negative correlation, meaning that institutional investors played a role in supervision mechanisms in the agent problem between managers and ownership. They (2002) further found institutional investors affected the structure of executive pay through their specific preferences. Cornett, etc. (2003) proved the relationship between the returns of companies operating cash flow and the proportion of ownership of institutional investors and the number of institutional investors were significantly related.

Of course, there are many scholars who doubt the positive role and functions of institutional investors participating in corporate governance. Hellman (2005) pointed out that institutional investors tended to use a small part of listed company information to action, Meanwhile,they tended to simplify their expectation formation process. If institutional investors in corporate governance has been placed in leadership roles, they rely heavily on external expert advice and over-emphasis on the behavior of quarterly reports, and the management of listed companies would have a negative impact. Webb,etc.(2003) questioned wether institutional investors in the UK play an active role in monitoring and strengthening corporate governance practicaly. If institutional investors continue to increase participation in corporate governance, which would interfere the effective functioning of capital markets, because institutional investors act as an agent not only to increase the social costs, but also caused the problem of free-rider. Bainbridge (2009) believed that existing U.S. law have severely limited the voting rights of shareholders, which affected shareholders in two ways: (1) preventing the formation of a large number of stocks; (2) hampering between shareholders communication and coordination.

3 Research Assumptions and Model Design

3.1 Assumptions and Model Design

The empirical researches show that the apperance of institutional investors in corporate governance will produce certain effect, which lead company management behaviour to change, making the company performance and market value consquently change. However, in view of the institutional investors in China' s listed companies' management, research results is still relatively few. This article is intended to study whether institutional investors have a significant impact on management incentives mechanism of listed companies in China and what impact it is, and demonstrate the effects of institutional investors in corporate governance.

Management incentives (including salary, equity and options) are a powerful tool to coordinating shareholders and managers' conflict of interest, and institutional investors are able to exert important influence on adjusting the incentive structure of managers. Hartzell and Starks (2003) taking 1992-1997 United States listed company as samples, found that ownership concentration of institutional investors and the sensitivity of managers' pay performance was positive related, which fully justified institutional investor's supervision and mitigated the conflicts of interest between shareholders and managers. Khorana (2005) found that the influence of institutional investors had an important impact on the salary policies of company managers, enabling the convergence of Manager and shareholder objectives.

Based on the above papers, institutional investors have a certain effect on reducing the agency costs, improving managers incentive efficiency and strengthening agent. This article will examine the role of institutional investors in monitoring executive compensation by empirical studies, making the following two research hypothesis:

H1: The stake of institutional investors have a significant negative impact on the salary levels of management.

H2: The stake of institutional investors have a significant negative impact on the stake of executives of the company.

3.2 Variable Design and Model Selection

In order to verify the relationship between institutional investors and management incentives, we design the two following models:

$$EC = a_0 + a_1 ISHP + a_2 LNSIZE + a_3 LSHP + a_4 TAT + a_5 ROA + a_6 LEVER + \sum_{i=1} INDi + \sum YEARi + e \ldots\ldots Model1 \tag{1}$$

$$ESHP = a_0 + a_1 ISHP + a_2 LNSIZE + a_3 LSHP + a_4 TAT + a_5 ROA + a_6 LEVER + \sum INDi + \sum YEARi + e.....Model2 \tag{2}$$

In Model 1, 2, we design institutional investors ' stake (ISHP) as explanatory variables, and the stake of executives (ESHP) and management compensation (EC) as explanatory variables. Models also includes some control variables, these control variables are: (1) company scale (LNSIZE) in terms of total assets of the company. The company scale was significantly associated with management incentive characteristics, the bigger the company scale is, the greater the management compensation is , so we forecast firm scale have a positive impact on management motivation level. (2) The stake of the largest shareholder (LSHP), showing in terms of the proportion ,which is showed the largest number of shares holding by the shareholder by the end of year proportioned total equity . The largest shareholder stake directly reflects the first shareholder influence and status of the corporate board of directors, and also have an impact on the voice of institutional investors in the enterprise. (3) Asset turnover ratio (TAT). The higher the enterprise's asset turnover is , the more efficiency of using its asset is. Practice has proved that the strength of business operations directly affects the ability of executive compensation levels, the stronger the normal operating capacity of enterprises are, the higher the level of executive pay are. (4) Return on assets (ROA), net profit divided by total assets of the company by the end of the year. The higher the level of profitability is, the higher the returns of its management have.(5) Financial leverage (LEVER), indicated by a debt-asset ratio. Jensen and Meckling (1976) confirmed that the pressure of debt finance helped to reduce the agent costs of Managers, which could improve corporate governance and constrain the manager's pay level.

3.3 Sample Selection and Data Sources

This article selected the 2006-2009 A-share listed companies in the non-financial category as initial samples. According to the following criteria,We eliminated same samples: (1) owing to the differences of financial characteristics and accounting system between financial companies listed and general companies listed, we eliminated financial and insurance industries from the listed companies sample; (2) we eliminated discontinuous data, lost data, and data with extreme value of deformity; (3) Avoided listing companies itself affecting institutional investors, we removed the market less than one year of the enterprise; (4)we eliminated ST and PT companies, whose "shell resource" properties may distort the company's value, and also restricted stock trading. Finally we got a sample 4837 observations. This paper data stemed from many professional database: structure of stock stemed from the wind datebase, governance data and the financial governance date of listed companies stemed from CCER database.

4 Empirical Analysis

4.1 Descriptive Statistics

Major results of variables of descriptive statistics show in Table 1: (1) In terms of executive pay (EC), the differences between each company is larger: the maximum value is 68,499,000 (LN logarithmic into 18.0423), the minimum value is 12,000 (LN logarithmic: 9.3926), and average values is 2,182,259 (LN logarithmic mean 14.1363), whose standard deviation reached 0.9644. (2)The differences of executives' stake ratio (ESHP) are large, whose maximum value is 78.38% and the smallest value is 0%. By contrast the differences of standard deviation is small, just for 0.1030, which shows that the overall trend of the situation and characteristics of executive stake holdings in listed companies in our country is stable. (3) Institutional investors holding ratio (ISHP) also has risen from the smallest of 0% to the largest of 98.51%, which is highly concentrated changed, and its proportion of average shareholding is 26.67%, meanwile, the standard deviation is also small, just 0.2271. The whole characteristics are relatively stable. Institutional investors in the 06-09 period is in greate development in the market, which the average stake is much higher than average stake executives, indicating that the influence of institutional investors in the Shanghai and Shenzhen markets is enormous.

Table 1. Descriptive statistics

Varibles	Average	Median	Minimm	Maximun	Standard deviation	Observation numbers
EC	2,182,259	1,418,000	12,000	68,499,000	0.9644	4387
LN(EC)	14.1363	14.1648	9.3926	18.0423	0.9644	4387
ESHP	0.0284	0.0000	0.0000	0.7838	0.1030	4387
ISHP	0.2667	0.2074	0.0000	0.9851	0.2271	4387
LSHP	0.3679	0.3550	0.0355	0.8642	0.1521	4387
LNSIZE	21.6740	21.5453	18.2658	27.8090	1.1409	4387
ROA	0.0501	0.0372	0.0001	0.8686	0.0490	4387
LEVER	0.4901	0.5038	0.0182	0.9730	0.1800	4387
TAT	0.8082	0.6484	0.0015	10.1793	0.6728	4387

4.2 The Regression Results and Analyses

From the regression results in Table 2 of model 1 , we can see that management compensation (EC) and the institutional shareholding (ISHP) is positively correlated ,and it is not only the opposite of hypothesis H1, but also it is opposite conclusions of the study of Hartzell and Starks (2000). In China, the institutional investors holdings only increased the level of executive compensation. We believed that effective supervision of institutional investors was a more complex issue, which institutional investors generally hire external managers to manage, and then the behaviour of the external managers in the process of goverance in the company is not necessarily consistent with the interests of shareholders. The external institutional managers and invested companies may be collusion. Levitz and Jennifer (2006) study found that mutual fund managers were often supported by investment firm's compensation plan and prevented the other shareholders who did not agree with compensation plan, which Showing that mutual funds participated in corporate governance enhancing interest conflict between shareholders and managers. In addition, monitoring costs would impede institutional investors on the restructuring of executive compensation to play a role.

Institutional investors investment preferences also can explain the positive correlation relationship. The institutional investors in China are more incline to invest large-scale and high-profit company (Ferreira and Matos, 2008). So institutional investors like to invest in larger-scale high-return companies, and the companies are in favour of high salary.

Table 2. Regression results

Variables	Expected Symbol	Model 1	Model 2
Intercept	?	7.0532*** (27.7163)	0.3230*** (10.4962)
ISHP	-	0.0100*** (16.5731)	-0.0001* (-1.9166)
LSHP	+	-0.9905*** (-11.5338)	-0.0570*** (-5.4904)
LNSIZE	+	0.3308*** (26.0101)	-0.0133*** (-8.6136)
ROA	+	2.0206*** (6.9293)	0.3257*** (9.2365)
LEVER	-	-0.3159*** (-3.8967)	-0.0093 (-0.9491)
TAT	+	0.0784*** (4.1202)	0.0068*** (2.9542)
IND		control	control
YEAR			
Adj-2		0.2669	0.0613
F-statistc		267.1444	48.7215
Sig.		0.0000	0.0000
N		4387	4387

Note: data in the table are the regression coefficients for their respective variables, the numerical brackets for T value, * * *, * *, * seperately significant level 0.01, 0.05, 0.10.

5 Conclusion

The article using data from the listed companies on China's A stock market for the period 2006-2009, has analysed the impact of institutional investors on management incentives. The empirical results indicated that the proportion of our institutional shareholding and management pay levels showed significant positive correlation, but it showed negative correlation with shareholding ratio by management. This showed that: in China institutional investors did not play efficiently supervision function in solving the agency problems between owners and managers, and there was no effective constraint on executive pay level, but in some extent it suppressed executives shareholding and did not significantly improve company management incentive mechanism. Generally speaking, in China, the institutional investors didn't play a expected role in improving companies.

References

1. Tang, Z., Gu, C.: Institutional investors participating in corporate governance: theoretical analysis, experience summaried and strategy suggestions. Jianghuai Forum 03, 37–42 (2005) (in Chinese)
2. Xie, Z.: Historic turning point in internal corporate governance - the involvement of institutional investors. Contemporary Manager 12, 87 (2003) (in Chinese)
3. Zhong, J.: The rise of active investors - why and how U.S. institutional investors participating in corporate governance and its implications for China. International Economic Review (9-10), 41–45 (2000)
4. Li, W., Li, B.: The empirical study of institutional investors involved in corporate governance - Based on the experience study of CCGINK. Nankai Business Review 11(1), 4–14 (2008) (in Chinese)
5. Gillan, S.L., Starks, L.T.: Corporate governance proposals and shareholder activism: the role of institutional investors. Journal of Financial Economics 57, 275–305 (2000)
6. Guercio, D.D., Seery, L., Woidtke, T.: Do boards pay attention when institutional investor activists "just vote no? Journal of Financial Economics 90, 84–103 (2008)
7. Florou, A., Pope, P.: Are boards and institutional investors active monitors? Evidence from CEO dismissal. Managerial Auditing Journal 23(9), 862–872 (2008)
8. Wahal, S., McConnell, J.J.: Do institutional investors exacerbate managerial myopia? Journal of Corporate Finance 6, 307–329 (2000)
9. Hartzell, J.C., Starks, L.T.: Institutional Investors and Executive Compensation. Working Paper, University of Texas at Austin (2000)
10. Cornett, M.M., Alan, J.: Marcus, Anthony Saunders, Hassan Tehranian. The Impact of Institutional Ownership on Corporate Operating Performance. Working Paper, NYU Stern Department of Finance (2003)
11. Niclas, H.: Can we expect institutional investors to improve corporate governance? Scandinavian Journal of Management 21, 293–327 (2005)
12. Robert, W., Beck, M., McKinnon, R.: Problems and Limitations of Institutional Investor Participation in Corporate Governance. Journal of Corporate Governance 11(1), 65–73 (2003)
13. Bainbridge, S.M.: Shareholder Activism and Institutional Investors. Research Paper No. 05-20, UCLA School of Law
14. Jensen, M.C., Meckling, W.H.: Theory of the Firm: Managerial Behavior, Agency Costs and Ownership Structure. Journal of Financial Economics 3, 305–360 (1976)
15. Levitz, J.: Do Mutual Fund Managers Back CEO Pay? —Study Finds Firms Failed to Use Voting Power in Favor of Linking Compensation to Performance. The Wall Street Journal 28, C.1(2006)
16. Ferreira, M.A., Matos, P.: The colors of investors' money: The role of institutional investors around the world. Journal of Financial Economics 88, 499–533 (2008)

Institutional Environment and Over-Investment – From the Empirical Evidence of Chinese a Shares

Xiya Luo

School of Business and Management, Ncepu
389272555@qq.com

Abstract. This paper uses all A shares of non-financial listed companies from the Chinese A-share market during 2001 to 2006 as the initial samples to study whether the institutional environment has a governance effect on corporate over-investment. The paper finds the following conclusions: marketization index and government intervention index can effectively inhibit listed company's over-investment impulses in the region, indicating that the differences in the degree of intervention made by local governments in various regions have different economic consequences. However, regional rule-of-law level can not have an effective impact on the company's over-investment. These evidences all provide a new way of thinking for improving china's external governance mechanisms.

Keywords: External governance mechanisms, Institutional environment, Over-investment.

1 Introduction

In the framework of new classical economics research, the companys' growth opportunities are the only motive of capital investment decisions. The companies continue to invest until the marginal revenues of investment are equal to the marginal costs of investment. Internal managers invest in the projects that whose NPV are positive, meanwhile return excess cash to the external investors, but because information asymmetry and the separation of ownership and management result in the manager's adverse selection and moral hazard, which makes managers have a goal but maximizing the value of the company. The company's investment decisions often deviate from the optimal level of investment, and the use of free cash flow for over-investment is an important way for managers to earn self-interests.

There are two mechanisms of corporate governance: the internal governance mechanisms and the external governance mechanisms, which together constitute a complete system of corporate governance structure. Overall the two are complementary, but both are not the same on the logical level. External governance is initiative, which is the primary condition and basic mechanism for corporate governance, however, internal governance is based on the external governance and it is the endogenous arrangement system of external governance. How the institutional environment influence governance structure should be the basis of the study of

Q. Zhou (Ed.): ISAEBD 2011, Part II, CCIS 209, pp. 239–245, 2011.

corporate governance(Williamson, 2000; Chen Xinyuan et al, 2004; Xia Lijun and Fang Yiqiang, 2005). This paper intends to study the instituional environment's effect on the micro - company's investment behavior.

Because of the effects of the governance logic that shareholders are supremacy, combined with establishing and improving the external governance mechanisms require a relative long process, so, for a long time, in our discussion of corporate governance, we often focus on the construction of internal governance mechanisms. However, the inefficiency or absence of external governance mechanisms will lead to a failure in building effective internal governance mechanisms. Therefore, in order to improve the efficiency of china's corporate governance, it is necessary to make a research on the construction of china's external governance mechanisms, and to enhance the company's investment efficiency and the shareholders' value.

2 The Theoretical Analysis and Assumptions

The most basic external mechanisms for the companies are legal environment, the degree of marketization and government administrative environment, which have a fundamental role on the the formation of institutional model of corporate governance, the company's investment behaviors and performances.

The traditional corporate governance research focus on the relationship between the corporate performance, corporate value and governance structure, but the idea of research ignores the more important, more fundamental factor behind governance structure, namely the institutional environment in which companies locate. In recent years, corporate governance research has gradually advanced to the level of analysis of relationship between institutional environment and governance structure. As the company is always in a specific institutional environment, and their behavior tend to draw on advantages and avoid disadvantages, adapting to their environment. Therefore, corporate governance structure is mainly born in the institutional environment in which the company was locate(Xia Lijun and Chen Xinyuan, 2007). La Porta et al (1997,1998,1999,2000,2002,2006,2007) published a series of academic papers concerning law and corporate finance, studying the strength of investor protection and the economic consequences under different legal systems by means of nationality comparison approach. They found that there exist the systematic differences in the ownership concentration, development of securities markets, dividend policy and the use of external financing and other issues among companies in different countries. These differences are closely related to the degree of legal protection for medium-and- small investors, so different legal systems can make different corporate governance structure modes.

Since 1978, China has started a reform and opening-up process and transformed itself from a planned economy to market economy. China's marketization process has made great achievements in 30 years, and the socialist market economy has been established and improved. Many countries have recognized China as a market economy country as a whole. However, because of China's vast territory, progressive reform and historical reasons, the marketization process of provinces are uneven, which is very obvious in both the administrative area and the industrial sector. Fan Gang, Wang Xiaolu, and Zhu Hengpeng(2007) studied the degree of marketization in many regions and obtained the marketization index and related subsidiary index in all provinces from 2001 to 2005. They found that the big differences of marketization degree in different provinces are mainly due to differences in resource endowments, geographical positions and national policies.

The third factor in institutional environment is the government administration. In fact, the government management factor is closely related to law environment and the degree of marketization. The better the law protection and the higher degree of marketization, the weaker government intervention's degree and motives. In the regions that law protection are poor and the degree of marketization are low, the government often exercise "grabbing hand" to intervene in the economy. The relationship between government and enterprises has always been a hot focus, especially for the state-owned economy as the main body of the economic transition countries. On one hand, as the administration of social affairs, the Government needs to carry out macroeconomic regulation and control daily, formulate appropriate laws and regulations to regulate and guide the behavior of market participants, namely the government playing a "referee" role; on the other hand, government is a shareholder and controller of many companies, even be directly involved in the daily operation and management of the company, playing a "player"role, which may easily lead to improper government intervention in the economy, often resulting in a negative impact on corporate governance and performances.

Currently, the government administration's impact on business is mainly developed through the relationship between government and market, government's intervention in the company, but the results specialize in government intervention's impact on investment behavior are few. In China, under the special fiscal decentralization system and officials examinational system, local governments have a strong motivation of intervention in their investment activities, and the depth and breadth of the intervention in the company is bigger than the central government's. Cheng Zhongming et al (2008) empirically tested the influence of government intervention and pyramid hierarchy on investment, who found that local state-owned listed companies have an over-investment phenomenon caused by government interference, and only weak evidences showed that government intervention has a positive correlation to the lack of investment. Yang Huajun and Hu Yiming(2007) found that local government control and local government intervention significantly increased the free cash flow of over-investment. Zhang Dong et al(2008) also found the less degree of intervention that local government has in the companies, the lower level of the region's over-investment. Based on the above analysis, we propose the following assumptions:

H1: The higher the degree of government intervention in which the company locates, the lower level of its over-investment is;

H2: The higher the degree of marketization in which the company locates, the lower level of its over-investment is;

H3: The higher the degree of legal protection in which the company locates, the lower level of its over-investment is;

3 Research Design

The paper's plan is as follows. First of all, learning from Richardson's(2006) model, we estimate the company's normal level of capital investment, then use the company's actual capital investment level minus expectations of the company's capital investment level, getting the company's over-investment levels(namely regression residual). Then, we use the over-investment value from regression analysis as the dependent variable, then guess each observation to examine the instituional environment's influence on the company's capital investment. Finally we will find which of the instituional environment has governance efficiency on inhibiting company's over-investment behavior? Which can not make a desired governance efficiency?

3.1 Variables of the Institutional Environment

This paper uses the data from(China's marketization index-report on the process of regional relative marketization in the 2006) as the proxy variables of the institutional environment(InstEnv), in which law level index(Lawind) is on behalf of the legal protection level in the region, the higher the value, the better the legal protection level; and marketization index(Marind) represents the region's marketization degree, the higher scores, the more developed the market is; and government intervention index (Intervind) is on behalf of the relationship between government and the market, the higher the score, the lower the degree of government's intervention. This paper uses financial marketization and the marketization of credit capital allocation to represent the region's financial development degree(Finind). The higher score of financial marketization (Finmar) and the credit capital allocation's marketization (Cremar), the higher degree of credit funds' allocation marketization in the region.

As the report only provides data from 2001 to 2005, so in modeling we use the data in 2005 to represent 2006's, because the marketization development in all regions has a certain inertia. So this method does not make substantial effect on conclusion. While there is too little data about all the Tibet Autonomous Region, so in modeling all the listed companies from Tibet were removed.

3.2 The Measurement of Over-Investment and Free Cash Flow

Over-investment refers to invest in the projects whose net present value(NPV) are negative(Jensen, 1986). This paper uses Richardson's(2006) measurement model, which defined the over-investment as the investment spending that more than maintaining the assets' existing state and financing the expected positive NPV of new investment. This model uses the explanatory variables growth opportunities GR, company age, financial leverage, cash stock, size, stock returns and the previous period's investment to estimate the normal level of investment. The regression's residual(namely Overin) is the company's over-investment level.

$$I = \beta_0 + \beta_1 GR_{t-1} + \sum Control \text{ Varibles} + \text{Overi}\, n_t, \quad (1)$$

According to the existing research, this paper select the free cash flow, state-owned as a control variable.According to Jensen's(1986) definition, we use operating cash flow (Ocf) minus expected cash flow(EI) as free cash flow: Fcf = Ocf-EI.

3.3 Institutional Environment and Over-Investment

According to the hypothesis proposed in this paper,we use the following models to test the related instituional environment's impact on the company's over-investment :

$$Overin_t = \alpha_0 + \alpha_1 Fcf_t + \alpha_2 InstEnv_t + \alpha_3 Fcf_t \times InstEnv_t + \Phi \quad (2)$$

3.4 Sample Selection and Data Source

This article uses the data in Shanghai and Shenzhen stock market from 2001 to 2006 of all A-share listed companies as the initial samples. First we eliminate the listed companies in the financial industry and companies in the face of financial difficulties such as ST companies; secondly, we eliminate the samples of related data missing, and thirdly, we eliminate samples of some extreme values, such as negative net assets, ROE are less than -100%, operating revenues growth rate is more than 1000%. Finally, we can get 4311 samples. The data used in this paper are from the CCER data system, and some data are from the CSMAR database. In the paper, calculation process uses Excel 2003 and SPSS Statistics 17.0.

4 Empirical Results and Analysis

4.1 The Variable Estimates and Descriptive Statistics

Table 1 reports the descriptive statistics results of main variables. From table 1, we can find that the marketization index(Marind), government intervention index (Intervind) and rule of law index (Lawind)'s are more decentralized, which are evidences of our more unbalanced economic development, and also provide the conditions for analyzing the unbalanced environment's impact on microscopic enterprise's investment behavior.

Table 1. The mean, maximum, minimum and standard deviation of main Variables

	N	Minimum	Maximum	Mean	Standard deviation
Overin	4311	-7.91E-01	1.92E+00	3.95E-05	0.112
Marind	4311	2.37	10.41	6.97	2.006
Lawind	4311	1.15	13.07	5.821	2.94
Intervind	4311	3.75	10.63	7.98	1.51
Finmar	4311	0.9	11.5	7.26	2.40
Cremar	4311	0	12.2	7.77	2.71

4.2 Institutional Environment and Over-Investment: Regression Results

Table 2 is the regression results of institutional environment and over-investment model. From the results, we find that interaction term of A and B every institutional environment agency variables and the free cash flow's are negative, consistent with their expected signs, indicating that on the whole, institutional environment is able to alleviate the problem of over-investment of free cash flow. Marind * Fcf, Intervind * Fcf are significantly negative correlated to each other at 10% level, and Cremar * Fcf is negatively correlated to at the 5% level, demonstrating marketization index, the government intervention index and marketization of allocation of credit funds can effectively inhibit the impulse to over-investment of listed companies in the area, and indirectly showing different economic consequences resulted from that local government's intervention in all regions' differences. Regression results support the hypothesis 2 and 3, however, Lawind * Fcf, Finmar * Fcf's interaction term of A and B are not significant, indicating that regional rule of law level can not have an effective impact on company's over-investment, which can't confirm hypothesis 1. On the whole, China do not have an adequate legal protection for external investors. Because of the characteristics that "economic reforms, political reform mainly slowed almost to a standstill" in our 30 years' reform and opening-up process, China lack a effective protection for external investors, so China is still lack a powerful weapon for protecting medium-and-small investors like Western capital market shareholders' lawsuit system.

Table 2. Empirical results of the institutional environment and over-investment

Variable	Model1:InstEnv is Marind	Model2:InstEnv is Lawind	Model3:InstEnv is Intervind
Intercept	.008	.007*	.010
	(1.087)	(1.676)	(.863)
Fcf	.222*	.135***	.282***
	(3.684)	(3.727)	(3.173)
InstEnv	6.554E-5	.000	.000
	(.066)	(.216)	(-.105)
InstEnv* Fcf	-0.15*	-.003	-.021*
	(-1.840)	(-.602)	(-1.915)
N	4311	4311	4311
Adj-R^2	0.013	0.012	0.013
Fvalue	20.325***	18.9***	20.31***

Note: The dependent variable is over-investment (Overin), and the upper part is a regression coefficient of the results, the lower part is the T value,***,**,* respectively indicating significant level 0.01,0.05,0.10.

5 Conclusion

This paper selected whether the institutional environment can alleviate company's over-investment as the main line of our research. In this paper, we use non-financial listed companies from 2001 to 2006 as samples, study whether the institutional environment has governance impact on company's over-investment. We can reach following conclusions: the regional marketization index and government intervention index allocation can effectively inhibit the listed companies' impulse to over-investment, indirectly showing different economic consequences resulted from differences in local government intervention's level in all regions. However, regional district rule of law level can not have an effective impact on company's over-investment .

References

1. La Porta, R., Lopez-de-Silanes, F., Shleifer, A., Vishny, R.: Legal determinants of external finance. Journal of Finance 52, 1131–1150 (1997)
2. La Porta, R., Lopez-de-Silanes, F., Shleifer, A., Vishny, R.: Law and finance. Journal of Political Economy 106, 1113–1155 (1998)
3. La Porta, R., Lopez-de-Silanes, F., Shleifer, A.: Corporate ownership around the world. Journal of Finance 54, 471–517 (1999)
4. La Porta, R., Lopez-de-Silanes, F., Shleifer, A., Vishny, R.: Investor Protection and Corporate Governance. Journal of Financial Economics 58, 3–27 (2000)
5. La Porta, R., Lopez-de-Silanes, F., Shleifer, A., Vishny, R.: Investor protection and corporate valuation. Journal of Finance 57, 1147–1170 (2002)
6. La Porta, R., Lopez-de-Silanes, F., Shleifer, A.: What works in securities laws? Journal of Finance 61, 1–32 (2006)
7. Richardson, S.: Over-investment of Free Cash Flow. Review of Accounting Studies 11, 159–189 (2006)
8. Williamson, O.E.: The New Institutional Economics: Taking Stock, Looking Ahead. Journal of Economic Literature 38, 595–613 (2000)
9. Chen, X., Chen, D., Zhu, K.: Ownership Structure and Corporate Performance: A Literature Review and Directions of Future Research. China Accounting and Finance Research 04 (2004)
10. Cheng, Z., Xia, X., Yu, M.: Government Intervention, the Pyramid Structure and the Investment of local State-owned Listed Companies. Management World 09, 3–10 (2008)
11. Fan, G., Wang, X., Zhu, H.: China's Marketization Index - the Report of Relative Process of Regional Markets in the 2006. Economic Science Press (2007)
12. Xia, L., Fang, Y.: Government control, management environment and corporate value. Economic Research 05, 3–11 (2005)
13. Yang, H., Hu, Y.: Institutional Environment and Overinvestment of Free cash flow. Management World 9, 2–6 (2007)

Empirical Analysis on the Regional Competitiveness of Telecom Industry Based on Principal Component Analysis

Yue Liu and XinLin Ouyang

Chongqing University of Posts and Telecommunications,
College of Economics and Management,
400065 Chongqing, China
liuyue@cqupt.edu.cn, ouyanglnp@163.com

Abstract. Telecom industry plays an important role in the modem economic and social development, in order to know China's telecommunications competitive situation. This paper builds the telecom industry international competitiveness evaluation index system from four aspects. Using principal component analysis we evaluate the competitiveness of telecom industry in 31 provinces of China, autonomous and municipalities from 2004-2008. Evaluation results show that the competitiveness of Shanghai, Beijing, Guangzhou ranks 1st,2ndand3nd. From the angle of each area ,the competitiveness of East is much higher than in the Central and West, Central area slightly higher than West, but East have the largest internal diversity, West and Central area have a small difference in internal diversity.

Keywords: Regional telecom Industry, Competitiveness, Principal component analysis.

1 Introduction

Market competition is the way to achieve optimal allocation of resources, economic participants must have certain competitive to survive in the market. The wave of economic integration makes the more intense competition between enterprises, industries and regions. The competition of regions, in fact, is the competition of industry.

With the development of telecommunication technology, Telecom industry became a pillar industry of the national economy . Meanwhile, it has the typical characteristics of the external economy, it's social benefits higher than economic efficiency. Therefore, telecom industry plays a decisive role in the modern economy. China's telecom industry developed rapidly in the past decade, In 2010, the total business reached 3.0955 trillion Yuan, business revenue is about 898.8 billion Yuan, completed 319.7 billion Yuan investment in fixed assets. Number of telephone users reached 1,153,390,000, Among them, about 859 million mobile phone users. However, in the long period of time, China implemented unbalanced regional economic policies, caused the gap between east, west and central regions. This imbalance of regional

Q. Zhou (Ed.): ISAEBD 2011, Part II, CCIS 209, pp. 246–252, 2011.

economic development not only led to the imbalance of the regional telecom industry, but also restricted to improve the international competitiveness of China's telecom industry. It is benefit to make rational policy to evaluate the competitiveness of the regional telecom industry. Therefore, research on the regional competitiveness of telecom industry has significance in theoretical and practical.

2 The Concept of Regional Competitiveness of Telecom Industry

Research on the competitiveness of the telecom industry can be divided into two main aspects: The First is the international competitiveness. The second is the regional competitiveness. Zhu Jinzhou (2006) [1]defined the regional competitiveness of telecom industry as: In the case of without increasing the burden on consumer in specific area, telecom industry's comprehensive capacity to create wealth.

Compared with other industries, telecom industry has public service and external economy characteristics . Thus the competitiveness of the telecom industry not only in the economic benefits, but also reflected in the meets consumer demand for telecommunications services and support the development of regional economic. This paper defines the regional competitiveness of telecom industry as: It is a Comprehensive capacity to provide efficient telecommunications services to consumers, support the development of regional economic, and then create economic benefits for own development.

3 Evaluation Indicator System

The competitiveness of the regional telecom industry is a comprehensive concept. Based on the previous study, this paper proposed a quantitative analysis model for evaluates regional telecom industry competitiveness, it contains four factors: Communication competence, Market competitivene- ss, Production competitiveness and Economic benefits.

On the basis of previous research results, we build up an evaluation indicator system on the principles of all-around perspectives, close relationship and data accessibility. It's a two levels indicator system, which consists of 5 first-level indicators, and contains 23 second-level indicators(Table1). Communication competence contains six indicators:X1-X6; Market competitiveness contains five indicators:X7-X11; Production competitiveness contains seven indicators:X12-X18;Economic benefits contains five indicators:X19-X23.

Table 1. The evaluation indicator system

Indicators	Variables
Length of fiber cable per capita	X1
Trunk switch board capacity per 100 persons	X2
Capacity of office telephone exchanges per 100 persons	X3
Capacity of mobile telephone exchanges per 100 persons	X4
Capacity of packet switched data network per 100 persons	X5

Table 1. (*continued*)

Number of internet broadband port per 100 persons	X6
Penetration rate of fixed-line telephone	X7
Penetration rate of mobile telephone	X8
Mobile subscriber growth rate	X9
Internet penetration	X10
Consumption expenditures on telecommunication per person	X11
The proportion of telecom industry employees	X12
Telecommunications service income per employees	X13
Investment in the fixed assets	X14
Total assets	X15
The profits of 100 Yuan assets	X16
Profit rate on costs	X17
Expenditures on research and development	X18
Telecommunications service income	X19
Business volume of telecommunications per capita	X20
Amount of profit	X21
Employee's average wage	X22
Telecommunications service income growth rate	X23

4 Empirical Analysis on the Regional Competitiveness of Telecom Industry

4.1 Method and Data

In this paper, the author calculated the weights of each index using principal component analysis. principal component analysis is a statistical procedure that transforms a number of highly correlated variables into a smaller number of principal components which account for most of the variance of the observed variables. These new principal components are irrelevant, and avoiding the deviations caused by overlapping information. We selected China's 31 provinces, autonomous regions and municipalities as evaluation object, collected data in 2004 -2008 of each index. The data are derived from statistics database of Guoyan website, China Information Industry Yearbook, China Statistical Yearbook and ministry of industry and information Statistics, both of them are published by the National Bureau of Statistics.

4.2 Analyzing Process and Results Analysis

We chose 2004 as the base year, calculated the weight of each index in 2004 and maintaining the same weight of individual indicators in 2005-2008, weights in short period of time will not cause significant deviation[3]. According the Principal component analysis, we use SPSS16.0 to analyze the original data of the 31 objects in

2004. The results show that the cumulative variance contribution rate of the first 4 principal components reaches 89.204%,and corresponding eigenvalues greater than 1, So that the first 4 principal components embody most of the information contained in all indicators. According to the component matrix, in accordance with the steps calculated the weight of individual indicators.

4.3 Regional Telecom Industry Competitiveness Analysis

As Table 2 shows,in2004-2008,the top 10 rank of average composite score are Eastern region provinces, the competitiveness of Shanghai, Beijing, Guangzhou ranks 1st,2ndand3nd,these areas score surpassed 0.7;Zhejiang, Jiangsu, Tianjin, Fujian, Liaoning and Shandong ranks 4th to 9th.Average composite score of these areas was

Table 2. The composite score of regional telecom industry competitiveness

Year / Region	2004	2005	2006	2007	2008	Average composite score	Rank
Shanghai	0.698	0.727	0.765	0.778	0.704	0.734	1
Beijing	0.735	0.755	0.756	0.727	0.655	0.725	2
Guangdong	0.778	0.676	0.699	0.746	0.646	0.709	3
Zhejiang	0.477	0.491	0.529	0.556	0.519	0.514	4
Jiangsu	0.364	0.371	0.440	0.446	0.412	0.406	5
Tianjin	0.381	0.405	0.404	0.380	0.348	0.384	6
Fujian	0.337	0.318	0.348	0.376	0.381	0.352	7
Liaoning	0.295	0.296	0.316	0.320	0.348	0.315	8
Shandong	0.288	0.280	0.325	0.330	0.289	0.303	9
Hebei	0.206	0.213	0.248	0.238	0.220	0.225	10
Shanxi	0.183	0.201	0.209	0.218	0.190	0.200	11
Shaanxi	0.184	0.189	0.203	0.208	0.198	0.197	12
Hainan	0.158	0.192	0.193	0.188	0.245	0.195	13
Sichuan	0.178	0.191	0.205	0.206	0.185	0.193	14
Henan	0.163	0.177	0.218	0.213	0.191	0.192	15
Hubei	0.176	0.201	0.200	0.195	0.187	0.192	16
Chongqing	0.190	0.174	0.200	0.190	0.181	0.187	17
Jilin	0.183	0.197	0.194	0.187	0.151	0.182	18
Heilongjiang	0.184	0.185	0.183	0.180	0.151	0.177	19
Hunan	0.156	0.196	0.182	0.180	0.160	0.175	20
Xinjiang	0.158	0.159	0.165	0.183	0.204	0.174	21
Neimenggu	0.152	0.165	0.172	0.177	0.175	0.168	22
Anhui	0.134	0.152	0.177	0.178	0.163	0.161	23
Guangxi	0.149	0.151	0.160	0.161	0.154	0.155	24
Xizang	0.173	0.131	0.140	0.149	0.158	0.150	25
Ningxia	0.154	0.157	0.146	0.140	0.148	0.149	26
Yunnan	0.142	0.137	0.157	0.151	0.134	0.144	27
Jiangxi	0.117	0.131	0.141	0.144	0.124	0.131	28
Qinghai	0.108	0.120	0.125	0.125	0.139	0.123	29
Gansu	0.094	0.090	0.104	0.102	0.095	0.097	30
Guizhou	0.086	0.094	0.107	0.107	0.091	0.097	31

more than 0.3,while telecom industry competitiveness of these areas have great gap with the top 3; Ranks in the middle of the provinces are Hebei, Shanxi, Hainan, Sichuan, Chongqing etc. Average score of these areas was 0.17~0.22, and no significant difference in telecom industry competitiveness; At the back of the provinces are Neimenggu, Anhui, Guangxi, Xizang, Guizhou etc .Most of them in the Western region, average score of these areas below the 0.17.

4.4 Comparative Analysis of East, West and Central Regions

For a long period of time, China implemented unbalanced regional economic policies, led to the imbalance of the regional economic. In accordance with the National Bureau of Statistics 2003 criteria for the region classification, calculate average composite score of Eastern, Central and Western areas(Fig.1).

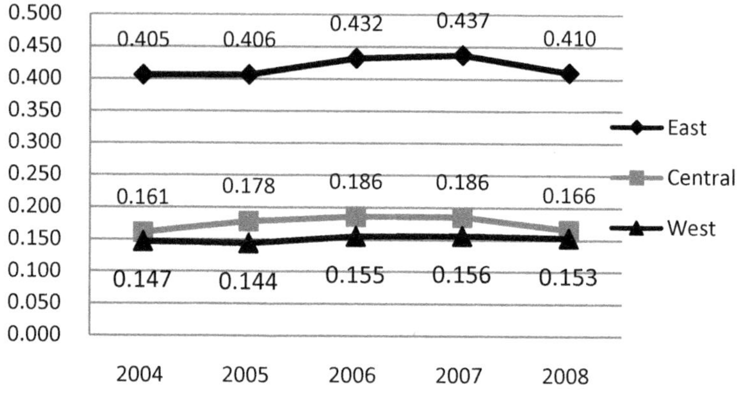

Fig. 1. The trends of regional telecom industry competitiveness

In the past five years, the three regions telecom industry have experienced increased stage in 2004-2007,while declined in 2008. Respectively, East's competitiveness average composite score was 0.405 in 2004,and increased to 0.437 in 2007,then decreased to 0.41 in 2008.The score of Central was 0.161, increased to 0.178 in 2007,and decreased to 0.166 in 2008.West's score was 0.147 in 2004, increased to 0.144 in 2007, and decreased to 0.153in 2008.So we can obtain the basic pattern of China telecom industry: Telecom industry competitiveness of East is much higher than in the Central and West, Central area slightly higher than West, but there is no significant difference between Central and West.

4.5 Comparative Analysis of Influence Factors

Factors are the reason for the difference of telecom industry competitiveness, therefore, to calculated the index of Communication competence, Market competitiveness, Production competitiveness and Economic benefits four aspects(Fig.2).

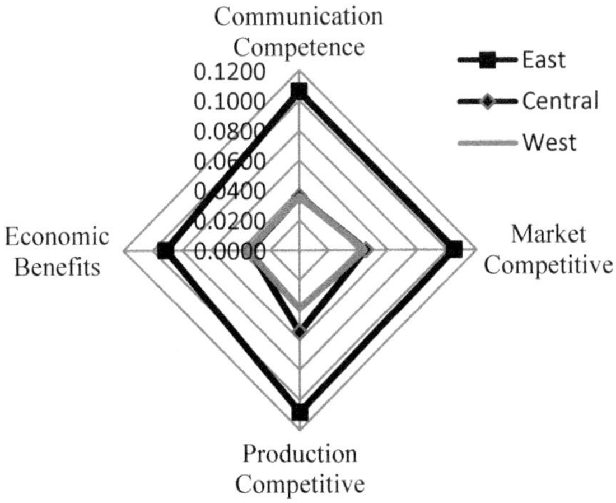

Fig. 2. Comparative analysis of influence factors in 2008

Compared with Central and Western, Eastern was superior in Communication competence, Market competitiveness, Production competitiveness and Economic benefits, the West's communication competence index and market competitiveness index almost equal to Central area.

The communication competence index of three areas are 0.106,0.036 and 0.036,proved that telecom infrastructure in West has reached the level of Central. The market competitiveness index of three areas are 0.105,0.045 and 0.044,the East is superior to Central and West. The production competitiveness index of three areas are 0.108,0.055 and 0.039, Economic benefits index are 0.091,0.033 and 0.035. The production competitiveness index of Central is superior to West, but the economic benefits of West is higher than Central.

4.6 Internal Diversity of Each Region

Internal diversity reflect regional coordinated development of telecom industry, coordinated development is benefit to improve regional telecom industry competitiveness. Usually, use the coefficient of variation(CV) to analysis the internal diversity (Table 3).

Table 3. Coefficient of variation of regional telecom industry

Year / Region	2004	2005	2006	2007	2008
East	0.55	0.52	0.49	0.50	0.44
Central	0.15	0.14	0.12	0.12	0.14
West	0.26	0.25	0.25	0.25	0.26

From Table 3,in the past five years, East have the largest internal diversity, followed by the West, and the Central have the smallest internal diversity. It is shows that although the East have unrivaled competitiveness, it's telecom industry disparate development. In 2004-2008,the CV of East showing a downward trend, CV of East was 0.55 in 2004,dropped to 0.44 in 2008.The CV of Central was small, and the west have a little change in CV, stabilized at 0.25, but over the central.

5 Conclusions

Through above research, we can drawn following conclusions: The gap between the East, West and Central in telecom industry competitiveness consistent with the differences in economic. The East is much higher than Central and West, Central area is slightly higher than West, but there is no significant difference between Central and West. Compared with Central and Western, Eastern was superior in Communication competence, Market competitiveness, Production competitiveness and Economic benefits, this is main reason caused the margin of telecom industry competitiveness. In terms of internal diversity ,Eastern have the largest internal diversity, but the overall level higher than the Central and West. The internal diversity of telecom in Central and West was small, but the comprehensive strength was weak, lack prominence provinces in telecommunications.

References

1. Zhu, J.: Telecommunications competitiveness. Beijing University of Post and telecommunications Press, Beijing (2006)
2. Zhang, L., Yuan, N.: Comparison and selection of index standardization method in linear comprehensive evaluation model. Journal of Statistics and Information Forum, 10–15 (2010)
3. Fan, G.: Marketization index of China's provinces. Journal of Economic Research, 9–18 (2003)
4. Telecommunications Research Institute.: The research report of China telecom international competitiveness (2002,2003,2004)
5. Qi, X.: Analysis on the China telecom international competitiveness. Journal of Qiongzhou University, 15–19 (2006)
6. Li, Z.: Evolution on the services international competitiveness. Master's degree thesis of Nanchang University (2006)
7. Zhang, Y., Wu, J.: Empirical research on telecom services international competitiveness based on factor analysis. Journal of Economic Forum, 101–103 (2009)
8. Porter, M.: National competitive advantage. Huaxia Press, Beijing (2002)
9. Zhang, J.: International competitiveness evaluation theory and method. Economic Science Press, Beijing (2002)
10. Bei, J.: Competitiveness economic. Guangzhou Economic Press, Guangzhou (2003)
11. Dunning, J.H.: Internationalizing Porter's Diamond. Management International Review, 7–15 (1993)

A Study of the State of Sports Consumption of University and College Students in China

Xiao-Dong Long, Yue-Feng Wang, and Xiao-Juan Liu

Jinggangshan University, Ji'an, Jiangxi, China 343009
Tel: +8613237068866, +8615979666111
lxd8307732@163.com

Abstract. The paper aims at the study of the state of sports consumption of university and college students in China to obtain some convincing views on the consciousness of sports consumption of the Chinese college students. The paper selects at random students from nine colleges and universities in China. By the research methods of questionnaire, literature, experts interviewing and mathematical statistics are applied to analyze the state of sports consumption of the Chinese college students. The conclusions can be obtained that: 1. the Chinese college students feel positive about sports consumption and they come to realize that sporting is a good way not only to strengthen their physical health but also to relax and entertain themselves. The college students accept sports consumption as a part of their life. 2. Sports clothing is a main aspect in colleges and universities students' sports consumption. 3. The average sports consumption of the college students is about 101-1200 yuan per year, which still keeps in a low level compared with the consumption of other groups. 4. 99.9% college students consume on sports under two or more motives --- real need as the primary motivation, entertainment as the next and knowledge acquirements as the last motivation.

Keywords: colleges and universities, college students, sports consumption.

1 Introduction

Since reformation and opening-up, China has made great achievements in economy, and the living standard of the Chinese has improved steadily. Sports, as a kind of everyday amusement, are accepted by more and more people. Many Chinese, especially contemporary college students, participate in various sports to enjoy the pleasures from sports. Therefore, the development of modern sports is closely related with that of economy. The rapid development motivates the development of sports, as well as the development of sports-oriented body-building and recreation, which enhance the awareness of sports consumption. In return, the enhancement of sports consumption and the development of sports promote the economic development. The development of modern sports has led to the formation of a huge consumption market which satisfies the dual need of health and amusement. The paper analyzes the state of

Q. Zhou (Ed.): ISAEBD 2011, Part II, CCIS 209, pp. 253–258, 2011.

sports consumption of the Chinese college students from the viewpoints of sports consumption awareness, sports consumption pattern, sports consumption level and sports consumption psychological motivation.

2 The Research Objects and Research Method

2.1 Research Objects

We selected at random from September to December in 2009 100 students from each of the nine colleges as the research objects. (Beijing Sports University, Renmin University of China, Tongji University, Xiamen University, Southeast university of technology, Hainan University, Nanchang University, Jiangxi Normal University and Jinggangshan University) Of the 900 questionnaires distributed, 835 questionnaires have been returned with a response rate of 92.8%. Among those returned, The total number of valid return was 789 (403 from male college students, and 386 from female college students) with a usability rate of87.7%

2.2 Main Research Methods

Questionnaire, literature, experts interviewing and mathematical statistics are applied.

3 Investigation and Analysis of College Students Sports Consumption

3.1 Investigation and Analysis of College Students' Awareness of Sports Consumption

The results of Fig 1 show: of the 789 college students investigated, ① 30.92% keep a normal sports consumption; ②19.77% spend money to buy health; ③49.31% hold that sports consumption reflects modern life style; ④ 77.31% keep a frugal sports consumption; ⑤22.69% keep a luxurious sports consumption. Accordingly, it can be analyzed that in general, college students take a positive attitude to sports consumption and regard it as a part of life-long physical health exercises. And 77.31% support frugal sports consumption, which reveals that the traditional concept of frugal sports consumption still bring important effects on college students. However, the traditional concept of frugal sports consumption is not in line with the economic development of modern society, and a new sports consumption concept is required.

index	*Male (numbers)*	*percentage%*	*female (numbers)*	*Percent tage%*	*Total percent tage%*
normal sports consumption	152	19.25%	92	11.67%	30.92%
Concept of spending moneyto buy health	103	13.05%	53	6.72%	19.77%
sports consumption as the embodiment of modern life	148	18.76%	241	30.55%	49.31%
Frugal sports consumption	126	15.97%	53	6.72%	22.69%
Luxurious sports consumption	277	35.11%	333	42.20%	77.31%

Fig. 1. Statistics of college students sports consumption concept （n=789）

3.2 Result Analysis of College Students Sports Consumption Pattern

The results of Fig 2show: of the 789 college students investigated,①Sportswear accounts for 57.79% ; ② Sports equipment accounted for 9.89% ; ③ sports newspapers and magazines and audio and video products account for 11.66% ; ④sporting performances and event tickets account for 5.32% ; ⑤consumption in fitness centers account for 10.52% ; ⑥expenses for sports training and health services account for 1.90% ; ⑦ expenses for sports lottery and others account for 2.92%。 It can be drawn from the analysis that : A major part of the expenses for sports is on sportswear. 57.79% college students spend money on sportswear, which is affected by the traditional consumption habits and consumption psychology of the Chinese people. 11.66% students spend money on sports newspapers and magazines and audio and video products. 10.52% students go to fitness centers. Only 1.90% students spend

index	*Male (num bers)*	*Percent tage%*	*Female (numbers)*	*Percent tage%*	*total percent tage%*
sportswear	153	19.39%	303	38.40%	57.79%
Sports equimpent	65	8.24%	13	1.65%	9.89%
sports newspapers and magazines and audio and video products	86	10.90	6	0.76%	11.66%
sporting performances and event tickets	39	4.94%	3	0.38%	5.32%
fitness centers	28	3.55%	55	6.97%	10.52%
sports training and health services	13	1.65%	2	0.25%	1.90%
sports lottery and others	19	2.42%	4	0.50%	2.92%

Fig. 2. Statistics of college students sports consumption pattern （n=789）

money on sports training and health services. Male college students sports consumption patterns are relatively decentralized, while the female students centralize their sports consumption on sportswear and fitness centers.

3.3 Analysis of the General Sports Consumption Level of College Students

The results of Fig 3 show: Of 789 college students investigated, the amount of sports consumption each year ia ①10.77% above 1201 yuan ; ②23.45% at 801-1200 yuan; ③ 30.80% at 401-800 yuan: ④22.18% at 101-400 yuan ; ⑤12.80% below100 yuan The results show that the sports consumption of each college students varies widely. The amount of sports consumption by male students is in general higher than that of female students. The total amount of sports consumption by male students is above 400 yuan and the total amount of sports consumption by female students is below 400yuan. The general amount of sports consumption by Chinese college students is at 101yuan per year—1200 yuan per year, which is shown that the consumption level of average per capita of sports is relatively low.

index	*Male (number)*	*Percentage %*	*Female (num ber)*	*Percent tage%*	*Total percent tage%*
above 1201 yuan	69	8.75%	16	2.02%	10.77%
801-1200 yuan	125	15.84%	60	7.61 %	23.45 %
401-800 yuan	142	18.00%	101	12.80%	30.80 %
101-400 yuan	46	5.83%	129	16.35%	22.18 %
Below 100 yuan	21	2.66 %	80	10.14%	12.80%

Fig. 3. Statistics of general sports consumption level of college students （n=789）

3.4 Analysis of Psychological Motivation of College Students Sports Consumption

He results of Fig 4 show: Of 789 college students investigated,①90.62% consume for the sake of real needs ; ②79.72% for the sake of body building ; ③57.03% for the sake of social interaction;④86.57% for the sake of entertainment and relaxation;⑤78.20% for the sake of aesthetic pursuit ; ⑥51.96% because of star effect ; ⑦21.30% because of sports achievement ; ⑧53.11% because of consumption comparison ; ⑨20.79% for the sake of knowledge acquisition。 Accordingly, it can be analyzed that: ①90.62% college students consume because of their real needs for sports, which corresponds to the current productivity development level in China and people's sports consumption concept. ② 86.57% college students are willing to consume on sports to satisfy their needs for amusement and relaxation, which can be revealed that compared with other groups, college students are more active in emotion. And the dull academic lessons may easily make the students feel bored. That is why college students require more pleasure and relaxation. ③79.72% college students consume on sports under the motivation of building their body, which reveals that under the current circumstances, college students shouldn't take health very seriously. While having certain consciousness of their health, they do not regard sports as a powerful means of keeping healthy.④78.20% college students consume on sports for the sake of aesthetic pursuit. Modern college students are characterized with passion, enthusiasm, imagination and curiosity. They are fond of innovation and they are perfectionists with a wish of being perfect in every way.⑤57.03% college students are willing to strengthen the interpersonal exchange by ways of sports, that is to say, sports is one of the best ways to improve interpersonal communication. This new social concept widens the road for the psychological development. ⑥53.11% college students consume on sports under the motivation of comparing with others, which shows that college students are driven in certain ways by the motivation of comparing with or even surpassing others. This kind of consumption is quite obvious among college students. ⑦51.96% college students consume on sports because of the star effect. College students are not only fascinated with watching sports-games, they are also crazy star chasers. ⑧21.30% college students consume on sports because of their own sports achievements. Some students are good at certain sporting events and they are willing to show to others their excellent sporting skills to achieve self satisfaction. ⑨20.79% college students consume on sports for the sake of acquiring knowledge. The motivations of male college students' sports consumption vary from real needs, body building, social interaction, amusement to star effect. Comparatively speaking, female college students consume on sports mainly because of real needs, body building, amusement and consumption comparison.

index	*Male (number)*	*percent age%*	*female (number)*	*percent age%*	*total percent tage%*
real need	362	45.88%	353	44.74%	90.62%
body building	373	47.27%	256	32.45%	79.72%
social interaction	287	36.37%	163	20.66%	57.03%
entertainment and relaxation	355	44.99%	328	41.58%	86.57%
aesthetic pursuit	249	31.56%	368	46.64%	78.20%
star effect	302	38.28%	108	13.68%	51.96%
sports achievement	131	16.60%	37	4.70%	21.30%
consumption comparison	83	10.52	336	42.59%	53.11%
knowledge acquisition	106	13.43%	58	7.36	20.79%

Fig. 4. Statistics of sports consumption motivation of college students (n=789)

4 Sugestions

1. The Chinese college students feel positive about sports consumption and they come to realize that sporting is a good way not only to strengthen their physical health but also to relax and entertain themselves. The college students accept sports consumption as a part of their life.

2. Sports clothing is a main aspect in colleges and universities students sports consumption.

3. The average sports consumption of the college students is about 101-1200 yuan per year, which still keeps in a low level compared with the consumption of other groups.

4. 99.9% college students consume on sports under two or more motives --- real need as the primary motivation, entertainment as the next and knowledge acquirements as the last motivation.

References

1. Li, R.: Verview of Sports Industry, p. 124. Beijing sport university press, Beijing (2005)
2. Wang, D.: Ew Consumer Psychology. Shandong People's Publishing House, Jinan (1996)
3. Wen, X., Ren, Z., Zhang, L.: Sumer Pychology. Tianjin University Press, Tianjin (1998)
4. Yin, S., Zhong, G., Xiao, F., Jie, G., He, L., Yan, J.: Hunan University Press, Changsha (2001)
5. Zhang, B.: Modern sports economics, pp. 217–226. Sun Yat-sen University Press, Guangzhou (2004)

On the Relationship between Corporate Sports Culture and Core Competence of Enterprise

Gan-Chen Tao

School of Physical Education, Jinggangshan University, Ji'an, China, 343009
Tel:+8613319333131
taoganchen@163.com

Abstract. This paper is a work based on documentary data methodology which elaborates the concepts of corporate sports culture (CSC) and Core Competence and explores the mechanism of CSC incentive on core competence formation and innovation; certain suggestions are herein given for developing Core-Competence-facilitating CSC. It is concluded that an enterprise determined in creation of new CSC needs to implant CSC philosophy in thoughts and put it into practice so that its time- and enterprise-specific CSC will be translated into cohesion, affinity and competitiveness that enhances its core competence.

Keywords: Enterprise, sports culture, core competence.

1 Introduction

In the world today characterized in explosion of high-technologies and accelerated globalization all countries are facing new political and economic prospects. And enterprises are facing challenges in an age of financial crisis and stock and real estate market upheavals. How can an enterprise comfortably handle market competition and its corporate management? One key lies in corporate culture, a new managerial theory and practice that provides important strategic resources for modern enterprises. As part of corporate culture, corporate sports culture (CSC) functions more than physical health; it influences multi-dimensionally on financial growth and culture formation. CSC development needs to be integrated into corporate culture at an underlying level so that it plays good roles in the formation of the latter[1]. Therefore, it is spiritual and cultural assurance beneficial for growth that an enterprise explores the CSC roles in the all-round enterprise development and the relationship between CSC and core competence.

2 Concepts of CSC and Core Competence

Corporate sports culture is daughter to both corporate culture and sports culture. It is a culture of mass or social sports. To corporate culture and sports culture, CSC is specific, that is, it shares some common features of the two, and possesses some particularities of its own. In other words, it is a specific culture developed in corporate

Q. Zhou (Ed.): ISAEBD 2011, Part II, CCIS 209, pp. 259–264, 2011.

sports activities carried out by staffs in their off-work time, through their physical activities and in way suitable to the corporate environment, for purpose of fitness and recreation, pursuing common values and communications, enthusiasm and ambitions. CSC functions both as a corporate culture and a sports culture, playing irreplaceable roles in an enterprise[2].

Core Competence is a core capacity inherent in an enterprise formed in its history, which makes up the enterprise's competitive superiorities in the past, present and future and ensures its initiatives on long-time competition. Specifically, it is a sustainable superiority developed and acquired in the process of supplementing, enhancing and strengthening of the existing core competence on condition that the competence matches the market opportunity handling capability. Core competence is developed through a course as follows:

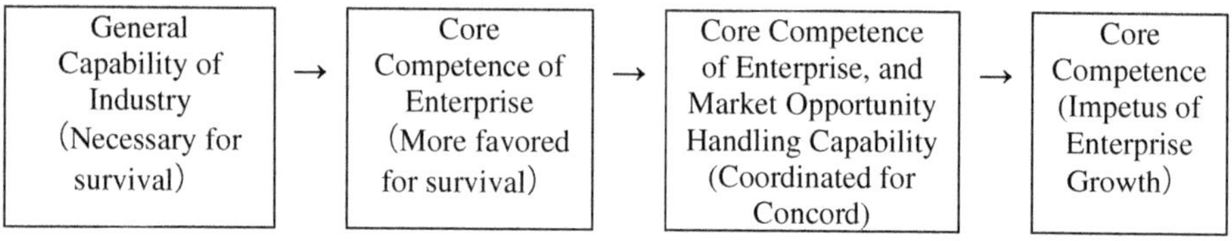

Fig. 1. Course of Core Competence Development

3 Mechanism of CSC Incentive on Core Competence Formation and Innovation

3.1 Functions of Corporate Culture

Firstly, corporate culture plays a role of orientation. It is the values shared by all staffs, which appeals the staffs and grows in them affinity and recognition to the enterprise, and pilots their individual goals and ideas towards those of the enterprise.

Secondly, corporate culture functions as adhesive that brings employees into cohesive one with definite and concerted targets, on basis that the enterprise is with proper essential aims catering interests of both the business and the most employees, both the collective and the individual.

Thirdly, corporate culture serves as incentive, a spiritual force. The culture develops an environment and value orientation by which employees are stimulated for more active, initiative and creative works through full play of their potential talents and capabilities, and by which enterprise sectors and their members have better self-management and operation.

The fourth function of corporate culture is restriction. By setting up correct orientations, it usually works as a kind of soft restraint on the behaviors which are harmful to long-run growth, thus rendering immunity for the enterprise. The restraint helps employees heighten their consciousness, enthusiasm and self-restriction, in addition to their understanding of the significances of their jobs.

The fifth effect of corporate culture is radiation. Once corporate culture grows in relatively stable mode, it not only influences internally, but also externally on communities through diverse channels. That is why publicizing of the corporate culture is beneficial for an enterprise to build its public identity, and why excellent corporate culture makes great differences to socio-cultural progress.

3.2 Functions of Sports Culture

As a first effect, sports spirits gives enterprise infinite dynamics to innovation. The spirits, *Swifter, Higher and Stronger,* encourages people's engagement in fair and just struggle that sublime themselves, a value agreeing with the inspiration of modern society that every person and every enterprise compete for maximal development.

Secondly, sports culture gives enterprise a spiritual essence of fair play. The consciousness of equality and fairness, which originated as basic rules in sports games, has been essential norms and requirements for modern enterprise. Rule-observance in competition has been normative to all social activities nowadays, and the fair play rule in sports is useful to facilitate enterprises towards market rules in a way humorous, natural, familiar and acceptable, expediting enterprise and its members to be a law-abidance entity recognizable and acceptable in the world.

Thirdly, sports culture gives enterprise vigorous and cooperative team spirits. In sports activities people contact, cooperate and encourage, arousing echoes in minds that improve inter-personal relation and team cohesion. By teaching people how to survive and how to live sports culture shows incomparable cohesion and affinity and gives people optimistic and aggressive spirits. Sports culture of an enterprise is reflection of its and its employees' values and common interests. By integration with corporate philosophies, targets, systems and spirits, it emits intangible and tremendous appeals to members and drives the enterprise to its destination. This is particularly true in the case of traditional Chinese sports culture which emphasizes "unity of body and mind", courtesy of combined "rite and righteousness", fair and equal competition, and struggle based on practice and facts—all of which being sources for corporate cohesion and incentive.

Fourthly, sports culture helps create favorable brand identity. Its application in enterprise, i.e. CSC, is valuable reflection of its extension in depth and broadness. CSC helps in rendering employees' welfare and health condition, uniting employees' talents, expanding communications between enterprise and its customers, media, public and governments, and establishing its identity[3]—enterprise with the Olympic spirits "Swifter, Higher and Stronger" will be of an identity globally acceptable.

3.3 CSC as Adhesives for Core Competence

CSC is adhesive to employees for their affinity, enthusiasm and creativity. An enterprise putting emphasis on sports spirits and its use as ethics, values and code of conducts will often succeed in arousing employees' efforts for development of the company and community. This is because only united talents, the most important resources a company has, can have full play of their genius and proficiency with a shared philosophy, thus enhancing the corporate competence which grows and develops into core competence after a long-time process. Based on the core competence other competences may be improved for the company's .competitive superiorities. In this way it is proper to say that CSC functions as driving incentive to talent genius and adhesive for core competence.

3.4 CSC as Activator of Core Competence

The roles of CSC in enterprise growth are played through internal growth force and the external identity innovation capacity.

Internally, as an environment for employees, CSC is beneficial both collectively and individually. In the enterprise, CSC works around "men", because every enterprise needs value beliefs and conduct tenets that bring the members together and spur them to work more enthusiastically, initiatively and creatively. The value beliefs, once internalized within the staff, will on one hand lay great social responsibilities on enterprise and require the enterprise's rectification of its conducts according to social and public welfare; on the other hand, the beliefs implant lofty significances in staffs' daily works, considering that employees always long for acknowledgement of his work by the collective and the society and for recognition and respect from the rest of the world through his performance. CSC is in one way aimed at creation of such a desirable work and living environment in which employees learn and feel with their heart. Certainly, every enterprise has its CSC. But one may has good one, while another has one less so good. Employees in a business without or with inferior CSC will be inflicted with an apparently bad feeling.

Externally, CSC also expands enterprise's space of existence. CSC is a highly community-radioactive sign of the enterprise's nature and operation approaches. Good CSC shows publics with great communicative affinity and attractions and builds positive corporate identity, popularity and reputation, creating an animating external space for survival and growth of enterprise.

The internal and external CSC-shaped environments are most important intangible wealth for the enterprise. Its employees' creativity and enthusiasm, as well as its identity and reputation, are transformable to product or service increment, which will in turn win for it the market, consumer, competitive competence and economic benefits. Profit organizations today are no more tech-economic complexes; rather, they are complexes of economy, technology, culture and psychology. They not only live in socio-economic context, but also in socio-cultural context. Excellent CSC helps enterprises keep balance and harmony in economy, technology and society and facilitate their smooth development and realization of operation goals. CSC is the united idealistic and spiritual pursuits of enterprise management and employees as well as historical enrichment developed in long process. It needs constant accumulation to yield proper social and economic benefits and to keep the enterprise moving forward.

4 Strategies for Core-Competence-Facilitating CSC Formation

4.1 Basic Principles for CSC Formation

First is the principle of objectives. Objective refers to the result expected to be realized in certain period. CSC ought to be assigned with objectives which are in line with the enterprise development. Management by objectives is an important thought and methodology in business management today, use of which may provide effective guide to sports consciousness and activities and bring about desirable stimulations.

Second is principle of adaptation. CSC in general should be adaptable to specific country, say, China where operate socialist market economy system and modern enterprise system, and suitable to specific enterprise's management style and general culture development program.

Third is principle of consensus. Consensus is a natural basis of corporate culture program. A culture lacking of consensus is one without core. Though CSC requires multi-orientated development, it needs more cultural consensus on the specificity of the enterprise.

The fourth is principle of performance. Performance is both end of a job and basis for a next move. The emphasis of performance helps shift people's focus from on "process" to on "end", thus excluding possible Pharisaism or doctrinarism in the process and meanwhile stressing CSC roles and functions.

4.2 Appropriate Entry for CSC Development

As enterprises are possibly of quite different background, industry, operation and status, it is necessary that an enterprise builds its modern CSC through an entry appropriate to its situations, in other words, proceeding from solution of the urgent primary contradictories towards establishment of rational operation mechanism, better work methods, correct values, sports behavior codes, and proper sports environment and ambience. In that way can the responses expected be aroused, and the role and values of CSC fully played.

4.3 Down-to-Earth CSC Development Design

Novel CSC development design requires analyzing, summarizing and evaluating of CSC situations, theoretical planning and feasibility analyses of the enterprise' values, fundamental philosophy, development objectives, operation mechanisms. The design also requires integration of theory, practice and cultural innovation which is source of progress. Additionally, the design requires combination of the generality and the individuality, of the uniformity and the diversity, because CSC is specific and individual to corporate culture, and only by integration into the latter, the more general, can it go into the macro-context social culture. Finally, CSC development design needs modifiability, considering that variations and uncertainties occur in real practice. Hence the final CSC design should be general guidance combined with innovations and flexibilities.

4.4 Multi-orientated CSC Practice

First, sports facilities are to be arranged under general corporate development plan, with increasingly perfected installations for recreation and sports, as well as material capitalizations on grounds, gymnasiums and fitness equipments that provide proper basis for employees' exercises.

Second, scheduled enterprise sports activities are to be rolled out, in which traditional sports games are kept, new ones developed and employees of all ages encouraged to take active part.

Third, diverse modes of sports activities are explored, including systematic sports competition, enterprise-community interaction, intra-enterprise sports club, enterprise-professional communication, etc. Thriving sports interior of enterprise, between enterprises and between enterprise and community helps to grow sports culture that strengthens corporate essence and shapes corporate identity.

5 Conclusions

Enterprise should build indigenous and reality-based CSC with new ideas and particularities, in a way that the CSC philosophies are both implanted and practiced. Therefore, such a process characterized in corporate-spirits -orientation, humanistic operation, honest operation and constant innovation will translate the time- and business-specific CSC into cohesion, affinity and competitiveness that enhances enterprise core competence.

References

[1] Ni, T. (ed.): Research on Management System and Operation Mechanism for Mass Sports of Grass Roots in China in Market Economy Context. People's Sports Press, Beijing (2002) (In Chinese)
[2] Xiao, Y., Lu, F.: A Survey of Corporate Sports Culture in Market Economy Context. Market Modernization 567, 315–316 (2009) (In Chinese)
[3] Zhang, J.-c.: A Study on Basic Concept of Sports Culture. Journal of Sports and Science 6, 12–14 (2003) (In Chinese)

Research on the Evaluation Model of Excellent Synchronized Swimming Athletes' Figure in China

Dong yue Wang

Zhengzhou institute of Aeronautical industry Management Henan Zhengzhou
hnxxwdy@yahoo.com.cn

Abstract. This paper takes 41 excellent synchronized swimming athletes in China as research objects, through the methods of documentary, questionnaire, mathematical statistics; experimental research, the author tries to build the evaluation model of excellent synchronized swimming athletes' figure by studying their figure indexes. The results shows: the excellent synchronized swimming athletes' figure can be divided into body gene, body component and body shape; the excellent synchronized swimming athletes should have a higher height, longer arms, wider palms and the "the inverse cone" streamline body shape. Whereas the requirement of under skin fat and body component is not high. This model may provide references for better selecting and scientific training of the excellent synchronized swimming athletes.

Keywords: Synchronized swimming, evaluation model, figure index, excellent athletes.

1 Preface

Synchronized swimming is an item which shows strength, endurance, flexibility, grace and artistry, and the result relies on the umpires' score, hence the athletes' figure may influence their achievements to certain extent. In recent years, we have made great improvement on competitive level of synchronized swimming, however, there still exits gap between China and world top teams like Russia, Spain etc. How to narrow the gap is one of the most important tasks for our research stuff to accomplish and consequently the study of the relevant factors which affect the competitive ability becomes urgent. The paper tries to provide scientific references of better selecting and scientific training of synchronized swimming athletes from the research of building the evaluation model and criterion of excellent synchronized swimming athletes' figure.

2 Objects, Method and Procedure

2.1 Objects

This paper takes 41 excellent synchronized swimming athletes in China national teams as research objects which 20 of them are under the age of 18. Among all of

Q. Zhou (Ed.): ISAEBD 2011, Part II, CCIS 209, pp. 265–272, 2011.

them, 5 are international master of sports, 29 are national masters of sports,2 are first grade and 5 are second grade and most of them have accepted special training for years. Their competitive level represents the highest level in China and can reflect the whole characteristics of our synchronized swimming athletes' figure and the number of the objects can also guarantee the accuracy of the research.

Table 1. Basic information

Team	Sports grade	no./n	average age/y	height/cm	weight/kg
National team1	international master of sport	5	22	169.8	56.6
	National master of sport	16	18.56	168.24	57.36
National team 2	National master of sport	13	16.69	166.54	54.1
	First Grade	2	16	165	54.25
	Second Grade	5	16.5	166	53.24

2.2 Methods

2.2.1 Documentary

Consulting and collecting the documentary of domestic and abroad research on athletes' figure, understanding the current research situation.

2.2.2 Questionnaire and Interview

By selecting the figure index which has close connection between the synchronized swimming and athletes' achievement the writer tries to build the evaluation model of excellent synchronized swimming athletes' figure. Based on consulting large amount of documentary, the writer interviewed with experienced coaches and experts on training which aims to the selection of athletes' figure index of synchronized swimming, and designed 9 expert questionnaire which including 2 professors, 1 associate professor, 6 coaches, the recovery percentage is 100%.

2.2.3 Testing

Centralized testing is carried on the selected athletes' figure index of national synchronized swimming team at the end of 2009. The testing time is Jan. 10, 2010 and the testing place is in the national swimming training gymnasium. During the test, the athletes all have their swimming costume. According to the standard testing method of domestic and abroad, the athletes were tested by professional figure testing equipment. The testing stuff is trained in advance and experts.

2.2.4 SPSS

Using SPSS method, the writer tries find out the most important factors which affect the whole figure by putting weight allocation on different figure indexes and thus achieve the aim of lowering down the index and calculating out the weight allocation of different indexes.

3 Result and Analysis

3.1 The Figure Index Selection and Confirmation

In order to simplify the component of figure index and find out the most useful index which benefits the research and analysis of figure characteristics of our excellent synchronized swimming athletes, the writer tries to confirm the system of figure index by the following procedures: firstly, consulting the relevant documentary and research achievements and selecting the preliminary index ; secondly, according to the preliminary index, the writer select the figure indexes which reflect the item based on the questionnaire and interview; thirdly, confirming the final index from the way of logic reasoning. The final indexes are: height, sitting-height, upper limb/height*100, palm size, pelvis/shoulder blade, Quetlet index, skin fold thickness.

3.2 Confirmation of Weight Factor of Figure Index

From the test of KMO variable of statistics and Bartlett, the KMO variable is 0.643≥0.5 which indicates that the figure index data we gathered satisfied the requirement of factor analysis.

Table 2. Explanation of population variance

	Initial Eigenvalues			Extraction Sums of Squared Loadings			Rotation Sums of Squared Loadings		
Component	Total	% of Variance	Cumulative %	Total	% of Variance	Cumulative %	Total	% of Variance	Cumulative %
1	2.492	35.597	35.597	2.492	35.597	35.597	2.170	31.006	31.006
2	1.494	21.348	56.945	1.494	21.348	56.945	1.798	25.680	56.686
3	1.175	16.782	73.727	1.175	16.782	73.727	1.193	17.042	73.727
4	.656	9.369	83.097						
5	.493	7.038	90.135						
6	.424	6.055	96.190						
7	.267	3.810	100.000						

Form the data and weight calculation we can find that weight factor 1 is 0.421, weight factor 2 is 0.348, and weight factor 3 is 0.231. Factor 1 includes height, sitting-height and palm size which named as body factor; factor 2 includes skin fold thickness and Quetlet index which named as body component factor; factor 3 includes length of upper limb/ height, shoulder blade index which named as figure factor.

Table 3. The load case of each factor after varimax orthogonal rotation

	Component		
	1	2	3
height	.853	.196	-.061
Sitting-height	.783	-.163	-.210
Palm size	.735	.241	.282
Sebum thickness	.070	.852	.039
Quetlet index	.462	.753	.153
Shoulder blade width	-.241	.615	-.506
Length of upper are/height	-.108	.059	.886

Table 4. Weight factors of figure index

Index	Factor1	Factor2	Factor3
height	0.262	0.068	0.029
height-sitting height	0.241	0.057	0.098
palm size	0.226	0.084	0.132
skin folder thickness	0.022	0.296	0.018
Quetlet index	0.007	0.262	0.072
Shoulder blade width	0.074	0.214	0.237
Upper limb/height	0.033	0.020	0.415

Table 5. Single index final weight and average model

index	weight	Mean and standard deviation
height	0.151	168± 3.77cm
height-sitting height	0.154	78.4± 5.81cm
palm size	0.164	131.6± 11.23mm
skin folder thickness	0.116	14.73± 3.12mm
Quetlet index	0.111	332.2± 21.4
Shoulder blade width	0.177	0.67± 0.05cm
Upper limb/height	0.127	43.5± 1.2cm

The aim of figure model is to confirm the weight allocation of the figure indexes and the weight allocation is achieved by the analysis of factors. Inferring from the analysis result of Table 2, it is certain that there are three major elements according to the eigenvalue and variance percentage. The accumulative variance percentage of these three major elements reaches 73.727% or more, which summarizes most information of specific body shape. Due to this, we may infer that except these three variables, others exert little influence to variance, so we take the first three as the major elements and then separate the body shape structure of our country's excellent synchronized swimming athletes into three factors. Due to the difference of each factor's eigenvalue and variance percentage, it takes different percentage in reflecting the body shape information of synchronized swimming athletes. The weight of each factor can be calculated according to the variance percentage.

3.3 Figure Index Weight Model and Mean Model

According to the load case of each factor after varimax orthogonal rotation as shown in Table 3: Factor 1 is named as Body- build Factor for indexes of it including Height, Height-Sitting Height and Palm Size, all of relatively high factor load, reflect the basic body shape of the synchronized swimming athletes ; Factor 2 is named as Body Composition Factor for indexes including Sum of Skinfold Thickness and Quetlet Index ,of relatively large load in Factor 2, mainly reflect the features of body composition of synchronized swimming athletes; Factor 3 is named as Somatotype Factor for indexes including Bone/Shoulder Breadth and Upper extremity length/Height are of large load in Factor 3.

Table 6 shows the weight of each body shape index calculated according to factor load with its calculating method explained in Formula (2). From the weight of each body shape index calculated by factor load, we may know that: in Factor 1, Height, Height-Sitting Height and Palm size Index have higher weights; in Factor2, Skinfold Thickness Index and Quetlet Index are of higher load; in Factor 3, Pelvis / Shoulder Breadth and Upper extremity length/Height are of higher load. Based on it, we can know that the weight of each factor's index matches with the factor' name property. Each index has a different weight in each factor which is also different from each other in weight. The final weight of each index can be calculated according to each factor and its weight of indexes for factor is the aggregate of indexes while index is the minimum unit to study weight.

Table 5 displays the weight model and mean model of excellent synchronized swimming athletes in our country. From the table, we may see that Pelvis / Shoulder Breadth is of higher weight , showing that streamline somatotype with relatively wide shoulder and narrow pelvis is required to every synchronized swimming athlete. This kind of somatotype can overcome the form drag when moving underwater, accordingly increasing the swimming speed and enhancing the strength in performing a complete set of movements, which also indicates the importance of inverted-cone body shape in synchronized swimming. Besides, Height, Height-Sitting Height and Palm size Index are of higher weight, indicating that synchronized swimming athletes should have the features of tall figure, relatively long reach of arms and wide palm which combines closely with stroke of swimming The research result identifies with the fact that the top-ranked Russian athletes are tall. Athletes from Russia and Spain keep tall build with an average height of 170cm or more. The weights of Sum of Skinfold Thickness Index and Quetlet Index indicate that the requirement on body composition is not very high.

3.4 The Establishment of Figure Evaluation System

The weight model and mean model of excellent synchronized swimming athletes in our country are built previously to provide a scientific reference for diagnosing the body shape structure of excellent synchronized swimming athletes. Individual evaluation standard and comprehensive evaluation system are specially established to further build an accurate evaluation system so as to perfect the body shape model. the marking of individual index adopts 5-mark evaluation system of percentile method with the following specific steps: find out four terciles of each body shape index including 10, 30, 70 and 90 and designate the level over 90% as excellent (assignment is 5 scores), level between 70% to 90% as good (assignment is 4 scores), level between 30% to 70% as average (assignment is 3 scores), level between 10% to 30% as bad (assignment is 2 scores) and level below 10% as inferior(assignment is 1 score), and the specific evaluation standards are as shown in Table 6.

Table 6. Single figure index evaluation criterions

index	5score	4score	3score	2score	1score
height	over 173.00	169.32-172.00	165.00-169.31	163.00-165.00	under 162.00
height-sitting height	over81.94	79.44-81.93	75.30-79.43	74.56-75.29	under74.55
palm size	over 145.31	136.84-145.30	125.02-136.83	116.88-125.01	under 116.87
skin folder thickness	over31.31	26.21-31.30	17.11-26.20	14.51-17.10	under14.50
Quetlet index	over361.71	341.52-361.70	321.21-341.51	303.71-321.20	under 303.70
Shoulder blade width	over72.63	68.93-72.62	65.72-68.92	63.32-65.71	under 63.31
Upper limb/height	over44.83	43.97-44.82	42.75-43.96	41.88-42.74	under 41.87

Evaluation standard of individual index only reflects one aspect of the athlete's body shape but not his integrate body feature, so it is necessary to establish a comprehensive index evaluation standard of excellent synchronized swimming athletes. The method to build a comprehensive evaluation standard of body shape is: firstly, transferring the testing index of every athlete into grade scores according to the individual evaluation standard of his body shape; secondly, multiplying each body shape index's weight by its scores and then add every product of multiplication all to get the comprehensive scores of the athlete's body shape; finally, regulating a comprehensive evaluation standard of body shape according to the method of percentile. The concrete procedures are: firstly, transferring each body shape index of an athlete into corresponding scores (5, 4, 3, 2 and 1);secondly, adopting formula (4) to calculate the total score of athlete's body shape according to his body shape index and its weight; finally, finding out the tercile of body shape index including 10,30,70 and 90 to complete the comprehensive evaluation on the body shape structure of excellent synchronized swimming athletes in our country.(as shown in Table 7)

Table 7. Whole figure index evaluation criterion

Criterion	Comprehensive score	grade
Over P90	over 3.49	excellent
P70-P90	3.20-3.48	better
P30-P70	2.19-2.54	medium
P10-P30	2.17-2.53	bad
Under P10	under2.16	worse

3.5 Retrospective Test to the Evaluation Standard of Body Shape

We make a comprehensive evaluation to the excellent synchronized swimming athletes of team 1 and team 2 with the specified evaluation standard in Table 7.

The evaluation results are shown in the Line Chart: the line chart's results of total scores of athlete from team 1 and team 2 indicate that the general distribution condition of athletes' total scores in body shape of team 1 is better than that of team 2, which identifies with the fact that the competitive ability of team 1 is superior to that of team 2. total scores of the athlete's body shape calculated according to the evaluation standard shown in Table 7 indicate that there are 3 athletes from team 1 whose total scores reach excellent level(account for 14.28%)and 7 athletes reach good level(account for 33.3%), and there is only 1 athlete whose total scores reach good level(account for 5%). The excellence and good rate of team 1 is obviously superior to that of team 2, fully showing that that evaluation model is appropriate to evaluate the body shape of excellent synchronized swimming athletes in our country.

4 Conclusion

1. From the analysis of figure index factors of our excellent synchronized swimming athletes, their figure can be divided into three factors: body factor, figure factor and body component factor. The reprehensive indexes are seven: height, height-sitting height, palm size, skin fold thickness, Quetlet index, shoulder blade and upper limb/height.

2. The evaluation model reveals that synchronized swimming athletes should have tall and thin figure, longer upper limb and larger palm size; the figure should be wider shoulder blade and narrow pelvis, the "the inverse cone" streamline body shape. Whereas the requirement of under skin fat and body component is not high.

3. To establish the single figure index evaluation criterion and whole figure index evaluation criterion of the item basing on the figure index data will provide references for better selecting and scientific training of the excellent synchronized swimming athletes.

References

[1] Wang, f.: Synchronized swimming on physical training of youth. Nanjing Institute of Physical Education (November 2008)
[2] Zhao, y.: Russia's physical training and test of the national youth synchronized swimming. Swimming (June 2007)
[3] Chen, c., Wentao, et al: Feature on muscle power of Guangdong synchronized swimmers. Guangzhou physical education institute (June 2003)
[4] Zhao, y.: Waist control training of synchronized swimming. Swimming (February 2005)
[5] Bai, m.: Problems and methods in power training of synchronized swimming on land. Swimming (May 2005)

The Research on Mobile Payment Marketing of China

Ling Ma and Yamin You

College of Economics and Management,Chongqing University of Posts and Telecommunications, CQUPT, Chongqing, China
maling1330@163.com, youyam@yahoo.cn

Abstract. As mobile phones are more and more popular in China, taking the mobile phones as terminal, the mobile payment business has a large market on the basis of wireless communication network. The essay analyzes the external environmental factors with the regard of the telecom operators at present, finds out the opportunities and challenges to develop mobile payment and poses the marketing strategies about the advancement of mobile payment based on the telecom operators.

Keywords: Mobile payment, environmental analysis, marketing strategy.

1 Analysis of General Environmental Factors to Mobile Payment

1.1 Technological Environment

China Unicom launched NFC technology, for China Telecom, SIM-PASS, and China Mobile RF-SIM technology, from the three operators in different regions of different technology-based mobile payment pilot, China's mobile payment market is in a "raising its head" stage. Although mobile payment is highly favored by experts, businesses, banks, operators and others, at the same time it brings convenience, it is lack of confidence by many consumers. So now security, encryption, real-time issues, identification and credit system are the major obstacles to the popularity of mobile payment.

1.2 Policy Environment

A country's payment system is the core of the financial infrastructure of the development of society and economy. In "Eleventh Five-Year " period, payment services has acquired diversified development, the supervision and management of payment system has increasingly improved, China's payment system has rapidly developed as basically realizing to the modernization.

At this stage, electronic payments become "Twelve Five" Plan highlights. "Twelve Five" Plan will take the electronic payment industry as a leader and the core of e-commerce services, and promote our country from the front-end retail e-business to the core of comprehensive e-business. With the publish of "Non-financial institution payment service management approach" and "Non-financial institution payment service management approach to the implementation details" by the central bank, the licenses of third-party payment have also been put on the agenda.

Q. Zhou (Ed.): ISAEBD 2011, Part II, CCIS 209, pp. 273–279, 2011.

1.3 Economic Environment

In macro level, 2011 is the first year of China's "second Five Year Plan", China will further speed up the development mode, promote strategic adjustment of economic structure and maintain stable and rapid development environment, implement the prudent monetary policy, further highlight the policy guidance of the adjustment to industrial and regional structures.

In micro level, in the current stage of development and popularization of information applications, the needs of mobile payment users trend towards the diversity, the entire, the rational and the fragmented directions. Learning from Yi Pai Consulting, in the view of age distribution, including the mobile payment users, the international service users are mainly between 18-34 years of age, educational level is generally higher, mainly to the population-based college education; to income view, mainly to low-income people; individuals' monthly income and expenses have greater contact, and the users of personal consumption expenditures on the 501-1500 per month are the most.

1.4 Social Environment

China's consumers have a strong dependence on cash transactions, it is the inherent understanding of consumption patterns and habits to bring natural limitations of mobile payments, people who have a greater concern of larger amounts business relatively believe small businesses, it will increase the operating costs of mobile payment.

2 Analysis of Industry Environmental Factors to Mobile Payment Services

2.1 Existing Competitors

Mobile payment has a large market. At this stage, all of the telecom operators, China Union Pay and the third party payment companies want to seize the mobile payment industry leading position on the chain to develop habits of users. Based on the user level, although the magnitude of China Mobile's users is far more than the other two, taking into account constraints of the habits and economic conditions, the number of users using mobile payment is not optimistic; in the field of mobile e-commerce business resource accumulation , third-party payment companies are more dominant; in the business qualification, the central bank has repeatedly made it clear that "electronic payment licenses cannot be issued to non-financial enterprises", "non-financial enterprises can't be authorized and engaged in mobile payment business", therefore, CUP have a greater advantage.

2.2 Threat of New Entrants

Mobile payment industry has higher entry barriers. Mobile operators have a large number of mobile phone customers, perfect communications infrastructure and strong R & D marketing capabilities; the financial payments industry has a huge financial user groups, the world's financial acceptance network across the country, even extending to the world, and the advanced payment and settlement systems; the third-party payment system has a wealth of business resources, combined with regulation and control of national policies on the payment industry. All these are barriers to the threat of new entrants.

2.3 Bargaining Power of Buyers

There are two basic factors determining the bargaining power of buyers: price sensitivity and relative bargaining power. At this stage, as a new mobile payment services, with a market introduction, consumer awareness is not high, price sensitivity is relatively low. In addition, the mobile payment industry can not yet form stable market competition, consumers have less choices, so there is low bargaining power of consumers.

2.4 Bargaining Power of Suppliers

There are a large number of mobile payment industry suppliers, many alternative and raw material that lead to low switching costs. However, in general, orders for communication equipment manufacturing industry have a longer contract period, operators should establish good relations with suppliers and develop a variety of supply channels that is the best defense.

2.5 Threat of Substitute Products or Services

The traditional means of payment contains traditional payment, online payments and mobile payments. The popularity of mobile Internet and mobile intelligent terminals will break the traditional limitations of e-business models, and lifts the restrictions of users on shopping and payment terminals. As a new service mobile payment will give users more and more efficient choice, which has small probability of being replaced.

3 Opportunities and Challenges to Develop Mobile Payment by Telecom Operators

3.1 Opportunities to Develop Mobile Payment by Telecom Operators

1) Based on the user level, telecom operators have a large user base to promote mobile payment with the relative concentration. They can quickly capture the market based on the infrastructure level, and they have convenient infrastructure to a high degree of information. In addition, operators have a wealth of value-added experiences in business operations.

2) Within the mobile payments industry chain, telecom operators as a "value distribution role" is an important bridge connecting users, service providers with financial institutions at the core of the value chain.

3) Standard uniform. The People's Bank of China and the three major telecom operators reached a consensus on the development of technology-based standards for 13.56MHz of mobile payment. With payment standards bottleneck being broken, the mobile payment market is expected to usher in blowout.

4) The advantages of mobile payment services. For telecom operators, the mobile payment has a huge role in the application of innovative telecommunications services, optimize the structure of telecommunications services and support the development of 3G services.

3.2 Challenges to Develop Mobile Payment by Telecom Operators

1) Users of low viscosity. According to the survey, about half the people have concerned about the security of payment transactions, user habits and confidence have not been established.

2) Pressure on users and business resources. Though operators are in hands of a large number of users of resources, in the payment field, relying on more than 80 financial institutions ,the CUP have an unparalleled advantage in whether terms of subscribers or user trust.

3) Business model is not clear. Currently, in order to achieve the purpose of controlling the industrial chain, telecom operators and financial institutions are all from the perspective of maximizing their own interests, have two-way penetration to make use of the advantage of funds, and have established their own industry standards.

4) Finance licenses. In the existing financial management system, lack of specific management ,non-financial institutions involved in financial business are confronted with potential risk, when the cross-industry business gets out of control, not only will it impact the existing monetary and financial systems, but also may even endanger the public funds.

4 Marketing Strategies of Promoting Mobile Payment Services

4.1 Product Strategy

1) Rapid penetration strategy

As a pilot of mobile payment services, in the early telecom operators can take rapid penetration strategy. Since mobile payment services market has a large capacity, consumers do not understand the product, but is very sensitive to price, using this strategy, telecom operators can pilot projects for regional markets, strengthen the stability of the payment platform, implement the low-cost and zero profit of the business promotion plans included bundling mature business or free charge calls. When the users recognize the advantages and convenience of mobile payment, it quickly goes into the growth stage, then the users have already accepted mobile payment services. Telecom operators can charge mode in the original reforms, and then gradually get profit.

2) Vertical product line extension strategy

In the early telecom operators expand the user, gradually introduce their characteristics of business in the late, and strengthen the cooperation of industry chain parties to form a healthy and orderly competitive environment. At this stage the Bank of China and Unicom signed a strategic cooperation agreement, China Mobile holds 20% stake in Shanghai Pudong Development Bank, the cooperation will improve the level of financial payment services based on the communication network and expand applications of banking services in the field of communications and electronic commerce, and deep mobile payment into the large payment field.

Table 1. The current situation of the 3 telecom operators' Mobile Payment

The current situation of the 3 telecom operators' Mobile Payment			
Telecom operators	Business Name	On-line time	Using the scale
China Mobile	Mobile Wallet	August 2003	National
	Silver ICT	2007	National
China Unicom	Mobile Banking	December 9, 2004	National
	Bank card phone recharge	June 14, 2006	Beijing□ Inner Mongolia
	Mobile Wallet	February 1, 2007	Guangdong□ Anhui
China Telecom	Phone Order	May 26, 2009	Shanghai
	Mobile Payment	May 26, 2009	Shanghai

4.2 Pricing Strategy

Currently, the mobile payment— "mobile wallet" services, include basic communications, functions and voice communication fee charges, business function costs isn't charged temporarily at this stage. As early mobile payment services are for small business promotion, it is wide coverage at the user, telecom operators can use penetration pricing to spread fastest in the business, and stimulate market demand for rapid growth.

In the profit model of mobile payment, the earnings of telecom operators are from two aspects, one is divided from the sales of businesses, the other is from user fee payment platform. This profit model promotes telecom operators to be the leader of mobile payment platform, in addition. there are also some hidden benefits, first it can stimulate more demand of data services form mobile users, prompt other mobile business development; second it can strengthen cooperation with financial institutions, from a certain sense, to expand the number of outlets of the mobile business; third it can make benefit from telecom operators to the stability of existing customers, attract new customers and improve the competitiveness of enterprises. There are revenue sharing and cost allocation issues in mobile payment industry value chain, we must take into account the interests of all parties of industry value chain, and operators can balance the profit model more clearly by taking moderate pricing strategy.

4.3 Distribution strategy

1) Channel integration strategy

The sales channels requires of communications business contain "multi-point contact, showing highlights, forming impulse, immediately pay, " as part of a unified marketing and sales, mobile payment services can be integrated to form multi-channel sales force. Multi-channel integration strategies, including: Message, outgoing calls and the integration of physical channel sales strategy, product line catalog and online sales platform for the integration of marketing strategies, physical channel integration strategy (terminal sales, business process, business experience platform of mobile payment, mobile promoters of the integration of payment services), etc, operators can flexibly use the above strategies to complete channel promotion of mobile payment.

2) Channel support strategy
Management support in the background, establish independent terminal supported by the self-management boss platform, establish mobile payment services sales management platform to statistics and evaluation, establish information management platform to inquire customer service, order status, user characteristics and user needs; marketing support in the foreground , allocate marketing specialist in order to experience zone of mobile payment services, as well as improve the efficiency of sales of mobile payment services.

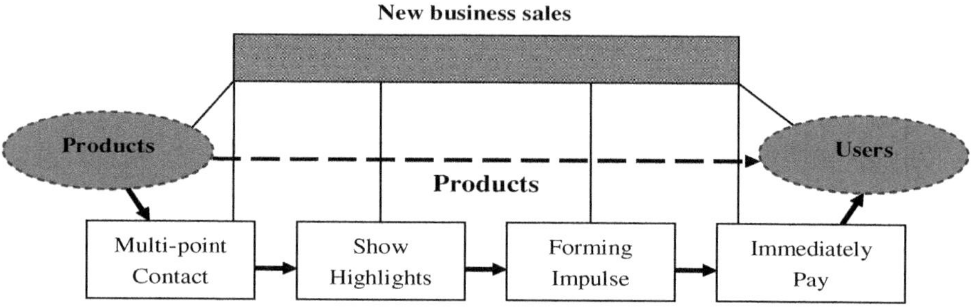

Fig. 1. The requirement of the channel to the new business sales

4.4 Promotion Strategy

1)Personal selling
Mobile payments are new products, Sales promotion is essential while the products are newly launched. Such as experiential marketing, salesmen promote the awareness, preference and finally make the purchase happen by letting target customers to watch, listen and try.

2) Advertising
Mobile advertising is targeted and is able to collected a large number of business information; DM has introduction related to mobile payment services, the specific circumstances of the major merchants, card issuing location and answers to frequently asked questions, which facilitate timely resolution of consumer doubts. Advertising in the media, can flat in the popular magazine advertisements; in the non-media advertising, can increase publicity through car ads and advertising light boxes. WAP PUSH, sent to the user the current new business ads address by SMS, the user can internet by WAP, then acquire the details of mobile payment services.

3) Sales promotion
The first is the way of sales promotion for the customers. Like making use of a mature package tied to mobile payment services on the stack, the free period and the sales awards to increase the user to customize the business momentum.

The second is the way of sales promotion for the agents, implement incentives when the agents complete the task over and pull in the market competition to the various channels and develop sales charts.

4) Public Relations

Firstly, using "self-promotion" strategy, operators leaflets issued in the major outlets, set up special counters for mobile payment business consulting and work experience, as well as start from internal staff, encourage employees to use mobile payment business; Secondly, strengthen the cooperation of the major merchants, such as areas of food shopping, beauty, hair, sports and fitness, so consumers can really feel convenience and benefits with the mobile payment services.

In recent years, mobile payment services are generally respected by the industry, but good application of business in other countries may face some obstacles and problems in the Chinese market. Therefore, the development of mobile payment need not only to learn from successful models abroad, but also the efforts of local industry, telecom operators and other mobile payment enterprises should work together, complement each other, set up win-win cooperation and bring about the rapid development of mobile payment services.

References

[1] 2009-2010 Development of Chinese Mobile Payment Market and Trend Analysis (2009), http://wenku.baidu.com/view/d0d83e12a2161479171128e3.html
[2] Zhou, H.: 3G era of Mobile Payment industrial chain model. Information and Communication 1 (2010)
[3] Shen, W.: Operation Mode of NFC mobile payment. Beijing University of Posts and Telecommunications, Beijing (2008)
[4] Zhou, B.: Analysis of Beijing Unicom mobile E-commerce marketing strategy. Hunan University 5 (2006)

The Test of Timeliness on China's Central Bank Open Market Operations

Sujuan Zhao and Yishuang Liu

School of Economics, Jilin University, Changchun, Jilin Province
juanqingsu1990@gmail.com, liuysh9045@gmail.com

Abstract. We used the VAR model to construct a new model in order to assess the impact of China's central bank note issuance and repurchase business on the overall price level of the market. We also used the impulse response function to analyze the impact of the base currency. The central bank invested it or withdrew it from circulation through the central bank note issuance and repurchase business, on prices and the time required producing such impact. We conclude that the impact of central bank bills on prices lasts a relatively long time and is relatively large; while repurchase can work more quickly, and then its impact will decline rapidly. Then, we propose the focus of open market operations in the present context of relatively high inflation.

Keywords: Open Market Operations, VAR Model, Impulse Response Function.

1 Background Introduction

A country's macro-economic policies to adjust the macro-economy include both monetary and fiscal policies. In China, monetary policies are developed and implemented by the People's Bank of China. Tools of monetary policy include open market operations, reserve, and the central bank loans--that is, the rediscount and interest rate policies in the economy[1].

Open market operations include both RMB and foreign exchange operations. The RMB operations are achieved with the primary dealers through treasury bonds, policy financial bonds and other trading tools. The open market bond trading business of China People's Bank mainly includes repurchase transactions, spot trading and issuance of central bank bills, considering transaction types. Among them, repurchase transactions can be divided into two kinds: repurchase and reverse repurchase. Repurchase refers to the transactions that the People's Bank of China sells securities to primary dealers, and agrees to buy back those securities on a specific date in the future; While reverse repurchase refers to the transactions that the People's Bank of China buys securities from primary dealers, and agrees to sell back those securities on a specific date in the future. Spot trading includes buyout and sell-off; the former means that central bank buys bonds directly from the secondary market, and the latter means that central bank directly sells bonds it already held. China central bank bills refer to short-term bonds issued by the People's Bank of China. The People's Bank of

Q. Zhou (Ed.): ISAEBD 2011, Part II, CCIS 209, pp. 280–285, 2011.

China invests and withdraws the base currency from circulation through these tools to influence the money supply, the price level and interest rates, and then the economic development. Based on the VAR model, we use impulse response functions to analyze the effectiveness of central bank bills and repurchase of open market operations.

2 The Basis of Theory

Consider Fisher's equation of exchange MV=PT. Where, M represents the quantity of money; V represents the circulation times of currency in per unit time, that is, the speed of currency circulation; P represents the commodity price levels; T represents the level of commodity trading. Because it is difficult to measure the amount of T, so in practical application, we can replace T with Y, that is, the real GDP. Then, PY will represent nominal GDP.

If the demand function of money changes, V will also change. To simplify the analysis, not general, we assume that V is a constant. Because the real GDP is determined by the productive capacity of economy, so the real GDP is an exogenous variable in this model. Therefore, the equation of exchange can be represented as

$$M\overline{V} = P\overline{Y} \tag{1}$$

Therefore, the increase in the quantity of money can be manifested as increased price level.

3 The Construction of Econometric Model

3.1 The VAR (Vector Auto-Regressive) Model

3.1.1 The Meaning of the VAR Model

VAR is based on the statistical properties of data to construct model. It takes each endogenous variable in the system as the function of lagged values of all endogenous variables in the system to construct model, so that it can promote the single variable regression model to the "vector" regression model consisting of multivariate time series variables.

3.1.2 Data Selection

Data adopted in this paper is monthly data from January 2008 to March 2011. The price level (P) uses China Commodity Price Index (CCPI)[2], carrying out its first-order differential treatment. Data about issuance of central bank bills (BN) comes from the Open Market Operations Report on the People's Bank of China website, however after treatment. The paper uses net issuance of the central bank bills each month, and a positive number indicates investment of base currency to the market while a negative number indicates withdrawal of base currency from the market. Data about the amount of repurchase (RP) has also been treated in the same way.

3.1.3 The Construction of the Model

$$Y_t = AY_{t-1} + BY_{t-2} + CY_{t-3} + DY_{t-4} + EY_{t-5} + FY_{t-6} + GY_{t-7} + \varepsilon_t \quad (2)$$

Where$Y_t = (P_t, BN_t, RP_t)$; ε_t is random disturbance term; A, B, C, D, E, F, G are parameter matrixes.

First, carry out the co-integration test on all elements of the vector sequence Y_t.The test results show that there are co-integration relationships among the three time series, that is, the long-run equilibrium relationship. Second, carry out the Granger causality test, and the results show that BN, RP Granger causes P. Finally, carry out LM autocorrelation test on the model, and the results show that there is no autocorrelation.

Therefore, VAR mode is applicable.

3.2 The Impulse Response Function

The impulse response function depicts the influence on the current value and future value of endogenous variables, when adding the impact of the size of a standard deviation to the disturbance term. The function can show how the impact of the size of a standard deviation influences endogenous variables and the time required to produce such impact.

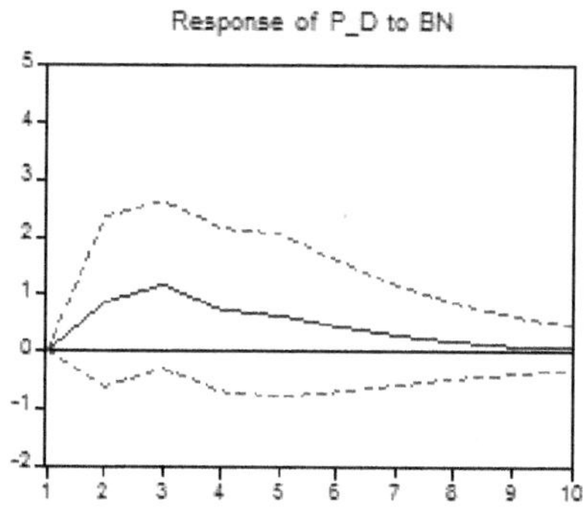

Fig. 1.

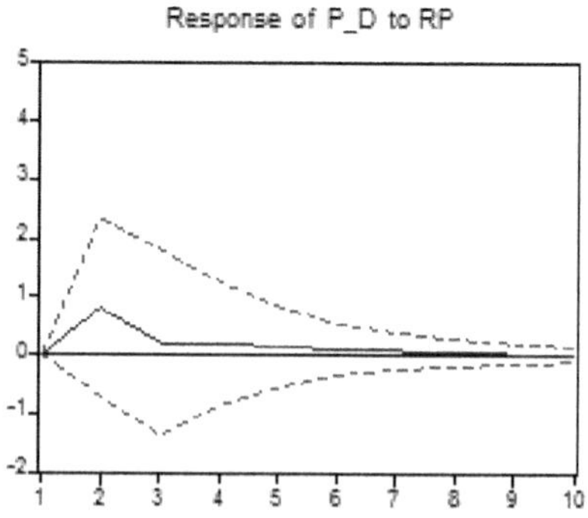

Fig. 2.

In period 0, add the impact of the size of a standard deviation to the random disturbance terms of BN and RP, respectively, to get the impulse response function of the first difference of price, as shown below:

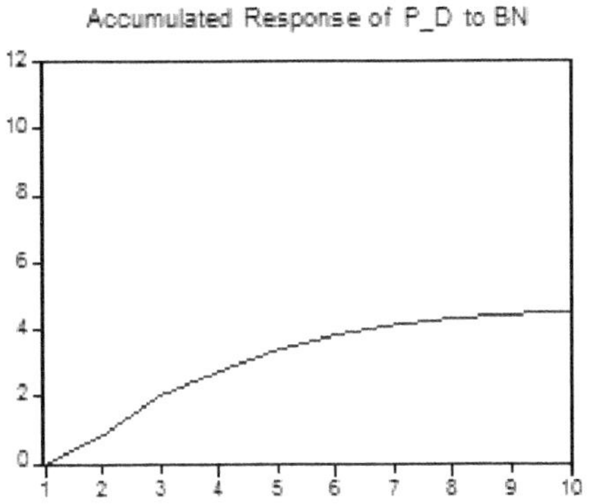

Fig. 3.

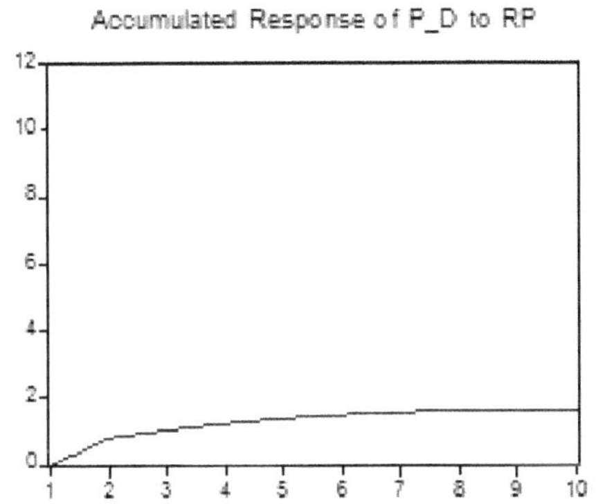

Fig. 4.

Figure 1 shows that, after giving BN a shock in the period 0, the price begins to increase from period 1 and reaches the maximum rate of increase, about 1 unit in period 3. After the period 3, the magnitude of price increase begins to decline. Until after the period 9, the price falls back to the original level. The above suggests that when the central bank invests the base currency into the market at the due of central bank bills, the price level will rise after 1 month, the growth rate will increase until it reaches the peak after 3 months, and then the growth rate will begin to decrease until about 9 months when the general price level won't increase any more. It also proves the economic point of view that "only continuous money supply shocks can lead to inflation". On the contrary, when the central bank withdraws the base currency from circulation through the issuance of central bank bills, the price level will decrease after 1 month, the decline rate will increase until it reaches the bottom, and then the decline rate will gradually decrease until about 9 months when the general price level won't decline any more.

Figure 2 shows that, after giving RP a shock in the period 0, the price begins to increase from period 1, the growth rate will increase until it reaches the peak in the period 2, and then the growth rate will begin to decrease until after about 6 months when the increase is close to 0 and the price is steady. Accordingly, when the central bank withdraws the base currency from circulation through repurchase, the price level will decrease after 1 month, the decline rate will increase until it reaches the bottom after 2 months. It takes approximately 6 months to recover to the steady state of the price level.

Figure 3 and Figure 4 shows that as for a shock from BN, the increase in price levels is much higher than that brought about by a shock from RP.

From the above analysis, we can see that the impact of central bank bills on prices continues a relatively long time and is relatively large; while repurchase can work more quickly, and then its impact will decline rapidly. So, in a relatively short period of time, if we want to make price change quickly, we should use more of the repurchase; and if we want to make substantial changes in prices, then we should use more central bank bills to adjust the money supply.

In the current context of massive price increase, in order to make a substantial decline in the price level, it is necessary to use more central bank bills to control money supply. However, the time required by the adjustment central bank bills is relatively long.

The above comprehensive analysis shows that the impact of central bank bills on the price will achieve the most value after 3 months and almost disappear after 9 months. Therefore, the central bank can conduct open market operations again after 3months and 9 months when it first withdrew the base currency from circulation. The central bank should also strengthen efforts to form a continuing impact on prices. Because of the short-term effects of repurchase, the central may consider high frequency operations.

4 The Shortages of the Model

First, the paper fails to consider other factors, including changes in deposit reserve ratio, interest rates and rediscount, except the open market operations of the central bank's monetary policy. Actually in China, the deposit reserve ratio is a very important monetary policy tool, especially in times of inflation, it changes more frequently. From January 2010 to March 2011, the deposit reserve ratio has been adjusted 9 times. The deposit reserve rate of large financial institutions increased from 15.5% in January 2010 to 20% in March 2011, a total increase of 4.5 percentage[3]. The adjustment of the deposit reserve ratio affects not only the supply of base money, but also affects the money multiplier; therefore, it has greater impact on money supply. Interest rate is also an important monetary policy, which can directly affect the money supply and money demand. In addition, China is an open economy, so changes in foreign exchange reserves will also affect the money supply. These factors will all impact on prices. In addition to these factors, there may also be imported inflation caused by the increase in international commodity, such as rising oil prices in the country. All of these factors influence the effect of central bank bills and repurchase, so, in practice, a variety of policy instruments are often used together.

Second, the data used in this paper is the result of calculation. As a result, errors may occur, affecting the results of the model and the accuracy of the model estimation.

Acknowledgement

1. Source: Monetary Policy Department of People's Bank of China. http://www.pbc.gov.cn/publish/zhengcehuobisi/619/1269/12696/12696_.html
2. China Commodity Price Index, referred to as "CCPI", based on "China's Circulation Industry Network " weekly spot prices of commodities databases, is calculated by the weighted average method of the fixed base index and it takes June 2006 as the base period. CCPI covers the energy, steel, minerals, metals, rubber, agricultural products, livestock, fuel oil, sugar, 9 categories and 26 major kinds of goods. http://www.e-circulation.cn/html//ccpi/intro/2009/11/25/1259118997564.html
3. Source: http://stock.hexun.com/2011-03-18/128046912.html

References

1. Chen, F., Zhao, X., Gao, T.: The Empirical Analysis of the Effect of Monetary-Policy Instrumental Variables in China. Quantitative & Technical Economics Research 19 (2009)
2. Ye, Y.: Policy Analysis on the Effectiveness of Current Monetary. China's Financial 12, 12–14 (2000)
3. Sun, X.: Effectiveness of Reserve Ratio on Monetary Policy. Friends of Science 09(26), 134–136 (2009)
4. Qian, X.: Review and Prospects of Open market operation in China. China's Financial 06 (1997)
5. Mao, D.: Delay Effect of Monetary Policy Analysis - Impulse Response Function and Variance Decompositio. Shanghai University 8(6), 562–564 (2002)

A Study on the Model of Work-Embedded E-learning

Hongli Cheng

School of Management, Xiangfan University
Xiangyang, Hubei, China
ch_hongli@126.com

Abstract. Work-embedded e-learning is a new learning model which not only replaces the age-old model of "learn-then-do" but also is the development of e-learning. The paper concluded two modes of work-embedded learning from literature and practice: one is bottom-up learning driven by problem and the other is top-bottom driven by competence and analyzed the means of knowledge acquisition in the two learning mode. Then we proposed a theoretical model, technical framework, application pattern, and ways of building up learning resource library for the work-embedded e-learning. At last, we addressed several issues worthy of attention in practice. The purpose of the study is to provide theoretical basis and practical advises on the development of e-learning and organization learning.

Keywords: e-learning, embedded learning, model study, knowledge management.

1 Introduction

Work-embedded e-learning is the development of e-learning which is integrated with the theory and method of knowledge management. In the maturity model of e-learning made by online-edu.org[1], Work-embedded e-learning lies in the highest rank which represents the development direction of e-learning.

IBM, which originally classified learning based on the relationship between work and learning as following: learning separated with work, learning based on work and work-embedded learning, is not only the practicer but also the provider of solutions. From 2005, IBM has made work-embedded learning as the main learning mode in the future and made personalized learning content embedded employees' desktop by intranet. With the development of collaboration technology, ubiquitous computing and mobile technology, work-embedded e-learning can be supported by more and more technologies and shows some basic characters [2]:

① Provides immediacy. Today's work environment is fast-paced and ever-changing, but formal structured learning events is time-consuming, Work-embedded e-learning system can immediately recommend personalized learning content or available experts according to work context anytime and anywhere.

② Stresses collaboration. Work-embedded e-learning emphasizes collaboration among employees, and provides a channel for obtaining organization's knowledge which is accumulated by learning and working.

Q. Zhou (Ed.): ISAEBD 2011, Part II, CCIS 209, pp. 286–293, 2011.

③ Employs non-learning technologies, such as email, instant messaging, intelligent search, and content management which can be easily and cost-effectively deployed to support work-embedded learning. But work-embedded e-learning can't be regarded as a simple "drop-in" solution [2], but requires these approaches tightly integrated with workplace tools.

④ Integrates learning with knowledge management. Knowledge management and e-learning belong to different fields [3]. Knowledge management originated from the management of knowledge enterprises. It emphasizes the knowledge innovation, store, sharing, utilization and informal learning approach to facilitate organization learning and the realization of organization strategy. E-learning developed from education field which stresses the usage of information technology and pedagogic approach, especially the design and arrangement of learning object. Schmidt A considered that both knowledge management and e-learning emphasize organization learning but take different paradigm to solve the problem so as to form two difference system. Furthermore he put forward that context-aware corporate learning can bridging the gap between knowledge management and e-Learning [4]. Work-embedded e-learning which provides a passage for obtain tacit and explicit knowledge in the work context is the best point of integration of knowledge management and e-learning.

2 The Driver of Work-Embedded Learning and Its Learning Mode

From the perspective of driving force and learning mode, there are two kinds of workplace learning: one is bottom-up learning driven by problem and the other is top-bottom learning driven by competence (see fig.1). In the two kinds of learning mode, not only individual learning cycle but also organizational learning cycle can be detected, it is to say that workplace learning is not only the combination of learning and work but also of individual learning and organizational learning.

Fig. 1. Two modes of workplace learning

2.1 Bottom-Up Learning Driven by Problem

Bottom-up learning driven by problem means learning takes place when there are problems in the task which mostly need somebody else to discuss or collaborate. When the problem is solved, the individual competence can be improved and the knowledge and experiences can be accumulated and stored in the organization, so the organizational competence can also be improved (see fig. 2). During this kind of learning, there are two major learning approaches:

①Communicate with others by face to face or using communication tools such as MSN, groupware etc. If there are tools embedded in the work environment which can recommend accessible experts according to the problem will facilitate learning.

②Search knowledge by all kinds of tools such as search engine, content management system and then learn self-directed. The knowledge obtained by this way is distributed and non-system and without didactical aid. So if the knowledge units are remarked with Semantic annotation, given pedagogic design and then connected and rearranged automatically by semantic web, the learning efficiency will be improved greatly.

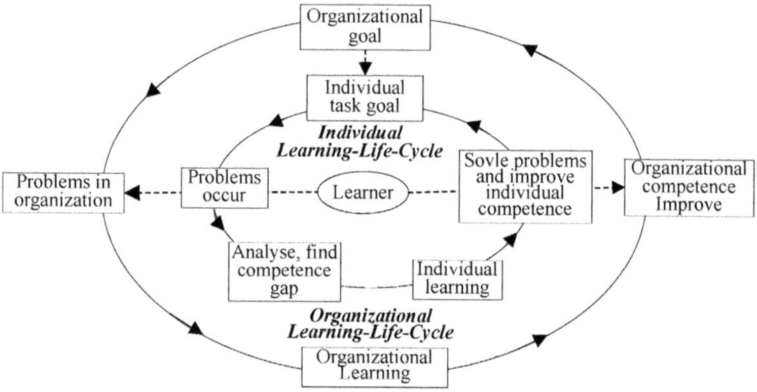

Fig. 2. Bottom-top learning driven by problem

2.2 Top-Bottom Learning Driven by Competence

Top-bottom learning driven by competence is activated by the competence gap between organizational strategy and present competence and performance. The individual learning goal is determined by organizational learning goal and individual career development, the circle life of learning see fig.3. Many kinds of ways of learning activities such as training, job rotation or take e-learning course can be chosen and then be checked by competence test or performance assessment. This kind of learning is based on job competence standard and is more systematic.

But as a usual way, traditional centralized training takes much time and money and the efficiency is low. Common e-learning courses are lengthy, time-consuming and lack enough individuation, so they can't meet the needs of the staff's personalized fast learning. So there needs to use the semantic deducing technology and personal competence ontology and design small grained learning objects which can be rearranged into learning units according to the learner's job and competence gap.

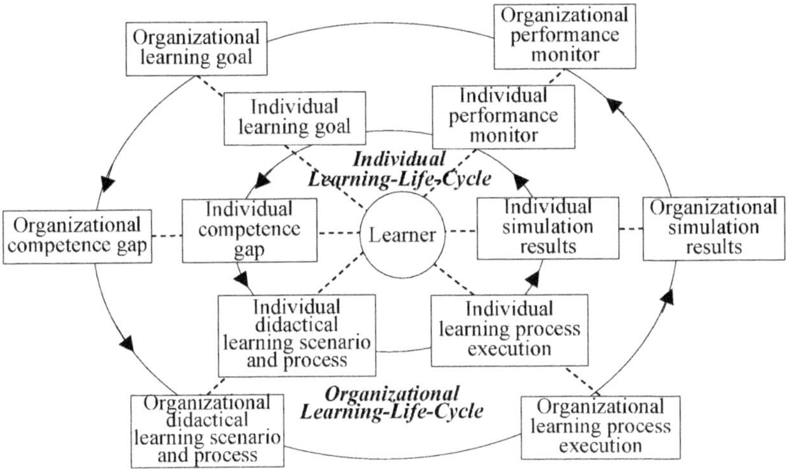

Fig. 3. Top-bottom learning driven by competence

3 The Model of Work-Embedded E-learning and Corresponding Technology Required

3.1 The Theoretical Model of Work-Embedded E-learning

According the foregoing analyses of the learning approaches and improving methods in the digital environment, the model of work-embedded e-learning can be brought forth as fig. 4.

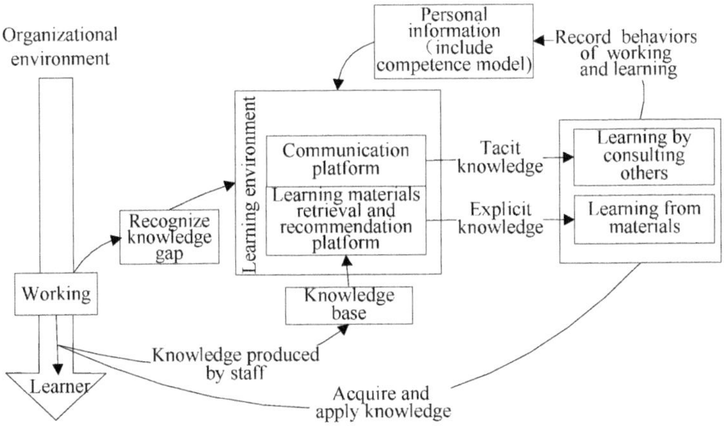

Fig. 4. The model of work-embedded e-learning

When employees meet some problems in the work or find him need to improve competence in some field, he can enter the e-learning platform which integrated into the work platform. The e-learning platform can passively recommend learning resources (include accessible experts or learning materials) to the learner according to the learner's asks or actively according to personal competence information and the job or task that he is doing. He can learn as he is working, and the knowledge produced during the learning and work can be store in the knowledge base. In the process of work-embedded e-learning, there are three characteristics deserve notice:

①Personal profile(including personal competence model) is embedded in the platform, which is not only the base of individualized information and knowledge service but also of the expert recommendation.

②The interactions between the employee and the platform(including learning platform and working platform such as software developing platform, document authoring system) are recorded which can be take as the base of analyzing the competence or knowledge requirement of the employees(can see reference [5]).

③The new knowledge produced in the process of working or learning (include the annotation) can be saved in the organizational knowledge base and be labeled and classified for retrieval.

3.2 The Model of Technical Platform for Work-Embedded E-learning

3.2.1 The Technical Framework of Work-Embedded E-learning

The technical platform for work-embedded e-learning is build on four layers which are hardware infrastructure, supporting layer of system integration, information resource layer and application.(see table 1.)

Table 1. Technical framework of work-embedded e-learning

Application layer	Application software or tools supporting working	Collaboration or communication tools	Application software or tools supporting learning
Information resource layer	Technology standard, documents, personal archives, web information and etc.		
Supporting layer of system integration	.NET Framework, SOA, XML, Web service, and etc. Operating system		
Hardware environment	Cable and wireless network technologies,devices and learning terminals such as laptops, handheld PCs etc.		

Hardware environment includes network technologies and corresponding learning equipment. The former includes Cable and wireless network technologies and the latter includes laptops, handheld PCs and so on. In the fast pace of modern society, mobile work or mobile office is becoming more and more universal. When the user leaves the desk and in the mobile, if he is unable to access their company's network resources and can't move to continue working, he may lose some business opportunities. Correspondingly the mobile learning is necessary for work-embedded e-learning.

Supporting layer of system integration includes technologies which can used for develop and integrate all kinds of resource and software such as .NET Framework, SOA, XML, Web service, and etc.

Information resource layer includes all kinds of information produced in working and learning.

Application layer includes application software or tools supporting working, collaboration or communication tools, and learning. Meantime collaboration or communication tools can be seen both as working tools and learning tools. At the same time learning system should be embedded in the working platform.

3.2.2 Application Pattern of Work-Embedded E-learning

According to the complexity of work-embedded e-learning, the technical platform can be classified into two types:

① Simple platform which can be easy to implement

Simple platform which can be easy to implement mainly implement three types of technologies:

◆Online communication and collaboration technologies such as IM, QQ, groupware, wiki and etc.;

◆The technologies of process learning materials. It can use usual knowledge management technologies such automatically indexing, classifying, organization techniques to make the original unstructured knowledge resources organized into easy usable knowledge base, then use the editing tools manually or the machine learning technology to produce learning object complying with the metadata standards Such as SCORM or LOM. Semantic annotation tools can be applied to denote the important concepts and their applying scenarios or to comment on the viewpoint of the materials to help learners understand.

◆Now the large units of digital course material which is expensive to produce and time-consumed to study is becoming obsolete, the small pieces of information unit, loosely connected and reorganizing dynamically, called micro-content are fit for the fast learning[6]. The micro-content can be a piece of text, a small audio or video clips, a little flash and etc.. It can accommodate just a theme, and at the technical level can suit for the screen of the mobile device. How to find the valuable micro-content and to extract, index and reorganize it according to the learner's need is the key problem to practice this kind of e-learning.

◆Individualized information retrieval and recommendation technologies. User Modeling and semantic matching are two kinds of core technologies. There are two simple user modeling mechanism, one is to let user input their own information, the other is to record user's information seeking behavior and then to model user information. Then information search and semantic matching technologies are used to provide personalized learning resources according to user model and user's task.

② Complicated platform which is function-enhanced.

Complex platform means using the expertise modeling and experts recommended technology, context awareness technology, semantic web technology, workflow-based knowledge recommended technologies and etc. to enhance the efficiency of learning. Now developing the complex platform using these technologies to enhance the workplace learning has become a research hotspot. The projects such as APOSDL, LUISA and PROLIX all used the semantic web technology, tasks modeling technology and individual competence modeling technology. They could deduce personal competence gap and learning objectives based on competence ontology, individual competence model (based on personal learning experience) and knowledge required in the working process, and then provide personalized learning materials.

3.3 The Approaches of Constructing Learning Resource Database

Building learning resources database is an important issue in the construction of work-embedded learning platform. To enrich the knowledge resources needed in learning, we can combine internal development and outsourcing strategies (see fig. 5).

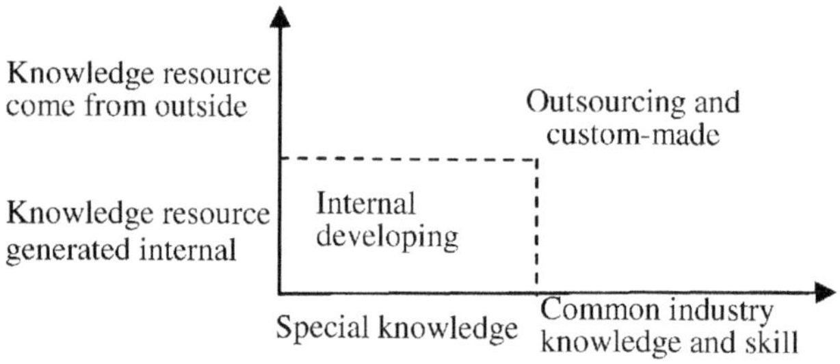

Fig. 5. The choice of ways of learning resource

①For some common industry knowledge and skills needed in the work, outsourcing or custom-made is the best way.

②Knowledge resources internally generated can be developed by internal experts and all the employees. By the comments or annotating tools which refer to learning object metadata standards and semantic annotation method at client side, employees could change long text into learning object or knowledge unit. Internal expert or other staff can make modification, supplement or evaluation on them so as to improve the quality of annotation through the collective wisdom.

4 Several Issues Worthy of Attention

In order to effectively implement work-embedded e-learning, it requires not only the support of technology platform, but also of strategy, management and other non-technical factors. The following measures are demanded to ensure the implementation of work-embedded e-learning:

① Placing work-embedded e-learning in the strategic position combined with organizational performance goals, talent development strategy and the goal of learning organization.

② Changing the role of the training sector. The role of the director of training should changed into chief Learning officer[7], whose main responsibility is to better understand the development of business, the future capacity required and then to build human resource strategy, learning strategy and appropriate solutions which suit for the corporate strategy and culture. The role of traditional trainers should be change into analysts, appraisers, consultants, manager or organizer of learning resource and so on.

③ Establish the evaluation and incentive mechanism for the employees' knowledge contribution and learning effect. It can combine the evaluation measures of knowledge management which usually by the amount and quality of knowledge contribution, e-learning which usually by testing and work performance which by the improvement of working outcomes. Base on the result of evaluation, incentives should be given to assure the effect of learning and knowledge contribution.

5 Limitation and Future Research Opportunities

Due to constraints of time, financing and objective factors, we only brought forward the theoretical model of work-embedded e-learning, analyzed the supporting technologies and approaches of constructing learning resource database, but didn't implement the model and methods to develop the e-learning platform or aid corporation to practise the work-embedded e-learning pattern. So the future research can be carried out in the following two directions:

① To develop prototype system. It requires us to collaborate with colleagues of school of mathematical and computer sciences.

② To investigate the practice of e-learning in corporations and help corporations practise the work-embedded e-learning pattern. It needs us to investigate the present state, problems and future requirement in corporation training and e-learning, and then collaborate with e-learning service providers to help corporations practise the work-embedded e-learning pattern.

References

1. Phpcms: From learning management to talent management analyze the mature model of e-Learning (October 30, 2010), `http://www.online-edu.org/e-Learning/content/02.html`
2. Littlejohn, M.: Embedded learning: is it learning or is work? Development and Learning in Organizations 20(5), 36–39 (2006)
3. Liu, S.Q., Xiang, G.X.: Research on the Integration of Knowledge Management and E-Learning. Modern Educational Technology 14(4), 10–14, 37 (2004)
4. Schmidt, A.: Bridging the Gap Between Knowledge Management and E-Learning with Context-Aware Corporate Learning. In: Althoff, K.-D., Dengel, A.R., Bergmann, R., Nick, M., Roth-Berghofer, T.R. (eds.) WM 2005. LNCS (LNAI), vol. 3782, pp. 203–213. Springer, Heidelberg (2005)
5. Cheng, H.L.: A Study on the Employees' Competence Modeling Based on the Personal Space of Information. In: 3rd International Conference on Information Management, Innovation Management and Industrial Engineering, vol. IV, pp. 539–554. IEEE Computer Society, Los Alamitos (2010)
6. Bruck, P.A.: What is Microlearning and why care about it? In: Proceedings of Microlearning Conference 2006, pp. 7–10. University Press, Innsbruck (2006)
7. Tao, L.: Learning Revolution: From the Training Director to the Chief Learning Officer (April 16, 2008), `http://berc.pku.edu.cn/bbs/viewthread.php?tid=3161` (September 20, 2010)

The Effect of Set-Aside Auctions

Xin Meng*

Southwestern University of Finance and Economics
Research Institute of Economics and Management
May 10, 2011

Abstract. I study the recent Canadian advanced wireless services (AWS) license auction in which 40 percent megahertz spectrum is set aside for new entrant firms in order to encourage the new entry. I show that spectrum set asides indeed result in inefficient allocation, since a new entrant firm (even though its valuation is lower than incumbents' will- ingness to pay) will enter the market. Moreover, this inefficient entry further reduces social welfare. But under some circumstance, I prove that a spectrum set aside increases the seller's revenue and consumer surplus. The simulation also gets the same result.

Keywords: Multi-Unit Auctions, Set-Aside, Social Welfare.

JEL Codes: D44, D82.

1 Introduction

In 2008, Industry Canada conducted the advanced wireless services (AWS) spectrum auction in which 40 percent megahertz spectrum is set aside for new entrant firms in order to encourage the new entry. Incumbents such as Telus, Rogers, and Bell Mobility, called for an open auction of all wireless spectrum to the highest bidder. They argued that a set-aside auction will result in inefficient allocation, reduce auction revenue and social welfare. Moreover, an open auction will promote market competition efficiently and make consumers better off. A spectrum set-aside auction can guarantee the new entry in the Canadian wireless services market and the price of wireless services will go down due to the intense competition. But the effects of a set-aside auction on revenue, consumer surplus, and social welfare are not clear. In this paper, I show that-unlike what Telus, Rogers, and Bell Mobility argued-under some conditions an auction with set asides may result in higher auction revenue and higher consumer surplus.

There are a few papers in set-aside auctions in the literature. Ayres and Cramton (1996) and Cramton et. al. (2008) study the incumbents bidding strategies in the FCC (Federal Communications Commission) set- aside auctions. They show that an

* I thank the participants of University of Manitoba Seminar Series and Hikmet Gunay, Ruqu Wang, Janet Hua Jiang, and Derek G. Brewin for their feedback. I acknowledge the financial support from Social Sciences and Humanities Research Council (SSHRC) in the form of SSHRC Doctoral Fellowship and from Southwestern University of Finance and Economics in the form of the Fund of "211" Project.

Q. Zhou (Ed.): ISAEBD 2011, Part II, CCIS 209, pp. 294–299, 2011.

incumbent firm took advantage of the set aside program and won the licenses originally reserved for small firms by creating a bidding front (a new small firm) to participate in the auction with set asides. In Canadian AWS auction, new entrants are defined as "an entity, including affiliates and associated entities, which holds less than 10 percent of the national wireless market based on revenue ". Therefore, three biggest national incumbents, Telus, Rogers, and Bell Mobility, cannot bid on the set aside spectrum licenses. It is impossible to be dominant in the set aside auction for national incumbents.

Crandall et. al. (2007) argue that set-aside spectrum for Canadian AWS auction will result in inefficient allocation and reduce economic welfare of consumers. Milgrom (2004) illustrates that an auction with set asides gener- ates higher revenue than an auction without set asides by using an example of four bidders with different exogenous valuation on licenses.

In contrast, I assume that bidders' valuation will be determined endoge- nously by the profits from the downstream market. Moreover, I show that expected revenue and consumer surplus from a set-aside auction depends on the cost asymmetry among bidders. That is, the expected revenue and consumer surplus from a set-aside auction may be lower than from a non set-aside auction. Hoppe et. al. (2006) illustrate the results with an example that set asides can lower social welfare due to inefficient market entry. They show that revenue is higher from a set-aside. In this paper, I find that a set- aside auction may decrease the seller's revenue, but social welfare is always lower in a non set-aside auction. Moreover, I show that as the market size increases, in other words, the cost asymmetry among bidders decreases, then the seller's revenue, consumer surplus, and social welfare for each auction will increase.

To summarize, in a model simplifying the recent Canadian advanced wire- less services spectrum license auction, I show that if the market size or cost asymmetry is moderate, both revenue and consumer surplus from an auction with a set-aside are higher than that from an auction without a set-aside. If the market size is big enough or the cost asymmetry is low enough, revenue will be lower, but consumer surplus will be higher with a set-aside auction. Social welfare is lower in all cases with a set-aside auction.

The chapter is organized as follows. I characterize a simple model with two incumbent firms and three potential entrant firms first. Then I simulate a two-license model with three incumbent firms and three potential entrant firms.

2 The Model

There are 2 licenses, license A and B for sale via a simultaneous ascending bid auction. The auction proceeds in rounds. Prices start from zero for two licenses and increase simultaneously and continuously until only one bidder is left on a given license. On that license auction, the last bidder wins that license at the stopping price. At the same time, the price on the other license will continue to increase, if there are more than one bidder.

The dropout is irreversible; once a bidder drops out of bidding for a given license, he cannot bid for this license again in the next round. The number of active bidders and the drop-out prices are publicly known.

There are 2 homogenous incumbent firms, denoted by firm 1 and firm 2 who are interested in new spectrum licenses to provide advanced wireless services, and 3 homogenous entrant firms, denoted by firm 3, firm 4, and firm 5, who want to win a license to enter the downstream cell-phone service market. Both incumbent and entrant firms' valuation for a single license is determined by the downstream market structure. I assume that if an incumbent firm wins a new license, her marginal cost will be C_L, otherwise, her marginal cost is C_H. We also assume that if an entrant firm wins a license, then her marginal cost will be C_H[1]. There is no fixed costs.

Moreover, I assume that the market demand function is $p(Q) = A - Q$, where A is the market size, and firms will Cournot compete with each other. I consider two types of auctions, auction without set-aside spectrum license and auction with set-aside spectrum license.

In a non set-aside auction, two licenses are open to two incumbents and three entrants. When incumbents' willingness to pay for a new license is higher than entrants' valuation, then two incumbents will win both licenses because they are identical, and pay the third highest valuation, that is, one of entrants' expected profit from the market.

In a set-aside auction, one of licenses will be set aside for three entrants and the other one will be open to both incumbents and entrants. Then, one of entrant firms will win one license and one of the incumbents wins the other license. Because spectrum set-aside guarantees the new entry and three entrants are homogeneous, one of entrants wins the license with expected zero profit. On the other license auction, incumbents will compete for only one new license. So one of incumbents wins the license with her willingness to pay when taking new entry into account, because incumbents are identical.

The following Lemma 1 shows that all the quantities are positive and incumbent firms' valuation is higher than entrants' valuation. Otherwise, two of three entrants will win both licenses in both auctions, there is no need to set aside for entrants.

Lemma 1: *When $2C_H - C_L < A < 14.4C_H - 13.4C_L$, incumbent firms' valuation is higher than entrants' valuation.*

When I compare a non set-aside auction with a set-aside auction in forms of seller's expected revenue, consumer's surplus, and social welfare, I find the following results.

Proposition 2:

a) When $2C_H - C_L < A < 6C_H - 5C_L$, then $ER_S > ER_{NS}$, $CS_{NS} > CS_S$;

b) When $6C_H - 5C_L < A < 8.5C_H - 7.5C_L$, then $ER_S > ER_{NS}$, $CS_S > CS_{NS}$;

[1] After winning a new license, incumbents' marginal cost is lower than entrants' because of their existing, well established customer base in previous generation wireless services.

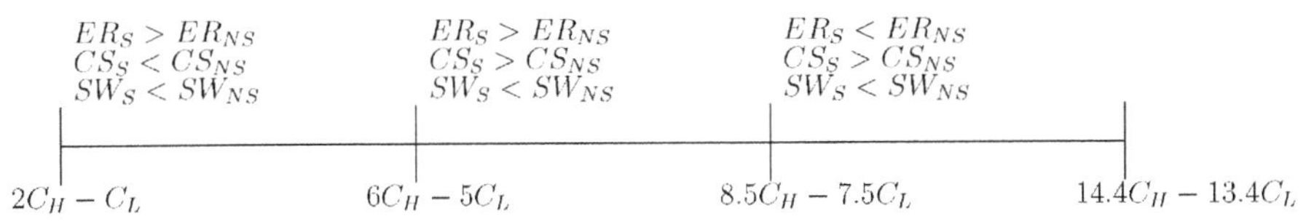

Fig. 1. Revenue,CS and SW Comparison

c) When $8.5C_H - 7.5C_L < A < 14.4C_H - 13.4C_L$, *then* $ER_S < ER_{NS}$, $CS_S > CS_{NS}$;

d) When $2C_H - C_L < A < 14.4C_H - 13.4C_L$, $SW_{NS} > SW_S$.

The seller's expected revenue functions in both a set-aside and a no set aside auctions are decreasing functions in cost asymmetry. When the cost asymmetry is high, the seller's expected revenue in a no set-aside auction decreases faster than that in a set aside auction. Thus, the expected revenue is higher in a set aside auction when the cost asymmetry is high enough.

In general, more firms in the market will benefit all consumers because more competition will result in lower prices. In this model, consumer surplus will depend on the relationship between the size of the market and marginal costs. In a set aside auction, one of the high type firms will enter the market. And this new entry will affect consumer surplus in two ways. On the one hand, if high type firm enters the market, then low type firm will produce fewer outputs because of competition. Therefore, there is a negative effect on total output and thus consumer surplus. On the other hand, if a high type firm enters the market, then the high type firm will produce outputs which are previously produced by the low type firm. Therefore, there is a positive effect on total output and hence consumer surplus. Thus, when the size of the market is big enough or the cost asymmetry is not significant, that is, a new entrant firm is relatively efficient, then the positive effect dominates the negative effect, total output increases and thus consumer surplus is higher in set-aside case. When the size of the market is small or the cost asymmetry is significant, that is, a new entrant firm is relatively inefficient, then the negative effect dominates the positive effect, total output decreases and thus consumer surplus is lower in set-aside case.

Social welfare is defined the sum of consumer surplus and producer sur- plus. A spectrum set aside has two different effects on social welfare. On the one hand, there is a positive effect on social welfare due to increased competition in the downstream market which further results in lower prices and higher consumer surplus. On the other hand, there is a negative effect on producer surplus. A spectrum set aside guarantees an inefficient entrant firm will win a license and enter the market. This will result in each firm's profits in the downstream market to decrease as the number of active firms increases. A spectrum set aside indeed lowers social welfare which means that the positive effect is dominated by the negative effect. Thus, this social welfare reducing effect of set asides is derived from the inefficient entry.

3 Results of Simulation

Now, if each bidder's marginal costs are different. I assume that there are two licenses for sale via a simultaneous ascending bid auction. There are three incumbents with differ ent marginal costs denoted by, a1 < a2 < a3, random drawn on [0.5,1] if they win new licenses, then their marginal costs be lower and denoted by, b1 < b2 < b3, random drawn on [0,0.5]. There are three entrants with marginal costs denoted by, c1 < c2 < c3 random drawn on [0.5,1] if they win a license. We run simulations with MATLAB. I find each revenue, consumer surplus and social welfare for a different market size. For each market size, I draw 200 observations, calculate revenue, consumer surplus and social welfare for each case and find the average of these results. From the results, I find that revenue from a set-aside auction will be higher when the market size is lower than 2, consumer surplus from a set-aside auction will be higher when the market size is lower than 4, social welfare is always lower in set-aside case because of inefficient entry. Therefore, I conclude the following observations:

Observation 1:

a) When $A < 2$, *then* $AR_S > AR_{NS}$, $CS_S < CS_{NS}$.

b) When $2 \le A \le 4$, *then* $AR_S < AR_{NS}$, $CS_S < CS_{NS}$.

c) When $A > 4$, *then* $AR_S < AR_{NS}$, $CS_S > CS_{NS}$.

d) When $1 < A < 5.5$, $SW_S < SW_{NS}$ *and as the market size increases, revenue, consumer surplus and social welfare will increase.*

4 Conclusion and Discussion

A spectrum set aside indeed results in inefficient allocation, since a new en- trant firm (even though its valuation is lower than incumbents' willingness to pay)will enter the market. Moreover, this inefficient entry further reduces social welfare. But under some circumstances, a spectrum set aside increas- es the seller's revenue and consumer surplus, even though the allocation is inefficient.

References

1. Ayres, I., Cramton, P.: Deficit Reduction Through Diversity: How Affirmative Action at the FCC Increased Auction Competition. Stanford Law Review 48, 761–815 (1996)
2. Cramton, P., Ingraham, A.T., Singer, H.J.: The Effect of Incumbent Bidding in Set-Aside Auctions: An Analysis of Prices in the Closed and Open Segments of FCC Auction 35. Telecommunications Policy 32, 273–290 (2008)
3. Crandall, R.W., Ingraham, A.T.: The Adverse Economic Effects of Spectrum Set-Asides. Canadian Journal of Law and Technology 6, 131–140 (2007)
4. Gunay, H., Meng, X.: The, Turkish Cell-phone License Auc- tion. Applied Economics Research Bulletin, Peer Reviewed Working Paper Series (2000) (forthcoming)

5. Hoppe, H.C., Jehiel, P., Moldovanu, B.: License Auctions and Market Structure. Journal of Economics and Management Strategy 15, 371–396 (2006)
6. Lahiri, S., Ono, Y.: Helping Minor Firms Reduces Welfare. The Economic Journal 98(393), 1199–1202 (1988)
7. Milgrom, P.: Putting Auction Theory to Work. Cambridge University Press, Cambridge (2004)
8. Rodriguez, G.E.: Auctions of licenses and market structure. Economic Theory 19, 283–309 (2002)

Dose the Weight Matter? An Empirical Study of Online Rating Systems in Buy-It-Now C2C Exchanges

Xianfeng Zhang and Nan Zhang

Department of Electronic Commerce
School of Economics and Finance, Xi'an Jiaotong University, China
zxf@xjtu.edu.cn; xfzhangchina@gmail.com

Abstract. This paper is to tell whether the weighted rating system is efficient to well distinguish the good sellers. It is designed to first test the relationships between weighted ratings and the sellers' sales – tagged price, charged price, sold probability and sold quantity, and then compare the stresses of the relationships under the weighed settings and the unweighted settings. The second biggest Chinese site paipai was chosen, and an identical prepaid card was selected for the study. It is surprising to find that the weight does not greatly matter: (1) the relationships between ratings and the sellers' sales conform to the results of prior literature; (2) no significant changes are made, though the sellers' tagged price showing a marginal slight decrease.

Keywords: C2C Marketplace, Online Rating System, e-Commerce.

1 Introduction

Binary online rating systems have been widely adopted in the C2C marketplace, as its generated rating indexes can be used as the signals to evaluate the sellers' trustworthiness. Through an easy coding of 1(positive), 0(neutral) and -1(negative), and a simple accumulation, a set of indexes are resulted, including the total rating and the positive feedback. Sellers with higher ratings have conducted trustworthy exchanges before, and will take the advantage of being believed to be trusted in the future transactions. However, many sellers find varieties of ballot ways to gain unfairly high ratings. The ballots are normally use intangible products to make fake exchanges with no products delivered, but some are real transactions. In view of the severity and notoriety of ballots, some C2C market runners introduce weighted binary rating systems to technically reduce the ballot possibilities. In the current practice, two elements, price and attribute, are normally considered in the weighted setting. Price-weighted settings consider the price of the exchanged products, and encode different weights on diverse categories of prices. The attribute-weighted settings distinguish tangible and intangible products, and provide disparate ratings.

Through the designing, it seems the weighted rating systems can effectively raise the capabilities of the traditional simple accumulative binary rating systems to discern the real good sellers. For one thing, it can eliminate the noise of small value ballot ratings. Traditionally, a seller who sold 1000 products less than 1 dollar can gain a rating of

Q. Zhou (Ed.): ISAEBD 2011, Part II, CCIS 209, pp. 300–306, 2011.

1000 if all the ratings are positive, however, in the price-weighted marketplace, the seller's rating will still be 0 if a weight of zero is set to exchanges lower than 1 dollar. For another, the ratings from exchanges of tangible or intangible products can be differentiated through attribute-weighted setting. Intangible products are easier to sale and are easier leading to ballot than tangible products. However, the system designers neglected one thing. Is the price-weight setting or attribute-weight setting really effective? How will the effectiveness show in the sellers' sales?

This paper is to explore the problem through an empirical study in the buy-it-now C2C marketplace. The remaining sections are organized as the following. The research hypotheses are proposed in section two with a brief literature review. Data sources and the collection procedures are reported in section three. Section four discusses the analyses results. Finally, a brief conclusion is followed in section five.

2 Research Hypotheses

Many researchers studied the value of binary reputation systems in auction-based C2C exchanges, and found that good reputation can bring higher price premium, entice larger numbers of bids, and engender higher sold possibilities (Ba and Pavlou 2002, McDonald and Slawson 2002, Dewan and Hsu 2004). But in the current practice, buy-it-now settings dominate the C2C marketplace, where buyers are in the position to directly take the price rather than to name a price. It is also found that under this setting, good-rated sellers have higher possibilities to sell their products, but the prices they tagged for sale are comparatively low. The prices they finally charged for the successful deals are also low, but not significant (Zhang 2009). It means in the buy-it-now setting, no price premium exists but price shrink involved.

Therefore, this research mainly concerns the buy-it-now exchanges. Two main questions are to be explored. First, how will the weighted rating systems affect the sellers' sales? Namely, what will be the relationships between weighted ratings and the sellers' sales like sold possibilities, sold quantities, tag prices, and charged prices? It is found in the former studies that the sellers' ratings are positively related with their sold possibilities and sale quantities, but negatively correlated with the tag prices and charged prices (Zhang 2009), we believe the relationships will be similar since the weighted treatments only change the calculation way, he underlying basic rating mechanisms are still the same. Regarding the detailed indicators in the rating system, there are multiple choices. A seller's total rating is the main indicator (McDonald and Slawson 2002, Dewan and Hsu 2004), while positive and negative ratings of different periods are also good pairs (Lucking-Reiley et al 2007). Dewally and Ederington (2006) even adopted the negative feedback in their research.

Second and the most important, will the weights change the above mentioned relationships? If not, will the relative stress be significantly different? It is logical to believe the stresses of the relationships are dissimilar since many c2c marketplaces have adapted to the weighted rating systems from the traditional simple binary rating systems. Accordingly the following hypotheses can be raised.

H1: The weighted ratings will have positive relationship with the sold possibility and sold quantity, and negatively correlate with the tag price and charged price.

H2: The effect's degree differs from the weighted ratings to the traditional ratings.

3 Data Source and Collection Procedure

After a brief review of the current c2c marketplaces in China, paipai.com is finally chosen for two reasons. First, no weighted systems are adopted in eBay – the worldwide famous runner and Taobao – the biggest runner in China. Second, paipai.com ranks the second with the second-highest traffic among Chinese C2C sites, and share comparatively larger market share than others (Pearl Research, 2007).

Paipai introduced its price weighted rating systems from the initial beginning. The exchanged prices are divided into five categories with four thresholds: 1, 200, 1000, 5000, and 5000 plus. It is regulated that exchanges valued under 1 yuan is weighed 0, and those between 1 to 200 yuan will be 1, and so on and so forth. The highest weight is 4, weighing those transactions charged greater than 5000 yuan. Paipai further adopted the attribute-weighted rating rule, through clearly indicating the proportion of tangible and intangible exchanges. From July of 2009, paipai totally turned the system into the double-weighted, with total ratings both price weighed and attribute weighed. Sellers can only select either tangible or intangible attribute as their main operation scope, thus buyers will see just the weighted rating of the selected operation scope.

The data collection was done in a 7 day period from January 17 to 23, 2010, since the c2c systems use 7-day or 14-day as the default listing duration. An identical 30-yuan prepaid game card is chosen for the research because of its identical traits. Besides, exchanges of prepaid cards may encounter the extremes, as many prepaid cards are less than 1. Searched listings are restricted to brand-new, buy-it-now prepaid game card for the "world of warcraft", with online instant sending as the shipping methods. During the period of the collection, there are averagely 1200 product listings for this product. We collected data of 1000 lists each day, from the listing page to the rating profile page.

A list of fifteen elements is obtained, ranging from the seller's ID, the listing name, price, ratings, and so on. In paipai, the half-year sold quantity is displayed. In order to reveal the real sales, the seller's sold quantity of the seven days is recalculated through the deduction of the first day's sold quantity from that of the last day. Then the number is averaged into daily sold quantity. Since the total ratings have been both price weighted and attribute weighted, a new variable is also calculated with the deduction of the total negative ratings from the total positive ratings. This new variable is to represent the unweighted rating, because the list of positive and negative ratings only records the sales history.

Therefore, nine variables are adopted for the research. Among them, three are for indicators of ratings, the total weighted rating (TRw), the unweighted rating originated from the deduction of the total negative rating from the total positive rating (TRu), and the positive feedback (PF). Three variables are to reflect the sales: price (P), sold probability (SPb), and daily sold quantity (SQd). Three other variables - Size, Visit and whether the seller enters the the customer protection program (CP) - are also selected as the control variables. The number of products the dealer sells in his or her online store is used to represent the Size. A larger number of visit numbers means that the seller attracted more potential buyers. Customer protection program is a trust-building mechanism paipai provided for their market buyers. Qualified sellers are asked to prepay a sum of money to enter the program, and related online seals will be placed with the sellers.

4 Data Analyses Results

4.1 Descriptive Statistics

Through the data collection, 736 samples are finally resulted. All those sellers with zero positive feedback are deleted, because they never sold before, and strictly can not be defined as valid sellers yet. Many sellers open varied sales for the same product during the period, so only one sale list is randomly selected to ensure no self-correlation exists. Missing value is checked, and absurd outliers are detected.

The descriptive statistics are reported in table I. The price of the 30-yuan prepaid game card ranges from 26.96 to 30, with the standard deviation of 0.34754. In the market, only 172 sellers sold their products out, and they sell the mean of 9.99 pieces daily, with the minimum of 0.2 pieces and the maximum of 585.2 pieces. Variables of weighted total ratings and unweighted total ratings are all skewed, with a respective standard deviation of 19003.4 and 21101.5. The positive feedback rates are left centered, ranging from 0.93 to 1. Not all sellers entered the customer protection program, resulting in a mean of 0.65. The minimum number of products the sellers have in their store is 1, and the maximum products one store can have are 7949, with the standard deviation of 557.232. The average visits are also skewed with a high standard deviation of 2471.2. Natural logarithms are taken to meet the normal distribution pre-requirements for variables of TRw, TRu, Size and Visits. We use TRw+1 and TRu+1 to do the logarithm, since 0 can't be taken a natural logarithm.

Table 1. Descriptive statistics

	N	Minimum	Maximum	Mean	Std. Deviation
TRw	736	0	258046	5634.7	19003.423
TRu	736	1	284389	6330.5938	21101.45601
PF	736	0.9297	1	0.998335	0.0053808
Price	736	26.96	30	27.6445	0.34754
SPb	736	0	1	0.23	0.423
SQd	736	0.20	585.20	9.99	52.365
CP	736	0	1	0.65	0.477
Size	736	1	7494	276.88	557.232
Visit	736	1	56739	382.07	2471.194
ln(TRw+1)	736	0	12.46	6.1378	2.53641
ln(TRu+1)	736	0.69	12.56	6.2971	2.49093
ln(Size)	736	0.69	8.92	4.8553	1.27674
ln(Visit)	736	0.69	10.95	4.1196	1.43098

4.2 Tag Price and Charged Price Estimation

In order to tell how the weighted rating system affect on tagged price and charged price, two sets of studies are conducted with weighted rating and unweighted rating as the main independent variable. Several control variables and due interaction effects are also considered. Therefore, sixteen sets of models are used during the estimation.

As the table 2 and 3 shows, all the eight models in tag price estimation are significant with a power above 0.9. But in the charged price models, only four fits well with the power above 0.75. The DW values are also good. Sellers' total ratings, regardless of weighted or unweighted, have significant negative relationship with their tag price. In the charged price model, negative correlations also exist but all are insignificant. Size significantly correlate with price in all models, which means the more sellers sell the higher prices they tag and charge. CP is negatively correlated with price, showing that those sellers who entered customer protection program usually tag and finally charge low prices. From this viewpoint, it is clear that no significant relational changes can be made through the introduction of weighted rating systems, so it is of necessity to further test whether the degree of the effects differ.

Table 2. Tag price OLS regression results (N=736)

IV	I	II	III	IV	V	VI	VII	Ⅷ
Ln(TRw+1)	**-0.029^{a}**	**-0.021^{a}**	**-0.019^{a}**	**-0.027^{a}**				
	(-5.807)	**(-3.114)**	**(-2.807)**	**(-3.881)**				
PF	-3.072	-2.817	**-10.407^{a}**	-2.995	-3.500	-3.048	**-10.566^{a}**	-3.300
	(-1.318)	(-1.207)	**(-2.869)**	(-1.291)	(-1.498)	(-1.302)	**(-2.909)**	(-1.416)
Ln(TRu+1)					**-0.027^{a}**	**-0.018^{b}**	**-0.015^{b}**	**-0.024^{a}**
					(-5.394)	**(-2.589)**	**(-2.182)**	**(-3.330)**
CP		-0.059	**-0.071^{c}**	**-0.074^{b}**		**-0.073^{b}**	**-0.094^{b}**	**-0.088^{b}**
		(-1.634)	**(-1.778)**	**(-2.043)**		**(-2.038)**	**(-2.328)**	**(-2.437)**
Ln(TRw+1)*CP			-0.007					
			(-0.453)					
PF * CP			**-16.619^{a}**				**-16.954^{a}**	
			(-2.773)				**(-2.822)**	
Ln(TRu+1)*CP							-0.013	
							(-0.855)	
LnSize				**0.035^{a}**				**0.033^{a}**
				(3.165)				**(3.011)**
F	**18.141^{a}**	**13.012^{a}**	**9.460^{a}**	**12.384^{a}**	**15.817^{a}**	**11.975^{a}**	**8.973^{a}**	**11.346^{a}**
R2	**0.047**	**0.051**	**0.061**	**0.063**	**0.041**	**0.047**	**0.058**	**0.058**
Power	**0.999**	**0.999**	**0.999**	**0.999**	**0.999**	**0.999**	**0.999**	**0.999**

Notes: a, b, c each means $p<0.01$, $p<0.05$, $p<0.1$; t value in the parentheses. the follow three table are same.

Table 3. Charged price OLS regression results (N=172)

IV	I	II	III	IV	V	VI	VII	Ⅷ
Ln(TRw+1)	-0.011	-0.019^{c}	-0.015	-0.003				
	(-1.205)	(-1.950)	(-1.516)	(-0.261)				
PF	-2.221	-2.771	-12.697	-2.157	-2.254	-2.796	-12.716	-2.144
	(-0.208)	(-0.262)	(-1.138)	(-0.206)	(-0.211)	(-0.264)	(-1.138)	(-0.205)
Ln(TRu+1)					-0.010	-0.018^{c}	-0.014	-0.001
					(-1.068)	(-1.820)	(-1.418)	(-0.118)
LnSize		0.041^{b}	**0.048^{b}**	**0.046^{b}**		0.040^{b}	**0.048^{b}**	**0.045^{b}**
		(2.090)	**(2.455)**	**(2.336)**		(2.047)	**(2.430)**	**(2.292)**
Ln(TRw+1)*Size			0.011					
			(1.587)					
PF * Size			**-29.828^{b}**				**-29.812^{b}**	
			(-2.276)				**(-2.273)**	
Ln(TRu+1)*Size							0.011	
							(1.631)	
CP				**-0.199^{b}**				**-0.207^{b}**
				(-2.236)				**(-2.332)**
F	0.753	1.968	**3.368^{a}**	**2.761^{b}**	0.597	1.802	**3.306^{a}**	**2.747^{b}**
R^2	0.009	0.034	**0.092**	**0.062**	0.007	0.031	**0.091**	**0.062**
Power	0.181	0.520	**0.908**	**0.769**	0.148	0.479	**0.905**	**0.769**

Paired T-test is adopted to compare the coefficients of the weighted ratings and unweighted ratings. It is found that the two series of coefficients are all significantly different at the alpha level of 0.05. The coefficients of the weighted ratings is -0.003 lower than that of the unweighted ratings in tagged price estimations, and -0.00125 lower in the charged price estimations. This means that ratings empower slightly stronger effects on prices after adapted to the weighted system, under which high-rated sellers may operate varieties of products, especially high-valued products, and accordingly possess smooth channels to offer trivially bigger discounts.

4.3 Sold Probability and Sold Quantity Estimation

The effects of weighted rating system on sold probability and sold quantity are also tested. Similarly, weighted ratings and unweighted ratings are adopted as the main independent variables. Accordingly, sixteen sets of models are estimated.

As the table 4 and 5 shows, no models are insignificant. Two sets of ratings all positively correlate with sold probability and sold quantity. The higher the ratings are, the bigger the sold probability and the sold quantity will be. The significant effects of the other variables show great similarity under the two systems. Visit plays a positive role. Price only shows direct negative effect on sold probability, but interactively affects sold quantity with ratings. CP does not significantly correlate with the two dependent variables, but displaying an interactive effect on sold probability. The degree of the affects is further tested with paired T-test. Contrary to the price estimation, the two series of ratings coefficients are found no significant differences.

Table 4. Sold probability logit regression results (N=736)

IV	I	II	III	IV	VI	VII	VIII	IX
Ln(TRw+1)	**0.365[a]**	**0.315[a]**	**0.229[a]**	-0.015				
	(74.525)	**(36.309)**	**(14.650)**	(0.046)				
PF	**110.035[b]**	**111.902[b]**	**98.416[b]**	**91.538[b]**	**112.217[b]**	**114.114[b]**	**99.827[b]**	**91.494[c]**
	(5.795)	**(5.870)**	**(5.690)**	**(3.492)**	**(6.046)**	**(6.104)**	**(5.871)**	**(3.485)**
Ln(TRu+1)					**0.363[a]**	**0.309[a]**	**0.209[a]**	-0.014
					(73.807)	**(35.055)**	**(11.555)**	(0.037)
CP		0.476	**1.117[b]**	0.419		**0.518[c]**	**1.254[a]**	0.415
		(2.457)	**(6.675)**	(1.398)		**(2.932)**	**(7.793)**	(1.382)
Ln(TRw +1)*CP			**0.487[a]**					
			(11.736)					
PF * CP			101.474				109.676	
			(1.772)				(2.095)	
Ln(SSRg+1)*CP							**0.529[a]**	
							(12.751)	
P				**-1.622[a]**				**-1.620[a]**
				(12.052)				**(12.033)**
LnSize				-0.135				-0.136
				(1.872)				(1.881)
LnVisit				**0.949[a]**				**0.948[a]**
				(76.883)				**(77.098)**
-2LogLike	**699.959**	**697.430**	**684.674**	**557.191**	**701.912**	**698.886**	**684.802**	**557.200**
HL test	**8.584[d]**	**11.909[d]**	**3.765[d]**	**12.098[d]**	**11.258[d]**	**12.567[d]**	**3.369[d]**	**12.162[d]**
CS R^2	**0.127**	**0.130**	**0.145**	**0.281**	**0.125**	**0.129**	**0.145**	**0.281**
N R^2	**0.192**	**0.197**	**0.219**	**0.424**	**0.189**	**0.194**	**0.219**	**0.424**

Table 5. Average sold quantity WLS regression results (N=172)

IV	I	II	III	IV	V	VI	VII	[redacted]
Ln(TRw+1)	**1.644[a]**	**1.531[b]**	**1.745[a]**	-0.496				
	(2.767)	**(2.492)**	**(2.797)**	(-0.440)				
PF	207.916	226.937	144.332	874.529	211.552	231.988	134.413	897.471
	(0.298)	(0.325)	(0.208)	(1.219)	(0.298)	(0.326)	(0.190)	(1.229)
Ln(TRu+1)					**1.637[a]**	**1.518[b]**	**1.787[a]**	-0.583
					(2.745)	**(2.445)**	**(2.814)**	(-0.517)
P		-5.215	**-17.710[c]**	-5.992		-5.091	**-17.841[c]**	-6.254
		(-0.730)	**(-1.949)**	(-0.836)		(-0.702)	**(-1.946)**	(-0.859)
Ln(TRw+1)*P			**-5.930[b]**					
			(-2.216)					
PF * P			-8603.675				-8718.233	
			(-1.245)				(-1.249)	
Ln(TRu+1)*P							**-6.020[b]**	
							(-2.256)	
CP				-3.667				-3.788
				(-0.802)				(-0.822)
LnSize				.099				0.159
				(0.066)				(0.103)
LnVisit				**5.659[a]**				**5.795[a]**
				(3.048)				**(3.098)**
F	**3.828[b]**	**2.722[b]**	**2.644[b]**	**3.010[a]**	**3.769[b]**	**2.669[b]**	**2.649[b]**	**3.028[a]**
R^2	**0.043**	**0.046**	**0.074**	**0.099**	**0.043**	**0.045**	**0.074**	**0.099**
Power	**0.701**	**0.668**	**0.819**	**0.914**	**0.701**	**0.668**	**0.819**	**0.914**

5 Conclusion

From the above analyses, it is found that weight in the rating systems do not greatly matter in the buy-it-now C2C marketplace. Though the prices the sellers tagged may show a marginal slight shrink in the weighted ratings systems, no significant changes exist in the sold probability and sold quantity. The charged prices in the successful deals also shrink, but insignificant. It is surprising to have the conclusion, since many C2C market runners transform to the weighted rating systems. If this really happens, new rating systems that can change the underlying rating mechanism should be designed to fit the buy-it-now C2C marketplace.

There is also possibility that the effect of the weight may differ for different categories of products. Therefore, tests with tangible products, especially those touch-and-feel products will be done in the future.

Acknowledgment. This research was supported by the National Science Foundation of China (70802049), and National Social Science Foundation (10BGL099).

Reference

1. Ba, S., Pavlou, P.A.: Evidence of the Effect of trust building technology in electronic markets: price premiums and buyer behavior. MIS Quarterly 26(3), 243–268 (2002)

Analysis of Evaluation about Regional Capacity of Science and Technology

Tan Heng

Zhongyuan Institute of Technology, Zhengzhou 450007, China

Abstract. This paper is from the input-output point of view, reflecting the innovation built environment, innovation input and innovation performance and the relationship between the three elements of a dynamic regional evaluation index system of regional science and technology innovation. We use related data of the Regional Technology Innovation in Henan in 9 years, using nonlinear weighted comprehensive evaluation of regional technological innovation ability of empirical analysis, then scientific and technological innovation to enhance regional capacity to provide basis for decision making.

Keywords: Regional Capacity, evaluation system, evaluation method.

1 An Evaluation Index System

Regional technological innovation ability evaluation index system is an important tool of the scientific evaluation of the actual level of regional science and technology innovation, and is a system innovation to build a summary of results of regional science and technology. Regional science and technology innovation is a systematic project, which is from the input-output perspective, regional science and technology innovation system is composed of the environment for innovation, technological innovation and scientific and technological innovation performance. These three elements, three elements are interdependent and influent each other and jointly promote regional scientific and technological innovation evolving. We use time series data to track changes in status of regional science and technology innovation, by building three elements which reflect the regional dynamic evaluation system.

In the evaluation system, the dynamic relationship between the three elements are: scientific and technological innovation policy, economic, information, human capital and other scientific and technological innovation environment, innovation is through investment in government and business, and result in innovative performance of economic performance and sustainable development, promoting regional economic development, regional economic development, and technological innovation policy, and economic, information, human capital and other environment will be further improvement and upgrading, but also promote the growing government and business investment in technological innovation further, then economic performance and greater development performance form a virtuous cycle of technology innovation system in a dynamic two-way. With the evaluation system, we need to select the index to the specific measure of regional scientific and technological innovation. In selecting indicators, the first from the innovation environment, innovation, and innovation

Q. Zhou (Ed.): ISAEBD 2011, Part II, CCIS 209, pp. 307–315, 2011.

performance connotation of the indicator elements of decomposition, while trying to avoid a large correlation between the indicators are included in the index system, to ensure that evaluation results will not be artificially magnified. Second, the operability of statistical data from proceeding to determine the elements needed to reflect the target. Finally, evaluation should also be considered representative of rationality; the data should be collected, and should be easy to compare values to ensure consistent evaluation of data-caliber from unified source.

Table 1. Regional Capacity Evaluation

First indicators	Secondary indicators	Third indicators	Unit
Environment for innovation (X1)	Policy environment (X11)	National science and technology projects(X111) Provincial science and technology projects(X112) Above the provincial level science and technology award(X113)	Items Items Items
	Economic environment(X12)	Per capita expenditure(X121) Consumption level(X122) Investment in Fixed Assets(X123)	Yuan Yuan Billion
	Environmental Science and Technology(X13)	Number of research and development per million people(X131) Number of patent applications per million people(X132) The number of papers and books per million(X133) Number of research and development company(X134)	Person/years Items/peopleArt icles/people person
	Information Environment(X14)	The number of mobile phone users(X141) The average number of families have computers at one hundred(X142) Internet users(X143)	Million Tai Hu
	Educational environment(X15)	GDP, the proportion of education funds(X151) the number of students in institutions of higher learning(X152) Per capita amount of public library(X153)	% person Book/person
Investment in technological innovation (X2)	Government investment in science and technology innovation(X21)	Total government investment in science and technology funds(X211) Government investment in science and technology funds accounted for the proportion of GDP(X212)	Billion %
	Business investment in technological Innovation(X22)	The amount of business investment in science and technology funds(X221) Enterprise Funds account for the main business technology share of income(X222) Business investment in technology to transform traditional industries(X223)	Million % Million
Technology Innovation Performance (X3)	Economic performance(X31)	New product output value(X311) New product sales(X312) GDP per capita(X313) Per capita revenue(X314)	Billion Billion Yuan Yuan
	Development performance(X32)	The number of invention patents per million people(X321) Tertiary industry GDP(X322) Industrial added value of energy consumption(X323) GDP, imports and exports accounted for(X324) Rate of increase of import and export(X325)	Items % Tons / million Yuan %

Drawing on previous research results and following the design principles based on the evaluation system, we constructed an index of regional Technology Innovation Evaluation System that contains 3 first indicators, 9 secondary indicators, 30 Third indicators(see Table 1), to make regional science and technology innovation on a more comprehensive and objective evaluation.

2 Nonlinear Weighted Application Comprehensive Evaluation

Non-linear weighted model for the comprehensive evaluation index has a strong correlation between, just for scientific and technological innovation ability evaluation index relatively strong correlation between the features. Non-linear weighted model is as follows:

$$y_i = \prod_{j=1}^{m} x_{ij}^{w_j} \qquad x_{ij} \geq 0 \tag{1}$$

y_i The object being evaluated, said the comprehensive evaluation value, x_{ij} Indicators for the evaluation of observations, w_j The corresponding index weights. Comprehensive evaluation of non-linear weighted as follows:

2.1 Evaluation of the Raw Data of the Dimensionless

For each index the original data dimensionless, as based on a comprehensive evaluation model of nonlinear weighted index of the observations of each request: $x_{ij} \geq 0$, Therefore, this thesis in the dimensionless value method used utility, utility value of the area [0,100]is provided, that the index value of 100 under the best and the worst value is 0, calculated as follows:

Efficiency indicators are calculated as the observed values:

$$x_{ij}' = \frac{x_{ij}}{m_j} \times 100 \tag{2}$$

$$m_j = \max_j \{x_{ij}\} \tag{3}$$

x_{ij} indicated that the observed value of each index, x_{ij}' said after the dimensionless indexes observations.

Observation of negative performance indicators calculated as:

$$x_{ij}' = \frac{m_j - x_{ij}}{m_j - n_j} \times 100 \tag{4}$$

$$m_j = \max_j \{x_{ij}\} \tag{5}$$

$$n_j = \min_j \{x_{ij}\} \tag{6}$$

x_{ij} indicated that the observed value of each index, x_{ij}' said after the dimensionless indexes observations.

The observations are valid indicators of the index means the greater the observed values, the higher utility value, such as per capita GDP, GDP, the proportion of tertiary industry, the number of invention patents and other people. Negative indicators of performance indicators is the observation that the greater the effectiveness of the lower. Technological innovation in Henan index of 30, only the yuan industrial added value is a negative energy efficiency indicators, other indicators have a positive effect on 29 indicators.

2.2 Determine the Linear Weighted Model Comprehensive Evaluation Index Weights

Weighted index were determined using the variance, the object being evaluated for m-, j-established indicators of the mean:

$$\bar{x}_j = \frac{1}{m}\sum_{i=1}^{m} x_{ij} \qquad j=1, 2, 3, \ldots, 30 \tag{7}$$

Variance can be obtained:

$$S_j^2 = \frac{1}{m}\sum_{i=1}^{m} (x_{ij} - \bar{x}_j)^2 , \quad j=1, 2, 3, \ldots, 30 \tag{8}$$

the weight coefficient of J-indexes is:

$$w_j = \frac{S_j}{\sum_{j=1}^{30} S_j} , \quad j=1, 2, 3, \ldots, 30 \tag{9}$$

2.3 The Evaluation Results Are Obtained

②,④data using standardized formula, the formula used to determine the weight coefficient⑨, ⑧,⑨substituted①Regional Capacity calculated evaluation value.

3 Analysis of Henan Science and Technology Innovation Comprehensive Evaluation

3.1 The Objects, the Year and Data Sources of Evaluation

(1) the year target of assessment and evaluation

Most previous studies focused on the evaluation of the object in a given year of a regional technological innovation ability of static analysis, ignoring the dynamic regional technology innovation trends. This study used time series data to track their own scientific and technological innovation in Henan changes. Identified in the evaluation year, the inspection-related national and Statistical Yearbook of Henan

Province, Henan Province before 2000 because the relevant data for statistical coverage issues and other issues related to missing data, and ultimately determine the evaluation year for the 9 years of data 2000-2008 .

(2) the underlying data sources

Evaluation of data from the national and provincial government released statistics, mainly in Henan Province Bureau of Statistics 2001-2009, compiled the "Statistical Yearbook of Henan Province", Henan Bureau of Statistics, Science and Technology Department of Henan Province and Henan Province Department of Education 2000-2008 Co-editor of the "Statistical Yearbook of Henan Science and Technology", Henan Science and Technology Agency's 2000-2008 series of "Henan Science and Technology Yearbook" and the official website of Henan Province Bureau of Statistics 2000-2008 and the national economy in Henan Province Social Development Statistics and other data.

(3)processing defect data

The statistical indicators in different years will have to adjust and change, such as the energy of the target before 2007, no statistics, began after 2007, so some data can not be obtained, we have done for the corresponding defect data processing, such as enterprise Number of research and development indicators (x134) data is used in large and medium industrial enterprises in research and experimental development personnel. From 2000 Statistical Yearbook of Henan Province is not in the statistics business research and experimental development personnel indicators, adopting a medium-sized industrial enterprises in the number of agency personnel office technology.

3.2 Data Collection and Processing

This data is based on selected years from 2001-2009, "Statistical Yearbook of Henan Province," 2000 to-2008 "Henan Science and Technology Statistical Yearbook" 2000 to-2008 "Henan Science and Technology Yearbook" and Henan 2000-2008 2001-2009 Provincial Economic and Social Development Statistical Bulletin and other order drawn, the original data entry into the SPSS17.0 (Statistical Package For the Social Science) software. As the dimensions of each index are great differences can not be used directly Henan Science and Technology Innovation Index comprehensive evaluation, therefore, first need to Henan Science and Technology Innovation Index of the raw data dimensionless. By the formula 1-2,1-5 observations of each index value after the non-dimensional treatment, to be able to make the observation model into the non-linear weighted evaluation.

3.3 Determination of Weights

Non-linear weighted model based on the comprehensive evaluation method, in addition to observations of each index for non-dimensional treatment, but also to determine the weight of each index, designed to reflect the evaluation's role in the evaluation system and the degree of importance. In order to avoid the error caused by the subjective weighting method, select the objective weighting method variance in the distribution of all the weight of each index, that is being evaluated for m-object, set the first indicators of the mean j:

$$\bar{x}_j = \frac{1}{m}\sum_{i=1}^{m} x_{ij}\quad , \quad j=1, 2, 3, \ldots, 30 \tag{10}$$

Variance can be obtained:

$$S_j^2 = \frac{1}{m}\sum_{i=1}^{m}(x_{ij} - \bar{x}_j)^2\quad , \quad j=1, 2, 3, \ldots, 30 \tag{11}$$

the weight coefficient of J-indexes is:

$$w_j = \frac{S_j}{\sum_{j=1}^{30} S_j}\quad , \quad j=1, 2, 3, \ldots, 30 \tag{12}$$

SPSS17.0 the original data entry after the first use of non-dimensional approach (using the formula to deal with ② and ④) of the original data dimensionless, and then use SPSS17.0 descriptive statistical analysis The indicators mean and standard deviation, and finally, the use of formula 1-9 obtained the weight of each index factor.

3.4 The Evaluation Process and Results

(1) Technology Innovation Capability Assessment Score

Environment for innovation, technological innovation and investment and technological innovation performance evaluation score of ①, the formula deduced by the formula. Environment for innovation is calculated as:

$$y_i = \prod_{j=1}^{16} x_{ij}^{w_j} \quad (i=1, 2, 3, \ldots, 9) \tag{13}$$

$x_{i1}, x_{i2}, \cdots, x_{i16}$ is the environment for innovation sub-indices of the observations, w_j the environment for technological innovation and the weight of each sub-index coefficient, calculated by the formula of technological innovation environment evaluation score of 2000-2008 (see Table 2).

Investment in technological innovation is calculated as:

$$y_i = \prod_{j=17}^{21} x_{ij}^{w_j} \quad (i=1, 2, 3, \ldots, 9) \tag{14}$$

$x_{i17}, x_{i18}, \cdots, x_{i21}$ is the scientific and technological innovation into the sub-index w_j observations for scientific and technological innovation into the weight of each sub-index coefficient, calculated by the formula of technological innovation into the evaluation score of 2000-2008 (see Table 2).

Technological innovation performance is calculated as:

$$y_i = \prod_{j=22}^{30} x_{ij}^{w_j} \qquad (i=1, 2, 3,\ldots,9) \qquad (15)$$

$x_{i22}, x_{i23}, \cdots, x_{i30}$ is the scientific and technological innovation performance indicators of each child observations, w_j scientific and technological innovation performance for the weight of each sub-index coefficient, calculated by the formula of technological innovation performance evaluation score of 2000-2008 (see Table 2).

(2)Technological innovation ability evaluation scores

Henan Science and Technology Innovation Capability evaluation scores obtained by the following formula:

$$y_i = \prod_{j=1}^{30} x_{ij}^{w_j} \qquad (i=1, 2, 3, \ldots, 9) \qquad (16)$$

x_{ij} is scientific and technological innovation capacity index of each sub-observation, w_j capacity for technological innovation sub-index weights of each factor. By the scientific and technological innovation formula comprehensive evaluation scores 2000-2008 (see Table 2).

Table 2. The environment for innovation, technological innovation and investment and technological innovation performance evaluation scores

Year	Environmental assessment score of Science and Technology Innovation	Investment in technological innovation Evaluation score	Technology Innovation Performance Evaluation score	Technology innovation Evaluation score
2000	5.1075	1.6642	2.8703	24.3969
2001	5.9473	1.6674	2.7820	27.5881
2002	6.4122	1.6954	2.8174	30.6293
2003	6.9524	1.7386	3.2053	38.7437
2004	7.4207	1.8218	3.3656	45.5003
2005	8.5456	1.8884	3.2642	52.6753
2006	9.2618	1.9236	3.6615	65.2346
2007	10.542	2.0076	3.9354	83.2865
2008	11.590	2.0142	4.1366	96.5640

4 Evaluation of Scientific and Technological Innovation in Henan Province

4.1 Technology Innovation Environment Impact Analysis of Technology Innovation

Environment for innovation to improve year by year, but growth is not balanced, in 2001 and 2005 increased more than 10 percentage points, respectively, 16.4% and

15.2%, the rest were less than 10% the year 2008 compared to 2002, an increase of 1.06 times. Annual growth rate of technological innovation is faster than the environment for innovation in 2006, 39.7%, but the fluctuations, in 2005 only 4% in 2008 compared with 2002, an increase of 3.6 times. By contrast we can see that the volatility of the environment for innovation will affect the ability of technological innovation, technological innovation environment of the ring than the higher rate of growth, technological innovation does not change at, but the environment for innovation than the rate of decline in the ring, then capability in the ring than the corresponding decline in growth, technological innovation and the environment contributed greatly to the scientific and technological innovation.

4.2 Investment in Technology Innovation Impact of Science and Technology Innovation

Fixed investment in technological innovation and the chain growth than the growth is very slow, and the annual growth rate of instability, combined with the results of factor analysis shows that enterprises are the main scientific and technological input in Henan, a serious shortage of government investment in science and technology, and business with science and technology investment will the economic and adjusted for changes in the economic environment, resulting in limited growth in science and technology investment and more volatile, and its ability to enhance scientific and technological innovation could not be fully effective.

4.3 Technology Innovation of Scientific and Technological Innovation Performance of Team

Technological innovation and scientific and technological innovation performance over-year change in the same direction, the most direct impact. From 2001 to 2008, technological innovation increases the changes are as technology innovation performance of the fluctuations with the fluctuations, most notably in 2005, technology innovation chain growth has seen the lowest value of 4% in the same year Technology Innovation significant increase in the environment, increase investment in science and technology innovation declined, but not decrease, but the performance of scientific and technological innovation have occurred 13% of the decline, technological innovation can be drawn down the most important reason is the impact of technological innovation performance, 2008 Technology innovation performance compared with 2000, also increased by 67.4%, improvement of scientific and technological innovation played a contribution to the role, but there is still much room for improvement.

4.4 Comprehensive Evaluation of Scientific and Technological Innovation in Henan Province

Information environment, policy environment and economic environment contributed greatly to the scientific and technological innovation, especially in the information environment, but the technology environment and the educational environment is poor, which greatly affected the Henan Science and Technology Innovations capability. Investment in technological innovation: the serious shortage of government investment, corporate investment instability, improvement of scientific and technological innovation is very restricted role. Technological innovation performance of scientific and technological innovation to enhance the most direct impact of the past few years, technological innovation and performance improvement of scientific and technological innovation has played a catalytic role, and there is still much room for improvement.

References

[1] Gang, H.: Study of Regional Capacity in Anhui Province. China's development 04 (2009)
[2] Dai, L.W.: SPASS for Windows statistical analysis. Electronic Industry Press, Beijing (2004)
[3] Statistical Yearbook of Henan Province and Henan Science and Technology Statistical Yearbook (2001-2009)

The Empirical Analysis on Industry Development and the Problems of Resources and Environment in the West of China

Xuemei Zhang and Shuang Wang

Associate Professor, Economics & Management School of Lanzhou University of Technology, 730050 Gansu, China

Abstract. The industries of the west have been increasing steadily but still lag behind the eastern region with the implementation of the west development strategy. From the perspective of sustainable development, this article discovers the problems such as weakened resources, poor environment's performance and serious environmental pollution in the resources-directional structure of the west industry. Meanwhile, according to the analysis of Environmental Kuznets Curve, "first pollution, last treatment" cannot work in the west. If the west still follows the traditional development mode, it would not appear the point of inflexion for the environmental improvement. Therefore, industry ecology will be the choice for the coordination of industries development with resources and environment in the west of China.

Keywords: The West of China, Industry Development, Resources and Environment.

1 Introduction

In the middle of 1950s, the relationship was hypothesized by Simon Kuznets between economic growth and income inequality that the difference of income first increased with economic growth till to a turn point and then decreased during the economic development. This result gave rise to an inverted U-shaped curve called "KUZNETS CURVE" relating economic growth to income inequality. Based on this hypothesis, a large amount of empirical research has been devoted to examining the relationship between economic growth and the environment. The Environmental Kuznets Curve (EKC) was first observed by Grossman and Krueger in 1995. They empirically describe a relationship between per capita income and certain indicators of environmental degradation in their investigation of the possible environmental impacts of a North American Free Trade Agreement (NAFTA).At early stages of development, the levels of certain pollutants rise with increases in per capita income (PCI), while at higher levels of development, environmental degradation is seen to decrease with further increases in PCI. These results give rise to an inverted U-shaped curve relating economic growth to environmental degradation.

Under the background of implementing the sustainable development strategy in China, this paper aims to study the industrial development of China's western region

Q. Zhou (Ed.): ISAEBD 2011, Part II, CCIS 209, pp. 316–323, 2011.

based on the EKC analysis, due to the west eco-system weaken, the decomposing ability of natural system lower than that of the eastern region and the environmental pollution easier to be diffused from the upper stream to other regions. A starting point is to summarize the characteristics of western industry and analyze the resources and environment problems noticeable in the industrial development. Then we choose indicators for the economic and environmental dimensions of regional development and use them for measuring the relationship between western economic growth and environmental degradation. Using the real data of the west, an empirical analysis will be employed to illustrate the shape of the western EKC. Finally, in terms of the result, some conclusions and proposals could be put forward and discussed on how to accelerate the coordinated development of industry and environment in China's western region.

2 The Industrial Characteristics and the Problems of Resources and Environment in Western Region

The industries of the west have been developing with high speed since 21st century. The output value of three industries has risen sharply and structural adjustment is getting faster whereas the disparity between the western areas and the developed eastern part of china is still widened.

2.1 The Industrial Characteristics of the West

During the Tenth Five-Year Plan period (2001-2005), the GDP increase of western areas has kept stable in the primary, secondary and tertiary industries. Particularly, the growth rates of secondary and tertiary industries are higher than that of primary industry. Of this total, the GDP of secondary industry has grown up from 743.058 billion RMB in 2001 to 1433.162 billion RMB in 2005 as well as that of tertiary industry being up from 698.479 billion RMB to 1323.706 billion RMB.

The industrial structure has been constantly adjusted and optimized in the past five years. The primary, secondary and tertiary industries accounted for 17.7%, 42.8% and 39.5% of the GDP in 2005, respectively. Compared with 2001, the proportion of primary industry dropped by 2.8%, that of secondary industry rose by 3.1%, and that of tertiary industry rose by 2.2%. At the first year of the Eleventh Five-Year period, separately, the contribution rate of three industries to the GDP was 8.26%, 58.72% and 33.02% and the drawing effect of those on the 13.1% growth of GDP came to 1.08%, 7.69% and 4.33% in which the role of secondary industry was most remarkable for the economic and social development of western areas.

The structural changes of the west industry are basically in line with the general law of industrial development at home and abroad so that the proportion of secondary and tertiary industries has gradually increased. However, compared with the eastern region, there is a big gap in such aspects as the GDP growth rate, three industrial output values and the rationality of the industrial structure. In 2005, the output value of eastern primary industry was 1087.445 billion RMB, which was twice more than that of western areas, the output value of eastern secondary industry was 6517.895 billion RMB, which was about five times of that in the west, while the output value of western tertiary industry was only one fourth of that in the east. In addition, the disparity between the west and the east is also reflected in the difference of per capita GDP depended on the industrial development. In 2007, the western region's per capita GDP was 13,212 RMB, lower than the national average of 18,934 RMB, while the eastern region's per capita GDP is about 2.5 times as much as that of the western region.

2.2 The Problems of Resources and Environment in Industrial Development

The natural environment and resources having the decisive effect on the formation of industrial structure in the west, but in the view of sustainable development, there are some resources and environmental problems increasingly prominent in its resource-based industries.

2.2.1 The Weakening of Resources Advantage

As heavy industries with energy and raw materials are in the prior position in the west while light, processing and equipment manufacturing industries are underdeveloped, industrial chains among them are broken, and the simple resource-based and high consumption industries become dominant and constraint the economic development of western region. For instance, since 1990's, owing to the scale expansion of industries such as aluminum and iron alloy with high consumption and a large number of raw materials continually, the great deal of electric power has been consumed by low value-added resource products. Thus, it greatly increases the pressure on energy supply and impairs the energy advantage as well. From 2000 to 2007, the intensity of energy consumption has been up from 1.75 ton of SCE per 10000 yuan to 1.95 ton of SCE per 10000 yuan, two times as much as that of eastern region. So, if the extensive development was not changed as soon as possible, it would accelerate the consumption of resources and weaken its resources endowment.

2.2.2 The Aggravation of Regional Pollution

As a general rule, the high-pollution industries concentrate on some high-consumption sector where sulphur dioxide (SO_2) and chemical oxygen demand (COD) are two major pollutants. In accordance with the proportion of high-pollution industries accounting for the total value of industrial output from different provinces in 2005, the high-pollution industries are mainly distributed in western region of Inner Mongolia, Gansu, Ningxia, Qinghai, Tibet, Yunnan and Guizhou province. Furthermore, the intensity of major pollutant discharge in the west is far higher than that of central and eastern regions because the industrial wastes always increase dramatically with the expansion of western industry. The intensities of SO_2 and COD are 2.1 times and 1.65 times of the national average level respectively, in particular, the intensity of solid wastes has become to 3.11 times of eastern region in 2007.

3 An Empirical Analysis of the Western EKC

3.1 Policy Implications of EKC

The EKC represents the inverted U-shaped relation between income and the concentration of waste gas, water and industrial residue pollutants. The thinking behind its emergence is the following: during the first stages of industrialization, pollution grows rapidly as priority is given to wealth accumulation. People are more concerned with their employment and their income than with the environmental quality. In more advanced development stages, people attach more value to the environment as soon as revenues increase and the environment is improved. Therefore, a country government can solve the environment degradation problems through accelerating its economic growth to reach the declining stage of the EKC as soon as possible. Many developed countries have followed the pattern of "pollute first and clean up later" reflected by the EKC such as Japan, the United Kingdom, and the USA in the past century. If the developing countries learn from their experiences and lessons and transform the economic growth mode, the top of the EKC would be crossed comparatively at smaller economic scale and lower pollution. This is showed by figure 1 where the abscissa is income per capita and the vertical is environment pollution. The changing curve of AEF, corresponding to the abscissa left moved and to the vertical moving down from the curve of ABCD, is the appropriate EKC for the developing countries.

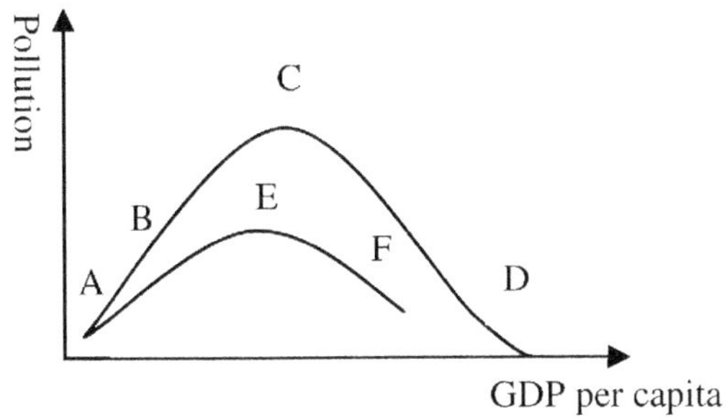

Fig. 1. EKC

3.2 Model Specification and Data Description

According to EKC hypothesis, we examine the relationship of three indicators of environmental degradation in the west to income per capita, as measured by real GDP per capita. The three environmental indicators —Volume of Industrial Waste Gas Emission, Volume of Waste Water Discharge and Volume of Industrial Solid Wastes— are chosen because they are available on a local basis and for the longest time period from 1986 to 2007. Moreover, the measures are standard indicators in every province of China and are widely used measures of environmental degradation. For all three measures, an increase in the indicator implies an increase in environmental degradation. We begin by estimating a standard reduced-form model of the relationship between environmental degradation and per capita GDP, and then evaluate the model using various econometric tests. The reduced-form model estimated using time-series data (see Table 1) of the west is given by Eq. 1:

$$Y_t = \beta_0 + \beta_1 \ln X_t + \beta 2 (\ln X_t)^2 + \beta_3 (\ln X_t)^3 + \mu_t \quad (1)$$

where:

Y = the natural logarithm of the measure of environmental degradation
lnX= the natural logarithm of real GDP per capita.

Table 1. The volume of the "Three Wastes" of industry in the west and GDP per capita (1986-2007)

Year	Volume of Waste Water Discharge(10000 tons	Volume of Industrial Solid Wastes (10000 tons)	Volume of Industrial Waste Gas Emission (100 million cu.m)	GDP per capita(us $)	ln GDP per capita
1986	562295	12687	15190	182.46	5.21
1987	583781	11834	16824	195.05	5.27
1988	592940	13744	18374	243.94	5.50
1989	522789	13045	17599	271.97	5.61
1990	514268	13731	18164	244.60	5.50
1991	495922	13935	22595	248.71	5.52
1992	500723	14623	19445	279.80	5.63
1993	453388	14905	21103	333.39	5.81
1994	457918	14567	21035	285.54	5.65
1995	506581	16028	23816	360.79	5.89
1996	430979	12750	25430	426.37	6.06
1997	410564	16889	27851	470.09	6.15
1998	426140	23162	28910	500.41	6.22
1999	451951	22282	30602	517.37	6.25
2000	447125	21842	31883	566.17	6.34
2001	443233	21740	34978	604.92	6.41
2002	450965	24229	39621	661.22	6.49
2003	482118	27617	44753	761.87	6.64
2004	489198	32197	59765	897.68	6.80
2005	535519	38073	59379	1136.5	7.04
2006	510878	44423	80285	1371.3	7.22
2007	554747	53142	104519	1737.5	7.46

Note: GDP exchanged to US dollar at average rate per year.
Source: Chinese statistics year book (1987-2008), Chinese environmental statistics year book 2007.

3.3 Estimation Results and Curve Figures

Ordinary least squares (OLS) estimates of the coefficients of Eq. 1 are presented in Table 2, together with a number of diagnostic statistics. The sample sizes range from 22 observations for these indicators. These results suggest that for all three measures of environmental degradation, the adjusted R^2 exceeds 0.7, implying that the reduced-form model explains much of the variation in the measure of environmental degradation. In view of F-tests, the overall regression of equation is significant. Thus the models, as a whole, appear to have explanatory power.

Table 2. Estimates of reduced-form model

Variable	Constant	lnX	$(\ln X)^2$	$(\ln X)^3$	Adjusted R^2	F-statistic
Volume of Waste Water Discharge	5128484.41	-1485353.5	117766.395	——	0.709	21.917
Volume of Industrial Waste Gas Emission	136004.132	——	-12772.65	1613.902	0.977	380.587
Volume of Industrial Solid Wastes	71810.554	——	-6450.652	820.636	0.97	294.053

Using estimates of reduced-formed model, we can graph the curve path that the environmental indicator is measured on the ordinate and the natural logarithm of real GDP per capita is measured on the abscissa(see figure 2, figure 3 and figure 4). On the contrary, the curve is different from the traditional EKC and shows "U" shape in the west where the volume of waste water discharge first decreases as GDP per capita rises, then increasing with GDP per capita, and respectively the volume of industrial waste gas emission and the volume of industrial solid wastes nearly take on monotonic increasing trend with GDP per capita.

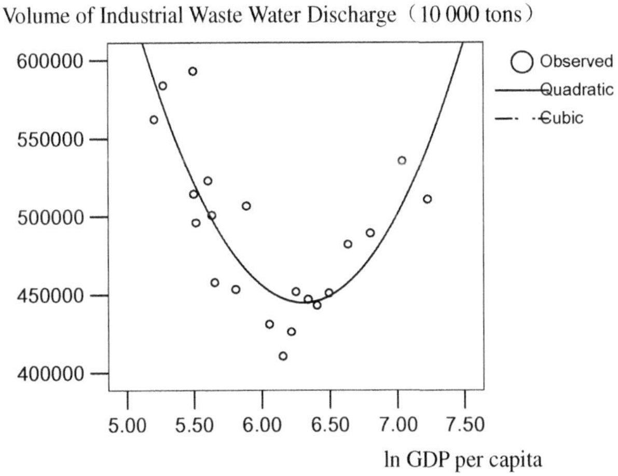

Fig. 2.

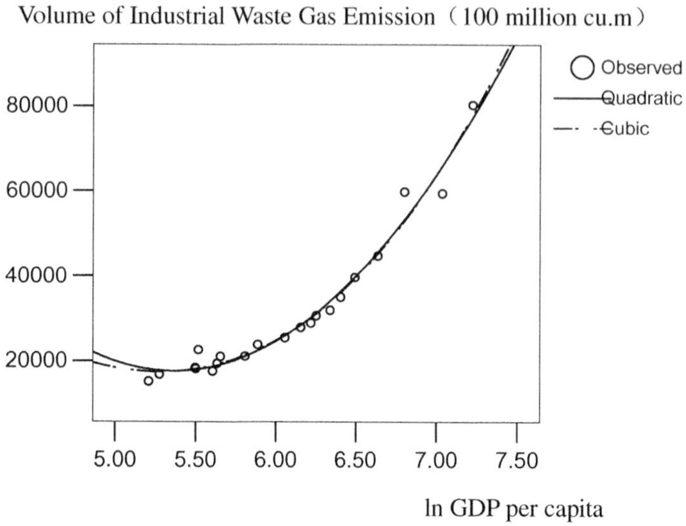
Volume of Industrial Waste Gas Emission（100 million cu.m）
Observed
Quadratic
Cubic
80000
60000
40000
20000
5.00
5.50
6.00
6.50
7.00
7.50
ln GDP per capita

Fig. 3.

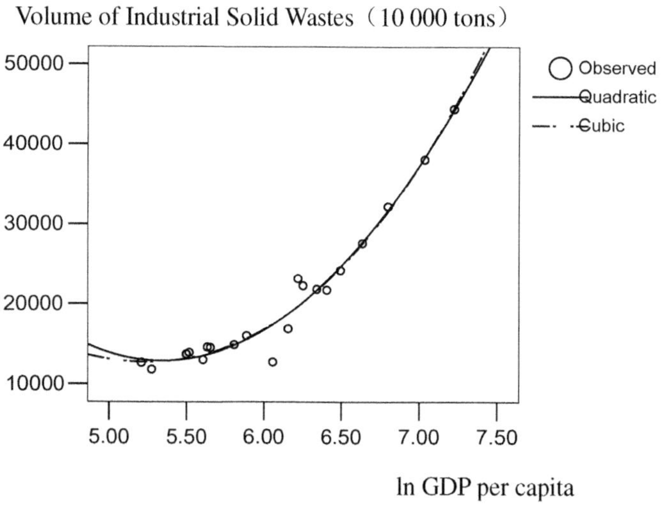
Volume of Industrial Solid Wastes（10 000 tons）
Observed
Quadratic
Cubic
50000
40000
30000
20000
10000
5.00
5.50
6.00
6.50
7.00
7.50
ln GDP per capita

Fig. 4.

4 Conclusions and Recommendations

It is estimated that the curve min value of waste water discharge and the natural logarithm of real GDP per capita is 6.31 in 1999 and 2000. The main reasons why the waste water discharge has raced up since 1999 is quite likely the implementation of west developing and the grads transfer of some heavy polluting and highly energy consuming industries from overseas and the domestic developed region to the west. Moreover, the estimated curve min values of industrial waste gas emission, industrial solid wastes and the natural logarithm of real GDP per capita respectively are 5.28 and 5.24 appearing in 1986 and 1988, which can explain the industrial waste gas emission and the solid wastes of the west rising with income increasing all the while. Consequently, it is found that the western region economy is fast growing at the expenses of environmental degradation. The west of China does not have the luxury of being able to grow out of its environmental problems. Thus, if we wish to prevent further environmental degradation it would seem that concerted policies and incentives are required to reduce pollution intensity per unit of output across sectors, to shift from more to less pollution-producing outputs and to lower the environmental damage associated with aggregate energy consumption. That means industry ecology and circular economy will be the choice for the coordination of industries development with resources and environment in the west of China.

Acknowledgement. The authors are grateful for the assistance and support on the research of industrial development of western China from the Youth Program of National Social Science Foundation of China and the doctoral fund program of Lanzhou University of Technology.

References

1. Grossman, G.M., Krueger, A.B.: Economic growth and the environment. Quarterly Journal of Economics 110(2), 353–378 (1995)
2. Prieur, F.: The environmental Kuznets curve in a world of irreversibility. Econ. Theory 40, 57–90 (2009)
3. Dasgupta, P.: The economics of non-convex ecosystems: introduction. Environ. Resource Econ. 26, 499–525 (2002)
4. Anton, N., Geoff, A.: The Environmental Kuznets Curve: A Literature Survey. South African Journal of Economics 3, 105 (2005)
5. China Council for International Cooperation on Environment and Development: The environment and development of China: Challenges and Choices. China Environmental Press, Beijing (2007)

Non-renewable Resources, Vertical Innovation and Economic Growth

Shuang Wang and Xuemei Zhang

Institute of Urban Economy, Tianjin Academy of Social Sciences,
Ph. D, 300191 Tianjin, China

Abstract. It is a controversy debate among economists that scarcity of resource might have a negative effect on economic growth. However, with available technology progress supported by innovation, especially by vertical innovation, its effect will be eliminated. In this paper, we use panel data to estimate the effect of resource on economic growth with vertical innovation. It shows that there are a few different results on the context of whether or not with innovation. When we run regression with innovation, the coefficients of resource reserves are mostly positive and significant, showing that innovation have conversed the negative effects which is seen in the regression without innovation into positive ones, that is to say, the scarcity of resources might not lead to the stagnated economic growth.

Keywords: Non-renewable resource, Vertical innovation, Panel data.

1 Introduction

Lots of recent growth theoretical literatures studied the relationship between resources and economic growth. Groth and Souch (2003) analyzed when non-renewable resources entered into "growth engine", i.e. non-renewable resources was treated as necessary inputs in the process of product, it will alleviate the effect of knife-edge which meant a small increasing of returns would cause explosive growth of output, because "the strain on the economy imposed by the need to extract successively smaller amounts of the resource might offset the potentially explosive effects of increasing returns to scale…".Smulders and Nooij (2003) added the technological effects when analyze the impact of resources on growth, they constructed a model with energy use and endogenous factor-augmenting technological change, they found that "with induced technical change, the reduction in energy inputs is offset by faster improvements in energy-related technology, which may mitigate the drop in per capita income…"So, they conclude that induced innovation could not decrease the using of energy and scarcity of resources would also affect long-run growth. Bretschger (2005) gave a great summary of the relationship between natural resources and technological change, and developed a model showing the effect of horizontal innovation on long-run growth with natural resources. He pointed out that technological change could compensate the scarcity of natural resources and showed

Q. Zhou (Ed.): ISAEBD 2011, Part II, CCIS 209, pp. 324–331, 2011.

how to model the effect of different technological change on growth with natural resources.

There are two types of innovation in the context of resources analysis, one is horizontal innovation, Gancia and Zilibotti (2005) gave the definition as "a discovery consists of the technical knowledge required to manufacture a new good that does not displace existing ones", which is represented as the increasing sorts of product. Grimaud (2001) studied the horizontal innovation model with natural resources in long-run growth to confirm the optimum growth path. Another is vertical innovation, which was given by Aghion and Howitt (1998), with the concept of "improvement of quality of product given the sort of that". Grimaud and Rougè (2003) developed a Schumpeterian endogenous model with non-renewable natural resource as an essential factor in "growth engine" under the framework of vertical innovation (or creative destruction).They applied vertical innovation of "`á lá Aghion-Howitt" to explore the possible steady growth path.

Since the stock of non-renewable resources is invariant, once it has been extracted, its quantity for using will inevitably decrease. However, we do need natural resources to produce what we need to sustain our lives. Without natural resources, especially the non-renewable resource which is still the main source that provides power, energy and fuel, we cannot produce mostly necessity of which we truly in need. With respect to its especial characteristic, what we can do to deal with its finite stock is depend on our technological process. Therefore, substitution of other renewable resources will be an available method, but it will expense to develop new resources which could perfectly take place of what we are using now. Enhance the efficiency of resources using or consumption might be a more direct and feasible alternative to alleviate the scarcity of natural resources. This paper will test the theoretical analysis that technological progress which be supported by innovation could ensure a steady growth rate with non-renewable resources as necessary inputs to growth.

2 Empirical Model

In this paper, we will develop a growth regression based on the previous literatures to study the impact of vertical innovation on long-run growth rate under the framework of non-renewable resource enter into "growth engine". We try to show the role of innovation when economic growth would be affected by resources scarcity. Our simple production function is:

$$g = f(p, k, l, s, r, z) \tag{1}$$

Where, g is the growth rate; p is the parameter of vertical innovation based on Grimaud and Rougè (2003); k is the capital stock; l is the labor; s is the resource capital which shows the resource endowment, we use the definition given by Wackernagel, Lewan, and Hansson(1999) to estimate it; r is the parameter presenting the resource efficiency, we focus on energy efficiency which be measured as energy intensity(energy using divided by GDP); z is the parameter of structure exhibits the natural resources abundance according to Ding and Field(2004).

Assume that our model is based on C-D growth model, we have:

$$g = p^{\alpha} k^{\beta} l^{\gamma} s^{\delta} r^{\varphi} z^{\tau} \tag{2}$$

Where $\alpha + \beta + \gamma + \delta + \varphi + \tau \geq 1$, which allows increasing returns to scale. Take logarithm on (**2**), it gets:

$$\log g = \alpha \log p + \beta \log k + \gamma \log l + \delta \log s + \varphi \log r + \tau \log z \tag{3}$$

Then, we transform (**3**) to a panel data model which is as follows:

$$\log g_{it} = C + \alpha \log p_{it} + \beta \log k_{it} + \gamma \log l_{it} + \delta \log s_{it} + \varphi \log r_{it} + \tau \log z_{it} + u_{it} \tag{4}$$

Where, g_{it} is the per capita growth rate of country i in period t. p_{it} is the current patents[1] in country i in period t. The reason why we choose patent to indicate vertical innovation stem from several previous studies. Dasgupta and Heal (1974)'s approach about optimal depletion of exhaustible resources, which argued that there is uncertainty connected with future technology, they treated the exact date of its coming as random but it would be bound to happen sometime in further. They pointed out that it was the increasing price of essential exhaustible resources that push entrepreneurs to invest on cheaper substitutes. Popp (2002) used U.S. patent data to analyze the effect of energy prices on energy-efficient innovations which had common characteristics of induced innovation with the same underlying implication of Dasgupta and Heal's discussion. Aghion and Howitt (1998) and Grimaud and Rouge(2003) all assumed that vertical innovations would arrive randomly with a Poisson arrival rate, which followed the thought of Dasgupta and Heal. Actually, we indeed have no idea on when will be new patents shown up, but we are sure about the fact that there must be patent in further which is compatible with the traits of vertical innovation. Therefore, we use patent to represent the vertical innovation in our analysis. k_{it} is the per capita capital in country i in period t, l_{it} is the labor in country i in period t, s_{ir} is the per capita natural resource capital of country i in period t, r_{it} is the resource efficiency of country i in period t, z_{it} is the structural variables of country i in period t. u_{it} is the error item, which has two cases:

I One-way error component model:

$$u_{it} = \mu_i + v_{it} \tag{5}$$

Where μ_i denotes the unobservable individual specific effect which is time-invariant and accounts for any individual specific effect that is not shown in the regression; v_{it} denotes the remainder disturbance which is independent and identically distributed IID$(0, \sigma_v^2)$.

II Two-way error component model:

$$u_{it} = \mu_i + \lambda_t + v_{it} \tag{6}$$

Where μ_i denotes the unobservable individual specific effect; λ_t denotes the unobservable time effect; v_{it} denotes the remainder stochastic disturbance with distribution of IID$(0, \sigma_v^2)$.

3 Data and Results

3.1 Date Description

Our data includes 66 countries over 32 years from 1970 to 2001, i.e. N=66, T=32. Except for 30 OECD countries, we add another 36 countries in the world to make sure our panel data sample has large N and with better representation. The dependent variables of left hand side in equation (**4**) we need to estimate are from below sources:

The patents of each countries we use "patent grants by patent office" from the data of WIPO Statistics Database (December, 2008) in countries level as an indicator of vertical innovation; The per capita growth rate which we drop from Penn World Table 6.2; The per capita capital stock is from EPWT 3.0(Extended Penn World Tables by Adalmir Marquetti); The labor we also use "number of employed workers" in EPWT 3.0; The per capita natural resource capital is measured by the three main non-renewable resources reserves, including oil reserves, natural gas reserves and coal production[2] averaged by population in country level, which from the database of EIA; We calculate energy efficiency as follows: we use energy use per capita divided by per capita GDP (total GDP divided by population) both from World Bank data, excluding Taiwan[3]; The resource structural variables we use SM(1997)'s definition, which is shown as share of resource export in GDP, still including three main non-renewable resources-oil, natural gas and coal export of each country from EIA divided by GDP in World Bank Database, where the oil export data of members of OPEC from OPEC database[4], coal export from EIA. 3.2.

3.2 Estimation Results

Firstly, we shortly summarize the estimation procedures which are related to our empirical work. It is the pooled OLS that we use to get the OLS estimations, which is probably to obtain efficiency with the large observations but they are likely to be biased because of the potential unobserved individual effects (i.e. individual heterogeneity). The alternative methodology is the FE estimation which takes into account the individual effects or both individual and time-specific effects across independent variables. Furthermore, the RE (random effect) estimation allows the individual or time-specific effects or both of them to be random which captures time-variant and time-invariant characteristic of explanatory variables. As to determine how to choose between FE and RE estimations, Hausman(1987) provide a Hausman test based on difference between FE and RE estimations which gave us a plausible method on model selection. Breusch and Pagan(1980) developed a Lagrangian multiplier test for significant of random effects. We apply all these tests in order to gain efficient and consistent estimations. We also report the MLE estimations of random effects to compare with GLS estimators.

We use this panel data to estimate two different types of models with individual effect and both individual and time effects separately. Assuming individual effect is fixed or random we get FE estimator or RE estimator, we also calculate OLS and MLE estimator of both effects, which shown as bellows.

Table 1. Panel Data Estimation of Model I

	OLS	FE Robust	RE Robust	MLE
Intercept	6.094135*	6.281726*	6.347289*	6.315129*
	(0.0742724)	(0.0179344)	(0.192153)	(0.1663588)
PATT	0.0611093*	0.1541297*	0.1384573*	0.1473199*
	(0.0088218)	(0.0189118)	(0.0147593)	(0.0105943)
PCAP	0.469264*	0.0789358*	0.1792259*	0.1242796*
	(0.0181554)	(0.0094535)	(0.0196634)	(0.0303213)
LABR	-0.1665185*		-0.0545281*	
	(0.0106536)		(0.0102005)	
POIL	0.0955915*	-0.0314807*		
	(0.0254279)	(0.0060843)		
PGAS	0.0353866*	0.0148732*	0.0171771*	0.0157441*
	(0.0057535)	(0.0175601)	(0.0055332)	(0.0065815)
PCOL				
RSEF		0.3427361*	0.2168008*	0.2815727*
		(0.0029481)	(0.0544703)	(0.1227365)
EOIL	-0.0252076*	-0.0228607*	-0.0238031*	-0.0232974*
	(0.0036145)	(0.0036594)	(0.0025306)	(0.0031667)
EGAS		-0.0106322*	-0.0099454*	-0.0103514*
		(0.0041777)	(0.0032987)	(0.0040029)
ECOL	-00190418*	-0.0433396*	-0.0410371*	-0.0424489*
	(0.0037937)	(0.1130768)	(0.0035826)	(0.0035198)

Note: Using the annual data over 1970-2001 for 66 countries, we estimate models (**4**) and (**5**) without time-specific effects, where the dependent variable is the logarithm of per capita GDP of 66 countries and the independent variables are ($p_{it}, k_{it}, l_{it}, s_{it}, r_{it}, z_{it}$)=(PATT, PCAP, LABR, POIL, PGAS, PCOL, RSEF, EOIL, EGAS, ECOL)it. The results of OLS are pooled OLS estimators. FE robust stands for robust fixed effect estimators, and RE robust shows robust random effect estimator. MLE is added to the results to report the random effect ML regression comparing with random effect GLS regression (i.e. robust random effect regression). Numbers in ($\cdot$) is the standard error. '*' denotes a significant coefficient at the 5% level. We use Breusch and Pagan Lagrangian multiplier test for random effects, which rejects the null that there is no random effect. We also run Hausman test on FE and RE to confirm whether there is correlation between explanatory variables and individual effects, the Hausman statistics rejects the null of no correlation between explanatory variables and individual effects.

Table 1 reports the One-way error component model that is shown as section 2. Based on Hausman test's result which shows that there exists correlation between explanatory variables and individual effect, we prefer to FE robust estimations. However, Breusch and Pagan Lagrangian multiplier test for random effects rejects the null that there is no random effect but not strongly. As in One-way error component model, FE robust estimations are significant at 5% confident level except for labor variable (LABR) and resources capital of coal (PCOL). The number of patent grants has a positive and significant effect on per capita GDP, which represents the vertical innovation that affects economic growth positively. The elasticity of patent grants on growth(PATT) is larger than that of per capita capital(PCAP) in our regression, showing the dramatic enhancement of innovation on growth rather than traditional factor—capital. Within the framework of non-renewable resources analysis, we add the resources as the essential factors that determine growth path. Except coal(PCOL), oil and natural gas reserves(POIL,PGAS) that are treated as natural resource capital all have positive effect on growth with the vertical innovation. Efficiency of energy usage(RSEF) appears to increase per capita GDP, although OLS estimator is not significant. Resources structural parameters(EOIL,EGAS,ECOL) are all significant but has negative effects on growth, the underlying meaning is related to the curse of resources, as the same results in SW(2001),saying that the countries exporting resources called "resources abundant countries" had poor economic growth. What is hard to explain is the negative effect of labor on economic growth in OLS and RE estimations and no significant in FE estimation, it is likely to reflect the endogenesis of labor supply which is probably decided by other factor which excluded from our model.

Table 2 shows the estimation results of Model II allowing time-invariant variables. There are a few notable discrepancies (mainly in the context of the RE estimation).

Table 2. Panel Data Estimation of Model II

	OLS	FE Robust	RE Robust	MLE
Intercept	5.593354* (0.1627034)	6.390211* (0.122208)	6.264076* (0.1968313)	6.345692* (0.1994417)
PATT	0.0888191* (0.0091767)	0.1573114* (0.0163101)	0.157482* (0.013694)	0.1578873* (0.0093956)
PCAP	0.4473* (0.0178271)		0.0787314* (0.020236)	
LABR	-0.1683733* (0.0103748)		-0.0538011* (0.0100299)	
POIL	0.1097615* (0.0247764)			
PGAS	0.0332273* (0.0057461)	-0.0165141* (0.0071289)	-0.0110974* (0.0062736)	-0.0148861* (0.0061959)
PCOL				
RSEF				
EOIL	-0.0133687* (0.0040122)	0.0094359* (0.0037011)	0.0058541* (0.0034563)	0.0082598* (0.0033991)
EGAS				
ECOL	-0.0112244* (0.0039602)	-0.0255666* (0.0042946)	-0.0250531* (0.0038105)	-0.0254539* (0.0033611)

Note: Using the annual data over 1970-2001 for 66 countries, we estimate models (**4**) and (**6**) with time-specific effects, where the dependent variable is the logarithm of per capita GDP of 66 countries and the independent variables are $(p_{it}, k_{it}, l_{it}, s_{it}, r_{it}, z_{it})$=(PATT, PCAP, LABR, POIL, PGAS, PCOL, RSEF, EOIL, EGAS, ECOL)it. The results of OLS are pooled OLS estimators. FE robust stands for robust fixed effect estimators, and RE robust shows robust random effect estimator. MLE is added to the results to report the random effect ML regression comparing with random effect GLS regression (i.e. robust random effect regression). Numbers in $(\cdot)$ is the standard error. '*' denotes a significant coefficient at the 5% level. We use Breusch and Pagan Lagrangian multiplier test for random effects, which rejects the null that there is no random effect. We also run Hausman test of random effect to confirm whether there is correlation between explanatory variables and individual and time random effects or both effects, the Hausman statistics does not rejects the null of no correlation between explanatory variables and individual and time random effects.

First, both Hausman test and Breusch and Pagan Lagrangian multiplier test are all showing more confidence of RE effect in this model. We then follow the results of RE robust estimation. Unfortunately, we figure out that two of three main resources capital, i.e. oil and coal are insignificant in growth regression (POIL, PCOL), as well as energy efficient parameter (RSEF) and share of natural gas export (EGAS) that surprise us, especially of the energy efficient parameter. We guess that energy efficiency might be determined by industrial structure, institutional environment, availability of substitute resource and national regulations on resource production transaction exclusively induce this result. However, we still get the significant and positive effect of innovation (PATT) and capital (PCAP) on economic growth, and the effect of innovation on growth still surpass the effect of capital, confirming our previous result. Differ from Model I, the sign of parameter of share of oil export (EOIL) differing from Model I which means the more export of oil increases per capital growth. The reason might be that we allow time-specific variance which emphasizes the violation of international oil market or the shocks to oil prices may affect the export-type economies diversely. Similarly, the effect of innovation represented by patent grants is still positive and significant, which could be additional evidence to the hypothesis in Section 1.

4 Conclusions

In this paper, we further the empirical analysis with the framework of non-renewable resources using 66 countries panel data to estimate the hypothesis that the potential effect of innovation on economic growth controls the resources depletion. As mentioned in theories of endogenous growth, resources, especially non-renewable resources are considered as inevitable input in the main production sectors, but the finite stock of resources might constraint their further consumption, which would be a negative factor possibly stagnate the rate of growth. To deal with this restriction, innovations then applied as available technologies play an important role in the process. Through application of innovations, the efficiency of resources usage will be improved, which allows us to extract less resource and leave more to next generation, it might be balance the intertemporal allocation of resources.

Acknowledgement. Thanks are due to Professor Mary E. Lovely and Professor David Popp in Syracuse University for their advices and language helps.

Annotation

1. We do not distinguish different type of patents thanks to the availability of data, it might be inaccurate. We ignore that in this study.
2. It should be the coal reserve, but we cannot get the complete 66 countries data, however, we choose to use this indicator.
3. This data of Taiwan from Taiwan Statistical Data Book 2008, which is obtained by "Final consumption of Commerical Energy" divided by GDP.
4. Here, OPEC members are Iran, Iraq, Kuwait, Qatar and Indonesia. And natural gas exports of Indonesia are also from OPEC database.

References

1. Bretschger, L.: Economics of technological change and the natural environment: How effective are innovations as a remedy for resource scarcity? Ecological Economics 54, 148–163 (2005)
2. Breusch, T.S., Pagan, A.R.: The Lagrange multiplier test and its applications to model specification in econometrics. Review of Economic Studies XLVII, 239–253 (1980)
3. Gancia, G., Zilibotti, F.: Horizontal innovation in the theory of growth and development. In: Aghion, P., Durlauf, S. (eds.) Handbook of Economic Growth, 1st edn., vol. 1, ch. 3, pp. 111–170. Elsevier, Amsterdam (2005)
4. Grimaud, A., Rougè, L.: Non-renewable resources and growth with vertical innovations: optimum, equilibrium and economic policies. Journal of Environmental Economics and Management 45, 433–453 (2003)
5. Grimaud, A.: Natural resources, knowledge and efficiency: beyond the Hotelling rule? Institut d'Économie Industrielle (IDEI), Toulouse, IDEI Working Papers (134) (2001)
6. Groth, C., Souch, P.: Can non-renewable resources alleviate the knife-edge character of endogenous growth? Oxford Economic Papers 54, 386–411 (2002)
7. Hausman, J.A.: Specification tests in econometrics. Econometrica 46, 1251–1271 (1987)
8. Popp, D.: Induced innovation and energy prices. American Economic Review 92, 160–180 (2002)
9. Sachs, J.D., Warner, A.M.: Natural resources and economic development the curse of natural resources. European Economic Review 45, 827–838 (2001)
10. Scholl, A., Semmier, L.: Sustainable economic growth and exhaustible resources: A model and estimation the US. Discrete Dynamics in Nature and Society 7(2), 79–92 (2002)
11. Stijns, C.J.-P.: Natural resource abundance and economic growth revisited. Resources Policy 30, 107–130 (2005)
12. EIA, Energy Information Administration, Official Energy Statistics from the U.S. Government, international statistics, `http://www.eia.doe.gov/emeu/international/contents.html`

Crude Oil Imports, Oil Price Volatility and Exchange Rate Adjustments: An Empirical Study Based on Monthly Data from 1995 to 2010

Chen Zhang

Department of World Economy, Economics and Management School, Wuhan University, 430072 Wuhan, Hubei, China

Abstract. Based on high frequency monthly data from 1995 to 2010, this study has employed VAR model to analyze the relationship between the international crude oil prices, exchange rate and China's crude oil imports. The Empirical results show that China's crude oil imports has a rather stable long term relationship with the international crude oil price adjustment and the RMB exchange rate fluctuations. The international crude oil price adjustment and exchange rate fluctuations have a relatively short-time delay in terms of their impact on China's crude oil imports; The international crude oil prices and the exchange rate of China's imports of crude oil appear as a one-way Granger causality. China's crude oil imports are the Granger cause of the international crude oil prices and exchange rate fluctuations.

Keywords: VAR, Oil Price Volatility, Exchange Rate, Crude Oil Imports.

1 Introduction and Literature Review

As one of the world's major energy resources, oil is widely applicable, scarcity and non-renewable. Since 1970s, as the two global oil crisis bought by oil price, home and abroad researchers began to work on the topic.

Hooker's study (1996) found that data collected after 1985 showed that the correlation between oil prices and economic activity is rather weak. His research suggests that there is strong evidence that oil prices since 1973 are no longer Granger causes of many economic indicator variable. OPEC oil prices did show a significant impact, but the economic impact of oil price decline in 1980s was small and difficult to characterize. Historical decomposition shows oil prices in 1973 has a large macroeconomic fluctuations, measurable impact, while the impact in 1979 is significant but cannot fully explain 1980-1982 recession. The macroeconomic analysis of the late 1980s shows that the relationship between oil prices and macroeconomics has changed and could no longer is simply presented by the asymmetry of price increase and decrease.

Abeysinghe (2001) studied and compared a dozen countries and regions (Indonesia, Malaysia, the Philippines, Thailand, Hong Kong, Korea, Singapore, China Taiwan, Japan, the United States and other OECD countries) in terms of the direct and indirect effects of oil price volatility's impact on their economies. Indirect effects take place mainly through economic and trade partners. Such as Malaysia and Indonesia are net oil

Q. Zhou (Ed.): ISAEBD 2011, Part II, CCIS 209, pp. 332–338, 2011.

exporters, and their major trading partners are Singapore. Singapore is a net importer of oil: when higher oil prices exert negative influence on its GDP growth, Malaysia and Indonesia will benefit from higher oil prices and increase their exports. This in turn will increase their imports from Singapore. Therefore, the size of negative influence of rising oil prices on Singapore depends on the size of these direct and indirect effects. Empirical results show that high oil prices' influence on Malaysia and Indonesia is positive, but they cannot escape the negative impact from its trading partners; therefore, in the long term, they still suffer from negative effects. Direct and indirect effects of other net importers are mostly negative, but Singapore is special – as a net oil importer, the impact of high oil prices in the beginning is slightly positive; but with Malaysia and Indonesia being negatively influenced by high oil prices, Singapore will also experience a relatively large indirect negative impact.

Qian et al (2005), through the analysis of relationship between changes in world oil prices and China's macroeconomic variables, found that there is a significant causal relationship between world oil prices and China's GDP, foreign trade and investment in fixed assets; oil prices have an negative effect on both China's GDP and import and export trade, and recent effect is greater than the longer-term, in which the greatest impact is on the import and export trade.

The remainder of the paper proceeds as follows: Section 2 lays out the variable selection and data illustration, including the source of the data and definition of variables. Section 3 is the part of empirical results and analysis. Section 4 contains the main conclusion.

2 The Variable Selection and Data Illustration

Three variables have been selected: the imports of crude oil (OI), crude oil price (OP) and the RMB exchange rate (Exchange), to be used to investigate the RMB exchange rate fluctuations and international crude oil prices to adjust with the interaction between China's crude oil imports.

The sample data used for empirical analysis are from January 1995 to March 2010 monthly data. Since 1993, China has been a net oil importer. In 1994, the RMB exchange rate system went through a major adjustment – shifting from pegging the US dollar as the single currency to adjustment based on a basket of currencies. Thus, choosing to focus on time periods after 1994 works better to test the interaction between these three variables. Crude oil imports data are from the China Economic Information Network database (http://www.cei.gov.cn), the RMB exchange rate data from the State Administration of Foreign Exchange (http://www.safe.gov.cn), and crude oil Price data from the Bloomberg database (http://www.bloomberg.com). In addition, to eliminate possible estimation error, all data have been made logarithmic. Empirical analysis and data processing are conducted via Microsoft Excel 2007 and QMS Eviews 6.1 software.

3 The Empirical Results and Analysis

This part will first examine the three stationary time series data, if the conclusions are stationary variables, then the stability based on the variable VAR model, the Johansen cointegration test sequences that may exist between the cointegration at the same time, the use of impulse response function analysis of crude oil imported by oil price volatility and exchange rate adjustment shock response. And further investigation using error correction model cointegration relationship between variables to maintain the adjustment efforts, and finally, the use of Granger causality test of the interaction between variables.

3.1 The Unit Root Test

If the variable is non-stationary, then the sequence contains a single integrated component, the difference required before estimation. The unit root tests for stationary time series of checks is very important. In order to better identify the variables that may exist between the cointegration relationships, the need for the relevant variables for unit root test, the test results shown in Table 1:

Table 1. Unit Test Results

Variables	Testing Form (C\T\K)	ADF	P-value	Results
LnOI	C,N,13	-1.5156	0.5234	Stable
△LnOI	C,N,12	-4.3991	0.0004*	Non-Stable
LnOP	C,N,0	-0.7781	0.8225	Non-Stable
△LnOP	C,N,0	-12.9803	0.0000*	Stable
LnExchang	C,N,3	-0.3853	0.9819	Non-Stable
△LnExchange	C,N,2	-3.7605	0.0040*	Stable

Notes: △ represents fires difference; C, T, K represent Constant, Trance and Lag in the testing N define None in Testing, K based on SIC criteria, and the Max lag is 10;"*" denotes rejection of the hypothesis at the 0.01 level.

The results show that international oil prices, crude oil imports and the RMB exchange rate are subject to I (1) process and thus there may exist a stable relationship among the three.

3.2 Johansen Cointegration Test

EG two-step method to the traditional two variables of the same order there are some limitations, so this requires the use of Johansen test to examine the stable relationship between three variables.

Jonhansen cointegration test is based on the VAR model, while the VAR model uses a number of simultaneous equations in the form of equations for each model, endogenous variables on the model of all the lagged endogenous variables return items to estimate the All the dynamic relationship between endogenous variables. Therefore, in the process of establishing the first model to determine the most appropriate lag k. By the LR statistic, FPE, SC criteria, AIC information criterion, HQ information criteria, we identified the establishment behind two of the VAR (2) model.

As Johansen cointegration test is the unconstrained VAR model was applied after the vector cointegration VAR model of restraint, so the chosen cointegration test should be equal to the lag order VAR model was unconstrained optimal lag order of minus one, thus confirming Johansen test of the lag order is 1. Table 2 shows the 5% confidence level, there are two cointegration equations, the three variables that exist between two cointegration relations.

Table 2. Johansen Cointegration Test

Unrestricted Cointegration Rank Test (Maximum Eigenvalue)				
Hypothesized No. of CE(s)	**Eigenvalue**	**Max-Eigen Statistic**	**0.05 Critical Value**	**Prob.****
None *	0.219579	44.62591	21.13162	0.0000
At most 1 *	0.086296	16.24466	14.26460	0.0240
At most 2	0.001133	0.204058	3.841466	0.6515

Notes:Max-eigenvalue test indicates 2 cointegrating eq(s) at the 0.05 level; * denotes rejection of the hypothesis at the 0.05 level ; **MacKinnon-Haug-Michelis (1999) p-values.

So, We obtains the Johansen cointegration function as the followed:

LnOI=--0.379272 (0.86594) LnExchange-0.574333 (0.10162)LnOP

Cointegration test results show that between China's crude oil imports, the international oil price fluctuations and the horizontal changes in RMB exchange rate, there is a negative correlation. If oil prices remain unchanged, a 1% change in the exchange rate will lead to reduction of 0.379 percent in crude oil imports. When the exchange rate remains stable, a 1% change in the international crude oil price will cause the domestic crude oil imports to fall 0.574 percent. Cointegration between the variables can only explain the long-term relationships and trends. In order to examine the response variable and short-term fluctuations between the short-term fluctuations and long-term equilibrium relationship we consider using the VAR model-generated impulse response function to do further study.

3.3 The Impulse Response Function Analysis

A stable VAR model is a prerequisite to conduct impulse response, as shown in Figure 1, the model of the characteristic roots are down in the unit circle; the model is stable. The VAR model is a non-theoretical model, in which variables do not need any a priori constraints. So when analyzing VAR models, the main focus are on a model error term change or a shock to the system by the dynamic image. This study looks into details of the response made by crude oil imports, when international crude oil prices exchange rate fluctuations go through a major shock. if give LnOP and LnExchange a positive unit-size impact respectively to gain an impulse response function of LnOI, it can be found that when exerting a positive impact on international crude oil prices in this period, Chinese crude oil imports will show a positive reaction in the next period, and then continues; and when exerting a positive influence on exchange rate in this period, the Chinese crude oil imports will show a modest positive reaction in the first four periods but shifts to a negative reaction in the fourth turn and continues. This shows that China's crude oil imports and the RMB exchange rate fluctuations respond very quickly to national price adjustments in oil.

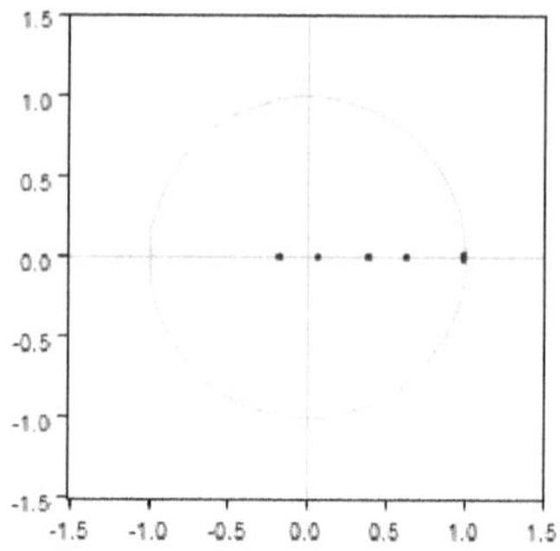

Fig. 1. Inverse Roots of AR Characteristic Polynomial

3.4 Error Correction Model

Engle and Granger combined cointegration with the error correction model to establish VEC model. As long as there is cointegration between the variables, VAR models can be transformed into VEC model. VEC model can be used to analyze the explanatory variables' adjustment speed and change direction after deviating from the equilibrium state. Table 3 shows that in the long-term cointegration relationship, D (LnOI)'s error

Table 3. Vector Error Correction Estimates

Error Correction:	D(LNOI)	D(LNEXCHANGE)	D(LNOP)
CointEq1	-0.373453	0.001413	0.046226
	(0.07618)	(0.00080)	(0.02981)
	[-4.90246]	[1.75554]	[1.55076]
D(LNOI(-1))	-0.156815	-0.001943	-0.036039
	(0.08028)	(0.00085)	(0.03141)
	[-1.95336]	[-2.29153]	[-1.14722]
D(LNOI(-2))	-0.108090	-0.000951	-0.035419
	(0.07296)	(0.00077)	(0.02855)
	[-1.48147]	[-1.23406]	[-1.24056]
D(LNEXCHANGE(-1))	6.442421	0.401077	-3.803512
	(7.01089)	(0.07406)	(2.74345)
	[0.91892]	[5.41576]	[-1.38640]
D(LNEXCHANGE(-2))	-3.606949	0.229536	1.078974
	(6.93240)	(0.07323)	(2.71274)
	[-0.52030]	[3.13453]	[0.39774]
D(LNOP(-1))	-0.193126	-0.002290	0.038250
	(0.19525)	(0.00206)	(0.07640)
	[-0.98914]	[-1.11033]	[0.50064]
D(LNOP(-2))	-0.039946	-0.000599	-0.043522
	(0.19696)	(0.00208)	(0.07707)
	[-0.20281]	[-0.28768]	[-0.56468]
C	0.014099	-0.000381	0.005538
	(0.01943)	(0.00021)	(0.00760)
	[0.72571]	[-1.85812]	[0.72850]

correction coefficient is negative, indicating that when deviated from the equilibrium state, it will make -0.3734 efforts to make the adjustment back to equilibrium.

3.5 Granger Causality Test

According to the results of cointegration test, the three variables have a long-term cointegration relationship. On this basis, we use Granger causality tests to look at three variables in the statistical interaction. From Table 4, we found that international crude oil prices, the exchange rate and China's crude oil imports all showed a one-way Granger causality. China's crude oil imports are the Granger cause for the international crude oil prices and exchange rate fluctuations.

Table 4. Granger causality test

Null Hypothesis:	Obs	F-Statistics	Prob.	results
LNOP does not Granger Cause LNOI	181	9.72662	0.0001	Accept
LNOI does not Granger Cause LNOP	181	0.33270	0.7174	Reject
LNEXCHANGE does not Granger Cause LNOI	180	3.49234	0.0326	Accept
LNOI does not Granger Cause LNEXCHANGE	180	1.80836	0.1670	Reject

4 Conclusion

This study has used high frequency monthly data to analyze the relationship between the international crude oil prices, exchange rate and China's crude oil imports. The main conclusions are as follows:

In the long term, China's crude oil imports has a rather stable relationship with the international crude oil price adjustment and the RMB exchange rate fluctuations. If the international crude oil prices remain unchanged, the exchange rate of 1% will cause China's crude oil imports to fall 0.379 percent. If the exchange rate remains stable, a change under the premise of 1% in international crude oil prices will lead to reduction of 0.574 percent of Chinese crude oil imports;

The international crude oil price adjustment and exchange rate fluctuations have a relatively short-time delay in terms of their impact on China's crude oil imports, which shows that China's crude oil imports have responded very quickly to the RMB exchange rate fluctuations and international crude oil price adjustments;

The international crude oil prices and the exchange rate of China's imports of crude oil appear as a one-way Granger causality. China's crude oil imports are the Granger cause of the international crude oil prices and exchange rate fluctuations. This shows that further increase in crude oil imports in China will lead to further appreciation of RMB and the upward adjustment in international oil prices, which will create new pressures for China's oil security.

References

1. Hooker, M.A.: What happened to the oil price-macro economy relationship? Journal of Monetary Economics 38(2), 195–213 (1996)
2. Abeysinghe, T.: Estimation of direct and indirect impact of oil price on growth. Economics Letters 73(2), 147–153 (2001)
3. Zheng Ming, Q., Peng Hui, G., Feng, G.: An Quantitative Analysis of the Impacts of WOP Fluctuations on China's Economy. Journal of International Trade 8, 21–25 (2005)
4. China Economic Information Network database, `http://www.cei.gov.cn`
5. State Administration of Foreign Exchange, `http://www.safe.gov.cn`

Financial Frictions Relevance during the Crisis: Czech Case

Jaromír Tonner* and Osvald Vašíček

Faculty of Economics and Administration, Masaryk University,
Lipová 41a, 602 00 Brno
{43121,osvald}@econ.muni.cz
http://www.econ.muni.cz

Abstract. In this paper, we estimate a small open economy dynamic stochastic general equilibrium model with financial accelerator. Our aim is to find a satellite model with financial block for imposing judgments on comprehensive models which lack direct financial variables. We choose the model originally developed by Mohamad Hasni Shaari [5] as our starting point. After the basic introduction to the model, we show results for a Bayesian estimation and a recursive Bayesian estimation on Czech data. Finally, we carry out an experiment which shows us that the reducing interest rates would probably be faster, bigger and longer lasting with a model, which in itself contains financial frictions. On the other hand, the risk of such a decision stems from the instability of estimated parameters.

Keywords: DSGE models, Financial accelerator, Bayesian methods.

1 Introduction

After the financial crisis, economists focus on developing models with a financial sector or, at least, they try to incorporate some financial variables into the current models. These extensions are welcome, but still it is not clear that the added complexity increases explanatory power of models or only satiate a demand for financial matter. That is why we decided to find a satellite model with financial block for imposing judgments on comprehensive models which lack direct financial variables.

To say a few notes about a technique, we believe that the Bayesian estimation is an important tool for checking a model's calibration (that our priors are in line with data) and providing an appreciable informative message about an economy. On the other hand, we are aware of considerable data uncertainty (short time

* Financial support of the Specific Research Fund and MSMT project Research centers 1M0524 at the Faculty of Economics and Administration and of the Research Project B2/10 at the Czech National Bank is gratefully acknowledged. The views expressed here are those of the authors, and do not necessarily reflect the position of the Czech National Bank. We are grateful to Miroslav Hloušek for many helpful comments and advices.

Q. Zhou (Ed.): ISAEBD 2011, Part II, CCIS 209, pp. 339–344, 2011.

series, structural changes in the data, frequent revisions, gradual convergence of the Czech economy etc.) and possible model misspecification that might potentially bias the estimation. That is why we also introduce a recursive Bayesian estimation to see a time-varying stability or instability of estimated parameters. Moreover, instability of the estimated parameters can disqualify some implications for monetary policy.

2 Model

The overall and detailed description of the model can be found in the thesis of Mohamad Hasni Shaari [5]. The model is based on the standard Gali-Monacelli model [4] and is extended by financial accelerator mechanism described in Bernanke, Gertler, and Gilchrist [1] (BGG hereafter). Here, we recapitulate only the main ideas of the financial accelerator[1].

In principle, the extended version of the basic Gali-Monacelli model incorporates two new equations in a log-linearized form.

Gross real return to investment for entrepreneurs $r_{K,t}$ is defined as a non-risk central bank real interest rate $r_t - \pi_{t+1}$, where π_t is CPI inflation, plus the cost for external funds where k_t is capital stock, q_t is price of capital in real terms and n_t is etrepreneur's net-worth.

$$r_{K,t+1} = r_t - \pi_{t+1} - \chi(n_{t+1} - k_{t+1} - q_t) \tag{1}$$

where $n_{t+1} - k_{t+1} - q_t$ is a leverage ratio and parameter χ represents the elasticity of the external finance premium to the leverage ratio.

The evolution of entrepreneurs net-worth n_t is defined as

$$\begin{aligned} n_{t+1} &= (\Gamma_5 + 1)\frac{\bar{W_E}}{\bar{K}} w_{E,t} + \\ &+ \zeta \bar{R}_K[(\Gamma_5 + 1)r_{K,t} - \Gamma_5(r_{t-1} - \pi_t) - \chi\Gamma_5(q_{t-1} + k_t) + \chi(\Gamma_5 + 1)n_t] \end{aligned} \tag{2}$$

where $\Gamma_5 = \frac{\bar{K}}{\bar{N}} - 1$, $\frac{\bar{K}}{\bar{N}}$ is the capital net-worth ratio in the steady-state, $\frac{\bar{W_E}}{\bar{K}}$ is a steady state wage-capital ratio of etrepreneur, $w_{E,t}$ is the share of the entrepreneur's real wage income from supplying labour for the production of household goods, $\bar{R}_K$ is a steady state value of the gross real return to investment for entrepreneurs, ζ is prob. that etrepreneur will survive into next period. In other words, net worth of entrepreneurs consists of two segments: the first one is the wage income from supplying labour for the production of household goods, the second is the net worth of entrepreneurs, who are still in business, from the previous period.

[1] We keep notation and equations' and variables' description from [5].

3 Estimation

In this section, we present results of the Bayesian estimation on quarterly Czech and Eurozone data and discuss the most interesting posterior values of model parameters. The posterior distributions are constructed with the Metropolis-Hastings algorithm[2] of the Dynare Toolbox [3].

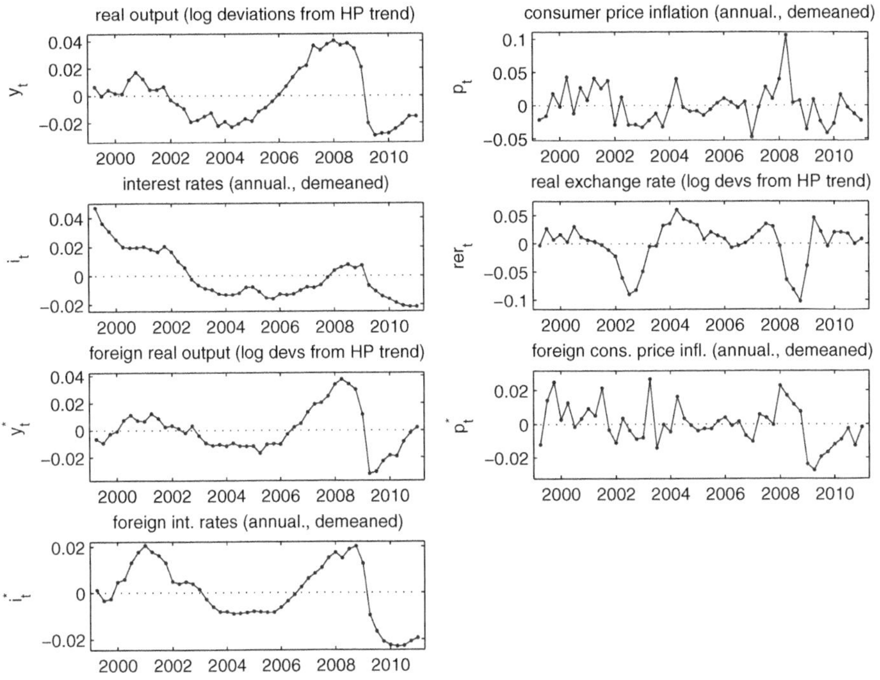

Fig. 1. Data

3.1 Data

The quarterly Czech data sample covers 60 observations from 1996Q1 to 2010Q4. We use seven time series as observables for the estimations. Seasonally adjusted national accounts data come from the Czech Statistical Office (CZSO). Namely, we use real volumes of GDP. The headline CPI inflation also comes from the CZSO. All series are seasonally adjusted to receive its trend-cyclical component. The exchange rate is the CZK/EUR and the domestic interest rate is the 3M PRIBOR. We use three foreign observables. The foreign interest rate is the 3M EURIBOR. The foreign inflation is the PPI of the effective Eurozone acquired from the Consensus Forecast. Finally, the foreign real economic activity

[2] 1 250 000 draws.

Table 1. Estimated Parameters

Parameter		Prior Mean	Dist	Posterior Mean	Lower and Upper Bound of a 90 % HPD interval
Preferences					
Habits	Υ	0.500	beta	0.5949	(0.4869 , 0.7015)
Elasticities of substitution					
Inverse of elasticity - labor supply	ψ	2.000	gamma	1.2644	(0.7593 , 1.7669)
Home/foreign	η	0.500	gamma	0.7031	(0.5495 , 0.8536)
Price and wage setting					
Calvo imp. prices	θ_F	0.650	beta	0.6398	(0.5892 , 0.6912)
Calvo dom. prices	θ_H	0.550	beta	0.5207	(0.4681 , 0.5717)
Indexation domestic prices	κ	0.500	gamma	0.2586	(0.1433 , 0.3690)
Monetary policy					
Taylor rule (int. rates)	ρ	0.650	beta	0.6647	(0.6096 , 0.7205)
Taylor rule (output)	θ_y	0.500	normal	0.5288	(0.3702 , 0.6823)
Taylor rule (inflation)	β_π	1.500	normal	1.4329	(1.2421 , 1.6307)
Financial market					
Financial accelerator	χ	0.070	norm	0.0269	(0.0108 , 0.0427)

is approximated by the foreign demand, acquired from the GDP of the effective Eurozone which stems also from Consensus Forecast.[3]

3.2 Calibration and Priors

We set values of standard parameters according to the literature (see [5]). Discount parameter $\beta = 0.985$, capital share in production $\alpha = 0.350$, depreciation rate $\delta = 0.025$, gross steady-state price markup $\mu = 1.20$, capital adjustment cost $\psi_I = 0.500$, elast. risk premium $\psi_B = 0.010$, prob. entrep. labour $\Omega = 0.990$, preference bias to the foreign goods $\gamma = 0.300$ are calibrated. We set means of the prior distributions for habit persistence $\Upsilon = 0.500$, inv. elasticity of lab. supply $\Psi = 2.000$, elasticity of substitution home/foreign goods $\eta = 0.500$, price indexation $\kappa = 0.500$, Calvo pricing - domestic goods $\theta_H = 0.550$, Calvo pricing - imported goods $\theta_F = 0.650$, HMT rule - smoothing $\rho = 0.650$, HMT rule - inflation $\beta_\pi = 1.500$, HMT rule - output $\theta_y = 0.500$. Especially, interest is devoted to setting of a prior for the parameter $\chi = 0.07$. The parameter of probability that etrepreneur will survive next period $\zeta = 0.9728$ and $\frac{\bar{K}}{\bar{N}} = 3.000$ are calibrated.

3.3 Posteriors

In this subsection, we present point estimates of some model parameters. Our objective here is to underline and discuss such parameter estimates which have relatively clear counterparts in the real economy. Point estimate of habit formation parameter is slightly bellow 0.6. The posterior thus exceeds our prior set

[3] The weights used in the calculation of the effective variables are the shares of the individual euro area economies in the foreign trade turnover of the Czech Republic. See Inflation Reports of the CNB [2].

to 0.5. Parameters ψ and κ are bellow priors, parameter η above the prior. The financial accelerator parameter posterior is 0.026 what is substantially bellow the prior (0.07). Other parameters are in line with out prior setting.

3.4 Recursive Bayesian Estimation

The stability or instability of estimated parameters can significantly affect the implications for monetary policy. That is why we also introduce a recursive Bayesian estimation. The Figure 2 shows the instability of the elasticity of the external finance premium to the leverage ratio. Economic policy recommendations must take this fact into account.

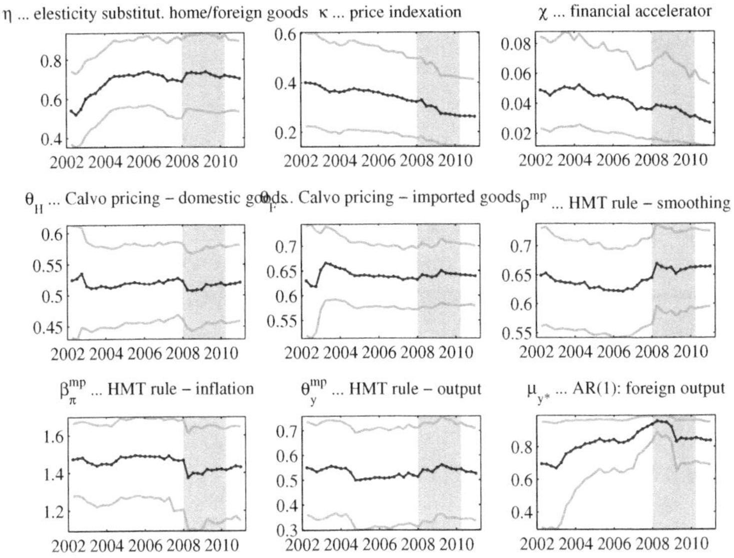

Fig. 2. Recursive Estimates

4 Monetary Policy Relevance

To find the implications of the introduction of financial frictions into the model, we can perform the following experiment. Suppose we are at the beginning of the crisis, as in the 3Q 2008. We have a model in which we can consider financing frictions. Suppose we are in a small open economy, i.e. all foreign variables on the forecast are entirely exogenous. We perform two experiments. In the first, we will predict the setting of interest ratest when assuming the existence of financial frictions and exogenous foreign variables over the forecast, in the second financial frictions are switched off. Figure 3 shows that if financial frictions would be considered, we would set lower interest rates of about 50 bp at the lowest point.

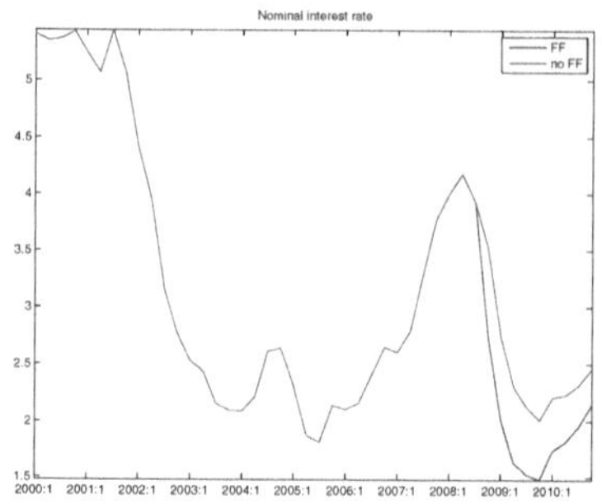

Fig. 3. Financial frictions and their monetary policy relevance

5 Conclusion

In the article, we estimate the model using Bayesian technique on the quarterly Czech and Eurozone data to obtain a sattelite model with financial block.

We return to the period before the crisis and carry out an experiment showing the effect of incorporation of financial frictions on forecast for interest rates. It turns out that reducing rates would probably be faster, bigger and longer lasting with a model, which in itself contains financial frictions. On the other hand, recall that the model structure is very simple and can not capture forecasting in central banks in their full complexity.

References

1. Bernanke, B.S., Gertler, M., Gilchrist, S.: The Financial Accelerator in a Quantitative Business Cycle Framework. In: Taylor, J.B., Woodford, M. (eds.) Handbook of Macroeconomics, vol. 1, pp. 1341–1393. Elsevier, Amsterdam (1999)
2. Czech National Bank Inflation Reports
3. Dynare, `http://www.cepremap.cnrs.fr/dynare/`
4. Gali, J., Monacelli, T.: Monetary Policy and Exchange Rate Volatility in a Small Open Economy. Review of Economic Studies 72, 707–734 (2005)
5. Shaari, M.H.: Analyzing Bank Negara Malaysia's Behaviour in Formulating Monetary Policy: An Empirical Approach, Doctoral thesis, College of Business and Economics, The Australian National University (December 2008)

Comparison between China and Germany in Financial Mode and Sports Mechanism*

Hua Pan[1] and Ying Fan-Zhang[2]

[1] Sports History Institute, Chengdu Sport University, Chengdu, Sichuan, China
huapan2002@yahoo.com.cn
[2] Foreign Language Department, Chengdu Sport University, Chengdu, Sichuan, China
grade03@sina.com

Abstract. For every countries and regions, financial mode influences and restricts all kinds of activities organized by functional organizations, that is to say "administrate via finance". By using literature review, mathematical analysis and logical deduction, etc., the paper compared the current financial mode and its corresponding sports mechanism in both China and Germany. Conclusion: the corresponding relationship between the financial mode and the sports mechanism, namely the State financial mode affect and restrict sports mechanism, and sports mechanism must adapt to the financial mechanism. Finally, the article also proposed China's sports mechanism should cope with current market-oriented financial mode.

Keywords: 1. sports industry, 2. Financial mode, 3. sports mechanism, 4. China, 5. Germany.

1 Introduction

The core of sports mechanism is the repartition of rights, responsibilities and profits of sports organizations at all levels and their mutual relationship, which has a certain historical and realistic value. The choice of sport mechanism is impacted and restricted by government financial mechanism. It is undesirable to do the simple "yes" or "no" judgments. Taking Germany as an example, the article does research on the corresponding relationship between the financial mechanism mode and sports mechanism. Why Germany was chosen? There are three reasons. First, it has distinctive characteristics in its financial mode. Second, its sports mechanism is also based on market economy. Third, it has same large population in sports and gets high level in competitive sports. Studying them will help us better summarize the principles of our sports mechanism and provide reference experience for the choosing of our own sports mechanism.

---

* This work is partially supported by Chengdu Sports University for doctoral station construction (Grant #: BSZX1013).

Q. Zhou (Ed.): ISAEBD 2011, Part II, CCIS 209, pp. 345–352, 2011.

2 The Financial Mode and Sports Mechanism in Germany

Finance means the science of funds management. The financial mode refers to the rules and regulations of profits distribution between governments at different level as well as government and enterprise. Germany is a typical federal state. There are three administrative levels: federation, state and region, and so does its financial mechanism. According to German "Basic Law", for the scope of disposal rights, the federal government is mainly responsible for federal affairs in administrative and financial management , diplomacy and international relationship, as well as national defense and national security service; the States government mainly engages on state's affairs in administrative and financial management, science and culture, as well as education, health, and sports, etc.; and the regional government is primarily in charge of maintaining local public order, and do medical care, etc.. By carrying the principle of "distribution and allocation", the governments at all levels determine the corresponding financial power according to the disposal rights , that means the governments at all levels bear its own administrative task and take its own costs and expenses. When the affairs are over the state financial burden, the federal government has the obligation to support by grants [1].

For the disposal rights of sports, the state government is responsible for the development of sports affairs. Accordingly, the state government sets up the departments related to sports, but for sports affairs overlapping scope of the state government, the federal government and state government will share investment in finance. First, let's study the official governing body. For the national level, interior Ministry is mainly responsible for nationwide competitive sports and the military sports, as well as providing supports in every aspect including funding and policy for German Olympic Sports Federation. And for the state level, the sports department has overall responsibilities for development of school sports, competitive sports and mass sports etc.. And the competitive sport is only part of their work. As for the regional and city government, the sports bureau only charges the venue construction. Then let us shift to non-government organization. German Olympic Sport Federation and its subordinate special associations mainly manage competitive sports. As two separate associations before 2006, German Sport Federation and German Olympic Committee merged into German Olympic sport Federation in May 2006[2]. The main tasks for German Sports Federation are : to formulate the policies and measurements for developing competitive sports, to maintain the common interests and public interests of sports organizations in all levels, to preserve the interests of sports organization in both domestic and international affairs, to coordinate the profits distribution among different associations. While, the German Olympic Committee belongs to the social sports organization. With no government funding, all the funds depends on public donations, business sponsorship and market operation [3].

3 The Characteristic of Sports Mechanism under the German Financial Mode

3.1 Rights Division

Involving people's affairs across the country, like diplomacy, national defense, German economic mechanism, financial mechanism and the division of their disposal rights was treated as the task of federal government. The states government is responsible for development of school sports, competitive sports as well as mass sports, while the regional and city government (mainly sports bureau) is mainly in charge of the venue construction. Thus, the disposal rights and financial expenditure are clear divided in the aspects of sports. For example, in 1990, the sports fee occupied 1.4% of GDP. For all the sports funding, regional and states government allocate 98%, which federal government only distribute 2%.

3.2 Distribution Principle

In Germany, principle of transferring the sports-related disposal rights to lower level is adopted. Governments at the lower level are responsible for sports affairs in local region. States governments manage the development of German mass sports, as regional and city governments do venue construction. As for the clerical work, like the specifically organization and direction of sports activities are bored by social groups and volunteers.

3.3 The Operating System

For the aspects of sports operating mechanism, based on sports clubs, German government launches varies forms of entertainment, fitness, as well as sports competition. In Germany, all kinds of sports, including competitive sports, mass sports and school sports, etc., are built based on the clubs. And especially, for the part of mass sports and nationwide fitness, German sports clubs play an active and effective roles [4]. In Germany, "member of Sports Club" becomes the synonym of "taking part in sports exercise". Sports clubs are the basic form of sports organization in Germany.

3.4 Source of Investment

The source of investment are varies for the competitive sports, military sports, and mass sports. Competitive sports and military sports are full fund by federal government. While fund of the mass sports comes from national finance, social donation, foundation assistance, member fees, sports lottery commission, company sponsor, as well as venue rent and ticket fee.

By analyzing the financial mode and sports mechanism in Germany, comes the conclusion that the organization setting, power distribution as well as operating mechanism of sports are governed and restricted under the certain financial mechanism. That is to say, national financial mode influenced and limited the sports mechanism. And the sports mechanism should cope with the financial mode. Only when sports mechanism is adapted to financial mode, the sports organization can operate effectively, and sports can develop fast and well develop.

4 Financial Mode and Sports Mechanism in China

Since the founding of People's Republic of China, a planned economic mechanism was carried out nationwide. The financial relations among governments at different level practice the principle of "uniform leadership and layered management", and carry the mechanism of "overall revenue, overall disburse". The governments at different level have it own sports administrative department to manage the sports affairs at their own level. Specifically speaking, the national sports administrative mechanism divided into two parts: one is the professional administrative mechanism taking former state sports commission as the highest; the other is non-professional administrative mechanism taking other related ministries (like the department of education and the department of health, etc.) as the top. As the functional organizations for managing sports in State department, the former state sports commission takes charge of leading, coordinating, supervising, as well as boosting the development of sports nationwide [5]. For the method of operating, government dominates the whole sports affairs. They distribute the goals and tasks of sports development by administrative method, deploy the sports resources by planed means as its goals and tasks, as well as pay sports fee through national finance [6]. For example, national governments pay for all the money for the sports group from the most basic amateur sports school to the highest National Team.

In 1992, the government proposed clear objectives of establishing the socialist market economic mechanism. That is to develop the market-related financial policy, under the background of establishing and consummating of market economy. And developing fiscal expenditure policy becomes a general trend. Under such circumstance, the States Department issued "The Decision on Implementing the Tax Division Management Mechanism" on 25, Dec 1993. Gradually form the economic mechanism with Chinese Characteristics, that is relative centralized in income, as well as relative decentralized in expenditure, and "top down" based transfer payments mechanism. It followed international trend [7]. With the changing of economic mode, Chinese Sports mechanism also changed from single system to multiple systems.

5 The Characteristic of Sports Mechanism under the China Financial Mode

5.1 Whole-Nation System

Followed east European sports mechanism, China carries the whole-nation system for competitive sports under the planned economy system. Whole-nation system is a kind of the management mode, which means concentrate all the people, money to develop competitive sports in uniform management and allocation. It is the results of socialism economy. And it does play a gigantic role in the process of advancement of Chinese society melting to enter international community. Compared to old whole-nation system, the system with Chinese characteristic lets government play the leading role and takes use of social and market value. And finally it becomes organic melting and coordinated operations among government domination, social self-government and market liberty.

5.2 Right Division

Right division is very important in the sports management. In different period, different guidelines, and policies are adopted. From 1949 to 1992, which is the period of planned economic, central government sets certain sports administrative department to manage sports. With highly concentration of rights, former national sports commission is the government administrative department mainly responsibly for national sports affairs. During the period of socialist market economy, in 1998, national sports commission was renamed as general administration of sport of China. Coming from former "cabinet member" of the State Council, it now becomes the organ directly under the State Council. It mainly focuses on the macro-manage, and transfers the right to the lower parts. And large part of transactional work was transferred to sports organization at lower level and specific sports association.

5.3 Source of Investment

The sources of sports fee are different in the time of planned economic system, and social market system. Due to the weak economic power, and the economic blockade from west countries, central government invests most of sports fees. For the time of social market system, government expands the sources of fund. Government develops sports industry rapidly, expands sports market greatly, and issues sports lottery. And now, based on the governments investing, the sources of sports fees become multi-channel, multi-layer structure.

6 Enlightenments

In German financial mode, the disposal right of sports is defined under the requirement of matching the financial expenditure and disposal rights, matching the administrative power with disposal power. In China, we carry two different economic mechanisms, which are planed economic mechanism and market economic mechanism. And coping with economic mechanisms, it carried mechanisms of" overall revenue, overall disburse" and "tax-sharing" mechanism in finance. For the "tax-sharing" mechanism, it asks for dividing the financial power and disposal rights between central government and regional government according to the expenditure scope of finance at different levels. For this part, our financial mechanisms and German financial mechanism has common points. But we still need utilize the German advanced experience in transferring the sports-related disposal rights to lower level, to distribute more financial profits to regional government, and let government at lower level respond regional sports affairs, and social sports organization run specific sports affairs.

6.1 Reasonably Divide the Rights

With the deepening of reform and the establishing of market economy, the responsibilities, profits and rights between central governments and regional, government and society are rearranged. First central government should separate power to regional government. Then central government mainly focuses on the enhancement of power of national competitive sports. In the parts of management and finance, the central government slopes towards competitive sports. And for the regional governments, they will do most works on the promoting of mass sports, and stimulating the initiative of whole society. Second, the governments at all levels separate power to sports associations. Sports administrative organs bear the function of macro-administration, while sports associations undertake the function of micro-administration, mainly operating specific sports affairs. The relationship between the sports associations and governments should be collaborative instead of being the leader to being the servant [8].

6.2 Clearly Arrange the Sport Expenditure and Rationally Allot Financial Profit

Now, our country carries "tax-sharing' mechanism in financial mechanism. National finance provides the expenditure for maintaining normal operation of state organs, and for promoting public welfare. It takes social public need, which means the basic requirement to reflect the social common interests, as a criterion. For the affairs related to social public needs, national finance will give monetary supports; and for those not related to, should not be invested by national finance, and can be carried out by market. And the regional sports administrative departments devote most of their attention to construct venue for mass sports, as well as push the development of mass sports.

As for the financial profits, theoretically, it needs to relocate the governments' profits under the promise of symmetry in disposal rights and financial rights. Actually, central governments over centralized much tax rights. That means central governments put many important taxes as central taxes and shared taxes as their source of income, and only separate few rights to regional government. At the same time, the expanding of executive capacity resulted in the deficit increasing in regional finance. First, due to the territoriality of the sports public products, regional governments need to construct their own sports venue, and sports equipment. Second, regional governments organize local sports fitness activity. All of them need enlarge the investment. In order to protect the supply of regional public sports products, more financial profits should be distributed to regional government to protect enough finance for local people's sports needs [9].

6.3 Multiple Investment Modes

In Germany, due to the market economy, the investment comes from varies sources including sports lotteries, government input, company sponsor, etc.. In China, because of the adopting of socialist market economy, the market operating system was also brought into the sports management. That means the investments come from both the government and society. Governments, by direct grant from finance, and indirect political support for sports lotteries, and sports funds, manage the sports management.

While the society, taking use of mass donation, member fees, company sponsor, raises money for the specific sports executives.

6.4 Classified Management of Sports

With the implementing of sports associations, various degrees of sports associations will be established in provinces, cities, regions, even counties, expect national levels. Association is the direct management department for all kinds of sports at all levels. National sports administrative department regulates the individual sports association. And all the individual associations regulate and direct the development of national and regional individual sports according to the prescriptions. The amateur training organizations and professional clubs, which meet the requirements of sports association, will take place of all kind of sports team at all levels. Under the management of associations, the clubs, as the independent legal or independent community organizations, organize competitive and training activities. It can be divided into amateur and profession. Through the leagues, organized by associations, the professional clubs enhance competition levels, and promote development. While taking part in sports activity organized by nation, region and professional association, the amateur clubs will enlarge their size, and quantities, to enhance the competitive level and promote the development of amateur clubs [10].

7 Conclusion

China should adopt what kind of sports mechanism? It is sill a question of Chinese Sports administrative reform. China is a developing country with socialist market economy as basis. Coping with the socialist market economy with Chinese characteristics, China adopts sports mechanism with multi-route, multi-methods. Specifically speaking, national sports administrative organ reinforce the macro-control on sports development plan, while market gives micro-control on specific sports execution.

References

1. Chen, J.: Comparison of Administrative Rights and Financial Expenditure Division of developed countries and its enlightens. Journal of Henan Business College 18(2), 1–3 (2005)
2. Liu, B.: Investigation on the Relationship between Sport Club Mechanism and Competitive Sports in Germany. Journal of Sports and Science 28(6), 65–69 (2007)
3. Li, X.D.: Comparison study of sports management mechanism between China and Germany. Sports Culture Guide 6, 53–55 (2005)
4. Pan, H.: Mass Sports in Germany. People's Sports Publishing House, Beijing (2011)
5. Wang, G.H., Huang, S.B.: Dualistic Structure of Sports Management under the Mechanism of Public Institution and Public Institution Character of Mass Sports. Journal of Chengdu Physical Education Institute 30(3), 1–5 (2004)
6. Liu, Y.W., Hu, X.M.: Research on China Sports Mechanism: History and Future. Sports Culture Guide 5, 19–22 (2006)

7. Li, G.Z.: Foreign experience for reference to perfect China's financial transfer payment mechanism. Public Finance Research 5, 64–66 (2005)
8. Liu, Z.Q., Huang, Y.Y., Li, L., et al.: Discussion on Chinese Sport Management Mechanism Innovation Inspired by the Chang of Sports Management of Eastern European Countries during the "Eastern European Shift" Period. Journal of Chengdu Sports University 36(1), 54–57 (2007)
9. Yang, H.Y., Fang, X.Y.: Financial Mechanism Model and Sports Mechanism among China and Germany. Journal of Chengdu Sport University 37(3), 6–10 (2011)
10. Liu, Q.: On the Mechanism of the Whole Nation and Innovation of Chinese Physical Education Mechanism. Journal of Southwest Jiaotong University (Social Sciences) 6(4), 90–94 (2005)

Factors Affecting Employment, Unemployment, and Graduate Study for University Graduates in Beijing

Jun Kong

School of Economics and Management, Northwest University,
Xi'an 710069, China
junkong555@hotmail.com

Abstract. The problem of unemployed university graduates has become serious in China, being a central issue regarding unemployment recently. This paper studies the factors that determine whether a Beijing graduate finds a job, cannot find a job or entering graduate school. The innovation of this paper is using a multinomial probit model for multi-objectives, covering college graduates' employment, unemployment and graduate study affected by three factors: reputation of college, major, and gender. This study indicates that the graduates find jobs faster and are more likely to study in graduate school if they come from higher reputation colleges. In addition, study shows graduates with engineering and business degrees find jobs more easily. Agricultural graduates have higher probability to go to graduate school. Finally, female graduates find jobs more easily than male graduates which is different from previous results, and they are more likely to go to graduate school.

Keywords: Employment Unemployment Graduate Education Factors Model.

1 Introduction

A number of university graduates continue to pursue higher academic qualifications, and others try to find suitable jobs after the completion of undergraduate study. The purpose of this paper is to apply a multinomial probit model to analyze the impact of three factors that determine which graduates continue learning at graduate school and which find employment in the market. In this paper, these factors are divided into two categories. The first category comprises the factor of a reputation and the second category comprises two personal factors, gender and undergraduate study majors.

Many scholars have pointed out that insufficient education is the main reason for unemployment in the United States (Sum, Harrington and Simpson, 1983; Norman, 1984; Stern, 1989 and Bratberg and Nilsen, 1998). Some scholars studied a case of Nordic countries and reached a similar conclusion (Bjorklund and Eriksson, 1996). However, other scholars have found that graduates from leading U.S. universities, who have high wage expectations, can experience an even longer duration of unemployment than graduates of ordinary colleges (Wolpin, 1987). In China, education level, or reputation of the university has only a slight impact on employment (Zhou, 2003). In addition, some research has shown that a strong university background, including

Q. Zhou (Ed.): ISAEBD 2011, Part II, CCIS 209, pp. 353–361, 2011.

leadership and personal academic performance in undergraduate study, correlate with ability to continue in graduate study (Mark Montgomery, 2000; Mark C. Berger and Thomas Kostal, 2002; Kelly Bedard and Douglas A. Herman, 2008).

With regard to the impact of gender on employment and unemployment, there is no final conclusion among academics. One faction thinks that male graduates find jobs more easily than female graduates (Zhou, 2003; Min et al, 2006; Ghazala, 2006; Rodokanakis, 2006; South Korea's statistics, 2008). Another faction believes that males from a prestigious college have a lower likelihood of employment than females from that college (Bradley and Nguyen, 2004). In addition, women are usually interested in pursuing a master's degree, rather than a Ph.D. (Perna, 2004). Few studies put the impact of majors on unemployment and graduate professional education as a priority. In China, it was difficult for the graduates to find jobs who came from law, computer science, and English education in 2008 (www.mycos.com.cn). In addition, more U.S. science graduates are likely to pursue a doctorate than other majors (Bedard and Herman, 2008).

The contribution of this research is the application of a multinomial probit model for multi-objectives, covering college graduates' employment, unemployment and graduate study affected by three factors: reputation of college, major, and gender. Previous studies mainly used logistic models to analyze the probability of a single target. In addition, previous studies focused on factors of business cycles, race, and family background that affect employment or postgraduate learning. Very few papers address the impact of major and gender on unemployment and graduate education in China.

This paper argues that, compared with graduates of three-year colleges, graduates of high reputation four-year universities and four-year colleges find jobs more easily. They are also more likely than graduates of three year college to enter graduate school to study. Secondly, engineering and business graduates find jobs more easily than other graduates. Law and science graduates have a higher risk of unemployment. The arts and social science graduates range between these two extremes. In addition, the probability that agricultural graduates enter graduate school to study is higher than other graduates, and the probability that business graduates enter graduate school to study is lower than other professional graduates. Finally, the female graduates find jobs more easily than male graduates, and they are more likely than male graduates to enter graduate school to study.

This paper is structured as follows: Section 1 is the introduction. Section 2 reviews literature. Sections 3 are the data description and summary statistics. Section 4 describes the empirical econometric model and estimation. The final section presents a conclusion.

2 Literature Review

Sum, Harrington & Simpson (1983), Norman (1984), Stern (1989) and Bratberg and Nilsen (1998) point out that U.S. high unemployment is mainly due to the lack of adequate education. Bjorklund and Eriksson (1996) find the same result by studying the case of Nordic countries. Wolpin (1987) reveals the opposite trend in the United States and that, although there is a higher level of education, a higher reservation wage will lead to a longer duration of unemployment. In addition, Bradley and Nguyen (2004) point out that the quality of schools has a greater impact on finding jobs than academic performance in the United Kingdom. They also find that it is more difficult for male graduates from high-quality schools to find a job than female graduates. Bratberg and Nilsen (1998) come to the same conclusion in Norway. However, Ghazala (2006) and South Korea Survey (www.korea.net) show that in Europe and Korea, male graduates find jobs more easily than female graduates.

In China, Zhou (2003) shows that the reputation of the university has a small effect on graduates' job searches. Zhou (2003) and Min et al (2006) also indicate that male graduates find jobs more easily than female graduates. In addition, the online educational consulting firm MyCos demonstrates that in China it is difficult to find jobs for law graduates, computer science graduates, and English education graduates in 2008 (www.mycos.com.cn).

In addition, Kalie, Oosthuizen and Westhuizen (2006) show that in South Africa, unemployment usually occurs because job-seekers have lower skills than the skills needed in the market. Rodokanakis (2006) indicates that in 1992 in Greece, women, unmarried persons and young people are more likely to be unemployed than men and married people, and college graduates are more likely to be employed than graduates of high school students. Borra, Gómez-García, and Salas-Velasco (2009) show that first, high graduates' comprehensive scores will speed up a job search, and second, internships or training also accelerate the process of looking for work in Spain. Consequently, any attempts for some new graduates to enter the labor market put them in a weak position because they have no work experience.

About the factors that influence post-graduate studies, Mark Montgomery (2000) uses a nested logit model to indicate that the prestige or ranking of an undergraduate college in U.S. News and World Report, the average GMAT, the average undergraduate GPA, have a positive and significant impact on the probability of post-graduate study. Berger and Kostal (2002) point out that in the United States, the state's average educational level and the popularity of university that graduates attend have a significant impact on the graduate admissions. Perna (2004) finds that women and men have different modes with respect to high education in the United States. She uses the National Center for Education Statistics Survey from 1992 to 1993 and 1994 to 1997, and finds that the proportion of undergraduate education for women is more than men (20% vs. 16%), the proportion of master's education for women is still more than men (23% vs. 16 %), but the proportions of doctoral education and first-professional program for women are lower than that of men (2% vs. 4%), and (5% vs. 10%), respectively. Bedard and Herman (2008) use a logistic model to indicate that in the United States, the higher grade point average individuals are more likely to enter the advanced degree program regardless of sex. In addition, graduate students are more likely to join the Ph.D. program from physical sciences, life sciences, computer sciences and mathematics.

3 Data Description and Summary Statistics

This dataset provides information of college graduates related to job-seekers, employment, basic work skills and vocational skills in 2007. This paper studies the variables including the reputation of colleges, undergraduate majors and gender. Different types of colleges and universities are used to define the reputation of colleges. There are high reputation universities, which belong to "211" universities regulated by Ministry of Education, China; ordinary colleges; and three-year colleges. The undergraduate majors can be combined into seven major categories including arts and social sciences, science, law, engineering, medicine, agriculture and business.

The numbers of employment, unemployment, and graduate studies are 7,619, 593 and 703 respectively, and the total number is 8,915. Moreover, the graduates of high reputation four-year universities reach 4,406 in employment, 351 in unemployment and 548 in graduate study, accounting for 83.05%, 6.62%, and 10.32% of the total number 5,305 for high reputation four year universities. The shares of employment, unemployment and graduate studies are 89.22%, 6.10%, and 4.68% for ordinary four-year colleges and 87.72%, 10.33%, and 1.95% for three-year colleges respectively. These ratios show that the graduates of ordinary four-year colleges find jobs in a higher probability, and the graduates of high reputation four-year universities are more likely to enter graduate school to study, while the graduates of three year colleges have higher probability of unemployment than the first two. Furthermore, most of the graduates employed are from arts and social sciences, engineering and business; the numbers of finding jobs are 2,034, 2,220 and 2,052 respectively. The business graduate employment rate is 89.57%, which is the highest percentage. On the contrary, the lowest rate of graduate employment is only 64.14% in agriculture, but they have the highest proportion of graduate study, reaching 31.03%. The law graduates have the highest unemployment rate 11.17%. Lastly, there are 3,899 female graduates employed, slightly higher than the number of male graduates with 3,720. The proportion of unemployed and the ratio of graduate study for female graduates are 6.18% and 8.96%, while these proportions for male graduates reach 7.15% and 6.71% respectively.

4 Empirical Model and Estimation

4.1 Empirical Model

The Multinomial probit model (MNP) is used to model a relationship between multiple dependent variables and multiple independent variables. The multiple dependent variables are discrete variables that represent different choices.

$$MNP\ (D) = \Pr(D) = \alpha + \beta_i X_i + \varepsilon_i$$

D stands for the category of employment, unemployment and graduate study, α is the constant, X_i stand for the explanatory variables including reputation of college, majors and gender, β_i are coefficients of the explanatory variables, and ε_i is a random variable with mean zero.

4.2 Estimation Results

The MNP model estimates impacts of the reputation of college, majors, and gender on employment, unemployment and graduate study. In an MNP regression, employment is the base category, while three-year colleges, engineering major and male gender graduate are treated as the omitted variables. First, the graduates of high reputation universities and the graduates of ordinary colleges find jobs more easily than the graduates of three-year colleges. Through the marginal impact analysis in Table 1, the probability of unemployment for the former two is reduced by 3.57% and 3.56% at the 1% significant level. However, there is no significant difference between the high reputation universities and the ordinary colleges in unemployment.

Moreover, the arts and social sciences, law, and science graduates are more likely to be unemployed than engineering graduates. Their probabilities of unemployment increases 2.42%, 7.92% and 6.50% respectively at the 1% significant level. At same time, law, and science graduates are more likely to be unemployed than business graduates. Their probabilities of unemployment increases 5.94% and 4.58% at the 1% significant level respectively. Compared with arts and social science graduates, the probability of unemployment for business graduates decreases 1.15% at the 10% significant level. There is no significant difference between engineering and business graduates for unemployment because we cannot reject the hypothesis that engineering equals business according to the F test. In addition, law and science graduates are more likely to be unemployed than the graduates of the arts and social sciences; their probabilities of unemployment increases by 4.33% and 3.12% at the 1% significant level. There is no significant difference between law and science graduates because we cannot reject the hypothesis that law equals science according to the F test. The unemployment probability for agriculture graduates decreases 3.73% at the 1% significant level and 3.18% at the 5% significant level compared with law graduates and science graduates. However, there is no significant difference between agriculture and other majors, except between law and science. We cannot reject the hypothesis that the effect of agriculture major equals those of arts and social science, engineering, medicine, and business majors respectively in terms of the F test. Therefore, the probability of unemployment for majors ranks from big to small as follows: law or science, arts and social sciences or agriculture, and business or engineering or agriculture. Meanwhile, there is no significant difference between medicine and above majors according to the F test. In addition, the marginal analysis shows that the probability of unemployment for female graduates declines 1.28% more than male graduates at the 5% significance level.

Second, the graduates of high reputation universities and the graduates of ordinary colleges are more likely to enter graduate school to study compared to the graduates of three-year colleges. Table 2 indicates that the probabilities of the graduates of high reputation universities and ordinary colleges entering graduate schools increase 9.18% at the 1% significant and 5.50% at the 10% significant level respectively compared with the graduates of three-year colleges. Meanwhile, the probability of post-graduate study for the graduates of high reputation universities is 4.61% at the 1% significant level more than the graduates of ordinary colleges. Furthermore, compared with engineering, arts and social sciences, agriculture, and business majors in the post-graduate studies have a significant effect at the 1% level. The probabilities of post-graduate study for the arts and social sciences, and business graduates are 1.80% and 3.36% less than engineering graduates. The probabilities for science graduates and agriculture graduates increase 2.38% at the 5% significant level and 16.33% at the 1% significant level compared to engineering graduates. There is no significant difference between engineering and law or between engineering and medicine because we cannot reject the hypothesis that engineering equals law, and engineering equals medicine according to the F test. If the arts and social science is the omitted variable, the probabilities that law, science, engineering, and agriculture graduates study further increase by 3.65%, 5.01%, 1.93% and 20.67% at the 1% significance level respectively. In addition, the probability of business graduates entering graduate school falls 1.74% at the 5% significance level. If law is the omitted variable, the probabilities of arts and social science and business graduates attending graduate school decrease by 3.00% and 4.47% at the 1% significant level, and the probability for agriculture graduates increase by 12.90% at the 1% significant level. We cannot reject the hypothesis that law equals science in terms of the F test. If science is the omitted variable, the probabilities of arts and social science, engineering, and business graduates entering graduate school decrease by 3.78%, 2.26% and 5.17% at the 1% significant level and the probability of agriculture graduates increases by 11.12% at the 1% significant level. If business is the omitted variable, the probabilities of arts and social, science, law, science, engineering, and agriculture graduates becoming graduate students increase by 1.91% at the 5% significant level and 6.14%, 7.72%, 4.03% and 25.43% at the 1% significance level. The probability of agriculture graduates increases by 16.97% at the 1% significant level when medicine is the omitted variables. The probability of medicine graduates entering graduate school decreases 5.85% at the 1% significant level compared to agriculture graduates. There is no significant difference between medicine and other majors except for agriculture. Therefore, the probability of post-graduate study in descending order according to majors ranking is as follows: agriculture; law, science, engineering or medicine; arts and social sciences or medicine; and business or medicine. Furthermore, female graduates are more likely to enter graduate school than male graduates. The probability of them entering graduate school increases 3.07% at the 1% significant level.

Table 1. Marginal Effects of Unemployment

	Comparison Variable		
	Three Year College	**Engineering**	**Male**
High Reputation University	-.0357*** (.0111)	---	---
Ordinary College	-.0356*** (.0097)	---	---
Arts and Social Science	---	.0242*** (.0087)	---
Law	---	.0792*** (.0159)	---
Science	---	.0650*** (.0146)	---
Female	---	---	-.0128** (.0055)

Table 2. Marginal Effects of Graduate Study

	Comparison Variable		
	Three Year College	**Engineering**	**Male**
High Reputation University	.0918*** (.0150)	---	---
Ordinary College	.0550* (.0212)	---	---
Arts and Social Science	---	-.0180*** (.0069)	---
Law	---	---	---
Science	---	.0238** (.0114)	---
Agriculture	---	.1633*** (.0352)	---
Business	---	-.0336*** (.0065)	--
Female	---	---	.0307*** (.0056)

The numbers in parenthesis show standard error. *** indicates 1% significant level, ** is 5% significant level, and * is 10% significant level.

5 Conclusion

This paper studies the effects of university reputation, undergraduate major, and gender on graduates' employment, unemployment, and postgraduate learning. The basic conclusions are first, that high reputation university graduates and ordinary college graduates find jobs more easily compared to three-year college graduates. This result differs from the conclusions of Zhou (2003) and Min et al. (2006), whose research shows that the effect of university reputation on finding work in China has only a slight impact. Meanwhile, high reputation university graduates have a higher probability of entering graduate school to study than ordinary college and three-year college graduates. This conclusion is similar to previous studies.

Secondly, engineering and business graduates find work more easily than other graduates. Law and science graduates have a greater likelihood of unemployment. Arts and social sciences graduates range between them regarding probability of unemployment. Their probabilities are 3.34% and 2.65% lower than those of law and science, but 2.42% higher than engineering. Meanwhile, business graduates have a lower probability of unemployment than arts and social science graduates by 1.15%. Agriculture graduates have lower probabilities of unemployment than law and science graduates by 3.73% and 3.18%, and no significant difference with other major graduates. Furthermore, medicine graduates have no significant difference from other major graduates in probability of unemployment. This conclusion is similar to previous studies in China. In addition, agricultural graduates have a higher probability of entering graduate school than other majors, and business graduates have a lower probability of entering graduate school than other majors except for medicine graduates. Law, science, and engineering graduates are more likely to enter graduate school than are arts and social sciences graduates, but there is no significant difference among law, science, engineering, and medicine graduates. Furthermore, there is no significant difference between medicine and arts and social science.

Finally, female graduates find jobs more easily than male graduates. This is different from the results that Zhou (2003) and Min et al. (2006) arrived at their studies. Their research indicates that it is difficult for women to find employment in China. In addition, female graduates are more likely than male graduates to enter graduate school. This result agrees to previous studies in the United States and China.

References

1. Bjorklund, A., Eriksson, T.: Unemployment in the Nordic Countries. In: Wadensjo, E. (ed.) The Nordic Labour Markets in the 1990's. Elsevier, Amsterdam (1996)
2. Bradley, S., Nguyen, A.N.: The School-to-Work Transition. International Handbook of Education Economics. Edward Elgar, Cheltenham (2004)
3. Bratberg, E., Nilsen, O.A.: Transitions from School to Work: Search Time and Job Duration, IZA, DP, No. 27 (1998)
4. Cristina Borraa, F., Francisco, G.-G., Manuel, S.-V.: Entry of Young Economists into Working Life: Analysis of the Determinants of First Unemployment Duration. Applied Economics Letters 16, 1483–1488 (2009)
5. Azmat, G., Guell, M., Manning, A.: Gender Gaps in Unemployment Rates in OECD Countries. Journal of Labor Economics 24(1) (2006)
6. Pauw, K., Oosthuizen, M., Westhuizen, C.: Graduate Unemployment in the Face of Skills Shortages: A Labor Market Paradox. Development Policy Research Unit, DPRU Working Paper 06(114) (2006)
7. Bedard, K., Herman, D.A.: Who Goes to Graduate/Professional School? The Importance of Economic Fluctuations, Undergraduate Field and Ability. Economics of Education Review 27, 197–210 (2008)
8. Perna, L.W.: Understanding the Decision to Enroll in Graduate School: Sex and Racial/Ethnic Group Differences. The Journal of Higher Education 75, 487–527 (2004)
9. Berger, M.C., Kostal, T.: Financial Resources, Regulation, and Enrollment in US Public Higher Education. Economics of Education Review 21, 101–110 (2002)
10. Mark, M.: A Nested Logit Model of the Choice of a Graduate Business School. Economics of Education Review 21, 471–480 (2000)
11. Min, W., Ding, X., Wen, D., Yue, D.: The Survey on the College Graduates in 2005. Guan Ming Observation (3) (2006)
12. Ministry of Education. Korea Labor Market for New Graduates, `http://www.korea.net/news/news.newsView.asp`
13. MyCos Company. Employment Report of China in 2006, `http://www.eol.cn/guo_jia_gwy.shtml`
14. Freeberg, N.: Factors Affecting Job Search Behavior and Employment Outcome for Youth, Final Technical Report, Educational Testing Service, Princeton, N.J (1984)

15. Rodokanakis, S.: Econometric Analysis of the LFS Micro-data: Exploring the Risk of Unemployment in Three Southern Greek Regions during the CSF-1. In: European Regional Science Association in its series ERSA Conference Paper with No ERSA 2006, p. 940 (2006)
16. Stern, S.: Estimating a Simultaneous Search Model. Journal of Labor Economics 7(3) (1989)
17. Sum, Harrington., Simpson.: Educational Attainment, Academic Ability, and The Employability and Earnings of Young Persons: Implications for the Planning And Design of JTPA Youth Programs. Northeastern University, Center for labor Market Studies, Boston, MA (1983)
18. Wolpin, K.I.: Estimating a Structural Search Model: The Transition from School to Work. Econometrica 55(4), 801–817 (1987)
19. Zhou, J.B.: A Study on Graduates' Costs in Job Hunting. Economics of Education Research (Beida) 1(1) (2003)

Theoretical Exploration on the Development Path of Sports Industrial Clusters in the Western Cities of China*

Liang Li

Sport Department of Chengdu Sports University, Chengdu, Sichuan, China
Liliang_626@163.com

Abstract. Based on the circumstances of the economy, regional and sports industry development of the city circle, belt and group in western. By using the methods of literature, expert interview and logic analysis etc. on the theory and practice exploration of the development of sports industry cluster general ideas, space layout, classification and regulation in the western cities of China. This paper results showed that the development ideas of sports industry cluster, which should be regional priority development, from "dot" to "face" integration development, provincial has conditions to developing step by step and small cities selectively key development in the western cities of China. Through the comparative studies and clustering analysis to the western sports industry clusters is divided into the primary stage, intermediate stage and advanced stage, and put forward the control strategy of the development of sports industrial cluster in each stage. According to the "HU Huan-yong line" and "the Kunlun Mountains", the sports industrial clusters divided into three regions in western cities, which are named "west triangle sports industry circle ". At last, this paper puts forward the sports industry in town towns and central towns, which is the key of the development of sports industry cluster in western towns.

Keywords: 1. the western region, 2. the city, 3. sports industry, 4. industrial clusters, 5. development path.

1 Puts Forward the Problems

Western China, including Chongqing, Sichuan, Guizhou, Yunnan, Guangxi, Shaanxi, Gansu, Qinghai, Ningxia, Tibet, Xinjiang, Inner Mongolia twelve provinces, municipalities and autonomous regions. The land area is 5,380,000 square kilometers, occupies 56% of the national land area; the population of western is about 287 million, occupies 22.99% of the national population. Western area has vast territory, sparsely populated and economically underdeveloped, needed to strengthen the development of the region. After the implementation of western development policy, rapid development of urbanization of the West, the cause of progress, economic strength has increased notably. At the end of 2003, there are 170 cities in the western region, of

* This work is partially supported by Chengdu Sports University for doctoral station construction (Grant #: BSZX1007).

Q. Zhou (Ed.): ISAEBD 2011, Part II, CCIS 209, pp. 362–369, 2011.

which there are four megacities, 28 mega-cities, 46 cities, 63 medium-sized cities, small cities have 29, and 7,088 towns. From the proportion of the urban system structure of the western region, medium and small cities accounted for 54.11%, higher than the national average of nearly 20 % points; but the proportion of the cities as regional economic center, or Secondary centers of large cities is too small[1]. Distribution of the western area of the city is that: the east-intensive, western-rare, North Line and South Line-intensive and middle rare; from south to north western area of the city mainly concentrated in two regions, namely Chengdu and Chongqing region, Guiyang-Kunming region and the Asia-Europe Along the Continental Bridge; however, in Qinghai-Tibet Plateau, Xinjiang desert region, city, very scarce [2]. The western region has a big gap compared with the eastern and central regions, no matter in number, density, structure, layout of the cities and towns in, or in economy, culture and education. Theory and characteristics of domestic and foreign industry proved that Industry clusters Strategy is the effective way to narrow the gap and foster regional competitiveness.. Zhejiang and Guangdong's economic development experience of recent years illustrates the overall effectiveness of the strategy to Industry clusters [3]. Industrial clusters as an economic phenomenon, was referred in Marshall's external economic theory and Weber's industrial location theory, but it may appear earlier. The first economist who study cluster is Alfred • Marshall, his main contribution is the discovery of the scale of industrial development and industrial areas has a lot of relationship, he believes that the cause of business cluster is due to external economies of scale; Harvard Professor Michael Porter presented the global economy of the industrial cluster theory, from a new perspective - the perspective of competitiveness, to treat and analysis the phenomenon of industrial clusters [4]. Industry cluster is a kind of phenomena that many enterprises and their support system is highly concentrated in a particular area of business and industrial. The cluster members including parts suppliers and other upstream and downstream channels and customers, offering complementary goods manufacturers and some other companies put together the relevant skills, technology or other industries, and also provide professional training, education, information, research and technical support of government or non-governmental organizations, such as universities, the quality of standards agencies, short-term training institutions and trade associations [5]. The competitive industries clusters is a kind of industry clusters which has special advantage in this region and cheaper production costs to complete a specific production compared with other regions, and has advantage in cost of the market share[6].

2 The General Concept of Development of Sports Industrial Clusters in the Western Cities

To accelerate the process of Western sports industry, space decentralization strategy, should be taken, focusing on the sports industry which the development of industry agglomeration and a high degree of concentration of urban areas to cities and towns. Therefore, the basic idea of sports industry the western road should be: concentration on spatial concentration and strategic focus on promoting. Vigorously promote the rural population and the sports industry to sports in an advantageous location, strong spatial accessibility, focus on the sports industry in the key urban areas of higher degree of industrial agglomeration and urban aggregation. Priority on the development of the sports industry on the major cities. Expand its scale of sports industry, to strengthen the division of labor and the degree of integration between the major cities, sports city and urban industry. Improve the urban spatial aggregation ability of the sports industry. And promote it develop towards urban sports circle, city sports industry belt, city sports industry Group and other new forms of urban space development of sports industry. Form the combination of the sports industry cluster of medium cities and small cities and towns. Expanding the scale of the Sports Industry Clusters in urbanization Area. Let several key areas of the western cities first achieve the level of developed coastal cities in sports industrial clusters. In order to raising the level of industrial clusters in the entire western region. The specific idea is:

1) The development strategy between the western regions. Priority to the development of the sports industry cluster in West Longhai - Lanxin Economic Zone, Chengdu-Chongqing Yangtze River economic belt, NGK area, Hubao - Baolan - Lanqing Line four key economic areas. Further strengthen the features of sports industry cluster of Chongqing, Chengdu, Xi'an as the largest western region, with inter-provincial regional. Play better as the economic, information, trade and cultural centers. And its role in the service in economic development, radiation and leading role in the sports industry in the western. Let Chongqing, Chengdu and Xi'an become the core population concentration and sports industry cluster of modern sports in western region and strategic support points.

2) From point to dimension integration development. Promote the development of industry cluster in the western region. Improve the degree of space polymerization for the sports industry. Promote the formation of urban sports circle, city sports industry belt, city sports industry group and the form of spatial organization of the sports industry. Change the sports industry in the process of urbanization from the traditional sports industry as a single urban core of the "point" of the cluster model to sports circle, sports industry belt, sports industry group and some new form of spatial organization of the sports industry as the center of the "face" or "group" gathering mode, form a broader set of area of sports industry. Strengthen the focus on regional medium cities and small cities, small towns' integration of the sports industry cluster, promote the coordinated development of sports industry in medium cities and small towns, and extend the sports industry chain. In improving the gather capacity of the sports industry in medium city, through the external demand as well as its capital, technology, the spread of radiation from outside. accelerate the integration of the sports industry cluster in medium cities and surrounding towns. Make the influence in industrialization and urbanization of the Sports Industry of the small towns surrounding the cities. To form a reasonable function division of labor in the sports industry between small towns surrounding and central cities and big cities. Form an spatial structure system of integrated city - town sports industry cluster.

3) Step by step conditionally development strategy in province region. Develop the sports industry in provinces (autonomous regions), areas and central cities, promote the formation of industrial clusters City Sports of provinces (autonomous regions), areas and central cities, developing a good momentum conditionally step by step. By adjusting and optimizing the sports industrial structure, improve the capacity of the sports industry cluster and the ability of radiation in sports industry on the surrounding area. To give full play to the sports industry an important role in economic development

in these cities in the region, make it the key regional industries in province (autonomous regions) and the sports industry cluster center that facing the inter-provincial border area.

3 Classification and Regulation of Cluster Development in West City Sports Industry

3.1 The Classification of Sports Industry Cluster Development in Western Cities

Sports industry cluster development can make coordinated development in the sports industry of cities and towns throughout the region and become highly innovative structure of the network industries, so it is the urgent choice of Western sports to response to industry knowledge economy, network economy, the development trend of economic globalization. The body of space accumulation closely linked through the criss-cross network, represent a new forms of space economic organization between the market and hierarchy. The Industry Cluster Development in Western China can basically form 8 major industrial clusters area. According to the law of development of sports industry, sports industry cluster development is from junior to senior. From analysis number of cities, sports population, rate of the sports industry, the proportion of sports industry share of total regional economic and other indicators. Through the comparative studies and clustering analysis to the western sports industry clusters is divided into the primary stage, intermediate stage and advanced stage.

1) The sports industry clusters in primary stage. There are 5 sports industry clusters in primary stage in western area: Intensive urban industrial ar areas, the central industry-intensive areas of Guizhou, Guangxi, South - North - Chin - anti-industry groups and industries in central Yunnan. The significant character of sports industry in this group is that the place occupied area of sports facilities and the sports population, sports unemployed population, the scale of the development of sports industry and the total economic value sports industry occupied in the proportion of this area are obviously lower than Guanzhong Plain City Sports Industry belt and Chengdu-Chongqing City Sports Industry Group. In fact, while there are a large number of sports population in the central city in Yunnan Province in sports industry, and large-scale development of sports industry, the total economic value sports industry occupied in the proportion of this area are higher, But its low level of industrialization, the serious polarization of the order of the scale level of the sports industry. Therefore, belongs to the primary stage of sports industry cluster.

2) The sports industry clusters in intermediate stage. There is 1 sports industry clusters in intermediate stage in western area: Guanzhong Plain City Sports Industry belt. the place occupied area of sports facilities and the sports population, sports unemployed population, the scale of the development of sports industry and the total economic value sports industry occupied in the proportion of this area in this stage are much higher than the 6 sports industry clusters, but it's obviously lower than Chengdu-Chongqing City Sports Industry Group.

3.2 The Developing Regulation Strategies of Sports Industry Clusters in Western Cities

Regulation means adjustment and control. The so-called control strategy is according to the corresponding situation to adjust established methods, and it is more used for policy decisions in education, communication and economic etc. In allusion to the classification of Western region urban sports industry clusters development we must have the corresponding control strategies.

1) The developing regulation strategies of the initial stage sports industry clusters. There were 6 such kind urban sports industry clusters, namely the North Slop city compact district sports industry cluster Of Tianshan Mountain, lanzhou -xining city compact district sports industry cluster, the sports industry cluster in middle Mongolia concentration area, guangxi south - north - khin - the city clusters sports industry cluster, guizhou middle city clusters sports industry cluster and yunnan middle city clusters sports industry cluster. The key point is to accelerate the coordinated development among urban sports industry clusters and the city sports infrastructure construction, it is also urgently needs to make full use of the great western development funds and the historic opportunity of policy inclination, take advantages of the "national fitness program (2010-2015) "and the mission of "the sports industry development guidance opinion" which by General Office of the CPC ,seize the opportunity given by the times about sports powerhouses strategic objectives construction. Through government-led to invest, give support focus development. The government plays an improving role through the association + club + company + all cooperation investment and take multilateral financing mode to widen the sports industry development space. What's more important is to coordinated urban sports infrastructure construction and regional economic development of sports industry, create excellent environment to promote the urban sports industry cluster grow. We should vigorously support public sports, accelerate the development of sports key projects industry, lead other cities in the area actively with the Primate City or regional central city, realize the urban sports industry cluster agglomerate development.

2) The developing regulation strategies of the Intermediate stage sports industrial clusters. There was only one such kind urban agglomeration: the Central Shanxi Plain Urban sports industry cluster district. The regulation strategies of these urban agglomeration sports industry uses develop as the main purpose, it means let market plays leading role, promote the integration development of urban agglomeration sports industry. Through the integration sports infrastructure construction which within urban agglomeration, guide urban and rural sports facilities construction, sports industry layout, sports industry resources factors flow; Breaking artificial barriers and administrative boundaries barriers and establish the integration market mechanism of sports industry. Promote the sports industry business and the effective flow of management personnel, capital, technology, information and other production elements and various physical sports products in the area, establish Shared urban agglomeration sports industry market system. Jointly develop sports industry cluster, sports services and sports fitness leisure entertainment to form competitive and energetic sports industry. Coordinate regional sports infrastructure construction between regional internal and interregional and trans-regional sports infrastructure construction, regional

public sports facilities construction, ecological environment protection etc, enhance the whole competitive advantage of regional sports industry clusters.

4 Distinguishment of the Development of Sports Industrial Clusters in the Western Cities of China

According to the "*HU Huan-yong line*" and "*the Kunlun Mountains*", "*HU Huan-yong line*"(Love fai - segmented line, namely Chinese population distribution line)was brought out in the 1930s by the famous geologist Mr. HuHuanYong, it shows the great differences about China's Eastern and western population distribution. At the same time, eastern and western area, internal western area's urbanization and economic development level have similar dense degree distribution with this line. Professor HuHuanYong wrote in the second phase "Chinese journal of population distribution" which published in "geographical journal "in 1935: "from heilongjiang province to make a straight line to southwest until yunnan. Divide the country as northwest and southeast two parts: the southeast area, is 400 million square kilometers, covers 36% of the whole country, northwest area is seven hundred square kilometers, covers 64 % of the whole country. As to the population distribution, the southeast has 4000040 million, accounts for about 96 percent of the whole population; while northwest has only 18 million accounts for about four percent of the country's population,." In this paper the attachment "Chinese lisarithmic map "was the first national lisarithmic map. This line is worthy of Geographical boundaries population, also was called Chinese population density line. The south of regions of kunlun mountains (here mainly refers to the kunlun mountains, qilian mountain and altun mountain ranges), average altitude of more than 4,000 meters, all the years frost and land reclamation rate is low, bad natural conditions , belong to the vast and sparsely populated region, it's not good for the formation and development of urbanization.

Through the analysis about western city clustering and contrast studies, use urbanization, population, geopolitical pattern as the main line, refer to the sports facilities area, the sports population and sports working population, sports industry development scale and the ratio of sports industry accounted for regional economic, economic develop speed, the humanities customs etc. divided the western city sports industry clusters into three regions: chengyu sports industry clusters which use chongqing as the center, guanzhong city sports industry cluster area with the center xian, lanzhou city center for sports industry district, known as the "west triangle sports industry circles". Although some scholars use three super-large center city chengdu, chongqing, xian as the strong point to divided the "west triangle sports industry circles" and forming a economic cooperation regional which connected the south and north of western area [8]. But based on the consideration of regional distribution of the western city, the authors think that we should combine chengyu and increase the XiLanYin which use lanzhou for center, would be more scientific. Thus formed the "west triangle sports industry circle" the article refers to.

Therefore, " west triangle sports industry circle " is a sports industry area across sichuan, shanxi, chongqing, gansu, and it will become the biggest sports industry cluster area in western China, compared with "long triangle", "pearl river delta" sports industry clusters, it is visible that put forward and establish "west triangle" is the inevitable process to promote western development and the urban sports industry in west. "West triangle" sports industrial clusters development, according to this city economic cooperation mode, can establish connecting sports industrial cluster district. It has important strategic significance and far-reaching influence to our urban sports in western China, the development of traditional sports industry, region economic development, regional national unity, natural ecological construction and integration development of east and west, harmonious to nations. From the developing experience of "long triangle", "pearl river delta" and "jing jin tang" three sports industry clusters, it is very difficult to isolate sports industry to develop. "West triangle" sports industry clusters was to complement each other's advantages, integrate resources, and reach common development, with "west triangle" sports industry clusters as the link, communicate southwest and northwest sports industry, finally become the fourth sports industrial clusters growth pole in china – which means the leader of west sports industry.

In western region, except town sports industry and non-agricultural industries of sports industry developed towns, namely town sports industry, there are some small towns sports industry can be effectively radiation driving regional development. This kind of small towns has less number, they could be 1-2 in small town, or 3-4 in big town, they are in the center of town, near several important transit interchange, has prominent geographical advantage, economic strength is stronger, exist reasonable industrial structure, the third industry is more developed than anyother[9] Therefore, it has a good foreground to become regional sports industry clusters center. Towns and cities type are mostly at an important traffic location, has prominent advantage, or at the people's governments ,or have a long history, or have good regional develop space. Its population scale and economic scale significantly higher than average, the third industry has certain base, infrastructure construction is better, has a great potential of development, and can drive around a large area's economic and social development. So town type sports industry and center town type is in a very special status in the development of county sports industry, plays an important role to improve the development of county sports industry. Therefore, we should abandon the balanced development strategy, emphasis and gives priority to the development of town and center town types sports industry, make them become "growth center" of the regional sports industrial economy , and through the accumulation effect and diffusion effects to promote rural regional sports industry and traditional sports development.

References

1. Chen, X.M.: The Research about Development Strategy for Competitive Industries in Western Cities – Use Qinghai for Example. People's Forum 8, 148–149 (2010)
2. Liu, X.Y.: The Discussion about The Important Way of Urbanization in Western Cities of China—the Boost of Urbanization of Sichuan Province and City Belt and Cluster. Journal of Southwest University for Nationalities (Social Science Edition) 24(1), 103–105 (2003)
3. Liu, X.Y., Zheng, C.D.: The Development Strategy and Advantage of Backwardness for Western Underdeveloped Towns in China–Take Sichuan Province for Example. Journal of Southwest University for Nationalities (Humanity Social Sciences Edition) 25(4), 1–5 (2004)
4. Liu, B.F.: The Trend of China City. China Economic Press, Beijing (2007)

5. Liu, Y., Liu, M.M.: The Research about Development of Sports Industry Clusters in Central Center Cities of China. Sports Culture Guide 2, 50–52 (2010)
6. Porter, M.: The Economics of Clusters and New Competition. Comparative Economic and Social Systems 2, 21–31 (2002)
7. Qiao, W., Jiang, W.Q.: The Studies about Measures for Accelerate Urbanization Process in Western Region. Rural Economy 2, 88–89 (2008)
8. Wang, J.C.: Innovative Space -Enterprise Cluster and Regional Development. Peking University Press, Beijing (2001)
9. Baidu Information, `http://hi.baidu.com/chaowang888666/blog/item/2b694b5540f494c6b645ae2d.html`

A Demonstrational Analysis of Relationship between FDI and Industrial Structure Upgrading in China

Yanfei Yin, Kai Li, and Yu Luo

Economics and Management School of Wuhan University,
Wuhan, Hubei Province 430072, P .R. China
yyfay@126.com

Abstract. FDI inflows in China has fluctuated in recent years. As labor and resource price rise, many foreign-invested enterprises gradually withdraw from China, while the current industrial structure and other economic changes further accelerated closure of many processing trade enterprises. In the context of the "double transformation" and the financial crisis, it is of great significance to conduct industrial upgrading and growth mode transformation. This paper uses cointegration analysis, dynamic variance decomposition, and other modern econometric approaches to conduct the empirical study on mutual influence between China's industrial upgrading and the FDI. The results indicate: the industrial upgrading and FDI have long-term stable relations and promote mutually, but the industrial upgrading changes more depend upon own change as well as forcesome foreign capitals to leave China and other conclusions.

Keywords: industrial upgrading, cointegration, variance decomposition, FDI.

1 Introduction

In recent years, Foreign Direct Investment (FDI) inflow and outflow in the volatile period in China. In 2010, FDI in China was 105.74 billion U.S. dollars which stands for the highest level. If we move the time span backward, foreign companies who has invested in China reached 51.06% average loss in the period of 2000-2006[1]. In these years, many foreign enterprises take divestment from China as a way of "escape in the middle night" .In 2009, the FDI has made the first significant decline in China. What the mechanism hidden behind FDI fluctuations in the short term? Is this phenomenon associated with the recent changes in China's industrial structure?

2008, the global financial crisis has impacted Chinese exports in a considerable degree. The exports account of United States and Europe occupied about 40% of Chinese total exports. Therefore, Chinese exports would inevitably be subject to the impact of weak demand of these industrialized countries, particularly the United States and Europe. For instance, a great number of processing trade enterprises orders dropped so sharply that some low-end enterprises have gone bankrupt. The fundamental reason is the low technology content of their products, resulting in low

[1] Refer to Wang Jinmeng "Why do foreign-invested enterprises gains large losses in China" ("World Economy"2008 vol. 1), the data refers to the National Tax Conference Paper (2007).

Q. Zhou (Ed.): ISAEBD 2011, Part II, CCIS 209, pp. 370–377, 2011.

value-added products, and many companies are in the bottom of the international industrial chain.The fact that many foreign companies moved to the middle and western provinces of China or Vietnam has convincingly proofed the above views. Many scholars believe the ‘withdrawal’ could not explain the deterioration of Chinese investment environment, but reflects the upgrading of industrial structure. There are also some scholars believe that this is the opportunity to promote Chinese industrial upgrading.

After years of reform and opening, China has become the largest country in attracting foreign investment. Chinese FDI has inflow 105.74 billion U.S. dollars in 2010. FDI has increased the Chinese domestic capital supply, trigger the domestic industry transfer, and promote the development of some new industries. In addition, most foreign direct investment enterprises possess advanced technology which is assist to filling the Chinese domestic blank. It has greatly promoted the transformation of traditional industries which is benefit for the adjustment of industrial structure (Yao Jun, 2005). If the influx of foreign investment has promoted Chinese industrial structure upgrade, then this upgrade process would force the low-tech and labor-intensive, high polluting and energy consumption foreignenterprises suffering from the upgrade impact,and then no choice but to withdrawal. What is the dynamic relationship exist between FDI and industrial upgrading? How much upgrading of industrial structure in China depends on foreign investment? Is the upgrade also driven by government industrial policies? These above questions are to be discussed in this paper.

2 Literature Review

There are an immense number of researches discussing on the influence of Foreign Direct Investment in host country'seconomic development. There are two effects of FDI in the host economy which including spillover effects and capital effects. The spillover effects can be divided into industrial structural effects, technology spillover effects and institutional change effects. (Jiang Jinfan, 2004). Borensztein, Gregorio and Lee (1995) used the data of 69 developing countries in the period of 1970-1989, tested the influence of OECD direct investment on developing countries’ economic growth. They found FDI is an important tool for technology transfer for making a positive contribution to economic growth, and the contribute rate is higher than domestic investment. ShenKunrong et al (2001) constructed endogenous growth model, considered the FDI can improve the host country's technological level and organizational efficiency via technology spillovers, thereby enhancing the economy's total factor productivity. Ni Yixuan, and Zhou Lei (2004), their analysis based on FDI and China's industrial upgrading correlation, showed that FDI has played in promoting the transfer of traditional industries. ChenLangnan (2001) considered the total fixed asset investment growth and economic growth have a significant linear correlation, the stock of FDI and industrial growth rate also have linear correlation. Chen Guohong (2008) used Engle-Granger cointegration test and Granger causality test, empirical studied the relationship between FDI, intellectual property protection and innovation capacity of 1991-2006. Their results showed the pairwise relationships between the three have long-term stability in China.

On the other hand, Ni Yixuan et al (2004) according to the product cycle theory, FDI investment pattern and capital return analysis, revealed some limitations of FDI Promotion to industrial upgrading in China.YadongLuo and Justin Tan (1998) did an empirical study on the impact of China's industrial structure to FDI. It concluded the industrial structure instability and the operational risks of foreign-funded enterprises are positively related, etc. Nigel Driffield (2001) has analyzed the impact of FDI to the British domestic industry concentration, and revealed that FDI inflows increased competitive pressures of domestic enterprises and reduce the excessive concentration of industry.

Kong Wen (1999) pointed out that there is no obvious effect of FDI in promoting the industrial structure advance in the development process. They based on the contradictions appearing when utilize the FDI in the industrial restructuring process, and then proposed policy recommendations. Wei Houkai and Chang-Chuan (2006) considered when the Reform and Open Policy has carried out , foreign investment has played an important role in promoting economic development while also brought many negative effects on private investment, international balance of payments, trade monopolies and national industrial development, resources and environment.

This paper is not bases on common logical reasoning to participate in the focus of controversy, but according to Chinese data contains the period of 1985-2010. It is using cointegration analysis, dynamic variance decomposition and other modern econometric techniques, then finished empirical research on relationship between Chinese industrial structure and FDI.

3 Data Description

We base on Chinese actual situation, using the increase in the proportion of tertiary industry as the standard to measure industrial upgrading[2]. FDI stock is accumulated of total FDI inflows, and then considering depreciation of assets, divestments and other factors, adjusted according to comparable prices.

In order to eliminate the dimension, the data were collected the logarithm as LnFDI, LnT. According to basic economic theory and data availability, we take the depreciation rate as 10%.We used annual data which involve the period of 1985 to 2010, limited by the space, the data of FDI inflows and outflows in China are omitted here. It can be available upon the request. These data sources are from China Statistical Yearbook and the SAFE website[3].

---

[2] Because the industrial structure upgrading is a difficult concept to quantify, different scholars have disputed. In this paper, via 30 years of reform and opening, the proportion of tertiary industry significant increase, so this proportion as a approximately indexpresents for industrial upgrading.

[3] There is disparity of caliber of foreign exchange and FDI between The National Bureau of Statistics and the State Administration of Foreign Exchange, our data in accordance with the SAFE website data.

4 The Model and Empirical Analysis

4.1 Single Integration and Co-integration Test

The main idea of cointegration test contains: if a linear combination of two or more same order time series vector can be combined a smooth sequence, these non-stationary time series has long-term equilibrium relationship. Only two variables which integrated of same order may existcointegration relationship. Therefore, we have to test order integrated of variables before the cointegrationtest. We use the Augmented Dickey - FullerTest (ADF) to test unit root sequence.

ADF test is based on the following equation:

$$\Delta x_t = a_0 + a_1 t + (\rho - 1)x_{t-1} + \Sigma\beta_i \Delta x_{t-i} + \varepsilon_t \tag{1}$$

Null hypothesis H0: $\rho = 1$, the alternative hypothesis H1: $\rho < 1$. Accepting the null hypothesis means that the time series contains a unit root. Test results in Table 1.

Table 1. Unit Root Test(1985—2009)

Variables	Intercept	Time trend	Lag phases	ADF statistic	Critical value (1%)	Critical value (5%)
LnT	Yes	Yes	3	-3.4821	-4.6205	-3.6992
Firstdifference	Yes	None	1	-2.8328	-3.1098	-2.6887
LnFDI	Yes	Yes	2	-4.3302	-5.3786	-4.0426
First difference	Yes	None	1	-3.9903	-3.9978	-3.1969

All variables are unit root exists, and their first differences are significant at the 5% level reject the unit root hypothesis. The variables are Integrated of Order One(I(1)) sequence, therefore, we can use it to do long-term cointegration. Two-step method has been proposed by Engle and Granger to estimate the cointegration vector. The cointegration parameter estimator which obtained by the EG two-step are trait with consistency and availability. In order to overcome the defect of EG two-step estimation in small sample situation, Johansen presented a dynamic distributed lag model (VAR) model to estimate the long-term equilibrium relationship, which availably to get valid unbiased estimates.

Initially, we base on the AIC, SIC information criteria to determine the final lag periods. In Table 2, we give the Log likelihood, AIC, SC values based on several lag intervals. Ultimately, we select the lag 2-order of VAR model, and the basic form is:

$$y_t = A_0 + A_1 y_{t-1} + A_2 y_{t-2} + \varepsilon_t \tag{2}$$

Which $y_t = (LnT, LnFDI)$

Table 2. Vector Auto Regression Estimates

Lag Intervals	Sample (adjusted)	Included observations	Log likelihood	Akaike information criterion	Schwarz criterion
1	1986-2008	23 after adjustments	27.8072	-1.1789	-1.0873
2*	1987-2008	22 after adjustments	27.8921	-1.9075	-1.2265
3	1988-2008	21 after adjustments	27.9079	-1.5803	-0.9128

Notes: the smaller AIC、 SC values, the better equation estimated.

After we estimate the proper Lag Interval, we shall do the VAR (2) model related tests to confirm the suitability for further integration and estimations. Table 3 shows the Autocorrelation LM Test and Residual Heteroskedasticity Test results. It conveys that:1- order, 2-order, 4-order, 6-order autocorrelation test and the heteroscedasticity test relatively fit the model, suitable for further integration and estimations.

Table 3. VAR(2) Model Evaluation Diagnostics

	Multivariate Diagnostic Test			
Autocorrelation LM Test (P values are in brakets)	LM(1) 2.1398 (0.1408)	LM(2) 4.4562 (0.1009)	LM(4) 8.1092 (0.0876)	LM(6) 11.8812 (0.0635)
VAR Residual Heteroskedasticity Tests		12.4120	(0.3397)	

Notes: The autocorrelation LM test and null hypothesis has no autocorrelation; heteroscedasticity test and the null hypothesis are no heteroskedasticity.

Then, we use cointegration tests to VAR (2) model by Johansen maximum likelihood estimation to confirm the variables equilibrium relationship in the long term. In the comparison of several results, we finally confirmed the test form: cointegration variables with a linear trend and intercept limited in the cointegration space. Johansen maximum likelihood estimate results have shown in Table 4.

Table 4. Johansen Maximum Likelihood Estimate Results

Eigenvalue	Likelihood Ratio	5 Percent Critical Value	1 Percent Critical Value	Hypothesized No. of CE(s)
0.5762	29.9910	25.61	32.37	None*
0.3901	8.8906	12.39	17.83	At most 1

Note: * indicates on 5% significance level reject the null hypothesis, the null hypothesis of Johansen test has no cointegration.

The table shows that: Johansen maximum likelihood estimate statistics is greater than the critical level of 5%, reject the null hypothesis, it reveals the cointegration. It exists long-term cointegration relationship between FDI and industrial upgrading.

4.2 Analysis of Variance Decomposition

The error variance of time series forecast is the interaction of disturbance of itself and the other disturbances within the system. The purpose of breaking down the impact of the mean squared error of the system is to decompose the contribution of each variance impact. We consider the existence of cointegration, decompose the △ LnT and △ LnFDI based on VECM.Results are as follows:

Table 5. The impact decomposition of △LnT and △LnFDI

	Variance decomposition of △LnT			Variance decomposition of △LnFDI		
Period	S.E.	△LnT	△LnFDI	S.E	△LnT	△LnFDI
1	0.250501	100.0000	0.000000	0.112978	11.02111	88.97889
2	0.319870	99.56953	0.430470	0.157404	10.98000	89.02000
3	0.357071	98.56206	1.437937	0.189710	8.849090	91.15091
4	0.379450	97.00261	2.997390	0.215372	6.631905	93.36810
5	0.394170	96.96855	3.031448	0.236557	5.333886	94.66612
6	0.404841	95.57669	4.423306	0.254418	14.96137	85.03863
7	0.413400	94.96280	5.037207	0.269666	18.52094	81.47906
8	0.420891	93.26031	6.739692	0.282790	22.0103	77.98097
9	0.427851	92.58408	7.415928	0.294147	30.46178	69.53822
10	0.434527	91.02168	8.978322	0.304013	35.85489	64.14511

According to the forecasting variance decomposition of △ LnT, the△ LnT changes can be largely explained by its own. △ LnFDI has relatively limit explanatory power to △ LnT ,however, the explanatory power of LnFDI gradually increases over forecast period. In contrast, it can conclude from the variance decomposition of △ LnFDI. In the first five period, most of the △ LnFDI growth can be explained by itself, △LnT have some weaker explanatory power to △ LnFDI. After the 5th period, the explanatory power gradually increases. In the 10th period even increases to 35.85%, and its explanatory power of LnFDI increases weaker.

5 Conclusion

5.1 Long-Term Stable Cointegration Relationship

The empirical results reveal the industrial upgrading and FDI variables are integrated of order one(1 (1)) process, that is first-order stationary. There exist long-term stable cooperative relationship. It also reveals from the variance decomposition of △ LnT and

△ LnFDI within which exist a synergistic interaction in long-term.Especially, the impact of △LnT to △ LnFDI becomes increasingly significant. In recent years, FDI rapid growth rate combined with high efficiency of industrial structure.

5.2 Majority of Industrial Upgrading Depends on Government's Industrial Policy

It can be seen from the △ LnT forecast variance decomposition: the △ LnTalters from 100%(in the 1st period) to 91.02%, can be fully explained the changes on its own.There is not a long time to establishment a market adjustment mechanism.It has failed to give full play to lead market in effective resource allocation. Industrial structure changes are the results of our government industrial policy, more obvious in short-term. But the △ LnFDI explanatory power gradually increases over time.

5.3 The Interaction between FDI and Industrial Upgrading

In the long run, the contribution of foreign investments in industrial upgrading will be growing. With a large number of investments select China as host country, foreign enterprises promoting and upgrading the Chinese industrial structure. For instance, it exerts technology spillovers effect, associated effect of host country enterprises, demonstration effect of production and management and the competitive effects.In addition, the forecast variance decomposition of the △ LnFDI can be interpreted that Chinese industrial structure upgrade promote the growth of foreign investment.

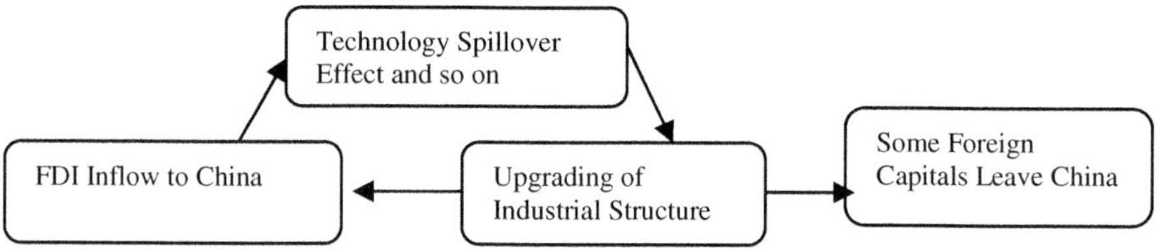

Fig. 1. The Relationship Between Industrial Structure Upgrading and Foreign Capital Changes

References

[1] Kunrong, S.: The Impact of Technology Transfer of FDI on the Quality of Domestic Economic Growth——A Test Based on China's Regional Panel Data. China Industrial Economy 272, 6–15 (2010)
[2] Chen, G., Tao, G.: Study on Relations Among FDI, Intellectual Property Protection and IndependentInnovation in Our Country. China Industrial Economy 4, 25–33
[3] Wang, l., Jiang, X., Lu, S.: Financial Crisis and China's foreign trade ——Research on Coastal Small Foreign Trade Enterprises. International Economic Review 7, 42–45 (2009)
[4] Nigeldriffield: Inward Investment and Host Country Market Structure: the case of UK. Review of Industrial Organization 18, 363–378 (2001)

[5] Jiang, J.: Foreign direct investment in China's economic growth mechanism. World Economics 1, 3–10 (2004)
[6] Jiang, X.: The Impact of Attracting Foreign Investment for Industrial Technology and R&D Capability in China. International Economic Review 3, 13–19 (2003)
[7] Wang, J., Mao, N.: Why do foreign-invested enterprises loss in China. World Economics 1, 23–35 (2008)
[8] Wei H., Liu, C.: Negative Effects of Foreign Funds Utilization in China and the Direction of Strategic Adjustment. Henan Social Sciences 5 (2006)

The Response of China's Economy to US Shocks

Xuelai Yang

Hubei University of Economics, No.1 Yanghu Road, Jiangxia District, Wuhan, China
yangxuelai0204@yahoo.com.cn

Abstract. Along with the opening up of China's economy, external shocks have directly influenced China's economy, and China's macro-economic variables volatility has been affected as well. Using structural VAR model, we look into China's economic variables volatility due to US shocks. According to the empirical results, US shocks can influence China's economy, though the degree is not very significant yet compared to domestic shocks. Among all the external shocks, US demand shock is the most important, while US supply shock has little contribution to China's GDP volatility, which means China GDP growth shows independence to US cyclical developments. For the transmission channel of US shocks, we estimate different China's variables volatility due to US shocks and find that Interest rate channel is the most important one.

Keywords: US shocks, international transmission, China's economic growth, SVAR model.

1 Introduction

Because of 2007-2008 turmoil, US shocks and its international transmission has recently returned to the focus of public interest. As a gradual opening economy, China's economic growth has also been influenced by external shocks. But to what extent and directions does China interrelated with US shocks, still remains a problem. This paper focus on international transmission of US shocks to China, and try to explain the linkages between US macro-economic variables volatility and China's economic volatility.

Nowadays, China has stepped into a new stage of openness, external dependency degree has improved a lot, this can be measured by foreign trade dependency degree (see figure 1). We can see that foreign trade dependency degree measured by goods imports and exports increases annually, as for year 2007, it has been raised to nearly 65%. Since 2003, China's GDP growth has kept annual growth rate over 10% for five years, higher than that of potential growth rate, and the economic growth relies on export heavily.Though because of external demand reduction after financial crisis of 2008, the share of foreign trade declined to about 45% in 2009, it was still a high level compared to other countries. FDI dependency degree measured by FDI stock also increases annually. The increasing integration with world economy may possibly make China's economy more infected by external shocks.

Q. Zhou (Ed.): ISAEBD 2011, Part II, CCIS 209, pp. 378–384, 2011.

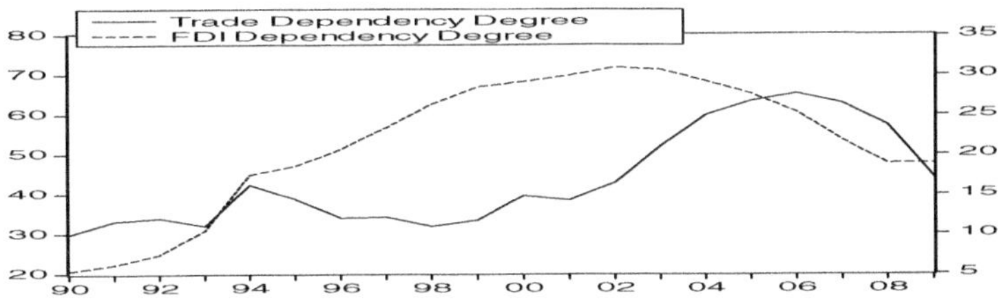

Fig. 1. External Dependency Degree of China (1990-2009) .Notes: data are in their percentage forms. The left axis indicates foreign trade dependency degree. The right axis indicates FDI dependency degree.

Since early 2008, a broader set of shocks has appeared, including various commodity price shocks, collapse of US housing bubble, global financial crises and the downturn of world economic growth. It can not be denied that shocks hitting the global economy seemed to be primarily US-based as US economy is often considered to play a pivotal role in global economy. We can also see the correlation of US real economic growth rates and China's real economic growth rates, at least in the recent period, China's economic growth has seen to be similar to the US and China can not be immune from external shocks.

This paper firstly reviews existing findings, then analyzes channels and mechanisms of how US shocks influence China macro-economic variables volatility, furthermore, we use SVAR model to measure the degree and direction that US shocks affect China's economic volatility. Finally, put forward our conclusions.

2 Review of Existing Findings and Studies

Economic growth volatility is influenced by a lot of macro-economic variables, which include foreign economic variables and domestic ones.

Foreign macro-economic variables' volatility results from cyclical factors can influence domestic economic variables through two main channels, trade channel and financial channel. Some literatures have focused on the spillover effect of country-specific—US shocks to other countries. A consensus appears to arise that spillover effects tend to run from North America to the rest of the world but not in the opposite direction (Dées and Vansteenkiste, 2007). US Monetary shock can be a most important source for macro-economic variables volatility. Based on traditional Mundell-Fleming model and intertemporal model equipped with sticky price, US monetary policy shock can be transmitted through exchange rate and interest rate fluctuation. It is US monetary policy that decrease world real interest rate, stimulate global excess liquidity and imbalance of global economy (Kim, 2001; Bems, Dedola and Smets, 2007; Bracke and Fidora, 2008).

Recent empirical researches on foreign shocks focus on global excess liquidity, world commercial prices fluctuation, US subprime crisis, etc. Such shocks have influenced domestic macro-economic variables volatility. Canova (2005) uses Bayesian VAR to estimate US economic shock transmission to eight Latin American countries. He finds that US monetary shock has strong influence on these countries, and the transmission pattern is quite different from that of developed countries. Mackowiak(2007) shows that external shocks are an important source of macroeconomic fluctuations in emerging markets. Because there is increasing trade integration, US shocks play an important role in economic growth of Asia (Pula and Peltonen, 2009). The open policy has strengthened the linkage between China's financial market and other market all over the world (Luo, Brooks and Silvapulle, 2011). As China has become the engine of growth in the world, it is important for us to understand how external shocks influence China's economic growth and the relative transmission channels.

Unlike other documents, we focus on US shocks and its transmission channels to China. SVAR model is used here and we also try to answer to what extent that US shocks influence China's economic growth, and we also observe the directions that US shocks infect China's macro-economic variables.

3 Method and Data

3.1 VAR Modelling

We assume that the economy is described by a structural form equation

$$B(L)y_t = u_t \tag{1}$$

where $B(L)$ is a matrix polynomial in the lag operator L, while y_t is a data vector that denotes economic variables. u_t is the structural disturbance vector, $E(u_t u_t^{'}) = I_k$.

The reduced form equation is

$$A(L)y_t = \varepsilon_t \tag{2}$$

Where ε_t is white noises vectors, $A(L)$ is a matrix polynomial in the lag operator L, we use traditional recursive schemes based on Cholesky decomposition. Within this framework, we identify four types of underlying disturbances in the basic model, respectively US supply shock, demand (spending) shock, monetary shock and common shocks denoted by non-fuel world commodity price index: $u_t^{'} = \begin{bmatrix} u_t^s & u_t^d & u_t^m & u_t^c \end{bmatrix}$, then we add China's economic variables one by one to the basic model which is called "marginal" method (Kim, 2001; Uligh, 2003).

3.2 Basic Identification Scheme

According to relative literatures and the purpose of this paper, we use an identification strategy similar to Peersman(2002), under the assumption that US economy is a big open economy, equation (1) can be rewritten as follows

$$\begin{bmatrix} y_t^* \\ p_t^* \\ R_t^* \\ wxp_t^* \end{bmatrix} = \left[B_0 - \sum_{i=1}^{n} B_i \right]^{-1} \begin{bmatrix} u_t^s \\ u_t^d \\ u_t^m \\ u_t^c \end{bmatrix} \quad (3)$$

Here, we use non-fuel world commodity price index (WXP_t^*) to denote common shocks, P_t^* denote US price level, federal fund interest rate (R_t^*) as proxy variable of monetary policy, and Y_t^* is US GDP growth. Small letters stand for the log form of the above variables. Thus, we can identify various US shocks with this simple model.

3.3 Extended System

To examine the effects of US shocks on China economic variables, the basic systems are extended to include additional variables, including real GDP (Y_t) and consumer price index (P_t); we use SSE composite index (SZZS) as proxy variable of equity prices. Other variables include short term loan rates R_t, real exchange rate FER_t defined as

$$FER_t = (P^*_t / CPI_t) \times FE_t$$

Where for each time t, FE_t denotes the nominal exchange rate, expressed as units of domestic currency per unit of US dollars. The data run from 1995Q1 to 2010Q2. Except for interest rate and foreign exchange rate all data are seasonally adjusted. All data are quarterly and in logarithm, except that the interest rates are in percentage points at an annual rate. The data series are from Guo Tai'an data base, Economic report of President, etc.

4 Econometric Analysis

By adding China's economic variables to the basic system marginally, we can observe the effect of US shocks on China economic variables. One lag is included in every system, the inverse roots of AR are all in or on the unit circle, which means the VAR system is stable.

4.1 US Supply Shock

US supply shock leads to a slight rise in China's real GDP of up to 0.1% in the first quarter, then will make China GDP rise up to the highest level at about 1.1% after fourteen quarters. Supply shock has effect on China commercial prices volatility, but the effect is not obvious. Exchange rate can be influenced by supply shock immediately, we can see an appreciation of RMB but the effect is not obvious. Supply shock leads to interest rate increase immediately. Supply shock can make equity prices rise two quarters after the shock, the peak is about 5.58% eleven quarters after the shock (see figure 2).

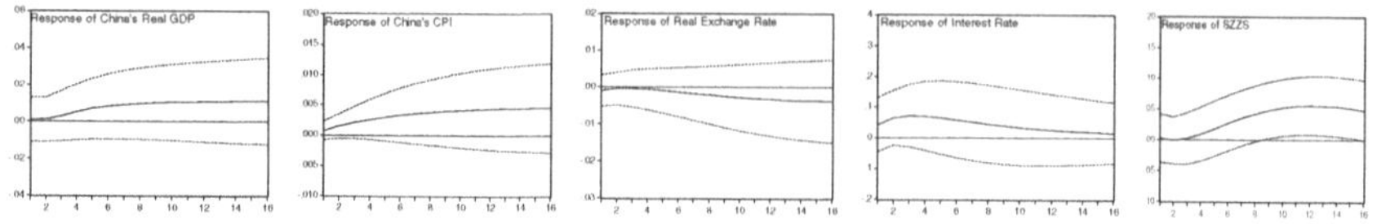

Fig. 2. Impulse responses of China's economic variables to US supply shock (one S.D. shock). Note: Intervals between the two dashed lines contain two standard errors.

4.2 US Demand Shock

US demand shock leads to a rise in China real GDP immediately, and can reach its highest to 1.8% at three quarters after the shock, which means that demand shock is much more important for China's GDP fluctuation than supply shock, while demand shock can leads to slight rise of China CPI. Demand shock can influence FER obviously, and leads to a rise of interest rate, the highest increase is about 5.44% six quarters after the shock, and then the interest rate will decrease. Demand shock leads to a rise of equity prices too (see figure 3).

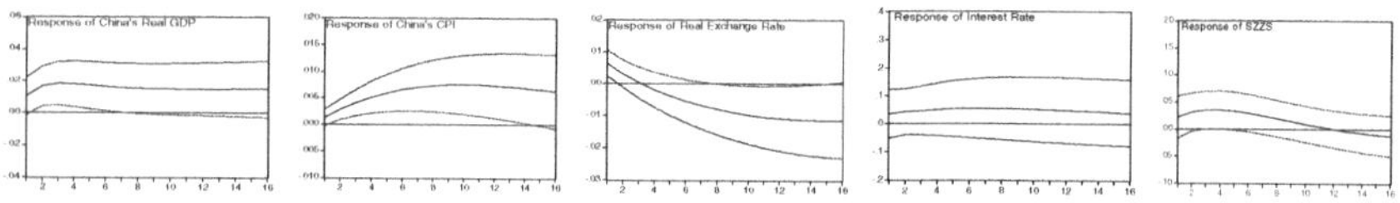

Fig. 3. Impulse responses of China's economic variables to US demand shock (one S.D. shock). Note: Intervals between the two dashed lines contain two standard errors.

4.3 US Monetary Policy Shock

Monetary policy shock leads to immediate rise in China's real GDP, then the contraction of monetary policy can make China real GDP decrease at the twelfth quarter after the shock. Contraction monetary policy shock leads to China's CPI decrease immediately, and the effect can only be seen in several quarters. Monetary contraction shock leads to RMB devalue immediately in the first quarter. Contraction of US monetary leads to a rise of SZZS with its highest level at about 5.8% in the third quarter (see figure 4).

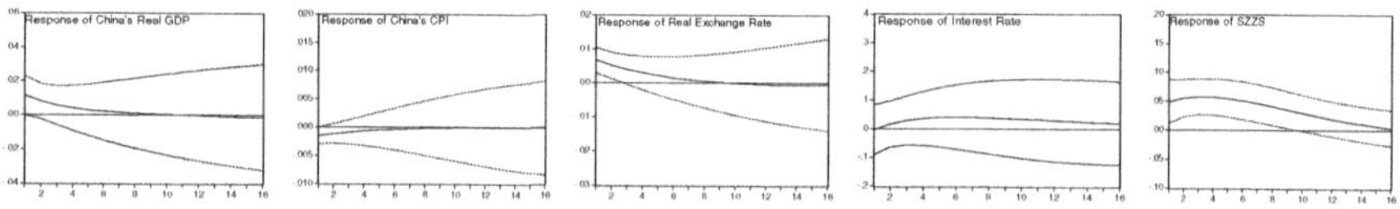

Fig. 4. Impulse responses of China's economic variables to US monetary shock (contraction with one S.D. shock). Note: Intervals between the two dashed lines contain two standard errors.

4.4 wxp* Shock

wxp^* shock leads to a rise of China's GDP immediately, which will arrive at the highest level about 1.98% at the eighth quarter. After a wxp^* shock, China's CPI rises soon, and the effect is long lasting. wxp^* shock leads to an appreciation of RMB and the peak increase (1.63%) is found in eleven quarter after the shock. After a wxp^* shock, China's equity prices increase in the first three quarters and then decline (see figure 5).

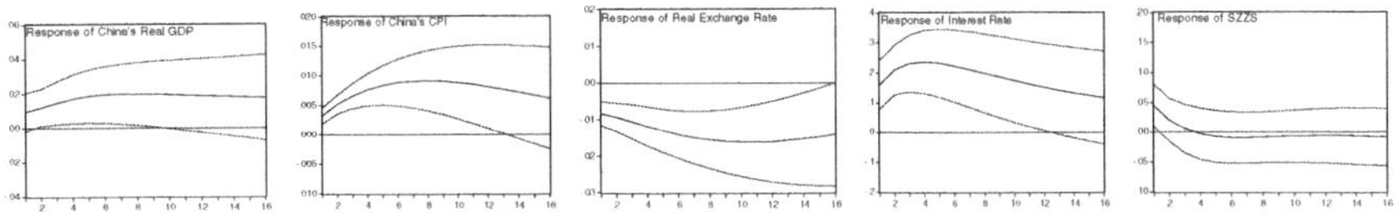

Fig. 5. Impulse responses of China's economic variables to wxp shock (one S.D. shock). Note: Intervals between the two dashed lines contain two standard errors.

4.5 Effects of US Shocks on China's Output

It may be better to examine the effects on all variables by considering interactions with external shocks and domestic shocks. We estimate the impulse responses and variance decomposition of China GDP with 1 lag for the ordering

$$\left(y^*, p^*, FFR, wxp^*, y, p, fer, R, szzs\right)$$

Table 1. China's GDP volatility due to US shocks

Source of disturbance	Horizon (quarters)	Fraction of the variance for China GDP volatility	Source of disturbance	Horizon (quarters)	Fraction of the variance for China GDP volatility
US shocks	1-2	18.58	FFR shock	1-2	6.73
	3-8	32.98		3-8	6.01
	9-20	38.65		9-20	5.19
y^* shock	1-2	0.05	wxp* shock	1-2	2.64
	3-8	0.11		3-8	6.5
	9-20	0.18		9-20	6.5
p^* shock	1-2	9.16			
	3-8	20.36			
	9-20	26.78			

Table 1 shows variance decomposition of China GDP due to US shocks (including all the shocks originated from US). US shocks still have limit contribution to China economic growth. And can reach its highest within 5 years. Among all the external disturbances, US demand shock is the most important, can account for average 26% for China's GDP volatility after two years, which means US spending can be an important external shock for economic volatility in China. This is identical to Chinese reality. China's GDP growth shows independence to US supply shock. wxp^* shock is more important compared to some US shocks for China's output, and contribute to China GDP volatility for about 6.5% after two year.

5 Conclusion

Along with the opening up of China's economy, foreign shocks have directly influenced China's economy, and economic variables volatility has been affected as well. As an important factor for global economy, US shocks can also influence China directly, though the degree is not very significant yet compared to domestic shocks. Among all the external shocks, US demand shock can not be overlooked, it is the most important factor among US shocks. US monetary policy shock has some contribution while supply shock has little contribution to China GDP volatility, which means China GDP growth shows independence to US supply.

References

1. Bems, R., Dedola, L., Smets, F.: US imbalances- the role of technology and policy. Journal of International Money and Finance 26(4), 523–545 (2007)
2. Bracke, T., Fidora, M.: Global liquidity or global savings glut. ECB Working Paper (June 2008)
3. Dées, S., Vansteenkiste, I.: The transmission of US cyclical developments to the rest of the world. ECB Working Paper (August 2007)
4. Ehrmann, M., Fratzscher, M.: Global financial transmission of monetary shocks. ECB Working Paper (April 2006)
5. Goodhart, C., Hoffmann: House prices, money, credit and the macro-economy. ECB Working Paper (April 2008)
6. Kim, S.: International transmission of US monetary policy shocks: evidence from VAR's. Journal of Monetary Economics 48, 339–372 (2001)
7. Llaudes, R.: Monetary policy shocks in a two sector open economy, an empirical study. ECB Working Paper (August 2007)
8. Luo, W., Brooks, R.D., Silvapulle, P.: Effects of the open policy on the dependence between the Chinese 'A' stock market and other equity markets: An industry sector perspective. Journal of International Financial Markets, Institutions & Money 21, 49–74 (2011)
9. Mackowiak, B.: External shocks, US monetary policy and macroeconomic fluctuation in emerging markets. Journal of Monetary Economics 54, 2512–2520 (2007)
10. Pula, G., Peltonen, T.A.: Has emerging Asia decoupled? An analysis of production and trade linkages using the asian international input-output table. ECB Working Paper (January 2009)

The Relationship between Financial Development and Economic Growth: An Empirical Study of Shanghai

Kefang Liu

Business School, Jiujiang University, Jiujiang, 332005, China
catheyun2004@yahoo.cn

Abstract. The best way to observe whether financial market has positive effect on the economic growth and the relationship between these two is econometric estimation. This paper uses unit root test, cointegration test, ganger causality, and the relative data from 1990-2009 to explore the relationship between financial development and economic growth in Shanghai. The results show no causal relationship between financial development and economic growth, but there exists long-term equilibrium relation between them. Shanghai should develop and deepen the regional finance via the finance reform to promote the economic growth.

Keywords: ADF test, Cointegration test, Granger causality test.

1 Introduction

Our finance and economy have developed quickly during the two decades. But financial reform still lags behind the economic reform. This phenomenon leads us to observe the relations between financial development and economic growth, which is not only the important theory about China's economic development but also the solution to the actual problems. At present, experts do lots of researches on the relations between financial development and economic growth in China but less empirical research on the relations in Shanghai. However, to some extent, finding out the relation between the two aspects is helpful to guide the economy growth in Shanghai. In this paper, we analyze the relationship between financial development and economic growth quantitatively and investigate the catalytic effect of financial development on economic growth according to the relative data of Shanghai from 1990 to 2009.

2 Indicators Selection

About the indicators selection, we use the growth ratio of the GDP to measure economic growth, and Financial Interrelations Ratio (FIR) and the interest difference between the deposit and loan (CDLC) to measure financial development. GDP is the best indicator to reflect a country or region's aggregate economic development capability, especially eliminating commodity price and population, which is RGDP. We use the financial scale metric and the financial intermediary efficiency metric to measure the level of the financial development. For the financial scale metric, we choose FIR, the value of (deposits + loans)/GDP. For the financial intermediary efficiency metric, it contains the

Q. Zhou (Ed.): ISAEBD 2011, Part II, CCIS 209, pp. 385–388, 2011.

operating efficiency and the allocating efficiency. Operating efficiency means the least cost and most deposit capitals. That is to say, it could be marked as CDLC. Allocating efficiency refers to the capability of transforming the surplus money into the loan. For this, we choose the ratio of deposits to loans of the whole financial institution, to present the ability of the financial intermediary to allocate the social sources. This marked as E. The specific data is shown in table 1.

Table 1. Finance development and economic growth in Shanghai (1990—2009)

Year	CDLC	FIR	E	RGDP	Year	CDLC	FIR	E	RGDP
1990	0.72	2.51	0.77	20.35	2000	3.6	3.48	1.29	9.91
1991	1.08	2.81	0.80	8.41	2001	3.6	3.80	1.32	10.30
1992	1.08	3.07	0.94	23.78	2002	3.33	4.28	1.33	9.08
1993	0	3.03	1.03	23.32	2003	3.33	4.55	1.32	13.67
1994	0	3.40	1.12	25.67	2004	3.33	4.33	1.34	14.11
1995	1.08	3.40	1.22	29.52	2005	3.33	4.34	1.39	13.70
1996	1.8	3.54	1.21	26.23	2006	3.6	4.26	1.42	11.77
1997	2.97	3.80	1.23	20.37	2007	3.33	4.16	1.40	13.37
1998	2.61	3.67	1.15	10.75	2008	3.06	4.25	1.47	7.70
1999	3.6	3.70	1.21	5.81	2009	3.06	4.94	1.50	11.71

Note: The data is the calculation results of the original data.

3 Empirical Analysis

3.1 Stationary Test of Variables

In order to avoid spurious regression, we need to conduct the stationary test for the data which is in time order. In this paper, we choose ADF test as the unit root test method. To enervate the process heteroscedasticity, we take the logarithm to various sequences data.

According to table 2, the primary time series are all un-stationary series. This shows no long-term stable relationship betweenRGDP and CDLC, ration of deposits to loans and FIR. But when we make first-order difference on these three series, the result tells us all of them are stationary, especially when they are above 5%, they are first order single, integrity sequences.

Table 2. Test results of ADF

Variables	ADF statistics	P-value	lags	Results
LNRGDP	-1.64439	0.0500	0	Not stationary
DLNRGDP	-3.19009	0.0007	0	stationary
LNFIR	-1.38048	0.0837	0	Not stationary
DLNFIR	-5.46725	0	0	stationary
LNCDLC	-0.54792	0.2919	0	Not stationary
DLNCDLC	-2.25484	0.0121	0	stationary
LNE	-1.51411	0.065	0	Not stationary
DLNE*	-6.51174	0	0	stationary

Note: The significance level is above 0.05. The significance level of DLNE* is above 0.10.

3.2 Cointegration Test

The purpose of cointegration test is to confirm whether we can get N-1 stationary sequences when two or more single integrity sequences combined. If the single integrity sequences can make up stationary sequences, we can call them cointegrated sequences. Cointegration focuses on the dynamic relation in time series. If sequences exists stationary sequences, they have long term relationship.

According to the ADF test, LNRGDP、LNCDLC、LNE、LNFIR are first-order single integrity sequences, in accordance with the same order. So, we need to give cointegration test to them to find whether they have long term relationship. The results are in table 3. From table 3, we can see that at the significance level of 0.05, all the null hypothesis are rejected, it indicates that there no long term relationship between FIR and RGDP, and between CDLC and RGDP.

Table 3. Unit root test results of LNFIR, LNE, LNCDLC and LNRGDP residual error

	ADF test statistic	10% level	5% level	1% level
LNFIR and LNRGDP	-3.604369	-3.310349	-3.733200	-4.667883
LNE and LNRGDP	-4.500548	-3.310349	-3.733200	-4.667883
LNCDLC and LNRGDP	-2.383769	-3.310349	-3.733200	-3.920350

From the cointegration test results, there is long term relationship between RGDP and E , the equation is LNE= 0.00980 + 0.84789LNE(-1) + 0.0197 LNRGDP.

3.3 Granger Causality Test

From the results of cointegration test, there exits long term relationship between the efficiency ratio of development in financial structure and the growth of economy, but others don't exist. However, we could not indicate which one affects on the other one. Because of this limitation, grander causality test is our choice for further development. Based on the former tests, we just use the Eview 6.0 to conduct this test. Results in table 4.

Table 4. Results of granger causality test

Lags: 1			
Null Hypothesis:	Obs	F-Statistic	Prob.
LNRGDP does not Granger Cause LNCDLC	18	2.38304	0.1422
LNCDLC does not Granger Cause LNRGDP		0.49919	0.4900

4 Conclusions

Firstly, from the results of causality test, financial development and economic growth do not exist causal relations. Secondly, there is no long term relationship exists between FIR and economic growth. Because of the special developing environment, increase in

FIR dose not present the depth of financial development but the restrain. Thirdly, long term relationship exists in financial efficiency and economic growth, and the elasticity coefficient is 0.02. The increase of financial efficiency promotes our economic growth, as economic growth is mainly stimulated by the investment in our country. Simultaneously, there is limitation of the expansion of financial efficiency, for it brings about pressure for environments, resources and goods prices. Relative departments should deepen the regional finance via the finance reform to promote the economic growth healthily and stably.

References

1. Jiang, T., Yu, W.: TRegional Financial Development and Economic Growth. Journal of Regional Financial Research (2010)
2. Rousseau, P., Wachte, P.: Financial Intermediation and Economic Performance Historical: Evidence from Five Industrialized Countries. Journal of Money Credit and Banking
3. Sun, P.:The Perspective of Size Effects to Study the Economies Growth and Financial Development in the Large Developing Countries.Nankai Journal (Philosophy, Literature and Social Science Edition) (2010)
4. Sun, P.: Financial Development and Economic Growth in Anhui Province: An Empirical Study Based on VAR and VEC Model. Statistical Education (2010)
5. Aghion, P., Howitt, P.: A Model of Growth through Creative Destruction. Econometrica (1992)
6. Liang, J.: The Relationship Between Financial Development and Economic Growth——An Empirical Study of Shaanxi Province. Journal of Xi'an University of Finance and Economics 7 (2010)

The Efficiency Evaluation of Resources Allocation in Mass Sport in China's Three Gorges Reservoir Area

Delong Dong[1], Yongping Yu[2], and Depeng Dong[3]

[1] Department of Physical Education, Southwest University, 400715 Chongqing, China
[2] The Primary School Attached to Southwest University, 400700 Chongqing, China
[3] The Company of Ark Human Resource in Weifang, 261041 Weifang, China

Abstract. The aim of this article is to analyze the efficiency of resource allocation on mass sport in Three Gorges Reservoir area in order to improve the level of development. Based on DEA models, the result shows that the effectiveness of its technical efficiency is less than 50%, but also presents the typical "inversion" phenomenon, that is to say, some cities what are strength in economic show obvious waste of mass sport resources, and others what is weak in economic maintain the effectiveness of technical efficiency. Therefore, adjusting the allocation of mass sport resource, optimizing mass sport resources, improve the institutional construction and enhance the effectiveness of overall technical efficiency will became an important point on mass sport development in the Three Gorges Reservoir Area.

Keywords: Three gorges Reservoir Area, mass sport, resource allocation, date envelopment analysis (DEA).

1 Introduction

The resource allocation of mass sport is one of the most controversial issues for some researchers, different researchers analyzed the question from different aspects (Stephen, W., 1992 & Clint, C., 2005), over the recent past, there has been enormous policy changes in china, for example, the overall development of mass sport in urban and rural was proposed in order to promote the level of mass sport (Yang, X.M., 2010). However, duo to economic and other reasons, the Three Gorges Reservoir Area is not equilibrium for resource allocation of mass sport in china, this is also the most factors for inequities in mass sport. Without any doubt, it will influence the Sustainable Development of mass sport in the Three Gorges Reservoir area.

Thus, the aim of the present paper is to explore the efficiency of resource allocation for mass sport in the Three Gorges Reservoir area in order to achieve the overall development of mass sport in urban and rural. For this purpose, DEA what is a mathematical programming approach development to measure the relative efficiency of units in an observed group of similar units was utilized in this article. By which, fifteen cities were analyzed in the Three Gorges Reservoir area, we hope that it can promote the overall development of mass sport and improve the efficiency of resource allocation.

Q. Zhou (Ed.): ISAEBD 2011, Part II, CCIS 209, pp. 389–394, 2011.

2 Methodology and Data

DEA Model. DEA (Date envelopment analysis) was developed by Charnes and Copper(1982), based on the definition of relative efficiency, it suppose we have a set n peer DMUs (decision making units), in which, the inputs and outputs for DMU_j are as follows:

$\chi_j = (\chi_{1j}, \chi_{2j}, \dots, \chi_{mj})^T > 0 \quad j=1,2,\dots,n$
$y_j=(y_{1j}, y_{2j}, \dots, y_{sj})^T \quad j=1,2,\dots,n$
also $x_{ij}>0$, $y_{rj}>0$, $\quad i=1,2,\dots m; r=1,2,\dots,s$

Whereas, according to the vector, for all $j_0 \in \{1,2, \dots, n\}$, when a DMU_{jo} is selected, we consider the following generalized DEA model (see Eq.1):

$$\begin{cases} \min \theta = V_D \\ \text{s.t.} \\ \sum_{j=1}^{n} \lambda_j X_j + S^- = \theta X_{j0} \\ \sum_{j=1}^{n} \lambda_j Y_j - S^+ = Y_{j0} \\ \lambda_j \geq 0 \quad j=1,2,\cdots,n \\ S^- \geq 0, S^+ \geq 0 \end{cases} \tag{1}$$

However, it is not an easy matter for application of EDA model, thus, BCC model was introduced in some article. In fact, The CCR model is the first DEA model, which has been provided by Charnes et al., and measures the efficiency under constant returns to scale assumption of technology. The BCC model has been introduced by Banker et al. also these models evaluate the units under variable, nonincreasing, and nondecreasing RTS (returns to scale) assumption of technology, respectively. Meanwhile, if the value of CCR was divided by BCC, The scale efficiency will be counted for the DMU. According to this, we can make the overall assessment of resource allocation for mass sport. The equation is as follows (see Eq.2)

$$\begin{cases} \min[\theta - \varepsilon(\hat{E}^T s^- + \hat{E}^T s^+)] = V_D \\ s.t \quad \sum_{j=1}^{n} \lambda_j \cdot \chi_j + s^- = \theta \chi_{j0} \\ \sum_{j=1}^{n} \lambda_j \cdot y_j - s^+ = y_{j0} \\ \lambda_j \geq 0 \quad j=1,2,\cdots,n \\ S^- \geq 0, S^+ \geq 0 \end{cases} \tag{2}$$

Here, $\hat{E} = (1,\cdots,1)^T_{1\times m}$ and $\hat{E} = (1,\cdots,1)^T_{1\times s}$ is the vector of m and s, when some units is 1.

$S^- = (S_1, S_2^-, \cdots, S_m)^T \quad S^+ = (S_1^+, S_2^+, \cdots, S_S^+)^T$

s_i^- and s_r^+ (i=1,2, ..., m ; r=1,2, ..., s) are slack variables

$\lambda_j (j = 1,2,\cdots n)$ is the weight for DMU, $\sum_{j=1}^{n} \lambda_j \chi_j$ and $\sum_{j=1}^{n} \lambda_j y_j$ are the inputs vector and outputs vector by weight count.

In addition, the evaluation rule is as follows:

if θ=1, $s^- \neq 0$ or $s^+ \neq 0$, then we say DMU is weakly efficient. It indicated that there are some unreasonable phenomenon for inputs and outputs.

If θ=1, s^-=0, and s^+=0, then we say DMU is efficient. It showed that there are no more efficient units than DMU_{j0}.

If $\theta < 1$, it supposed that there exists an unreal DMU, that is to say , The DEA model is not efficient.

Research index. When DEA model was used, the inputs and outputs for DMU_j should be established. As far as resource allocation of mass sport is concerned, the most important thing is to promote the efficiency of mass sport in urban and rural. Therefore, combine with others research (Yu, T., 2009; Li, Q.J., 2005), we construct the index system of resource allocation for mass sport in the Three Gorges Reservoir area (see table 1).

Table 1. The index system of resource allocation in mass sport in Three Gorges Reservoir area

Classification	Index1	Index2
Inputs index	Financial inputs	The total funding of mass sport (ten thousand)
	Human inputs	Sport instructor (n)
	Property inputs	Sport foundation (m^2/per person)
Outputs index	Direct output	Sport population (%)
	Output effect	The pass rate of physique (%), sports business income(ten thousand)

(Note: all data are from the statistical yearbook of Chongqing in china and internet.)

3 Results

By utilizing the DEAP2.1 software, all outputs index of table 1 were subjected to empirical analysis in this study, then DEA provides a comprehensive evaluation of overall performance, table 2 and 3 present the CCR efficiency scores under constant return to scale(CRS), and technical efficiency scores, scale efficiency scores under variable return to scale. The results show that (a) as far as technical efficiency under constant returns to scale is concerned, six cities (i.e., Fuling, Kaixian, Yuyang, Wushan, Wuxi, and Shizhu) are relatively efficient, their efficiency scores are all equal to 1 and all slack variable is 0. that is to say, it indicated that they make the maximum output under the minimum investment. And we can see that the effective cities are less than the fifty percent in Three Gorges Reservoir area; (b) The average BCC technical efficiency (under variable returns to scale) used to measure the efficiency of resource allocation is 0.933, meanwhile, the deviation is very large, Thus, it suggested that there exists mainly some unbalance phenomenon in Three Gorges Reservoir area, rather than technique; (3) the scale efficiency scores as defined by the ratio CCR/BCC show large differences in Three Gorges Reservoir area, but compared with BCC technical efficiency, of the 15 cities, 5(Jiangjin, Changshou, Fengdu, Wulong and Zhongxian)have low BCC efficiency scores and relatively high scale efficiency scores, meaning that the overall inefficiency of the resource allocation on mass sport is caused by inefficient BCC efficiency rather than scale inefficiency, meanwhile, of 15 cities, 4 (Banan, Yubei, Wanzhou and Fengjie)have BCC efficiency scores equal to 1 and relatively low scale efficiency value, this can be interpreted as indicating that the CCR inefficiency values can be mainly attributed to disadvantageous conditions.

Table 2. The Efficiency scores for DEA models

DMU	CCR Efficiency	BCC Efficiency	Scale Efficiency	Efficiency variable
Banan	0.573	1.000	0.573	drs
Yubei	0.541	1.000	0.541	drs
Jiangjin	0.579	0.745	0.777	drs
Changshou	0.871	0.874	0.997	irs
Fuling	1.000	1.000	1.000	-
Fengdu	0.868	0.883	0.983	drs
Wulong	0.798	0.809	0.986	irs
Wanzhou	0.960	1.000	0.960	drs
Zhongxian	0.687	0.690	0.997	irs
Kaixian	1.000	1.000	1.000	-
Yunyang	1.000	1.000	1.000	-
Fengjie	0.888	1.000	0.888	drs
Wushan	1.000	1.000	1.000	-
Wuxi	1.000	1.000	1.000	-
Shizhu	1.000	1.000	1.000	-
Mean	0.851	0.933	0.913	

(*Note*: irs, - and drs are scale efficiency increasing, unchanged and decreasing respectively).

Table 3. The slack variable of resource allocation on mass sport in Three Gorges Reservoir area

DMU	s_1^-	s_2^-	s_3^-	s_1^+	s_2^+	s_3^+
Banan	0	0	0	0	0	0
Yubei	0	0	0	0	0	0
Jiangjin	23.113	0	0.120	0	0.059	0
Changshou	28.901	0	0.058	0	0.012	44.725
Fuling	0	0	0	0	0	0
Fengdu	3.060	0	0	932.188	0	0
Wulong	16.153	1.093	0	32.091	0	63.073
Wanzhou	0	0	0	0	0	0
Zhongxian	1.458	0.280	0	123.681	0	95.833
Kaixian	0	0	0	0	0	0
Yunyang	0	0	0	0	0	0
Fengjie	0	0	0	0	0	0
Wushan	0	0	0	0	0	0
Wuxi	0	0	0	0	0	0
Shizhu	0	0	0	0	0	0
mean	4.846	0.092	0.012	72.531	0.005	13.573

4 Conclusions

In this study, the efficiency of resource allocation on mass sport was analyzed in Three Gorges Reservoir area, we find that 6 cities are relatively efficiency, and the results were scale efficiency and BCC efficiency, that is to say, the total rate of efficiency is less than fifty percent, Therefore, this can indicated that the efficiency of resource allocation in mass sport is low in this area. Meanwhile, integrated with the BCC efficiency value and scale efficiency, we can also find that some cities should pay attention to the BCC efficiency, because the BCC efficiency is lower than scale efficiency (i.e. Jiangjin and Zhongxian, et al.), on the contrary, some cities should strength the scale efficiency (i.e., Banan and Yubei, et al.). in addition, of 15 cities, 6 exhibit constant returns to scale, 6 exhibit decreasing returns to scale, this show that these cities improve their efficiency of resource allocation by decreasing their size. Of 15 cities, 3 exhibit increasing returns to scale, they can improve their efficiency of resource allocation by increasing their size. Summary, the results of this research can help those involved in managing these resource allocation understand their relative efficiency and, therefore, respond by adjusting the input and output items in order to achieve the overall development of mass sport in urban and rural.

Acknowledgements. The research was funded by "2009 the young project of philosophy and social science in Chongqin", china (Grant No. 2009ZH12).

References

1. Stephen, W., Raudenbush, Chinnapat, B.: The Distribution of Resources for Primary Education and Its Consequences for Educational Achievement in Thailand. International Journal of Educational Research 17(2), 143–164 (1992)
2. Clint, C.: The Vital Role of Strategy in Strategic Human Resource Management Education. Human Resource Management Review 15(3), 200–213 (2005)
3. Yang, X.M., Tian, Y.P., Wang, H.: Theoretical Basis and Current Conditions for Coordinating Development of Mass Sports in Urban and Rural area. Journal of Guangzhou Sport University 1, 41–45 (2010)
4. Charnes, A., Cooper, W.W.: A Multiplicative Model of Efficiency Analysis. Socio-Economic Planning Sciences 16(5), 223–224 (1982)
5. Yu, T.: An Analysis on the Ttheory of the Framework of Resource Allocation of Mass Sport. Journal of Beijing Sport University 12, 16–19 (2009)
6. Li, Q.J., Wen, G.X.: The Current Situation and Countermeasures of Mass Sport in Three Gorges Reservoir Area. Journal of Southwest University for Nationalities 8, 377–378 (2005)

Research on Compensation Issues of Urban Resettlement in China

Gui-sheng Chen[1,2] and Li Tian[2]

[1] College of Resources Science and Technology, Beijing Normal University, China, 100875
[2] School of Public Administration, Tianjin University of Commerce, China, Tianjin, 300134

Abstract. The demolition of urban housing is of vital importance to urban construction planning. In today's society, house demolition compensation disputes are not rare occurrences, of which the most essential issue is the lack of protection of the legal rights of those whose houses are removed. Based on the system of compensation for house demolition, real estate appraisal system and government behavior, the paper puts forward some suggestions on perfecting the resettlement compensation law and improving assessment of market and regulating government behavior in order for a harmonious society.

Keywords: Resettlement, Compensation, Public interest.

1 Introduction

Urban resettlement compensation system is in the ownership of land ownership and housing built on the basis of separation, which is a unique system in our country. All the territory is owned by all the people in our country, so the urban land belongs to the state. Whereas many foreign countries have not set up a special urban resettlement compensation system, where the compensation range is stated in the land collection system.

1.1 Laws on Urban Resettlement Compensation in Developed Countries

France is the country who first implemented administrative compensation system. In 1789 the Universal Declaration of Human Rights announced: "Property is a inviolable and sacred right, except when the public needs to be legally determined is necessary, and the fair and advance compensation under the condition of anyone's property shall not be deprived."In 1977, "The French Code of expropriation" specifies that: "Compensation must include all the losses related to public collection, with an account of the direct, the materialized and the determined."[1] On the basis of the combination of French law with practice of executive compensation it can be learned that the basic administrative compensation of France reached the stage of full compensation.

Article 14 paragraph 3 of German Basic Law sets: "For public interest, the property can be levied. Public collection shall be in law or based on law and the law must also stipulate the type of compensation and the scope. Levy compensation shall be

Q. Zhou (Ed.): ISAEBD 2011, Part II, CCIS 209, pp. 395–401, 2011.

determined by the interests of the both on reasonable measure."[2] The law fully considers the dismantlers' legitimate rights and interests, and it fully reflects the fair compensation principle.

Provisions of the United States Constitution Fifth Amendment: "Except the proper procedure, government shall not deprive anyone of his life, liberty, or property. The reasonable compensation shall not expropriate private property for public use." American property law defines property rights as including real property rights and property future interests .Any damage to the real rights must make compensation ,which is reasonable compensation under the Constitution. From the relevant laws it can be seen that the American "reasonable compensation" principles are mainly in accordance with market price, including the current value of the property and the future profitability of the value. Ding Lin, a scholar in our country, said: "The principle is that the United States make reasonable compensation to the level that the original owner voluntarily sell their real estate property."[3]

1.2 On Urban Resettlement Compensation in China

Generally speaking, China's urban resettlement compensation analysis comes mainly from legal and sociological studies.

1.2.1 Legal Perspectives

The starting point in the relocation compensation, the demolition of the drawbacks of regulations is the core of public interests and commercial interests are not clearly defined. Xiao Yi think, " Thus ,in the name of public interests, local governments often Levy citizens of land and property ,then batch to developers and seek their own unfair interests, resulting in practice damaging the legitimate rights and interests of the right holder. " [4]Dou Xingxing says, "Public interest is the premise of the existence of executive compensation. Due to the lack of public interest criteria and identifying procedures , many land uses of non-public interests are likely to seek requisition collection in the name of public interest."[5]

Thus, to make our cities truly achieve a reasonable compensation, we must define the fundamental issue of the public interest and commercial ones. However, these scholars focused on the legal practice of the demolition, they failed to carry out enough in-depth study and research on theory.

1.2.2 Sociological Perspectives

Li Huai thinks, "Demolition means the occurrence of the migration process within the city. The dismantlers will be away from the full geopolitical they once lived with intimate relationship of acquaintances and community. So in that sense, the demolition has become way of life and sense of community which cannot be calculated in monetary level. "[6]Liu Yang says, "Those Demolished do not get reasonable compensation, which not only brings psychological imbalance, but is a source of disruption. It is difficult to implement the minimum living guarantee. "[7]Tang Daizhong and Ma Weifeng say that, "The problem is mainly that the compensation mechanism is unreasonable, the standards for compensation should be related to the degree of support from the residents."[8]

Chinese scholars have conducted many research and made lots of achievements, but meanwhile, thy have some disadvantages. The main problems, such as urban demolition of land use rights, opportunity costs, indirect costs and the real issue of compensation, are not fully resolved.

2 Problems of Urban Resettlement Compensation

In recent years, housing compensation disputes occur frequently, and even some people lost their lives to safeguard their legitimate rights and interests. The compensation problems are analyzed mainly from compensation system, evaluation system and government behaviour.

2.1 The Resettlement Compensation System

2.1.1 Unclear Definition of Public Interest

In 2001"Urban Housing Demolition Management Regulations" Article 1sets:"In order to strengthen the administration of urban house dismantlement, to safeguard the lawful rights and interests of the parties and to ensure that the construction projects proceed smoothly, this regulation is formulated. "We can see from the Ordinance that the main purpose of the demolition is to protect the construction project going on, without clear explanation of the use. Likewise, the lack of strictly defined public interests and commercial interests of dismantlement behavior cause some developers and some local governments to satisfy its self-interest, under the name of public interests, and to remove urban house.

2.1.2 Limited Scope of Compensation

The urban house dismantlement administrative regulations of our country urban-house removing compensation scope includes the premises and appendages, housing benefits and relocation expenses four aspects. But these four compensation scopes far not offset the dismantlers' loss. First, our country has the ownership of urban land. Citizens enjoy independent use right of state-owned land. No one should obtain this right for free through dismantlement. However, the existing regulation does not compensate for the land use right .The dismantlement didn't put good relationships among neighbors, convenient traffic, developed medical service and high quality education and other intangible assets as independent loss compensation.

2.1.3 Unreasonable Compensation Standard

According to Article 24 "Urban Housing Demolition Management Regulations", "Amount of monetary compensation should be determined according to the location of housing demolition, use, construction area." But, in practice, due to business interests and that of the local government, compensation standards are often lower. The most typical practice is to put the dismantlers housing evaluation price too low, and the evaluation price of the relocation housing too high, leading to the lowering-down of the living standards of demolition residents. This creates a large gap with foreign countries in reasonable, just and proper compensation .

2.2 Aspects of Real Estate Appraisal System

2.2.1 Lack of Reasonable Assessment Methods

In urban-house removing compensation, to different demolition and different house that is to be demolished, real estate appraisal method should be different .For example residential houses and profit-making room, the specific real estate appraisal method should be used to balance the dismantlement legal relationship of the interests of both parties. For this the existing laws and regulations do not have specific expression. In reality, due to different understandings and different parameters, large difference about report results by different rating agencies occur .Therefore, we must choose specific provisions of assessment methods to ensure that legal and orderly conduct of the work. This is the loophole in legislation. [9]

2.2.2 Lack of Independence on the Part of Rating Agencies

Most real estate development companies have some close and subtle relationship with real estate administrative agencies, especially some state-owned development company. In this way, the real estate rating agencies make friends with the demolition of real estate management and development company .Unscientific nature of the mechanism make the rating agencies favor the interests of the real estate development companies. They thus lose independence, not to mention fairness, impartiality or justice.

2.3 Government Behaviour

2.3.1 Excessive Improper Government Intervention

For most Chinese people, the house is their most important property .However, in maintaining their legitimate rights and interests the dismantlers face the power of the government's intervention. Through the issuance of dismantlement permit, determining the compensation price and even the adoption of some compulsory measures, the government damage the dismantled' interests, placing the dismantler a strong position, making it impossible for those dismantled to negotiate equally with the dismantlers. [9]

2.3.2 Government Compulsory Demolition

Urban Housing Demolition Management Regulations" make it clear that the dismantling institutions are those with house demolition permit. But in reality, demolition by the government department directly is quite common. Compensation and resettlement does not reach the designated position, houses inferior in quality, discontent widespread among those dismantled. Many of those dismantled are not opposed to dismantlement, they are just not contented with the settlement. Regulations not complied with, the illegal and compulsory dismantlement with government acquiescence or support arouse agony among the public. [10]

3 Suggestions on Constructing Perfect Compensation Mechanism

As compensation for house demolition in the city's legal practice, the relocation compensation standard mechanism is imperfect. Unfair real estate assessment, improper intervention by government, the shortage of house supply for the demand of those dismantled, and other reasons cause the occurrence of many disputes, which results in social instability and problems in development. To this end, the following suggestions are put forward in the hope of relocation compensation as soon as possible to resolve problems arising.

3.1 Strictly Defined Public Interests

A clear distinction between public interest and commercial interest should be drawn and the government intervention and compulsory demolition should be strictly limited to the demolition of public interest. China can learn from the relevant foreign law to modify the "Urban Housing Demolition Ordinance." as soon as possible. It should be clearly defined that only in the following situations can the government practice compulsory demolition: State or military use, urban infrastructure and public welfare undertakings, the infrastructure supported by the state land and legal provisions of other public land .Only through strictly defining the public interest can the commercial use of land by the name of the public be eliminated.

3.2 To Establish and Improve Urban Resettlement Law

Urban Housing Demolition Management Regulations is only the State Council' administrative rules and regulations, which has no legal effect. It does not make specific provisions about standard for compensation and the compensation principle .In practice, there are many legal loopholes, causing the demolition disputes. Therefore, our country is now in urgent need for the establishment of the urban house dismantlement laws, not only to improve the use of land compensation standard, to expand sphere of compensation, to concretize the compensation standard , but also to develop detailed rules and conditions of compensation method .Only in this way can those who dismantle be prevented from using the loopholes in the law to harm the interests of those dismantled, reducing the relocation disputes.

3.3 To Establish and Improve Assessment System

Improve the real estate assessment in a market-like method. Our current legislation on evaluation method lack clear and unified regulation on assessing method, which leads to differences in assessment due to the application of different methods. Therefore it's necessary to legislate the assessment methods .In real life, the market comparison method is a way close to the market price, we should set up an assessment system with market comparison as principle and the supplement of other assessment methods.

Establish the legal liability system of rating agencies and their staff. If found prior consultations with the dismantler, the relevant agent or agency should be published according to law. If Less serious, the one who is responsible should not be allowed, within a few years, to take the industry and pay the damage to those dismantled. In serious cases, he will be criminally responsible.

3.4 To Transform Government Function and Establish Limited Government Liability

Under the condition of market economy, the government should be limited one, whose function should be to provide public materials which market can not. In city construction, the government should play the basic functions such as the land use planning and land use control .Only for certain public need, can an individual citizen be deprived of his private land use rights. Even for specific public need, if the problem can be solved through negotiations with the citizen, market methods should be applied to obtain private property.

3.5 Perfecting the Resettlement Program

In the demolition process, those dismantled have no opportunities and chances to express their opinions, and many relocation issues are decided entirely by the government or even by developers. Thus, China's relocation compensation hearing system should be introduced and those dismantled should be fully listened to so as to ensure that they have the right to participate in the demolition process with the supervision of public opinion.

3.6 Introducing Foreign Public Development Systems

The public development system extensively used in western countries weakens commercial color and emphasizes the government's public development activities .Many countries strictly distinguish the purposes of land use .The land for commercial use does not adopt administrative collection to obtain, only for the public interests, can the government get involved.

Public development system established in China will not only help the people to understand and support the demolition work, improve the urban reconstruction of economic and social benefits, but also can regulate government behavior to avoid the abuse of power. Therefore, we should consider making our urban house dismantlement system for the public development policy. [8]

4 Conclusion

Compensation for urban resettlement is a very important issue, along with the construction of our democratic rule of law. Therefore, it is very important to improve the house demolition compensation system. The compensation would be very unfair if they can not reach their original standard of living. Thus, conflicts can not be fundamentally resolved. Therefore, we should further improve the compensation of house demolition regulations, formulate unified compensation standard to execute fair compensation, which is important to the social stability in our country.

Acknowledgement. This paper is a periodical achievement of Research on Inter-government Relationships in View of Regional Cooperative Governance: A Case Study of Capital Metropolitan Economic Area, a project funded by China Postdoctoral Science Foundation(No.20110490013).

References

1. Wang, M.: French Administrative Law, pp. 366–393. China Politics and Law University Press, Beijing (2003)
2. Maurer, H., Guo, J.: (traanslation): General Part of Administrative Jurisprudence, p. 689. Law press, Beijing (2000)
3. Lin, D.: Dismantlement in the United States. Community 15, 33 (2005) (in Chinese)
4. Xiao, Y.: Chongqing City of Compensation for House Demolition. Master Thesis. Southwest university, Chongqing, p. 28 (2007) (in Chinese)
5. Dou, X.: Talk About the Our Country Urban-house Removing Compensation System Consummation. Journal of Jiangxi University of Finance and Economics 4, 120 (2009)
6. Li, H.: Social Demolition of Conflict of Interest: A Sociological Analysis. Northwestern National Research 3, 57 (2005)
7. Liu, Y.: Administration of Urban House Demolition Compensation System. Master Thesis. Anhui: Anhui University, pp. 21–41 (2007) (in Chinese)
8. Tang, D., Ma, W.: Based on Evolutionary Game Theory of Urban-house Removing Compensation Mechanism Study of City. Finance and Trade Research 6, 25–28 (2007)
9. Wang, K., et al.: Legal Problems of the Urban House Demolition. The China legal system publishing house, Beijing (2007)
10. Shen, K.: Executive Compensation Study, p. 245. Law press, Beijing (2004)

Key Issues in China's Sustainable Urbanization

Gui-sheng Chen and Yun Mei

School of Public Administration, Tianjin University of Commerce,
China, Tianjin, 300134

Abstract. Sustainable urbanization is an important measure to ensure the harmonious development of China's economy and society. However, many problems exist in the process of urbanization, such as misunderstanding of the functions of city government, deteriorated urban ecosystem, lacking of rational planning of urban land, the urban-rural dual system, uncoordinated urban and rural construction, and so on. Therefore, corresponding system must be improved to ensure the rapid and rational development of sustainable urbanization.

Keywords: sustainable urbanization, ecological environment, functions of government.

1 Introduction

Urbanization on economic and social progress in developed countries has already been evidence in promoting. It is becoming China's regional economic growth and source, as the main theme of modernization. Urbanization in China is in a period of accelerating development and in the world is facing Increasingly, the pressures of the rare population, resources and environmental and the impact of globalization. Under resources, environment, population and many other restricted condition, whether China can go out of the road of a healthy development city or not ,which is only related to the realization of building overall well-off society goal ,but also China's major contribution to global sustainable development.

China's future economic and social harmonious development still depends on the rapid development of urbanization, and thus which is bound to call for China's urbanization to go its sustainable development pattern. Sustainable urbanization is to meet in the city contemporary and future and each generation people's demand as their goal. But with the passage of time and the continuous development of the city, the content and level of human needs will continue increasing and improving Therefore, the sustainable urbanization itself implied constantly dynamic evolution process from low level to high level. The essence of sustainable urbanization is grasping and solving the coordinative development of social economy between a natural and subsystems, and between urban system and the surrounding areas such as external systems and achieving urban complex ecosystem optimization development, which ultimately improve people's welfare and quality of life [1].

Q. Zhou (Ed.): ISAEBD 2011, Part II, CCIS 209, pp. 402–408, 2011.

2 Key Issues of Sustainable Urbanization

Sustainable urbanization is not only related to the quality, the degree and level of China's economic and social development, but also to the information society and the construction of a harmonious society. The progress of human civilization and the result of sustainable urbanization of developed countries suggest that if it unswervingly follow the road of sustainable urbanization, it can meet the needs of people continuously improving the material life and spiritual and cultural life, which achieve the necessary scientific approach of overall national objectives. Therefore, we mustefforts to recognize key problems existed during the development process and puts forward the corresponding solutions.

2.1 Misunderstanding in China about Sustainable Urbanization

Currently, in the process of sustainable urbanization in China there are four major misunderstandings: (1)It is thought that urban development will inevitably lead to urban and rural isolation and speed up the dual structure of society. (2)It is thought That urban development must cause a "urban disease". (3)It is thought that the development of large cities must be strictly controlled. (4)It is thought that the result of urbanization should not be distinguished in urban and rural areas and balanced distribution and blossom everywhere. [2]

2.2 Inaccurate Functions of City Government

Full play the functions of cities also depends on the reasonable position of government functions and full implementation: The main functions of city government should also assume five roles: (1)the development of sophisticated urban planners, (2)effective public goods and services providers, (3) governance by a strong public order, (4)noble spirit of the advocate and protector of the city cultural characteristics, (5)active agents of foreign cooperation and exchange.[3]

However, these functions have not been in the city government functions effectively achieved. Currently, cities across China to speed up the development momentum of the large, according to incomplete statistics, nearly a hundred cities across the country put forward the goal into an international metropolis. Therefore, in many places at the city the huge amounts of money is spent on cities of the planning and construction, blindly expanded the city scale, pursued the number of large cities and the urbanization is turned into Zaochengyundong. In some places in order to expand the city limits, but through administrative means, not through market means, simply withdraw from County to City, county to change the area. Thus, scale of the city have been expanding at the same time, the city's industrial clustering functions, business transactions function, social services, economic radiation function has not improved accordingly; In addition, the city government also failed to effectively provide excellent infrastructure, well-developed market service system, adequate resources for education, good public order and other services.

2.3 Urbanization, Environmental Pollution and Destruction of Urban Ecosystem

Sustainable urbanization requires people to resource conservation and environmentally friendly according to the requirements of production and lifestyle adjustments, within the ecological carrying capacity to determine their consumption standards, continue to reduce the pressure on resources and the environment.

A prerequisite for a sustainable urbanization environment is that it should not pose a threat to current or future users. And the objectives commonly associated with the idea of sustainable urban development are reduction of threats to personal health and the natural environment are [4]. Ecological conditions based on the survival of both cities, but also the fundamental quality of modern cities. Urbanization should protect the natural environment, and create a pleasant living environment. However, some places pursuit One-snidely in the pace of urbanization, increased long-term reliance on investment and material input of the extensive economic growth mode, resulting in urban ecological environment coming up, such as the growing shortage of water resources, a significant increase of sewage and waste ,abnormal climate change, emissions and noise pollution remains high, many cities discharge of pollutants exceeds greatly the environmental capacity. [5]Ecological carrying capacity was close to the limit, urban ecosystems have been severely damaged. Environmental pollution and ecological damage in some areas has become a harm people's health, impede economic development and social stability is an important factor, as the process of urbanization must be given to resolve the outstanding issues. So how in the rapid urbanization and the implementation of sustainable urban development has become one of the key strategies.

2.4 Lack of Rational Planning in Land Use

At present, the acceleration of urbanization in China, making China's urban land rare in the world is facing a severe environment. On the one hand, the state is in the acceleration of industrialization and urbanization stage of development, urban land expansion is the inevitable demand of economic development and improving people's quality of life On the other hand, urban expansion will inevitably have to take the land resources that in China are very scarce and valuable.

Land use issues of China's urbanization are highlighted in some areas:(1) Extensive land use, land-use efficiency is low. In an old historical town, there are a lot of idle and unused places, and use greatly the levy phenomenon of extensive land. (2)City land transfer is more prevalent, but lack of legal basis to give guidance. In practice, the city's collective land transfer more common. However, the existing legal basis and practical needs is a big vacancy. Laws and regulations of land management have lagged behind the actual social and economic development. (3) Structure of using Land is irrational and layout of the building is messy. The survey found that layout confusion of using land space is more common, Unction partition is not obvious, Industrial, administrative, commercial, residential, storage and other types of land interspersed, staggered, mutual influence and interference with each other .In particular, some heavily polluting factories mixed in between the living space, which is dirty, chaotic and poor problem highlighted.[6]

2.5 "Dual Structure" of Urban and Rural Areas

Urbanization in China started in the early day, overall resources in the community are extremely limited, only the expense of the development of agriculture raises the high investment in heavy industry.

This was indeed achieved results, but due to the continuation of related systems, the formation of urban and rural social structure resulted in the weak of agricultural development. Urban-rural dual structure led to division of the land system, the household registration system, administrative system, the social security system and the traditional concept of production and life impeded the flow of the wider population and concentration, which limited developing of capabilities of towns, but also wasted a great of land and other public resources, and in turn, has constrained the development of industry concentration. In addition, in the process of rapid urbanization, with the urban infrastructure and industrial projects take a lot of land, which result in more and more farmers losing their jobs and lands .As constraints of the level of farmers knowledge and technology , it is very difficult to the employment for those farmers of stability, resettlement land-lost .Thus setting effective management systems, solving the urban-rural dual structure is further resolving the employment problem good land-lost farmers. Helping farmers find self development way out is not only the economic issue, but also related to social stability.

2.6 Uncoordinated Urban and Rural Construction

The purpose of speeding up the urbanization builds not more cities, but promotes the coordinated development of urban and rural areas.However, in real developing, some developed areas of the city absorbed a lot of strong labor force in rural areas and imported technical talents of many rural, which has left many sick and elderly of villagers in rural areas. In addition, each district speed up construction of new countryside and had made some achievements but owing to lack of local financial resources and social capital, rural transformation and environmental improvement of villages are still not ideal. Metro construction of the city is changing fast, but new rural country is still relatively backward. The new rural development and urban construction is a big gap. Therefore, urbanization should coordinated and with new rural construction to achieve the common development of urban and rural [3].

3 Measures for Sustainable Urban Development

3.1 Priorities to Citizens, Ecology and Environment

Sustainable urbanization construction needs to explore "people-oriented" principle and to satisfy demand of people's all-round development as standard of the construction measure and change the past "GDP first", "see things but not people " the disadvantages. City as a product of development of human society, its development is built around the social main body to launch Industrialization, urbanization, social modernization is actually the process of civilization evolution of the Trinity, so one of the ultimate goal of the city is to create the most appropriate living environment. Therefore, in the process of urbanization, we need to reference lessons of the world sustainable urban development and adhering to the principle of "ecological and environmental priorities" promote urban development, environmental protection as an important value orientation. We can not sacrifice the expense of the environment, to pursuit blindly economic growth. Only putting the "ecological and environmental priorities" into the "people first" philosophy being can ensure sustainable development.

3.2 Establishment of Government System in Urbanization

Sustainable development itself is fundamental changes of a development model, which must be accompanied by innovation of technological and system. As the distribution center of various elements, the city often means market competition of more intense and human resources of more quality, which to some extent, help the power and ability of stimulate system and technological innovation. Therefore, we need to further deepen the reform, transformation of government functions, improve system innovation and protection mechanism, play the market in a fundamental role of the allocation of resources, realize resource to flows through regions to promote the urbanization development and rational division of each city [7]. Simplify and reduce setting standards of the urban, so that small towns are upgraded to a city to provide the scientific threshold; actively cultivate new cities and system of linking urban and rural areas, and create economies of scale. Through institutional innovations to promote the rational allocation of production factors, the development of economic and social and resources and environmental protection has been a win-win.

3.3 From Extensive Mode to Intensive Mode of City Development

Urban construction begin with the Combination way of production factors, the structure and as soon as possible from the existing track, or "freeze" of the extensive development get out, to achieve gradually intensifying development.

Through technological progress and improve management, improve quality and efficiency of factors of production to achieve economic growth, the assembly of combination of the elements, coordination and optimization, conductive the implementation of adjustment of economic restructuring, promoting technology level, promoting policies and measures of urbanization, pursuitting efficiency and effectiveness of development achieving the overall improvement of the level of development. With the advance of industrialization, there has been the increase dramatically raw material costs, energy, land costs, wage labor costs, environmental costs, and social costs. So, extensive mode of growth can only be changed by technological innovation and industrial upgrading to absorb costs, which can improve the ability of market changes. Through the allocation of coordination of resources form a coordinated industry and industry structure.

3.4 The Positive Role of Market in Urbanization

Market is the main means of vector of the factor of production, intermediate products and final consumer goods distribution, configuration, exchange To break the urban-rural dual system, eliminate elements of production between urban and rural areas to the free flow of various institutional and policy barriers, unified rural markets with urban markets, construct integrations factor market of the urban and rural.[8] In addition, in the process of urbanization, we need to properly handle the relationship between the question of government and market, and resection for the laws of the market and playing the role of government guidance. Strengthening the Government's service functions create an environment focused, and by improving infrastructure to develop human resources, taxation, finance and other related policies, vigorously develop modern service industry, strengthen regional planning and management for blocks together of the comprehensive service function, and rational distribution, dislocation development.

3.5 Compound Urbanization

Urbanization and urban development has its own track and regular pattern and should follow the urban to development regular pattern、rules of market economy, environment optimizing rule and law of social development, and to diversify the city complex development path. In the urban system construction, we must not artificially encourage or restrict certain types of urban development, as long as the law is in line with the urbanization should support. Faced characteristics of stage of the current economic and social development, the government should encourage and support a positive number big, middle development of the city. Through the function of urban improvement form a reasonable large, medium and small urban layout so that playing different the role of the sizes of different cities. In particular, encourage the population of the city in more than 100 million development of content-type. In addition, in the urban function and construction of spatial layout, through the industrialization achieve urbanization of the employment structure That is through deepening and industrialization to solve conversion of the vast majority of the rural population and to solute the city's total employment capacity and population issues so that achieve conflicts and contradictions of the urban population, resources, environment and economic growth to promote sustainable development of various types of cities.

4 Conclusions

Sustainable urbanization is dynamic process of orderly of an urban ecosystem structure, processes, and functions from simple to complex, from unsustainable to sustainable. If the construction of new cities in China is mainly producing goods for other countries, these cities will be unsustainable and will lead sustainable of the whole society. If urban production is mainly used to meet their own needs, they will be more sustainable.

With the concept of sustainable development to guide the practice of urbanization, we should recognize that: (1)Urbanization in line with the requirements of sustainable development, (2)The city's aggregate effect Focus on the effectiveness of sustainable development, (3)Metropolitan is the basis layer for achieving sustainable development Faced process of rapid urbanization and the forecasts the optimistic urbanization, we need to calmly consider whether the city does have enough resources to carry so much of the population or not. That is mastering the rhythm of the City to avoid "urban disease." of big cities.

Sustainable urbanization takes into account the modernization of infrastructure, modernization of management, modern lifestyle and a series of integrated system. Concerned about the pace of urbanization in the same time, we should pay more attention to the sustainable development of urbanization, Among population, land and water to reach the rational allocation, it protect rational structure, process efficient, perfect function of urban ecosystem, and promote sustainable development of economic and social, and construction of harmonious society.

Acknowledgement. This paper is a periodical achievement of "On Paradigm of Regional Governance In the framework of Comprehensive Reform", a project funded by National Ministry of Education(NO.10YJCZH009).

References

1. Cui, S., et al.: Theoretical thinking on urbanization and sustainable urbanization. Urban Studies 3, 19 (2010)
2. Niu, W., Li, Q.: The understanding of strategy of new Chinese urbanization. Impact of Science on Ssociety 1, 16–17 (2010)
3. Yang, J., Zhao, S.: Study on orientation of Chinese city governments' functions basing on urban basic functions. Chinese Public Administration 1, 88–90 (2008)
4. Cozens, P.M.: Sustainable Urban Development and Crime Prevention Through Environmental Design for the British City. Towards an Effective Urban Environmentalism for the 21st Century. Cities 19(2), 131 (2002)
5. Zhao, H., Wen, M.: On irresistible trends of Chinese urbanization development. Social Sciences in Ningxia 9, 82 (2009)
6. Tingting, S., Anna, S.: The research into issues of land utilization extension in urbanization. Social Sciences Review 10, 69 (2009) (in Chinese)
7. Zhou, Y.: The characteristic description, analysis and assessment on Chinese urbanization. Gansu Social Sciences 3, 138 (2010)
8. Cai, W.: The approach innovations in rural industrialization and urbanization sustainable development in China. Productivity Research 12, 34 (2009)

Measuring the Development of Life Insurance Market with the Adjusted Life Density: An Empirical Study on China's Regional Markets

Lina Yu[1] and Yan Guo[2]

[1] School of Finance, Renmin University, 100872, Beijing, China
lina.yu@ruc.edu.cn
[2] School of Management, Tianjin University, 300072, Tianjin, China
yanguo@tju.edu.cn

Abstract. China has seen rapid growth in its insurance market over the last 30 years. But how to measure the development of its many regional markets properly has yet to reach a consensus. This paper investigated the issue by introducing a new indicator- Adjusted Life Density. It is built on the basis of a panel-data regression where factors forcing the markets can be recognized. The idea behind is that a well developed insurance market is not the one who realized large amount of premium but who is well integrated with the local economic and social environment. Under the new indicator the common judgment that Eastern China is doing better than the central and the western parts does not hold. On the contrary Adjusted Life Density tells the eastern has been left behind.

Keywords: Life Insurance Market Development, Adjusted Life Density, China's Regional Markets.

1 Introduction

China's insurance market has been growing vigorously over the last 30 years. In 2010 the market reached 1.45 trillion RMB while the life sector realized 1.05 trillion. However when we look at this countries' many regional markets, it turns out to be a different picture i.e. the markets' variances are significant according to those popular indicators—insurance premium, insurance density and insurance penetration. Take 2010 for example, Guangdong province got the first place with 123.2 billion in premium, While Qinghai remained last(Tibet excluded) due to its relatively tiny market, i.e.2.6 billion.

But is the judgment reasonable? It might not be the case. We should first ask what we are actually talking about when we consider the development of a life insurance market. Is it simply the market volume or something more meaningful? In this paper we suggest a new indicator in measuring the development of the life insurance market under which the adaptability of the market with local economic and social environment is of the most concern. And in this way forces driving the markets, such as income level, mortality rate, dependency ratio, etc. can be recognized and analyzed.

Q. Zhou (Ed.): ISAEBD 2011, Part II, CCIS 209, pp. 409–414, 2011.

This paper is structured as follows: Section 2 identifies the factors determining the development of China's regional life insurance markets using a panel data regression. Section 3 constructs the new indicator—Adjusted Life Density based on the results in Section 2 and ranks the regional markets according to the new indicator. Finally Section 4 presents the conclusion.

2 Factors Determining the Development of Life Insurance Market

2.1 Life Insurance Market Determinants

In this section we describe the theoretical underpinnings of our empirical study and different forces hypothesized to drive the development of life insurance markets.

Income. Life insurance consumption should rise with income for several reasons. First, typically higher income leads to higher consumption, thus creating a greater demand for insurance to safeguard the income potential of the insured and the expected consumption of his or her dependents. Second, higher income can result in higher level of saving, thus greater desire for life insurance. Finally, increasing income may enable people to allocate a larger share of their income to retirement-related life insurance product. Several studies have shown a positive relationship between life insurance and income (Beck& Webb(2003);Sen and Madheswaran(2007); Outreville(1996); Browne& Kim(1993).Here we take GDP per capital as a proxy for income and assume it is positively correlated with insurance consumption.

Expected inflation rate. Expected inflation rate is typically negatively correlated with the life insurance consumption as insurance benefit and the return on life insurance products are both subject to inflation uncertainty especially in the long run. Browne and Kim (1993), Li and others(1990), Outreville(1996 and Beck and Webb(2003) find a negative relationship between expected inflation rate and life insurance consumption. In this paper we use the inflation rate over the prior 3 years as a proxy for expected inflation rate and assume it is negatively correlated with the life insurance consumption.

Risk aversion. Higher level of risk aversion results in greater demand for life insurance coverage to safeguard the possible interruptions of income and consumption. In this paper we take higher education enrollment ratio as a proxy for risk aversion and assume it is positively correlated with life insurance consumption.

Mortality rate. Lower level of mortality rate means reduced costs of mortality-risk related insurance products, thus may encourage life insurance consumption. Further lower mortality rate is another way of saying longer life expectancy, so we may assume a rise in the saving-related insurance products and annuities. In this paper we assume mortality rate is negatively correlated with life insurance consumption.

Young dependency ratio. A higher young dependency ratio may increase the demand for mortality coverage and decrease the demand for saving-related insurance. Beenstock and others(1986), Browne and Kim(1993),and Truett and Truett(1990) find that young dependency ratio is positively correlated with life insurance consumption.

While Sen and Madheswaran(2007) shows there's no significant relationship between the two. In this paper we assume young dependency ratio is positively correlated with life insurance consumption.

2.2 Model Specification and Empirical Findings

The empirical study is based on a set of panel data of China's 30 provinces (Tibet excluded) over 11 years ranging from 1999 through 2009. We use life density as the measure of life insurance consumption. The regression equation takes the log-linear form and is specified as followed:

$$\begin{aligned} \ln lifdens_{it} &= \beta_0 + \beta_1 \ln percapGDP_{it} + \beta_2 \ln expinf_{it} \\ &+\beta_3 \ln edu_{it} + \beta_4 \ln mort_{it} + \beta_5 \ln ydep_{it} + u_{it}\,. \end{aligned} \tag{1}$$

Where, $lifdens_{it}$ = density of life insurance in province i in year t,
$percapGDP_{it}$ = GDP per capita in province i in year t,
$expinf_{it}$ = expected inflation rate in province i in year t,
edu_{it} = rate of higher education in province i in year t,
$mort_{it}$ = mortality rate in province i in year t,
$ydep_{it}$ = young dependency rate in province i in year t,
u_{it} = random error term.

Table 1 reports the estimated parameters and corresponding t-statistics. The income variable (which is GDP per capital) and the risk aversion variable (which is measured by the rate of higher education in the population) are statistically significant and positively correlated with life insurance consumption which is consistent with our assumption. As income increases, life insurance product becomes more affordable. And people with higher education are more likely able to identify risks and understand the insurance policies, thus protect themselves with insurance products against any possible interruption in their income.

Table 1. Determinants of the Development of Life Insurance in a Panel, 1999-2009, Full Sample, Fixed Effects

Variable	Parameter	T-Statistic
Constant	-3.86***	-3.07
percapGDP	0.98***	14.13
expinf	1.72	1.20
edu	0.25***	4.21
mort	0.15	0.65
ydep	-1.05***	-6.88
Adjusted R-squared	0.97	
F-statistic	307.72	

*** Significant at 1 percent level.

The young dependency variable is reported statistically significant but negatively correlated with life insurance consumption which is not consistent with our assumption. But it is reasonable anyway since young dependency rate may have mixed effects on the life insurance consumption. Higher young dependency rate may lead to less savings due to a relatively smaller portion of working population, thus make the insurance products less affordable.

The model shows the expected inflation rate and mortality rate are not statistically significant correlated with the life insurance consumption.

3 New Indicator Construction and Ranking

3.1 Constructing the New Indicator—Adjusted Life Density

A new indicator in measuring the development of life insurance market is built based on the results above. The idea is we can not only look at the market volume when considering the development of life insurance markets. Since the markets have been evolving to date as a joint effort of several forces, i.e. the income level, risk aversion and dependency rate etc., according to the empirical analysis above. Focusing on any single factor can lead to misunderstanding, especially when comparing the differences across the many regional markets.

Here we introduce a new indicator—Adjusted Life Density, which can better embrace the determinants driving the markets and is able to measure whether the insurance market is adaptable to local economic and social environment or not. It is computed as followed:

$$\text{Adjusted Life Density} = \text{Life Insurance Density}/\text{Estimated Life density} \quad (2)$$

Where, the estimated life density is the fitted value of life density obtained from the regression in section 2. The fitted value implies the level of development of the life insurance market which is adapted with the underlying economic and social environment thus can be seen as "the market potential". In this way the new indicator is a measurement of the variance between the actual market development (which is depicted by the life density) and the market potential. Therefore, a market with a higher value of the Adjusted Life Density is considered doing better than one with a lower value.

3.2 Ranking Based on Adjusted Life Density

In order to better understand the development of China's life insurance market, we look at the variances of its 30 regional markets measured by the Adjusted Life Density. We are to see which province has a better suited insurance market in the context of local economic and social environment. Table 2 reports the ranking under the Adjusted Life Density in comparison with that under the traditional indicators, say the life premium and the life density in the year 2009.

Table 2. Rankings comparison in 2009

Province	Adjusted Life Density	Life Density	Life Premium
Hebe	1	10	6
Chongqing	2	8	18
Sichuan	3	16	8
Henan	4	18	7
Anhui	5	22	12
Hunan	6	23	11
Shanxi	7	9	14
Heilongjiang	8	13	15
Shandong	9	12	5
Yunnan	10	26	21
Gansu	11	24	26
Guizhou	12	30	27
Xinjiang	13	19	23
Hubei	14	14	10
Jiangxi	15	25	20
Shanghai	16	1	4
Guangdong	17	5	1
Guangxi	18	28	25
Fujian	19	11	16
Jilin	20	15	19
Beijing	21	2	3
Liaoning	22	7	13
Hainan	23	27	29
Jiangsu	24	3	2
Ningxia	25	20	28
Zhejiang	26	6	9
Shaanxi	27	17	17
Qinghai	28	29	30
Neimeng	29	21	24
Tianjin	30	4	22

Here we come to several interesting findings. First, contrary to the traditional understanding, those mega-cities as Beijing and Shanghai are not on the top of the rankings at all, but in the middle and lower-middle classes most of the time. It indicates that the development of the insurance markets in these cites are not compatible with their potential which can be determined by the income level, higher education, dependency rate etc. Second, provinces in the central and western parts of China as Sichuan, Henan, and Shanxi etc. have seen great developing in their life insurance markets respectively. Despite their relatively smaller volume, the markets are actually doing well in the way that they are quite suited to the local economic and social development.

4 Conclusion

In this paper we introduce a new measurement of the development of life insurance markets, i.e. the Adjusted Life Density. The idea behind is that a well developed insurance market is not the one who realized large amount of premium but who is well integrated with the local economic and social environment. Under the new indicator we reach several interesting conclusions: First, contrary to the traditional understanding, those mega-cities as Beijing and Shanghai are not among the best players at all, but in the middle and lower-middle classes most of the time. Second, provinces in the central and western parts of China as Sichuan, Henan, and Shanxi etc. have seen great developing in their life insurance markets respectively.

These results have important implications for the market and the regulatory body as well. The life insurance carriers may reallocate their resources geographically to take advantages of those markets who have yet live to their "market potential", i.e. to better stress the markets who've got low scores on the Adjusted Life Density. And China's insurance authority can be equipped with a better tool in assessing the development and variances of China's regional life insurance markets, thus may place itself in a better place in making regional policies and guidelines as well.

Acknowledgement. We are deeply grateful to Professor Bo Hu for his instructive advice and useful suggestions on this paper. And we are happy to any further discussion on this topic. Yan Guo is the corresponding author, her e-mail is yanguo@tju.edu.cn.

References

1. Beck, T., Webb, I.: Economic, Demographic, and Institutional Determinants of Life Insurance Consumption across Countries. The World Bank Economic Review 17(1), 51–88 (2003)
2. Browne, M.J., Kim, K.: An International analysis of Life Insurance Demand. The Journal of Risk and Insurance 60(4), 616–634 (1993)
3. Lewis, F.D.: Dependents and the Demand for Life Insurance. The American Economic Review 79, 3 (1989)
4. Outreville, J.F.: Life Insurance Markets in Developing Countries. The Journal of Risk and Insurance 63(2), 263–278 (1996)
5. Sen, S., Madheswaran, S.: Are Life insurance Demand Determinants Valid for Selected Asian Economies and India? In: 11th Annual Meeting of APRIA (2007)
6. Truett, D.B., Truett, L.J.: The Demand for Life Insurance in Mexico and The United States: A Comparative Study. The Journal of Risk and Insurance 57(2), 321–328 (1990)

Residential Demand, Investment Demand and Property Price in China

Yu Guan[1,2]

[1] School of Economics, Huazhong University of Science and Technology
[2] School of Economics and Management, Heilongjiang Institute of Science and Technology
TangchangStr. 1, Songbei district, 150000 Harbin, China
1269033590@qq.com

Abstract. This paper investigates the relationship between property demand and property price in China. Using a unique database that includes information for 29 provinces, autonomous regions and municipalities from 1998 to 2009, the author finds evidence that residential demand is the basic driver of Chinese property price rise, which is more obvious in lower per capita GDP area than in higher one. Therefore, the author believes that "Limit to Buy" can only work in a short time, but in a long run it is effective to increase supply.

Keywords: property price, investment demand, residential demand.

1 Introduction

To stabilize property price, Chinese government has launched a lot of policies in recent years, including recent "New Eight Terms" and "Limit to Buy". But the result is not ideal. Thus, it is meaningful to deeply analyse the causes of property price rise and help to adjust policy timely and effectively.

Earlier researches on the relationship between macroeconomics and property price commonly used simple or composite indicators, such as Gottlieb(1976) , Mankiw and Weil(1989). But, simple or composite indicators are lack of solid theoretical basis.

Since 1990, Stock-Flow Model and Representative Agent Model has been two important models to analyse the relationship. Their Reduced Form Models are alike in form. Downs(1993), Ortalo-Magné and Rady(2004), Gavin etc.(2006), Major etc.(2008) and Oriol Aspachs-Braconsetc (2010) all studied based on the two models. They investigated the relationship between property price and population, income, age structure, credit limit, space, subprime debt quantity, mortgage loan scale etc..

Domestic studies about property price are mainly after 2000 and follow abroad, such as Shen Yue and Liu Hongyu (2004), Zhou Jingkui(2005), Liang Yunfang and Gao Tiemei(2007), Yi Xianrong(2009) and Zhang Ming(2009).

This paper investigates the relationship between property demand and property price, tries to reveal the basic driver of property price rise in China, using regional data from 1998 to 2009 and applying a Fixed-Effect panal data model, for the purpose of more effective regulation.

Q. Zhou (Ed.): ISAEBD 2011, Part II, CCIS 209, pp. 415–421, 2011.

2 Model and Data

The Reduced Form Models of Stock-Flow Model and Representative Agent Model are similar. The basic model is equ.(1). P, the property price. INC, per capita income. POP, population. VAC, vacancy. UNE, unemployment rate. COST, housing construction cost. X, other exogenous variables.

$$P = f\ (\text{INC},\ \text{POP},\ \text{VAC},\ \text{UNE},\ \text{COST},\ X)\ . \tag{1}$$

This paper also uses the basic model, with the emphasis on residential demand. The model is equ.(2). The dependent variable is P_{it} representing average commercial housing sale price or average residential housing sale price. INCI, urban per capita disposable income. INCO, rural per capita net income. POP, Chinese population.

$$P_{it} = f\ (\text{INCI}_{it},\ \text{INCO}_{it},\ \text{POP}_{it},\ \text{CR}_{it},\ \text{CLF}_{it},\ \text{INVE}_{it},\ \text{SH}_{it},\ \text{LB}_{it},\ P_{it}/P_{it-1}) \tag{2}$$

CR, urbanization rate which equals urban population divided by total population. CLF, urban land user tax. INVE, house developing investment. LB, loan balance of financial institutions. P_{it}/P_{it-1}, expected revenge rate of property investment. SH, commercial property or residential property sale area. Data comes from “The New China 60 Years Statistics Compiled”, CCER financial database and 1999-2010 national and local statistics.

Average commercial property sale price and average residential property sale price are the most complete regional data from 1998 to 2009. Their difference is the former includes the retail property etc., while the latter does not.

Liang Yunfang and Gao Tiemei(2007) substituted per capita GDP for per capita income. It’s of shortcomings. One hand, after the reform and opening up, Chinese per capita income growth is far behind per capita GDP, so the substitution may affect the accuracy of analyse. Another, GDP is a macro economic indicator and closely related with many factors, thus it could make it difficult to explain the result of regression. Therefore, the paper simply uses urban per capita disposable income and rural per capita net income, which also facilitates comparison of their influences on house price.

Population growth and urbanization could influence property demand. House developing investment is one of the most important factors deciding directly housing supply and also could be an indicator of housing development cost which is more comprehensive than pure construction cost.

Housing is durable. So, the change of long-term supply and demand will change the housing stock and lead it to an equilibrium, which is the core idea of Stock-Flow Model. The paper incorporates housing sale area into the model. Many studies substituted housing sale area for the housing stock in practice, such as Liang Yunfang and Gao Tiemei(2007) . The paper does so, too.

China's property market development is influenced by administrative power very much. Local governments take land revenue as an important fund sourse. At the same time, GDP is one of the important indicators of local government achievements and property industry promotes considerably GDP. The author takes urban land user tax into the model to try to analyse local governments' work on property price.

Virtual economic factors' influences on property price were emphasized by many scholars, such as Major etc.(2008), Oriol Aspachs-Bracons etc.(2010), Liang Yunfang and Gao Tiemei (2007) and Zhang Ming(2009) etc.. Credit and expectation are two important virtual economic factors.

Chinese property investment depends on loan very much. A large part of housing demand is investment demand, which may due to expected high yield. Therefore, loan balance and anticipated revenge rate are coorperated into the model.

Chinese market-oriented reform of interest rate has not been completed and interest rate can't reflect the actual demand yet. At the same time, the annual average loan real interest rate of all regions are in scarce. So, interest rate is not in the model. Chinese house leasing market is not developed, while its market share is very small and the real rent can't accurately reflect house user cost. Therefore, rent is not in the model, either.

The paper uses a unique database that includes information for 29 provinces, autonomous regions and municipalities from 1998 to 2009. Hong kong, Macao, Taiwan, Tibet and Chongqing are not included. All variables and dependent variables are logarithm, so the estimators are elastic coefficients. Except for SH, POP and CR, all variables and dependent variables are changed into real value with CPI based on 1998 price. The paper uses the stable parameters panal data model and tests the stability of all variables and dependent variables with the common unit root LLC (Levin-Lin-Chu) test (levin, lin and chu, 2002) and individual unit root Fish-ADF test (Maddala and Wu,1999). The results show that POP, CR, P_{it}/P_{it-1} are I(0) process and the others are I(1), but Kao (Engle-Granger Based) tests show that all I(1) sequences in the model are cointegrated.

3 Method and Result

The paper uses Fixed-Effect panal data model and makes an OLS regression.

Because Chinese property market was opened totally in 1998, the sample interval is short, so the effectiveness of time series analyse is not very good.

Chinese property market development is not balanced. Fixed-Effect panal data model can effectively reduce every region's individual effect by applying virtual variable on the cross section, so its result is more reliable than a mixed OLS panal data model and Random-Effect panal data model.

For a further inspectation into various factors' influences on property price in different areas, besides the analyse on the basis of national data, the paper divides 29 regions into two groups based on per capita GDP (one group 14 and another 15, different regions in the two groups shall not affect the analytical results) and estimates the same model by the same method.

OLS is the most theoreticaly mature and commonly used method to regress and enough to achieve the analyse target. The result is shown in tables below.

Table 1. Total regions

Variables	Commercial	Residential
P_{it}/P_{it-1}	0.517（0.000）	0.557（0.000）
LB	0.153（0.001）	0.184（0.000）
POP	0.37（0.043）	——
CR	0.159（0.018）	0.15（0.026）
INCI	0.348（0.000）	0.394（0.000）
INCO	——	——
CLF	0.051（0.000）	0.07（0.000）
SH	-0.083（0.002）	-0.092（0.001）
INVE	0.065（0.002）	0.058（0.007）
R^2	0.962	0.963
Ajusted R^2	0.957	0.959
F	196.06	211.42
SC	-1.35	-1.31
Samples	319	319

Table 2. Higher per capita GDP area

Variables	Commercial	Residential
P_{it}/P_{it-1}	0.507（0.000）	0.523（0.000）
LB	0.222（0.000）	0.246（0.000）
POP	0.663（0.005）	0.613（0.010）
CR	——	——
INCI	0.242（0.044）	0.228（0.558）
INCO	——	——
CLF	0.07（0.000）	0.082（0.000）
SH	-0.073（0.059）	-0.068（0.058）
INVE	0.043（0.053）	0.043（0.057）
R^2	0.973	0.974
Ajusted R^2	0.969	0.97
F	239.25	248.74
SC	-1.5	-1.47
Samples	154	154

Table 3. Lower per capita GDP area

Variables	Commercial	Residential
P_{it}/P_{it-1}	0.472 (0.000)	0.547 (0.000)
LB	-0.125 (0.05)	-0.131 (0.053)
POP	-0.785 (0.003)	-1.058 (0.000)
CR	0.228 (0.009)	0.265 (0.004)
INCI	0.447 (0.003)	0.54 (0.001)
INCO	0.36 (0.011)	0.466 (0.002)
CLF	——	——
SH	-0.086 (0.036)	-0.087 (0.046)
INVE	0.122 (0.005)	0.091 (0.042)
R^2	0.92	0.926
Ajusted R^2	0.907	0.915
F	73.64	80.97
SC	-1.62	-1.5
Samples	165	165

Note: Estimate using Eviews6.0, coefficients out of brackets, P value of T test in brackets, "——" indicating not significant.

Population, per capita income and urbanization rate influence property price in whole country significantly.

Urban per capita disposable income's effect is significantly positive and big, all in whole country and different groups. The coefficients are more than 0.3 in whole country, higher than 0.2 in higher per capita GDP group and higher than 0.4 in lower one. The rise of urban residents' income has more pushed property price up in lower per capita GDP group than in higher one.

Rural per capita net income and urbanization rate's influences are limited in lower per capita GDP group but big. Two coefficients are both more than 0.2 and their sum is about 0.6. This furtherly shows that real economic factors and property price are more related to each other in lower per capita GDP group than in higher one.

The population's effect is sophisticated. Its influence is significantly positive on commercial property price but not significant on residential property price in whole country. In higher per capita GDP group its influences are significantly positive and the coefficients are over 0.6, while in lower one its influences are significantly negative and the coefficients are less than -0.75. It may be because in the latter, population growth lowers seriously purchasement ability while not in the former.

Expectation's influences on property price are significantly positive all in whole country and different groups. The coefficients are more than 0.45. This shows that the expectation is important. So, one of the keys to control property price is the management of expectation.

Loan increasement pushes property price up in whole country, but its influences are different in two groups. Its influence in higher per capita GDP group is significantly positive and the coefficient is more than 0.22, while significantly negative in lower one and the coefficient is less than -0.12. This is probably because in the former, a larger part of loan flows into the property market and pushes house price up by increasing demand or other means. While in the latter, loan largely flows into the outside of property market.

Expectation and loan increasement's work indicate that in higher per capita GDP group investment demand for house is more important than in lower one. Population, income and urbanization's effects also stand by the opinion.

Urban land user tax's coefficients are significantly positive both in whole country and in higher per capita GDP group, which shows that local governments play a role in property price rise. But the coefficients are small, less than the above-mentioned factors', which shows local governments' role may be less important than we imagine. But local governments' work must be sophisticated and only one index may be not enough to reveal local governments' work.

In this paper, property developing investment and property price are not related negatively but positively. This is probably because property demand is larger than supply very much, which causes that supply follows demand. Therefore, property developing investment is basicly driven by demand and reflects development cost rather than supply.

Commercial and residential property have not obvious differences in whole country. The reason may be residential house takes a large part of commercial house. But in lower per capita GDP group, population and income have different influences on commercial and residential property. The absolute difference of the coefficients is more than or equal to 0.1, which shows that residential property price is more influenced by real economic factors. This also supports the opinion in lower per capita GDP area residential demand is more important than investment demand.

4 Conclusion

Population, urbanization rate and income influence house price more than loan and land user tax, while property investment and property sale area have impacts but less than loan. Therefore, the author believes residential demand caused by real economic factors are the basic driver of housing price rise. Expectation is important, but it plays its role based on residential demand in medium-long term.

Urbanization rate and per capita income's influences on house price is more obvious in lower per capita GDP group than in higher one. Commercial property price and residential property price react to per capita income and expectation more differently in lower per capita GDP group, too. Expectation and credit' effects on house price are more significant in higher per capita GDP group than in the other. These support that in lower per capita GDP group residential demand is more important than in higher one. Therefore, "Limit to Buy" might be more effective in higher per capita GDP area.

In general, residential demand is the basic driver of Chinese property price rise, especially in lower per capita GDP area. So, the key is to increase the valid supply which is in public purchasing ability to meet residential demand. But this opinion still need more powerful evidence to support.

Acknowledgement. This paper draws on research carried out for a project ("How does Heilongjiang province participate in financial cooperation in North-East Asia") funded by Heilongjiang Institute of Science and Technology (HIST). We would like to thank Lu Yong Heng in HIST for very helpful comments. All errors and omissions remain my own.

References

1. Gottlieb, M.: Long Swings in Urban Development. Columbia University Press for NBER, NewYork (1976)
2. Mankiw, N.G., Weil, D.N.: The Baby Boom, the Baby Bust and the Property Market. Regional Science and Urban Economics 19, 235–258 (1989)
3. Perron, P.: Test Consistency with Varying Sampling Frequency. Econometric Theory 7, 341–368 (1991)
4. Downs, A.: Property and Long-Wave Cycles, National Property Investor (1993)
5. Pierce, R.G., Snell, A.J.: Temporal Aggregation and the Power of Tests for a Unit Root. Journal of Econometric 65, 333–345 (1995)
6. Maddala, G.S., Wu, S.: A Comparative Study of Unit RootTests with Panal Data and A New Simple Test. Oxford Bulletin of Economics and Statistics 61, 631–652 (1999)
7. Levin, A., Lin, C.F., Chu, C.: Unit Root Tests in Panal Data: Asymptotic and Finite-Sample Properties. Journal of Econometrics 108, 1–24 (2002)
8. Ortalo-Magné, F., Rady, S.: Boom in, Bust out: Young Households and the Property Price Cycle. European Economic Review 43 (2004)
9. Cameron, G., Muellbauer, J., Murphy, A.: Was There A British House Price Bubble? working paper (2006)
10. Coleman IV, M., LaCour-Little, M., Vandell, K.D.: Subprime Lending and the Property Bubble: Tail Wags Dog? Presented at the ASSA Meetings, New Orleans (January 2008)
11. Aspachs-Bracons, O., Rabanal, P.: The drivers of property cycles in Spain. SERIEs 1, 101–130 (2010), doi:10.1007/s13209-009-0010-y
12. Shen, Y., Liu, H.: Housing Prices and Economic Fundamentals: A Cross City Analysis of China for 1995—2002. Economics Research Journal 10 (2004)
13. Zhou, J.: Excessive Financial Support and the Real Estate Bubble, vol. 5. Peking University Press (2005)
14. Liang, Y., Gao, T.: Empirical Analysis on Real Estate Price Fluctuation in Different Provinces of China. Economics Research Journal 8 (2007)
15. Yi, X.: Researches on the Rational Boundry of Credit Expansion and the Fluctuation in Real Estate Price. In: Address at the Seminar on Monetary Policy and Asset Prices (2009)
16. Zhang, M.: Irrationality of Bank Credit and Real Estate Market. Studies of International Finance 4 (2009)
17. Kuang, W.: Expectation, Speculation and Urban Housing Price Volatility in China. Economics Research Journal, Volume 9 (2010)

Analysis of and Research into Foreign Factors That Drive China's Ice-Snow Tourism

Zhaoyuan Huang and Liangzhu Zhang

Physical Culture Institute of Changchun Normal University, Changchun,
Jilin Province 130032, China
hzy1353160@sina.com

Abstract. The paper deals with the foreign factor in China, Vasaloppet International Skiing Festival in Changchun, and its influence on China's ice-snow tourism. The document-data method and the logic analysis method are used for systematically analyzing the current development of the ice-snow tourism in China. According to the research, the foreign factor has activated the ice-snow tourism and brought new opportunities to the development of the ice-snow tourism.

Keywords: Foreign factor, Ice-snow Tourism, Activate.

1 Introduction

When visiting China in 2003, Swedish Vasaloppet international headquarter was attracted by the unique natural landscape and the entironment of Jingyuetan in Changchun and considered it similar to Northern Europe and that it was the best place for cross-country skiing. So it entered into a coordination agreement with Jingyue Tourism Economic Development Zone in Changchun to hold Vasaloppet International Cross-Country Skiing Sports at Jingyuetan, Changchun, China. Thereafter, such foreign factor as Vasaloppet International Cross-Country Skiing Festival that has more than 80 years of history came to China and settled at Jingyuetan in Changchun. European Broadcasting Union has made a special TV program on Vasaloppet in China for four years continuously to promote Changchun around nearly 30 countries and regions, thus establishing Changchun's position as a famous ice-snow sports place in the word.

Vasaloppet International Cross-Country Skiing Festival is for both professional players and the public with its tenet of "Champion of the festival being the public". Now, driven by the foreign factor, Vasaloppet International Cross-Country Skiing Festival involving the public, the commonly seen ice and snow in northeast China has become a valuable resource in winter in north China. Seen from Changchun Ice-snow Tourism Festival to Jingyuetan Vasaloppet International Skiing Festival, from ice-snow art and culture to ice-snow events and sports, and to the infinite business opportunities arising out of ice-snow tourism and trade, Changchun has converted their cold resources into a hot industry through several years of efforts since 2003 when the first Vasaloppet Skiing Festival was held in China. Through the participation of the public, the great natural wealth has become a great capital and

Q. Zhou (Ed.): ISAEBD 2011, Part II, CCIS 209, pp. 422–427, 2011.

information flow. Just as the Chinese saying says that "Ice and snow are resources and coldness is the advantage", the silver chain made up of ice-snow sports, ice-snow tourism and nice-snow trade and so on exposes the ice-snow economy, which plays an important role in driving the industrialization of ice and snow tourism.

2 Current Development of China's Ice-Snow Tourism

Sports industry is called a rising sun industry, and the annual output of the sports industry in the world amounts to more than USD 400 billion and increases by about 20% every year. The sports industry has become one of the hot industries for investment that develop fastest in the world for its great attractiveness and capability of integrating transnational resources and driving economy, which is the most prospective industry. Accordingly, the ice-snow industry, as one part of sports, also has a broad space for development. Ice-snow sports industry mainly consists of the tourism and is the efficiently combined ecologic-economic complex where the first industry, the second industry and the third industry develop in a coordinated way. Ice-snow tourism is viewable, for participation by the puiblic, exciting and challenging, which is attractive to tourists with great value in ice-snow products.

There are more than 600 ski stadiums all over the world, which are mainly in Europe and North America. Every year, there are up to 400 million skiers in the world with the revenue from ice-snow tourism up to USD 70 billion. Currently, far behind the world's ice-snow sports industry, China's ice-snow industry, develops quickly though in these years, is not so attractive to investors as a complete industry. However, it also promises a great space for making profits from China's ice-snow sports industry.

With China's ice-snow tourism represented by northeast China, the ice-snow festival promoted by Changchun, Jilin Province, the ice-snow exhibition and the ice-snow painting and calligraphy art exhibition held in Harbin, Heilongjiang Province, are very popular with tourists. After the prosperous ice-snow tourism in northeast China, some other areas in China began to recognize the business opportunities hidden in ice-snow tourism. In recent years, ice-snow tourism programs are also launched in Xinjiang, Ningxia, Inner Mongolia, and even some areas in the south. Currently, the ice-snow tourism booms all over China and industries relating to ice-snow tourism become larger and larger. Hundreds of ski stadiums have been established in dozens of cities. According to incomplete statistics, as of 2005, newly 50 cities have moved their focus onto the potential ice and snow industry which is fiercely competed for, and the ice-snow tourism becomes well developed from the preliminary stage.

3 Introduction of Foreign Factor-Vasaloppet International Cross-Country Skiing Festival-Into China

3.1 Origin of the Foreign factor-Vasaloppet International Cross-Country Skiing Festival

In Sweden, Vasaloppet Skiing Festival has a long history and tradition dated back to 500 years ago, namely, 1521 when Swedish Crown Prince Gustaf Vasa went through

Dalarna County to seek for the public's help to revolt against Christian II, the king of Denmark then, who ruled Stockholm, the capital of Sweden then. Through great efforts, Gustaf Vasa finally succeeded in recovering the independent Kingdom of Sweden and became the king of Sweden. In 1922, in memory of Gustaf Vasa and what he had made, the yearly 90 kilometer skiing competition was initiated along the same route as Vasa had walked along then, which then became the current Vasaloppet Skiing Festival.

Swedish Vasaloppet Cross-Country Skiing Competition has more than 80 years of history with more than 40 thousand participants every year, which now has become the largest cross-country skiing event in the world.

3.2 Introduction about the Development History of the Foreign Factor-Vasaloppet Skiing Festival in Changchun

On January 2, 2003, Changchun People's Government sponsored the first Changchun Vasaloppet Skiing Festival in China together with Nordicways from Sweden.

On January 2, 2004, the second Jingyuetan Vasaloppet International Cross-Country Skiing Festival was held at Jingyuetan in Changchun, China, and more than two thousand athletes from 15 countries participated in it. In 2004, Swedish Vasaloppet International Headquarter signed a ten-year coordination agreement with Changchun Municipal Government in good faith, and Changchun Jingyuetan Vasaloppet International Cross-Country Skiing Festival became the first pioneering event that held outside Europe.

On January 2, 2005, the third Changchun Jingyuetan Vasaloppet International Cross-Country Skiing Festival began in China as an important constituent for Changchun Ice-snow tourism festival. The three-day skiing festival included events of different groups ranging from 3 kilometers to 50 kilometers. The most important event was the 50 kilometer group held on January 2, followed by the student group, the 25 kilometer group, the 10 kilometer group and women Vasaloppet. In addition, the top Chinese and European performing artists also provided the crowning touch for the entire event.

On January 2, 2006, the fourth Jingyuetan Vasaloppet International Cross-Country Skiing Festival started at Jingyuetan National Forest Park in Changchun. The festival attracted tens of thousands of professional and amateur skiers from all over the world, and numerous spectators for its wonderful live entertainment, tense and exciting skiing events by International Ski Federation, shocking skiing event for the handicapped, the public interesting skiing events.

On January 2, 2007, the fifth Changchun Ice-snow Tourism Festival and Jingyuetan Vasaloppet International Skiing Festival (abbreviated as "the Ice-snow Festival") began at Jingyuetan National Forest Park in Changchun when 30 thousand participants and spectators turned the opening ceremony into the sea of joy and happiness. CCTV-4 and CCTV News Channel live broadcasted the opening ceremony. More than 30 thousand tourists were attracted, including more than 1200 ones from Northern Europe, 400 more than that in the previous festival. China and Changchun become more known to the world through the Ice-snow Festival. Gong Wenbin, director of Jingyuetan Tourism Development Group Co., Ltd, said that they would invite more national professional athletes to the next ice-snow festival, and list the annual skiing event for the handicapped onto the formal schedule, and they would also introduce regulated children skiing events for children 8-15 years old next year in order to keep in line with the children event of Swedish Vasaloppet Skiing Festival. Gong Wenbin further said that with the rapid development of Vasaloppet in China, China's Vasaloppet would surpass Swedish Vasaloppet that had tens of years of history in five to eight years.

4 Analysis of the Foreign Factor That Activates China's Ice-Snow Tourism

4.1 Features of Ice-Snow Tourism

The ice-snow tourism has the two major aspects of participation and entertainment, and attracts a great many fans for its features.

1) Worthiness of Watching

Ice-snow events are well worth watching for its artistry, high skills, difficulty to do, breathtaking and fiercely competitive scene, which feel aesthetic and exciting, and bring great artistic experience and mental experience to sports tourists as well as attract more tourist participants.

The ice-snow events have changed ice and snow into valuable, and linked ice with snow. The large snow carved parks and the large ice carved parks have become unique new focuses and improve the cultural connotation of ice-snow activities. The organized winter swimming exhibition matches, American snowboarding performance, on-ice chess south-north contest, ice and snow short track car pull challenge and so on are well worth of watching. The Large Snow at the Temple of Heaven and the Ice Chess South-north Contest at 2004 Shenyang Ice-snow Festival have applied for Guiness Records.

2) Wide participation

The public actively participate in the ice-snow tourism: the public may carve the snow; and dozens of new popular events such as winter swimming, climbing ice and overhead cable, on-ice shooting, snowboarding and so on have been added based on the original popular ice-snow events, thus involving more tourists.

3) Novelty of events

The ice-snow events are full of varieties, include both wonderful performance and professional events, both ice and snow entertainments and food and shopping, which combine stillness with motion, and combine participation with entertainment, thus meeting the requirements of groups of different ages for participating in ice and snow tourism events.

4.2 Climateness Factor for the Development of Ice-Snow Tourism in China

The three provinces in the northeast of China that are the main places for ice snow tourism have climate appropriate to viewing ice lanterns, ice sculpture, snow sculpture, playing in the snow, skating and skiing. The average temperature of Harbin is 12.2 degrees centigrade below zero with the average ice-snow term of 113 days; that of Changchun in winter is 9.7 degrees centigrade below zero with the average ice-snow term of 101 days; that of Shenyang is 6.8 degrees centigrade below zero with the average ice-snow term of 70 days. Due to the appropriate climate and the clean air, the snow in Shenyang and Changchun is softer and whiter, which is the best material for snow sculpture. However, Harbin is the best for ice sculpture.

4.3 Geographic Advantage for Ice-Snow Sports in China

Changchun is located in the center of northeast China with more than 20 ice-snow tourism attractions such as Jingyuetan, Lianhuashan, the Great North Lake in Jilin Province, Qipanshan Mountain in Shenyang, and the Ice-snow World in Harbin and so on within 300 meters from Changchun. Changchun is the optimum tourism center for its geographic advantages because it has integrated the ice-snow tourism resources of the four cities in northeast China and has created optimum paths for ice-snow tourism in northeast China. In addition, Changchun government has engaged an international famous expert to redesign the cross-country skiing course, which is a professional cross-country skiing course that is accredited by the international snow federation second to Sapporo in Japan in Asia just 18 kilometers from downtown area and not far away from the skiing field in Lianhuashan Mountain. By contrast, Yabuli Ski Resort in Harbin is 195 kilometers from the downtown area, and Erlongshan Ski Resort is 65 kilometers from the downtown area. In this way, the tourists may experience the snow and ice in north China, local conditions and customs of north China.

4.4 People's Support for Launching the Ice-Snow Sports in China

In the 1960-70s, an event called "Millions of People Skating on Ice" was launched in north China, and almost every school, institution, factory and mine has their own ice stadium in Heilongjiang and Jilin Provinces. In winters, skiers of all ages gather at the ski stadiums, which becomes a peculiar scene of body building activities involving the public in northeast China. With the quick development of Chinese economy, more and more people start to have ice-snow sports. Just in Beijing suburb, dozens of ski stadiums have appeared in recent years. According to reports, the ski stadiums in Beijing are full of people every weekend, in particular on the New Year's Day and during the Spring Festival this year.

5 Conclusion- Foreign Factor Has Activated China's Ice-Snow Tourism

5.1 Changchun Jingyuetan Vasaloppet Skiing Festival Being the Activator for the Mass Process of Ice-Snow Sports in China

It is not only ice-snow sports, but also an industry integrating resources in economy, culture and arts and so on, which will become a part of Chinese life. Different skin colors and different clothes act in the same way and show the same passion. The colorful crowd storm surge onto the glaciers and the white plains quickly…Thousands of people including professional athletes, and skiers ranging from 70-year old men to young children are spiritually interpreting the infinite charm of the ice and snow world.

Changchun Jingyuetan Tourism Development Group is training students from 17 universities and colleges in Changchun on skiing to involve more people in skiing, and it is predicted that more than 10 thousand university students will participate in skiing. The trained university students will have a matching at the opening ceremony and participated in the cross-country skiing event on December 24, 2006.

5.2 Changchun Jingyuetan Vasaloppet Skiing Festival Has Activated the Silver Chain, the Ice and Snow Sports Industry in China

The ice-snow tourism includes the six aspects of eating, accommodation, moving, traveling, shopping and entertainment, which is associated with more than six industries. According to the principle of economics, the tourism revenue of 1 Yuan will bring the revenue of at least 10.3 Yuan to associated industries, and one job in tourism will bring at least additional five jobs in other industries. Since December, 2006, the occupancy rate of hotels and inns in Changchun kept rising and many hotels above three-star ones have an occupancy rate of 100%. Some tourists also have meals and are accommodated in the farmhouses nearby, thus benefiting the peasants.

By introducing the foreign factor, namely, holding Changchun Vasaloppet International Skiing Festival in China, Changchun has been listed in the ice-snow map of the world and become a brand city of ice and snow as well as created its ice-snow brand internationally. It not only promotes the construction of ice-snow project in Changchun, has explored the connotation, expands Changchun's ice-snow tourism market, promotes the popularization of the public skiing sports, but also expands Changchun's foreign exchange and improves its fame both inside and outside China. Changchun is developing aiming at the world skiing center to become the focus of the world sports and ice and snow tourism in winter. Changchun Vasaloppet International Skiing Festival has become a great event in China's ice-snow tourism, which significantly drives the tourism economy and activates the silver chain, the ice-snow sports industry in China.

References

1. Dong, S., Wang, W.: Current Development of China's Ice-snow Sports Industry and Research into the Measures. Science and Management 6 (2006)
2. Continuous Popularization of Ice-snow Events, Ice-snow Sports Is Coming into the Public Life (January 31, 2007), http://www.singtaonet.com
3. Jiang, L.: Thinking About Developing the Winter Sports Tourism in Heilongjiang Province. Ice-snow Sports 3 (2001)
4. Changchun Ice and Snow Bring Gold, Innovation and Making Great Achievements (2006-02-22) 09:29:42, http://travel.163.com

Analysis on the Factors of Affecting the Sticky Behavior of Net Users

Nan Zheng and Yang Chen

College of Economic and Management Xi'an University of Post and Telecommunication Xi'an, China
zn20102@126.com, chen89yang@126.com

Abstract. Online Stickiness is a new concept derived from the growth of cyber economy, which is one of the key factors affecting the competitiveness of organizations. This paper gives a comprehensive picture of the affecting factors on online stickiness in terms of six aspects: personal factors, user experience, social factors, economic factors, cultural factors, and political factors, aiming at providing some theoretical references for the growth of cyber economy through studying the psychology and behavior of net users.

Keywords: net user, online stickiness, sticky behavior, factors analysis.

1 Introduction

As the information technology dramatically developed, a new economic era has approached to us, which is characterized by globalization, informatization, network and digitalization. This is information-transitory world in which net users increasingly diversify their needs. The population of net users in China is continuously increasing. Meanwhile, the network plays a more and more influential role in the life of net users who become unceasingly dependable on the Internet. By Dec 2010, 457 million people have been available to the Internet, increasing by 73 million in comparison with 2009. The Internet popularization rate amounted to 34.3%, rising by 5.4%.

The utilizing behaviors of net users show some features. Firstly, that the degree of commercialization is rapidly improved. Secondly, the recreational bias is maintained and thirdly, the values of communication and information tools are deepened in cyber world. By the first half year of 2010, varied Internet applications have been more popular among net users who are enlarging in a sustaining way. The commercial application in particular stand out, the consumers of online payment, online shopping and online bank growing respectively by about 30%, although the net users of social communicating websites, network literature and searching engine rapidly expand. The access rate of online shopping, online payment and online bank are respectively 33.8%, 30.5% and 29.1% and the size of users in half year is amplified by 31.4%,

Q. Zhou (Ed.): ISAEBD 2011, Part II, CCIS 209, pp. 428–434, 2011.

36.2% and 29.9%. The net users' behavior has gradually demonstrates stickiness to Internet.

2 Definition on Online Stickiness and Sticky Behavior

Online Stickiness is a new concept derived from the growth of cyber economy, which is still in preliminary stage for the researchers abroad. At present, there is not standard definition on online stickiness. But it essentially means retaining the online customers and prolonging their duration online. The degree of online stickiness will vary according to the frequency, the mental dependency, the immoderation and the physiological performance.

Broadly speaking, the stickiness is that people are attracted by the external and appear to be some changes in psychology and behavior. These changes may occur in any situations of daily life. They're not absolutely related to the consumer or the online behavior. In a narrow sense, the stickiness is that consumers pay excessive attention to some kind of products and services, which essentially leads to the changes in their psychology and behavior. While in the network platform, stickiness is that the net users insist on repeatedly visiting and using their favorite websites in the future, even if there is the potential to cause switching behaviors of the scenarios and marketing efforts (Lietal, 2006). Online stickiness is the ability that websites have in order to draw and retain users from their emergences. Online user's stickiness is a repetitive visit to and use of a preferred Web site because of a deeply held commitment to reuse the Web site consistently in the future (Wang hai-ping, 2010). When Internet visitors and even prior customers have many if not hyper competitive commerce choices, overcoming purchasing objections and indifference distills to site "stickiness" (Martin Nemzow, 2010). Customer's loyalty requires a strong desire by the customer for a product for which several product vendors are available (Ramakrishnan Ramanathan, 2010). In this paper, stickiness is defined as a continuous contact between the net users and network products and their services. And the online sticky behavior is caused by the appearance of online stickiness. Apparently, it is a continuously using behavior, which in fact is caused by the change of the net users' psychology.

3 Factors Analysis

The factors affecting online sticky behavior mainly include personal factors, user experience, social factors, economic factors, cultural factors and political factors (Fig. 1 shows an example).

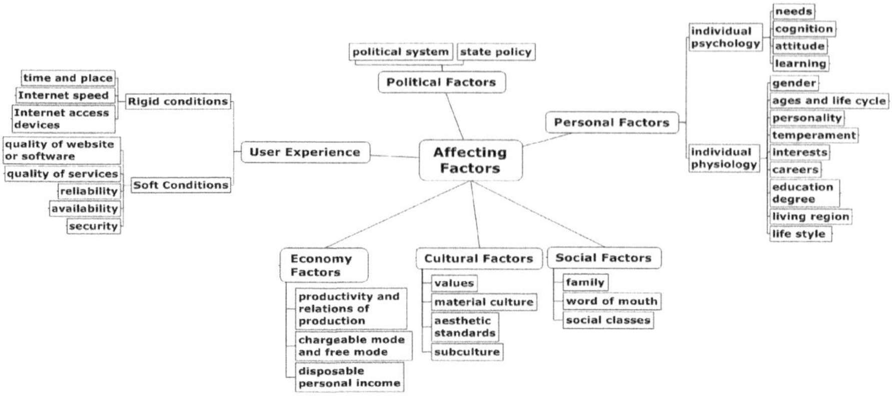

Fig. 1. Affecting Factors Analysis

3.1 Personal Factors

This paper classifies the personal factors that affect the sticky behavior of net consumers into two categories: individual psychological factors and individual physiological factors.

Individual Psychological Factors

The sticky behavior of net users is dominated and controlled by their mental activities. The major elements influencing the mental process of net users are needs, cognition, learning and attitude.

Firstly, needs reflect the anticipation of net users for the sustaining and developing the objective world in a certain cyber environment. Psychology study indicates that the needs of net users are kind of unbalance against the peripheral network environment because net users themselves lack a certain psychological or physiological factors. The needs of net users identify the target of their cyber behavior. Therefore, needs are the internal driving force. Secondly, the net cognition is made up of perception and consciousness, memory and thinking from net users on various products and services provided by Internet. Perception and consciousness refer to a personal or a general cognition by people through their sense organs to the Internet as well as its derivatives, which belongs to the forming phase of cognition. Thirdly, the attitude of net users refers to their response tendency (i.e. the emotional bias, affirmation and negation) to the internet and its relevant things while they use the net services and products. The net users who have affirmative attitude would form and sustain their net sticky behavior, and vice versa. Last but not the least, human acquires other behaviors by learning from outside world except the internal instinct-driving behaviors like being hungry, being thirsty and having sex, etc. The learning of net users is a process through which they unceasingly gain knowledge, experiences and skills, and meanwhile continuously improve their using behavior when net users purchase and use the internet and its derivatives.

Individual Physiological Factors

The innate factors like gender, ages and life cycle, personality, temperament, and interests unavoidably contribute to the online sticky behavior. In addition, some acquired disposition factors like careers, education degree, living region and life style also play an important part in the online sticky behavior.

3.2 User Experience

User experience has an influence on the online sticky behavior of a net user from both rigid and soft conditions. Rigid conditions, including time and place of surfing the Internet, Internet speed and Internet access devices three aspects. Rigid conditions affect the convenience of surfing the Internet. If a user (that has Internet experience and certain stickiness to the net) surfs the Internet inconveniently, his online sticky behavior will not be affected by the inconvenience in the short term. But in the long run, it will inevitably lead to his loss of interest to the Internet. At the aspect of Internet access devices, portable degree of the terminal, screen size, mouse control, system functionality (complexity) and quality, system design and even the interface details, will affect the willingness of his continuously using behavior. These rigid conditions above have long-term effects on the online sticky behavior through the experience of the user from outside.

Soft conditions, including the quality of website or software and its service, reliability, availability, security and other conditions, have an influence on the level of net users' satisfaction and trust, which are precisely the direct influencing factors of online sticky behavior.

3.3 Economic Factors

In this section, economic factors are discussed from three aspects: social productivity and production relations, chargeable mode and free mode, and disposable personal income.

Social Productivity and Production Relations

In the history of human development, each of technical revolutions led to huge improvement of productivity and great transformation of production relations. And the development of relations of production requires the growth of productivity. As a representative of information technology revolution, computers made the productivity step on a new height stage and the relations of production go with it. Apparently, change of productivity contributed to great change of production relations. Change of productivity and relations of production can lead to changes in national economic structure, industrial structure and employment structure in macroscopic view. They will have effects on people's work, study and life. So will they from microscopic view. For example, in the 20th report of July 2007, CNNIC concluded that 99% of people who had contacted with the Internet would continue to surf the Internet. Therefore, the information technology revolution creates necessary conditions for the occurrence of online sticky behavior from the microscopic view.

Chargeable Mode and Free Mode

As disposable personal income of net users within a certain period of time is limited and the services based on the Internet always appear at a certain price in the market, thus, net users must make a choice to meet their needs according to how much the disposable income is, whether the service of different site or software charges or not, and the fee amount if it charges. Once the issue of charging mode and free mode becomes an important factor in decision-making net users, it will reflect switching costs. The cause of switching costs is that future options for people, in a large extent, lock into and even depend on the choice of present and past. Once a net user pays for some service on the Internet, a high switching cost is produced.

Disposable Personal Income

Every net user that can be free to certain income belongs to net users with disposable personal income, such as working people and Chinese college students. Because these people, no matter their disposable incomes at hand come from personal work or family sponsorship, all have independent consuming ability. The amount of personal disposable income will affect the decision in the process of net users' online trading commodities and services, thereby affecting the online sticky behavior.

Some chargeable services of sites or soft wares (such as QQ VIP of yellow diamond and green auger, etc.) are rare choices for net users with low disposable personal income. And the Chinese net users have been accustomed to "free". But nowadays, more and more people are willing to pay for the content and service that have high quality and are different from others'. Once this value-added service is formed, it must further the established online sticky behavior.

3.4 Social Factors

Social factors affect online sticky behavior from three aspects:

Family Members

Couples live together, so their living habits and preferences will become increasingly similar through the running. Thus, it indirectly affects each other's behaviors, certainly including the behavior of surfing the net. Children are easy to be affected by parental behaviors and prone to imitation. For example, a father engaged in advertising design often browses design class of websites, so his children are easy to put their attention in such websites, and thus the probability of occurrence of the online sticky behavior increases for them.

Word of Mouth

It is a verbal tribute to the people, and generally propagated by the reference groups, which as a direct (face to face) or indirect reference affect the online sticky behavior. It is called membership group that have a direct influence, including primary groups (family, friends, neighbors, colleagues and others) and secondary groups (religious organizations, professional organizations and Allied Workers and other sub-groups). As a result of herd mentality, net users are easy to be affected by these reference groups who give verbal praise to those websites and services that they've used for long. They form the habits that have an influence on the online sticky behavior as well.

Social Classes

Social classes divide members of society into a number of social levels, according to certain social standards, such as income, education, occupation, social status and prestige, etc. People in the same social class tend to share common values, lifestyles and ways of thinking and life goals. That is the reason social classes affect the online sticky behavior. For example, when browsing information online, designers are more concerned about design-related information, while sports journalists pay more attention to sports-related news. Another example is that college students prefer social networking websites such as the Facebook, while the professional managers prefer to enter the circle of managers.

3.5 Cultural Factors

Traditionally, culture generally refers to human wisdom, belief, art, moral, law, aesthetics, customs, language as well as the capabilities and habits man has acquired in social life. However, this paper mainly focuses on the net culture, which means the cultural activities and cultural products characterized by the network community. In addition, the net culture is network spirit creation based on the invention and growth of cyber substance, computer technology and information network technology, and cyber economy. It includes some net activities such as working, learning, communicating and entertaining, etc. The social values and social mentality are reflected as well during these activities, basically deciding the anticipation and behavior of net users. Therefore, the net culture imperceptibly influences net users in terms of values, material culture, aesthetic standards and subculture.

3.6 Political Factors

The political factors are primarily involved in political system and state policy. The former is defined as the social political institution pursued by a nation or an area, which plays influential role in the consuming way and the net behavior of net users. The net users in China should utilize the Internet within the framework of the socialism politics as well as the principle of culture and morality. The latter, as a policy form, regulates the Internet consuming behavior by what a nation synchronously advocates and opposes. Various policies will be formulated and adopted according to different cyber behavior, which is specifically related to commercial transaction, Internet entertainment, Internet communication and information acquisition.

4 Conclusions

One research indicates that online stickiness has positive and negative output effects. The customer satisfaction and loyalty represent the positive effect, but the Internet addiction and Internet dependency represent the negative effect. The online sticky behavior among net users has become increasingly prominent in recent years. Therefore, it has been a practical issue to minimize the negative effect on customers' real life while they can benefit from the powerful information, entertainment and transaction function provided by network. In conclusion, this paper gives a comprehensive picture of the affecting factors on online stickiness in terms of six aspects: personal factors, user experience, social factors, economic factors, cultural factors, political factors, aiming at providing some theoretical reference for the growth of cyber economy through studying the psychology and behavior of net users.

Acknowledgments. This article has been funded by the National Social Science Foundation of China under Grant 10BGL099 and the General Project of Humanities and Social Science Research of The Educational Ministry under Grant 10YJC630268.

References

1. CNNIC: The 27th report of China Internet development and statistic (2011) (in Chinese)
2. Dong, L., Gong, Y.: The Factors Affecting Consumers' Behaviors. J. Chongqing Vocational & Technical Institute 13(3), 80–81 (2007) (in Chinese)
3. Su, Q., Zhao, L., Cui, Y., Chen, T.: An Empirical Analysis on the Antecedents of Internet Customer Behavior. Systems Engineering 25(2), 1–6 (2007 (in Chinese)
4. Huang, S., Wu, Y.: On the Status Quo of Internet Behavior Study. School of Philosophy and Sociology. Lanzhou University (Social Sciences) 35(2), 32–38 (2007) (in Chinese)
5. Haiping, W.: Research on online consumers' stickiness. Ms D Thesis. Shandong University, China (2009) (in Chinese)
6. Menon, S., Kahn, B.: Cross-category effects of induced arousal and pleasure on the internet shopping experience. Retailing 78(1) (2002)
7. Ulaga, W., Eggert, A.: Relationship Value and Relationship Quality. European Journal of Marketing (2006)

The Improved Performance Evaluation Model for Non-profit Organizations

Hong yu Zang and Chong Wu

School of Management, Harbin Institute of Technology, Fayuan 17, 150001 P.R. China
zanghongyu@hit.edu.cn

Abstract. Non-profit organizations (NPOs) play an important role in society. The purpose of this paper is to set up a relative assessment model to improve existing NPO evaluation method. The advantage of the model is dynamic, and takes the context of statues into the evaluation which is suitable for the characteristic of NPO in China. The model adopted optimal frontier re-assessment method into fuzzy DEA that overcomes the limitation of re-assessment built on groundwork, and neglects the progress made by those with poor condition of NPOs at beginning. The result shows that the performance evaluation of NPO becomes more objective and equity. It encourages NPOs with poor condition to seek for development and NPOs with superior conditions strive to keep position. To date, little research has been carried out to analyze the issue and this study will provide valuable insight to academicians and business professionals.

Keywords: Performance evaluation, Non-profit Organizations (NPOs), Fuzzy DEA, secondary relative benefits.

1 Introduction

Non-profit Organizations carry important mission for wellbeing of society, including education, sanitation, scientific research, environmental protection and helping the poor. NPOs are called "the third department of the society", and undertake the welfare task which can not achieved well by government and market[1]. The resources NPOs used are mainly come from government financial allocation and donations from society. So, high quality and low cost are economic goals for NPOs to achieve. In order to attract more support form government and society. It is very important for NPOs to provide favorable performance record. In China, there are different statuses for NPOs, for those NPOs with government background usually have good financial support and it is easy to keep good performance position. On the other hand, for those NPOs without government background, it is hard to have good performance position for the existing evaluation method. And these grass roots NPOs urgently need admission of society to attract support. Unfortunately the evaluation model is based on original settings does not reflect the change brought by hardworking for poor conditioned NPOs. The performance evaluation loses its fairness and equity. To overcome the shortcoming of the present evaluation method and create a reasonable development environment, it is very urgent to improve the method and set up a rational model.

Q. Zhou (Ed.): ISAEBD 2011, Part II, CCIS 209, pp. 435–440, 2011.

There are methods for assessing performances of organizations, and fuzzy DEA assessment is one of them. Performance evaluation of NPOs can be divided into two types: fuzzy DEA effective (including pessimistic fuzzy DEA effective and optimistic fuzzy DEA effective) and non-fuzzy DEA effective (including non-pessimistic fuzzy DEA effective and non-optimistic fuzzy DEA effective). For non-fuzzy DEA effective units, abundant management decision information can be obtained. This is helpful to estimate the level of relevant effectiveness according to the distance to effective frontier, and more over, it is useful to analyses the reasons of ineffectiveness and make relevant improvement proposal [2]. But for fuzzy DEA effective units, especially pessimistic fuzzy DEA effective units, it can only be estimated as effective or weak effective and it can not be differentiated further[3]. The information shortage of these fuzzy DEA effective units is obviously unsatisfied for valuators, especially even when many or all of the decision units being assessed as fuzzy DEA effective, DEA assessment information gained is very limited. Some studies adopt other non-DEA methods to re-assess DEA effective units [4].

At present, NPO performance re-assessment often adopts the assessment models either based on weight or estimated principle. For assessment method based on weight, each decision unit has the same title in making index weight. But there is large difference for each decision unit on scale, power and representation. The "voice power" they hold is naturally different in deciding index weight [5]. Take them as the same is actually neglect the difference exist among units, and the assessment result is hardly to be scientific. The method based on estimate principle adds certain estimate principle into original DEA model, and the added principle is equivalent to increase restrictions. This may make part of DEA effective units become ineffective units and the number of DEA effective unites decreases. To solve the problem, this study discusses the NPO re-assessment issue based on production frontier of fuzzy DEA method. Through the way of establish production frontier to deal with shortage and to make performance evaluation more rigorous.

2 Assessment Method Based on Optimal Frontier

Decision unit DEA effective means assessed unit lies on effective production frontier constituted by present product possibility set. But for the dots on the same effective production frontier, DEA can not differentiate them further. If a new production frontier is established and it may make assessed DEA effective unit do not located on the frontier, then DEA effective unit can be distinguished[6]. Following this idea, researchers put forward DEA effective unit re-assessment method based on optimal frontier and based on critical frontier.

For DEA effective unit, if a new production frontier is established and make it lie over the new production frontier. When DEA effective unit turns to non-DEA effective unit, it means the decision unit lie over the new frontier is more effective than original decision unit[7]. In order to establish more effective new decision unit, some research have borrowed thought of establishment for ideal solution from the multi-goal decision method -- TOPSIS (Technique for Order Preference by Similarity to Ideal Solution), and establishes following virtual ideal decision unit:

Suppose there are n production decision units, each decision unit DMU_j has m input index and s output index:

$$X_j = (x_{1j}, \ldots, x_{mj})^T > 0, Y_j = (y_{1j}, \ldots, y_{nj}) > 0, j = 1, \ldots, n.$$

In order to make effective rank order for all units, establishes a new decision unit DMU_{n+1}, let decision unit's input is the minimum value from all of the decision units, and the output is the maximum value of all of the decision units, that is

$$x_{i,n+1} = \min(x_{n,} \cdots, x_m), i = 1, \cdots, m;$$

$$y_{r,n+1} = \max(y_{r1,} \cdots, y_{rm}), r = 1, \cdots, s$$

Define 2.1. Two production probable sets Z_m and Z_n constituted from m and n decision units, if $Z_m \subset Z_n$, and there is maximum one DEA effective unit $DMU_j \in Z_{m,}$ in Z_n. Then, Z_n is optimal production probable set of Z_m.

Define 2.2. The effective frontier Z_m constructed by production probable sets of Z_n is named as optimal frontier of Z_n.

Obviously, new established decision unit is not worse than any decision unit of the original production possibility set, and it constitutes the new production probable sets with original decision unit becomes optimal production probable sets of original production possibility set. We can take optimal production probable sets frontier -- optimal frontier as standard to measure original decision DEA effectiveness. DEA effective unit re-assessment model based on optimal production frontier is:

$$\min \theta$$

$$s.t. \sum_{j=1}^{n+1} \lambda_j X_j + S- = \theta X_0$$

$$\sum_{j=1}^{n+1} \lambda j Y j - S^+ = Y_0$$

$$\lambda j \geq 0, j = 1, \cdots, n+1$$

$$S^- \geq 0, S^+ \geq 0$$

There are several ways to establish virtual decision unit. The operation situation of these virtual units is recognized relatively ideal.

3 Discussion and Case Analysis on Optimal Frontier Model

DEA effective unit re-assessment is proved effective and feasible [8]. The reason that most, even all of the decision units may assessed DEA effective in DEA assessment is apart from each decision unit confirm index weight from the benefit from itself, more over, DEA assessment is only a relevant assessment and not "absolute assessment" [9]. That means the effectiveness for excellence or inferior from the assessed unit is relevant only with units in the reference set, and irrelevant with others.

3.1 Discussions at the Application of the Model

The characteristic of DEA can only use on relevant effective assessment may generate a question on the emergence of many effective units[9]. More over, it may generate following two questions:

(1) There is requirement for certain amount of numbers for assessment units. It is only used for relevant assessment and difficult to make "absolute assessment" for each decision unit.

(2) Because DEA is to assess relevant efficiency for each unit, if all of the assessed units are low in efficiency in fact, then DEA will not be able to distinguish, but it can select several effective decision units from them.

Two questions above are practically significant for NPO service management assessment. For the first question, there are actually not NPOs attending the assessment each time, especially when the NPOs are conducting self assessment, and there would no reference set. The character of DEA is equivalent to increase the condition for the implementation of assessment, and decrease the serviceability of assessment method. For the second question, there is no certain that there are the high effective units for each assessment. If all of the units for assessment are low in efficiency, it is hard to find the problems exist in the assessed NPOs.

To solve the problem that DEA is only applicable for relevant effective assessment and hard to conduct "absolute assessment" for single NPO, and can not conduct "effective identification", this study put forward the method of "reference set selection". That is, sanitation department conducts large scale of NPO assessment and select several NPOs as representatives for reference set for NPO assessment later on.

3.2 Numerical Example

To illustrate the model, we chose data from nine public welfare foundations in 2009 and 2010 to measure their performance situations. To simplify the calculation process, four factors are used to indicate the order for performance condition. The factors are fundamental condition, management system, governance structure and external inspection. As the condition the bigger the better for index factors, we take four indictors of fundamental condition, management system, governance structure and external inspection as integrated output, substitute DEA model which only has output.

First step, according to the performance index system, we invite specialists to give marks. Then, we take two principles as standard for assessment. The principles are pertinency and accuracy. Second step is to give the weight of factors by variation coefficient method. Third step is to obtain integrated results using weightmean calculated in 2009 and 2010. The last step is to calculate the performance effectiveness according to the integrated evaluation result of the two years and obtain the final result shows in table 1. below.

The example shows a different picture for performance grading for nine foundations in two years with general evaluation method. The new model describes the change brought by endeavor which is very meaningful for survive and development of NPOs at all levels.

Table 1. Measurement of performance effectiveness

Order	2009	2010	leading surface	performance effectiveness	Evaluation result
1	0.9487	0.9051	0.9746	0.9287	6
2	0.9429	0.9057	0.9704	0.9334	5
3	0.9696	0.8606	0.9898	0.8695	9
4	0.9662	0.9044	0.9873	0.916	8
5	1	0.9875	1.0011	0.9863	2
6	0.9789	0.9173	0.9965	0.9205	7
7	0.9837	1	1	1	1
8	0.9439	0.9159	0.9711	0.9431	4
9	0.9738	0.9385	0.9928	0.9453	3

4 Conclusion

Traditional evaluation of Absolute Progress Effectiveness (APE) on performance of management has been adopted ratio of total comparative index. This paper really reflects the effective progress based on the same reference in NPO management, evaluates Relative Progress Effectiveness (RPE) depend individual relative progress index and individual valid exerting degree by Data Envelopment Analysis method, which so beneficial for NPOs to conduct stage-evaluation and regulation department to offer fair assessment, to improve the social effectiveness and acknowledgement for NPOs. Based on the effectiveness index of subjective efforts to measure the progress effectiveness, depended on three-time relative evaluations as technical index, and adopted the method of Data Envelopment Analysis. The model provided by this paper considers the final result of management efficiency, meanwhile, pays attention to the effective management effort for NPOs. The results show that the new model takes the referring period data as assessment base, receive individual progress indicators through the data comparison between base period and current period. To measure the relative progress level from overall point of view has provided the effective progress measurement under the similar references for NPOs.

Acknowledgments. This work is supported by Ministry of Education: Humanities and Social Science Fund of China No.10YJA630198, and Innovation Foundation of Harbin Institute of Technology: HIT. NSRIF. No.2010087.

References

1. Wu, J.B., Han, Y.Z., Liu, C.Q.: Application of Fuzzy Assessment Method in NPO Performance Management. Chinese NPO Administration 4, 37–39 (2006)
2. Szamosi, L.T., Duxbury, L.: Development of a Measure to Assess Organizational Change. Journal of Organizational Change Management 15(2), 184–201 (2002)
3. Alexander, J.: Organizational Diagnostics: Integrating Qualitative and Quantitative Methodology. Journal of Organizational Change Management 15(2), 156–168 (2002)
4. Friedman, L., Stern, Z.S.: Scaling Units Via the Canonical Correlation Analysis in the DEA Context. European Journal of Operational Research 100, 629–637 (1997)
5. Sueyoshi, T., Ohnishi, K., Kinase, Y.: A Benchmark Approach Forbaseball Evaluation. European Journal of Operational Research 115, 429–448 (1999)
6. Chiclana, F., Herrera, F., Herrera-Viedma, E.: Integrating Three Representation Models in Fuzzy Multipurpose Decision Making Based on Fuzzy Preference Relations. Fuzzy Sets and Systems 97, 33–48 (1998)
7. Ren, M., Wang, L.: DEA Effective Two Stage Method on Assessment Decision Unit. Forecast 22(6), 75–77 (2003)
8. Forrester, R., Drexle, A.B.: A Model for Team-based Organization Performance. The Academy of Management Executive 3, 429–444 (1999)
9. Feng, Y., Dawei, W.: Performance Management and Management Efficiency. Chinese Soft Science 4, 132–136 (2003)

The Effects of Sudden Celebrity Deaths on the US Stock Market

Zhiping Chen

Zhengzhou University of Light Industry, Dong Feng Rd.5,
Zhengzhou, China
chenzhipingiec@yahoo.cn

Abstract. In contribution to behavior finance studies opposing the efficient market hypothesis, this report tests the null hypothesis that sudden deaths of celebrities are economically-neutral events which do not have a significant impact on United States stock markets. The underlining logic being that although economically-neutral events reflect no financial information, it can alter the decision making process of financial professionals by affecting investor mood, confidence, risk aversion levels and emotional states. This in turn, influences the financial markets. Examining index returns with sudden deaths of celebrities nominated on the Hollywood Walk of Fame as a dummy variable, this paper finds no significant evidence against the null hypothesis. Hence, from this perspective, the US financial market is efficient.

Keywords: Event Study, efficient-market hypothesis, Celebrity Death, Impact, the US Stock Market.

1 Introduction

It is unbelievable how strong the influence of a celebrity can be, especially when died. One example is Michael Jackson, the superstar who left the world in June, 2009. As the news flooded online, web traffic jumped up by at least 20 percent of normal traffic, causing many major websites, including TMZ, Twitter and the Los Angeles Times to slow or even crash from user overload. When his memorial was held on July 7, 2009, at the Staples Centre in Los Angeles, more than one billion audiences worldwide estimated to watch the broadcast. The audience in the US alone was estimated to be 31.1 million, a scale similar to that of the burial of former president Ronald Reagan and the 1997 funeral for Princess Diana. This is not a unique event. Similar circumstance occurred in December 1980 when the singer of The Beatles, John Lennon, was shot dead [5].

The impact of celebrity suicides, and other sudden deaths, has been studied by many researchers. Such research has documented a range of different impacts, including minor influences like depression and lack of confidence in individuals, to deeper impacts like increased automobile accidents and, in extreme cases, higher suicide rates. It is clear that such deaths affect the ordinal life of individuals. Correspondingly, there may also be an impact on financial markets. This report

Q. Zhou (Ed.): ISAEBD 2011, Part II, CCIS 209, pp. 441–447, 2011.

examines this issue, testing the null hypothesis that sudden deaths of celebrities are economically-neutral events which do not have a significant impact on United States stock markets. That is, that the financial market are efficient.

2 Theoretical Background and Literature Review

There has been a long running debate among investors and researchers regarding the efficient-market hypothesis. That is, the hypothesis claiming that all information regarding the future economic aspects of an asset is reflected in its price, thus, proposing that asset prices are rational. In contrast, behavioral economists argue the financial markets are imperfect, providing evidence of a number of cognitive biases such as the overconfidence, overreaction and human errors in price reasoning and information processing. This suggests that asset prices will deviate from their intrinsic value, as would be the case in an efficient market. One implication of the irrational market view is that financial-market participants can be psychologically impacted by events which are economically-neutral, events which reflect no financial information but can nevertheless alter investor mood, confidence, risk aversion levels and emotional states.

Various economically-neutral events have been documented in previous articles, including the weather, sleep patterns, accidents, disasters and sports events. For example, Saunders (1993) [4] finds evidence against the rational market hypothesis by studying the relationship between NYSE and AMEX prices and the local weather in New York City. From a market perspective, weather is an economically-neutral factor, containing no market information. While the weather can influence certain stocks in the agriculture sector, this effect is unsystematic and should be eliminated through diversification. If the market prices rationally, asset prices should not be systematically affected by the local weather.

However, previous research finds that meteorological variables such as temperature, relative humidity, precipitation, wind, sunshine, and the percentage of cloud cover do have significant psychological effects. These findings are consistent with the theory that market participants, like floor traders gathering in the same location daily, have their mood affected by the local weather.

Sleeping disorders have also been found to be a reason for numerous accidents [7]. Around daylight saving time clock shifts, researchers have found a statistically significant increase in automobile accidents, irrespective of the direction of the daylight saving time shift. A number of striking tragedies in human history have also been linked with sleep imbalances due to work shift changes.

Studies have also shown that sports results have a significant effect on a person's mood. Losing results can lead to an increase in heart attack, crime and suicide rates [10] [11]. It is therefore reasonable that sporting losses can also affect stock market returns. Edmans et al. (2007) [3] investigate the effect of international soccer matches on the stock market via changes in investor mood. The paper finds significant evidence that losing results negatively affect stock returns but no such evidence is found with respect to winnings.

Similarly, Kaplanski and Levi (2010) [6] find significant evidence that stock prices are negatively affected by large-scale aviation disasters, studying 288 disasters within a 58 year period from 1950 to 2007 using data from the Aviation Safety Network of the Flight Safety Foundation database and the NYSE Composite Index. In terms of monetary impact, the indirect loss caused by sentiment change is 60 times bigger than the actual loss of the aviation disaster, less than $1 billion per disaster on average.

These studies support the theory that stock returns are affected by economically-neutral events through their influence on investor psychology. Market participants, upset and anxious from these events, tend to be more pessimistic regarding future stock returns and have a lower tolerance of risk. As a result, their decision making process are by the negative sentiment, in turn affecting stock return.

Five market reactions occur consistently throughout these studies, serving as indicators that negative sentiment has affected market participant decision making. First, sharp declines of stock prices are commonly followed by reversals. Price declines associated with actual economic losses are unlikely to be consistently followed by a price reversal. Thus, these reversals are an indication that the market is not efficient. When events first happen, prices are driven down by panicked investors. When more informed investors exploit the mispricing, a reversal takes place. Second, the effects of the economically-neutral event are larger for smaller firms, firms in more unstable industries or firms with more volatile stocks. Third, the scale of the impact is correlated with the speed at which news of the event travels and the amount of media coverage on the event. Fourth, the event is also found to affect the perceived risk of companies, supported by increases in implied volatility while actual volatility remains unchanged. Fifth, there is no significant evidence that capital flowed out of the stock market enter into the bond market following an economically neutral event.

Edmans et al. (2007) summarizes three key characteristics an economically-neutral event (variable) must satisfy to rationalize studying its link with stock returns:"First, the given variable must drive mood in a substantial and unambiguous way, so that its effect is powerful enough to show up in asset prices. Second, the variable must impact the mood of a large proportion of the population, so that it is likely to affect enough investors. Third, the effect must be correlated across the majority of individuals within a country."

One additional criterion is the degree of media coverage, raised by Phillips (1974) [9], who documents the phenomenon that suicide rates increase following a suicide story with newspaper publications. Media coverage played an important role here as the increase in suicide rates occurred mainly in the region the story was published in. Media coverage is the vehicle that delivers the events to the general public and can influence all three characteristics above in some degree depending on the view and aggressiveness of the news.

Sudden deaths of celebrities generally have a powerful impact on a large proportion of the population and the emotional orientations of the impact on individuals are similar. Further, the deaths of well know celebrities attract attention of media as breaking news, meaning there is no lack of publication. Since all four criteria have been met, impacts of celebrity sudden deaths as economic-neutral events on the stock market are expected to be significant.

3 Data

A celebrity data set, with a corresponding popularity ranking is necessary for the study. Such a popularity ranking must consider a number of factors such as personal achievements, frequency of public exposure and media coverage. As a museum of celebrities who had great contribution to the American entertainment industry, the Hollywood Walk of Fame [1] provides the ranking. It is located in Hollywood, Los Angeles, with more than 2,000 pink five-pointed stars to commemorate influential celebrities. The sample initially consisted of 2439 celebrities holding more than 2000 stars on the Hollywood Walk of Fame. The difference between stars and celebrities arising as some stars are awarded to bands. Several fictional characters such as Mickey Mouse and Donald Duck have been removed from the sample. Furthermore, stars have been granted to people whose deaths are not expected to be economically-neutral, they have been removed from the sample as well. This includes Ronald Reagan, a former president of America whose death was striking news to the world.

Biographic data was collected for each celebrity, including date of birth, date of death, place of birth, place of death, age and the cause of death. The majority of the information is collected from Wikipedia, a free, web-based, collaborative, multilingual encyclopedia. The cause of death data is double checked using Google with the full name of celebrities and the phrase "cause of death" as key words.

Among these celebrities we identify 1483 deaths. Cancer and heart attack are the two most common causes of death. 754 deaths were categorized as sudden death, 500 as non-sudden death and 229 with no cause of death found.

For the purpose of this report, a sudden death is defined in the following way. If the cause of death is an accident such as airplane crash, gun accident or suicide, it qualifies as sudden death. If the cause of death is a health issue, then the illness must be acute. Of the celebrity deaths classified as a sudden death, 42 percent died from heart failure, 11 percent from pneumonia, 9 percent from stroke, 5 percent from respiratory or cardiac arrest, 4 percent from non-heart organ failures and 3 percent from emphysema. Accidents account for 8 percent of our sample. They include murder and suicide (27 cases), plane crashes (11 cases), traffic accidents (6 cases), drowning (3 cases), and other incidents (12 case). 139 deaths (18 percent) are attributed to other reasons which caused unexpected death.

The market impact of death of young celebrities is unlikely to be comparable to the death of older celebrities. For example, health conditions tend to deteriorate with age and as such, when an individual close to the average age of the population, contracts an illness or meets an injury, a lower impact is expected. Consider the death of Marilyn Monroe (5th of August, 1962, died at age of 36) and Charlie Chaplin (25th of December, 1977, died at the age of 88), the former is more shocking to the world. The sample used in this report includes celebrity deaths from beginning of the 20th century. With reference to the average population age at that time, this report only includes celebrities who had died at the age of 50 or younger. This further reduces the sample to 114 observations.

Financial data is available from the daily closing price of four major indices in the US. They are the Dow Jones, the NASDAQ, the NYSE and the S&P500, accessed from globalfinancialdata.com. The S&P500 data is used for this report as it provides data from the 31st of December, 1927, the earliest among the four indices.

4 Methodology and Empirical Results

Both the Ordinary Least Squares (OLS) test with a continuous dependent variable and the binary test method are employed in this paper to test the null hypothesis that sudden deaths of celebrities are economically-neutral events which do not have a significant impact on United States stock markets.

Equation 1 presents the first OLS model, based on the regression used by Saunders (1993).

$$R_t = \beta_0 + \beta_1 R_{t-1} + \beta_2 D_t + \beta_3 J_t + \beta_4 M_t + \beta_5 F_t \quad (1)$$

R_t is the simple return calculated from closing stock prices. A series of returns are calculated for the following event windows: (0), (-1, +1), (-1, +2) and (-2, +2). The model is run using each of the identified event windows.

D_t is a dummy variable that equals 1 when there is a sudden death of celebrity on that day and equals 0 when there is none. If the death occurred on a non-trading day (e.g. weekend) then the death is assigned to the closest trading day after the death.

R_{t-1} represents the lag (1) index return. For return periods longer than one day, it stands for the return of the previous return period.

J_t is the January dummy with value equal to 1 for returns in January and 0 for other months. This dummy variable is included to account for the January Effect, a calendar related anomaly in the financial market where abnormal return in January are larger compared to the remaining eleven months [8].

Mt is a dummy variable with value equal to 1 for returns calculated on a Monday and 0 for other days. Similarly, Ft is a dummy variable with value equal to 1 for returns calculated on a Friday and 0 for other days.

Regression results for model (1) are shown in Table 1.

Table 1.

Return Period	**Daily**	**(-1, +1)** ****	**(-1, +2)** ****	**(-2, +2)** ****
Lag	0.0349 ***	-0.0114	0.0023	-0.0127
Death Dummy	-0.0005	0.0004	0.0003	0.0004
January	0.0003	0.0006	0.0008	0.0011
Monday	-0.0019 ***	-0.0017 ***	-0.0011 ***	-0.0003
Friday	-0.0001	-0.0006 **	-0.0011 ***	-0.0008 ***
R^2	0.0050	0.0018	0.0008	0.0005
Adj. R^2	0.0047	0.0015	0.0006	0.0003
F - Test	21.6714	7.7451	3.6489	2.1525

* = significant at 10% level
** = significant at 5% level
*** = significant at 1% level
**** = using Newey-West HAC Standard Errors

According to the regression, the Death dummy Dt is not statistically significant.

As well as ordinary OLS test, a binary test has also been employed in this paper following Boyle and Walter (2003) [2]. This model uses a dummy variable as the dependent variable. The dummy value is equal to 1 if the stock return is positive the trading day after the event and equal to 0 if the stock return is negative the trading day after the event.

$$Sign_t = \beta_0 + \beta_1 R_{t-1} + \beta_2 D_t + \beta_3 J_t + \beta_4 M_t + \beta_5 F_t \qquad (2)$$

Again, there is no significant evidence supporting the influence of sudden celebrity death.

5 Conclusions

To conclude, this report presented an event study, following behavioral finance research, which tests the efficient market hypothesis. Motivated by prior research into the impact of economically-neutral events on the financial markets, this paper tested the proposition that sudden deaths of celebrities have a significant impact on the United States stock markets. The underlining logic being that although economically-neutral events reflect no financial information, it can alter the decision making process of financial professionals by affecting investor mood, confidence, risk aversion levels and emotional states. This in turn, influences the financial markets.

The sample used in this report consists of 114 sudden deaths of celebrities taken from the Hollywood Walk of Fame who died at the age of 50 or under. The stock returns used were the daily closing price of the S&P500 index for the period from the 1st of January, 1928 to the 31st of December, 2009. Index returns over five periods (0), (-1, +1), (-1, +2) and (-2, +2) were calculated and used in separate models for the study.

OLS and binary tests were employed in this report. Regressing the index returns against the sudden deaths dummy variable, the lagged index return, the January effect dummy, the Monday dummy and the Friday dummy, this paper found no significant evidence supporting the sudden celebrity death effect. Hence, the null hypothesis cannot be rejected.

The finding that stock market returns are not influenced by the economically-neutral event is consistent with the efficient market hypothesis, although the results are in contrast to those of early studies such as Saunders (1993) and Kamstra et al. (2000). One possible reason for this contradiction is that although there is some emotional impacts of celebrity sudden deaths, the magnitude of them are too weak to significantly influence stock returns. Boyle and Walter (2003) supplied another explanation when studying the effects of sports match results. They claim that the glory of the fans supporting the winning side is the pain of the fans supporting the losing side. Hence the overall impact on stock return is minimal. Such an explanation is inappropriate in this context as the sudden death of a celebrity is expected to raise either a negative or neutral response in individuals.

It is possible that only certain types of sudden death, such as suicide and murder, have a pronounced impact on the stock market. However, since these two causes of death only make up 11 deaths in the sample. Therefore, no reliable regressions can be conducted. Further studies need to be carried out in this direction based on a broader database.

References

1. List of stars on the Hollywood Walk of Fame (2010), `http://en.wikipedia.org/wiki/List_of_stars_on_the_Hollywood_Walk_of_Fame` (retrieved May 31, 2010)
2. Boyle, G., Walter, B.: Reflected glory and failure: international sporting success and the stock market. Applied Financial Economics 13(3), 225–235 (2003)
3. Edmans, A., García, D., Norli, Ø.: Sports Sentiment and Stock Returns. The Journal of Finance 62(4), 1967–1998 (2007)
4. Edward, M., Saunders, J.: Stock Prices and Wall Street Weather. The American Economic Review 83(5), 1337–1345 (1993)
5. Elliott, A.: Celebrity and Political Psychology: Remembering Lennon. Political Psychology 19(4), 833–852 (1998)
6. Kaplanski, G., Levy, H.: Sentiment and stock prices: The case of aviation disasters. Journal of Financial Economics 95(2), 174–201 (2010)
7. Kamstra, M.J., Kramer, L.A., Levi, M.D.: Winter Blues: A SAD Stock Market Cycle. The American Economic Review 93(1), 324–343 (2003)
8. Keim, D.B.: Size-related Anomalies and Stock Return Seasonality. Journal of Financial Economics 12, 13–32 (1982)
9. Phillips, D.P.: The Influence of Suggestion on Suicide: Substantive and Theoretical Implications of the Werther Effect. American Sociological Review 39(3), 340–354 (1974)
10. Trovato, F.: The Stanley Cup of hockey and suicide in Quebec. Social Forces 77(1), 105–126 (1998)
11. Wann, D.L., Dolan, T.J., Mcgeorge, K.K., Allison, J.A.: Relationships between spectator identification and spectators' perceptions of influence, spectators' emotions, and competition outcome. Journal of Sport and Exercise Psychology 16, 347 (1994)

The Factor Analysis Regarding High Price Tendency of Commercial Housing in Third-Tier Cities of China

Liqiao Ma and Qian Li

School of Management, Xi'an University of Architecture and Technology,
No. 13 Yanta Road, Xi'an, China
maliqiao@qq.com

Abstract. With third-tier cities' housing prices rising higher the more, it impacts national economy a lot. This paper aims to find out the factors which cause third-tier cities' housing prices too high. Take Baoji City as an example, we study on residential housing component costs, cities' GDP and income of urban residents, by applying data from National and Baoji City Bureau of Statistic over the years to summarize general trend in higher residential housing prices. From empirical research in conjunction with multiple linear regression analysis on economic and non-economic factors, we forecast residential housing prices trend of Baoji.

Keywords: Third-tier cities, Baoji City, Residential housing price, Multiple linear regression analysis and modeling, Discriminant analysis.

Introduction

Since 2004, tier and second tier cities' residential housing prices are rising too fast in China. So far from 2009, this trend has spread to third tier cities and become worsen. The sharp rise in residential housing prices in major cities makes a very heavy burden to local residents. On the one hand, with urban population growing, rigidity demand for housing is increasing, which changed arable land of outskirts into residential land while new arable land was not added promptly, on the other hand, for hedging against inflation, speculators invest huge capital in real estate industry, this behavior led to a large number of vacant houses while lower income residents can't even afford a small one to live in.

As third tier cities involved in this predicament, it's essential to find out these factors which lead to the contradiction between supply and demand. This paper takes Baoji City as an example, because it has some basic features as a third-tier city like convenient transportation, pleasant environment, lots of tourist attractions, etc.

1 Summary of Residential Real Estate Prices

1.1 Concept of Residential Real Estate Prices

Residential real estate prices are defined as the actual transaction price of houses developed by qualified real estate company. It consists of costs, taxes and profits etc.

Q. Zhou (Ed.): ISAEBD 2011, Part II, CCIS 209, pp. 448–453, 2011.

It is subject to the location, floor, direction, quality, material difference in price and other factors. In general, it consists of several components[1],that is land use right fee, development costs and expenses for the period, profits and taxes.

1.2 Criterion of Reasonable Residential Real Estate Prices

1.2.1 Real Estate Price Index

Real estate price index reflects price of different periods of the real estate market trends, in the form of percentage to reflect the range of different periods of ups and downs. It only reflects prices change caused by market supply and demand, and also the purchasing power of money, excluding other changing factors[2] . It is widely used to determine whether the price is reasonable or not.

1.2.2 Ratio between Housing Prices Than Income

Ratio between housing prices than income is an indicator to judge the reasonableness of the residential housing price. The ratio presented by Word Bank is 5:1, United Nations is 3:1. According to data analysis announced by government, this ratio of Baoji City is much higher than UN target, which is 12:1 ~ 15:1. Some experts believe, as a risk evaluation criterion, ratio between housing prices than income is an efficacious criterion. But in terms of the current situation of the country, it's better to consider it as a constraint on purchasing a house for working families.

1.2.3 Gross Domestic Product

Gross domestic product is a total measure of a country or region's all resident economic units final product in the accounting period. It's an important indicator of economic condition. When the ratio between real estate sales prices and GDP growth of a city is less than 1, then it is acceptable[3].

2 Factors Affect Residential Real Estate Prices

2.1 Impact of Consumer Price Index

Consumer price index is an inflation indicator. It reflects price variation of families purchasing on consumer goods and services expenditures. At present, according to State Statistical Bureau's report, domestic CPI contains 8 major categories, including food which weight is 34%, alcohol and tobacco(4%), clothing(9%), household equipment and services(6%),health care(10%),transportation and communication (10%), entertainment and education(14%), residence(13%). From this report, we know that residential consumption only takes 13%of the total, is it true? Actually, the percentage is much lower than it is, because sample data obtained so little that can't fully reflect the actual situation. This lead to a lower CPI, further caused low interest rates. So speculators swarm into the rest estate market, push up housing price by using bank credit of low interest. Then the price is higher and higher.

2.2 Influence of per Capita Income

In economics, effective demand is generated by consumer demand and the ability to make payments[4]. Under normal circumstances, the capacity to pay depends on income levels. As incomes rise, people are willing to pay more to improve the living conditions of existing. From the perspective of the marginal effect, the influence of increase income on housing prices is also differentiated. When people's income is in subsistence stage, the consumption of basic needs is increasing, but limited impact for residence. When income reaches a certain level which is sufficient to meet daily needs, it will lead to a further increase of housing demand, its marginal effect on housing prices will be more obvious. Therefore, the increase of per capita income is another economic factor makes high price trend.

2.3 Impact of GDP

Under the current rules of statistical, residential property prices accounted for half of the total domestic consumption in 2009 is not included in CPI, nor included in PPI. Thus, the amount increased by housing prices will be fully included in the GDP that year. For example, sold one million square meters when the price is 5000 Yuan per square meter may create a GDP of 5 billion Yuan, and if the price reaches to 20000 Yuan per square meter, correspondingly, the GDP is 20 billion Yuan. Area did not increase, but people need to pay more 15 million Yuan. There is no change in total output, but GDP has increased by 15 billion Yuan. It is based on the pursuit of increased GDP and fiscal revenue motives, local governments may be more willing to see the residential real estate prices at a high level. It's simple and effective to increase local revenues by selling land for third-tier cities which is lack of investment. All of this led to high prices.

The following data comes from Baoji Statistical Information Network 2004~2009, Baoji City National Economic and Social Development Statistic Bulletin, x_1 is an increase in consumer prices, x_2 for the per capita income, x_3 for the city's GDP, y is housing prices in center of Baoji City. From table1, housing prices increased evidently year by year when GDP is rising.

Table 1. Distribution of 2004~2009,housing prices in Baoji City

Year	x_1 (%)	x_2 (Yuan)	x_3 (billion Yuan)	y (Yuan/m²)
2004	3	8700	32.03	2423.1
2005	0.9	11247	41.579	2541.8
2006	1.6	12642	47.693	2696.9
2007	4.8	15439	58.016	2909.9
2008	6.0	18992	71.407	3008.8
2009	1.0	21525.5	80.656	3300

3 Modeling Based on Linear Regression Analysis

3.1 Modeling

According to general formula of multiple linear regression model ,

$$\hat{y} = b_0 + b_1x_1 + b_2x_2 + b_3x_3 . \tag{1}$$

Let

$$Q = \sum(y - \hat{y})^2 = \sum (y - b_0 - b_1x_1 - b_2x_2 - b_3x_3)^2 . \tag{2}$$

According to data from table 1,sum every column to caculate each item,we get the following results:

n=6, $\sum x_1$=17.3, $\sum x_2$=88545.5, $\sum x_3$=3313.81, $\sum y$=16880.5, $\sum x_1^2$=72.4, $\sum x_1x_2$=266034.2, $\sum x_1x_3$=9973.9, $\sum x_1y$=49192.28, $\sum x_2^2$=1424411108.3, $\sum x_2x_3$=53372664.1, $\sum x_2y$=256866030.1, $\sum x_3^2$=1999956.3, $\sum x_3y$=9617555.9.

Use the least squares method to determine b_0, b_1, b_2, b_3 to make Q smallest. Ternary function by the necessary condition for extremum of the standard equations can be deduced as follows:

$$\begin{cases} nb_0 + b_1\sum x_1 + b_2\sum x_2 + b_3\sum x_3 = y \\ b_0\sum x_1 + b_1\sum x_1^2 + b_2\sum x_1x_2 + b_3\sum x_1x_3 = \sum x_1y \\ b_0\sum x_2 + b_1\sum x_1x_2 + b_2\sum x_2^2 + b_3\sum x_2x_3 = \sum x_2y \\ b_0\sum x_3 + b_1\sum x_1x_3 + b_2\sum x_2x_3 + b_3\sum x_3^2 = \sum x_3y \end{cases} \tag{3}$$

Solving the equations above, we can get the results as follow:

b_0=1901.6656, b_1=-11.52, b_2=-0.1331, b_3=5.2678, take them into general formula, then the ternary linear regression model is:

$$\hat{y} = 1901.6656 - 11.52x_1 - 0.1331x_2 + 5.2678x_3 . \tag{4}$$

Fitting curve between price and time is described as Figure1:

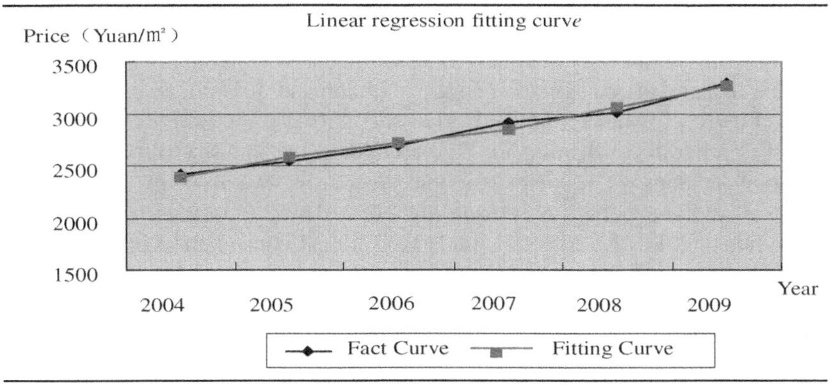

Fig. 1. Fitting curve between price and time

3.2 Model Fit Test

1. Coefficient of determination, denoted by R^2,

$$R^2 = \frac{U}{L_{YY}} = \frac{\sum(\hat{y}_i - \bar{y})^2}{\sum(y_i - \bar{y})^2} \tag{5}$$

Use the data above to calculate, R^2=0.9998, the literature[5] shows that the closer R^2 to 1,the better the model fit.

2. Estimated standard error denoted by S_Y,

$$S_Y = \sqrt{\frac{Q}{n-2}} = \sqrt{\frac{\sum(y_i - \hat{y})^2}{n-2}} \tag{6}$$

Use the data above to calculate, S_Y=51.6481, according to literature[5],the smaller S_Y is, the better the model fit.

4 Results Analysis

In regression analysis, the influence coefficient of CPI on housing price has reached to -11.52, it's consistent with chain reaction which is caused by fluctuations in the CPI index, lower CPI induces lower interest rates which make the speculators take advantage of bank credit to push up residential real estate prices more easily. In addition, per capita income effect on the price is very small, only -0.1331, of course, prices can be reduced for the reason of per capita income increasing, but compare to the other two factors, the amount of reduce is minimal. Meanwhile, with the improvement of living quality, developers have to provide high quality house in order to meet market demand, and rising costs make the price rise at the same time. Moreover, the government departments also expected housing prices could maintain a high level in order to facilitate the city's GDP. In view of this, housing prices in third-tier cities will naturally rise year by year. We infer this trend will go on in future.

5 Conclusion

To sum up, in a similar third-tier city like Baoji, in rapid progress of urbanization process, the recent real estate market supply and demand does not occur significantly improved. Future pressure on upward price still persists. We propose the following advices to improve the situation: Firstly, strengthen the industry, service and other real economy to improve residents' income. Secondly, speed up the social security system to ensure residents' retirement benefits. Thirdly, increase investment in affordable housing. Lastly, correctly guide the rational consumption of the residents, change their notion of living, 'own' to 'rent'.

Acknowledgments. I would like to express my gratitude to all those who helped me during the writing of this thesis. My deepest gratitude goes first and foremost to associate Professor Qian Li, my supervisor, for her constant encouragement and guidance. Without her consistent and illuminating instruction, this thesis could not have reached its present form.

References

1. Liu, C.: Budget Estimate of Civil Engineering, pp. 9–21. Wuhan University of Technology Press, Wuhan (2000)
2. Cao, Z.: General Theory of Real Estate Economics, pp. 156–161. Peking University Press, Beijing (2003)
3. Run, Z.: GDP and FDI Effects on Real Estate Prices in China Empirical Analysis. Economic Research Guide (1), 177–179 (2007)
4. Li, L., Dong, Z.: Economic Applied Statistics Tutorial, vol. 7, pp. 254–293. Economic Daily Press, Beijing (2005)
5. Liu, Y.: Mathematical Model of Multiple Linear Regression. Journal of Shenyang Institute of Engineering 128, 38–39 (2005)

Study of Customer Segmentation in E-Business

Ling Tian and Guangwen Ren

School of Management, Beijing Union University,
100101 Beijing, China
glttianling@buu.edu.cn,
gltguangwen@buu.edu.cn

Abstract. Along with the network popularization and e-business in-depth development, customer relationship management has attracted attention from a wide variety of professions. Segmenting customers effectively is the premise and guarantee to realize the targeted customer relationship management. Given that customers' dynamic and virtual characteristics under network environment, this article further details the conventional RFM index (Recency, Frequency, Monetary) after studying the conventional customer segmentation. As the standard of customer segmentation, the refined RMF receives a better result as it establishes a customer segmentation index system which fits various characteristics of e-business.

Keywords: E-business, CRM, Customer Segmentation, RFM, Index System.

1 Introduction

With the popularization of the internet and the development of e-business, much more business is conducted via the internet. Internet provides mutual, direct and interactive communication, which allows the enterprise to shorten the distance between them and their customers. The use of internet in business challenges and greatly influences the traditional concept of marketing strategies as well as customer body. The increase of business information via internet brings more options to the customers, and thus requires more dynamic interaction between the enterprise and the customers. The explosive growth of customer data increases difficulties for understanding the customers. Moreover, the e-business model requires agile service, quality product, quick response and accurate identification, which are caused by the personalized and much more matured needs of the customers.

These changes shift the enterprise's focus from the product to the customer, and thus, establishing a long-term cooperative relationship with the customer has become an essential key for the business' continuous, steady and long-term development. As a result, how to effectively manage the relationship with the customers has become an important issue that attracts attention from various industries.

Q. Zhou (Ed.): ISAEBD 2011, Part II, CCIS 209, pp. 454–459, 2011.

2 Customer Segmentation in CRM

Customer relationship management (CRM) is to obtain, maintain and increase value to customers. The priority is to take effective way to segment customers into different major classes or types. And according to the importance degrees, the enterprise assigns limited resources to different classes of client unequally, to save corporate resources, to improve enterprise level of services, to increase customer loyalties, and ultimately maximizes corporate profits and the interest of customers.

2.1 CRM and Customer Segmentation

Customer Relationship Management (CRM) is to obtain, maintain and increase the number of valuable customers. The primary concern is to take effective method to segment customers into different classes or types according to their degree of importance and which allows the enterprise to assign its limited resources unequally. As a result, the enterprise is able to save its limited resources, improve the level of customer service, enhance customer loyalty and ultimately maximize corporate profits and the interest of customers.

2.2 The Conventional Indexes of Customer Segmentation

As shown in Figure 1, in a conventional environment, indexes that often being used to segment customers include.

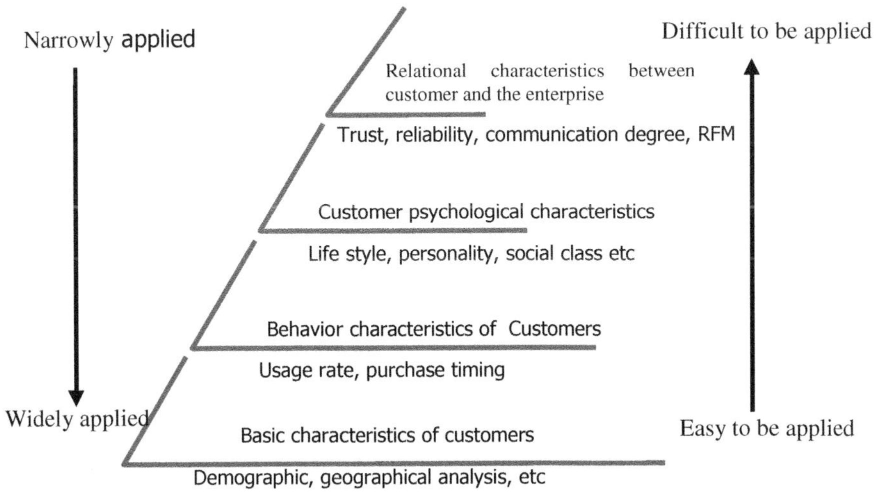

Fig. 1. The conventional indexes of customer segmentation

The conventional indexes of customer segmentation are: demographic and social factors, geographic area factors, psychological factors, customer benefits, behavior factors, product and customer value and etc. All these factors could be classified into four major index categories: basic characteristics, psychological characteristics, behavior characteristics of customers and the relational features between customer and enterprise (as shown in Figure 1).

There are four major index categories in customers' segmentation (as shown in Figure 1):

1. Customer basic characteristics

This type of indexes is based mainly on humanities statistics and geographical analysis and it is the most commonly used and most convenient index being used so far. This index includes factors such as demographic statistics, geography and contextual factors, for example the age, gender, income, occupation, education, religion, geographical location and social environment etc.

2. Customer behavior characteristics

This type of index reflects different perception and reaction from customers towards the product or service. Usage rate, purchase timing, media preference and marketing mix factors are mainly considered. Since this kind of customer data can be obtained easily, this index is widely used in practice.

3. Customer psychological characteristics

This type of index embodies activities, interests and perspectives through some particular customer psychological characteristics and specific environment features, such as life style, personality, social class and etc. Since it is difficult to collect such kind of data, the application range of this index is relatively narrow.

4. Relational characteristics between customer and the enterprise

This type of indexes mainly emphasizes a multi-related relational structure between customer and the enterprise. It is the most difficult index to measure, yet providing the most accurate measurement result and therefore is being used in the minimum application range. This index includes factors such as the sense of trust, reliability, communication degree, RFM (Recency, Frequency, Monetary), and etc.

3 Study of Customer Segmentation Index System in E-Business

In view of the changes brought from the network environment and e-business in-depth application to enterprise and customer and also the various characteristics of customer value and behavior such as multi-channel nature, complexity, diversity, mutability and virtuality, it is certain that the accurate customer segmentation is not a problem to be solved by a single index, a method or a factor. Therefore, this article uses the most easily quantifiable, accurate, and easy-to-use RFM index raised by direct marketing expert Bobby Stone as the foundation. The index is based on many other database marketing study experience and to use the detailed RFM index as the segmentation standard, establishing the index system (as shown in table 1).

Table 1. Customer segmentation index system in e-business

Index	Detailing	Detailing method and implication
1st- Recency	R_1	The ratio between a particular customer's average customer recency value and the total customers' recency value. It measures long-term customer behavior from a macroscopic view and being used as the basis for analyzing customer loyalty and satisfaction.
	R_2	The ratio between a particular customer's latest recency value and his/her historical recency value. It measures the latest abrupt change to his/her dynamic behavior from a microscopic view and thus identifies the signal of losing this customer.
	R_3	The ratio between a particular customer's latest average recency value and the total customers' average recency value. It measures the variation trend of the customer's latest dynamic behavior and his/her potential value from a macroscopic view. Thus enables the enterprise to predict customer satisfaction and potential value.
2nd- Frequency	F_1	The ratio between a particular customer's average frequency value and the total customers' average frequency value. It examines the customer's long-term connection with the enterprise from a macroscopic view and thus indentifies customer loyalty and satisfaction. It helps to find the customers who have the closest connection with the enterprise.
	F_2	The ratio between a particular customer's latest frequency value and his/her historical frequency value. It examines the customer's short-term behavior abrupt change and his/her variety trend from a microscopic view.
	F_3	The ratio between a particular customer's latest average frequency value and the total customers' average frequency value. It examines the variety trend of a customer's latest behavior abrupt change and his/her potential value from a macroscopic view.

Table 1. (*continued*)

3rd-Monetary	M_1	The ratio between a particular customer's total monetary value and the total customers' average monetary value. It measures the customer historical value from a macroscopic view.
	M_2	The ratio between a particular customer's latest monetary value and his/her historical monetary value. It identifies a customer's variety trend and his/her potential value from a microscopic view.
	M_3	The ratio between a particular customer's latest monetary value and the total customers' average monetary value. It identifies the customer's current value from a macroscopic view.
	M_4	Customer value-added potential, valued by experts through evaluating the customer's overall strength. It identifies the market growth and potential value of customers from a microscopic view.

In conclusion, the above index reflects various factors including static, dynamic, long-term, short-term, macroscopic and microscopic factors. All these factors form the customer segmentation index system together in e-business. It considers comprehensively of customer value (historical, current and potential value etc) and customer behavior (transaction change and trend of running away etc).

It analyzes each type of customers' characteristics more accurately (customer growth and etc), and therefore enables the enterprise to come up with various coping strategies after segmenting customers (as shown in Figure 2).

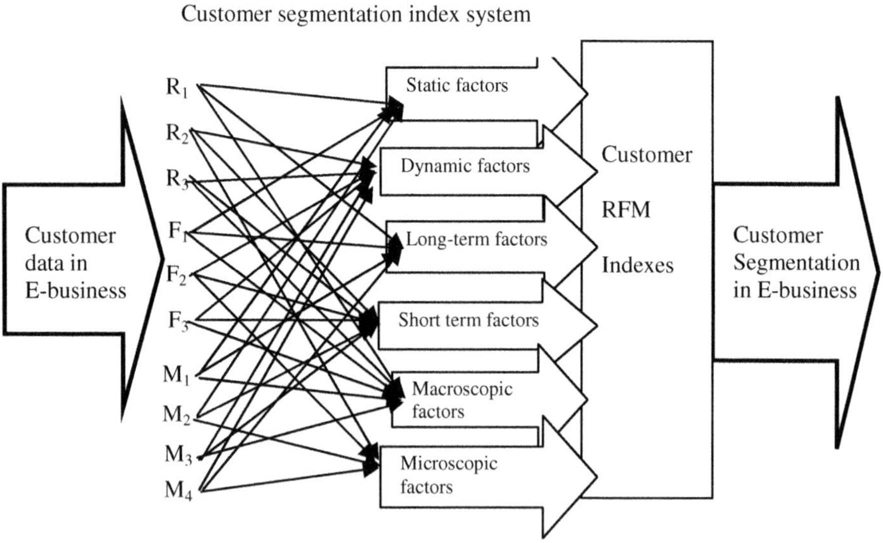

Fig. 2. The process of Customer Segmentation in E-business

4 Practice and Experimental Verification

Compared with other segmentation indexes, this article not only considers customer values (static factors such as historical, current and potential values), but also integrates customer behaviors (dynamic factors such as transaction change and trend of running away).

Also, this index system measures the current value of the customer as well as the growth and potential value of the customer which fits the real situation in e-business customer management more accordingly.

Moreover, this index is easy to be measured and quantified; it also eliminates artificial factors which increase the authenticity of the measuring result, making it more feasible and possible to achieve success customer segmentation.

Overall, e-business enterprises can get a more practical segmentation result after analyzing their customer data using this index system. This has certain research value and practical significance.

5 Conclusion

This paper focuses on customer segmentation index system in CRM, because segmenting customers effectively is the premise and guarantee to realize the targeted customer relationship management. Given that customers' dynamic and virtual characteristics under network environment, this article further details the conventional RFM index (Recency, Frequency, Monetary) after studying the conventional customer segmentation. As the standard of customer segmentation, the refined RMF receives a better result as it establishes a customer segmentation index system which fits various characteristics of e-business.

Acknowledgement. This work reported in this paper is supported by the Natural Science Research Project form Beijing Union University, Beijing, which is from "Study of Marketing Strategies in Beijing's Small and Medium Sized E-business Enterprises" (SK200944X); please allow me to express my gratitude here.

References

1. Newell, F., Li, A., (translate): The customer relations manage in the Internet age. Huaxia Press, Beijing (2001) (in Chinese)
2. Fan, z., Wang, J., Chen, Y.: Comments and forecast for customer relations manage (CRM). Systems Engineering 20(6), 1–8 (2002) (in Chinese)
3. Wu, K.: An analysis on customer segmentation method. Industrial Technology Economy 22(6), 95–96 (2003)
4. Tsai, C.Y., Chiu, C.C.: A purchase-based market segmentation methodology. Expert Systems with Applications 27(2), 265–276 (2004)
5. Jedid-Jah, J., Nanda, P.: Joint optimization of customer segmentation and marketing policy to maximize long-term profitability. Expert Systems with Applications 27(2), 159–168 (2004)
6. Tian, L.: The study of customer relationship management in e-business age. Intellectual-Property Press, Beijing (2009) (in Chinese)

Statistical Data Analysis of Typical Silk Enterprise Based on BP Neural Network

Cen Feng[1,2], Bingdi Liu[1], Hai Liu[1], and Lun Bai[1,2,*]

[1] Soochow University, Suzhou, 215006, China
[2] National Engineering Laboratory for Modern Silk, Soochow University, Suzhou, 215123, China
fengcen@suda.edu.cn, Liubingdi_111@163.com, 20094215012@suda.edu.cn, bailun@suda.edu.cn

Abstract. The topic used BP network to make positive analysis on silk, satin and clothing export sales to get full commodity export predictive value. At the same time, adopted Time Series to set up corresponding models, and then made comparison between their results to get suitable fluctuation analysis in silk export market. The method use will supply the producer and the operator with feasible quantification target for studying dynamic change as well as predicting the future.

Keywords: BP Neural Network, Full Commodity Export Sales, Models.

1 Introduction

Silk industry is one of the Chinese traditional industries and a typical export-oriented industry with obviously regional characteristics. Silk, satin and clothing exports accounted of total world trade for 90%, 70% and 60% respectively. Within the years of data statistics and collection process in silk industry, subsequent judgment and qualitative judgment caused hysteresis and the lack of quantification in the market management and policy establishment. In order to obtain an appropriate method of analyzing the silk export market volatility, this paper based on the actual data of the typical silk enterprises' exportation, studied the predictive analysis using BP artificial neural network, and compared the result with the one made of time series modeling prediction. This paper aimed to provide one viable quantitative parameter to the producers and the operators for researching the dynamic change and predicting the future development.

* Corresponding author.

Q. Zhou (Ed.): ISAEBD 2011, Part II, CCIS 209, pp. 460–466, 2011.

2 BP Artificial Neural Network Model of the Typical Silk Enterprises' Export Data

2.1 Full Commodity Exports' Data Collection of the Typical Silk Enterprises

This paper selected 84 groups of full commodity exports' data spanning from January 2003 to December 2009 monthly. The data were derived from the actual operating results of the China National Silk Import and Export Corporation in recent years. The impacts of the full commodity exports were silk exports, satin exports and clothing exports. Fig.1 is the statistical data curves of the full commodity exports and its factors.

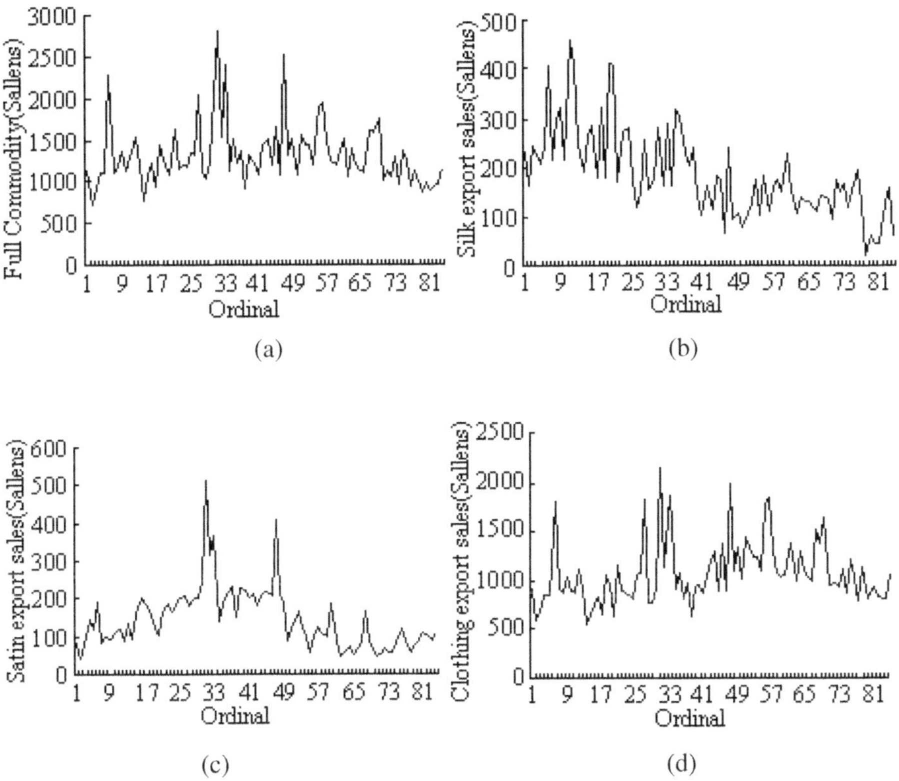

Fig. 1. Statistical data curves of the full commodity export and its factors (The data are from the China National Silk Import and Export Corporation)

2.2 Full Commodity Export Sales Prediction Based on BP Artificial Neural Network

The topic made use of BP Neural Network predictive thinking on condition of existing data, took full commodity export sales as well as its influencing factors as studying sample, determined the relationship between them according to BP Neural Network, and then forecast the full commodity export sales with future value of its influencing factors future value.

Set up a BP Neural Network, the first layer for input, input vector are influencing factors of full commodity export sales, the hide layer is in the middle, made approximation to annual of full commodity export sales for our country by means of adjusting neuron weight, the last layer is for output, and input vector are full commodity export sales, made some corresponding treatment for output network and got the predictive value [1-2].

Thought 1-72 team's data as training sample, 73-84 as test sample to analyze. Analyzed silk export sales, satin export sales and clothing export sales respectively by dint of BP Neural Network. Considered 12 team's data as input of network data in turn, and the latter 12 team's as output of network data, which is also named target data, arranging them in the rolling type and forming the training sample for neural network.. Determined the hidden neuron numbers corresponding to the minimum err for the network and the most rapid training in the light of cut-and-trial to increase the hidden neurons. The comparison results for silk export sales of different hidden neurons are shown in Table 1.

Table 1. Results of different network comparisons for silk export sales

Hidden neurons	Times	Iterative-number	Hidden neurons	Times	Iterative-number
4	4	3.62×10^{-7}	17	2	6.24×10^{-6}
5	3	5.93×10^{-6}	18	3	3.27×10^{-11}
6	4	3.26×10^{-7}	19	3	1.43×10^{-10}
7	3	2.35×10^{-6}	20	3	3.44×10^{-9}
8	3	5.29×10^{-6}	21	3	1.04×10^{-10}
9	3	8.72×10^{-10}	22	2	2.51×10^{-7}
10	3	1.32×10^{-8}	23	3	1.87×10^{-11}
11	3	8.59×10^{-9}	24	2	3.61×10^{-6}
12	3	1.08×10^{-11}	25	2	1.24×10^{-7}
13	3	1.14×10^{-9}	26	2	8.44×10^{-6}
14	2	1.40×10^{-6}	27	3	5.29×10^{-11}
15	3	4.25×10^{-8}	28	2	1.33×10^{-6}
16	3	4.57×10^{-10}	29	2	3.20×10^{-6}

According to Table 1, we can see that hidden neurons for silk, satin and clothing are 12,29,and 24. Then made fitting for the network, in the end, obtained their predictive value. By the way, their fitting results are shown in Figure 2.

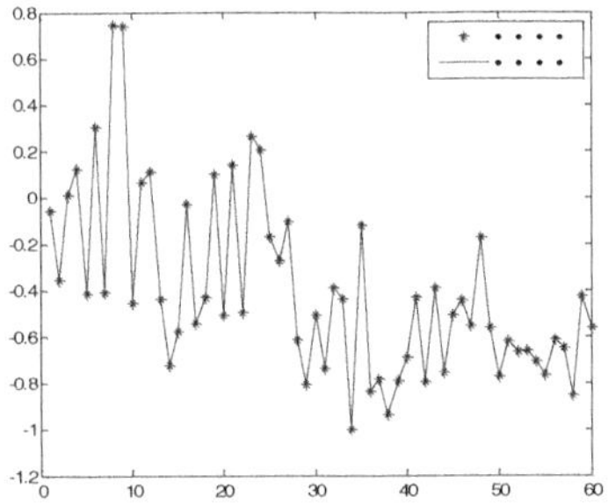

(a) Fitting for silk export sales

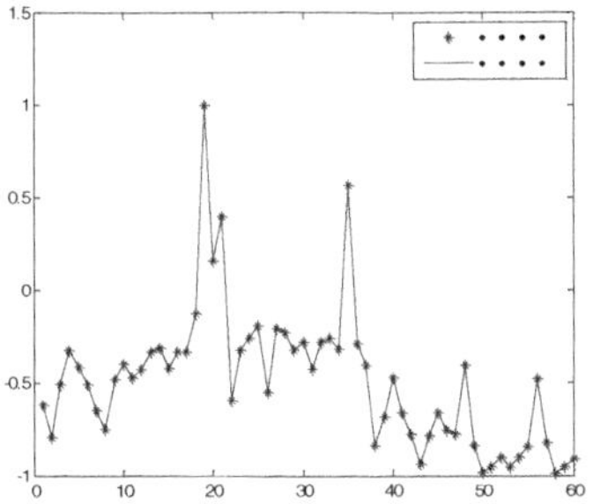

(b) Fitting for satin export sales

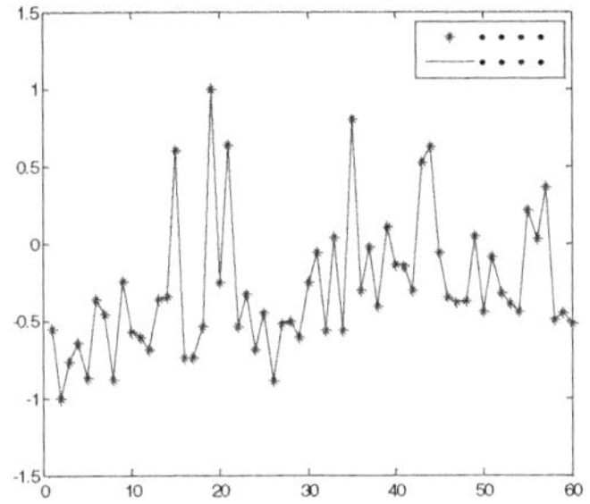

(c) Fitting for clothing export sales

Fig. 2. BP Neural Network fitting for silk, satin and clothing export sales

Table 2. Comparison of actual and predictive value of full commodity export sales

Ordinal	Actual (Sallens)	Predictive(Sallens)	Absolute error	Relative error(%)
1	1283.5500	1312.0718	28.5208	2.2220
2	958.6700	891.5581	67.1119	7.0005
3	1365.1100	1386.2811	21.1711	1.5509
4	1270.2900	1444.8415	174.5515	13.7411
5	923.9900	1013.1744	89.1844	9.6521
6	1134.2300	1133.0833	1.1467	0.1011
7	865.5400	1222.0701	356.5301	41.1916
8	974.3800	908.1968	66.1832	6.7923
9	891.8700	1034.3591	142.4891	15.9764
10	939.8500	1067.2954	127.4454	13.5601
11	959.0300	790.9005	168.1295	17.5312
12	1168.1500	1253.3674	85.2174	7.2951
Average error			110.6401	11.3845

It's suggested that BP Neural Network is suitable for analysis and prediction silk, satin and clothing export sales. At the same time, on account of comparison of actual and predictive value of silk, satin and clothing export sales in Table2, the mean absolute error and relative error are: 110.6401, 11.3845%, 88.6155%, judged from 12 predictive indicator that predictable accuracy is higher for short-term forecasting.

3 Time Series Models Building for Typical Silk Export Enterprise

Made smooth Conversion on full commodity export sales time series and drew autocorrelation and partial correlation figure, judged whether there is auto-regression different variance effect in the time series by LM test [3-6]. At last, built AR(3) model according to full commodity export sales feature. Got the auto-regression coefficient of Dy_t time series and interference terms with least squares, the Dy_t model is:

$$Dy_t = -0.7141(Dy_{t-1} + 2.5031) - 0.3442(Dy_{t-2} + 2.5031) - 0.3239(Dy_{t-3} + 2.5031) + 2.5031$$

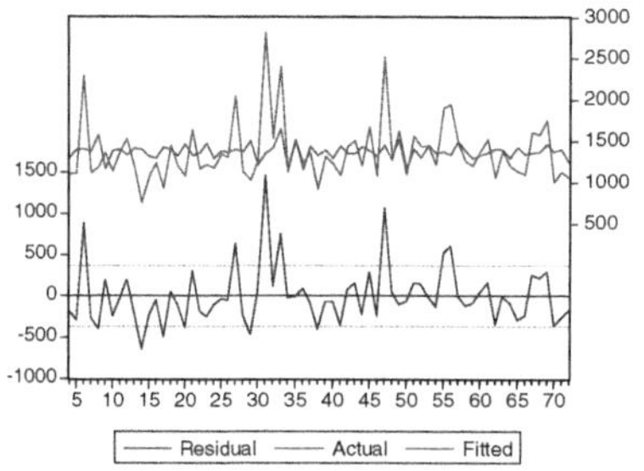

Fig. 3. Fitting of time series

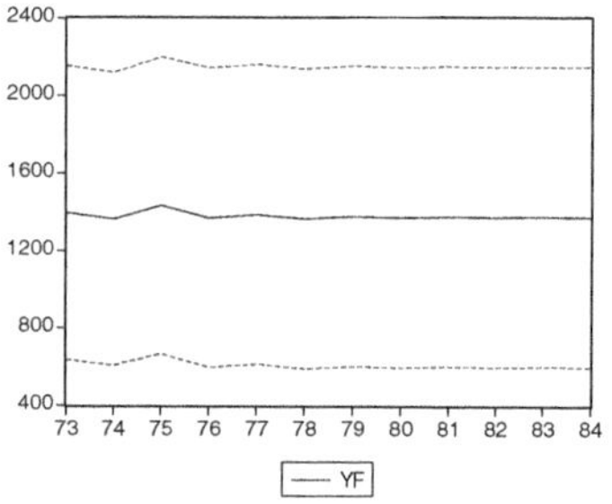

Fig. 4. Prediction of time series

Table 3. Comparison of actual value and fitting of full commodity export sales

Ordinal	Actual (Sallens)	Predictive(Sallens)	Absolute error	Relative error(%)
1	1283.5500	1318.0187	34.4687	2.6854
2	958.6700	1124.8584	166.1884	17.3353
3	1365.1100	1203.4487	161.6613	11.8424
4	1270.2900	1137.1709	133.1191	10.4794
5	923.9900	1225.9710	301.9810	32.6823
6	1134.2300	1165.8843	31.6543	2.7908
7	865.5400	1205.6523	340.1123	39.2948
8	974.3800	1175.1405	200.7605	20.6039
9	891.8700	1208.6633	316.7933	35.5201
10	939.8500	1188.3113	248.4613	26.4363
11	959.0300	1207.1499	248.1199	25.8720
12	1168.1500	1195.8089	27.6589	2.3678
Average error			184.2483	18.9925

The fitting and prediction of full commodity export sales are shown in Figure 3 and Figure 4. In Figure 3, initial data is changed between 1000 and 3000, and fitting error is from -500 to 500, which is in coincidence with confidence interval. In Figure 4, the real line signifies dependent variable prediction, the two dotted lines on the top and bottom are forecast close to 95% confidence interval, error is increased little by little approximately; what is more, variation trend of predictive value is in accordance with actual value. In addition, the Comparison of actual value and fitting of full commodity export sales are shown in Table3. The average absolute error, average relative error and accuracy are : 184.2483, 18.9925%, 81.0075%.

4 The Comparisons of the Two Methods for the Statistical Data of Typical Silk Company

Figure 5 shows the pattern description of comparisons among actual data, BP predictive data, time series data for full commodity export sales. Table 4 shows every evaluation of estimate of prediction by BP Neural Network as well as Time series, which contains MAE, SSE, MAPE, A and so on.

Table 4. Comparisons of evaluation of estimate between two methods

Indicator	MAE	SSE	MSE	MAPE	A
BP Neural	110.6401	247758	20646.4994	11.3845%	88.6155%
Time Series	184.2483	545256.8151	45438.0679	18.9925%	81.0075%

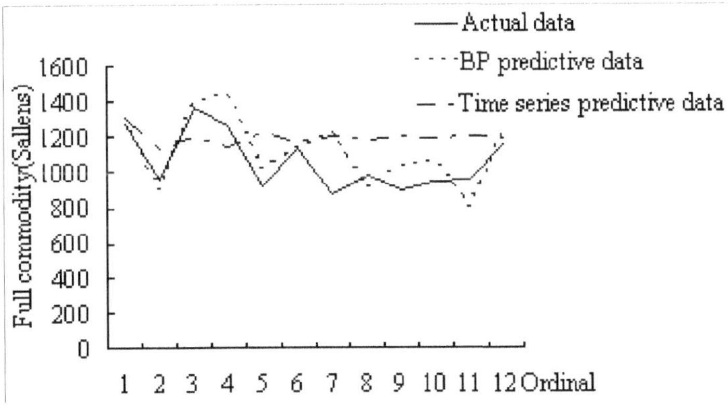

Fig. 5. Comparisons among actual data, BP predictive data, time series data

According to comparisons among evaluation value, we can find that both BP Neural Network and Time series maybe used for full commodity export sales prediction, besides, branch predictor by BP Neural Network is better than Time series, which can fit actual data better. Judged from Table 6, MAE, SSE, MAPE by BP Neural Network are less than that by Time series. The positive analysis prove that, thanks to human factors taking parting in the BP artificial neural network prediction, it can develop subjective activity of the statistical personnel, and has the ability of intervening the market on the prediction, nevertheless, for the time series, after the data is determined, it only can express and forecast the future passively under the mathematical theory model state. Consequently, in terms of full commodity export sales being influenced by many factors, BP Neural Network has more advantage for using on the modeling and prediction, which can help deciders in silk industry with judging and analyzing new circumstance and new problems in export trend as well as economic development for silk products, adjust policy for company in time to carry out expected target for the enterprise.

5 Conclusions

(1) Took advantage of BP Neural Network to make positive analysis on market fluctuation data for silk, satin and clothing based on shared pool of typical silk export company, took the relationships between full commodity export sales and its influence factors into account, used predictive value of its influence factors to predict full commodity export sales. At last, the predictive precision is 88.6255%, which shows that BP Neural Network is fit for short-term forecasting.

(2) Made use of Time series to analyze and predict full commodity export sales, making smooth conversion on raw silk price time series, drawing autocorrelation and partial correlation figure, judging whether there is auto-regression different variance effect in the time series by LM test, built corresponding time series model, and the predictive precision is 81.0075%, which shows that Time series is available for full commodity export sales prediction, but the relative error is larger appreciably.

(3) The predictive results by two methods show that BP Neural Network is superior to Time series on MAE, SSE, MAPE and A, which is more suitable for prediction and analysis for actual statistical data, and can supply feasible quantized indicator for producers as well as operators to work over trends changes and predict the future.

Acknowledgements. Financial support for this work was provided by the Project for National Engineering Laboratory for Modern Silk of Jiangsu (KJS0916) and Creative Research Project for Graduate Students of Jiangsu Province (CX10B_037Z) and A Project Funded by the Priority Academic Program Development of Jiangsu Higher Education Institutions.

References

1. Dai, D.: The Research on BP Neural Network Used on market forecasting. Wuhan University of Technology, Wuhan (2006)
2. He, Q.b.: Back propagation Neural Network and Applications. Chongqing Jiaotong University, Chongqing (2004)
3. Wang, Z., Hu, Y.: Application of time series analysis. Science Press, Beijing (2007)
4. Feng, C., Nie, B., Liu, B.-D., Bai, L.: Time Series Modeling and Analysis on the Silk Crape Satin Product. In: Advanced Material Research (EI 2011), vol. 175-176, pp. 412–417 (2011)
5. Zhang, X.: A Guide to Using Eviews. China Machine Press (2007)

Measuring Independent Innovation Capability of Advanced Material Industry in the Yangtze River Delta Area: Scale Development and Validation

Rong Wang, Lianghua Chen, and Yan Li

School of Economy and Management, Southeast University, Nanjing, China
wangr6899@163.com

Abstract. Independent innovation capability of advanced material industry (AMI) has been highly valued in recent research. This paper developed a scale for evaluating independent innovation capability of AMI from the external view of government manager. The result of survey shows that independent innovation capability of AMI consists of several facets such as innovation strategy, innovation technology, innovation funds, innovative talents, innovation environment and innovation culture. In addition, our results demonstrate that independent innovation capability of AMI in the Yangtze River Delta Area need to upgrade. The practical implications are discussed in the end.

Keywords: Independent innovation capability, Scale development, Advanced material industry.

1 Introduction

It is extraordinary important to recognize and measure the independent innovation capability of the industries in China (The concept of independent innovation is newest put forward by Chinese experts and scholars. Overseas similar concept is endogenous innovation and integration innovation), which has been the strategic basis of the science and technology development and the key link in adjusting the industrial structure and transforming the economic growth pattern [1-3]. The Yangtze River Delta is one of the most dynamic industry clusters in China or even the world. The study in measuring the independent innovation capability of the Advanced Material Industry (AMI) in this area by scale development [4] is thus put forward.

The AMI (Advanced Materials are new and developing materials with traditional materials not available in excellent performance and special function. Some key materials satisfying the development of high-tech industry generally belong to the category of advanced material.) is the pilot and foundation of many other industries, which were known as one of the three major promising industries. The most prominent characteristics of the AMI are technology intensiveness, high investment on R&D and remarkable economical benefits. The independent innovation capability is the capability on the original innovation, integrated innovation and the introduction of further absorption of innovation, whose essence is not only a kind of technology capability, but also ability to self-integrated and gain competitive advantage by the application of

Q. Zhou (Ed.): ISAEBD 2011, Part II, CCIS 209, pp. 467–473, 2011.

various technical knowledge comprehensively. The correlation researches in home and abroad have given many definitions on independent innovation capability. Burgelman & Madique (1988) assisted those aspects would be available resource, ability to understand the competitors and environment, organizational structure and culture, strategic management ability; While Barton (1992) thought it should be considered in such aspects as technology manager, creative management, technology system, technology consciousness; WEN Ruijun (2005) pointed out that it was shown by research & development ability, manufacturing ability, value realization ability and autonomous management ability.

In order to fully cover the definition of the IIC (independent innovation capability) in AMI, based on the existing results [5-11] and the characteristics of AMI, this paper generalizes the composition of IIC in six aspects as innovation strategy, innovation technology, innovation funds, innovative talents, innovation environment and innovation culture. It is necessary to develop an indexes library which can totally cover these six parts firstly, then classify those overlapping indexes on the basis of positive analysis.

2 Index Development and Validation

It is emphasized that the system of evaluation would be found from the external view of government manager. Therefore, referring to Churchill's index develop procedure (1979), this paper develops a project library composed by 68 indexes at the first, 20 indexes are extracted by exploratory factor analysis (EFA) and confirmatory factor analysis (CFA) on the basis of preliminary investigation and the first empirical analysis. Thereafter, the second empirical test is put forward on the indexes system's reliability and validity by enlarged sample data. PASW Statistics (SPSS) 18.0 & LISREL8.8 are used in this article.

2.1 Index Screening

The preliminary investigation at the very first aimed 20 experts in the area of industrial economy, through which the most overlapping and less-validity indexes were eliminated, and 32 indexes were generated to cover the comprehensive property of IIC in AMI. Based on that, we developed the first exploratory investigation on some AMI enterprises in South Jiangsu (Suzhou, Wuxi, Changzhou, Nanjing, Zhenjiang) by questionnaire on those 32 indexes. 95 copies of valid questionnaire were recalled, all indexes were measured in Likert 7 Scale. (7=totally agree; 1=totally disagree) Through Kaiser-Meyer-Olkin Test and Bartlett Test by 95 samples, we confirmed factor analysis could be used here. After measuring the unidimensionality & reliability of the 32 indexes, EFA was employed on the samples, as a result, 6 factors were extracted by the method of oblique rotation. In order to get the valuable factor, the screen standards in this paper are: (1) Index's minimum loading value on each factor is 0.4; (2) the least factor intersection load value; (3) the same index's intension on the same factors. Under these procedures, 23 indexes were kept still, and 70.34% variance can be explained.

2.2 Index Test on Reliability and Validity

A series of CFA are employed by Lisrel 8.8 to examine 23 indexes' reliability, validity and structure, and, 3 indexes which may weaken corresponding factor's internal consistency are eliminated. After analysis, the measuring model made by remaining 20 indexes came out the fitting degree value as χ^2=332.28, GFI=0.75, NFI=0.73, NNFI=0.79, CFI=0.82, IFI=0.82, SRMR= 0.091, RMSEA=0.11, and the range of factor loading was 0.590-0.959. Furthermore, the index system is with superior reliability and validity in measurement because most factor loading value over 0.7 and all Alpha coefficients over ordinary acceptable standard—0.7.

2.3 Index Validation on Applicability

We expanded investigation area into the Yangtze River Delta Area for test the exist 20 indexes' measurement accuracy and applicability, and got 320 copies of questionaire. With which, 20 indexes and the index system were updated, the corresponding fitting degree values are χ^2=1316.848, GFI=0.9, NFI=0.92, NNFI=0.92, CFI=0.93, IFI=0.93, SRMR=0.057, RMSEA=0.088 (as indicated in Table 1). It is shown that 20 indexes generates 6 factors as "innovation strategy, innovation technology, innovation funds, innovative talents, innovation environment and innovation culture", with each index's factor load highly significant and all Alpha coefficients over 0.7. The system's reliability, validity and the applicability in AMI are thoroughly proved.

Table 1. CFA analysis (*n*=320)

Factor	Index	Factor Load	T value	Alpha coefficient
innovation strategy	A1	0.762	24.367	0.848
	A2	0.770	26.806	
	A3	0.611	15.094	
	A4	0.619	16.314	
innovation technology	B1	0.844	31.996	0.719
	B2	0.810	27.390	
	B3	0.748	25.255	
	B4	0.730	20.746	
innovation funds	C1	0.702	18.912	0.807
	C2	0.863	33.585	
	C3	0.644	17.872	
innovative talents	D1	0.695	17.785	0.799
	D2	0.783	25.550	
	D3	0.826	32.347	
innovation environment	E1	0.850	35.320	0.791
	E2	0.783	26.534	
	E3	0.806	27.974	
innovation culture	F1	0.828	29.365	0.817
	F2	0.928	37.552	
	F3	0.921	36.350	
Fitting Degree of our Model	χ^2=1316.848, GFI=0.9, NFI=0.92, NNFI=0.92, CFI=0.93, IFI=0.93, SRMR= 0.057, RMSEA=0.088			

3 IIC Evaluation on AMI in Yangtze River Delta

High or low IIC directly determines the innovative performance, therefore, in order to get further evaluation the IIC of AMI in the Yangtze River Delta, we took the average score(from original evaluation data) in each factor as six independent variable and took the average score of "innovative performance" as dependent variable (from four assessment project of innovative performance)to get further study. We can see the result in Table 2.

Table 2. Descriptive results on IIC evaluation

Variables	Mean	Standard Deviation	T value
Factors			
innovation strategy	3.532	0.462	21.781*
innovation technology	4.023	0.817	25.452*
innovation funds	3.129	0.459	12.905*
innovative talents	3.055	0.655	11.573*
innovation environment	5.555	0.683	34.685**
innovation culture	5.983	0.991	37.925***
Results			
innovative performance	4.985	0.467	

Note: *, **, *** separately represent significant level 0.05, 0.01 and 0.001, two tail test. (the same below).

A multi-variable linear regression model was set up to analyze the relationship between IIC and innovative performance in AMI. Also, we took six factors as independent variable and took "innovative performance" as dependent variable to examine the significance by Stepwise Method. Multiple altogether linear examination showed, all VIF(Variance Inflation Factor) in our model are far less than 10, in other words, the Tolerances are much higher than ordinary standard 0.1. Furthermore, Durbin-Watson residual sequence correlation index is near to 2, which proved our model error serial irrelevant. The result was shown in Table 3.

Table 3. The regression analysis on IIC to innovative performance

Variables	β	T value	VIF
innovation strategy	0.204	21.781*	1.315
innovation technology	0.244	25.452*	1.363
innovation funds	0.165	12.905*	1.079
innovative talents	0.164	11.573*	1.074
innovation environment	0.330	34.685**	3.159
innovation culture	0.387	37.925***	3.673
Adjusted R^2	0.798		
F-test	1660.216		
D-W	1.942		

Note: β represents standardized partial regression coefficient.

We can draw a comprehensive conclusion that all the six factors have significant positive effect on innovative performance through multiple regression analysis and descriptive statistical analysis. And there are details below:

(1) Innovation culture contributes most to AMI's IIC in the YRD(Yangtze River Delta), which indicates that the Advanced Material Enterprises(AME) in YRD have fully upheld the enterprise culture of innovation. The AME in Jiangsu and Zhejiang Province, different from those in Pearl River Delta with plenty of foreign capital introduction and those in the areas surrounding Bo Sea who formed by research institutes' restructuring, developed from township enterprises and private enterprises and grew out of nothing, from infancy to maturity. In the course of development, the advocating innovation enterprise culture came into being, which provides excellent humane conditions for the enterprises to explore advanced material R&D and strengthen industrial capability of independent innovation.

(2) Innovation environment comes after innovation culture in contribution. This empirical analysis results proved that good external investment, financial and business environment created by the government for the high-tech enterprises in YRD could improved the AMI's IIC dramatically.

(3) The third contributive factor is innovation technology. The consequence that innovation technology contributes less to AMI's IIC in YRD comes from the AME's development endogenous mode in YRD. Different from the AME's "exogenous mode" in Pearl River Delta and Bo Sea Rim, those in YRD developed rely on its own strength and formed "endogenous mode". Although the mode helps them with powerful motivation, its deficiencies of nature will erect barriers to improve AME's IIC.

(4) Innovation strategy is the fourth one. The AME's manager in YRD are Lack of foresight in some certain, which determines the less contribution innovation strategy have to enhance their IIC of AME in YRD.

(5) Innovation funds have less effect on the IIC in YRD. Because of AMI's characteristics of high upfront input, long development cycle and big investment risk, most enterprises won't prefer high investment in advanced material project, which causes the lack of the innovation funds in this area.

(6) The factor of innovative talents is the least helpful there. Even though a lot of advanced material technology talents gather in YRD, the specialists' power is still very weak. In YRD, senior and experienced advanced material R&D technicians are badly in need.

4 Conclusions and Suggestions

The measurement of industry's IIC is being regarded increasingly. Especially, the IIC of AMI is a very important condition to improve the competitiveness of a enterprise, an industry or even a country. Based on analyzing the latest newly published articles and the investigation, this paper develops a scale composed by 20 indexes who can evaluate the AMI's IIC precisely. The study shows that IIC of AMI can be covered by 6 dimensions such as innovation strategy, innovation technology, innovation funds, innovative talents, innovation environment and innovation culture. The scale's high consistency reliability has been proved, and most requests in deep connotation (content, focus & rules) and empirical aspects were considered here.

Rely on our study, innovation culture & innovation environment are the most crucial dimension in AMI's IIC evaluation in YRD, followed by innovation technology & innovation strategy, and innovation funds & innovative talents the least. In order to have high-level tech innovation ability, the government and enterprises must focus on promoting advanced material innovation strategy, gaining more innovation funds, attracting highly talented personal, forming favorable innovation environment & culture. These strategic move's effect must be positive in improve the AME's IIC in YRD.

During our analysis, the AMI's IIC in YRD still needs to be further deepened and enhanced. The government & the enterprise manager could enhance them by following methods: (1) "The endogenous mode" implemented by most AME in YRD makes the development of IIC limited, so, the effective solutions to reinforce the IIC will be enhancing cooperation and coordination between enterprises and research institutions home & abroad; (2) Due to the lack of innovation funds, high risk and long development cycle, the government should aggressively promote broadening the AME's financing channels, enhancing the mechanism for venture investments to attract more risk investments. Besides, the AME's managers in YRD ought to put forward financing positively by themselves; (3) In order to improve AMI's talent level in YRD, relevant authority could construct comfortable environment to attract high-level talents in R&D of AMI and enhance the AMI's development potential; (4) The administrator could also provide the latest international information of AMI and create the professional information communication platform to raise our AMI's strategic position to some extent.

Acknowledgments. The work is supported by humanities & social science foundation of the Ministry of Education. (Grant No. 2007jjd790130)

References

1. Rothwell, R.: Successful Industrial Innovation: Critical Factors for the 1900s. R&D Management 22(3), 221–239 (1992)
2. Anderdassen, R., Nardini, F.: Endogenous Innovation Waves and Economic Growth. Structural Change and Economic Dynamics 3, 1–18 (2005)
3. Guan, J.: Innovative Capability and Export Performance of Chinese Firms. Technovation 9, 737–747 (2003)
4. Devellis, R.F.: Scale Development: Theory and Application. Chongqing University Press, Chongqing (2004) (in Chinese)
5. Nelson, R.R., Nelson, K.: Technology, institutions, and innovation systems. Research Policy 31, 265–272 (2002)
6. Burgelman, R.: Strategic Management of Technology and Innovation. McGraw-Hill, New York (2004)
7. Wei, J.: The definition of technology innovation capability and the correlation with core competence. Research Management 6, 12–17 (1998)
8. Wei, R.: Research on the evaluation independent capability of enterprises. Group Economic Research 9, 68–69 (2005)

9. Hefa, S.: Research on independent Innovation and innovation measurement. China Soft Science 6, 60–66 (2006)
10. Liu, F.: Evaluation of regional independent innovation capability based on set pair analysis. China Soft Science 11, 83–92 (2005)
11. Zhou, J.: The linkage between independent innovation and intellectual property. Management Review 11, 41–45 (2005)

Appendix: Measuring Indexes

A1: The innovation ability at present is the key factors to determine if advanced material product should be developed; A2: The ideas of advanced material innovation product is always the entire enterprise strategic drive; A3: Advanced materials development strategy and the new decisions are expounded by enterprise strategy clearly; A4: Top managers are always willing to provides resources for advanced materials innovation development project; B1: Our enterprise is always continued advanced materials technology's reformation; B2: Our enterprise's advanced material product technical craft is advanced; B3: Our enterprise's key technology in advanced material production is in a leading level; B4: Advanced materials technology is always developed by our enterprise independently; C1: Our enterprise invests a lot in advanced material R&D each year; C2: The R&D funds in advanced materials is in large proportion each year; C3: The R&D funds increases year by year; D1: Existing technology talents are the main undertaker of product innovation; D2: Technology innovation personnel is in large proportion to the total number of enterprises staff; D3: Our enterprise is always able to introduce needed senior talents; E1: Industry informatization level greatly promotes advanced material product development and information transfer; E2: Government always support the development of our advanced materials product; E3: The financial institutions always support the development of our advanced materials product; F1: Our enterprise encourages entrepreneurship development and taking risks; F2: Our enterprise insists on the development and innovation of advanced material project; F3: Our enterprise emphasizes human resources and gives extra bonus in advanced material development projects.

Research on Relationship between Knowledge Sharing and Team Performance in R&D Team

Zhichao Cheng and Cui Li

College of Economics and Management, Beijing University of Aeronautics and Astronautics
BeiJing 100191
qingniaoabc@163.com

Abstract. This paper discusses the relationship between knowledge sharing and team performance in R&D team. We analyze the antecedents of knowledge sharing and its influence on group performance team performance. By using statistical tools such as SPSS and AMOS, we validate this relationship. The results which we showed in this paper are obtained. These results will be significant for management practice.

Keywords: R&D team, Knowledge sharing, Team performance.

1 Introduction

In recent years, our country proposed the status of technological innovation that will be strategic. R & D team is the main organization form of technological innovation. So R & D team performance related to knowledge innovation level. However, in knowledge economy, knowledge innovation's become more complexity. So the knowledge sharing in team becomes more necessary, which can not only achieve more complex missions, but also enhance the organization R&D level and members' innovation ability. Therefore, within this background, it is of significance meanings for modern organizations to research on the relationship between knowledge sharing and R&D team performance.

This paper focuses on antecedents of the knowledge sharing in R&D teams and the relationship between knowledge sharing and team performance. The purpose of this paper is to provide some theoretical suggestions for a benign knowledge sharing in the R&D team, which can improve the team performance.

2 Research Plan and Theoretical Assumptions

2.1 Introduction

In recent years, our country proposed the status of technological innovation that will be strategic. R & D team is the main organization form of technological innovation. So R & D team performance related to knowledge innovation level. However, in knowledge economy, knowledge innovation's become more complexity. So the knowledge

Q. Zhou (Ed.): ISAEBD 2011, Part II, CCIS 209, pp. 474–481, 2011.

sharing in team becomes more necessary, which can not only achieve more complex missions, but also enhance the organization R&D level and members' innovation ability. Therefore, within this background, it is of significance meanings for modern organizations to research on the relationship between knowledge sharing and R&D team performance.

This paper focuses on antecedents of the knowledge sharing in R&D teams and the relationship between knowledge sharing and team performance. The purpose of this paper is to provide some theoretical suggestions for a benign knowledge sharing in the R&D team, which can improve the team performance.

3 Research Plan and Theoretical Assumptions

3.1 Research Plan

In the process of team knowledge sharing, knowledge, team members and Situation constitute the team knowledge sharing system. Therefore, this paper designs these three parts as elementary factors influencing team knowledge sharing. According to the previous research, knowledge sharing is measured by three dimensions: process satisfaction, knowledge innovation and knowledge internalization. Meanwhile, the team performance is also measured by three dimensions: task performance, team satisfaction and knowledge& skill improvement.

3.2 Theoretical Assumption

(1) Knowledge trait

Abstractness denotes knowledge is difficult to be observed and expressed. Most of knowledge exists in the form of tacit knowledge. Many researchers considered that tacit knowledge would limit knowledge sharing (Szulanski, 2000; Bresman, 1999). Knowledge expressivity means the extent what knowledge can be written by language and the spread by media. According to the empirical study by Cummings &Teng(2003), the more difficult knowledge express, the more difficult knowledge sharing. knowledge embedability means knowledge is produced under some specific situation and embedded in a certain scene (Argote&Ingram, 2000). Because of organizations' knowledge embedded in processes, paths and structures, the knowledge can not transfer successfully without the whole work groups and work nets transfer (Teece, 2000) [1], particularly in R&D team. So we propose the following assumptions:

Hla: the extent of knowledge abstraction has a negative impact on knowledge sharing in R&D team.

Hlb: knowledge embedability has a negative impact on knowledge sharing in R&D team.

(2) Members' factors

Sharing intention means the extent knowledge owners would like to share knowledge with other members [2]. Szulanksi (1996) considered that when lacking of motivation factors, knowledge owner could not take the initiative to share knowledge. [3]. Communication skills include knowledge owners' teaching skills and knowledge receptors' absorptive abilities. Teaching skills refer to the abilities choosing an appropriate way to express knowledge and promote knowledge learning. Absorption abilities refer to identifying knowledge value, knowledge absorption and knowledge exploitation. Knowledge gap indicates significant differences among team members in education background, knowledge stocks, work experience and so on. Von Hippel (1994) believed knowledge sharing may be influenced by the experience and skill of knowledge receptors [4]. Otherwise it would increase the learning steps and the difficulties of knowledge sharing [5]. This paper proposes the following assumptions:

H2a: Sharing intention has a positive impact on knowledge sharing in R&D team.
H2b: Team members' communication ability has a positive impact on knowledge sharing in R&D team.
H2c: Knowledge gap between team members has a negative impact on knowledge sharing in R&D team.

(3) Situation factors

Knowledge owner would maintain their knowledge in the organization, but organization wants members to share knowledge. Effective incentive mechanism can resolve this contradiction. On the other hand, the success of knowledge sharing depends on better channels support. The channels include not only the team knowledge management system but also other support, such as common langrage ,other communication signals. Smooth and stable sharing channels can make members get different knowledge, and improve the knowledge integrating abilities. In addition, team culture can generate some practices and customs, which are beneficial to team corporation and Operating mechanism, then become the basis of knowledge sharing (Wolfgang Scholl et al.,, 2000)[6]. We proposed assumptions:

H3a: Perfect incentives mechanisms have a positive impact on knowledge sharing in R&D team.
H3b: Better sharing channels have a positive impact on knowledge sharing in R&D team.
H3c: Team culture has a positive impact on knowledge sharing in R&D team.

(4) Knowledge sharing and team performance

So far, researches on the relationship between knowledge sharing and team performance is relatively scarce, but there are also some scholars paying attention to this issue in some degree. JallZ, et al., (1997) did an experiment on R&D team performance factors and found that knowledge sharing was a mediator between team interdependence and team innovation performance. When the interdependence is higher, the knowledge sharing is better. This process improves work efficiency and team performance [7].Meng-Lei et al., researched the relationship between knowledge share and service innovation performance in hotel team. This study found that team culture atmospheres, knowledge share and service innovation performance had a significant and strong inter-relationship by a scurvy on 621 international tourist hotel employees [8]. Zhou Mi, Zhao Xi-ping (2006) took R&D team as an example and researched the relationship between the individual contextual performance and the effectiveness of knowledge sharing. The consequence indicated that they had positive correlation [9]. So paper proposes the following assumptions:

H4a: knowledge sharing has positive effects on the team task performance .
H4b: knowledge sharing has positive effects on team satisfaction .
H4c: Knowledge sharing has positive effects on team knowledge & skills improvement.

4 Empirical Research Designs

Questionnaires used in this article were formed on the basis of a large number of literatures, interviews. First, we reviewed relevant literatures and absorbed related indicators in these papers, then formed the preliminary research structure. Second, we asked for the views of experts, modified the original scale and formed a revised questionnaire. Third, the revised scale was used for pre-test to verify questionnaire. Then we absorbed feedback opinions and formed the final questionnaire.

The sample survey method is more suitable for empirical data collection and analysis, so this paper adopted this method. For reaching the research purpose, this paper raised series of requirements on the subjects. First, they must be a member of team. Second, the subjects must be have engaged in the R&D work. We selected more types of organizations to test the relationship, such as enterprises, universities or research institutes. We put out a total of 500 questionnaires, got back 213, and 165 valid questionnaires. The questionnaire validity is about 76.1%. Because of the length of article, this paper neglected the difference between different types of corporations.

5 Data Processing

5.1 Reliability Test

This paper analyzes reliability using Cronbach's α coefficient. Generally, when Cronbach's α coefficients range from 0.7 to 0.98, the reliability is high. 0.35-0 .7 for the reliability is acceptable. If it is less than 0.35, the result should be rejected. However, the exploratory research can be given a more lenient standard. In this paper, Cronbach's α values of latent variables are more than 0.7 and Item-Total correlation values are greater than 0.5, which accord with the standard above.

5.2 Confirmatory Factor Analysis (CFA)

This research model is based on the theoretical support, and the relationship assumptions are proposed based on the literature, so CFA is more appropriate.

(1) Factor analysis of knowledge sharing influence factors
Using the software AMOS 7.0, we calculated the key fit index to reflect the fitting degree of hypothesis model and the observed data, including χ^2/df , GFI , IFI , TLI , CFI and $RMSEA$. In general, χ^2/df less than 3 is appropriate; GFI value should be greater than 0.9; IFI value should be greater than 0.9; TLI value greater than 0.95; CFI value should be larger than 0.9 and $RMSEA$ value should be less than 0.06. (Table 1)

Table 1. CFA model fitting results

	χ^2/df	*GFI*	*IFI*	*TLI*	*CFI*	*RMSEA*
Knowledge trait CFA	1.250	0.990	0.922	0.951	0.933	0.051
Members factor CFA	1.451	0.931	0.938	0.915	0.925	0.043
Situation factors CFA	1.790	0.901	0.910	0.947	0.973	0.039

(2) Factor analysis of knowledge sharing and team performance

Table 2. CFA model fitting results

	χ^2/df	*GFI*	*IFI*	*TLI*	*CFI*	*RMSEA*
knowledge sharing CFA	2.225	0.912	0.910	0.949	0.958	0.021
Team performance CFA	1.163	0.964	0.971	0.984	0.993	0.042

As it is shown in Table 2, the model fitting results are acceptable. Measurement model fit results meet the requirement.

5.3 Structural Equation Analyses

(1) Knowledge sharing based on the structural equation analysis
In this paper, antecedents of knowledge sharing are divided into three categories: knowledge trait, members' factors and situational factors; and eight items: abstraction degree, embedding degree, sharing intention, communication skills, knowledge gap, incentive mechanism, the sharing channels and team cultural. Table 3 shows the significant test results about standard estimated value of path relationship coefficient, C. R. and path relationship coefficients.

Table 3. The standard path parameter estimation about knowledge sharing factors

Path	Path parameter	S. E.	C. R.	P
knowledge sharing <--- knowledge abstract	-.530	.106	3.076	.002
knowledge sharing <--- knowledge embedded	-.060	-.028	0.673	.601
knowledge sharing <--- sharing intention	.590	.154	4.380	.000
knowledge sharing<---communication abilities	.640	.149	3.466	.000
knowledge sharing <--- Knowledge gap	.140	-.021	0.369	.507
knowledge sharing <--- incentives mechanisms	.560	.290	3.010	.003
knowledge sharing <--- sharing channels	.700	.191	2.038	.004
knowledge sharing <--- team Culture	.590	.121	2.433	.000

We can see from the Table 3, the absolute values of path coefficients in hypothesis H1a, H2a, H2b, H3a ,H3b, H3c are greater than 0.5; C. R. values are greater than recommended standard 1.96 and significance levels are less than 0.05, so the hypotheses are supported.

H1b hypothesis testing: the path coefficients absolute values from knowledge embedded degree to knowledge sharing is -0.060, C. R. value (0.673) is less than recommended standard value (1.96), significance level of path coefficient is 0.601. H1b is not tested support. Similarly hypothesis H2c test also is not supported.

(2) Knowledge sharing and Team Performance based on the Structural Equation Analysis

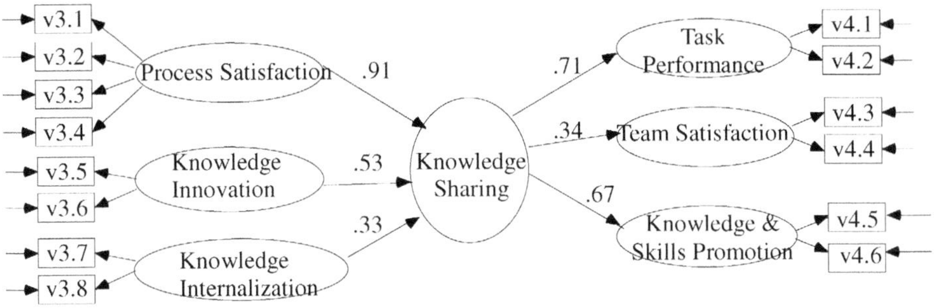

Fig. 1. Relationship model between knowledge sharing and team performance

Table 4. Relationship model fitting index between knowledge sharing and team performance

χ^2/df	*GFI*	*IFI*	*TLI*	*CFI*	*RMSEA*
1.66	0.913	0.925	0.963	0.935	0.032

As it is shown in Table 4, model fitting degrees are acceptable. As it is shown in Figure1, all path coefficients statistical tests are significant; the standard regression coefficient of latent variable path coefficients is shown in table 5:

Table 5. The standard path parameter estimation about knowledge sharing and team performance

Path	Path parameter	S. E.	C. R.	P
Task performance<-knowledge sharing	.710	.180	1.879	.040
Team satisfaction <-- knowledge sharing	.340	.204	2.511	.012
team knowledge & skills promotion<--knowledge sharing	.670	.210	4.128	.000
knowledge sharing <- process satisfaction	.910	.139	4.221	.000
knowledge sharing <-knowledge innovation	.530	.195	3.236	.000
knowledge sharing <--knowledge internalization	.330	.163	2.248	.004

According toe the table 5, we can see that, the path coefficients absolute value of hypothesis H4a、H4b、H4c are greater than 0.5; C. R. is greater than the standard value(1.96); significance level is less than 0.05, so all hypothesis are supported.

6 Results and Discussing

Except hypothesis H1b, H2c, the rest hypotheses are supported in this paper. This paper finds that knowledge sharing has greatest impact on team task performance, the secondary impact on knowledge and skills improvement and the smallest impact on team satisfaction. In the knowledge sharing process, team members cooperate to complete team task and improve team task performance. At the same time, team members improve their knowledge and skills. Through learning from each other, team members create lots of new ideas and new work models, which enhance the team's knowledge and experience levels. As for the team satisfaction, knowledge sharing has lower impact on team satisfaction because team satisfaction is an integrated psychological feeling which is influenced by many factors. These factors include work factors and other complex factors which are not controlled in this study model. Therefore, the effect is not significant.

References

1. Xu, J.F., Xu, Q., Gu, J.L.: Context—based model of knowledge transfer in firm. Science Research Management (03), 54–60 (2003)
2. Shu, L.B.: Research on the process mechanisms of knowledge transfer and influencing factors in team. In: Zhou, H. (ed.) Zhe Jiang University (2006)
3. Szulanski, G.: Exporing internal stickiness: impediments to the transfer of best practice within the firm. Strategic Management Journal 17(2), 27–43 (1996)
4. Von Hipple, E.: "Sticky Information" and the Locus of Problem Solving: Implications for Innovation. Management Science 40(3), 429–439 (1994)

5. Hamel, G.: Competition for competence and inter-partner learning within international strategic alliances. Strategic Management Journal 12(4), 83–103 (1991)
6. Deng, J.Y., Zhou, X.D.: Analysis of Influences of Corporate Culture on Knowledge Sharing. Science of Science and Management of S.& T (9), 82–85 (2005)
7. Wang, Q.: Research on the impact factors of Knowledge Worker's Performance. Zhe Jiang University (2006)
8. Monica Hu, M.-L., Horng, J.-S., Christine Sun, Y.-H.: Hospitality Teams: Knowledge Sharing and Service Innovation Performance. Tourism Management 50, 41–50 (2008)
9. Zhou, M., Zhao, X.P., Li, H.: Study of Relation between Individual Contextual Performance Knowledge Transfer Success and Team Performance of R & D Team. Science of Science and Management of S.& T 12, 138–143 (2006)

Management Standard: A Survey and Analysis of College Students' Mental Health and Personality Traits

Bingwei Wang[1], Honglan Lü[1], Minglu Xu[1], Lan Wang[2], and Xingyu Qiu[1]

[1] Henan Institute of Science and Technology, Henan, Xinxiang, China
[2] Henan Normal University, Henan, Xinxiang, China
wangbingwei@yahoo.cn, 834856219@qq.com, xuminglu@hist.edu.cn, 345451371@qq.com, Qxy585@163.com

Abstract. Objective: To study the psychological health and character of freshman and carry out pertinence management. Methods: The conditions of the psychological health and character of 3540 persons in grade 2010 freshmen were investigated by using Symptom Checklist 90 and Eysenck Personality Questionnaire. Results: In SCL-90, The total score and different factors values were markedly lower than the college norm （$P<0.01$） . The level of total score, somatization, obsessive-compulsive, interpersonal sensitivity, depression, anxiety, phobic anxiety, additional itemsobsession， sensitive, depressed, anxiety, horrible, psychotic of female were significantly higher than that of male($P<0.05$). In EPQ, the scores female and male got in P and N items are both lower than norm, while in E and L items, the scores are higher than norm. The score that female got in P item is lower than those the male got, while in N and L items, the scores are both higher. The contrast is statistical. The analysis are as follows, SCL-90 and P （r=0.26-0.36, N （r=0.47-0.67 positively related） E （r=-0.40--0.40） , L （r=-0.40--0.27） ($P<0.01$ negatively related). Regression analysis shows, P （β=0.075） ,E （β=-0.103） ,N （β=0.562） So the results are useful to prognosticate the mental health. Conclusions: The conditions of the mental health of female were worse than male. We should set up an idea that to give students' psychological guidance according to their gender and special strengthen the psychological education for woman. We should adjust the management according to the gender and take more care of female students, enhance the personality training.

Keywords: Symptom Checklist 90, Eysenck Personal Questionnaire, mental health, personality, freshman.

1 Introduction

Mental health refers to a kind of good state based on the normal development of intelligence, when internal psychological coordination complies with external individual behavior. In psychology, the personality usually refers to the unique psychological reflection that is the total of the different trending psychological characteristic. To explore their mental health in college students, their personality traits, and the relationship between the two, to provide the basis for student

Q. Zhou (Ed.): ISAEBD 2011, Part II, CCIS 209, pp. 482–487, 2011.

management, to strengthen students management and make it effective, we have had investigated in 3540 freshmen of 2010 grade, studying their psychological health and personal characteristics. The reports are as follows.

2 Objects and Methods

2.1 Objects

Here are 3540 freshmen aged 17-22 years old of 2010 grade.

2.2 Tools and Conducting Methods

2.2.1 Symptom Checklist 90 (SCL-90)

The Symptom Checklist-90 (SCL-90) is a relatively brief self-report psychometric instrument (questionnaire) published by Pearson Assessment. It is designed to evaluate a broad range of psychological problems and symptoms of psychopathology. Responses were made on scales from 1 (never/not at all) to 5 (always/very much), which involve ten Symptom Checklists such as, somatization (SOM), obsessive-compulsive(O-C), interpersonal-sensitivity(I-S), depression(DEP), anxiety(ANX), hostility(HOS), phobic anxiety(PHOB), paranoid ideation(PAR), psychoticism (PSY), additional items(ADD). The higher the score is, the more serious psychological problem is.

2.2.2 Eysenck Personal Questionnaire(EPQ)

Eysenck Personality Questionnaire (EPQ) is a questionnaire to assess the personality traits of a person. EPQ includes Extroversion/Introversion(E), Neuroticism/Stability (N), Psychoticism/Socialisation (P), Lie(L)4.

2.3 Data Analyses

Statistical analyses were performed using programs available in the Statistical Package for Social Sciences (SPSS for Windows release 11.0). The significance of observed associations and/or differences between variables was tested using the Student's t test, analysis of variance (ANOVA, F test), Pearson correlation coefficient, and Regression. A difference was considered to be statistically significant if $P<0.05$.

3 Results

3.1 Comparison of the SCL-90 Factor Score of Freshmen with the Youth Norm and the College Norm

In freshmen of grade 2010, students who get higher score in Obsessive-Compulsive, Psychoticism are youth norm. Students who get lower score in Somatization, Interpersonal Sensitivity, Depression, Hostility, Paranoid Ideation are youth norm. The contrast is statistical ($P< 0.05$) , while several other factors are relatively poor without statistical significance ($P>0.05$) . College students who got lower score than youth norm have better mental health than the rest college students. The contrast is of statistical significance ($P< 0.001$) .

Table 1. Comparison of the SCL-90 factor score of freshmen with the youth norm and the college norm(M±SD)

factor	youth norm (n1=781)	college norm (n2=4 141)	freshmen (n=3 540)	t1	t2
SOM	1.34±0.45	1.45±0.49	1.24±0.35	5.813b	21.808b
O-C	1.69±0.61	1.98±0.64	1.79±0.57	-4.059b	13.932b
I-S	1.76±0.67	1.98±0.74	1.63±0.57	5.181b	23.572b
DEP	1.57±0.61	1.83±0.65	1.43±0.49	5.816b	30.314b
ANX	1.42±0.43	1.64±0.59	1.43±0.46	-0.702	17.373b
HOS	1.50±0.50	1.77±0.68	1.37±0.45	6.815b	30.971b
PHOB	1.33±0.47	1.46±0.53	1.33±0.44	-0.104	11.584b
PAR	1.52±0.60	1.85±0.69	1.40±0.46	4.862b	33.474b
PSY	1.36±0.47	1.63±0.54	1.40±0.42	-2.112a	21.145b
ADD			1.38±0.43		
TOTAL			129.96±36.09		

Note : "a", P<0.05 ; "b", P<0.01。

3.2 Comparison of the SCL-90 Factor Score between Male and Female

The total score the female got in somatization, obsessive-compulsive, interpersonal sensitivity, depression, anxiety, phobic anxiety, additional items is higher than that the male got. The contrast is statistical (P<0.05). While the score the male got in hostility, paranoid ideation, psychoticism is higher than the girls got, it has no obvious difference (P>0.05).

Table 2. Comparison of the SCL-90 factor score between male and female(M±SD)

factor	male n=1538	female n=2002	*t*	*P*
SOM	1.24±0.35	1.24±0.35	0.082	0.935
O-C	1.75±0.57	1.81±0.58	-3.358	0.001
I-S	1.59±0.56	1.65±0.58	-2.895	0.004
DEP	1.38±0.46	1.47±0.51	-6.299	0.000
ANX	1.40±0.44	1.46±0.47	-4.084	0.000
HOS	1.38±0.47	1.36±0.43	1.574	0.116
PHOB	1.26±0.38	1.39±0.47	-10.365	0.000
PAR	1.42±0.46	1.40±0.45	1.296	0.195
PSY	1.35±0.40	1.36±0.39	-0.883	0.377
ADD	1.36±0.42	1.39±0.43	-2.321	0.020
TOTAL	127.78±35.41	131.59±36.51	-3.523	0.000

3.3 Comparison of the EPQ Factor Score of Freshmen with the College Norm

The results showed that the original scores in P E N L items, which are got by investigated boys and girls, are very different from the college norm. In P and N items, the scores they got are both lower than norm. while in E and L items, the scores are higher.

Table 3. Comparison of the EPQ factor score of freshmen with the college norm (M±SD)

gender	factor	n1	freshmen	n	college norm	*t*	*p*
male	P	1538	3.53±2.28	140	7.27±3.11	-13.891	0.000
	E	1538	14.40±4.13	140	10.92±4.59	8.655	0.000
	N	1538	8.09±5.17	140	10.75±5.21	-5.778	0.000
	L	1538	13.19±3.59	140	10.08±3.89	9.104	0.000
female	P	2002	3.26±2.19	72	6.90±3.43	-8.942	0.000
	E	2002	14.23±4.06	72	10.41±4.37	7.306	0.000
	N	2002	8.99±5.33	72	12.15±5.14	-5.113	0.000
	L	2002	13.84±3.40	72	11.07±2.98	7.693	0.000

3.4 Comparison of the EPQ Factor Score between Male and Female

The result shows that the score in P item that the female got is lower than that the male got, while in N and L items, the scores are bother higher than those the male got. The contrasts are both statistical ($P<0.01$). Score in E item has no difference($P>0.05$). Please refer to Tab 4.

Table 4. Comparison of the EPQ factor score between male and female (M±SD)

factor	male n=1538	female n=2002	*t*	*P*
P	3.53±2.28	3.26±2.19	3.590	0.000
E	14.40±4.13	14.23±4.06	1.210	0.225
N	8.09±5.17	8.99±5.33	-5.042	0.000
L	13.19±3.59	13.84±3.40	-5.484	0.000

3.5 The Relationship between Mental Health and Personality

From table 5, it can be seen the correlation coefficient between the total SCL - 90, each factor for EPQ.

Table 5. The correlation coefficient of SCL-90 and EPQ Factors

factor	P	E	N	L
TOTAL	0.36	-0.36	0.66	-0.38
SOM	0.30	-0.23	0.47	-0.27
O-C	0.26	-0.34	0.58	-0.33
I-S	0.33	-0.40	0.65	-0.34
DEP	0.36	-0.41	0.67	-0.35
ANX	0.32	-0.32	0.60	-0.33
HOS	0.36	-0.20	0.58	-0.40
PHOB	0.27	-0.30	0.49	-0.24
PAR	0.32	-0.19	0.54	-0.37
PSY	0.32	-0.28	0.54	-0.33
ADD	0.31	-0.26	0.54	-0.29

Note: In this table, all indexes have been inspected by statistic, $P < 0.01$.

3.6 Regression Analysis Affecting Mental Health Personality Factors

Take college students' mental health as the dependent variable, four factors of personality characteristics as the prediction variables, we have forecasting analysis by using Stepwise Multiple Regression. The result is shown in table 6.

Table 6. Coefficients and values of the Regression of EPQ on SCL total score (a)

Independent variables	Unstandardized Coefficients		Standardized Coefficients		
	B	Std. Error	Beta	t	P
Constant	112.380	7.011		16.028	0.000
P	1.153	0.473	0.075	2.439	0.015
E	-0.873	0.249	-0.103	-3.504	0.000
N	3.692	0.221	0.562	16.725	0.000
L	-0.525	0.299	-0.056	-1.757	0.079

a Dependent Variable: SCL-90 total score.
Model Summary: R=0.68, R^2=0.46, $\triangle R^2$=0.45, F=24.73, P=0.000.

4 Discussion

The scores in different items that the freshmen in our school got are all lower than college norm. They are in good mood with the joy and expectation to college life. Compared with the courses in high school, the pressure and the assignments are lighter. Some of them have not realized the employment in future. Psychological health of female college students is poorer than that of the male. The psychological symptoms for female are more obvious and widely than that of the male. This is the same as the research by Hanqian and Liu Baiqiao. Judging from the personality characteristics, the degree of extraversion and diffidence in male and female is no different. The female is more neurotic than the male. This is different from the research by Wang zhen, but the same as the research by Yu Xiuli. The result conforms to the female characteristics that we observed. In addition, it is the same as other researches, which affirm that neurotic characteristics play the most important role in all the factors affecting the mental health.

5 Conclusions

The results of research remind us students' managing should be based on their psychological health and personality. First, "Teaching should be based on the sex". The difference between the male and the female should be admitted and valued. In order to offer them help and guidance, special education should be given to the male and the female according to different traits. Second, the psychological health and the positive development of personality for the female should be cared and emphasized much because of their weaknesses and problems in psychological health and personality. Third, when we intervene and guide the students, not only should we manage from the superficial symptoms, but also we should do from the deep personality background, especially the development of self-awareness. To freshmen, we must foster their good personality and transform their bad one, making them have the conscious choice such as self shaping, self exercising, and self-optimization, which will positively affect the psychological health.

References

1. Wang, X., Wang X., Mahong, et.: Rating scales for mental health (M(.Beijing: Chinese Mental Health Journal, 1999.33-37.
2. Gong, Y.: Eysenck Personal Questionnaire Handbook, vol. 2, p. 31. Hunan Medical College publishing company, Changsha (1993)
3. Han, J.: The Investigation of Freshmen,s Mental Health. Journal of Sichuan College of Education 11, 17–19 (2009)
4. Liu, B.: Survey on the Mental Health Status of 2007 Freshman. China Journal of Health Psychology 16(10), 1117–1118 (2008)
5. Wang, Z.-y., Wang, W.-z., He, G.-h.: A study of the relationship between mental health and personality characteristics of freshmen. Medical Journal of Chinese People s Health 12, 3057–3059 (2009)

The Application of English and American Literature Input in Reading Class Teaching of English Major

Honglan Lü, Bingwei Wang, Xinyu Wang, and Yan Su

Henan Institute of Science and Technology, Xinxiang, Henan, 453003
834856219@qq.com, wangbingwei@yahoo.cn
wxy@hist.edu.cn, suyan2004@hotmail.com

Abstract. Taking extensive reading textbooks of English major, Extensive Reading (Higher Education Press, the edition of 2006, total editor: Huang Yuanshen), as an example. This article analyzed the significance of English and American literature input in reading class teaching of English major. English and American literature input were carried in such ways, preview before class, input in class, extensional reading after class and so on. It greatly stimulates students' interesting of English reading, helps students to improve the understanding of general knowledge of English and American literature, lays the foundation for students majored in English to learn English and American literature in grade three and at the same time it enhances literature quality of students majored in English.

Keywords: English and American literature, input, English major, reading teaching.

1 Introduction

Extensive reading is a very important course for the student whose major is English, it belongs to basic language skills training. The teaching task of Extensive Reading is very heavy, for the students have high pressure to pass TEM4 and TEM8. There are kinds of articles are complied in extensive reading textbooks, for example, *Extensive Reading* (Higher Education Press, the edition of 2006, total editor: Huang Yuanshen). In four books of Extensive Reading, there are 12 units involving English and American literature in 60 units. Units concerning with literature account for 20% of all reading materials. Besides, in other basic English teaching courses, the students also will meet many English and American writers and their works, they need to know a lot of knowledge about English and American literature. So as the English teacher of Extensive Reading, he shouldn't neglect the colorful resource of English and American literature.

2 The Significance of English and American literature Input in *Extensive Reading* Teaching

English and American literature input means: during the process of extensive reading teaching, the teacher timely and moderately stretches or adds some auxiliary teaching

Q. Zhou (Ed.): ISAEBD 2011, Part II, CCIS 209, pp. 488–493, 2011.

content of English and American literature corresponding to the text content, such as introduction of some famous works of English or American writers, showing some photos of the writers and their famous novels and plays, the appreciation of some pieces of works about English and American literature, and so on. In this way, it can cultivate the students to become interested in English and American literature and western civilization, stimulate them to have the aesthetic needs and reading desire, so they can learn English voluntarily, and then reach the aim of improving students' English application ability.

2.1 Stimulating the Students' Interesting of English Reading

In the textbooks of Extensive Reading (Higher Education Press, the edition of 2006, total editor: Huang Yuanshen), although there are 12 units involving English or American literature in overall 60 units, there are many other styles of reading material, such as narrative, explanation, essay, and so on, especially those articles involving popular writings. Some times, these articles are long and difficult for students to read, many students felt it was boring to read this kind of reading materials all the time. English and American literature input during the process of extensive reading teaching can arouse the great interest of the students to read English. Because literary language has the characteristics of vitality, musicality, fluency, integrity, etc. It can improve the expressive ability of general language, contains writers' psychological experience, for example, rich consciousness, emotion, imagination and so on, it can bring the readers into feeling world. "Literary language is not a rigid text language, it is not a floating signans sport either. It is a lively verbal behavior, and is anchored in survive experience and world of human being. ... it can surpass the limitation of 'human language', let us remove the shackles and overshadows of rationalism. "[1] If the teacher properly input English and American Literature not only enlarge students' knowledge of English and American literature, but enhance students' English application ability. For example, in Book I of *Extensive Reading*, Unit 3 is about Young William Shakespeare. Before letting the students read the material, the author introduced William Shakespeare and his 4 tragic plays and 4 comedies. The author also showed students one poem of Shakespeare's sonnets and some famous sentences of Hamlet's monolog "To be, or not to be, that is question......" on multimedia. When the students read the reading material, they showed much more interest to know the life of young William Shakespeare. After class, some students asked the author to list some plays for them to read in their leisure time.

"Deep-rooted learning motivation has no direct relation with the future and economic benefit of learners, learning motivation comes from learner's interest to English language and culture... the best way to stimulate the deep-rooted learning motivation of students is to strengthen the interest of language, make students really understand the specificity of language use and make the students to master language under the natural language context. All of these requirements need the teacher to pay more attention of literariness of works during the process of teaching and emphasize the process of literature input."[2] Thus it can be seen that literature input plays an important role to stimulate the students' interest to English reading. If the students have the interest to read more literary works in English, it is easy and natural for them to remember many new English words and it is very helpful to improve their English reading ability.

2.2 Helping the Students to Know about Literary Knowledge of English and American Literature

There are many kinds of literary works appear in *Extensive Reading* textbooks, during the process of teaching, if the teacher timely and properly input some knowledge about English and American literature it can greatly enlarge the students' literary knowledge. For example, in Book 2 of Extensive Reading, Unit 2 is a short story "A Very Special Goose", it belongs to science fiction. Many students knew little about science fiction. The author gave three definitions to students of what is Science Fiction, what is Magical Realism and what is Fairy Tale. After that, the author listed some names of works, such as *One Hundred Years of Solitude*, *Harry Potter*, *The Hen that Laid Golden Eggs* and *Around The World in Eighty Days*, the students have no trouble distinguishing them. The author also introduced The Father of Science Fiction, Jules Verne, listed four famous works of him. Then the author told the students to read "A Very Special Goose" more carefully, because of it has the characteristics of science fiction, it is long, full of scientific terms. But many students had a desire to read this short story. In this way of literature input, the students knew more literary knowledge. Unit 15 of Book 2 of Extensive Reading is the selection reading of *The Old Man and the Sea*, the introduction of Ernest Hemingway and his famous works also can greatly improve the student's knowledge about American literature and some thing about Nobel Prize.

2.3 Laying the Foundation for Students to Learn English and American Literature in Grade 3

In China, in many departments of foreign language of colleges, Extensive Reading course is designed in Grade 1 and Grade 2, English literature and American literature are designed in Grade 3. Comparing Extensive Reading and Intensive Reading, the reading materials in the former are longer and more difficult than those in the latter. Many literary works appearing in the text books of Extensive Reading will be helpful for students to know about some information about English and American literature. In the author's 18 years of teaching experience, many students majored in English in grade 3 had read few full-length novels. Because of the pressure of passing TEM4, they were willing to spend more time in reading the short articles relating to improve their comprehensive reading ability. Some students thought it would waste a lot of time to read novels written in English. So when they learned English and American literature in grade 3, many students were not familiar with some famous English and American writers, not along to know their works. The teacher of English and American literature must spend a lot time introducing the background of writers and their famous works. There are so many works, and so many writers in English and American literature books, the teacher always feels there is not enough time to give lectures in teaching English and American literature. In the process of Extensive Reading teaching, if the teacher can input more information about English and American literature, it can lay the foundation for students to learn English and

American Literature in grade 3. For example, in Book 3 of Extensive Reading, Unit 7 is "A Room of One's Own", Virginia Woolf was a very famous writer of modernism; in Book 4 of Extensive Reading, Unit 15 is "The Chrysanthemum", John Steinbeck was a famous American writer during the great depression of America. So, if English and American Literature input arouses the students' interest to read many literary works of these writers, they will not say they never hear of these famous writers name and their works in grade 3.

2.4 Improving the Students' Literary Quality

Literature always gives people wish and hope, and makes people's spirit and wisdom be given full play. It can make sure the emotion communication between people, consequently create a special human language environment, and improve people's personality and literary quality. The proper English and American literature input can lead students to read, recite, get into character, get into the emotion world of the author of the work. Through experience and reading, the students can get into the character of true-life, and improve their literary quality.

3 The Ways and Means of English and American Literature Input

During the process of inputting English and American literature in Extensive Reading teaching, the author advocated combining preview before class, introduction, watching movie and discussion in class and extensional reading after class. Classroom teaching takes the students as "the center", the teacher as "leading factor", and "the cooperation of teacher and students" as the teaching idea. Using PowerPoint and net resource to make English and American literature input animated and stretching. During the practical teaching process, literature input can be carried concretely in the following three ways.

3.1 Preview before Class

Literature input can decrease anxiety of learners, which is helpful to language acquisition. Foreign language anxiety is the special phenomenon of language learning. "it is related to classroom learning, which appears in the process of language learning. It is the unique and complex self-awareness, conviction, emotion and behavior." [3] In order to remove the anxiety of students when they read the reading material about English and American literature, the best way is to let the students to preview before class. The teacher can provide information relating to the text, ask the students to look for corresponding information in library, on line. For example, in Book 2 of Extensive Reading, Unit 15 is *The Old Man and the Sea*, before class, the author asked the students to list Ernest Hemingway's famous works, find the reasons why Ernest Hemingway won the Noble Prize, recite the famous saying of Hemingway in *The Old Man and the Sea* "A man is not made for defeat. A man can be destroyed but not defeated. " and explain what is the image of "tough guy" in Hemingway's novels. After the students previewed, the teacher input properly some knowledge about Hemingway in the class, it was found that the students had less anxiety to read the selection of *The Old Man and the Sea,* and their accuracy rate of comprehension exercises was higher than that of other texts. Therefore, preview before class plays an important role for the teacher to input literature knowledge in class.

3.2 Introduction, Watching Movie and Discussion in Class

In the classroom teaching, the teacher can introduce the background of the writer, his or her literature status, the summary of the novel in the textbook, and so on. The teacher also can show some pictures about the writer and his works in the way of PowerPoint, or let the students to watch movie clips. After that, the students can discuss the novel or film with each other. At last, the teacher can make a summary of the students' conclusion. This kind of literature input teaching mode has the characteristic of Multi-dimension, as it was shown in figure 1. [4]

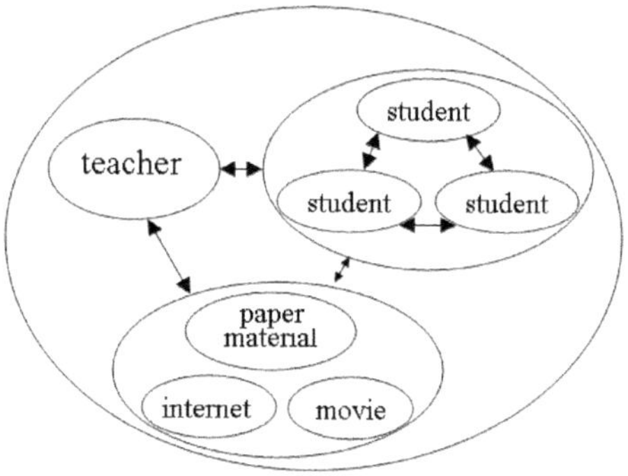

Fig. 1.

3.3 Extensional Reading after Class

At first, the teacher should give students some tasks to read more English and American literary works after class. For example, after reading the selection "The Old Man and the Sea", the teacher can ask students to read *Farewell to Arms* of Hemingway after class. The teacher should guide the students to search material on line, such as, Google, Yahoo, Infosee, Baidu and so on. Let the students know how to use Web Browser and Metsites to browse all webpages. Teach the students to evaluate the credibility of online information, so that the students can make a correct acceptation or rejection. In this way the students will have interest to widen their range of reading, in a natural way to improve their English reading ability.

4 Peroration

In short, it is necessary and feasible to input English and American literature in the extensive reading class. Through the author's many years of teaching practice, it indeed had the satisfactory teaching effect. But it needs to make a careful arrangement on input material, time, object, methods, etc. In the process of teaching, English and American literature input will be adjusted according to classroom situation. At the same time, the teacher should fully consider the drawbacks aroused by inputting literature knowledge in extensive reading class. For example, long time of literature input will make students tired, this need the teacher input literature in a new perspective; during the process of literature input, especially, its content is consistent to the teacher's research direction, sometimes the teacher can not stop his lecture, this needs the teacher to follow his teaching plan in the class. In a word, English and American input in extensive reading teaching is a kind of method and a kind of supplement. Only the teacher inputs properly, timely, fittingly and moderately, can English and American literature input put a cherry on the top and get twice the result with half the effort.

References

1. Fan, Y.: On the Foundation of the Ontology of Literature Speech. Journal of Guizhou Normal University(Social Science) 4, 75 (2010)
2. Li, L., Sun, y., Wu, Y.: English and American Literature Input and College English Teaching Reform. The Border Economy and Culture 11, 152 (2010)
3. Horwitz, E.K., Horwitz, M.B., Cope, J.: Foreign language classroom anxiety. The Modern Language Journal, 70 (1986)
4. Zhang, H.: The Alias Studiotools of English and American Literature Multi-dimension Culture Input. Journal of PLA University of Foreign Languages 11, 47 (2006)

The Reciprocal Impacts of the Senior Executives' Pay and the Corporation's Performance in the Publicly Listed Companies in China

Xin Bi[1], Mingche Su[2], Chucong He[3], and Yuanyuan Yang[4]

[1] College of Business, Jilin University
[2] College of Computer Science and Technology, Jilin University
[3] College of Business, Jilin University
[4] College of Economics, Jilin University
bixinyes@163.com, sumingche@gmail.com,
littleshusong@yahoo.cn, betty.y.bj@gmail.com

Abstract. This paper aims to study the reciprocal impacts of the senior executives' pay and the corporation's performance with 3079 publicly listed companies as the research subjects. The research data between 2006 and 2008 are used in this article to evaluate the impacts of the corporation size, the proportion of the stock shares held by the senior executives and corporation locations on the senior executives' pay and corporation's performance. The results show that the senior executives' pay and corporation's performance are positively related to each other and have different impacts on the corporations that are in different regions. In addition, the senior executives' pay and corporation's performance have a bigger impact in those under-developed regions.

Keywords: Senior Executive's Pay, Corporate Performance, Mutual Effects.

1 Introduction

To address these three disparities, this paper bases on the prior domestic and international theory and research works to study the correlation between the senior executives' pay and the corporation's performance via the qualitative and quantitative analysis and a combination of the theoretical and empirical methods and provide a practical guidance for a reasonable compensation incentive mechanism in the publicly listed companies. This paper makes contributions in several areas as follows. First, the paper proposes a comprehensive model to systematically study the reciprocal impacts of the executives' pay and the corporation's performance and avoids the more limited single factor analysis which was used by many prior research papers. Secondly, this paper carefully chooses a comprehensive set of variables that can reflect the latest pay and corporation performance data without resorting to the old and out of date research data that cannot represent the current economy situation in China.

Q. Zhou (Ed.): ISAEBD 2011, Part II, CCIS 209, pp. 494–500, 2011.

2 Literature Review

There have been a lot of research works done in the area of executive compensation strategy internationally. Among them, the tournament theory and behavioral theory are the two most representative theories.

2.1 Tournament Theory

The tournament theory uses the game theory method to study the agent relationship and believes that an agent's remuneration can be determined according to its marginal production when there is a low cost and reliable monitoring mechanism.

2.2 Behavioral Theory

An Empirical Study of the Incentives and Corporate Performance in Listed Companies" used the linear regression method to examine the relationship and revealed that there is a significant relationship between the executives' pay and the corporation size. Zhou Zhaosheng (2003) examined 911 sample listed companies and concluded that the annual salary, equity income and job promotion are positively correlated to the corporation's performance. He also inferred the numerical correlation model in which the corporation's revenue would be increased by 1 million Yuan when the manager's pay is increased by 83.17 Yuan and the stock shares' net value is increased by 1,012 Yuan.

3 Theoretical Analysis and Proposed Assumptions

According to the tournament incentive theory, there is asymmetric information flow between the company operator and the owners. The company owners will base the executive's pay on the corporation's performance in order to reduce the agency costs. In contrast, the behavioral theory believes that the smaller pay gap between the company employees will improve company performance. This article bases on the unique financial system in China and the prior preliminary research results to study the impact of the regional difference in the capital markets, financial situation, corporation size, proportion of the stock shares held by the executives and other key factors on the pay of the senior executives and contribute new findings to this research area. This article proposes the following hypotheses that remain to be verified:

3.1 The Impact of the Corporation's Performance on the Senior Executives' Pay

An appropriate pay is intended to reward the employee's achievements and motivate them to deliver better performance. Therefore, the corporation's performance is generally regarded as an alternative index of the executive's pay in most cases. This article studies the impacts of the economy development of the corporation's area, corporation's size, financial leverage and the proportion of the stock shares held by the executives on the executives' pay. Based on these above factors, this paper proposes the following hypotheses:

Hypothesis 1-1: The executive pay and annual corporation performance are positively correlated.

Hypothesis 1-2: The economy development of the region that the corporation is located is related to the annual corporation's performance and therefore related to the executive's pay.

Hypothesis 1-3: The corporation size is related to the executive's pay.

Hypothesis 1-4: The corporation's financial leverage is related to the executive's pay.

Hypothesis 1-5: The proportion of the stock shares held by the executives is related to the executive's pay.

3.2 The Impact of the Senior Executives' Pay on the Corporation's Performance

The corporation cannot ignore the role of the incentive for the executives on the corporation's performance which can be explained using the agent theory as a higher incentive would motivate the executives to work harder to improve the business performance. Therefore, this article also adopts the corporation's performance as a interpreted variable to study the effects of the incentive on the corporation's performance improvement. At the same time, we also consider the impacts of the corporation's size, the proportion of the stock shares held by the executives and the proportion of state-owned stock shares on the corporation's performance. Therefore, the following hypotheses are proposed:

Hypothesis 1-1: A high executive pay would motivate the executives to improve the corporation's performance.

Hypothesis 1-2: The corporation performance is related to the proportion of the stock shares held by the executives.

Hypothesis 1-3: The corporation performance is related to the corporation's location.

Hypothesis 1-4: The corporation performance is related to the corporation's size.

Hypothesis 1-5: The corporation performance is related to the proportion of state-owned stock shares.

4 The Study Scheme

4.1 Sample Selection and Data Sources

This article uses the executive's pay data from the annual salary report disclosed by the corporation and the top three pays for the senior executives (including base salary, bonuses and allowances) in the CSMAR database are used as the evaluation indicators. The corporation selection criteria we use are as follows: (1) Exclude those corporations which are labeled as ST and PT and have a negative net asset return rate, negative profit and negative net profit; (2) Consider those listed companies only with A shares but no B or H shares; (3) Exclude the corporations that were listed after January 1, 2007; (4) Exclude those corporations with incomplete disclosed financial data.

4.2 Variables Definitions

Salary (AC)

This article only considers the top three senior executives remuneration packages which include the fixed remuneration (basic salary) and short-term compensation (variable pay).

Corporation's Performance (ROA)

The total asset return rate reflects the profitability of a corporation. This indicator is positively correlated to the corporation's profitability.

Area (DQ)

we use the hierarchical clustering method (SPSS10.0 software) to classify Shanghai, Beijing and Guangdong as the developed areas among the 31 provinces and autonomous regions in China. The synthetic variable DQ indicates whether the location is in underdeveloped areas (0 value) or developed areas (1 value).

Corporation Size (SIZE)

Since the corporations with varying sizes will give out different remuneration packages, this paper uses the total asset as an indicator of the corporation's size.

Financial Leverage (DEBT)

A large number of previous research results show that appropriate financial leverage will greatly improve the corporation's performance. Therefore, this article considers it as a control variable.

4.3 Model

The model for evaluating the impact of the corporation's performance on the executive's pay is as follows:

$AC = \beta 0 + \beta 1ROA + \beta 2SIZE + \beta 3DEBT + \beta 4MH + \varepsilon i$ (Model I)

The model for evaluating the impact of the executive's pay on the corporation's performance is as follows:

$ROA = \beta 0' + \beta 1'AC + \beta 2'SIZE + \beta 3'GYBL + \beta 4'MH + \varepsilon i'$ (Model II)

4.4 Analysis and Study Methods

First, simple descriptive statistics are applied on the collected data to calculate the maximum, minimum, average and standard deviation and to analyze the samples' characteristics and understand the variables' distribution. The regression analysis is conducted on the independent and dependent variables to confirm the regression model and proposed hypothesis and illustrate the relationship between the independent variables and the dependent variables.

5 Empirical Results and Analysis

5.1 Descriptive Statistical Analysis

Table 1 shows the statistical descriptions about all the variables in the model and the results show that the average executive compensation in developed regions is much higher than that in underdeveloped regions while the average corporation size in the developed regions is much larger than that in underdeveloped areas. In addition, the difference between the maximum and minimal performance of the corporations in the underdeveloped regions is bigger and more fluctuating than that in developed areas.

Table 1. Descriptive Statistics of the Sample Variables

variable		number of samples	minimum	maximum	mean	variance
all samples	AC	3079	0.0000	17040000.0	1010568.1	1077758.3107
	ROA	3079	0.0003	1.9916	0.051410	0.056644
	SIZE	3079	107883703.4	994092000000.0	7084837499.3	38021253522.6
	MH	3079	0.0000	0.6420	0.002691	0.028693
	GYBL	3079	0.0000	0.8629	0.271982	0.2362388
	DEBT	3079	0.0091	9.3232	0.489218	0.2539679
developed regions	AC	665	101000.0	17040000.0	1406845.5	1413230.90804
	ROA	665	0.0004	0.5605	0.054631	0.0468447
	SIZE	665	135406683.2	994092000000.0	11665218442.2	57651377837.2
	MH	665	0.0000	0.6420	0.002917	0.0328414
	GYBL	665	0.0000	0.8629	0.284550	0.2416382
	DEBT	665	0.0207	9.3232	0.485024	0.3877277
under-developed regions	AC	2414	0.0000	15720900.0	901403.095149	936424.857447
	ROA	2414	0.0003	1.9916	0.050522	0.0590365
	SIZE	2414	107883703.4	994092000000.0	5823050702.7	30365133851.6
	MH	2414	0.0000	0.6420	0.002629	0.0274479
	GYBL	2414	0.0000	0.8629	0.268520	0.2346622
	DEBT	2414	0.0091	5.4936	0.490373	0.2022400

5.2 Correlation Analysis

According to the statistical data, the tolerance for all independent variables are all above 0.5 and the VIF value is below 1.2. Therefore, the variables used in the model do not contain the collinearity problem and the independent variables explanatory power on the dependent variable is not affected. The analysis results obtained from these data are scientifically sound and convincing.

5.3 Regression Analysis

The Impact of the Corporation's Performance on the Senior Executives' Pay.

The results of the regression analysis for the model 1 are shown in Table 2. As can be seen from Table 2, the corporation's performance is positively correlated to the executive's compensation. AS for the control variables, the three groups of samples have shown that the corporation size, proportion of stock shares held by the executives and proper financial leverage are all positively correlated to the executive's pay. In addition, the results also imply that the corporation's performance in underdeveloped areas has a bigger impact on the executive's pay than that in developed areas.

Table 2. The Impact Effect of the Corporation's Performance on the Senior Executives' Pay

variable	samples		developed regions		underdeveloped regions	
	Coefficient	t value	Coefficient	t value	Coefficient	tvalue
ROA	0.149***	8.418	0.113***	2.929	0.171***	8.468
SIZE	0.189***	10.803	0.182***	4.792	0.180***	9.117
DEBT	0.026	1.476	0.001	-0.022	0.048**	2.377
MH	0.023	-1.339	0.028	-0.718	0.024	- 1.195
Adjusted R Square	0.060		0.043		0.063	
F	49.703		8.461		41.378	

Note, the symbols *, **, *** represent 10%, 5% and 1% significance level respectively.

The Impact of the Senior Executives' Pay on the Corporation's Performance Table 3 provides the regression analysis results for the impact of the executive compensation on the corporation's performance. As can be seen from this table, the corporation's performance has positive impact on the executive's pay and is significant at the 1% statistical level. In addition, it can be seen that the corporation size and the proportion of the stock shares held by the executives both have significant positive impact on the executive's pay in both developed and under-developed areas.

Table 3. The Impact Effect of the Senior Executives' Pay on the Corporation's Performance

variable	samples		developed regions		underdeveloped regions	
	Coefficient	t value	Coefficient	t value	Coefficient	t value
AC	0.150***	8.304	0.115**	2.939	0.166***	8.144
SIZE	0.022	1.185	0.046	1.148	0.016	0.796
GYBL	-0.004	-0.221	-0.004	-0.090	-0.005	-0.223
MH	0.079***	4.443	0.133***	3.452	0.067***	3.328
Adjusted R Square	0.029		0.028		0.031	
F	23.983		5.832		20.555	

Note, the symbols *, **, *** represent 10%, 5% and 1% significance level respectively.

6 Conclusion

For the investors, they need to take into account the executives' compensation in addition to the accounting information or other relevant financial information when choosing the investment objectives and making investment decisions.

Suggestions to the Senior Executives in the Corporation More and more performance incentive systems will be used in the corporation as the main factors to determine the executives' compensation. This research work found that the executives' compensation is more sensitive to the corporation's performance in the less developed areas. Knowing this point will help the executives better evaluate themselves and position them for the right jobs in the right companies.

References

1. Li, Z.: Incentives and Corporate Performance. Accounting Research (2000)
2. Zengji, S., Zhongyi, Z.: Listed Company Compensation and Firm Performance An Empirical Study. Chongqing University (2002)
3. Wang, K.: The Executive Pay and Corporation's Performance Correlation Analysis. Capital University of Economics (2007)

The Interaction between China's Foreign Trade and Environmental Quality

Yujing Wang

School of Economy, Tianjin University of Commerce
Jinba Road, Beichen District, Tianjin, 300134, PR China
yjwang0303@yahoo.com.cn

Abstract. Though China's foreign trade has developed increasingly, the main export structure is still resource intensive and labor intensive industries. Exporting pattern like this depletes resources and causes high emissions and high environmental pollution. The paper analyzes the relationship between the major export industries trade volume and the "three waste emissions" of major industries. Evidences prove that the increasingly expanding foreign trade has accelerated the negative effects on China's environmental quality. The last part of the paper points out it is necessary to integrate trade development with environmental protection.

Keywords: Foreign trade, growth, environment, waste emission.

1 Introduction

Trade is the engine for economic growth. However, with the rapid development of international trade and the increasing environmental problems trigged by trade, the research concerning the relationship between the trade and environment has drawn much attention. Trade activities influence ecology and environment through production, logistics and consumption. Theoretically, environmental protection and trade can develop harmoniously since environment is the base for the development of trade. However, controversies and conflicts do exist between international trade and environment in reality.

2 The Interactive Relationship between China's Foreign Trade and Environment

The relationship between the growth rate of manufactured exports and that of "three industrial wastes" from 1996 to 2008 is reflected in Fig 1. The growth rate of manufactured exports volume fluctuates between 1.4% and 37% and the growth rate of industrial three wastes shows upward tendency. In general, the changing tendency of "three industrial wastes" complies with the growth rate of manufactured exports volume after 2001. Figures prove that positive correlation exists between the expanded manufactured exports and the deteriorated environmental quality.

Q. Zhou (Ed.): ISAEBD 2011, Part II, CCIS 209, pp. 501–507, 2011.

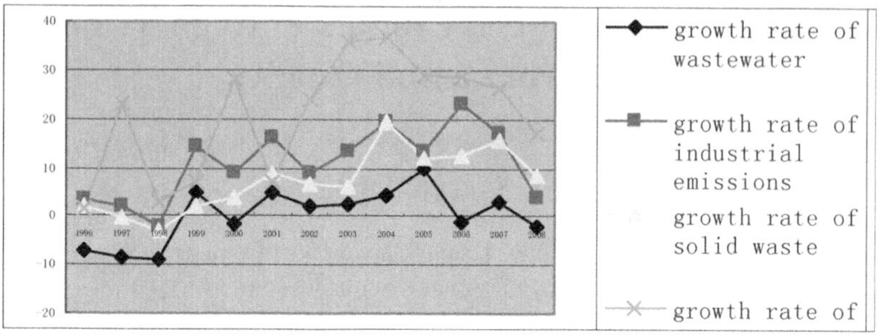

Fig. 1. The relationship between growth rate of manufactured exports and industrial wastes Source: calculated according to China Statistics Report (1996-2008)

Major Industries Export Trade Volume

Table 1 illustrates the major industries export trade volume and their ranks in the whole trade volume. In most years, the top 10 export industries are: machinery and electronic equipment, textiles materials and products, metal manufacturing, chemical material and manufacturing, ferrous metal and manufacturing products, extractive

Table 1. Export trade volume of major industries and the rank in total export volume (Billion US dollar)

Sectors	2002	2003	2004	2005	2006	2007	2008
Extractive industries	98.4 (5)	127.4 (6)	165.7 (6)	209.2 (6)	213.9 (7)	235.9 (7)	364.9 (6)
Food beverage tobacco industries	67.0 (9)	77.0 (9)	94.12 (9)	112.0 (9)	138.0 (9)	164.7 (8)	182.1 (9)
textiles material and products	578.5 (2)	733.6 (2)	887.7 (2)	1076 (2)	1381.0 (2)	1658 (2)	1797 (2)
leather fur and feather products	93.3 (7)	115.7 (7)	136.7 (6)	156.1 (8)	153.8 (8)	163.6 (9)	182.7 (8)
paper industry	23.4 (10)	30.30 (10)	38.0 (10)	51.14 (10)	69.0 (10)	91.9 (10)	103.9 (10)
chemical raw material and manufacturing	146.1 (4)	185.3 (4)	245.8 (5)	318.5 (5)	377.5 (5)	510.9 (5)	688.7 (5)
ferrous metal manufacturing	97.0 (6)	128.6 (5)	252.1 (4)	341.2 (4)	519.2 (4)	766.2 (4)	1019 (4)
metal manufacturing	1891 (3)	251.2 (3)	437.4 (3)	570.9 (3)	853.0 (3)	1155 (3)	1440 (3)
Plastic industry	80.4 (8)	99.8 (8)	131.1 (8)	177.8 (7)	222.2 (6)	264.0 (6)	298.1 (7)
machinery and equipment	1571.0 (1)	2273 (1)	3233 (1)	4267 (1)	5494 (1)	7011 (1)	8229 (1)

Source: calculated according to China Statistics Report (2000-2009).
Note: number in bracket is the rank.

industry, leather fur and feather products, plastic industry, food beverage tobacco manufacturing and paper industry. Among these, the top 3 are machinery and electronic equipment, textiles and metal manufacturing since 2000. According to SITC trade categories, pollution intensive industries consist of industrial chemicals, paper and pulp, non-metallic minerals, iron and steel and non-ferrous metals. It is obvious that pollution intensive industries occupy majority in the top 10 exporting industries.

The Export Trade Volume of Major Opening Areas and Three Industrial Waste Emissions

The export trade volume of major costal cities and regions has been increasing rapidly and accounted for 79.8% in 2008. According to the data in China Statistic Bureau, it is easily proved that the "three industrial wastes" gradually increase with the growth of the exports in these areas (see Fig. 2, Fig.3, Fig.4, and Fig.5).

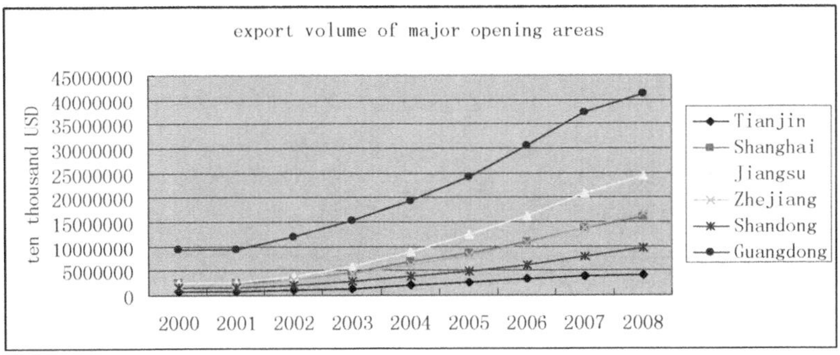

Fig. 2. Export volume of major opening up cities and provinces

Source: calculated according to China Statistics Report (2000-2008)

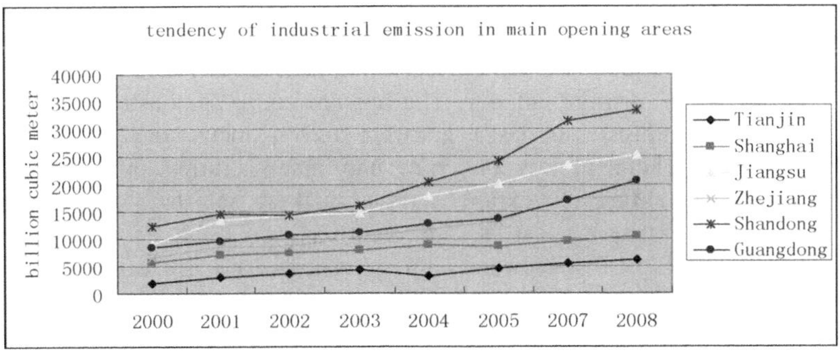

Fig. 3. The changing tendency of industrial emissions in opening up areas

Source: calculated according to China Statistics Report (2000-2008)

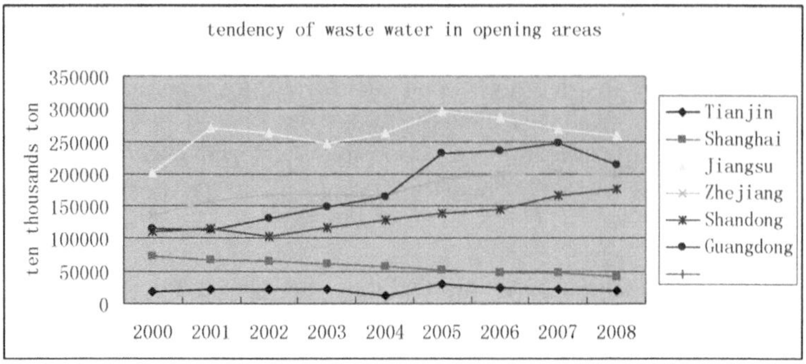

Fig. 4. The changing tendency of wastewater in opening up areas

Source: calculated according to China Statistics Report (2000-2008)

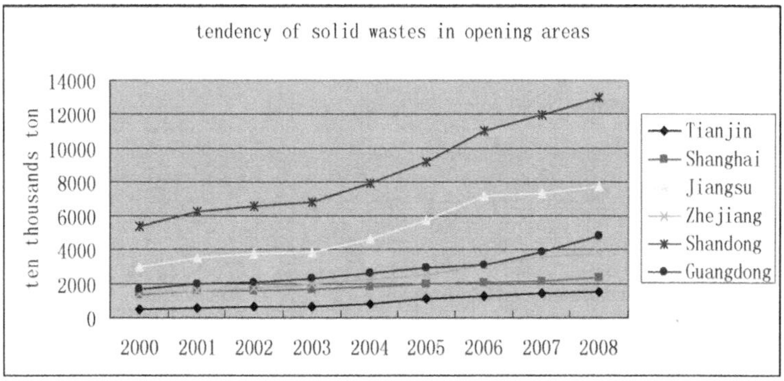

Fig. 5. The changing tendency of solid wastes in opening up areas

Source: calculated according to China Statistics Report (2000-2008)

Three Industrial Wastes of Major Industrial Export sectors

Figure 6 is the industrial waste gas of major industrial export sectors during 2000 to 2006 and shows the raising tendency. The upward curve demonstrates that the fast emission growing industries in past years were: ferrous metal smelting, non-metallic mineral products, chemical raw materials and manufacturing products and non-metallic mineral smelting. The export volumes of these industries occupy top 10 in the export volume of major industrial export sectors.

The fast increasing of wastewater emissions industries are extractive industry, textile, paper and paper products industry, and chemical raw materials and manufacturing products (Fig 7). In the top 4 export sectors, wastewater emissions have been upward tendency in recent years.

Figure 8 reflects that the solid waste of extractive industry and ferrous metal increased fast in these years. And the export volumes of these sectors stand in the top rank of total export volume of manufacturing products.

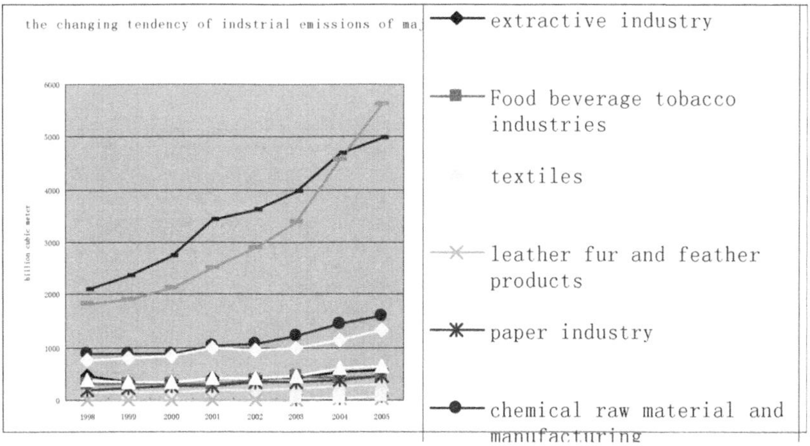

Fig. 6. The changing tendency of industrial emissions of major industries (1998-2006)

Source: calculated according to China Statistics Report (1998-2007)

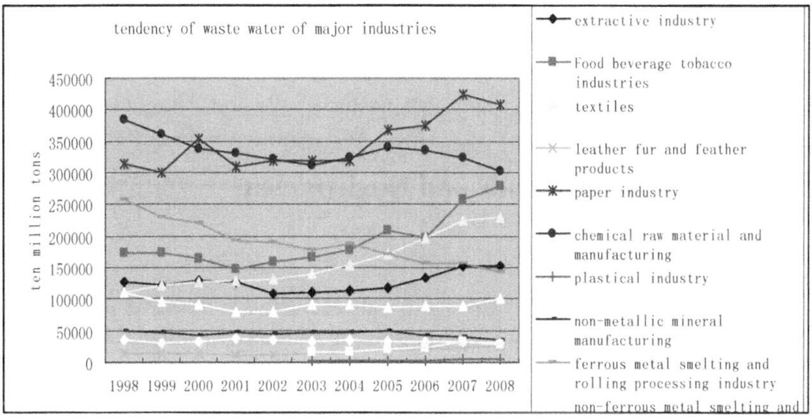

Fig. 7. The changing tendency of wastewater of major industries (1998-2006)

Source: calculated according to China Statistics Report (1998-2007)

From the above statistics and diagrams, it can be concluded that the export comparative advantages of China's manufacturing sectors are pollution intensive and environment sensitive industries. With the expanding of exports, the growing of foreign trade will exacerbate the negative impact on environmental quality.

In addition, this export commodity structure is prone to be affected by environmental technology measures or b arriers. The effect of environmental TBT on China's export is more than \$20 billion every year. The direct loss of TBT is almost \$36 billion in 2006, accounting for 3.71% of the export volume. The major influenced sectors are machinery and electronic equipment, agriculture products, chemical and mineral products, plastic and textiles. The environmental technical barriers mainly include environmental standard, packing material reuse, limitation on toxic materials and protection of ozone layer of controlled substances, pesticide residues and other food and clothes safety requirement.

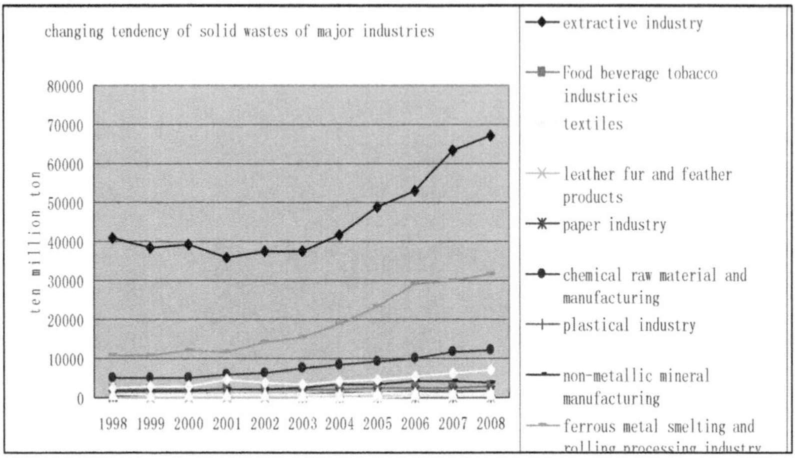

Fig. 8. The changing tendency of solid wastes of major industries (1998-2006)

Source: calculated according to China Statistics Report (1998-2007)

3 How to Harmonize Trade and Environment

3.1 Implement Cyclic Economy

Cyclic economy is a new pattern of economic increase and is based on the principle of the efficient utilization of resources and protection of the environment. Different from the traditional economy, a unidirectional linear economy from resource to waste, cyclic economy is a closed-loop system. The theme of cyclic economy is the exchange of materials where one facility's waste, including energy, water, materials - as well as information - is another facility's input. Cyclic economy integrates clean production, optimal use of resources, ecological design and sustainable consumption, constructing the production mode of low depletion, high utilization and low emission. The nature of cyclic economy is ecological economy, since it advocates the notion of "from cradle to cradle" and regards the wastes as resources. The basic principle of implementing cyclic economy is reducing, reusing and recycling. Start-of-pipe-control, the focus of cyclic economy, highlights reducing input in the process of design and production and decreasing disposal in using, as well as recycling the waste.

3.2 Environmentally Sound Technology Innovation

Cyclic Economy's development depends on the technology innovation; especially environmentally sound technology (EST). EST comprises technologies that have the potential for significantly improved environmental performance and is characterized by using resources in a more sustainable manner and recycling their wastes and products. Environmentally sound technology innovation (ESTI) integrates the ideas of EST and innovation and is the dynamic process from R&D to production and to technology innovation diffusion. ESTI comprises clean energy technology, clean production and technique, end-pipe pollution disposal and recycling. It involves environmentally sound product innovation, environmental process innovation and environmental management innovation. ESTI is not a mere technological concept but reflects the ecosystem-centered value and coordinates the technology innovation to the ecological system so that the firms can harmonize economic and ecological benefit and can achieve sustainable development.

3.3 Actualizing Environmental Labeling

The certification criteria of environmental labeling system include resource and energy allocation, technology, waste disposal and recycling. It not only requires the corporation to eliminate the pollution as much as possible at the production stage but also minimizes the environmental damage when disposing wastes. Implementation and adopting of environmental labeling in trade has the significant role on the enforcement of corporation environmental responsibility and protection of environment.

4 Conclusion

The growth of foreign trade is confronting with increasing pressure from environmental management and social responsibility. To reduce the environmental pollution of foreign trade, updating industrial structure and implementing environmental technology innovation are the effective ways. In addition, it is necessary to strengthen environment regulations on traded goods in order to achieve the sustainable development of trade and the improvement of environmental quality.

Acknowledgments. The author is indebted to Tianjin Social Science Project (No.TJYY10-2-381) and Humanities and Social Science Projects in Tianjin Universities (No. 20082411).

References

1. Busse, M.: Trade, Environmental Regulations and the WTO: New Empirical Evidence. World Bank Policy Research Working Paper, No. 3361 (2004)
2. Chen, J.G.: Improving Quality and Standard of China's Manufacturing Industry (02-1-2008), http://www.cei.gov.cn
3. Li, J.W.: Analyzing Effect of Circular Economy on China's Foreign Trade. Journal of Shi Jiazhuang Economic College (12), 69–72 (2010)
4. Liu, J.J.: Strategic Measures of China's Foreign Trade and Circular Economy. World Economy Research 8, 26–30 (2009)
5. Zhou, J.W., Lu, J., et al.: The Study on Changing Growth Mode of China's Foreign Trade. Economic Study 6, 23–28 (2010)

Impacts of Monetary Policy on Prices in a Country without Own Currency

Martinho De Matos Silvestre and António Manuel De Almeida Serra

Center of African and Development Studies (CEsA)
martinhosilvestre@gmail.com,
aserra@iseg.utl.pt

Abstract. This paper estimates a model for Consumer Price Index (CPI) of East Timor using monthly data from 2003 to 2010. The approach followed in the formulation of the econometric model is based on the Quantity Theory of Money and uses stationarity and cointegration tests. The policy implications of the paper are the following: the control of inflation requires the Public Expenditure to be bounded; some Public Expenditure should be used for formation of Human Capital and Fixed Capital; there is evidence supporting the Quantity Theory of Money in East Timor.

Keywords: Consumer Price Index, Budgetary Policy, Quantity Theory of Money, Inflation, Stationarity, Cointegration.

1 Introduction

The recent increase of inflation in East Timor has motivated the design of a model to estimate the consumer price index (CPI) of this country. The CPI is a weighted average of the prices of a specified set of goods and services purchased by consumers. This index allows the measurement of the inflation rate, which has been rising without restraint since 2008 [21].

This conjuncture is particularly dramatic, since the increase of inflation implies a drop in the purchasing power of East Timor households. In turn, governmental injections of money worsen an already overheated economy. The process becomes self-perpetuating, i.e., a snowball effect, which can only be stopped by controlling inflation [26].

Due to the fact that East Timor does not have its own currency, controlling inflation calls for public expenditure to be bounded. However, public expenditure has experienced an exponential rate of growth: for example, the increase was 130% from 2007 to 2008. At the same time, the money supply (M2) has also been increasing: for example, the increase from 2009 to 2010 was 38% [10]. As it is well known, the supply of money is one of the most common explanations of price increases, i.e., the "Quantity Theory of Money" [7].

Based on this theory, and using stationarity and cointegration tests, we developed the first macroeconomic study for East Timor resulting in a model that

Q. Zhou (Ed.): ISAEBD 2011, Part II, CCIS 209, pp. 508–517, 2011.

may help the Central Bank of East Timor advise the government on its most appropriate policy options.

The remainder of the paper is organized as follows: Section 2 presents a survey of the literature; Section 3 describes the contextual setting; Section 4 develops the theoretical framework; Section 5 presents the data and results; Section 6 discusses the results; and Section 7 concludes the paper.

2 Literature Survey

In this section, we conduct a brief survey of some relevant literature on East Timor and inflation and the application of the Quantity Theory of Money.

Brouwer (2001) [4] considers the decision to dollarise (by which a country decides to introduce another country's currency as its own) and concludes that East Timor should adopt a firmly fixed exchange rate (US dollar or the Australian dollar). Jacome and Lonnberg (2010) [16] identify key aspects related to dollarisation which must be addressed by countries intending to dollarise officially. They analyze, in particular, the experiences in adopting dollarisation of countries such as Ecuador, El Salvador, Kosovo, Montenegro and East Timor.

Concerning papers studying the targeting of inflation in emerging countries, Amato and Gerlach (2002) [1] conclude that inflation targeting (IT) is a useful policy strategy for emerging market economies. Mishkin (2000) [23] stresses the implications of inflation targeting for emerging market economies and concludes that it may not be appropriate for many emerging market countries. Fraga et al. (2003) [11] discuss the policies appropriated to make inflation targeting successful; Otero and Ramirez (2006) [24] analyze the inflation in Colombia, before and after central bank independence with a vector error correction model (VEC).

Finally, we consider some empirical papers on the Quantity Theory of Money. Bullard (1999) [5] conducts a large review of papers on long-run monetary neutrality and (super) neutrality propositions and emphasizes that while there is, in general, evidence in favor of the neutrality proposition, no clear-cut inferences can be drawn from the international evidence of (super) neutrality. Geweke (1986) [13] uses a century of annual US data as well as postwar monthly data supports the neutrality of money for the US economy; King and Watson (1997) [18] investigate various long-run neutrality propositions using postwar US data and conclude that the data contain little evidence against the long-run neutrality of money and suggest a very steep long-run Phillips curve.

3 Contextual Setting

The Democratic Republic of East Timor is a small country in South-east Asia, as shown in Figure 1. Before its independence, East Timor had suffered harshly for more than two decades following the Indonesian invasion and occupation, which began in December 1975. Liberated in late-1999, the country achieved independence in May 2002 [6]. Thus, an independent East Timor is quite recent, which explains the relative paucity of data and some lack of organization in this

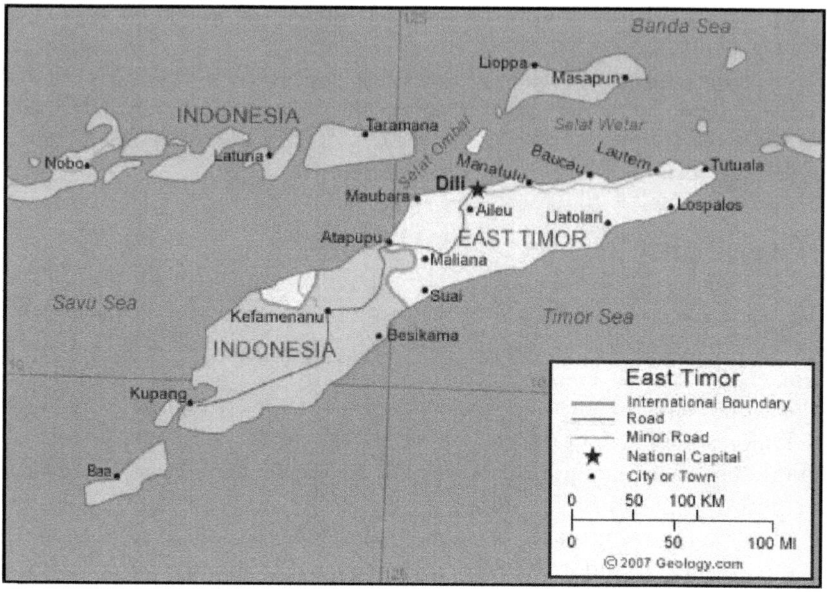

Fig. 1. Map of Indonesia and East Timor

respect. Nowadays, the Banking and Payments Authority of East Timor acts as the monetary authority, which, in accordance with the country's Constitution, is to be replaced by the Central Bank of East Timor in the near future. One of its main purposes will be price control.

East Timor does not have its own currency, which limits its ability to influence inflation [27]. East Timor was obliged to adopt the Indonesian rupiah in July 1976, replaced by the US dollar in 2003. However, in November 2003, the replacement of US dollars by a new national currency was discussed. As we can see, the conditions to make monetary policy are highly unstable, which may make long-run analysis difficult [16]. Finally, the money supply (M2) has been increasing exponentially, for example, the increment from 1-10-09 to 1-01-10 was 38%. As is well known, the money supply is one of the most common explanations for price increases, as asserted in the Quantity Theory of Money.

Concerning the budgetary policy, public expenditure has grown strongly in recent years[1]. The wage increases in the public sector, which is the country's largest employer, create an "output gap" that pressures prices upwards [25]. Moreover, we found more effects of the expansionary policy that worsen the inflation scenario, such as an increase in private consumption. To sum up, not only has government policy contributed to inflation by raising public expenditure, but

[1] The increase was 130% from 2007 to 2008.

it has also incited private consumption and the stock of money[2], which have the same effect.

Lastly, the market structure in the country is characterized by "asymmetric information". Consumers have little access to economic information. The power of oligopolies is, in some way, responsible for the extraction of profits at rates above what is economically and socially justifiable.

4 Theoretical Framework

We based our empirical model on the Quantity Theory of Money (QTM). According to this theory [12]:

$$P = \frac{M}{Q} \times V \tag{1}$$

Applying logarithms to the identity of Quantity Theory of Money we may write:

$$\log(P) = \log(M) - \log(Q) + \log(V) \tag{2}$$

Let us consider that prices (P) are represented by CPI, money supply (M) by M2, the quantity of goods (Q) by GDP at constant prices and the velocity of money (V) as a constant. We can now use econometric software to estimate an econometric model for the explanation of the CPI of East Timor.

For a better interpretation of the results, we use the variables measured in indexes based on the value in January 2003. It is important to note that GDP is typically measured annually, whereas all the other variables are observed monthly, so we formulate an appropriate hypothesis: the monthly growth rate of GDP is constant within the year.

Before the model can be estimated, the properties of the data must be investigated. Therefore, unit root and cointegration tests must be conducted. Figure 2 shows that the variables[3] have a similar trend during the time period under analysis. Since the variables have a similar increasing pattern, we expect that there is a cointegration relationship. For more details on cointegration, see Gonzalo (2010) [14].

We seek the existence of a cointegration relationship between CPI, M2 and GDP (in logs), although we concede that our time series are too short to run the available tests of cointegration. Nevertheless, we will consider the Engle-Granger methodology.

Finally, if cointegration is assumed, the model to be estimated later is as follows:

[2] Because East Timor does not have its own currency, the increase in public expenditure indirectly "injects" money into the economy.

[3] For more details on the data, see Appendix A.

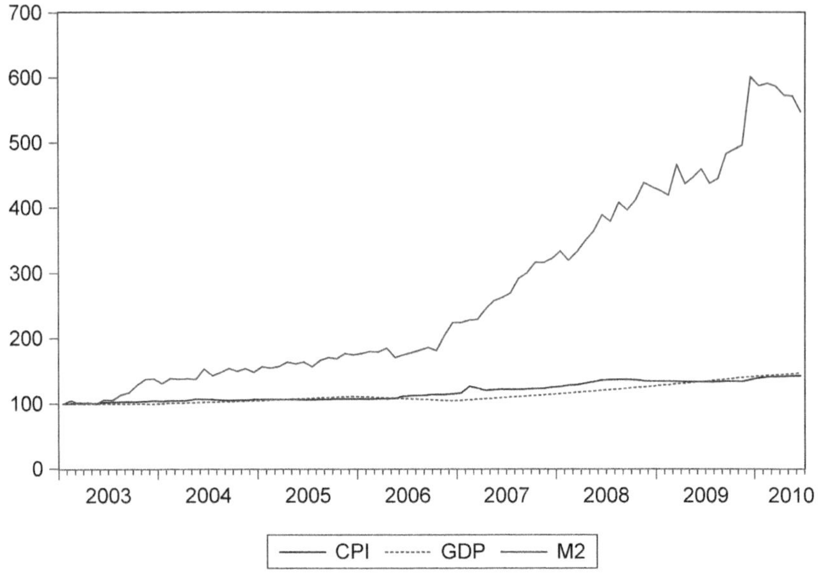

Fig. 2. Evolution of the explanatory variables during the interval 2003-2010

$$\log(CPI_t) = \beta_0 + \beta_1 \log(M2_t) + \beta_2 \log(GDP_t) + \delta t + u_t \tag{3}$$

Where u_t is the error term of the model, verifying the usual assumptions of the linear regression model, and t a temporal variable that excludes the trend effect. With regard to the expected signs of the coefficients:

$$\beta_1 > 0 \text{ and } \beta_2 < 0.$$

5 Data and Results

We started by confirming that all series have a unit root and then applied a unit root test to the residuals of the estimated regression, leading to the conclusion that a cointegration relationship exists [9]. These tests can be viewed in Appendix B.

In order to test the variables for a unit root, we used the Dickey and Fuller unit root test and concluded that all the series presented a unit root [8]. These results led us to the study of cointegration. For the application of the Engle and Granger test, we estimated the following equation: [9]

$$\underset{}{LCPI_t} = 4.272 \underset{(0.06)}{-0.177 LGDP_t} \underset{(0.028)}{+0.243 LM2_t} + 3.441 \times 10^{-05} t$$

In this equation, the numbers in parentheses are the standard errors of the coefficients, LCPI is the logarithm of CPI, LM2 is the logarithm of M2 and

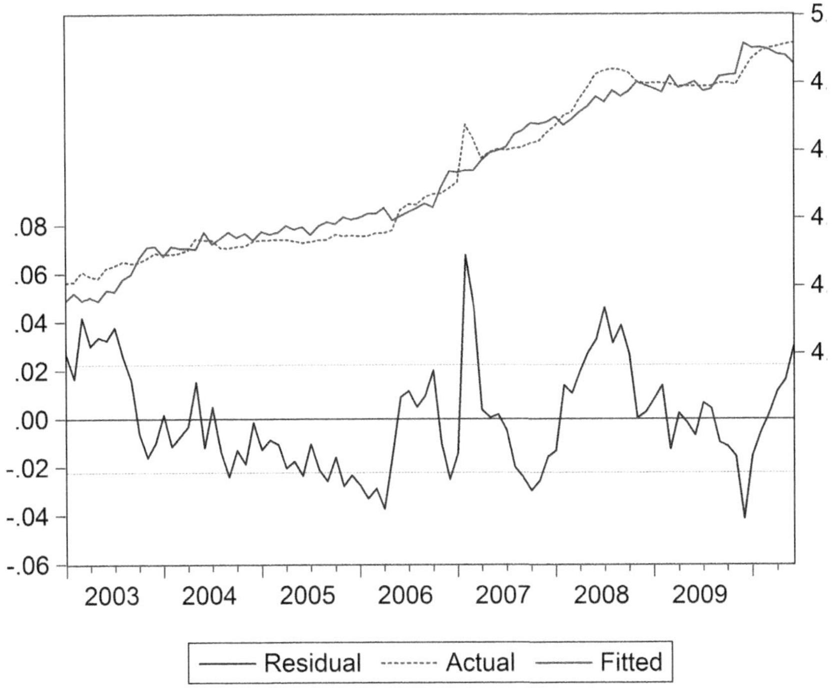

Fig. 3. Residuals of the model

LGDP is the logarithm of GDP at constant prices. Observing the signals of the coefficients, we find that they all conform to our expectations. Therefore, we find no reason to believe that we are dealing with a spurious regression. Nevertheless, we conducted the Engle and Granger test to confirm the existence of a cointegration relationship [15]. The result of this test leads to the conclusion that the null hypothesis of existence of a unit root should be rejected, so that this regression appears to model a cointegration relationship, as you can see in Appendix C. However, the test result may differ for the same variable, in levels and logarithms. For further details on this subject, see Lee and Jong (2010) [19]. Thus, this is the model adopted for our analysis.

Through the analysis of the residuals, serial correlation could also be suspected, so the Breusch-Godfrey serial correlation test was performed, which confirmed our suspicions [3]. In order to correct the serial correlation, lags of the variables should be included [17]. However, we chose not to do so, as this would be contrary to the Quantity Theory of Money. Moreover, this model is well fitted to the data, with an R-squared of 0.96 and is appropriate for forecasting, given its Root Mean Squared Error (RMSE) of 0.022.

6 Discussion of the Results

In this section, we interpret the results of our study and compare them with other published research. In relation to the marginal effects of explanatory variables, we found, as expected, a negative effect of GDP. According to the estimated value of this effect, on average, a rise of 1 percentage point of GDP implies a fall in the CPI equal to 0.177 percentage points. However, the effect of M2 is quite different. We estimated that, on average, a rise of 1 percentage point in M2 leads to a rise in the CPI equal to 0.24 percentage points.

Although East Timor has no monetary policy, the effect of M2 is very high. Since East Timor does not have his own currency, we can assume M2 as a proxy for public expenditure. This means that the only way for the government to inject money into the economy is by public expenditure. To verify this theory, we computed the correlation between Budget Execution (a proxy for public expenditure) and M2, discovering a very high value of 0.93.

In addition to the empirical relation, there is an economic explanation. In fact, East Timor imports a very significant part of the goods that it consumes. The healthy financial situation of the country and its ability to import is due to the fiscal income received from the oil production in the East Timor Sea. Thus, whenever the government decides to raise public expenditure, it is indirectly injecting money into the economy. Hence, from now on, we will refer to public expenditure rather than M2.

Aslan and Korap (2007) [2] found similar results concerning cointegration and the sign of the coefficients, but the magnitudes of the effects are quite different. They found values for the coefficients close to one, thus verifying the Quantity Theory of Money (QTM). Although our coefficients are very low (close to zero), we still support the QTM.

However, since our aim is to analyze the influence of the budgetary policy on inflation, let us turn again to the model. As is well known, the first difference of the logarithm of a variable is approximately equal to the growth rate of the variable. Thus, we have the following relation between the growth rate of CPI and the growth rate of M2 and GDP:

$$\Delta LCPI = 0.243(\Delta LM2) - 0.177(\Delta LGDP) \tag{4}$$

For the economy to be in a sustainable condition, inflation caused by the economic agents should be bounded. By so doing, it is ensured that the economy does not overheat nor becomes deflationary, what must be avoided if an economy is to remain healthy.

For example, in order to have an inflation rate of 3%, with a GDP growth rate of 8% (value of 2010), the growth rate of M2 should not exceed, approximately, 18%. It is now possible to forecast the rate of inflation that would result from an increment of 21% in the public expenditure[4].

[4] From 604 million in 2009 to 730 in 2010.

7 Conclusions

Firstly, unit root tests were conducted in order to confirm the conditions of the cointegration relationship. After confirming that all the variables had an unit root, we tested for cointegration using the Engle and Granger methodology. Finally, we concluded that the series were indeed cointegrated. Thus, the conditions to estimate our model were guaranteed.

When the model was estimated, we found that there was serial correlation, which could be solved using some lags of the variables. However, since it was our intention to test QTM, we did not include any lags. Thus we ignored this problem and focused solely on the QTM. Despite the low value of our coefficients, our results still support the QTM.

Finally, we computed the correlation between M2 and Budget Execution and found a very high value (0.93). Therefore, as East Timor does not have its own currency, we assumed M2 as a proxy for public expenditure. We were thus enabled to offer some suggestions on budgetary policy. For example, if an inflation rate of 3% is sought, the growth rate of public expenditure should be 80% of the growth rate of GDP at constant prices.

Our findings emphasize that public expenditure must be bounded in order to sustain the purchasing power of the economic agents (particularly households). If inflation continues to increase with no bounds, there will be long term problems in the economy. However, East Timor need more than that. In order to control the inflation in the long run, the economy must be more productive. The natural way to do it is to invest in human resources and fixed capital. So the Public Authorities should start by diverting some of the funds applied in Public Expenditure to productive investment [20]. But it is also possible to turn the economy productive by attracting foreign investment. However this requires the creation of some conditions, as we can see in Wang (2001) [28].

Other authors have followed a similar methodology, as Aslan and Korap (2007) [2], and found similar results concerning cointegration and coefficients sign for Turkish Economy. However, the magnitudes of our coefficients are very low, so our results are not very robust. This way we should not forecast the inflation using this model. We may use ARIMA models to maximize goodness of fit and forecast the phenomena [22].

References

1. Amato, J.D., Gerlach, S.: Inflation targeting in emerging market and transition economies: Lessons after a decade. European Economic Review 46(4-5), 781–790 (2002)
2. Aslan, O., Korap, L.: Testing quantity theory of money for the turkish economy. Journal of BRSA Banking and Financial Markets 1(2), 93–109 (2007)
3. Breusch, T.: Testing for autocorrelation in dynamic linear models. Australian Economic Papers 334–355 (1979)
4. Brouwer, G.: Currency and monetary arrangements for East Timor. Australian National University (April 2001)

5. Bullard, J.: Testing long-run monetary neutrality propositions: Lessons from the recent research. FRB of St. Louis Review, 57–77 (1999)
6. Candio, P., Bleiker, R.: Peacebuilding in east timor. The Pacific Review, 63–84 (2001)
7. Cecchetti, S.G., Debelle, G.: Has the inflation process changed? Economic Policy, 311–352 (2006)
8. Dickey, D., Fuller, W.: Distribution of the estimators for autoregressive time series with a unit root. Journal of the American Statistical Association 74, 427–431 (1979)
9. Engle, R., Granger, C.: Co-integration and error correction: Representation, estimation, and testing. Econometrica, 251–276 (1987)
10. Fabrizio, S., Mody, A.: Can budget institutions counteract political indiscipline? Economic Policy, 689–739 (2006)
11. Fraga, A., Goldfajn, I., Minella, A.: Inflation targeting in emerging market economies. National Bureau (2003)
12. Friedman, M.: Quantity Theory of Money. The New Palgrave: A Dictionary of Economics (2008)
13. Geweke, J.: The superneutrality of money in the United States: An interpretation of the evidence. Econometrica, 1–21 (January 1986)
14. Gonzalo, J.: The making of "estimation of common long-memory components in cointegrated systems". Journal of Financial Econometrics, 174–176 (2010)
15. Greene, W.: Econometric Analysis. Prentice-Hall, Englewood Cliffs (2002)
16. Jacome, L., Lonnberg, A.: Implementing official dollarization. IMF (2010)
17. Johnston, J., Dinardo, J.: Econometric Methods. McGraw-Hill International Editions, New York (1997)
18. King, R., Watson, M.: Testing long-run neutrality. FRB of Richmond Economic Quarterly, 69–101 (1997)
19. Lee, J., Jong, R.: Cointegration in logarithms versus cointegration in level. Ohio State University (2010)
20. Lim, J.: Central banking in the philippines: from inflation targeting to financing development. International Review of Applied Economics, 271–285 (2008)
21. Luintel, K.B.: Exogeneity of money and its policy implications for price control: Evidence from south asia. Pacific Economic Review, 505–517 (2002)
22. Meyler, A., Kenny, G., Quinn, T.: Forecasting irish inflation using arima models. Tech. rep., Central Bank and Financial Services Authority of Ireland (1998)
23. Mishkin, F.: Inflation targeting in emerging-market countries. American Economic Review 90(2), 105–109 (2000)
24. Otero, J., Ramirez, M.: Inflation before and after central bank independence: The case of colombia. Journal of Development Economics, 168–182 (2006)
25. Sheriff, E.: Inflationary memory as restrictive factor of the impact of the public expense in the economic growth. working paper, Universidad Privada Boliviana (2010)
26. Sovacool, B.: The political economy of oil and gas in southeast asia: heading towards the natural resource curse? The Pacific Review, 225–259 (2010)
27. United Nations: Regulation on Banking and Payments Authority of East Timor. Jornal da República 6, Series II (2001)
28. Wang, H.: Informal institutions and foreign investment in china. The Pacific Review, 525–556 (2001)

A Data

Statistics	Mean	Median	Max.	Min.	Std. Dev.	Description
CPI	117.96	113.63	142.36	100	3493	Consumer Price Index
BEC	305.52	165.34	947.66	100	6976	Budget Execution Code
GDP	113.80	108.65	146.46	99.64	4845	Real Gross Domestic Product
M2	268.40	185.38	601.51	99.60	7946	Monetary Aggregate M2

B Unit Root Tests

Variable	n	Model	ADF *Hamilton test statistic*	*p-value*
LCPI	89	c	0.02	0.96
LCPI	89	c,t	-1.99	0.59
DLCPI	88	c	-8.90	0.00
LGDP	89	c	-0.35	0.98
LGDP	89	c,t	-1.77	0.71
DLGDP	88	c	-9.83	0.00
LM2	88	c	-0.08	0.95
LM2	88	c,t	-1.89	0.65
DLM2	88	c	-11.91	0.00

Note that *c* denominates the intercept and *t* the trend.

C Cointegration

Augmented Dickey-Fuller test

t-statistic	-3.651593
Prob.*	0.0311

Included observations 89 after adjustments

*MacKinnon (1996) one-sided p-values

Study on the Generation of Collar Curve Based on 3D Point-Cloud Data

Xu Xiao-hui[1,2], Gu Bing-fei[1,2], Su Jun-qiang[1,2,3], and Liu Guo-lian[1,2]

[1] National Engineering Laboratory for Modern Silk
[2] College of Textile and Clothing Engineering, Soochow University Suzhou, China
[3] Changzhou Textile & Garment Institute
jstxgbf@yahoo.com.cn

Abstract. In this paper, non-contact anthropometry is done on the female bodies, and the 3D point-cloud data is got by 3D scanner, and then the collar curve of female tight prototype is generation by data processing on point-cloud figures using reverse engineering software. The collar curve can be divided into the front and back collar curve. The characteristic points of the front collar curve are points of side neck and front neck, and the characteristic points of the back collar curve are points of side neck and back neck. By making the cross sections of the above points, the depth and width of the front and back collar curves are got, and according to the principle of equant depth four related points are inserted in the front collar curve, and three related points are inserted in the back collar curve.

Keywords: point cloud data collar curve; side neck point; front neck point; back neck point; insertion points.

1 Introduction

With the garment CAD / CAM technology development and its specific application in the garment industry, apparel design and production into an automated, high-efficiency time. Non-contact body measurement system makes the emergence of tailored clothing and personalized production become reality [1]. 3D human point cloud data from Non-contact body measurement system can reproduce 3D characteristics of the human body provided the conditions for the deep development.

Shi Xi-Fen, Lin Yi offered a method of connecting free curves which based on fairness principle, and a curve form which based on quartic spline is constructed which can be applicated in CAD [2]. Shi Jian-Feng and Li Zhong extracting border of neckline points then uses the non-uniform cubic B-spine curve to interpolate them and calculates the length of each boundary[3]. Liu Geng-Xin study the digital features of NURBS curve in application of the garment prototype armhole spline curve,and then offer that uses NURBS curve fitting garment prototype curve[4]. This paper research3-D body point cloud data by reverse molding software Imageware, first determination the basic frame of collar curve,then insert relevant point by using the collar depth halving method, finally formation the female tight prototype collar curve.

Q. Zhou (Ed.): ISAEBD 2011, Part II, CCIS 209, pp. 518–524, 2011.

2 Experiment Process

Measuring objects: Female students (20-25 years old) of Soochow University
Measuring environment: T:25±2°C, RH: 65±5%
Measuring location: Measuring laboratory of 3D scanner in Soochow University
Measuring method: Non-contact anthropometry
Measuring announcements: The measuring objects should wear undervest in order to avoid the experimental results.

This study uses non-contact 3D body scanner Symcad of Telmat, which automatically completes the whole body scanning in 20s to capture half a million data points of human body, and has 0.2cm measurement accuracy. Meanwhile, the scanner can also output scattered point cloud data of the body surface, which are namely 3D human data.

3D point cloud data can acquire the whole information of body surface, and they can be read by reverse engineering software Imageware. Cutting out the cross sections, simulation of curves, length measurement of curves and other operations can be done by choosing or inputting 3D coordinates of points.

3 Data Collection and Analysis

3.1 Determination of Depth of the Front Collar Curve

In the tight prototype of garment, the vertical cross-section C1 is done crossing the point of side neck, and the horizontal section C2 is done crossing the point of front neck. The contour lines of the two sections are intersected in point A, and the depth of the front collar curve is the length of the curve between point A and the point of side neck in the contour line of section C1.(The length of the curve is measured in the side figure of human body.)

In the figure of 3D point cloud, the depth of the front collar curve is determined, which is shown in Figure 1.

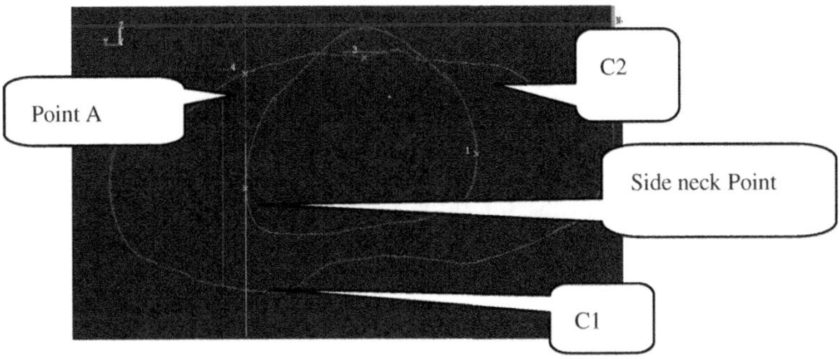

Fig. 1. The depth of the front collar curve

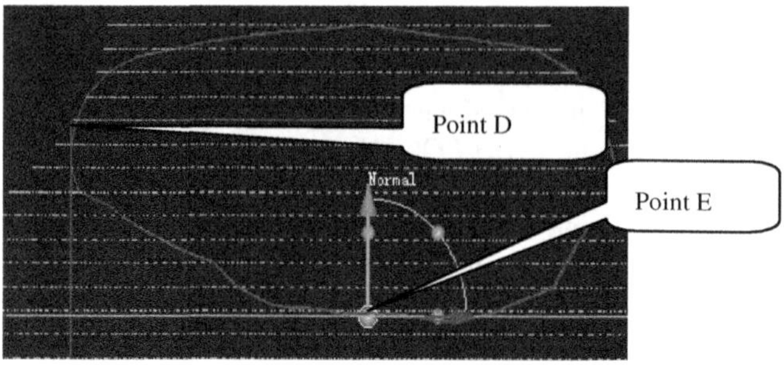

Fig. 2. The obligue section of the front collar curve

3.2 Determination of Width of the Front Collar Curve

In the tight prototype of garment, the vertical cross-section C1 is done crossing the point of side neck, and the horizontal section C2 is done crossing the point of front neck. The contour lines of the two sections are intersected at point A, and the width of the front collar curve is the length of the curve between point A and the front neck point in the contour line of section C2.In the figure of 3D point cloud, the width of the front collar curve is determined, which is shown in Figure 1.

3.3 Methods of Insertion Points of the Front Collar Curve

After determination of the depth and width of the front collar curve, several related points should be inserted in order to get more accurate front collar curve. The specific methods of insertion points are as follows:

The first step: The basic cross sections should be done, such as the horizontal section crossing the point of side neck, the vertical section crossing the point of side neck, and the horizontal section crossing the point of front neck.

The second step: The obligue sections are done crossing the point D of side neck and the point E of front neck and the required section can be regarded appreciatively as the contour line of the front collar curve, shown in Figure 2.

The third step: Quartering is done on the measured depth of the front collar curve. Because the curve transition of the fourth part is a little large, the fourth part can be cut in half once more, and the mark should be done. From top to down, the point of the first part can be marked as insertion point F1, and the point of the second part can be marked as insertion point F2, and the point of the third part can be marked as insertion point F3, and the middle point of the fourth part can be marked as insertion point F4, shown in Figure 3 and Figure 4.

The fourth step: In the front figure, quartering is done on the measured depth of the front collar curve. The horizontal lines can be done crossing the marked points, and the distances between the marked points in the horizontal lines and the contour line of the front collar curve. The distance between point F4 and point G on the contour line is shown in Figure 5.

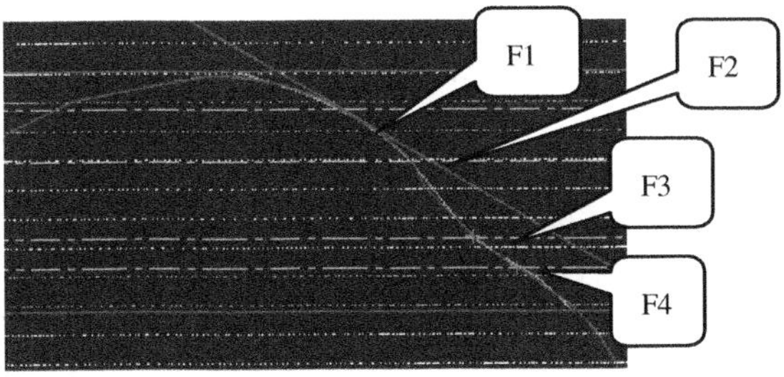

Fig. 3. The marked points in the side figure

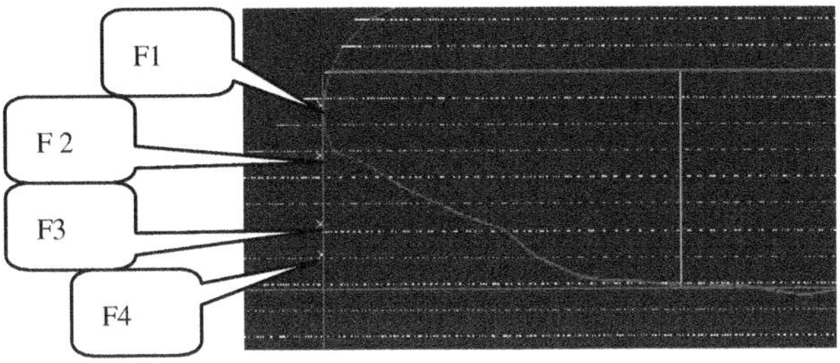

Fig. 4. The marked points in the front figure

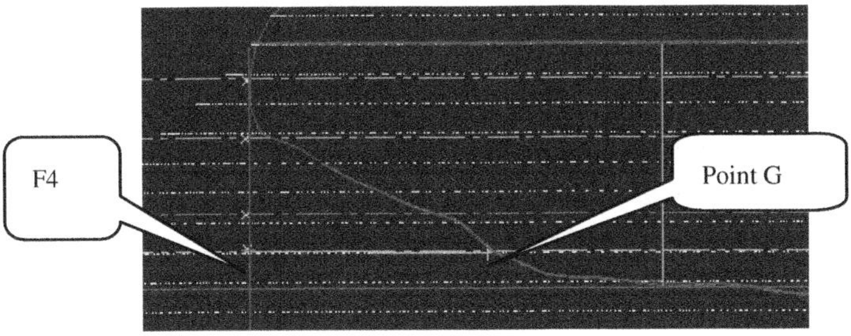

Fig. 5. The distance between point F4 and point G

3.4 Determination of Depth of the Front Collar Curve

The horizontal section C1 is done crossing the point of side neck. Because the seventh cervical point is not enough protuberant in the body surface, especially the very fat or thin people, whose bones extrude not very obvious, another horizontal section C2 is done in the location which is 0.5cm below the point of side neck, according to that the seventh cervical point is 0.5cm below the point of side neck measured by 2D photos, shown in Figure 6. The vertical section C3 is done crossing the point of side neck and the two contour lines of C3 and C2 intersect in the point A, and then the depth of the back collar curve is the distance of the curve between the point of side neck and point A, shown in Figure 7.

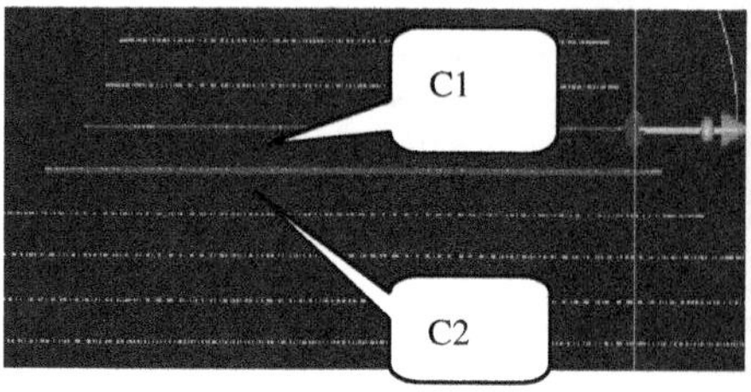

Fig. 6. The horizontal section at side neck point

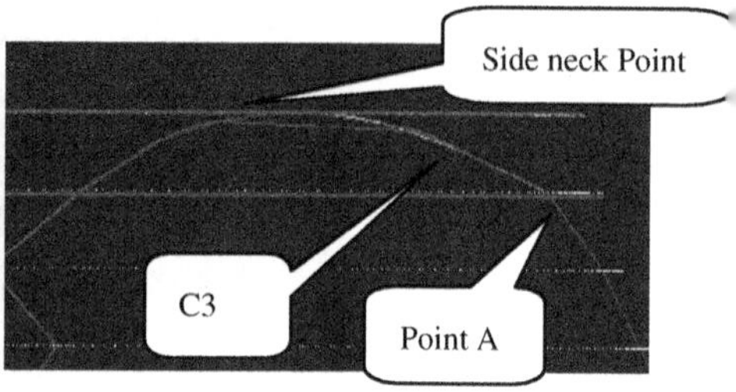

Fig. 7. The side figure of depth of collar

3.5 Determination of Width of the Back Collar Curve

In the tight prototype of garment, the vertical cross-section C4 is done crossing the point of side neck, and the horizontal section C5 is done crossing the point of back neck. The contour lines of the two sections are intersected in point B, and the width of the back collar curve is the length of the curve between point B and the point of back neck in the contour line of section C5, shown in Figure 8.

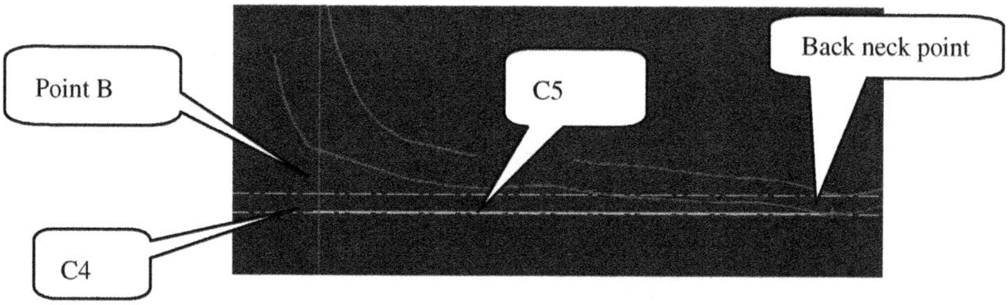

Fig. 8. Width of the back collar curve

4 Result Analysis

In this paper, taken the front collar curve as an example.

4.1 The Basic Framework

The vertical coordinate system is done, in which the vertical axis Y shows the depth of the front collar curve, and the horizontal axis X shows the width of the collar curve. According to the mean of the measured values, the necessary distance of the depth and width of the front collar curve are cut out separately on the axis X and Y.

4.2 Inserted the Related Points

Eight same parts are divided the depth of the front collar curve into eight same parts. The height of the first point is 3/4 of the depth of the front collar curve, and the height of the second point is 1/2 of the depth of the front collar curve, and the height of the third point is 1/4 of the depth of the front collar curve, and the height of the fourth point is 1/8 of the depth of the front collar curve.

In this paper, the point of the first part is the first point A, and the point of the second part is the second point B, and the point of the third part is the third point C, and the middle point of the fourth part is the fourth point D. The length between the each point and the line of neck depth is the horizontal ordinates of each point.

Table 1. The ordinates of each point

Top point	First point	Second point	Third point	Fourth point	Bottom point
(0,8.4)	(0.4,6.3)	(1.3,4.2)	(3.2,2.1)	(5,1.1)	(7.2,0)

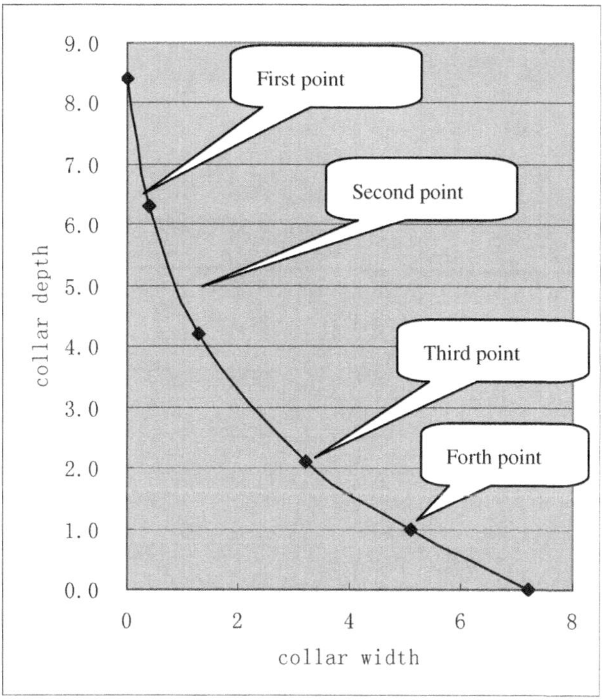

Fig. 9. The basic configuration of the front collar curve

Acknowledgement. Funded by the First Phase of Jiangsu Universities' Distinctive Discipline Development Program for Textile Science and Engineering of Soochow University.

References

1. Lin, D.-j., Sun, X.-d.: Technique of Measurement Extraction Based on 3D Human Body Scanning Data. Computer Center of Beijing Institute of Clothing Technology 09, 36–41 (2005)
2. Shi, X.-f., Lin, Y.: Algorithm of uniting quartic free curves based on energy method. Computer Engineering and Applications 07.2, 131–133
3. Shi, J.-f., Li, Z., Hu, J.-L., Jin, Y.: Boundary extraction and editing on 3-D garment mesh models. Journal of Textile Research 1, 129–133 (2010)
4. Liu, G.-X.: Study the NURBS curve in Application of the Garment Prototype. Guangxi Textile Science and Technology 3, 34–37 (2007)
5. Zhang, Y., Zhou, F.-Y.: Principle and Application of Three-dimensional Body Measurement Technology. Journal of Zhejiang Institute of Science and Technology 20(4), 310–314 (2003)
6. Shan, Y.: The Technical Basis of Imageware reverse molding, 1st edn. Tsinghua University Press, Beijing (2006)

Study on the Generation of Armhole Curve Based on 3D Point-Cloud Data

Xu Xiao-hui[1,2], Gu Bing-fei[1,2], Su Jun-qiang[1,2,3], and Liu Guo-lian[1,2]

[1] National Engineering Laboratory for Modern Silk
[2] College of Textile and Clothing Engineering, Soochow University Suzhou, China
[3] Changzhou Textile & Garment Institute
jstxgbf@yahoo.com.cn

Abstract. In this paper, non-contact anthropometry is done on the female bodies, and the 3D point-cloud data is got by 3D scanner, and then the collar curve of female tight prototype is generation by data processing on point-cloud figures using reverse engineering software. The armhole curve can be divided into the front and back armhole curve, this paper mainly on the front armhole curve. The characteristic points of the front armhole curve are points of shoulder point, armpit point and chest width point. By making the cross sections of the above points, get the depth and width of the front armhole curves and according to the principle of equant depth three related points are inserted in the front armhole curve.

Keywords: point cloud data armhole curve, relevant point, correlation analysis.

1 Introduction

3-D human point cloud data from Non-contact body measurement system can reproduce 3D characteristics of the human body provided the conditions for the deep development. Liu Geng-Xin study the digital features of NURBS curve in application of the garment prototype armhole spline curve,and then offer that uses NURBS curve fitting garment prototype curve, and through VBA programming can achieve curve automatic fitting [1].

Shi Jian-Feng and Li Zhong extracting border of neckline and cuffline points then uses the non-uniform cubic B-spline curve to interpolate them and calculates the length of each boundary[2]. Shi Xi-Fen and Lin Yi offered a method of connecting free curves which based on fairness principle, and a curve form which based on quartic spline is constructed which can be applicated in CAD[3]. San Tian Ming Zi analyses the sleeves shape of coats, jackets, shirts for woman, and divide armhole lines into three classes. This three results are valuable for sleeve-lines, and for establishing standards for the development of basic-pattern blocks for individuals items[4-5].This paper research3-D body point cloud data by reverse molding software Imageware, first determination the basic frame of front armhole curve, then insert relevant point by using the front armhole depth halving method, finally formation the female tight prototype armhole curve.

Q. Zhou (Ed.): ISAEBD 2011, Part II, CCIS 209, pp. 525–531, 2011.

2 Experiment Process

Measuring objects: Female students (20-25 years old) of Soochow University.
Measuring environment: T:25±2℃, RH: 65±5%.
Measuring location: Measuring laboratory of 3D scanner in Soochow University.
Measuring method: Non-contact anthropometry.
Measuring announcements: The measuring objects should wear undervest in order to avoid the experimental results.

This study uses non-contact 3D body scanner Symcad of Telmat, which automatically completes the whole body scanning in 20s to capture half a million data points of human body, and has 0.2cm measurement accuracy. Meanwhile, the scanner can also output scattered point cloud data of the body surface, which are namely 3D human data.

3D point cloud data can acquire the whole information of body surface, and they can be read by reverse engineering software Imageware. Cutting out the cross sections, simulation of curves, length measurement of curves and other operations can be done by choosing or inputting 3D coordinates of points.

3 Data Collection and Analysis

3.1 Determine the Depth of Front Armhole Curve

Analysis the original point cloud data from 3-D body scanner that each human point cloud data are composed of five sub-point cloud: the left and right upper, and left and right lower limbs, trunk and head. As shown in Figure 1.

This paper uses the function of software Imageware show/hide point cloud, just show the trunk and head point cloud for further research, as shown in Figure 2. In the front view, determine the shoulder point and armpit point and attach these two points, then choose the midpoint A that shown in Figure 3.

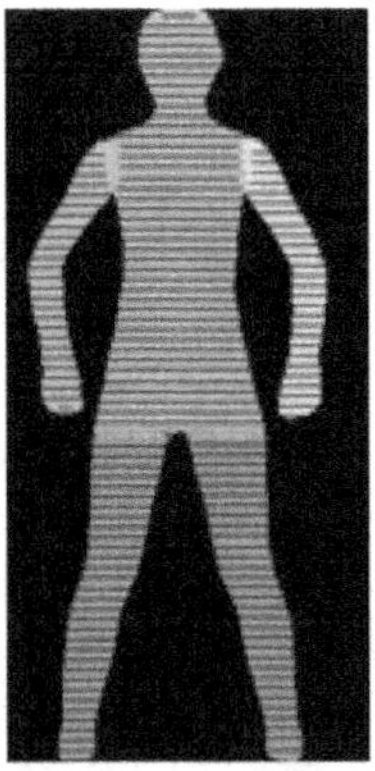

Fig. 1. Point cloud data

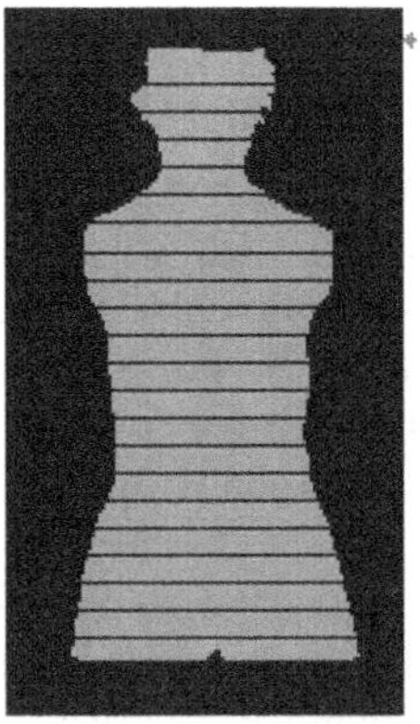

Fig. 2. The head and trunk point cloud.

As the chest wide point is the midpoint of intersection line that between the arms and torso (shown in Figure 3 the Intersection L). When just show the trunk point cloud ,the level line via point A and the intersection L intersect at point B, that, s to say the point B is chest width point, make vertical cross-section is done crossing the chest width point.

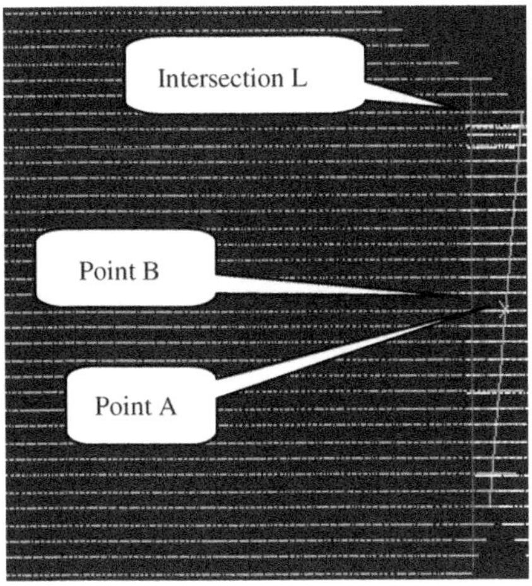

Fig. 3. Vertical cross-sections crossing the chest width point

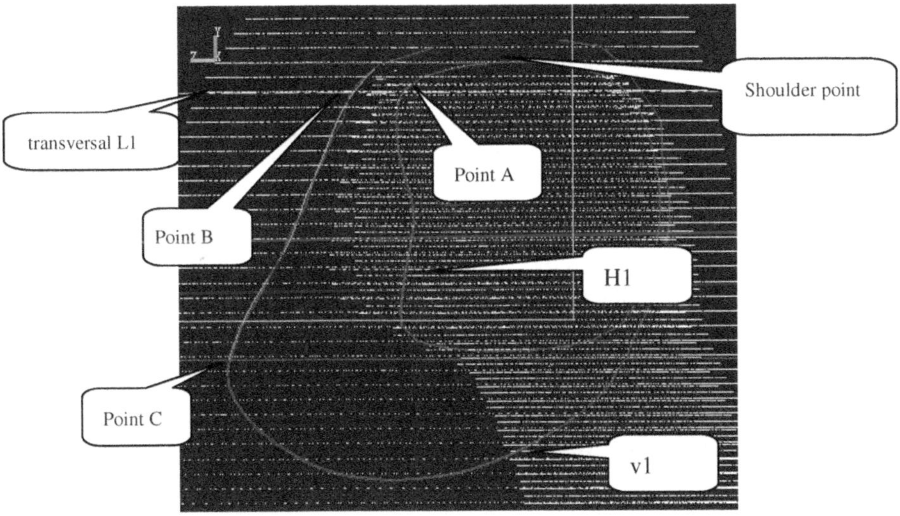

Fig. 4. Determine the depth of front armhole curve

The vertical and horizontal cross-section are done crossing the shoulder point, and the vertical cross-section V1 is done crossing the chest width point (shown in Figure 4). From Side view at front armhole curve, there is a point has the biggest curvature at the contour line of the vertical cross-section are done crossing the shoulder point, it is point A as shown in Figure 3. Make the level line via point A and the contour line of V1 intersect at point B. Measure the distance between shoulder point and point A at the vertical section crossing shoulder point(with Bessel curve fitting),marked as the length S1.

The depth of front armhole curve divides into two parts: the first is S1.

The second part: ①the horizontal cross-section are done crossing the armpit point (H1), the vertical cross-section are done crossing the chest width point (V1).

②Take the V1 plane as the datum, cuts the -Z axis direction unnecessary part at H1 plane, obtains transversal L1, the L1 and the contour lines of V1 intersect at point C; ③then the curve length of point B and point C in the contour line of V1, just the second part of the depth of front armhole curve, marked as the length S2.

The width of front armhole curve divide into upper wide and lower wide.

3.2 Determine the Lower Wide of Front Armhole Curve

First make three section: the vertical cross-sectionV1, and the vertical cross-section crossing armpit point (V2), and the horizontal cross-section crossing the armpit point (H1).The contour line of V1 and H1 intersect at point F, that's to say the length between point F and armpit point at the contour line of V2 just the lower width of the front armhole curve, as shown in Figure 5.

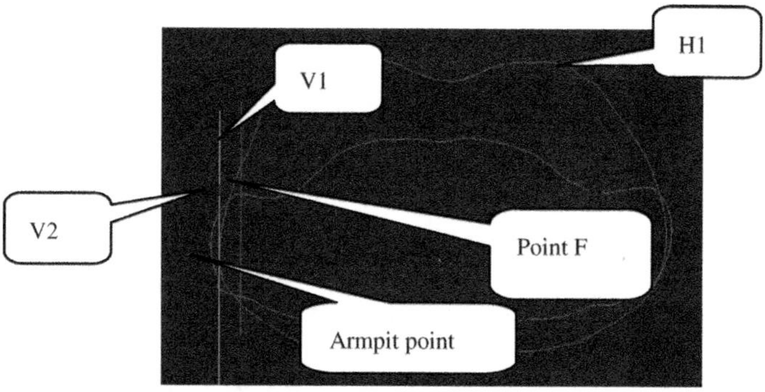

Fig. 5. The lower wide of front armhole curve

3.3 Determine the Upper Wide of Front Armhole Curve

In the front view the contour line of V1 and H2 intersect at point H, that's to say the straight line length between point H and shoulder point just the upper wide of front armhole curve, as shown in Figure 6.

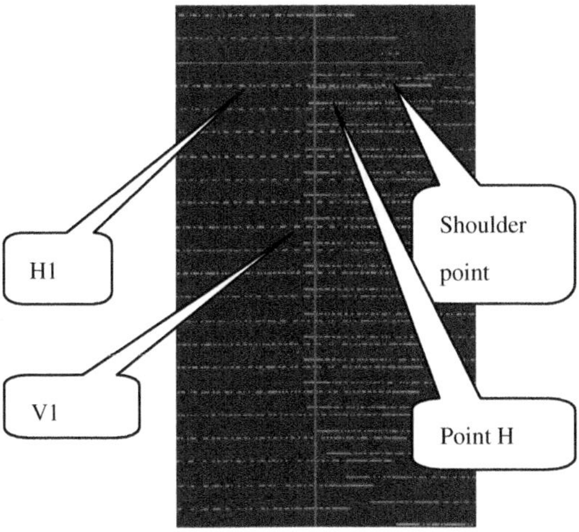

Fig. 6. The upper wide of front armhole curve

3.4 Insert Relevant Point at Front Armhole Curve

Determine the depth and width of front armhole curve, aim to get more accurate front armhole curve, must insert several relevant point. The following is the specific method of inserting relevant points

First step: divide the depth and width of front armhole curve into four quarters, and divide the fourth depth into three equal pieces. For simple, record this three points as four -zero point, four -one point and four –two point. As shown in Figure 7.

Second step: In the top view the contour line of the horizontal sectionV3 cross four -zero point, and the contour line of the vertical section cross the chest width point, these two contour line intersect at point I; the contour line of the V3, the contour line of the vertical section cross armpit point, these two contour line intersect at point J. That's to say the length between point I and point J at the contour line of the horizontal section cross chest width point just the upper width of four –zero point, as shown in Figure 8.

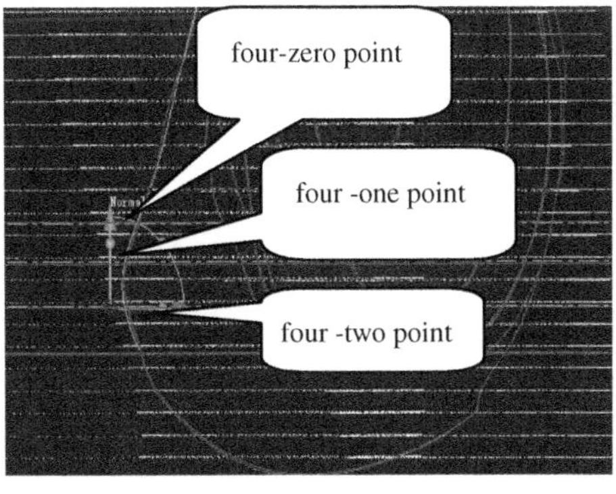

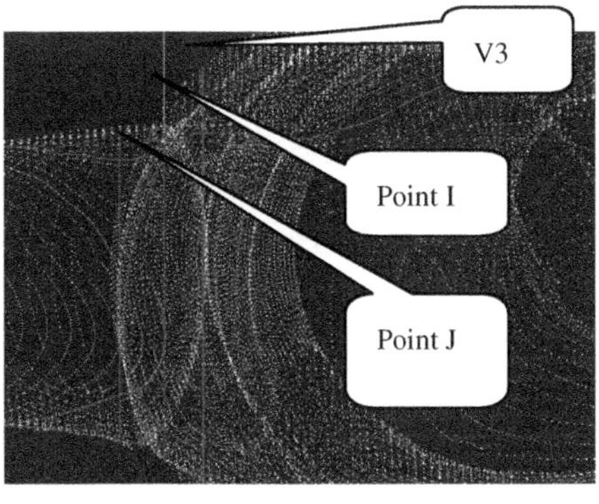

Fig. 7. Three cross-sections

Fig. 8. Insert relevant point at front armhole curve

4 Result Analysis

This paper research mainly on the curve of tight prototype, if measure each human body that's will time-consuming and energy-consuming. So establish the front armhole curve rulers to provide basic rulers to automatically generated clothing pattern.

The correlation analysis among the depth of front armhole curve(front depth), the width of front armhole curve, chest circumference, height is done by SPSS, (measuring unit: cm).

Table 1. Correlation analysis of front armhole curve

		front depth	height	chest circumference
	Pearson Correlation	1	.316(**)	.763(**)
	Sig.(2-tailed)	.	.000	.000
height	Pearson Correlation	.316(**)	1	.218(**)
	Sig.(2-tailed)	.000	.	.000
chest circumference	Pearson Correlation	.763(**)	.218(**)	1
	Sig.(2-tailed)	.000	.000	.

** Correlation is significant at the 0.01 level (2-tailed).

From the table 1, the front depth has significant correlation with chest circumference and height at 0.01 reliability analysis. the lower width also has significant correlation with chest circumference ,height and front depth at 0.01 reliability analysis .The upper width also has significant correlation with front depth at 0.01 reliability analysis.

From SPSS multiple linear regression, work out front depth with these two principles.

front depth =0.151*chest circumference+0.49 （1）

front depth =0.144*chest circumference+0.029*height-3.6 （2）

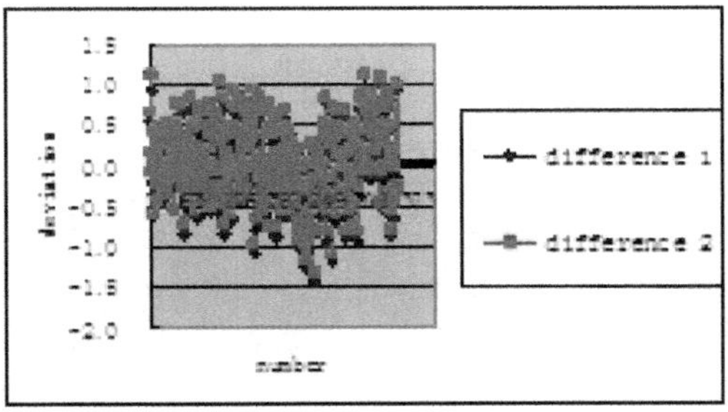

Fig. 9. Compare the difference

For simple, calculate the difference between formula(1) and front depth, mark as difference 1; calculate the difference between formula(2) and front depth, mark as difference 2; compare this two differences, as shown in Figure 9.

In difference 1,the deviation range is -1.27-1.27. the deviation range at 0.5cm about 219/356=62%,the deviation range at 0.7cm about 271/356=76%,the sum of error absolute value is 181.6。

In difference 2,the deviation range is -1.30-1.16. the deviation range at 0.5cm about 213/356=60%,the deviation range at 0.7cm about 282/356=79%,the sum of error absolute value is 179.

The precise of formula(2) is superior than formula(1),so take the formula(1) to simulate front depth: front depth =0.144* chest circumference +0.029*height-3.6.

Acknowledgement. Funded by the First Phase of Jiangsu Universities' Distinctive Discipline Development Program for Textile Science and Engineering of Soochow University.

References

1. Liu, G.-x.: Study the NURBS curve in Application of the Garment Prototype. Guangxi Textile Science and Technology 3, 34–37 (2007)
2. Shi, J.-f., Li, Z., Hu, J.-i., Jin, Y.: Boundary extraction and editing on 3-D garment mesh models. Journal of Textile Research 1, 129–133 (2010)
3. Shi, X.-f., Lin, Y.: Algorithm of uniting quartic free curves based on energy method. Computer Engineering and Applications 07.2, 131–133
4. San, t.m.z.: Research on the Typification of Armhole Line for Clothing Design. Japan Research Association for Textile End-uses, 124–139 (2007)
5. San, t.m.z.: Research on the Typification of Armhole Line for Clothing Design. Japan Research Association for Textile End-uses, 124–139 (2007)
6. Zhang, Y., Zhou, F.-y.: Principle and Application of Three-dimensional Body Measurement Technology. Journal of Zhejiang Institute of Science and Technology 20(4), 310–314 (2003)
7. Shan, Y.: The Technical Basis of Imageware reverse molding, 1st edn. Tsinghua University Press, Beijing

Cross-Border M&A and Industrial Safety of Equipment Manufacturing Industry in Liaoning, China*

Xiaonan Fan, Xiaocheng Sun, and Yuehua Dong

Dalian Polytechnic University, China
catfxn@sina.com

Abstract. There are increasing M&A in equipment manufacturing industry by multinational enterprises in Liaoning Province, which bring negative effects on the industrial safety. In order to evaluate the effects, we developed a model covering industrial growth, competitiveness, and control power. We find that cross-border M&A don't make industrial safety deteriorated, but there are still some problems in industrial safety.

Keywords: Cross-border M&A, Industrial Safety, Equipment Manufacturing Industry.

1 Introduction

Since 1980s, Cross-border Mergers and Acquisition (cross-border M&A) by multinational corporations have deeply affected globalization. As the first big pillar industry, the equipment manufacturing industry supports the economic growth and the process of industrialization in Liaoning province. In recent years, foreign investment has also permeated this industry. Although the cross-border M&A brings capitals, technologies, brands and international marketing channels, we must also be aware that the rising proportion of foreign capital and the increasing number of cross-border M&A by multinational corporations will threat the industrial safety of equipment manufacturing industry in Liaoning province. Therefore, it is of theoretical importance and practical significance to study on the effects of cross-border M&A on the industrial safety in equipment manufacturing industry in Liaoning province.

2 Cross-Border M&A of the Equipment Manufacturing Industry in Liaoning Province

2.1 Amount and Scale of M&A

With the deepening of economic globalization, cross-border M&A turns to leading enterprises in important industry. From 2002 to 2008, there are more than 20 cases in cross-border M&A in equipment manufacturing enterprises in Liaoning province,

* Sponsored by Liaoning Province Education Department(2009 B023) .

Q. Zhou (Ed.): ISAEBD 2011, Part II, CCIS 209, pp. 532–538, 2011.

mainly occurring in Shenyang and Dalian, and the leading enterprises in equipment manufacturing become the victims.

The M&A scales are quite different due to different enterprises' registration capitals and scales. Among them, the maximum amount of accumulative total acquisition is $5750 million, which happens in the M&A for Jinbei Automobile by GM. There are five cases in M&A, whose scales arranging from $20 million to $30 million, however, the capital mainly focuses on around $10 million. There also exist cross-border M&A capital investment paying in installment; some multinational companies use technology as investment.

2.2 Means of M&A

Cross-border M&A is comprised of cross-border merger and cross-border acquisition, and cross-border acquisition includes asset acquisition and stake purchase. Multinational corporations mainly buy equipment manufacturing enterprises by making equity acquisitions in Liaoning province, see table 1.

Table 1. Means of cross-border M&A

Means	Percentage
Minority stake purchase	42%
Majority stake purchase	33%
Wholly owned stake purchase	8%
Asset acquisition	4%
Cross-border merger	13%

Stake purchase refers to an enterprise's purchase of another enterprise, thus obtains part or the whole ownership of the target enterprise. When the multinational companies want to purchase the enterprises which have difficulties in production and management, they usually will take this way, and also they will increase their capital and enlarge their stake to force Chinese companies to give up majority stake or dilute Chinese shareholding proportions, with the result of controlling the target enterprises. For example, after the joint venture between Shenyang Storage Battery Factory and Japan Panasonic, Panasonic took the advantage of the tight budget in that factory and increased additional capital and expanded their stake. In the end, Shenyang Storage Battery Factory's share was diluted to 5% and eventually lost their control power.

Asset acquisition is a market transaction that an enterprise purchases all or part asset of another enterprise, making it as a part of itself, and actually obtaining all or part of control power. This way is often used when the target enterprise is in crisis or in asset restructuring, and the multinational corporations will ultimately get the ownership and control of the target enterprise.

Cross-border merger refers to the combination of assets and operations between two different companies from two countries and forming a new company, with the target enterprise as an independent economy no longer exists. The equipment manufacturing enterprises in Liaoning province that were merged by multinational corporations are those with worsening management and in heavy debt burden, such as Dalian Electrical Machinery Factory.

3 The Impacts of Cross-Border M&A on Industrial Safety

3.1 Impacts on Industrial Growth

Cross-border M&A may cause direct financial loss from equipment manufacturing enterprises. In recent years, due to obscure property rights and fuzzy responsibilities in state-owned enterprises, the state-owned assets of the target enterprises haven't been checked standardized in M&A cases, which caused the underestimate of the state-owned asset value and the loss of it. For example, the previous Dalian Electrical Machinery Factory was bought by Singapore Westwood at the price of 100 million RMB, while the actual value of it was at least two to three times. Multinational corporations took high quality assets and left only debts, thousands of employees' resettlement to government, which makes the government back a heavy burden.

The cross-border M&A also affects the development of local brands. The profit-seeking nature makes multinational corporations always consider their global strategies. After becoming the shareholder of the equipment manufacturing enterprises, some foreign companies utilized the production capacity and channels to promote their brands and gradually reduced or even stopped using Chinese brands, leading to the decline of reputation and value of Chinese brands; and some foreign companies stipulated to forbid Chinese brands, causing the replacement of Chinese brands with foreign brands.

3.2 Impacts on Industrial Competitiveness

Cross-border M&A in a certain degree brings Chinese enterprises with advanced technology, but actually it does not promote the development of industrial competitiveness. The overall level of equipment manufacturing industry in Liaoning province is still at the stage of mechanization, with low level of technological equipment, while the developed countries have entered into automatization stage with computer control flexibility and intelligent integration. And for the structure of products, there are still some problems, such as the convergence of moderate and low products and lack of high-tech products. The majority of enterprises don't have their exclusive technology, and their products are lack of technical contents and unique competitiveness. Besides, the multinational corporations only transfer some second-rate even third-rate, outdated technology. And most of the multinational corporations control their technology strictly and take all measures to prevent their technology, especially the core technology from spillovers.

3.3 Impacts on Industrial Control Power

Cross-border M&A threaten the control power of Chinese enterprise. The leading equipment manufacturing enterprises in Liaoning were purchased by multinational corporations in the past few years, involved in global production system to produce low value-added products under the domination of global strategies of multinational corporations. Therefore, they can not form their own independent industry system, and the control power is transferred to the foreigners. In the M&A cases of Dalian electrical Machinery Factory and Shenyang Rock Drilling Machinery, the foreign companies first gained some amount of stock through joint venture, and then by bad running they achieved 100% stock, which makes Chinese enterprises lose their control power and their controlling position.

4 The Evaluation of Impacts of Cross-Border M&A on the Industrial Safety

4.1 Model Construction

Referring to the multi-indicator system that is presented by Lausanne International Institute of Management and Development in Swiss, the most authoritative research institution on international competitiveness, and the World Economy Forum (WEF), we developed the evaluation model:

$$S=\alpha X+\beta Y+\gamma Z \tag{1}$$

S – The impacts of cross-border M&A on industrial safety
X – The impacts of cross-border M&A on industrial growth
Y – The impacts of cross-border M&A on industrial competitiveness
Z – The impacts of cross-border M&A on industrial control power

α, β and γ are the coefficients of each first index, and according to the importance they are given corresponding weights whose sum equals 1. Among them, industrial growth is the basis for sustainable development of industry, and industrial competitiveness and industrial control power complement each other. Therefore, the weights for industrial growth, competitiveness and control power are 0.4, 0.3 and 0.3 respectively.

4.2 Evaluation Index Selection

We select industrial growth, industrial competitiveness and industrial control power as first indices, and then select six representative secondary indices to analyze, which are shown in table 2.

Table 2. Evaluation index system

First index	Secondary index
Industrial growth	Industrial value-added rate
	Sales revenue, total asset and employee growth rate
Industrial competitiveness	Domestic market share
	Industrial profit rate
Industrial control power	Foreign capital dependence
	Industrial asset-liability ratio

The evaluation method is to give weights to corresponding indices first, then to analyze the secondary indices quantitatively to get evaluation values, and then to multiply the evaluation values with their own weights, and at last to calculate the sum. The sum is the numerical value to measure the impacts of cross-border M&A on industrial safety. If the sum falls in the intervals of [85%, 100%], [65%, 85%], [45%, 65%], [25, 45%] and [0%, 25%], it means that the industry is very unsafe, unsafe, basically safe, safe and very safe respectively.

4.3 Pact Evaluation

The impacts of cross-border M&A on industrial safety are evaluated from the aspects of industrial growth, competitiveness and industrial control power. According to *State Statistical Yearbook* and *Liaoning statistical Yearbook*, the evaluation results are organized as Table 3.

Table 3. Evaluation of secondary index system

Industry	Industrial add-value rate	Sales revenue growth rate	Total asset growth rate	Employe e growth rate	Market share	Profit rate	Foreign capital dependenc e	Asset-liability ratio
Metal product	28.86%	39.88%	46.44%	25.11%	48.96%	41.1%	6.31%	45.55%
General equipment	32.50%	49.19%	52.52%	35.10%	74.81%	35.75%	6.77%	64.87%
Special-purpose equipment	32.49%	37.67%	29.03%	24.18%	82.08%	-9.66%	22.31%	73.63%
Transportation equipment	23.38%	84.39%	45.37%	40.98%	66.39%	34.60%	21.47%	86.45%
Electric machinery and equipment	28.81%	14.01%	13.20%	17.98%	54.89%	-16.01%	27.66%	94.17%
Communication equipment, computer and other electronic equipment	25.76%	-12.97%	-5.29%	15.64%	51.46%	-8.78%	54.38%	70.15%
Instruments, cultural and office machinery	37.67%	-9.18%	-2.36%	-1.35%	45.42%	-5.78%	29.63%	57.32%
Standardized value	29.92%	29.00%	25.56%	22.52%	60.57%	10.17%	24.08%	70.31%

Data sources: *State Statistical Yearbook, Liaoning Statistics Yearbook*

Table 4. Evaluation of the impacts of cross-border M&A on the industrial safety

First index	First index weight	Secondary index	Secondary index average	Secondary index weight	First index value	Impacts of cross-border M&A on industrial safety
Industrial growth	0.4	Industrial add-value rate	0.2992	1/2	0.2781	0.3589
		Sales revenue growth rate	0.29	1/6		
		Total asset growth rate	0.2556	1/6		
		Employee growth rate	0.2252	1/6		
Industrial competitiveness	0.3	Market share	0.6057	1/2	0.3537	
		Profit rate	0.1017	1/2		
Industrial control power	0.3	Foreign capital dependence	0.2408	1/2	0.4720	
		Asset-liability ratio	0.7031	1/2		

Then, we calculate the sum of the product of the average of secondary indices and their weights and obtain the values of first indices, multiplied with their weights, and then we get the impacts of cross-border M&A on the industrial safety of the equipment manufacturing industry in Liaoning province.

From Table 4, we can see that the value that measures the impacts of cross-border M&A on industrial safety in the equipment manufacturing industry in Liaoning is 35.89%, belonging to the interval of [25%, 45%]. So we can draw the conclusion that by December 2008, the equipment manufacturing industry in Liaoning province is safe.

From analysis, cross-border M&A didn't make industrial safety deteriorated, but we have to admit that there are some problems in industrial safety of the equipment manufacturing industry in Liaoning province. On one hand, for the state-owned or shareholding enterprises that undertake the task of modernization of the equipment manufacturing industry in Liaoning province, they have weak profitability, heavy debt burden and depend on foreign capital greatly, so they have disadvantageous position in market competition; on the other hand, the equipment manufacturing industry in Liaoning is lack of technology R&D and innovation ability, and some companies tend to introduce foreign technology, ignoring digestion and innovation, which affect their international competitiveness negatively. In addition, there are malicious M&A by multinational corporations, who usually adopt the mode of "joint venture – loss – single proprietorship" to scramble for the control power.

5 Suggestions to Ensure Industrial Safety

5.1 Enhance the Deepness and Extent of the Industrial Development

The equipment manufacturing enterprises in Liaoning should integrate production and research resources. First, we should develop midfield industry. Midfield industry produces components and parts, which is between raw material and final product manufacturing industries. Through reorganization and transformation, we should develop some large-scale and specialized equipment manufacturing companies to become national and global suppliers, and form the cluster effects of this industry.

And we should pay attention to develop the new service industry extended from the equipment manufacturing industry. Developing new type service is the new path to revitalize the equipment manufacturing industry, which can promote the selling and increase the added value.

5.2 Strengthen R&D and Innovation Ability

The equipment manufacturing enterprises in Liaoning should make the technological innovation as the central task of enterprise development, paying attention not only to original innovation, but also to introduction, digestion and innovation. Through technological innovation, the enterprises will hold their own brands with independent intellectual property. Especially for the advantageous industries, such as NC machine tools, shipbuilding, aircraft manufacturing, power supply, and large metallurgical equipment, etc., the enterprises should pay much attention to R&D, the supporting core components and the integration of processing systems. And the equipment manufacturing industry should develop in coexistence of foreign capital and thus realize the ascending progress in global value chain.

5.3 Beware of Multinational Companies' Malicious M&A

The ultimate goal of multinational corporations is to capture the emerging markets and obtain monopoly profits. Therefore, for the enterprises, they should be aware of the true purpose of cross-border M&A; while for the joint venture companies, Chinese should never easily lose control power, and should insist on holding 51% share or Chinese acting as the general manager with the right of drafting contract. Meanwhile, we should pay close attention to company's stock market, and if there is something abnormal, we'd better be on guard and do some investigation so as to respond as soon as possible. For the government, they should fully play the role in checking M&A, especially in the aspect of industrial competitiveness, and improve the industrial safety evaluation index system and evaluation methods. The government should define their position, policies, principles and procedures to cross-border M&A through legislation, regulate the evaluation and supervision of state-owned assets of equipment manufacturing enterprises.

References

1. Han, S.K., Li, Q., Han, A.Q.: 'The Effects of Cross-border M&A on Development. Business Times 17, 56–61 (2003)
2. Nie, M.H., Yan, X.H.: The Tendency of Sole Proprietorship of Foreign Investment in China. Social Science 12, 33–34 (2006)
3. Jing, Y.Q.: The Evaluation Index System of Industrial Safety. Economist 2, 70–76 (2006)
4. Song, Q., Chen, C.Y.: 'The Effects of Cross-border M&A on Economy and the Countermeasures. Review of Economic Research 1, 3–10 (2002)
5. Liu, Z.H., Cui, J.: The Position and Function of Government in Utilizing Foreign Investment and Maintaining Economic Safety. Economic Research 4, 25–28 (2005)

Research on the Transition of the Service Mechanism of the University Library

Ke Wang and Jin Xu

Department of Library Huazhong Normal University
Wuhan, China
tongwang889@TOM.COM

Abstract. This paper discussed the Service Mechanism of "human-oriented" in university library, which is an essential requirement and the prevailing trend for university library development today. According to the practical problems, this paper from four aspects proposes some relevant suggestions for the transition of Service mechanism in university library, thus provide a reference for current university library.

Keywords: university library; human-oriented; service mechanism; transition.

1 Introduction

University library as one of three pillars, it is shouldering the assignment of inheriting civilization, spreading knowledge and fostering talents. In firmly establish and fully implement the scientific concept of development today, the library requires a comprehensive, coordinated and sustainable development, it is necessary to provide the humanized service for readers. It is no exaggeration to say that the establishment of "reader-oriented" Service Mechanism in university library is an essential requirement and the prevailing tread for university library development today.

2 Results

The trends of the transition of the service mechanism of the university library are as follows: (1) the humanization of Environmental Layout; (2) the comprehension of the readers' education and propaganda;(3) high-level service of information knowledge for humanistic glycosylated;(4) readers self-service.

Firstly, Library environment is an important window of schools, reflecting their hardware of teaching. Besides, it also takes an important part in material civilization of the campuses. At present, with the insufficiency of library buildings and the increasing demand of readers, many universities have been built or are going to build new high-tech libraries. This is because they have fully realized that a good library environment has a good influence on the teaching and humanistic atmosphere. Indeed, they firmly believe that only combining with environment, teaching, supervising and service, can complete century's great cause of teaching.

Q. Zhou (Ed.): ISAEBD 2011, Part II, CCIS 209, pp. 539–543, 2011.

Modern Library is also a high-tech library, this is the times required. When the readers enter the library, they begin to feel the high-tech library in our eyes. After going by computer-controlled access control system identification, the reader walk into the library building, and start to accept computer monitor in the same time, the central air conditioning let readers feel warm in winter and cool in summer naturally, the computers which is used to search and look up can be seen everywhere, and then what each needs traveling by the electric elevator entrance reading room in the light of. Needless to say, hi-tech library give the readers convenience and comfort, however, we need to know ignore the human charm and green environment, the library is a library without a soul, university library building should be a green library, it should be the natural objects of human creation and integration of the unity of perfect harmony.

Secondly, The readers' educational work of university libraries is one of important content of the university library reader services, is also the important content of higher education reform in college students' quality education. At present, the reader education work continues to be able to take seriously, to explore and develop, but at the same time, the reader's bad behavior is still common occurrence. Readers fails to return the book even stealing books which lead to a serious loss of library books, the books are outlined, tore dug that is to let person painfully unceasingly; Reading room 's cell phone rings upsurge. Reading room cell phone rings upsurge, Do not use allograph board, throw and put books everywhere commonly, computer parts of the electronic reading room were malicious damage; which is not surprising; disrespect and slander staff events occurred occasionally.

Along with the innovation of library work, many libraries began to introduce all the open-shelf service, Indeed, which not only can reduce labor intensity of finding the book, but also improve the utilization of library materials. But, with those whether bring more books confusion, loss phenomenon? The new situation, the new period to the reader, which undoubtedly put forward higher request to staff, library reader education is a task which already have no delay.

The library propaganda work of the readers is one of the activities that library carried out the purpose to make full use of all kinds of literature resources, cultivate the information quality for readers. The library lack propaganda work of readers is lifeless, empty buildings. The real utility of library Just being shallow mining, library real utility was just a small mining, New performances into the library doesn't know how to acquire literature and the senior grades students who lack information literacy will only to simple access book s or Use of the library self-study learning environment.

As is known to all that every year the university library will pay majority of money for buying rich and diversified information resources that including books, newspapers and electronic resources, if we use inadequate of the resources not only cause tremendous wasteful but also unfavorable to the cultivation of information talent. In the current digitized era, the social need high information quality talents and need to be able to obtain information, control, using information and reproduction of information talents, and these ability should be develop at the initial contact information of the university library.

Propaganda work of the readers needs us from the passive service steering active push. Propaganda work of the readers should be diversified, sustainability, we should intensify propaganda of the library, through advocacy and guide make readers to fully understand and master the function and information resources and promptly issued " bulletin of information resource", provide training of search, database Introduction Seminar, user educate course, online consulting, vigorously developing library "publicity week" and "publicity month" and other activities. We guides the student to make full use of library information resources, increase their consciousness of access the information, cultivate their scientific research and innovation ability and make their lifelong benefit.

Thirdly, Scientific research plays a very important role in the development of Universities. In China Universities scientific innovation competitiveness evaluation, Evaluation of the comprehensive competitiveness of Chinese universities, for scientific research strength of comprehensive evaluation are included, it can said that the research level of the Universities largely represents its overall level and overall strength. As college information resource center of library, comprehensive, professional, continuous updated collection resources and relatively complete, the characteristic database ought to bear the task to provide the information resource guarantee for the entire school teaching and research.

In recent years, various colleges and universities are increasing investment into library's construction, purchase large and professional purchasing database and some of them to build new high-tech library buildings, hardware has turned from the traditional library to digital library. However, most of staff in the library still in traditional understanding passively find information and data, they lack of understanding of teachers and students of scientific research and rarely participate in teachers' and students' scientific research activities and they think that good working attitude for its lending services is the best service for readers.

In the information era today, the dependence of scientific research on information strengthened day by day, the urgency and innovation of university scientific research has brought new challenges for library work. The scientific research work demands of its obtain the amount of information and was expanded to information Range and information quality requirements are increasingly high, so scientific research work not only need the library, database etc. become its solid backing for conducting scientific research and information service and still need library around discipline research development of the high quality information resources. All of these needs the library staff take certain innovation service pattern, for scientific research provides high-level information knowledge service.

University library's service research object is teachers who has scientific research task of each professional, they has a tight schedule, need large amount of information that from research need background materials and frontier knowledge to reference material of scientific research among needs at any time complement. What they need is a comprehensive system, widely and deeply information resources, which requires us to no longer is mechanically passive provide information, but actively carry out "personalized" service, that is when the scientific research in understand familiar with user task, according to user's information needs to search, screening and delivery information.

Personalized service way is based on user needs and formulate a variety of form of a variety of services that Web books appointment on research, scholars launched "borrowing special passage" and information customization etc. belong to personalized service. High-level "personalized" information service is based on the user's information required and must pass professional background workers search, screening, after extraction of the information recommendation. For instance scientific novelty searching service, it is the information consulting service form of Basis to provide documentation as searching certain literature information source, for evaluation of scientific research project, achievements, patents, invention of novelty, advancement and practicability and it is prerequisite for scientific researcher certain subject research. For example, the subject librarian service, it is information services of the form that selected with certain professional background of librarians responsible for the same or similar specialized subject information needs, the latest timely inform the library resources, and timely feedback to listen to the demand of teachers, researchers and students. In addition, still can establish scientific research scholar on these files, track subject service and understand the subject of scientific research achievements of social repercussions, etc. Undeniable, development high-level information resource service is difficulty for college library service work, but only truly achieve high-level "personalized" of information services, it can fundamentally strengthening library's service function and contribution for scientific research strength and can inject new vitality for library.

The last but not least, Library self-service is a kind of service mode served by readers themselves according to their different individual demands. Currently, the most common modes of readers' self-services in library include online renewing and reserving books, and online self-accessing electronic resources, etc.

Self-services are usually of the characteristics of humanity, flexibility, and autonomy. So, readers can use the library resources without the limit of time, location and completely according to their own tastes and demands. In a certain sense, self-service increases readers' self satisfaction, improves the utilization of library resources and expands the library's physical space. At the same time, it also reduces work load of library staffs, breaking through the traditional mode of all the library services arranged by staffs. Hence, this service further embodies the "people-oriented" service ideas of modern libraries, which is deeply popular with the mass readers.

However, though the library provides the readers with self-services, it does not mean that the focus of library work is transferred. Even though the self-service is popular with the readers, we have to think about how to deepen the services and how to take the best advantages of them. First of all, as for the readers' quality of information, we should strengthen the training the skills of retrieving information; in the propaganda, we should get more readers to know what self-services we provide and how to carry out them; in the library hardware, we should timely introduce advanced automation equipment and realize the integration in order to make readers borrow and return, and pay some charges at any time; On the network, apart from purchasing the database to provide digital resources, professional staffs can also upload the information of various subjects to the websites based on the classification of different majors, or even build a database by themselves to provide useful information for self-service readers according to the demands.

3 Conclusion

Under the current background of studying and implementing the scientific development view, the core of library work is "people-oriented"; the root of the creation of library service system is “readers-oriented”, which is the basis of libraries’ existing, development and innovation. The "reader-oriented” service concept is to transfer the library work from emphasizing preserving books to highlighting the use of reader so as to meet readers’ demands and realize the real values of library staffs and books reflecting the humanistic care. “Readers first, service upmost” becomes the subject of everlastingly pursuit and constantly explored by the university library. But, it will be endowed with different meanings in different phases of different times.

References

1. Liu, J.: Research on Cultivation of Information Quality of Contemporary College Students. Library Work in Colleges and Universities 2, 4–6 (2003)
2. Zhao, W.: Research on Service Innovation of Harmonious Society in Libraries. Journal of The National Library of China 2, 76–78 (2007)
3. Sun, Z.: On the Orientation of Architectural Design of Modernized Libraries in China. Library 5, 38–39, 62 (1998)
4. Qin, J.: The Ideal and Practice of Human Service in Libraries. Library 5, 46–48 (2004)
5. Peng, F.: Scientific Research and Development in Information Security. Wuhan University Press, Wuhan (1998)
6. Wu, X.: The Effect of User Self-service Modes on Library Information Service. Information Studies:Theory & Application 5, 441–443 (2003)

Research on the Operational Mechanism and Development of Commercial Horse Racing: Taking Wuhan, Hubei Province as an Example*

Qingshan Hu and Cheng Yang

College of Physical Education, Huazhong Normal University
Wuhan, China
hu_yeahe@126.com

Abstract. Through the investigation and research of commercial horse racing operation situation, this paper discovered the existing system problems and obstacles about the commercial horse racing in Wuhan. Combined with the current situation of Wuhan horse racing development, proposed the operation mode and operation mechanism suit for Wuhan commercial horse racing. The studies suggested that the problems mainly displayed in the law, which is not perfect, short of standardized format imperfect competition, the low degree of industrialization and social involvement, lack of the Chinese characteristics business operation mechanism and so on. At last, based on the corresponding ideas and solutions discussed above, in order to provide certain theoretical basis to accelerate the "Wuhan horse" development.

Keywords: Commercial horse race, operating mechanism, development, research, Wuhan.

1 Introduction

Commercial horse racing is a new huge industry, which include many kinds of elements, such as commerce, tourism, culture, leisure sports, agriculture and so on. And Wuhan have a unique advantage of location and economic .It continuously held the 7th world horse racing festival from 2003 to 2009.The world horse racing rapidly promoted the development of Wuhan's economic, culture, city construction and had the positive effect for promote the Wuhan city's influence in the world. After years of cultivating, Wuhan horse racing has walk from regional into international. It's not only became the country which has high influential horse racing festival activities, but also acquired the higher attention in the international. Along with the NPC and CPPCC, Wu Han city central center held the success of pilot city instructions. Commercial horse racing undoubtedly is an important "a very" development of sports industry and social public sports .Currently, China's commercial horse racing has not yet won the approval of relevant state departments, there are many reasons and the reasons are rather complicated. But there is a bit we have to mention is that China's commercial horse

* This work is supported by Wuhan Social Science Fund (whsk10026).

Q. Zhou (Ed.): ISAEBD 2011, Part II, CCIS 209, pp. 544–548, 2011.

racing operation system has not yet been constructed. Even if foreign commercial racing developed countries have mature operation system, we also cannot copy .Because China has the special national conditions and national related laws of the special policy. So, It have great significance to seminars and constructing China's commercial horse racing operation mechanism and institutional problems .The reason why we discussing the Commercial horse racing operation mechanism is to promote China's commercial horse racing development smoothly "on horse ", and to provide decision-making reference and the suggestions for the relevant competent administrative departments to help the commercial horse racing promotion and development in our country. And also In order to provide the running horse sports lottery practice guidance, to fight the private color and underground gambling activities, and also play an important role to help maintain the social stability.

2 Methods

Take Commercial horse racing operating mechanism as object of study, look up the relevance document, policy, document and treatise, work out the investigation inquiring into a questionnaire and carrying out demonstration, be tied in a classic documentation, analytical Commercial horse racing match makes and manages system, try to find Commercial horse racing restraint factors launching a pilot project in Wuhan and, submit corresponding countermeasure and suggestion according to our national condition and reality.

3 Results

2008 Beijing Olympic Games is not heat back, re-ignited the 2010 Guangzhou Asian Games sports event on the enthusiasm of people. With the deepening of economic reform in China all-round social progress, China has in the sport, economic, technological, and military, including a number of social and cultural fields has made rapid development, especially in the Beijing Olympic Games is made in China excellent results of the first gold medals, no doubt today's China has become a sports power. The world level of sports development of a country to rely on players not only fruitful results and the development of mass sports is also an important measure. Needless to say, every sports person tireless dedication to the ultimate goal of silence is to serve the greatest majority of the general public, so that every member of society to enjoy the benefits brought by the national sports development and the interests of our country, shifting our country whose athletes' competitive level is at the top-grade, to a country which is based on community sports, with competitive sports as a guide and whose overall level of all sports fields is at top-grade in the world, becoming a world sports power.

Currently, leisure sports and healthy sports has gradually become the mainstream consciousness of society and people's pursuit of goal. Commercial horse racing is slowly approaching the people's attention, which has a huge industrial chain and the popular sports industry is composed by many related fields such as agriculture, animal husbandry, education, real estate development, leisure and tourism, culture and entertainment, commercial investment, business investment and so on.

It is self-evident that commercial horse racing industry, which is not only undoubtedly a highlight of the new development of mass sports, but also a huge commercial profits body, should become an important sports industry in our province. At the same time, Wuhan City as the country's "two sessions" instruction in the middle of center city, has a unique geographic advantages and economic advantages, no doubt to provides the commercial horse industry a good external environment. From another perspective, Wuhan City Should develop and consolidate the status of central cities in central area, and play full demonstration of the advantages of the pilot, commercial horse racing industry also will have a great role in promoting. Governor Hongzhong-Li in Hubei Province in “two sessions" the government work report in 2010, made clear that "this year, the Hubei Provincial Government in 2010’s main development objective is to accelerate industrial upgrading, do a good job of Wuhan City Circle and the Western Hubei '1+8' ecological, cultural Circle construction, to meet the public’s diversity and multi-level needs. Develop initiatively cultural, sports, convention and other new services, build a number of competitive fitness and recreation and athletic performances as well as other cultural and sports industry base. "Obviously that the Government address clearly the direction of the sports industry for commercial horse racing industry in our province provides an important guide and leader.

Commercial horse racing industry in the world had not been a new thing, commercial horse racing industry in the United States is second only to baseball's being the second largest sport. The U.S. is the world's third Derby lottery state, with strong national power and rich resource, has the world's largest horse farm, horse farmer and high-quality, ultra high-quality horses, and has a large middle class and wealthy classes of the horse owners groups. Commercial horse racing in the states have legal status, which are recognized and protected by local laws. In Chinese commercial horse racing, it is Hong Kong’s Jockey Club that has successful precedent and takes the forefront in the world, although it is the only company in the world and has a charitable non-profit racing organization, but still give the Hong Kong rapid economic growth has brought a great impetus and objective economic value. But in the vast land of China Mainland, commercial horse racing industry for many people is still very strange, especially in Wuhan, and just a few place names such as Wan Guo, Yue MaChang, MaChangJiao remind each person of when the Wuhan Jockey drummed all day, turned out the brilliant history. Mr. Zunwen-Qin Lottery experts on horse racing, had boldly predicted if the correctly direct the commercial horse industry in Hubei, it will be on an enormous impact on society. Relying on commercial horse racing sports lottery, will achieve sales of 1,000 billion per year and turned over 400 billion tax revenue, job creation 3000000. This is what came to be widely cited, and to annotate Lottery on horse racing energy of the "143" digital combination. Commercial horse racing industry not only can expand domestic demand, but also promote agriculture, animal husbandry, the media, tourism, education, industry and other industries, as well as promoting the sports industry in Hubei Province and the industrial structure adjustment of agriculture animal husbandry.

Commercial horse racing sports lottery in the world has become a trend, but in China is relatively backward, the relatively low degree of development of the entire horse racing industry, the lack of core commercial pulling power, low level of commercial operation which makes it difficult to form a polarization effect , leading to a rigid or break horse racing industry chain and hard to influence the related industries, away from public life, just like high-altitude hypoxia, which seriously impede the rapid growth of horse racing industry; because our country's long-term restrictions on the gaming industry since the founding of our country, the horse racing industry long-term restrictions on the horse racing industry awareness of social is low, advocacy efforts, not enough depth and breadth of commercial horse racing Sports Lottery lack of mass base cannot stimulate the enthusiasm of society, industrial development is difficult to accumulate more extensive social resources and public support; domestic commercial operation of horse racing pilot repeatedly sports lottery failure, lack of effective internal management system of commercial horse racing, horse racing in China not long history there have been several scandals, the existing policy of race walking a fine line to play more industrial development, the relevant legal provisions and policy is not perfect, the lack of comprehensive industrial development legislation and effective monitoring mechanisms, development of commercial horse racing is not the appropriate legal basis and guarantee mechanisms, is difficult to diversify.

4 Conclusion

Commercial horse race management system must be led by the government to ensure the credibility, so we are supposed to establish the law items to protect the development of horse racing as soon as possible.

We should consider the local conditions and build a board which contains the participation of government, folk organization and horse racing party, and the board is authorized to supervise, monitor and manage the whole process of the horse racing or the publishing of sports lotteries. Therefore the "Elite-led race" and "balanced power" can prevent all the corruption and fakes.

And that can also ensure the payout can be paid back fairly and mentally satisfied. We can still have psychological aid for the gamblers who are lost in the field. At the same time, we must fight against the illegal gambling about horse-racing, and make sure that all the fund we gained can be invested to the programs and projects for public good.

Let's build up a correct and positive direction of public opinion, make full use of the value produced by the Asian Games held in Guangzhou to stimulate and motivate the whole society's participation; and let's boost the horse-racing and related industries with various ways such as the advantage of Wuhan urban circle and the restructuring of rural industry. Therefore we can give full play to the propulsive effect of entertainment, sports and tourism in Wuhan urban circle, and expand our radiation and influence in the tourism of our country.

References

1. Qing, Z.: U.S. horse racing industry experience and Implications for China. Jianghan Forum 12, 51 (2008)
2. Qing, Z.: Wuhan Jockey lottery prospects and problems to be solved——Wuhan issue of race lottery poll. Contemporary Economic 2 (2009)

3. Li, H.: Guess the pilot issue of the necessity and feasibility of the lottery race. Shanghai Institute of Physical Education 2 (2009)
4. Cheng, Q.: Wuhan "society" How should the construction industry transfer abroad. Foreign Trade Practice 4, 23, 25 (2009)
5. Wu, Y.: Wuhan Science and Technology Analysis of Resource Allocation and Optimization. Technology Progress and Policy 26(5), 11–15 (2009)
6. Lu, D.: Wuhan Economic Transformation: Comparing the traditional and sometimes to the competitive advantage. Economic Survey 5(2), 18–20 (2008)

Estimation of the Non-market Value Generated by 2009 Shanghai ATP Masters 1000 : A Case Study of the Value of Civic Pride

Haiyan Huang and Hanqi Gao

Sport Events Research Center
Shanghai University of Sport
Shanghai, China
huangyy11@163.com

Abstract. Non-market values are main representation of the social influence of holding sports events. At present, the Contingent Valuation Method is the most extensive and developed valuation method for the non-market values of sports events. The case analysis of the civic pride valuation is carried out with the Contingent Valuation Method for the 2009 Shanghai ATP Masters 1000.The results indicate that several factors have influence on the civic pride and WTP for the 2009 Shanghai ATP Masters 1000, including gender, education qualification, annual family income, aggregative indicator of product of annual family income and education qualification, and the average WTP value for the 2009 Shanghai ATP Masters 1000 is 24.2 Yuan; and then the civic pride valuation for this sports event is between 84,157,900 Yuan and 337 million Yuan.

Keywords: Non-market Value, Sport Events, Civic pride, ATP 1000.

1 Introduction

As sports events have distinctive external and public features, the accompanied non-market values are obvious. Due to an absence of relevant price benchmarks, there are only sporadic descriptions of the non-market values of sports events at present. However, with the development of economic research, some methods have laid quantitative foundation for the non-market values of sports events, such as the Contingent Valuation Method, the Travel Cost Method and the Asset Value Method.

In recent years, economists employ the Contingent Valuation Method (CVM) to assess the values of public products in sports activities (the non-market values) for the identification of the factors that determine the individual willingness to pay for the sports products. Johnson & Whitehead and some others are the first to use this method. In 2000, they employed the Contingent Valuation Method respectively to investigate and compare the residents' willingness to pay for a basketball stadium built for NCAA in a large city, and a baseball stadium built for a minor baseball league in a small city; in 2001, they made an assessment of the non-market values created by the American Hockey League; and recently, they made investigations of the residents' willingness to spend money in two cases. In addition, some other scholars conducted similar researches: Carlos Pestana Barros investigated the residents' willingness to pay for the

Q. Zhou (Ed.): ISAEBD 2011, Part II, CCIS 209, pp. 549–554, 2011.

2004 European Football Championship in Portugal, and made an analysis of the findings via the Tobit regression model; Harry Walton and others investigated the potential the non-market values of the 2012 London Olympic Games. And still others, such as Fenn & Crooker (2003), Rappaport & Wilkerson (2001),Siegfried & Zimbalist (2000) conduct relevant researches.

The social influence of holding sports events is mainly represented by non-market values, which has always been a focus of China in its development of sports undertakings, building of city images, constructing of the residents' cultural life and so on. At present, except for the sporadic descriptions of the social influence of sports events, there is a general lack of in-depth analysis and research on specific sports subjects. A case analysis of the civic pride valuation is carried out here with the Contingent Valuation Method for the 2009 Shanghai ATP Masters 1000.

2 Methodology

The design of the questionnaire borrowed the major CVM components summarized by Mitchell and others. To increase the CVM reliability, we made improvements through several pre-investigations. The questionnaire research consisted of three parts: (1) the investigation of the residents' recognition of the social influences of 2009 Shanghai ATP Masters 1000; (2) the investigation of the civic pride valuation and WTP for 2009 Shanghai ATP Masters 1000; (3) the investigation of the respondents' social and economic situations.

After the completion of the questionnaire design, a short-term training was held for the investigators. Other measures included making preliminary investigations of the target groups, conducting pretests about the questionnaire quality, and making corresponding amendments to the questionnaire.

Face to face investigation was used according to the 25 principles of NOAA. The street investigations were made in crowded places such as subway stations, entrances to the supermarkets and the residential quarters. Random sampling was adopted in the districts of Pudong, Xuhui, Baoshan, Jing'an, Yangpu, Zhabei, Jiading, Hongkou, Minhang and Changning. As a result, this questionnaire research met the broad representative requirement of the CVM research.

The investigation was held during May and June in 2009. The total sample size was 1800. Among the 1,732 recovery copies, there were 1,630 valid ones, excluding 102 copies with a very low answer rate. It made a collect ratio of 90.5%. High reliability was achieved due to a total error range of 2.06% here. A significant increase of sample size would be required for a higher statistical accuracy, which would have cost gigantic labor and material resources. This was rather unnecessary. Therefore, the sample size was decided according to the 95% veracity for the research.

3 Result and Analysis

A. The Statistics of the Basic Questionnaire Information

Among the 1,630 valid questionnaires in this investigation, 601 respondents did not know the sports event while the other 1,029 respondents did, among whom, 656 people responded positively by selecting "You feel pride in holding Shanghai Tennis Masters Series" but 135 of them expressed no willingness to pay.

It is common that a great quantity of zero WTP appears in the CVM questionnaire research. In this case, there are several major explanations: (1) protest answers; (2) some respondents with no income, low income, or heavy economic burdens; (3) some respondents think that the sports events should not be funded by government, as they are operated by enterprises(reflecting the respondents' hitchhiker attempt) and so on. Only 521 respondents expressed positive WTP with varied payment patterns, i.e.: (1) to pay fixed annual taxes to the government; (2) under the condition of stable family finances, to help the government relieve the financial pressure, donate fixed amount of money to the funds of official sports events; (3) to make direct contributions to sports operating enterprises.

B. The Distribution of WTP

The statistical result did not exceed expectations, as the WTP distribution curve was neither smooth nor normal. Almost all the WTP of these respondents were below 500 yuan. There were five main distribution values: 20 yuan, 50 yuan, 100 yuan, 150 yuan and 200 yuan. Among these values, 50 yuan was the dominant one with a proportion of 26.8%.

C. The Average WTP

WTP1 was the mathematical average value of the positive WTP. It was 75.9 yuan per person. Considering the respondents who did not know the sports event, expressed no willingness to pay, and those who thought that "this sports event will not bring civic pride", the accurate average WTP value would require econometric calculation. Since the calculation principle of an average WTP for payment questionnaire is similar to the open-ended questionnaire, Kristrom's Spike model, effective to both open-ended and dichotomous questionnaires, is applied in this research. After a little adjustment, the average willingness to pay WTP2 equals to WTP1 multiplying the proportion of positive WTP to the total valid questionnaire samples. Therefore, WTP2=75.9×(521/1630) =24.2 yuan / person.

D. The Regression Analysis

The dominance of zero WTP is a common issue in the CVM evaluation. For dichotomous questionnaires, the two-step regression analysis model in other countries is more popular. It provides two processing methods for zero WTP: The first method takes zero WTP as the result of random factors, excluding it from regression analysis; the second method takes zero WTP as valid finding, replacing it with relatively small WTP value in regression analysis. This paper adopts the second method in regression analysis.

Due to differences between WTP patterns caused by payment card questionnaire and dichotomous questionnaire, the first-step probability model in regression analysis of dichotomous questionnaire is omitted. Zero WTP is replaced by a relatively small WTP value (one yuan), and the analysis proceeds to the second-step of logarithmic transformation least-square model. In the analysis, the variable WTP depends on the respondents' paying ability, which is associated with such factors as gender, age, occupation, education qualification, income level, and so on. Based on the research experience of Johnson & Whitehead, Harry Walton and others, the following factors of gender, age, education qualification, income level, product of income and education qualification are selected as the independent variables to form the multivariate linear regression equation: $InWTP = \beta_0 + \beta_1(Gen) + \beta_2(Age) + \beta_3(Edu) + \beta_4(InInc) + \beta_5(In(Inc * Edu))$

In this formula, InWTP is the natural logarithm of the respondents' WTP; β0 is the constant term; β1, β2, β3, β4, β5 are the evaluated regression coefficients; Gen refers to the respondent's gender : male = 1, female = 2; Age refers to the respondent's age: below 20=1, 20-30= 2, 31-40= 3, 41-50= 4, 51-60= 5, above 60= 6; Edu refers to the respondent's education qualification: below high school student=1, junior college student=2, undergraduate=3, graduate = 4, Ph.D. = 5; InInc is the natural logarithm of respondent's annual family income (ten thousand yuan / year); In(Inc*Edu) is the natural logarithm of the product of respondent's annual family income and education qualification. The result of the statistical analysis is shown in Table 1. Due to some uncertain factors in investigation, the result of t testing indicates significant variations of variables except age (it is omitted in Table 1). This feature is similar to other relevant researches outside China. The determination coefficients R2=0.607, F=2.865(α=0.05).

To establish hypothesis for testing H0: β1= β3=β4=β5

And k=4, n=1029. If α=0.05, Fα (k,n-k-1)=F0.05 (4,1023)=2.37, F>Fα, the original hypothesis H0 can be denied, i.e., the regression equation is significant. This indicates the linear relation between InWTP and the independent variable.

Table 1. The result of multiple regression analysis

Coefficient	Regressed Value (Standard Deviation)	t Testing Value (Significance Level)
β0	40.243 （0.013）	2.743(0.01)
β1	-1.472(0.716)	-2.286 （0.05）
β3	1.572 （1.036）	1.863 （0.10）
β4	3.531 （1.394）	2.873 （0.01）
β5	5.308 （1.267）	2.417 （0.01）

E. The Factors That Influence WTP

According to the result of model calculation, when other conditions are kept constant, the following several factors should generate influence on the residents' sense of pride and WTP for the 2009 Shanghai ATP Masters 1000: (1) Gender has influence on the residents' WTP. The gender coefficient is significant at the level of 0.05 with a negative value, which indicates a higher WTP of male than female; (2) Education qualification has great influence on the residents' WTP. The education coefficient is significant at the level of 0.10 with a positive value, which indicates a higher WTP of residents with higher education qualification; (3) The annual family income has a significant positive effect on WTP. The income level coefficient is important at the level of 0.01 with a positive value, which indicates a higher WTP of residents with a higher annual income level; (4) The aggregative indicator of product of annual family income and education qualification has great influence on the residents' WTP. This coefficient is significant at the level of 0.01 with a positive value, which indicates a much higher WTP of residents with both a higher education qualification and annual income level.

F. The Civic Pride Valuation for the 2009 Shanghai ATP Masters 1000

In above analyses, the average WTP for 2009 Shanghai ATP Masters 1000 has been worked out for this essay. The total valuation of civic pride can be obtained by multiplication of the average WTP and aggregate population. According to Shanghai economy almanac, by the end of 2008, the number of registered population of Shanghai was 13,910,400. Therefore, the total valuation of civic pride for 2009 Shanghai ATP Masters 1000 can be expressed as: CVMWTP1=24.2yuan/person*13,910,400persons=337 million yuan. Of course, this is an upper limit value. The target objects of this investigation were individuals, yet the respondents were likely to express the WTP on family basis. Assuming that the average family population in Shanghai is 4, then the lower limit value of civic pride for 2009 Shanghai ATP Masters 1000 can be expressed as: CVMWTP2=24.2yuan/person*13,910,400persons/4=84,157,900 yuan.

Thus, we can reach the following conclusion: The total valuation of civic pride for the 2009 Shanghai ATP Masters 1000 is between 84,157,900 yuan and 337 million yuan.

4 Conclusion

(1) Several factors have influence on the civic pride and WTP for the 2009 Shanghai ATP Masters 1000, including gender, education qualification, annual family income, aggregative indicator of product of annual family income and education qualification. When other conditions are kept constant, the male WTP is higher than the female WTP; the residents with higher education qualification have higher WTP; the residents with higher annual income level have higher WTP; the residents with both higher education qualification and annual income level have much higher WTP.

(2) The average WTP value for the 2009 Shanghai ATP Masters 1000 is 24.2 yuan; and then the civic pride valuation for this sports event is between 84,157,900 yuan and 337 million yuan.

References

1. Douglass Shaw, W., Rogers, J.: Review of Non-market Values Estimation for Events and Festivals: A Discussion Paper. Draft report submitted to the Ontario Tourism Board by Research Resolutions Ltd. Inc., Toronto, Canada (August 2005)
2. Johnson, B.K., Whitehead, J.C.: Value of public goods from sports stadiums: The CVM approach. Contemporary Economic Policy 18, 48–58
3. Johnson, B.K., Groothuis, P.A., Whitehead, J.C.: The value of public goods generated by a major league sports team: The CVM approach. Journal of Sports Economics 2, 6–21
4. Barros, C.P.: Evaluating Sport Events at European Level: The Euro 2004. International Journal of Sport Management and Marketing 1(4), 400–410 (2006)

5. Walton, H., Logo, A., Dawson, P.: A Contingent Valuation of the 2012 London Olympic Games: A Regional Perspective. Journal of Sports Economics 9(3), 304–317
6. Fenn, A.J., Cooker, J.R.: The Willingness to Pay for a New Vikings Stadium. Western Economics Association Meetings, Denver (2003)
7. Rappaport, J., Wilkerson, C.: What are the benefits of hosting a major league sports franchise? Federal Reserve Bank of Kansas City Economic Review, First Quarter, 55–86
8. Siegfried, J., Zimbalist, A.: The economics of sports facilities and their communities. Journal of Economic Perspectives 14(3), 95–114

Research on the Supply of the Sport Facility

Yuanxin Chen and Jian Wang

College of Physical Education
Huazhong Normal University
Wuhan, China
chenpaths@126.com

Abstract. This dissertation mainly focuses on the supply of the sport facility in China. By using the methods of the documents, the questionnaire, the expert interview and the statistics, it analyzes the basic issues which concern to the supply of the sport facility, such as the theoretical foundation of the supply, the supply status, the existing issues of the sport facility, the financial status, the private supply model, and role of the government played in the supply, and so on. It thinks that the privatization supply is the mainly direction for the future supply of the sport facility and the university will play an important role in the supply of the sport facility. Then, it put forward some suggestions in order to promote the supply of the sport facility.

Keywords: the sport facility, supply, the privatization, government-guided, suggestions.

1 Introduction

The sport facility is the premise and necessary physical foundation for applying the great events. Due to the 2008 Olympic game and the 2010 Asian games which holding in our country and the implementation of the applying system on the great games such as the national games and the city games, the demand of the sport facility becomes higher. However, given the restrictions of the inadequate in the theoretical research on the sport facility supply, the features of the sport facility and the poor finance of the government, the sport facility supplied inadequately and existed many issues in practice, the paper has important theoretical and real significance on researching the issues of supplying sport facility.

2 Results

The theory of public goods, privatization idea and the new public management theory which had a great and positive impact on the reform of the sport facility supplying system, and laid the premise for the marketing supply of the sport facility, they are the theoretical foundation of the supply and diversifization.

From the time before the liberation, the government and the voluntary organizations had played a great role in the sport facility supply. Objectively, the import of the new

Q. Zhou (Ed.): ISAEBD 2011, Part II, CCIS 209, pp. 555–558, 2011.

sports, the concern which the government put on the construction of the sport facility and great games promoted the supply of the sport facility. The change course of the supply objects and methods which from the single to the diversity would be the historical change from the time after the founding of the new China, and the course of introducing the marketing system. The integrated and great events have been the promoter of supplying the sport facilities.

The supply status of sport facility was that there were so many kinds of the supply object, but the school was the main supply object, the indirect supply model by the government was the mainly supply model of the sport facility, the private positively participate the supply of the sport facility, the fund for the supply came from different source, the process of affording and producing the sport facility merged together, the market system was introduced into the process of affording, the quantity and the investment of the sport facility increased quickly, and so on.

There are some problems existed in the sport facilities supply, including the great inadequate supply and the local surplus, the single supply objects and the outdated methods, the mixed provider and producer, the poor operating efficiencies, the sluggish course of the market supplying the sport facilities and the unscientific supply decision .

The financing status of the sport facilities was that the more financing demand and the lower investment, and the simple of the investment object, the source of the funds and the model of financing, the lower efficiency of investment and the lack of the investment in the operation, which results from the impression of the traditional financing system, the old concept of the government and the quality of itself.

The market failure of the sport facilities supply was caused by the nature of the quasi-public goods, for its externality, natural monopolies and the asymmetric information in the supply. All of these mainly can see from several aspects, the market objects do not want to join in the supply, and the number of the sport facilities supplied by the market was so small that can't meet the demand of the society. The government failure which caused by the poor finance, the subjective decision and short sight of the governors, the incomplete decisive information, the provider who is lack of the motive for obtaining surplus and the producer who is lack of the competition and the supervision on the fund mainly showed by the way of government's poor investment, the wrong supply decision, the higher cost and the low productive efficiency. The sport facility supplying which has the great externalities be showed from expanding the city space, improving the layout of urban space, promoting the transformation of the old downtown and revaluation of the surrounding land, promoting regional economic recovery and the development of the third industry, speeding up infrastructure construction, enhancing the view and the fame of the city and so on。The sport facilities of Chinese mainland adopted the measure of the government supply, the Pigouvian tax and the enterprise merger to subsidize the externalities. Adopted the measure of the government regulation, the enterprise merger and the Coase theorem, the mode of China sports has properly subsidized the externalities, offered a good way for the private capital participating the supply of the sport facilities. It is the ideal mode to correct the externalities of the sport facility.

The privative supply of the sport facility should be the activity that the private institute of the public to meet the social demand. The course of the privative supply of the sport facility in Chinese mainland was showed that partly sport facility supplied by the privative model and the commissioned management and the outsourcing services were not universal and so on. The major main of privative supplying the sport facility was the government, the market and the voluntary organizations, and whose major model was the governmental provision and the non-governmental provision. The former contents the governmental direct provision and the indirect provision, and the latter contents the market provides and the voluntary organizations provide. The major produce models of the sport facility were the governmental produce, the market produce and the public-private partnership. The paper analyses put forwards that the PPP, BOT and derivative way, governmental grants, the governmental supply, outsourcing services, commissioned operation were the feasibly systemic arrangements of privatization in our country. Then it put forward some issues which should catch our attention were protecting the right of worker, avoiding lose of the public assets, implying the interest of the society and rightly recognizing the privatization.

The government plays as a main role in the sport facilities supply. While the important position is reflected by plan-making, supply decision, coordinating services, policy-supporting, resource ration, market managing, operation services, rights and interests protecting, etc. It is very necessary for the privatized sport facilities with the management by the government. The contents of such management mainly include the management of the plan and design, the management of the capital of the quality of the project, the management of the construction, the management of the standard, the management of the price, and the management of the service quality, etc.

The method of college-supplying sport facilities can ease the shortage of the sport facility supply, promote the supply, mitigate the sport facility's operational difficulty which emerged in the late period, increase the using rate and solve the problem of sport facility oversupply in some area. This method is with characters of unique function design, sole supply objective, multiform serving targets and function, and public used production. At present, the trend of college-supplied sport facility supply towards to the cooperation between the college and the government, the college self financing its needed capital, the professional of the college sport facility operation, and the college becoming the important supply objective of the sport facility.

3 Suggestions

On the basis of the above research, it put forward some suggestions to promote the supply of the sport facility. First of all, it believed that the government should make a good understand of its own duty, increase its investment on the supplying of the sport facility, which is the obligation of the government. Secondly, it should depend on the occasion of holding the major events to promote the supply of the sport facility. The local governments pay more attention to the major events and expend so much money on constructing the infrastructure and the major events was the promoter of the supply of the sport facility, especially the great stadiums and arenas. Thirdly, it should build up the system of scientific decision to improve the supply decision. The most important is built up the cooperation system between the government and the school, especially the university, because the university becomes the important object to supply the sport facility for the major events step by step. The university could deal with the existing issues of the operational difficulty after major events, and it also had a hurry demand for constructing the sport facility, which can save the money for constructing the repeated sport facility. Fourthly, it should setup the cooperation system between the government and the market to promote the private supply of the sport facilities. On one hand, the government should put forward some positive policy to attract the private to participate the supply of sport facility, on the other hand, it protect the legal rights and interests of the private. Fifthly, it should introduce the competition system into the market, set up the encourage system, reduce the supply cost and give an important position to the effect of the college-supplied sport facilities. It also gives some advices included cooperative supply supported by the government and the college to promote the effective supply.

References

1. Swindell, D., Rosentraub, M.S.: Who benefits from the presence of professional sports teams? The implications for public funding of stadiums and arenas. Public Administration Review 58, 23–47 (1998)
2. Fried, G.: Managing sport facilities, pp. 20–72. Human Kinetics Publishers (July 2005)
3. Xianpeng, L.: The stadiums construction and the city regeneration (unpublished)
4. Yuanxin, C.: A research on the supply of the great sport facility (unpublished)
5. Jian, M.: Research on the systemic obstacle of the big sport facility (unpublished)
6. Groothuis, P.A., Johnson, B.K., Whitehead, J.C.: Public funding of professional sports stadiums: Puilic choice or civic pride? Eastern Economic Journal 30(4), 78–104 (2004)

The Road of Growth of Self-alienationed Modern People Who Breakthrough to Humanity

Zhuang Xiaoman

Qiongtai Teachers College, Haikou, Hainan, 571127, China
zhuangxmye@126.com

Abstract. Human civilization steps towards the 21st century, in this new century rely on technology to improve civilization process, human harvest rich material wealth through making inventions and innovations. Modern people get more and more material meet, but the pressures of life is more and more heavy, modern people have hindered the natural growth of human nature. Regress into humanistic maybe the only way that modern people's "breakthrough" to find their well-being.

Keywords: modern people, self-alienation, human growth, humanistic regression.

Human civilization steps have toward the modern technology society, science and technology to be powerful productivity and brings fancy "gift" for human material civilization continuously, when people found that to have these novel "gift" can make themselves into the prince, giants, immortality people, they would try their best to find a way to occupy more "gift". Later on, people get more and more "gift", piles of "gift" gradually covered themselves, owns numerous "gift" will let people feel their own existence, the self will be safe, strong and happy. People living for more "gift", human growth has lost the direction, this phenomenon is essential for modern people's self alienation.

1 Human Growth and Self-alienation

The essence of human growth. Humanism humanity consider: the psychogenic organism growing is the same with biological organism growing which have to undergo a gradually grow up process gradually. For newborn baby, everything are chaotic(does not exist divisional between self and others, inner self and external self, true or false), they are born to be good nature and self-actualization trend. In the process of the self growth, individual needs the help of keen intuition and experience to out of chaos. Human nature is divided from self body, "I" soberly aware of own emotions, self ideal and pursuit.

The essence of human nature growth is self development, self can be divided into the subject self and object self. The former is the main active and observer, refers to person's behavior and mental experience; the latter is passives and observed, refers to views and ideas that people for themselves. The individual organism appraisal process

Q. Zhou (Ed.): ISAEBD 2011, Part II, CCIS 209, pp. 559–564, 2011.

giving directions to self growth, rely on the guidance of appraisal process, self gradually valued and conceptualized within continuous open experience. The ideal development mode of human nature is self suffer airframe appraisal process lead people to self actualization.

Self-alienation. Self-alienation refers to people's self activities and its products become alien force, which in turn againsting or dominating, ruling man himself. Such as human self deformed development, personality fission and mental deviation.[1]

According to the phenomenological theory, analysis human growth must analysis the realistic environment of self growth at first. If human lived in a chaotic and pure world which is similar to Eden, perhaps humanity can completely depend on individual to be good, self-realization to guide the individual growth, because in the similar Eden world, the psychogenic organism growing can synchronous development with biological organism growing gradually, means individual self-concepts coincident and collaborative with body experience. Biological organism growing has phased, sequence, irreversible as other life, although psychogenic organism growing show period, certain sequence, but this is not absolutely, some stimulus appears at the moment in complex environment, when it being considered as their phenomenal field by individuals, will lead to psychogenic organism jumping development and even reverse development, the retreat in psychoanalysis therapy is an example of reverse development.

2 Human Self-alienation in Modern Society

Modern living environment is a technological civilization, science and technology in this society has become the main productivity improving civilization process. With the powerful transmission of network, the influence of science and technology presents explosive enlarging trend, technology update speed shorter than before, change into actual productivity quicker than before, and broadly spread, it means that human beings have entered a era that people almost is omnipotent. Based on scientific and technology, on the land, human beings have deservedly become god of all things, who can run faster than the cheetah, can move thousands of elephants one time; In the sea, human beings can exceed all the fish swim the fastest, dive in the deepest; In the sky, human beings have no wings but fly higher than proud eagl. Modern people as one of the creatures of the earth, it had been armed by technology and alienated as "biological alien" out of the earth's ecological circle.

Husserl once aptly described the characteristics of this era:"With the expanding and improving of people's cognition power to the world, human can also effective control outward of people's practice with each passing day, and this outward is progressing and expanding unlimitedly. This also involves to the control of human themselves which belong to the true world, means control himself and his partner have greater strength to control his own destiny, so people really become the imitator human also can say, 'God is infinite distant people.'"[2]

The development of science and technology make people's heart cast off the heavy outer form, tThe heart can breathe in greater space. Human become god of all things gradually, they can go into various creatures world, to understand the family life of a pround lion or a little ant, they also can feel the world changes from the eyes if dragonfly. Unfortunately, technological progress can only help people understanding their body deeper, but can't help people to understand themselves' soul.

Technology development provides unlimited possibilities to satisfy human desire, which encourages the human desire to inflation. The development of human technology have forgotten our ancestors' original intention, ancestors research on aircraft are only to enjoy the freedom of birds fly in the sky, research on submarine just to visit the fish's house, research car only to race with horses, our ancestors' rich imagination prompted them managed to exile their soul to a broader space. However, all imagination became realistic nowadays, the plane, submarine, and car ancestors looked forward are not the luxury satisfied human's soul, but appendant in human life. Without them, human survival will be difficult, it means that in modern society, many appendants such as airplanes and cars have become people's living necessities.

The original intention just want to increase the spirit space gradually became black holes of desire, human aspire more necessities endlessly. Therefore, human living in a the environment filled with materials, the relationship between "human" and "environment" is not harmonious in here. This unharmonious outstanding performance is the developing boundless material possessive, external conditions of material can easily capture human. After human born, they began to accept them to be a part of themselves gradually, and finally themselves became their appendant then dominated by these necessities. Like a happy kid like parents buy toys for him, because of toys can icing on the original happiness, if his parents don't buy new toys for him, he couldn't find happiness, in order to let himself be happy, he would endlessly required his parents to buy new toys for him.

Conditional evaluation screened self assessment, people began to get locked in their vaults and stay. Using high-tech products, human individual may stronger than any of their ancestors, their hands can stretch longer, ears can hear farther, feet can run faster, even fly higher, whether the brawn who shoots vulture or the hero who shoots tigers cannot compare to the top ancestors. Person's individual powerful in this form is conditional, as if a warrior rely on various advanced and strong equipments to make himself and others recognised his powerful. This conditional evaluation are commonly recognized by individuals and all others, it inevitably leads to human self-inflation, which caused unharmonious relationship between "I" and "others". This unharmonious outstanding performance is "I" used technological product as armour to armed as "false me", and then show off the powerful to "others"(Includes not only their own kind, but also includes other creatures on earth), despised even trampled "others" dignity, let "false me" drunk to substance-desire and lust-desire, at the same time build a solid defense mechanism to prevent "others" detect the weakness of "actual me". At the moment, social evaluation is the conditional evaluation beyond the overt resources possession, inner valuations have been concealed that cannot play the leading role in human growth.

Biological organism can be replicated and recombined make the beauty value of human growth challenged. Technological advances let human come into other creatures territory without restraint, more and more natural secret was revealed as well as biological nature of human. The map of human's gene is interpreted, research on human cloning technology, the obtain of human's longevity methods, have let some people began to despise birth and death which are seemed as the most sacred and mysterious thing by human from of old. It means that human needn't fear the birth and death in the future society, they can play birth and death at the palm just like the most brilliant magician, biological organism can be replicated and recombined like children playing transformers.

Nevertheless, biological organism can be replicated ,but psychogenic organism cannot. From the moment when human delighted for their biologic gene can be replicated, they began to have a nightmare that reproductions replace themselves. Biological organism can be replicated and recombined subverted the standard of true, good and beauty on organism."I" is really or shadow is true? "The new" is beautiful or "the original" is beautiful? Whether use "new" instead of "old" is for good or not? All this leaves the appraisal process more confused and chaotic, so human's psychogenic organism produced more defense mechanism to protect themselves.

Marx once described the alienation of human growth in high-tech society: Machine has the magic power to reduce human labor and make labor more productive, but caused hunger and excessive fatigue. New source of the wealth become poverty for some strange and incredible magic. Technology victory seems to be get based on the cost of moral taint. As people controlling nature increasingly, individual seemed to be others slave or slaves for their own despicable behavior."[3] Nevertheless we should be aware of that technology is like a Pandora's box which disseminated evil and kept hope after being opened.

3 Modern People Regress to Humanity, Human Growth after "Breakthrough"

Rogers' enlightenment about human growth and self-alienation. Humanism scholars Rogers considered that individual growth began in chaos, free grown with human nature to be good and self-actualization trend. As self differentiation, self-concept appeared and makes people pay attention to the relationship between "reality me", "ideal me" and environment. The behavior of individual motive is not blindly for "career" or "business", but for interpersonal relationship to the person's promise. "The natural tendency that human care about others not I take care of you just because you and I are the same" but"I appreciate you and cherish you, because you and I are different".[1] Thus he put forward the main mechanism of self development are unconditional positive attention and conditional positive attention, under the unconditional positive attention, self-concept is consistent with body experience, the relationship between "I", "others" and "environment" is harmonious, individual can grow free depend on organism appraisal and drive to be good, self-fulfilling.

Under the conditional positive attention, there maybe two kinds of cases: One case is conditions tally with organism appraisal, "I", "others" and "environment" remained harmonious, self remains free developing. When the conditions of conditional positive attention is not conform to organism appraisal, humanity will change into alienation. At this moment others take environment conditions as attention farmar, sharpen others in relationship, destroyed harmonious relationship between "I", "others" and "environment", organism experience and self-concept are not in balance, this kind of unharmonious show as anxiety and self chaos, it must adjust self-concept in order to restores balance, self made concessions and give up the concepts tally with organism appraisal(the guidance of organism appraisal process), accept external experience(conditions proposed in conditional positive attention).

For this reason, in the modern materialistic society, remain simplicity of organism experience in humanity growth process and organism appraisal are always the impulsion of self growth, this is the prerequisites of humanity growth.

Humanistic therapy of "breaking through" regression. The goal of humanistic therapy is "eliminate the false and retain the true". "False" is various embedded additional conditions piled up when human alienated, the influence of individuals as follows:individuals seemed the process of pursuing additional conditions as pursuing self-actualization, but he often unaware of this pretend. "True" is the demand of "I" free development, the influence of individuals as follows:individuals know exactly what they need, pursuit the process of self-actualization by the organism appraisal(of course don't expel use defense mechanism sometimes).

People-centered therapy emphasizes the role of interpersonal relationship, the change of human alienation to high-tech society, the expand of this relationship, expanded to human-human, human-environment-human relationships. Also is to treat human self-alienation, eliminate the false and retain the true needs to return to innocence. The therapists should provide an original life camp for patients(a place where people completely depend on their own stamina to engage in the production of labor, without any science and technology to improve production efficiency), lead patient remove the error estimates that original technology effects on human abilities by devoting to practice, to understand their own physical strength, find their potential, establish self confidence and find the real organism experience. Once more, let patients' organism appraisal play the guide role on humanity growth through understanding group therapy.

In the pure environment specially designed by therapist, patients' organism appraisal began to play a role, but this cannot prove that patients have found themselves and have the ability to face the real technology social life. The key to solve this problem is to help patients build self-concept based on coordinate self value and social value. Therefore, couldn't maintain absolutely value neutrality in the process of humanistic therapy, should conduct necessary value interference. When analysis conditional attention, Rogers talked about if conditional attention consistent with organism appraisal, then the condition can be individual internalised as part of his self-concept. As a result, the therapist can target of patients' original mistake values, guide patients to compare the experience in two different living environment, Through the consultant's understanding of patient's organism experience, implante new values step by step, combined with the group discussion, encourage patients discussing the conflict of new values and old values, and finally patients decide where their souls go. So the treatment process does not exclude real life situation, but let patients continue to review, compare and reflect the experience in real life, eventually help patients find a point use "true me" to face the real life.

In the variety of modern society, Confucius's way——"I has self-examination three times a day" expresses to modern people:any time and any place, people should keep a self-examination heart that they'll not lose the direction of humanity growth.

References

1. Che, W.: Humanistic Psychology. Zhejiang education press (2003)
2. Husserl, E.(eds.) Zhang, Q. (translate): European Science Crisis and Transcendentalism Phenomenology. Shanghai Translation Publishing House (1988) (Germany)
3. Marx and Engels Selections, vol. 1 People's Publishing House(1995)
4. Wenbing, W.: Humanity Conscientious of High-tech Times. Studies in Dialectics of Nature 11 (2005)
5. Li, Q., Wu, S.: Value Neutrality or Value Participation: Never-to-be-Evaded Problem of Psychological Counsellor. Chinese Mental Health Journal 11 (2005)
6. Zhao, D.: The Western Humanism Tradition and Marx's Human-Ooriented. Journal of Beijing University (philosophy and social science edition) 11 (2004)

Study on the Development of Martial Arts Industry in China

Fang Hui

Zhengzhou University of Light Industry, Zhengzhou, Henan, China
fang2247@tom.com

Abstract. The fundamental that why culture industry is different from others is that it is based on culture as the basis and core, it revolves the culture whether for cultural significance creation and sales or cultural products reproduction and transmission. The Martial Arts Industry in China has represented a significant advancement. It shows as below: firstly, development concept of martial arts industry update; secondly, sound policies and regulations of martial arts; thirdly, the martial arts culture industry with government leading forms; fourthly, Concentrate the strength of social sports organization, produce the resultant force to develop Chinese martial arts industry; fifthly, speed up the exploitation of martial arts intangible assets; finally, pay attention to martial arts culture industry personnel training and team-building

Keywords: Of South Korean Culture Industry.

1 Cultural Deposits Is the Development Foundation of South Korean Culture Industry

The fundamental that why culture industry is different from others is that it is based on culture as the basis and core, it revolves the culture whether for cultural significance creation and sales or cultural products reproduction and transmission. The development of cultural industry needs to have a full cultural resources, South Korean culture industry development is based on its cultural deposits.

The formation and development of South Korean culture is the results from comprehensive effect of its political, economic, social, environmental factors. South Korean traditional culture is developed from the interaction with Confucianism culture and South Korean government learning (The politics of geography environment). South koreans codes of conduct and values by Confucianism influence. South Korean norms and values were influenced by Confucianism. An important factor of the rise of East Asia is Confucius Culture effect, Confucianism advocates such as filial piety and view, charity harmony view, diligent and frugal view, the positive factors such as humanity, justice of the Confucian ethics are the key factors which support economic development. As an important country in the circle of East Asia, South Korea is typically in the practice of the Confucianism ethical absorption and application, the views including true patriot love, value family, emphasize organization of coordination among the members of the cooperation, unity and harmony all deeply influenced every

Q. Zhou (Ed.): ISAEBD 2011, Part II, CCIS 209, pp. 565–571, 2011.

aspect of society economy and life in South Korea. This kind of cultural factors deeply rooted in the values of whole social, code of conduct, mental attitude, educational thoughts and enterprise culture. The Confucianism order which maintained by group socialist principles is supported by loyalty and filial piety, formed a unique overall called on mechanism, enhance the cohesion and solidarity of society. Meanwhile, it helps to form the government power, makes state intervention realized smoothly. South Korean culture was directly influenced by Confucian culture, deal with contemporary issues with the Confucian ethics and values, use the positive factor of Confucian culture to develop the social economic, formed a good social culture atmosphere which plays an important part in promoting the economic development and maintaining social stability. This relatively deep-rooted culture become an inexhaustible source and strong power of South Korean culture industry.

Financial crisis grows great development of cultural industry. The material resources of South Korea are not rich, under the circumstances, there are many restrictions in the traditional model of economic development, even will cause serious consequence. The Asian financial crisis of the late 20th century sounded the alarm of South Korean economic development model, which made the development of the South Korean economy had a profound impact. In order to promote its economic development, Out of the quagmire of financial crisis, South Korea began to look to the cultural industry. It is not excessive to say that culture industry promoted the development of South Korean national economy, South Korea out of financial turmoil cannot without the help of online game's cultural industry. Video game industry have sprung up everywhere, and quickly became South Korea's new economic growth point. After the Korean economic crisis, a large number of people unemployed. Some people got 5,000 million won severance payments, and input the money into Internet cafes and game entertainment, that the Korean Internet cafes have mushroomed developed. At the same time the South Korean government also set up educational institutions of game, established more than 20 cultural industry universities, game college and game school. In 1998, South Korea Game Industry Revitalization Center was set up, it promoted the export of cultural products vigorously. This strategic priority to the cultural industry development has received significant results. Such as the digital game designed for home computer, the output growth doubled since 1998 because of that it was identified as national strategic industry in South Korea. The most prominent game is "Nintendo", it is not only popular in Asia, but also forms the three-way confrontation together with Microsoft and Sony in the world gaming market, even promotes the development of e-commerce in other areas, gradually push "South Korean manufacturing" into "South Korean Writing". In 1999, the Ministry of Culture and Tourism, the Ministry of Industry and Resources and the Ministry of Information &Communications Technology cooperated, and established the respective affiliate "game integrated support center" (competent game industry park construction and management), "game technology development center" (competent game industry technology development), formed a cohesive force, focus on supporting the game industry. The high speed developing of South Korean game industry made Korean quickly out of the 1997 Asian financial turmoil shadows.

2 The Development History and Current Situation of South Korean Culture Industry

After South Korean suffered the Asian financial crisis, the culture industry was determined to be the pillar industry of national economy in 21st century, many departments of South Korean government downsizing, only the cultural sector increased rather than decreased. In 1998, the south Korean government officially proposed "cultural lines"policy, take the culture industry as the strategic pillar industries to developing national economy. Established cultural industry bureau in the Ministry of Culture and Tourism Board, which responsible for managing the publishing and newspaper, radio and advertising, film and video, interactive media and other content of cultural industry, formulated "cultural industry revitalization of basic law" aims to promote the development of cultural industry, and increased the budget input. In 1999-2001 has formulated the "5 years plan of cultural industry development", "21 cultural industry outlook" and "cultural industry promotion plan", cleared the culture industry development strategy as well as medium and long term development plan, detrusion a series of major measures which vigorously promoted the development of cultural industry. The South Korean government consolidate step by step, built an all around strong cultural industries.

The development plan of South Korean culture industry as follows: since 2001, use 5 years to increase the South Korean output of cultural industries in the world market share from 1% in 2001 to 5% (710 million), overseas exports to 100 billion U.S. dollars, the South Korean cultural industry become the world's five major powers, the ultimate goal is build South Korea to be a country of culture and knowledge of economic power in 21st century. In the ensuing years, the South Korean government put forward various measures, provided support and assurance to the development of culture industry.

The first "5 years plan of cultural industry development" implement by 3 stages from 1999 to 2003: The first stage is lay the foundation for the development of cultural industries in the legal, financial, personnel, organization; the second stage focus on developing export-oriented products, exploit overseas market, improve the international competitiveness; the third stage is pay close attention to build a number of cultural industry, form a set of spinning, the scale of industrial operation. By the implementation of 5 years plan, build a framework for the revitalization of the cultural industry and lay a solid foundation for further development.

The basic strategy to promote South Korean cultural industry is: First, focus on developing an internationally competitive, high-quality cultural products; Second, focus on cultivating a strategic cultural industries, concentrate on key sectors and important projects; Third, strive to make the national support policies have the greatest overall effectiveness. Now the South Korean culture industry has became the second largest export industry just second to automobile industry. Behind these achievements is the strong support of Korean "Culture Nation" strategy. We can not simply rely on the market that only the "invisible hand" to promote the development of culture industries, what's more, the effects of government's Macro regulation and rational guidance on cultural industries can not be ignored.

3 The Inspiration South Korea to Chinese Martial Arts Industry Development

Development concept of martial arts industry update. In the early time when South Korea supported to develop culture, the first is clear the development direction of industry: First, the manufacturing of cultural products, such as books, newspapers and printing industry, the imaging industry, etc.; the second is the wholesale and retail trade of cultural products; Third, cultural services, such as mass entertainment, theatrical performances, information services and so on. This classification shows that the country valued entity, the physical basis of the development of cultural products, and for the more abstract and difficult to direct perception of "cultural value", "cultural significance" of the "invisible" and "services" category for further processing. Our perceptions of martial arts industry should refer to South Korean advanced concepts in the development of cultural industry. For the traditional national culture and regional cultural elements, is the main source to develop ideas. Martial arts is the excellent and typical representative of Chinese traditional culture, it's a kind of cultural phenomenon itself, martial arts in modern developing has formed certain scale of the industry (such as martial arts literature industry, martial arts film industry, martial arts tourism industry, martial arts performances industry, etc), especially in recent decades, martial arts industry is developing fast, not only the exploit of traditional martial arts cultural elements is more and more abundant, but also combined with the latest high-tech tightly, its industry scale are getting more and more serious which presents the obvious characteristics of the martial arts creative industry. The rich and unique martial arts cultural elements of Chinese martial arts should be the creative core of the ideological line, based on modern high-tech, formed an industry which can produce great economic benefits in the protection of intellectual property rights. Martial arts creative industry with Chinese characteristics has become an important part of the creative industry. Chinese martial arts as Chinese national traditional sports typical delegate, its long history and contemporary value has the advantages to become localization, mondialisation.

Sound policies and regulations of martial arts. Martial arts as a cultural form, the performance of its resources are the material culture connotation resources and the martial arts system culture resources based on the material and cultural basis. In the socialist market economy, the performance of these resources exploitation and utilization is the establishment of martial arts market with the rules in various system and legal documents. The legal trend of South Korean culture industry obviously, which emphasize according to law constraint market order, according to laws and regulations clear market orientation, give the green light to industry development in the basic of industry regulations. Laws and regulations of martial arts industry should be laid down in the early market development. Market economy is legal economy which determines seeking the development of martial arts industry in the market economy environment must have legal norms and safeguard, Will the martial arts and economic can not tightly integrated or connect with market without the legalization of martial arts industry. Because of the market economy has prompted the various independent sports industry investment diversification and interest difference obviously, all aspects of social relations such as investment in the behavior of the sports industry norms, the main protection oflegitimate rights and interests, to fulfill obligations that could no longer mainly directly intervening by the administrative department,it only can be replaced by the adjustment of legal means. But for some sports organizations such as professional sports association, sports joint-stock company, private sports clubs, etc. Various kinds of sports entity organization system, leading system, leading organization generation method and responsibility and authority, legal status, with government relations and sports leadership as well as what's the effects in sports undertaking, should provide guidance in the law; For the define of professional sports, the operation of sports show market, athletes production and management, etc, are clearly stipulated by law urgently. Only under the premise that obeying the principle of market economy to establish sports management mechanism which adapted to market economy, establish a competition rules in conformity with market economy and a good competitive environment, with appropriate administrative intervention to guide the martial arts industry always in the right and health direction.

The martial arts culture industry with government leading forms. The government plays an important role in the development of South Korean culture industry. In order to promote and develop culture industry, South Korea strengthen mechanism construction gradually in various aspects such as organization management, capital support, production management, talent cultivation, etc, and implement systematic support to product research and development, manufacture, distribution and export. Mainly take: develop international market vigorously; strengthen surveying market to develope suitable products; concentrate on developing brand-name products; establish "forward stronghold" in the cultural exports strategic areas; develop transnational production cooperation actively; host and participate in the international exhibition negotiation activities; concentrating funds to support key export projects; create an incentive system; build a multi-faceted overseas marketing network, and other important initiatives. Our government should study from South Korea, seeing from the structure of our martial arts industry organization management system, it includes the State Sports General Administration, the National Martial Arts Institute and other macro-leading organ, besides a variety of martial arts association, martial arts hall, martial arts schools, and other micro-structures. Consequently, under the planned economics system regardless of manage and found, the mode that make a strategic decision by government must be reformed, the diversity of running subject, request the mechanism of martial arts industry management must have a multivariate comprehensive decision-making system, then can formulate the target, activity of the scheme, policies and strategies, and major measures of martial arts services business activities multi-level flexibly. To guide into market economy moving mechanism on all sides in meant to transform martial arts from a public welfare undertaking into a relatively independent economic industry, with the adjustment of the mechanism of market economy according to the characteristics, through constant innovation, fully exavate and meet market demand, for their own survival and development, fully participate in resources and consumer purchasing power competition. For this reason, the government authorities should reform the unsuitability management system, convert their functions, instead of undertaking various events, plan and manage the specific activities directly, clinching required investment and expenses, but perform the functions well such as the long-term planning, standardize order, supervision and control, macro coordination and services guidance, policy support, etc.

Concentrate the strength of social sports organization, produce the resultant force to develop Chinese martial arts industry. It's not enough to develop martial arts industry only depends on local sports organization strength. The arrangement that

South Korean government manoeuvre enterprise into the cultural industry development reminded us that we should play the leading role of local government, set up and provide a platform, give some guide and support in funds and policy, establish investment and financing system; to mobilize the enthusiasm of social aspects, encourage social sectors participate extensively to drive the development of relevant industries, such as hotel, airline service industries. The local government coordinate, give preferential policies, support related industries that industries can join hands, exploit local martial arts competition and culture to achieve a win-win or win more goals. Take the advantages of local place, identify the conjunction point between martial arts and social economy development, construct cultural tourism city or town with the characteristic of martial arts, make management system, break resource department management rules, implement the management mode which is standardization and modernization, according to the principle of the strict protection, rational development and sustainable utilization, martial arts industry resources integration and development all over. Utilize this characteristic of martial arts to catch the eyes outside the region, vigorously promote local martial arts industry develops rapid and healthy, make martial arts industry become a new growth point and new luminescent spot of local sports industry and national economy step by step.

Speed up the exploitation of martial arts intangible assets. South Korean culture industry attaches great importance to intangible assets, with comprehensive arrangements. One is the production of the cultural industry intangible assets, it established a special cultural heritage protection agency. Another is established corresponding non-material cultural development institutions. Ensure the intellectual property belongs of the country culture. According to Korean successful experiences and effective measures in this aspect, in the future development of domestic martial arts intangible assets, we should on the basic of improvement and implement intellectual property first, to maintain a good momentum of development of martial arts industry in several key aspects, to develop its high quality derivatives hardly, extended industry chain, enlarge industrial scale; Through some policy assistance, encourage and facilitate all localities and departments developed unique martial arts culture industry and its derivative products, to increase their industrial sectors andproduct categories.

One side soil inoculate one side culture, one side cultural influence one side economy, make one side social customs. China is a country with a long history, a vast multi-ethnic, geographical environment and humane factors are extremely abundant. As a result of history and nation, there are some differences in each region between economic and cultural development, so formed a number of small distinctive inland very early, for example: Zhongyuan culture area, Qilu culture area, Guanlong culture area, Yue culture area, Bashu culture area and Minnan district, Lingnan culture area, as well as subsidiary Jingpai culture area and Haipai culture area, they all have distinct regional characteristics. Actually, the traditional martial arts culture is derived from these regional culture, and these are the best "material" to form the industry characteristics and develop industries intangible assets.

Pay attention to martial arts culture industry personnel training and team-building. For a long time, the Chinese sports talent cultivation is always planned according to economic mode, the sports management talent who has comprehensive quality in economic, legal, management, planning, marketing, public relations and intermediary didn't listed as training objective, with the shunt of our sports undertaking and the rise of the sports industry, appear a phenomenon lack of martial arts management talent seriously which constrain the martial arts industry development in our country. The important reason why South Korean culture industry successful is that the country has a large number of professional teams in industry planning, management and product development. They play an important role in remaining the chain of industry development. Therefore, pay attention to train talents who possesses modern sports management ability, and master the basic sports and national preach knowledge and skills is the urgent matter to promote the martial arts in our country. Operationally, speeding up improving martial arts talent education projects, establishing martial arts teaching and scientific research personnel center, select professional foreign aid workers for the domestic and international wushu organization, institutions and schools; Speed up training of the martial arts doctors, masters and bachelor of education, adjust and reform the martial arts professional curriculum, additional economic, legal, and planning, marketing, public relations, intermediary courses, strengthen the training on martial arts students' management and entrepreneurial ability; Secondly, set sports economy, sports tourism profession or professional direction in comprehensive university and sports colleges, with the basic of sports science (including the national tradition sports) and the industry and commerce management courses, cultivate trained personnel who engaged in sports industry management, resolve the problem lack of talents fundamentally.

References

1. Yan, C.-S.: Korean audio-visual industry development, management and reference to our country. China Radio & TV Academic Journal 7, 34–37 (2003)
2. Korean network game will establish the new standards of the game industry `http://dynamic.sohu.com/template/news/print.jsp?NTITYID=219842904&Dynamic=yes`
3. Korean strategy: The comprehensive construction culture industry, International Cultural Development Report
4. Zhang, X.-m., Hu, H.-L., Zhang, J.-g.: Chinese culture industry development report, pp. 56–57. Social Sciences Academic Press (2006)
5. Song, K.: Korean culture industry development background, features and the enlightenment. The Heilongjiang Social Science (January 2007)

Research on Emotional Labor: Review and Prospect

Ding Junwu[1,2]

[1] Anhui Normal University Wuhu, China
[2] Huazhong Normal University Wuhan, China
j.ding89@yahoo.cn

Abstract. As the coming of the service oriented society, employees should exert themselves to manage their emotions in the workplace to conform to the expectations of customers and organizations, which is called emotional labor. Emotional work focuses on the internal regulatory processes in order to express the appropriate feelings consisting with the job requirements. Emotional work is an important factor that influences the job performance and organizational goals. It may be a powerful predictor of job performance, job satisfaction and emotional exhaustion et al. The article reviews some important studies in this research field. It elaborates the concept, the definition, the structure, the emotion work strategies, the measurement, the antecedents, the consequences and the possible mediator of emotional labor. On the basis of a comprehensive review, the article points out the limitations of existing research and the future research directions.

Keywords: Emotional labor/work, Review, Prospect.

1 Introduction

Emotional work can not be ignored in the individual life and organizational work. For a long time, emotional issues in organizational behavior researches have been neglected by the reason-dominant orientation of Cognition. Under the conditions of modern economic life, as the expanding of service industry in the economic structure and the "humanism" of the organization contacting with the public, the level of the emotional characteristics of the staff has become a constraint and an important factor to achieve job performance and organizational goals. Therefore, Hochschild first presented the concept of emotional labor (or emotional work) in organizational behavior research in 1979. The concept emphasizes that the expression and regulation of mood is indispensable in the employees' work and influence the employees' performance greatly. [1] In the subsequent two decades, the value of emotional work was valued by psychologists, who launched a series of studies focusing on the concept, characteristics, and mechanisms of emotional labor and accumulated a certain amount of research results. Today, the emotional issue has caused wide concern by academics and practitioners and has become the forefront of organizational behavior research. This paper sorts out the status of this research area, points out the problems and shortcomings, and outlooks the future research directions.

Q. Zhou (Ed.): ISAEBD 2011, Part II, CCIS 209, pp. 572–578, 2011.

2 The Concept of Emotional Labor

Emotional work is a multi-dimensional concept. The meaning of emotional work can be summarized into two main categories. The first category could be called vocational definition that emphasizes the regulation of emotional expression in accordance with job requirements and organizational expectations. For example, Ashforth and Humphrey held that emotional work is based on job requirements to express the appropriate emotion under the occupational rules; [2] Morris and Feldman held that emotional work is the efforts to regulate and control the emotional expression in the process of interpersonal interaction. [3] The second category can be called mental processing definition that defined emotional work from the point of view of inner psychological processing. For example, Grandey defined the emotional work as "carrying out the necessary psychological adjustment of emotion to meet the expectations of the organization ". [4] That is to say, emotional work is internal mental activities of target recognition, planning, monitoring and feedback. Diefendorff and Gosserand defined emotional work as the process of continuous emotion monitoring and regulation from the point of view of psychological control, that is, emotional work is "to monitor the differences between the feeling expression and the expression rules and try to adopt strategies to reduce the differences". [5]

Both of the two definitions, although in somewhat different focus, but in fact are interrelated with each other, complement each other, and help us understand the nature of emotional work from different angles. Of course, we must also note that the differences of the two types of definition indicating that researchers have understand emotional work from the analysis of phenomena to the depth of mechanisms.

3 The Theoretical Model of Emotional Work

A. *Morris and Feldman's causal model*

Hochschild first proposed the definition of emotional work in 1983, but did not operationalize the concept. It results in measurement difficulties. To better understand the role of the emotional work and to explore the relevance between the emotional work and other variables, Morris and Feldman first proposed a "causal relationship model of emotional work," including a number of antecedent variables and consequences variables. [6] Organizational characteristics, job characteristics and individual differences are the antecedent variables. Emotional exhaustion, job satisfaction are the result variables. Morris et al defined emotional work as "the individual's efforts, planning and control of emotion in the process of interpersonal interaction to meet the organization's expectation", and divided emotional labor into four dimensions: frequency of emotional display, attentiveness to required display rules, variety of emotions required to be expressed, and emotional dissonance. Meanwhile, Morris presented assumptions on the antecedents and assumptions and pointed out that the above four factors have relation to emotional exhaustion and job satisfaction.

Although Morris et al described the contents and the connection between antecedent variables and consequent variables, but there are some framework problems in the model. First, Morris believed that emotional work is a kind of "effort, planning and control," but in addition to mood disorders, other three contents are all behavioral indicators of emotional work. Second, Morris listed the antecedent variables, but in addition to gender, the majority variables involved the role and duties of the job, lacking of information of personal characteristics. In fact, follow-up studies showed that individual characteristics have an important impact on the emotional labor. [7] Thus, on the whole, the model can not fully explain the dimensions of emotional work, but the model provides inspiration for the construction of emotional labor model.

B. Grandey's causal model

Based on the emotion regulation theory and Hochschild's concept of emotional labor, Grandey proposed a causal model of emotional labor. [8] In this model, the antecedent variables of emotional labor were divided into four categories, the consequences variables were divided into 2 categories. In terms of antecedent variables: 1) job requirements on emotional labor of employees including the frequency of emotional expression, attention to rules of emotional expression and emotional expression level of diversity can predict the level of employees' emotional labor; 2) the emotional events itself including positive and negative emotional events in work or life impact on staff's emotional labor; 3) personal factors such as gender, age, intelligence, emotional sensitivity can predict employees' emotional labor; 4) organizational factors such as job autonomy, organizational support will affect the emotional labor of employees. In terms of outcome variables, the emotional labor has impacts both on the organization and the individual to a certain degree: 1) on the organization, staff emotional labor can predict organizational performance and vitality; 2) on the individual, the emotional labor of employees can predict employees' burnout and job satisfaction. Grandey's causal model explores the antecedents and the outcomes of emotional labor more comprehensively and provides a reference for further study (to construct emotional labor model).

Following Morris and Grandey, scholars proceeded to construct theoretical model of emotional labor in order to reveal the psychological process of emotional labor. Totterdell and Holman made an emotional adjustment process model of emotional labor; [9] Diefendorff and Grosserand proposed a psychological control model of emotional labor; [10] Fischbach presented an emotional self-regulation model of emotional labor. [11] Overall, however, these models are far from perfect level and can not describe the psychological process of emotional labor comprehensively and sufficiently. To construct a mature model of emotional labor still needs a long time.

4 Emotional Labor Strategies

Since the concept of emotional labor was presented and the idea of emotional commercialization was made by Hochschild, emotions evolved as important as the rational elements of psychology. Up to now, Researchers have undertaken extensive research around the concept of emotional labor, mechanisms, dimensions, measurements, strategies, antecedent variables, consequences variables et al, of which the study of emotional labor strategy is one of the focuses.

Hochschild believes that emotional labor is similar activities such as actors engaging in emotional acting, who perform in the front but cover up the true feelings. Accordingly, Hochschild divided emotional labor strategies into three categories: the surface acting, the deep acting and the genuine acting. [12] Surface acting is the regulation of the visible aspects of emotion expression when the emotional feeling and performance rules are inconsistent, resulting in emotional behavior changes in accordance with the requirement of the rules. At this time, the individual's internal emotion does not change. The behavior of surface acting is kinds of temporary pretend emotions. Deep acting is emotion regulation when the deep feelings and the performance rules is inconsistent. At this time, individuals adopt strategies through positive thinking, imagination, memory and other internal psychological process to arouse or suppress certain emotions, so that the performance of the real emotional experience and emotional requirements consistent. This time the individual's internal experience and external behavior change jointly. Genuine acting is the real mood of the individual feelings when the internal emotions consistent with the performance rules.

In addition, Zapf reputed that there is another case of emotional labor. That is, in some situations there are different rules for emotional expression, these rules require individuals should not only show the appropriate emotion, but also to maintain a neutral inner feelings (calm and cool). Zapf called this case the deliberative dissonance acting. [13] In the basis of comprehensive studies, Zapf proposed three levels of emotion regulation: acting strategy, experience strategy and internalization strategy. Acting strategy is the formation of the emotional expression script in routine situations in the long-term process of work. Employees can use the procedural script to perform specific feeling to meet the requirements on emotions; experience strategy means that staff regulate their feelings to maintain good mood in someone else' place or through the experience transfer means; internalization strategy is that employees will internalize specific emotional rules and requirements into their own achievement goals, and then be able to work spontaneously and obtain self-fulfillment.

Diefendorff examined the expression of real feelings as an independent strategy of emotional labor, and examined the relationship between the three types of strategies and the variables of individual differences, situational variables and surface behavior. [14] The results demonstrate the expression of real emotion is not surface acting of low level as described in the past. It together with the surface acting and deep acting constitute the constructs of emotional labor. Moreover, the research also found that individuals demonstrate the genuine emotions more frequently in the work, rather than feeling changes by deep acting or feeling camouflage through the surface acting.

In addition to previous concern about the surface acting and the deep acting, Mikolajczak pointed out that emotional labor strategy should also include "positive consonance" and "negative consonance" categories. [15] Positive consonance refers to the consistency of individual's emotional feelings, emotional expression and emotional requirements. Negative consonance means that the expression and experience of feelings are consistent, but the expression of feelings and the organizational requirements on emotion are inconsistent. That is, the staff intends to violate the emotions rules and express their inner real feelings. Mikolajczak et al found that positive consonance has nothing to do with emotional exhaustion and mood disorders, but negative consonance will induce mood disorders and emotional exhaustion. Cukur's study further confirmed that negative consonance is a separate dimension of the emotional labor strategies. He called it the emotional deviation. [16]

In summary, the researchers have summarized four types of independent emotional labor strategies: surface acting, deep acting, emotional deviation, and the expression of real emotion by the analysis of verification. Each motional labor strategies require different emotional efforts or psychological energy and influence the result variables of emotional labor (such as job performance, job burnout, stress, satisfaction, mood disorder, etc.) to different extent and in different directions.

5 Measurement of Emotional Labor

In-depth study depends on the innovation of research methods and the development of research tools. For the research on emotional issues, it is essential means and effective methods to develop emotional scale to measure the psychological process of emotional labor. The first emotional labor scale was compiled by Adelmann according to Hochschild's concept of emotional labor. The scale involves six aspects of emotional labor, such as mood induction, emotional restraint, surface acting and deep acting. Ashforth and Humphrey proposed that real feeling expression is another emotional labor strategy. Zapf called this kind of emotional labor automatic emotion regulation. Diefendorff et al thus developed a scale to measure emotional labor, including three dimensions: surface acting, deep acting and automatic emotion regulation. [17] Glomb et al proposed that the general emotional expression requirement is to stir up positive emotions and restrain negative emotions. Whereby they developed the DEELS scale (the Discrete Emotions Emotional Labor Scale) to measure emotional expression, emotional camouflage and emotional repression. [18]

From the "job requirements" point, Morris and Feldman divided emotional labor into three dimensions: frequency of interaction, interactive persistence and mood disorders (who also produced a three-dimension emotional labor scale). However, Grandey and some other scholars believe that emotional requirement is actually the antecedent variables of emotional labor and can not be confused with the emotional labor itself. Brotheridge & Leea combined both Morris and Grandey's point of view and developed an emotional labor scale containing both features of job requirement (on emotion expression) and emotion regulation. [19]

Overall, with regard to the measurement of the emotional labor, some scholars emphasize to measure the process of individual's emotional labor at work, and some others pay attention to the emotional labor requirements. Brotheridge and Grandey accordingly distinguished the measurement of emotional labor into two categories. One is employee-focused emotional labor research, and another is job-focused emotional labor research. [20] On the term of the issue itself, the staff-focused studies may represent the development direction of emotional labor research.

6 The Limitations of Existing Research and the Prospects of Future Research

A. The Connotation of the Concept and Theoretical Basis

Scientific constructs would evolve following a predictable sequence of three developmental stages: concept introduction, concept augmentation, and concept consolidation. The construct of emotional labor has survived the first two stages; however, the disagreements on operationalizing emotional labor impede the progress of emotional labor research.

In addition to the content and structure of emotional labor is not yet full consensus, the theoretical basis of emotional labor is still debatable. Can resource conservation theory, social interaction theory, emotional motivation theory, self-regulation theory and emotional cybernetics be used to explain the theoretical model of emotional labor? Unclear concept and weak theoretical foundation can not form a convincing and comprehensive emotional labor model.

B. The Problem of Research Methods

Early studies on emotional labor are qualitative research and researchers have proposed many hypotheses. In recent years, scholars begin to carry out empirical research and some of the assumptions have been verified. However, these studies are mostly correlation research and regression analysis. Correlation research can not indicate a causal relationship between variables and regression analysis can only explain the predicted effect between variables to some extent. Thus, future research may take the path analysis method to verify the causal relationship between the antecedent variables and the consequent variables of emotional labor, and then use structural equation modeling to build the emotional labor models in different occupational groups.

C. The Problem of Ecological Validity

Emotional labor is a management of emotional experience and expression, but also a cultural phenomenon. Although overseas studies indicate that emotional labor and its function have a good cross-cultural consistency. But we should seriously deal with this "conclusion". It is necessary to develop research tools appropriate to their nation's culture (such as emotional labor scale) under the guidance of relevant emotional labor model.

D. The Issue of Emotional Labor Mediator

Many studies abroad on emotional labor have been carried out to explore the relationship between emotional labor and its consequent variables, but whether there are adjustment variables or not between emotional labor and its consequences (such as emotional intelligence, self-efficacy, job autonomy etc.) still need to be clarified. Similarly, we should also carry out empirical research on the antecedent variables of emotional labor (such as gender, age, etc.) to demonstrate its impact on the emotional labor itself and work performance through emotional labor.

E. The Issue of the Development of Emotional Labor Skills

For the high emotional work occupations (such as tour guides), emotions play an important role in the work and directly affects the work quality and customer's satisfaction. Therefore, future research should consider emotional factors in job analysis, job design and job evaluation. At present, those researches should be urgently undertaken to develop individual's skills of emotional labor.

References

1. Hochschild, A.R.: Emotion work: feeling rules, and social structure. American Journal of Sociology 85, 555–575 (1979)
2. Ashforth, B.E., Humphrey, R.H.: Emotional labor in service roles: The influence of identity. Academy of Management Review 18(2), 88–115 (1993)
3. Morris, J.A., Feldman, D.C.: The dimensions, antecedents, and consequences of emotional labor. Academy of Management Review 21(4), 966–1010 (1996)
4. Grandey, A.: Emotion regulation in the workplace: A new way to conceptualize emotional labor. Journal of occupational Health Psychology 5(1), 95–110 (2000)

5. Diefendorff, J.M., Gosserand, R.H.: Understanding the emotional labor process: a control theory perspective. Journal of Organizational Behavior 24, 945–959 (2003)
6. Morris, J.A., Feldman, D.C.: The dimensions, antecedents, and consequences of emotional labor. Academy of Management Review 21(4), 966–1010 (1996)
7. Kruml, S.M., Geddes, D.: Exploring the dimensions of emotional labor. Management Communication Quarterly 14(1), 8–49 (2000)
8. Grandey, A.A.: Emotional regulation in the workplace: a new way to conceptualize emotional labor. Journal of Occupational Health Psychology 5(1), 95–110 (2000)
9. Totterdell, P., Holman, D.: Emotion regulation in customer service roles: testing a model of emotional labor. Journal of Occupational Health Psychology 8(1), 55–73 (2003)
10. Diefendorff, J.M., Gosserand, R.H.: Understanding the emotional labor process: a control theory perspective. Journal of Organizational Behavior 24, 945–959 (2003)
11. Fischbach, A.: Determinants of Emotion Work. University of Gottingen, Germany (2003)
12. Hochschild, A.R.: The Managed Heart: Commercialization of Human Feeling. University of California Press, Berkely (1983)
13. Zapf, D.: Emotion work and psychological well-being: A review of the literature and some conceptual considerations. Human Resource Management Review 12, 237–268 (2002)
14. Diefendorff, J.M., Croyle, M.H., Gosserand, R.H.: The dimensionality and antecedents of emotional labor strategies. Journal of Vocational Behavior 66, 339–357 (2005)
15. Mikolajczak, M., Menil, C., Luminet, O.: Explaining the protective effect of trait emotional intelligence regarding occupational stress: Exploration of emotional labor processes. Journal of Research in Personality 30(1), 1–19 (2007)
16. Cukur, C.S.: The Development of the Teacher Emotional Labor Scale (TELS): Validity and Reliability. Educational Sciences: Theory & Practice 9(2), 559–574 (2009)
17. Diefendorff, J.M., Croyle, M.H., Gosserand, R.H.: The dimensionality and antecedents of emotional labor strategies. Journal of Vocational Behavior 66(2), 339–357 (2005)
18. Glomb, T.M., Tews, M.J.: Emotional labor: a conceptualization and scale development. Journal of Vocational Behavior 64(1), 1–23 (2004)
19. Brotheridge, C.M., Lee, R.T.: Development and validation of the Emotional Labor Scale. Journal of Occupational &Organizational Psychology 76, 365–379 (2003)
20. Brotherdge, C.M., Grandey, A.A.: Emotional labor and burnout: Comparing two perspectives of “people work”. Journal of Vocational Behavior 60(1), 17–39 (2002)

Impact Study of Aerobics to Develop the Students' Self-confidence and Innovation Ability

Li Ya-nan

Henan Chinese Medicine Institute, Henan 450003, China
liwangmy@163.com

Abstract. Aerobics as a new sports items, it's an important form, method and content to conduct a comprehensive quality education for students, through the aerobics not only can nurtures the body but also have the function of moral education, intellectual education, aesthetic education, it has an great significance in improving the students' self-confidence and innovation ability. This paper mainly explore the influence of aerobics on students self-confidence and innovation.

Keywords: aerobics, student, self-confidence, innovation.

1 The Concept and Characteristics of Aerobics

The definition of aerobics. Aerobics originate from aerobic exercise, which is a sport event that fused together gymnastics, dance and music, aspire comprehensive and artistic of the human body health and beauty, through unarmed and using equipment to carry on the movement, it was created by absorbing the characteristics of basic gymnastics, artistic gymnastics, modern dance, disco and so on, made up of individual action, joint action with set movement that can accepted by the majority of people, it has a unique double-effect on fitness and heart health.Its form is new and lively, content is rich, pace can be fast or slow, with the accompaniment of harmonious music to achieve the mold character, entertainment, fitness purpose, it is a "blending exercise with pleasure". Aerobics as an aerobic exercise, it has all functions that aerobic exercise has, such as improve the physical quality, improve cardiopulmonary and muscular endurance, promote coordination and operation of each tissue organ, to achieve the best functional status.Moreover, It differs from other items of aerobic exercise is that it is an easy, graceful sport, at the same time of fitness, it brings people art enjoyment, make people feel happy, reveling in the joy of exercise, reducing psychological stress and promote physical and mental development, which greatly enhances the fitness results. Aerobics not only can enrich the emotions, cultivate people's sentiments, encourage the human spirit, amuse the mind and body, but also can develop the person aesthetic psychology, form good personality and moral quality. Therefore, calisthenics teaching also favored by the students, it has an extremely vital significance in improving the student's psychological quality.

Q. Zhou (Ed.): ISAEBD 2011, Part II, CCIS 209, pp. 579–583, 2011.

2 The Characteristics of Aerobics

High artistic. Aerobics art is mainly reflected in its project characteristic "health, strength and beauty", "health, strength and beauty" is the highest position of physical condition that people aspired in human history. But in aerobics, whether fitness aerobics, or competitive aerobics, all have demonstrated the "rehabilitation, force, beautiful" feature, contains high artistic factors that makes aerobics different from other sports, and this is the right reason why people love aerobics. The action of aerobics is coordinate, smooth and elastic which makes practicer not only exercise the body, enhance physical fitness, but also get the "beauty" enjoyment, and improve the aesthetic consciousness and artistic accomplishment.

Strong rhythmic.Rhythm is an indispensable constituent part in any sports, and this characteristic of aerobics is more marked. Aerobic exercises usually accompanied by music, but the characteristics of aerobics music are powerful and melodic rhythm with the function of heightens the atmosphere, cultivate physical and mental. When the aerobics fully manifested through music, the music became a good way to inspire the mood effect. The reason why aerobics is favorite by people as follow: in addition to the effect of exercise itself, the period feel of action, the very important factor is the modern music has brought vitality to aerobics; aerobics movement and the strong rhythm of music make aerobic exercise more appealing and entertaining.

Wide adaptability. Aerobic exercise in various forms, the amount of exercise is changeable and easy to control, the requirements of cite equipment is not high, so it suitable for the people in different ages, different genders, different physical quality, or different skill levels, all kinds of people can find the best way in aerobic exercise and have fun. As the old people can choose low-intensity aerobic exercise, to exercise, entertainment, and stay healthy; but for young people who has a good physical quality and want to improve, they can choose more difficult and large amount competitive aerobics as their exercise methods, it not only training the body but also improve skill levels through competitive aerobics exercise, meet their ambition requirements. Therefore, the aerobics is wide adaptability.

Fitness safety. The sports load and movement rhythm designed by aerobics are fully considered the feasibility about a series of stimulating results from sports, to make the aerobic range suitable for everyman's physique even the weak people. They are in flat floor, with the joyful music, and exercise follow the rhythm of paces which are very safe and effective. Its convenience and security also the important reason why many people choose and like aerobics.

3 The Influence of Aerobics on Students' Self-confidence

Aerobics besides the characteristics of highly artistry, the strong rhythm, wide adaptability and fitness security, its sports load and difficulty can be choose freely, the requirements of cite equipment is not high, safe and convenient to practice, that deeply general student's affection. Therefore, many schools will offer the aerobics as a sport event for student to choose and practice.Meanwhile, the function of aerobics on students' all aspects of body and mind development, particularly plays an important role in promoting students' self-confidence. Self-confidence is the self-value expression of one person, the important psychological basis for one person's success and development, the stable inner experience of one's recognition and evaluation on his own strength. PE teaching has a special function in cultivating students' confidence that other subjects doesn't have. Every student has the desire to succeed, the aerobics teaching disintegrate the skilled movement, easy to difficult, strengthen the auxiliary practice, complete assorted movement. When the former exercise completed successfully, students could engender confidence to impact a new height on the basis of the success, it can make students with greater desire and willpower to complete the next exercise task, enhance self-confidence with successful experience. As a student said: "I have confidence obviously when I walked high up, I feel nothing is impossible, I have courage and confidence to overcome the difficulties when I do high intensity exercise, because I have realized that I can succeed as long as I can insist on". Aerobics cultivate and promote students' self-confidence, mainly through the performance of the following three aspects:

1) Stimulate the expression of students, thereby enhancing self-confidence. Aerobic exercises are skilled physical activities, it has a significant differences in learning progress compared with other disciplines is that learners should have a strong at least a positive performance desire, because only performance can strengthen the aerobics skills. In college aerobics teaching, not only let students to master aerobics basic movement, pace, but also show their vigor and enthusiasm: if someone want to complete the entire movement perfectly and to show effects of health, strength, beauty, make people have a beautiful enjoyment, that needs practice has a strong expressive and appealing of his body movements and facial expression, besides accurate movements and obvious rhythm. In the process of student performance, action failure always happen because of many kinds of factors, and then, teachers should guide students challenge to difficulties; teach learning skills when students in wrong learning methods; adjust when students feel weakness; point the way when students puzzled; give spiritual encouragement when students fear; to achieve good emotional control, improve the ability of self-expression, so that the students build a stronger self-confidence and stir up the enthusiasm, to make the movement more attractive.

2) Keep good volitional quality, so as to enhance self-confidence. Volition is the psychological process that people determined purpose consciously and dominated action to overcome the difficulties to realize. Aerobics is an aerobic exercise program which is mixed music, dance and gymnastics together to pursuit of human fitness. It is based on the human body itself as an object, according to the body's anatomy and the requirements of comprehensive development, incorporates the function of promote health, shape one's body, cultivate spirit with purpose and pertinence. So, we should keep a certain practice time and exercise load, we will have physical fatigue and muscle pain when practice, it's difficult to keep going and come into effect without good self-control ability and strong volition. Athletic training is the unification of physical strength and volition cultivate, for this reason, aerobics as a sport which can enhance physique and improve skills, it also cultivate practice's volition, develop their perseverance of quality. With the strong volition, students will have more possibility and hope to do anything, and their self-confidence will higher with a hard striving hope.

3) Establish a good interpersonal relationship, so as to enhance self-confidence. In aerobics exercise, the contact between classmates is close that combine with some familiar or unfamiliar students at any time, expanded the scope of communication, learned to collaborate and help, and experienced the joy of being help and helping others. Help students learn the normal interpersonal communication, coordinal relationships and learn to get along with others to improve interpersonal and social adaptability. Various forms of aerobics competitions proposed the requirement for participants to communicate to enhance mutual emotion. With the interpersonal relationship promoted and strengthened, the evaluation of students themselves will be more positive and optimistic. Good interpersonal relationship will also makes students feel happier and more popular, this psychological feeling has great impact and help to promote their confidence.

4 The Influence of Aerobics on Students' Innovative Ability

The innovative ability is the demand of the development of future society and knowledge economy, China's development relies on innovation, the key to creation and innovation lies in human resources, whose development depends on education. Innovative education in our country is in the early stage, how to carry out the innovative education is a significant research topic. Aerobics pass into class in our country with its unique charm and fitness function as a new sport, and has a positive significance on students' innovative ability. Aerobics innovation is multifaceted, has great development space, innovation is the development trend of aerobics, innovation is a kind of spirit, a kind of thinking, also a kind of learning process, which is need technical knowledge accumulation. Consequently, innovation process is organized, time series, irreversible and path dependence. Concretely speaking, the influence of aerobics on students' innovative ability performance in the following two aspects:

1) Improve students' innovative abilities by cultivating the skills of aerobics innovation. Students' skills innovation has its own natural path. Although a skill innovation happens at one time, however, we back up, the student who realized skills innovation must have had a long period to accumulate and learn the technical knowledge, students' skill innovation will be the castles in the air without such knowledge accumulation and learning process. Innovation is the life of aerobics, the ultimate purpose of aerobics learning is not learn to jump several sets of simple movement, but master the scientific fitness methods and do some simple movement creation by study. Creating use the learned knowledge, proceed new design and exploration through the processing of thinking and imagination, to create new ideas and improve the ability to create new movement. It can be said that is difficult to have the creativity of aerobics activities without aerobics skills, in creative activities, higher skills can produce more new ideas and new activities. Consequently, we should inherit aerobics study but cannot regard it as natural and synthetic, what we should to do is to cultivate students from different aspects to explore the value of knowledge, have the courage to think, imaginative, improve the innovative ability.

2) Improve students' innovative abilities by cultivate the innovative thinking. Aerobics is complete sets of learning, improve from one to six level by level, but there are seven kinds of basic movement, each level is made up of different movements combination with arm, orientation, route changes. In practice, let the students to understand the inner link of the knowledge, improve the ability from perceptual knowledge to rational knowledge. Know what it is and know why, understand correctly and use freely. Aerobics helps to improve students' attention, working memory, thinking and imagination, etc, to promote the development and utilization of the brain, strengthen the function of nervous system, promote the brain blood circulation, improve respiratory function, make the brain gets more nutrition's which is benefits for the memory and imagery thinking of brain. Moreover, it can eliminate the fatigue due to brain work to a certain degree, improve the learning efficiency and fully excavate and developing the learning potential. These are extremely advantageous to enhance students' innovative consciousness and thinking of aerobics, aerobics innovation consciousness training process is a process of training comprehensive abilities, innovation is the source of life of aerobics, and learns from thought, diligent in thinking is the key to develop the innovative ability. We would improve students' innovative ability steadily if we can arouse the motivation and consciousness of study; stimulate students' creative thinking with maximum limit in aerobics teaching and practice.

5 Conclusion

The new century calls for the talents who is brave in to develop, dares enterprising and innovating, and this kind of new-style talents must have the quality of self-confidence and creativity, there will be a force with confidence that will be brave to face frustrations and difficulties, there will never have a power failure that will push the success have obtained to victory again. The future college aerobics education is pay more attention to spiritual level, body and mind health, external beauty combined, and rich thought, which is based on the development of skills and physical, its charm is not only cultivate a body external posture beauty, but what important is to develop the personality, innovation and artistic expressions of the aerobics practitioners. Through the aerobics, it can practice students' volition, promote their intelligence and self-awareness, improve interpersonal skills, it has great benefits to strengthen the students' self-confidence and promote their innovation ability which is worth energetically advocate.

References

1. He, Y.-f.: Discussion the Introduction of Creative Thinking to College Aerobics Teaching. Journal of Guangzhou Physical Education Institute 5 (2002)
2. Hong, X.-s.: How to Implement the Innovation of College Physical Education. Journal of Beijing University of Physical Education 4 (2002)
3. Zhang, M.-x.: Innovative Education of Sports. Journal of Neijiang Teachers College 2 (2005)
4. Xiao, G.-l.: Aerobics, 1st edn. People's Education Press, Beijing (2004)

Discussion on the Connotation of Olympic Culture

Li Yanan

Henan Chinese Medicine Institute, Henan 450003, China
liwangmy@163.com

Abstract. Using literature data and other research methods, the paper analyzed on the connotation of Olympic culture, resolved the feature of Olympic culture.The research carried out that the connotation of Olympic culture is very rich,it not only covered the Olympic Games, but also management,systems, rituals,ceremonies,education,art, architecture,technology and the mass media etc. during the Olympic Games.The Olympic movement, concept, ideal and everything about it is human's cultural heritage.

Keywords: Olympic Games, the Olympic Culture, Connotation, Heritage.

Modern Olympic Games have become a social and cultural phenomenon, she has rich cultural connotation and completely not limited to sports field, although she takes sport as main content. Olympic ranging from material to spiritual civilization, from individual to social, from concrete to abstract all aspects, fully reflect the rich cultural connotations of Olympic Games. There are different explanations about the Olympic culture connotation; all things originated from Olympic Games can became Olympic culture. Olympic Games is a special kind of sports culture forms, and has its own cultural expression. Olympic Cultural not only contain Olympic Games, but also covered management system, etiquette and ceremony, education art, architecture technology and mass media, etc. One of the ideas, ideals, specific activities and all things surrounding the Olympic Movement are humanity's cultural heritage.

1 Management and System

Ideological system of the Olympic Movement Ideological system of the Olympic Movement is mainly made up of olympism, Olympic tenet, Olympic spirit, and Olympic motto. The system made Olympic Games has solid ideological basis and clear guidelines.

Olympism "Olympic Charter" in the definition of Olympism made clear: "Olympism is to enhance the body, will and spirit and to the overall development of a philosophy of life. Olympus-led party socialist buck for a blend between sport with culture and education, to create a life-style that seeks joys in effort, play a good example of basic education value and respect social morality principles". Olympism connotation is very rich, Olympism is a philosophy of life, the life philosophy, it emphasizes that to make people get the body, mind and spirit integrated development through enhanced physique, temper and cultivate noble sentiment. Olympism

Q. Zhou (Ed.): ISAEBD 2011, Part II, CCIS 209, pp. 584–591, 2011.

promotes people's physical, moral and spiritual development and improvement through the combination of sports and culture and education, it emphasizes that sport give service to harmonious development of human being to promote the creation of a harmonious society.

Olympic tenet. About the goal of the Olympic movement, the "Olympic Charter" mentioned that "through without any discrimination, has the Olympic spirit - the friendship, solidarity and fair spirit of mutual understanding - sports activities to educate the youth, so as to contribute to create a peaceful and better world". The goal of the Olympic movement specific can reflect for: to make sport for the harmonious development of human services to enhance human dignity; to friendship, solidarity and fair play and promote better mutual understanding of youth that help to build a better world of peace; the world's athletes in each a grand festival every four years - the Olympic Games get-together. Olympic tenet can be highly summarized as: "peace, friendship and progress".

Olympic spirit. About the Olympic spirit, "Olympic Charter" said the Olympic spirit is the spirit of mutual understanding, friendship, solidarity and fair competition. The historical process of modern Olympic movement development, is the process of the Olympic spirit connotation has been improved and enriched. It not only contains the narrow sense of "mutual understanding, friendship, solidarity and spirit of fair competition", but also in the Olympic movement's purpose, motto, slogan and image tag, also includes athletes self defeating, to challenge the limits and the pursuit of harmony between man and nature unity, the spirit of promoting world peace. "Participation is more important than winning," the Olympic movement widely circulated saying, is the belief in the Olympic Games. 1908 July 24, Coubertin was in London attempting the 4th Olympic Games, the British government held a reception banquet, he quoted a paragraph from Pennsylvania bishop in athletes awarded ceremony organized in Sao Paulo in his speech:"to the Olympic Games, it more important to participate than to win."Coubertin also made insightful explanation to this sentence:"the important thing in our life is not the triumph but the struggle, its essence is not to win but to make human beings become more courageous, more robust, more cautious and more graceful. This is our guiding ideology of the International Olympic Committee."

Olympic motto .The Olympic movement's motto is "faster, higher, stronger". This motto is come up with Coubertin's friend Henry Martin Didone. He proposed this motto and made it as the school motto of his own PE school. Coubertin appreciates this motto completely, the International Olympic Committee members were also appreciated it. After that, Coubertin proposed to write this motto into "Olympic Charter" in 1913. "Faster, higher, stronger" as a part of the International Olympic committee emblem at the 6th Congress of the International Olympic, in 1913, this motto became a part of the Olympic logo.

At the beginning of Rogge took office, he proposed Olympic motto:"Cleaner, more humanity, more united". "cleaner" embodied human's firm belief to carry forward sports ethics and resolution to maintain fair competition of the Olympic movement; "more humanity" is the supreme ideal of the pursuit of human nature, human values, human dignity and human power would be perfectly embodiment and hold highly; "more united" is human's deep calling for the Olympic ideal of peace, expected the Olympic family members with a more unprecedented unity to promote peace and development of human society in the new century. Olympic new motto represent that the new century Olympic movement has a direction that people oriented, fair competition with civilization, unity and progress, man's all-round development is the soul of the new motto.

The organization system of Olympic movement. The organization system of Olympic movement includes three parts: the International Olympic Committee(containing each subsidiary body), International Sports Federations, and National Olympic Committee(Figure 1).

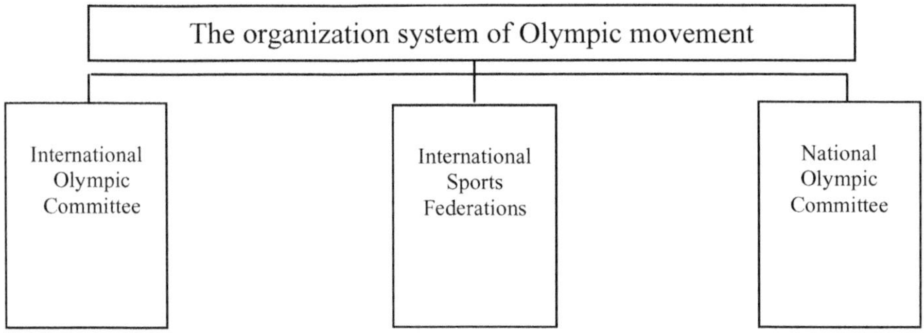

Fig. 1. The organization system of Olympic movement

The International Olympic committee referred to IOC, it's the supreme authority of the Olympic Games. International Olympic Committee's Organizational Structure including plenary meeting, executive council, headquarters and special committee. International sports federations refers to administer one or several individual sports in the worldwide, admit the Country and regional unofficial and international organizations which are administer one or several individual sports. International Sports Federation consists of monomial associations of each country or region. National Olympic Committee referred to NOC. It was set up according to "the Olympic Charter", it's the organization got the IOC's admission to take charge of a country or region to carry out the Olympic Games, the agent of the International Olympic Committee in different countries all over the world, its regulations should consistent with "the Olympic Charter". NOC is the only legal organizers and leaders of Olympic Games in country or region, the only organ who have the rights to choose athletes to take part in the Olympic Games, and the only organ who have the rights use the Olympic rings, badge and logos.

Activity system of Olympic Games. Olympic Games includes a lot of periodical and aperiodic activities. There are 8 types in modern Olympic Games: Summer Olympics, Winter Olympics, Paralympics, Summer Special Olympics, Winter Special Olympics, Deaf Olympics, World Transplant Games and Youth Games. In addition, people hold various Olympic mass sports activities, the Olympic education, scientific and cultural activities, as well as the Olympic cultural activities, etc.

Olympic volunteerism. Olympic volunteer play an increasing role in the Olympic Games organization and the embodiment of the Olympic spirit. With the developing of Olympic Games, more and more volunteers involved. Olympic volunteers as a broad concepts, it refers to all people who contributed their labor, technology and time for the development of Olympic Games[1]. Olympic volunteerism embodies the highly fit with olympism and volunteer spirit.

There were 900 volunteers in the first modern Olympics, volunteer began to do some skilled work in the 1952 Helsinki Olympic Games, and the organizing committee have volunteer training for the first time, laid a solid foundation for the following volunteers training work. Olympic organizing committee began to take volunteer service into the agenda and the committee's overall planning in 1980, Lake Placid, Winter Olympics. 1984 Los Angeles Olympics organizing committee has established a special volunteers department. The concept of Olympic volunteers first clear defined according to the official reports in 1992 Barcelona Olympics:"Olympic volunteer is the person who in their own personal selfless participation, try their best to cooperate, finish to his task, and don't accept payment, or seek other anything in return in the Olympic hosting process." Form then on, Olympic volunteer developing in the direction of organization, specialization, and individuation.

2 Etiquette and Ceremony

Modern Olympic etiquette is the behavior rules and norms followed by a complete set of performance respect, education and aesthetic significance when people participating in the modern Olympic Games activity process [2]. The modern Olympic etiquette object is Olympic ceremony; mainly have the opening ceremony, the torch relay ceremony, the awarding ceremony, and the closing ceremony, etc. These ceremonies not only bring strong festal atmosphere, but also a solemn and sacred grade to the Olympic Games, which makes it has a strong artistic appeal.

The opening ceremony. At the opening ceremony, the representative team from various countries as a part of the team step into the stadium. To commemorate the origin of the modern Olympic Games, Greek team always enter the stadium first. Host team is always the last to enter the stadium. The modern Olympics has evolved into a grand ceremony, including music, speeches, entertainment and various makeup parade and many other content. At the opening ceremony, The Olympic flag gradually rising which is represents Africa, the Americas, Asia, Australia and European nation together gradually rising.

The torch relay ceremony. The torch relay ceremony first appeared in the Olympic Games in 1936 Berlin Summer Olympic opening ceremony. The Olympic torch flame symbolizes the Olympic spirit from generation to generation from ancient Greece until today. The torch was lit in Olympia, Greece first, and then by a number of torch relay to the host city in the next period of time. After the final torch bearer lit the Olympic torch in the Olympic main venue, the head of the host country announced the official opening of the Olympic Games, and then flying pigeon symbolizes the hope for world peace.

The awarding ceremony. The awarding ceremony is the ceremony after the end of each event. At the ceremony admiral MEDALS awarded the top three. Winners mount the rostrum accept gold, silver and bronze MEDALS. The winner of three countries where national flag is raised, and played the title belongs to the country's national anthem.

The closing ceremony. In the early Olympic ceremonies have another parade, however, in the 1956 Melbourne, Australia Summer Olympic Games, athletes disrupted formation, shaking hands, hug each other to celebrate this moment. This freedom celebrate form fixed from then on, and continue to use so far. IOC President will invite athletes and spectators reunion at the next Olympics, when the athletes assembled celebrating in the main Olympic stadium. After that, IOC President announced the games ended, and the Olympic flame is extinguished.

Spectator Etiquette. Spectator Etiquette is an important part of the Olympic etiquette. In different competition have different kind of viewing etiquette. For instance, in the process of fencing, the athlete will choose sword, attack mode according to the characteristics of other athletes, when the audience should not cheer up any more so that athletes can think and make moves better. In addition, the audience can't cheer or applause when the referee send password so that athletes can hear the referee password clearly. The audience can cheer or applause after the light on. In the tennis match, after you go into the tennis court, you should turn off you phone or tune the ring into vibration, you can't speak aloud and camera may not use a flash during the match process. In badminton, table tennis competition, the whole competition terrain should keep quiet when athletes ready to serve; the audiences should shout cheer and applause after the first serve.

3 Architecture and Technology

Olympic Architecture Every building is an ever popular music, passed down silently touched the hearts of the people; every one of the buildings are historical scroll of a human creation, standing silently around the world to witness the great historical events of mankind. Olympic Architecture is the grand epic of silent music of the Olympic Culture. Olympic Architecture keeps the Olympic orchestra music permanent for the host countries. Every Olympic Park, every Olympic Stadium is like an open Olympic history books, many history, many legends, and many cultural solidificated among them. Olympic Stadium, Olympic Village, Olympic Sports Park are represent the Olympic host humanities style and urban architectural style, the Olympic Architecture merge the modern science and humanities concern together perfectly, make it become the human eternal chapter. Modern Olympic Architecture is wonderful in the development history of world architecture and technology. Olympic Architecture embodies the Olympic spirit, making the Olympic architecture engraved different signs from simple sports building. One Hundred Years of Olympic architecture consistently reflected the modern sports, culture, technology, economic aspects of achievement.

Olympic Technology. Technology has been promoting the development of the modern Olympic Games. Overview the 100 years development of the Olympic Games, the Olympic Games is not only the experimental field of science and technology development, but also provide a platform for the exhibition and communication of science and technology. The use of technology in the Olympic including stadium, exercise, safe, traffic, communication, energy and environment, etc. Specifically, in the construction of Olympic Stadium, the technological innovation, lightning protection and seismic technology of stadium, etc; in sports,

sports competence evaluation, nanotechnology, doping detection technology, etc; in the Olympic security, urban monitoring, identification, food safety detection, etc; in the area of transportation, intelligent transportation system construction, electric vehicle application and accurate weather forecasts the use of technology, etc; in communications, the next generation Internet, 3G technology, wireless broadband technology; etc; in the energy utilization, solar, geothermal, photovoltaic energy technology has widely used in People's Daily life gradually ; in environmental protection, preventing sand, water conservation, waste treatment and flowers cultivating [3]. It can be seen that penetrates the power of modern science and technology, from the innovation of sports technical and tactical, to the changes of sports equipment and field; from design concept of the Olympic architecture and the use of new materials, to the intelligent information of the tournament organization management; even a small torch in the Olympics.

4 Education Art

"Olympic Charter" pointed out: "Olympic activities are global and continuously. The highest level of activity is to gather all athletes in the world in the Olympic Games which is a grand sports festival." This "global and continuously" means the mass sports, education activity, culture and art activities. Olympic movement is not only the Olympic Games, its scope includes often mass sports and cultural education and artistic activities [5].

Education is the core of Coubertin sports thought, as well as the Olympic movement. Olympic education is the education of the Olympic movement itself, propagandize and spread the Olympism education in a certain sense, also the education that carry forward the Olympic spirit and the Olympic ideal. It is an ideological and political education, and the scientific research improved and developed Olympism theory. This kind of education and research is indispensable for the global development of Olympic Games, it's very necessary for the countries and cities who host the Olympic Games.

Compared with other sports, Olympic Games besides sports, also contains culture, education and art. Sports competition does not represent the entire content of the Olympic Games, cultural art is the indispensable important component. As Mr. Samaranch said: "Olympic doctrine is beyond athletic sports, especially in the most extensive and most complete sense, it is not to separate with education. It will makes the sports activities integrate with art and mental, and tend to be a whole person."

Olympic art form can be said a colorful picture, including not only the Olympic stamps, medals, souvenir badge, anthem, literature, film, sculpture, painting and other things, but also including the large-scale cultural performances of the opening and closing ceremonies, and the Olympic festival, Olympic Arts Festival and other celebrations. Especially the large-scale cultural performances of the opening and closing ceremonies in modern Olympic Games, it always the most programs attracted people's view, the most beautiful flower of human civilization that Olympic movement dedicated to the world, and what is more, it pull the Olympic culture and art to the extreme. These touchable, seeable, audible art forms enriched the connotation of Olympic Games immensely; add the happy festive atmosphere to the

Games, makes the Olympic Games every four years in the long cycle was full of the rich Olympic culture atmosphere, which reflects the progress of human civilization and promoting the development of human society [6].

5 The Mass Media

The Olympic Games had an indissoluble bond with the mass media when it came into the world. In today's era of information and knowledge economy, economic globalization trend is clearly, civilization has a trend that spreading and developing in cross-cultural and multi cultural ways, Olympic movement and the mass media are getting closer, the two complement each other, promoting each other, can be said that symbiotic relationship.

The mass media are mainly carrier of the Internet, newspapers, the news agency, radio, TV, news and news journal record film, etc. The revival of the Olympic Games can not without the publicity of mass media. All awash with mass media publicity reported from the difficult start of modern Olympic Games to became the global event. The mass media played an important advocacy and decisive role in promoting the Olympic Movement and Olympic ideals. Especially in resent years, with the coming of information ear, people's world cognition is influenced by mass media. Olympic Movement in the context of globalization and cultural cross-cultural communication has swept the world, the mass media contributed.

6 Conclusion

Olympic Culture has become the mainstream of world sports culture, it not only realize the development for all countries and nationalities culture, and also themselves cultural connotation in richer at the same time. With the changing times, the advancement of technology, humanities, promoting the development of Olympic Culture will also keep pace with the times. Particularly in the situation of world multiple culture cross-cultural development, the impact of the Olympic Games increasing, cultural deposits becoming more and more profound. Olympic Culture is the common heritage of human civilization, as time went on, she also constantly enrich the connotation, has increasingly become an important area of human cultural innovation.

References

1. Song, Y.-f.: The Olympic volunteer management study. Journal of Sports Science 25(2), 86–94 (2005)
2. Fan, D.-y.: The definition and characteristic analysis of modern Olympic etiquette. Journal of Chengdu Sports College Journal 1, 22–25 (2005)

3. Science daily, and the Olympic technology, action plan leadership group, the science and technology commission of the 29th Olympic Games. Walk into Scientific Olympics vol. 11. Guangxi People's Publishing House, Nanning (2008)
4. Li, Y.-c.: The technology innovation of competitive sports and science: expound Beijing science and technology Olympics. Beijing Sport University Press, Beijing (2008)
5. Luo, S.-m., Tan, H.: The Olympic Science. Higher Education Press, Beijing (2007)
6. Wu, Z.-l., Wang, Z.-j.: Read the Olympic. Art roll, 11th edn. Jiangxi Fine Arts Publishing House, Nanchang (2007)

Research on Influence of Aerobic Dancing and Tennis Exercises on Middle-Aged Women's Bone Mineral Density of Calcaneus

Bao He[1], Li Qin[2], and Wang Jinan[3]

[1] Hubei Communications Technical College, 430079, China
[2] Central China Normal University, 430074, China
[3] Wuhan Institute of Technology, 430073, China
He_bb22@163.com

Abstract. In order to find out the influence of aerobic dancing and tennis exercises on middle-aged women's bone mineral density of calcaneus, we select the healthy middle-aged women aged 30-50 as test subjects. We use quantitative ultrasonic bone imaging and measurement system to test the subjects' bone mineral density of calcaneus. The result shows that the stiffness and bone mineral density of aerobic dancing group and tennis group is higher than that of control group. The difference between aerobic dancing group and control group is not obvious, however, the difference between tennis group and control group is very significant ($p = 0.000$). The risk degree of fracture of aerobic dancing group and tennis group is lower than that of control group, but the aerobic dancing group and control group have no obvious difference, while the difference between tennis group and control group is very obvious, which indicates that the role of playing tennis is better than taking aerobic dancing in enhancing stiffness and bone mineral density and reducing risk degree of fracture.

Keywords: aerobic dancing, tennis, bone mineral density.

1 Introduction

Women have the special physiological phenomenon – menopause. It leads to postmenopausal osteoporosis which has already drawn the widespread attention of medical workers. There are many researches on osteoporosis of postmenopausal women, and the main study population is postmenopausal and perimenopausal women. The studies of Garn [1] show that even after 20 years, the bone mass still completely relates to the initial bone mass. Therefore, the effect of preventing bone mineral density from declining of the middle-aged women on preventing osteoporosis can't be neglected. The main methods for the middle-aged women to prevent the bone mineral density from declining are filling calcium and sports exercises, among which, the effect of sports exercises is better.

During sports exercises, calcaneus is easy to be stimulated, especially during onshore programs. Almost all the sports will produce stress stimulation to calcaneus,

Q. Zhou (Ed.): ISAEBD 2011, Part II, CCIS 209, pp. 592–597, 2011.

and the structure of calcaneus is similar to that of vertebra, which is mainly cancellous bone. Metabolism refresh rate of cancellous bone is 8 times that of cortical bone, which can mostly reflect the effect of various factors on bones.

This research selects the healthy middle-aged women as test subjects, divides them into aerobic dancing group, tennis group and control group (non-exercises group) according to their sports habit and use quantitative ultrasonic bone imaging and measurement system to test the subjects' bone mineral density of calcaneus. The purpose is to find out the respective influence of the two activities on middle-aged women's bone mineral density through tasting and comparing, and to provide some valuable information for many women to prevent osteoporosis by taking sports exercises.

2 Research Contents and Methods

2.1 Research Object

We screen 60 subjects at the age of 30-50 from the questionnaires and divide them into three groups according to their sports habit.

(1) Aerobic dancing group: there are 20 middle-aged women who take part in more than three times aerobic dancing every week, each time lasts about 1 hour, and the exercise period is 1 year.

(2) Running and tennis group: there are 20 middle-aged women who take part in exercises more than three times every week, each time lasts about 1 hour, and the exercise period is 1 year.

(3) Control Group: There are 20 middle-aged women who usually hardly participate in any sports activities.

All the test subjects are voluntary for the test and healthy, who don't have major disease and family history and don't take calcium tablet for a long term.

2.2 Experiment Equipment

UBIS5000 QUS (quantitative ultrasound) bone imaging made by French and measurement system.

2.3 Test Principles and Methods

(1) Test principles: the main structure of calcaneus is cancellous bone, which is similar to that of vertebra. Calcaneus is the place which is mostly like to be fractured. Furthermore, there are two parallel surfaces of calcaneus which is only surrounded by a little soft tissue. So it's idea for the ultrasonic to spread. Ultrasonic is a kind of elastic wave, which will attenuate when it encounters resistance during spreading though bones. The scanning system draws the image of calcaneus according to the attenuation degree of ultrasonic. The scanning pixel of UBIS5000 quantitative ultrasonic bone imaging and measurement system id 1mm2, and the size of scanning

zone of Broadband Ultrasound Attenuation (BUA) is 60mm×60mm. After drawing image, the system will automatically orientate the return-on-investment (ROI) and proceed with the calculation of related indexes.

(2) Test methods: the study objects wipe both sides of heel and the corresponding parts with calcaneus with alcohol swab till the sebum is basically cleansed. Then they put their feet into test slot motionlessly, and the technicians test them after entering the objects' number, name, sex, birth date, height, weight, and test limb into computer. The test result can be directly showed in the display, at the same time, it can also be printed as test report through background printer.

(3) Test indexes: bone stiffness index (STIM), bone mineral density index (OP), and risk degree of fracture (RRFM).

2.4 Statistics Methods

Make T test and univariate ANOVA for each index of bone mineral density by using SPSS statistics software. We take $p < 0.05$ for significant level, and $p < 0.01$ for quite significant level.

3 Results and Analysis

3.1 Results

After conducting statistic and analysis of the test date, we get the following result:

Table 1. The Statistic Result of Bone Quality before Experiment

n=60			
	STIM	OP	RRFM
Aerobic dancing group A (M±SD)	105.31±17.57	105.53±4.66	99.32±23.14
Tennis group B (M±SD)	105.23±19.24	106.58±5.83	98.76±13.53
Control group C (M±SD)	104.11±10.36	106.32±3.91	101.72±58.64
PA－B	0.37	0.34	0.32
PA－C	0.22	0.45	0.18
PB－C	0.24	0.33	0.13

Note： ＊ represents P < 0.05， ＊＊ represents P < 0.01。

Table 1 shows that the bone stiffness, bone mineral density and risk degree of fracture among the three groups before experiment don't have significant difference. But after one-year exercises, the stiffness and bone mineral density of aerobic dancing group and tennis group is higher than that of control group. The difference between aerobic dancing group and control group is not obvious, however, the difference between tennis group and control group is very significant ($p < 0.01$). It indicates that aerobic dancing and tennis exercises play certain role in improving bone stiffness and bone mineral density, but the effect of aerobic dancing is not obvious. The risk degree of fracture of aerobic dancing group and tennis group is lower than that of control group, but the aerobic dancing group and control group have no obvious difference, while the difference between tennis group and control group is very obvious ($p < 0.01$), which indicates that aerobic dancing has certain use in reducing risk degree, but the effect is not significant, whereas tennis exercises have an obvious role in reducing risk degree of fracture. Comparing tennis group with aerobic dancing group, we can find that bone stiffness and bone mineral density of tennis group are significantly higher than that of aerobic dancing group ($p < 0.05$), while the risk degree of fracture of the former is obviously lower than that of the latter ($p < 0.05$), which shows that the effect of tennis exercises is better than that of aerobic dancing on improving bone stiffness and bone mineral density, and reducing risk degree of fracture.

Table 2. The Statistic Result of Bone Quality after Experiment

n = 60			
	STIM	OP	RRFM
Aerobic dancing group A（M±SD）	115.24±18.63	106.56±9.02	108.31±120.26
Tennis Group B （M±SD）	127.90±18.84	113.78±8.12	35.99±20.97
Control Group C （M±SD）	102.81±12.67	104.29±5.49	112.32±62.22
PA－B	0.039＊	0.011＊	0.012＊
PA－C	0.18	0.343	0.895
PB－C	0.000＊＊	0.000＊＊	0.000＊＊

Note： ＊represents $P < 0.05$， ＊＊represents $P < 0.01$。

3.2 Analysis

There are feedback mechanisms during bones' reaction process to different sports stimulation. When the exercise load increases, the bone strain will increase, which will make the bone mass increase, the bone structure change and the skeletons sustain the corresponding strain. Within a certain range, sports intensity is proportion to the increasing of bone mineral density. At this time, the process of bone remodeling is in positive balance, that is, on one hand, the absorption of inner cavity bone of cortical bone reduces, the sectional surface increases, and the volume increases; on the other hand, the amount of bone trabecular increases and the bone mineral density buildups. Frost [6] puts forward that the process of remodeling can change the building mode and shape of bones to adapt to the needs of loading under the stimulation of appropriate stress. He proposed that the strain that daily activities can make bone generate is bout 200-500με (micro-strain). In order to produce a positive balance of bone remolding to increase bone mass, the mechanical load should make bone generate strain of 1500-2500με. While studying the relation between strain and strain frequency during bone remodeling, Rubin [7] finds that it only needs four times load stimulation every day can achieve the maintenance of bone when the dynamic strain is 2000με, 0.5Hz. When the strain reduces to1000με, 1Hz, it needs 100 times mechanical load stimulation every day to maintain sclerotin. While the frequency changes to 200με, 30Hz, it needs 1800 times load stimulation to maintain sclerotin.

Aerobic dancing is one kind of fitness program which has high popularizing rate and is much loved by middle-aged women in our cities. With the accompaniment of music, the exercisers get fit with trippingly dance steps. The subjective feelings during exercises are relaxed or rather relaxed, the corresponding heart rate is about 110 times per minute, the exercise intensity is 35%VO2max, the strain stimulation to the bone is among 500—1000με, and the remodeling process of bones is in slightly positive balance, so the various indexes of the exercisers have no significant difference with that of control group, but are slightly improved. Therefore, taking part in aerobic dancing more than three times a week, each time 1 hour, and continuing to exercise for 1 year has great effect on bone mineral density of calcaneus of 30-50-year-old middle-aged women, though the effect is not significant. Because the exercise period of our test objects is 1 year, whether the accumulative effect of long-term exercises is better needs further study.

Tennis exercise is kind of fitness and entertainment program springs up with great improvement of people's living standard, which has been very popular in recent years. During the race, the opponents with significantly different strength can end one game in 10 minutes or so; while the opponents with equal strength may play quite a few hours. In the mass sports, exercisers can choose playing intensity and length of time according to one's own conditions. During the whole exercise period, the subjective feelings of exercisers is little strenuous, the corresponding heart rate is about 130 times per minute, the exercise intensity is 50% VO2max, the strain stimulation to the bone is among 1500—2000με, and the remodeling process of bones is obviously in positive balance, so it can improve the exercisers' bone mineral density effectively. It also shows that it can improve the bone mineral density of calcaneus of 30-50-year-old middle-aged women in a short period (1 year) if they take part in tennis exercises more than three times a week and each time will last about 1 hour. As aerobic dancing, its effect of long-term exercises still need further study.

4 Conclusion

(1) No matter for aerobic dancing or tennis exercises, if people can take part in more than three times per week, each time about 1 hour, and can continue for I year, the bone mineral density of their calcaneus will be improved. However, the effect of aerobic dancing is not significant, whereas the effect of tennis exercises is quite significant.

(2) For the physical exercises aiming at improve bone mineral density, the effect of tennis exercises is better than that of aerobic dancing, and the long-term effect still need further study.

References

1. Garn, S.M., et al.: Continuing bone expansion and increasing bone loss over a two-decade period in men and women from a total community sample. Am. J. Hum. Biol. 4, 57 (1992)
2. Zhang, X., Wei, L., Yang, X.: Clinical Significance of Ultrasonic Testing of Elderly People's Calcaneus. Modern Rehabilitation 5(2), 95–96 (2001)
3. Sun, C., Ding, R., Li, H.: Combination of Traditional Chinese Medicine and Western Medicine on preventing and treating Osteoporosis. Journal of Chinese Trauma 1(3), 82 (1999)
4. Lu, H., Dai, K.: Gene and Primary Osteoporosis. Chinese Journal of Orthopedics 19(8), 500 (1999)
5. Wu, X., Liao, E.: Application and Development of Evaluating Bone Quality by Quantitative Ultrasonic. China Medical Tribune (June 17, 1999) (third edition)
6. Frost, H.M.: Skeletal structural daptation to mechanical usage (SATMV): 1.Redetining Wollff's Iaw: the modeling problem. Anat. Rec. 226, 403–413 (1990)
7. Rubin, C., Mcleod, K.: Promotion of body in growth by frequency specific, low amplitude mechanical strain. Clin. Orthop. Rel. Res. 298, 165 (1993)

Research on Measurement of and Evaluation Criterion for Female Boxer's Special Physical Quality

Bu Xiangui

Shangdong Institute of Physical Education and Sports,
Rizhao, Shangdong 276800, China
buxgye@163.com

Abstract. On the basis of the reality and special characteristics of female boxer, by means of the Delphi Method to measure indexes of physical quality and by setting Shandong provincial female boxing team as the research object, this paper designed a standard system of evaluation criterion for female boxer's special physical quality which provides a scientific basis for special physical training of female boxer.

Keywords: female boxing, physical quality, measurement index, evaluation criterion.

1 Introduction

Female boxing in our country has made significant progress since it was introduced into China in 1997. Especially in 2010, Chinese female boxers topped the medal tally by winning 1 gold medal, 3 silver medals and 3 bronze medals in the 6th World Women's Boxing Championship. Permitted by the OCOG, Women's boxing will be included in the London Olympics in 2012. It is an urgent issue to seize the opportunity and expand the advantage to promote the development of Chinese women's boxing. Until now, tactics and skills of women's boxing has enhanced substantially on the international level, which posed a higher requirement for the athlete's physical training. It has been proved that good physical quality is crucial to win the competition. Thus, athletes, coaches and sports scientific personnels all paid much attention to physical quality in training.

Scientific evaluation of boxer's physical quality is very important in athlete selection, training plan formulation, training process regulation and training results evaluation. According to documentation and experts, at present evaluation indexes and criteria for female boxer's physical quality are various and have considerable differences. It would be more pertinent to evaluate athletes in line with age, training level and special characteristics. While it is difficult to provide valuable information for training if evaluation criterion broke away from the actual situation of athletes. Based on the Shandong provincial women's boxing team, this research designed evaluation criterion and testing indexes of physical quality according to athletes' practical situation and special characteristics. Thus it provides a scientific basis for special physical quality training of female boxer.

Q. Zhou (Ed.): ISAEBD 2011, Part II, CCIS 209, pp. 598–603, 2011.

2 Research Object and Method

2.1 Research Object

30 athletes were selected from in random Shandong provincial women's boxing team. All of them are between 18 and 23 years old with training life over 4 years.

2.2 Research Method

Literature Consultation: By applying document retrieval tool such as CNKI, WangFang, Weipu etc. and consulting relevant books in Shandong Sport University library, the author collected a large number of documentation related to the research, which provided theory basis for the research.

Questionnaire: 15 questionnaires of *Measurement and Evaluation Criterion of Female Boxer's Special Physical Quality* were designed in order to sift through 8 testing indexes of Shandong provincial women's boxing team. All questionnaires have been taken back. The completion rate is 100%.

Mathematical Statistics: Statistical methods such as conventional method of descriptive statistics, deviation method and percentile method etc. were applied to process these collected questionnaires. All the data were analysed by SPSS11.4 and verified the its reliability and validity.

Experimentation: When experts selected physical quality indexes after the questionnaire, test of different conners and repeated test of the same conner were conducted in Shandong provincial women's boxing team so as to verify the reliability and validity of the indexes and methods.

The Delphi Method: Through a series of concise consult tables and controllable feedbacks, the most reliable agreement of expert panel was obtained and the physical quality index was concluded after three round of Delphi method questionnaires.

2.3 The Selection of Test Indexes of Boxers' Special Physical Quality

According to the event- group theory, the boxing is a contact event of technology-led class in terms of leading factor of competitive ability; the boxing is an event of variant combination in terms of movement structure; the boxing is an event of winning class by hit scoring or knockout; the boxing is an mixed load event of balanced exercise intensity and amount. From the boxing special features, the boxers' sports qualities (the strength, speed, endurance, sensitivity, flexibility showed by boxers during the trainings and competitions on the basis of good control of weight) play a crucial impact on evaluating the athletes' competitive level.

In terms of the energy supply of athlete organism, the boxing needs higher capacity of aerobic and anaerobic metabolism. By observing Kinematics features on the spot, we find the quick start, the sensitivity of action, the coordination ability to complete the various complex technical movements, the quality of endurance and strength to persist in the longtime and high-intensity confrontation all influence the athletes' technical and tactical performance. Based on the above theoretical analysis, eight test indexes of physical quality concerned with special features chosen primarily are: ①20s straight punch; ②20s hook punch; ③20s barbells bench press(45kg); ④20s upper hook; ⑤20s sit-ups; ⑥1min vertical and horizontal push-ups; ⑦standing triple jump; ⑧10m×4 shuttle run. And then the expert questionnaire survey and experiments are performed (chart 1). In the four tests that have highly approval rate by fifteen coaches, 20s straight punch is highest, 97%; followed is 20s hook punch, 93%; 1min vertical and horizontal push-ups and 10m×4 shuttle run, 87%. Therefore, the four indexes selected have higher effectiveness in terms of test of female boxers' special physical quality. The reliability coefficient was calculated by product moment method using the test results from the repeated experiments under the same conditions. The highest reliability coefficient is 0.98 and the lowest is 0.90, which reflects that the selected tests can measure the true developing level of female boxers' physical quality accurately. So, we believe that the four selected tests can be used as the indexes of female boxers' special physical quality.

Chart1 the Expert Questionnaire Survey and Experimental Results

	20s	10m×4	1 Min	20s
	Straight punch	shuttle run	vertical and horizontal push-ups	hook punch
Number of approval	14	12	12	13
Approval rate %	93	80	80	87
Reliability coefficient	0.98	0.90	0.90	0.95
Test property	upper limb speed	reaction and flexibility	explosive force of upper and lower limbs	flexibility of upper limbs

2.4 The Standard Setting of Individual Test Score of Special Physical Quality

The evaluating indexes of female boxers' special physical quality are determined from Delphi method. The raw score of diversity index was obtained in strict accordance with standardized tests (chart 2).

Chart 2 the Tests Results of Female Boxers' Special Physical Quality

	20s	10m×4	1 Min	20s
	Straight punch/ times	shuttle run/s	vertical and hook punch/times	horizontal push-ups /times
Average	48	5.6	36	40
Standard Deviation	4.1	0.38	6.28	4.52
Max	58	6.0	45	46
Minimum	42	49	31	32

According to the degree of dispersion of individual test score distribution, the X±2s test score is selected. The average of individual score is set 50 points by departure method. The standard score of index that has the higher test score the better is presented by T, that is 50+50 (x -x)/2s ; the standard score of index that has the lower test score the better is presented by T, that is 50-50 (x -x)/2. The standard score of individual test score is calculated. The average, standard deviation, max and minimum of standard score are in chart3.

Chart 3 the Four Tests Score Standard Grading of Female Boxers

	20s Straight punch/ times	10m×4 shuttle run/s	1 Min vertical and hook punch/times	20s horizontal push-ups /times
Average	50.22	48.9	51.24	49.8
Standard Deviation	13.4	14.68	15.94	15.8
Max	98.92	95.6	94.8	95.4
Minimum	11.8	12.7	10.86	1088

From the test score, the score range of plus-minus standard score is from 0 point to 100 points all covering the highest and lowest test scores.

2.5 The Evaluation of Integrative Development Level of Female Boxers' Special Physical Quality

The physical quality of female boxers includes speed, explosive force, endurance and flexibility. The single test score of physical quality is hard to measure the overall development level of the athlete's physical quality. According to the above standard score of individual test score, the average and standard deviation of total score are calculated. And then according to the fundamental principle of normal distribution, the integrative development level of female boxers' special physical quality is intended: the high level accounts for 25% and the low level accounts for 25%. The assessment standard of the integrative development level of female boxers' special physical quality is set up (chart 4). According to the standard, if the total score of individual test score of the athlete's physical quality can't reach 211.58 points, the coach should pay attention to the training of the athlete's physical quality.

Chart 4 the Assessment Standard of the Integrative Development Level of Female Boxers' Special Physical Quality

Total score	Evaluation Grading
>268.89	high level
268.89-211.58	necessary level
<211.58	low level

2.6 The Evaluation of Individual Development Level of Female Boxers' Special Physical Quality

According to the above standard score of individual test score of physical quality and the fundamental principle of normal distribution, the individual development level of female boxers' special physical quality is intended: the high level accounts for 25% and the low level accounts for 25%. The assessment standard of the individual development level of female boxers' special physical quality is set up (chart 5). According to the standard, if the individual score of the athlete's physical quality can't reach the necessary level point, the coach should pay attention to the training of the individual physical quality.

Chart 5 the Assessment Standard of the Individual Development Level of Female Boxers' Special Physical Quality

	20s	10m×4	1 Min	20s
	Straight /times	shuttle run /s	vertical and hook punch/times	horizontal push-ups /times
High level	>56.1	66.52	>52.84	>55.32
Necessary level	56.1—39.0	66.52—42.5	52.84—38.4	55.32—34.2
Low level	<39.0	< 42.5	< 38.4	<34.2

We can use the assessment standard of the female boxers' special physical quality from the research to arrange the training program reasonably in accordance with the athletes' actual situation. Summary, the assessment standard of the athletes' physical quality from the research can provide a reference for the boxing coaches to scientifically arrange the training of athletes' special physical quality.

3 Conclusions

3.1 The research results indicate that there are four indicators to evaluate the special physical quality of female boxer:20s straight punch, 10m×4 shuttle run,1 min vertical and horizontal push-ups,20s hook punch and so on, which have a high test validity, reliability and objectivity.

3.2 Evaluating the individual level of development of physical quality of female boxer with the grading standard of test scores of individual physical quality from the research, the coach should improve the development of the athlete's individual physical quality when the individual score is lower than the necessary level.

3.3 Evaluating the overall level of development of physical quality of female boxer with the grading standard of test scores of overall physical quality from the research, the coach should improve the development of the athlete's overall physical quality when the total score is lower than 211.58.

References

1. Yu, Z.: Scientific Selection of Athletes. University of Traditional Chinese Medicine Press, Shanghai (2006)
2. Fengdao, J.: The Basic Training of Boxing. People's Sports Press, Beijing (2003)
3. Tian Maijiu Sports Training. People's Sports Press, Beijing (2002)
4. Huang, M.: Sports Experimental Design and Scientific Quantitative Methods. Higher Education Press, Beijing (2003)
5. He, G.: Practical Statistics Methods and SPSS Operating Essentials. Press, Wuhan (2001)
6. Boxing Coach Learning Materials. People's Sports Press, Beijing (1998)
7. Wang, R.: Exercises Physiology. Sports Press, Beijing (2003)
8. Yang, X.: The Research on Principles of Selection Assessment of Boxing Athletes' Individual Movement Qualities. Nanjing sports Institute Journals 5 (2006)
9. Pan, D.: Brief Comment on the Constraint in the Development of Boxing in China. PLA Institute of Physical Education Journals 5 (2002)

Author Index